D1134872

Library of Congress Catalog Card Number: 60-60000

First Printed 1960—CMH Pub 5–7

UNITED STATES ARMY IN WORLD WAR II

Stetson Conn, General Editor

Advisory Committee
(As of 15 March 1959)

Elmer Ellis
University of Missouri

Maj. Gen. Hugh M. Harris
U.S. Continental Army Command

Samuel Flagg Bemis
Yale University

Brig. Gen. Edgar C. Doleman
Army War College

Gordon A. Craig
Princeton University

Brig. Gen. Frederick R. Zierath
Command and General Staff College

Oron J. Hale
University of Virginia

Brig. Gen. Kenneth F. Zitzman
Industrial College of the Armed Forces

W. Stull Holt
University of Washington

Col. Vincent J. Esposito
United States Military Academy

T. Harry Williams
Louisiana State University

Office of the Chief of Military History

Col. Warren H. Hoover, Acting Chief

Chief Historian
Chief, Histories Division
Chief, Publication Division
Editor in Chief
Chief, Cartographic Branch
Chief, Photographic Branch

Stetson Conn
Lt. Col. Joseph Rockis
Lt. Col. E. E. Steck
Joseph R. Friedman
Elliot Dunay
Margaret E. Tackley

iii

. . . to Those Who Served

Foreword

In the capture of the southern Marianas, including the recapture of Guam, during the summer of 1944, Army ground and air forces played an important, though subordinate, role to that of the Navy and its Marine Corps. Marine personnel constituted the bulk of the combat troops employed. The objective of this campaign was "to secure control of sea communications through the Central Pacific by isolating and neutralizing the Carolines and by the establishment of sea and air bases for operations against Japanese sea routes and long-range air attacks against the Japanese home land." Its success would provide steppingstones from which the Americans could threaten further attack westward toward the Philippines, Formosa, and Japan itself, and would gain bases from which the Army Air Forces' new very long range bombers, the B–29's, could strike at Japan's heartland. Recognizing and accepting the challenge, the Japanese Navy suffered heavy and irreplaceable losses in the accompanying Battle of the Philippine Sea; and the islands after capture became the base for all the massive air attacks on Japan, beginning in November 1944.

In the operations described in the present volume, landings against strong opposition demonstrated the soundness of the amphibious doctrine and techniques evolved out of hard experience in preceding Pacific operations. Bitter inland fighting followed the landings, with Army and Marine Corps divisions engaged side by side. The author's account and corresponding Marine Corps histories of these operations provide ample opportunity to study the differences in the fighting techniques of the two services. Dr. Crowl also deals frankly with one of the best-known controversies of World War II, that of Smith versus Smith, but concludes that it was the exception to generally excellent interservice co-operation.

With team effort among the military services the order of the day, this record of the Army's experience in working with the Navy and the Marine Corps should be particularly valuable both now and in the future.

Washington, D.C.
16 March 1959

WARREN H. HOOVER
Colonel, U.S.A.
Acting Chief of Military History

The Author

Philip A. Crowl, who has an M.A. from the State University of Iowa and a Ph.D. from the Johns Hopkins University, taught History at the Johns Hopkins University and at Princeton. Commissioned in the Navy in World War II, he became a lieutenant (senior grade) and commanding officer of an LCI gunboat that was in action at Leyte Gulf, Lingayen Gulf, and Okinawa. From 1949 through 1956, Dr. Crowl was a historian with the Office, Chief of Military History. He was awarded the James V. Forrestal Fellowship for 1953–54 to study command relationships in amphibious warfare in World War II. Since 1957 he has been in Department of State Intelligence. Dr. Crowl is author of *Maryland During and After the Revolution* (1943) and coauthor of *The U.S. Marines and Amphibious War* (1951) and *Seizure of the Gilberts and Marshalls* (1955).

Preface

This volume is a companion piece to *Seizure of the Gilberts and Marshalls* by Philip A. Crowl and Edmund G. Love, also published in the Pacific subseries of the UNITED STATES ARMY IN WORLD WAR II. Together, the two volumes cover the beginning and climax (although not the conclusion) of the Central Pacific phase of the war against Japan, with special emphasis, of course, on the U.S. Army's contribution to the victories won in that area.[1] Specifically, *Campaign in the Marianas* treats of the capture of Saipan, Tinian, and Guam in the southern Marianas; the strategic and tactical plans leading thereto; supporting operations by naval and air units; and the final development and exploitation of these islands as bases for furtherance of American joint operations against the Japanese homeland.

The word *joint* cannot be overemphasized in connection with any consideration of U.S. operations in the Central Pacific. It was predominantly a U.S. Navy theater under the command of Admiral Chester W. Nimitz. The main burden of the amphibious and ground fighting in the Marianas, as in the Gilberts and Marshalls, fell on the shoulders of the U.S. Marine Corps, whose troops far outnumbered those of the U.S. Army. The author recognizes this and recognizes also that, by concentrating on the activities of the Army, this volume in a sense presents a distorted picture. The distortion is deliberate. The book represents, by definition, one segment of the history of the U.S. Army in World War II. Excellent official and semiofficial histories of U.S. Navy and U.S. Marine Corps operations in the Marianas have already been published. The present narrative of Army activities should add in some measure to what has already been written about the campaign. The reader may also gain additional insight into the nature of joint operations and interservice co-ordination.

Because the number of Army troops participating in the Marianas Campaign was comparatively small, it has been possible to devote more attention here to small unit actions than in the volumes of the series that deal with the movements of great armies and corps over large continental land masses. In much of this narrative the spotlight centers on the infantry company. Ideally, as much attention should have been devoted to equivalent artillery units, especially since Army artillery played a major role in the Marianas Campaign. Unfortunately, the records kept by artillery units during the campaign were—to understate the matter—terse. Unfortunately also, Army field historians who

---

[1] The conclusion of this phase of the war is covered in Roy E. Appleman, James M. Burns, Russell A. Gugeler, and John T. Stevens, *Okinawa: The Last Battle,* UNITED STATES ARMY IN WORLD WAR II (Washington, 1948).

accompanied the troops and who were to supplement and correct the official records by conducting on-the-spot interviews, mostly neglected the artillery in favor of the more mobile infantry.

No really adequate acknowledgment can be made to the many kind and industrious people who helped to bring this book to completion. On substantive matters of strategy and tactics, Dr. Louis Morton, Chief of the Pacific Section, Office of the Chief of Military History, during the preparation of this volume, was a tireless and able critic. On questions of literary style, Dr. Kent Roberts Greenfield, formerly Chief Historian, Department of the Army, was the same. The final editing of the manuscript was performed by Miss Mary Ann Bacon, whose eye for detail is remarkable. None of them is responsible for any errors of fact and interpretation or gaucheries of style I may have persisted in despite their stern warnings. To all I am very grateful.

I owe a special debt of gratitude to Mr. Wsevolod Aglaimoff whose services went far above and beyond the call of his duties as Deputy Chief Historian for Cartography. His maps speak for themselves. What is not so apparent is his meticulous scrutiny of the written narrative presented here and his expert advice on all matters tactical—advice based on almost a half-century's intensive study of military tactics.

Maj. Gen. A. C. Smith, formerly Chief of Military History, Col. George G. O'Connor, formerly Chief of War Histories Division, and the military members of their staffs were liberal in their technical assistance and made it possible for me to have access to the classified source material upon which this volume is based. Mr. Thomas Wilds is responsible for unearthing, in some cases translating, and in most cases interpreting the widely scattered and often obscure Japanese source material upon which is based the account of enemy plans, defensive preparations, and combat activity. Miss Margaret Plumb began and Mr. Stanley L. Falk completed a highly useful study of the Guam phase of the campaign. Mr. Falk's excellent draft narrative of the operations of the 77th Infantry Division on Guam forms the basis for the account of that division's actions presented here. Loretto Carroll Stevens was copy editor for the volume and Norma Heacock Sherris was responsible for the selection of photographs. The Index was compiled by Nicholas J. Anthony. Mr. Israel Wice, Chief Archivist, General Reference Branch, and his staff and Miss Lois Aldrich of the World War II Records Division, NARS, were unfailingly patient and courteous. The debt to officers of the Army, Navy, and Marine Corps who read and criticized various portions of the manuscript or corresponded with the author is acknowledged in the Bibliographical Note appended to the volume.

Since so much of this volume deals with Marine Corps operations, I have been particularly dependent on the co-operation of members of the Historical Branch, G–3 Division, Headquarters, U.S. Marine Corps. Special thanks are due to the late Lt. Col. Frank O. Hough, USMCR, Lt. Col. Harry Edwards, USMC, Lt. Col. Carl W. Hoffman, USMC, and Maj. O. R. Lodge, USMC.

Washington, D.C.   PHILIP A. CROWL
16 March 1959

Contents

PART ONE

Introduction

PART TWO

Saipan

PART THREE

Tinian

PART FOUR

Guam

PART FIVE

Conclusion

Tables

Charts

Maps

Illustrations

Photographs are from Department of Defense files with the following exceptions: photographs on pages 37 and 38 from the personal files of Col. Robert C. Richardson, III; the photograph on page 418 from the Bishop Museum, Oahu, Hawaii; and that on page 444, by J. R. Eyerman-Life. (c) 1950 Time Inc.

PART ONE

INTRODUCTION

CHAPTER I

Background of Strategy

On 15 June 1944 American forces invaded the island of Saipan thus piercing the first hole in the inner line of island fortifications that the Japanese had laboriously constructed in order to defend their homeland, their empire, and their recent conquests in the western Pacific and in Asia. Saipan is 1,270 nautical miles from Tokyo, 1,430 from Manila, 1,640 from Shanghai, and 3,350 from Honolulu. Located in the southern portion of the Marianas chain, it was the most heavily fortified of that group of islands and was considered by the Japanese to be a keystone in the defensive system for the homeland.

After twenty-four days of strenuous battle and much bloodletting on the part of both victor and vanquished, Saipan was conquered. On 1 August the little island of Tinian, just a few miles to the south, fell to U.S. forces, and in the same month Guam, the southernmost of the Marianas chain, was recaptured from the Japanese, who had wrested it from the Americans during the first days of the war.

Speaking of the fall of Saipan, Fleet Admiral Osami Nagano, Supreme Naval Advisor to the Emperor, could only remark, "Hell is on us."[1] Premier Hideki Tojo publicly announced, "Japan has come to face an unprecedentedly great national crisis." The following month Tojo resigned in disgrace along with his entire war cabinet. His resignation marked a major turning point in the war. Up to that time the military clique, led and symbolized by Tojo, had been in secure control of the machinery of government and had dictated Imperial policy without any effective restraints. Thereafter, an opposition party with strong inclinations toward terminating the war made gradual but steady inroads into the councils of state, until at last it was able to persuade the Emperor to surrender. The loss of Saipan and the overthrow of Tojo gave this peace party its first opportunity.[2]

The spark that set off this interesting train of events was a directive issued by the U.S. Joint Chiefs of Staff on 12 March 1944.[3] This body—consisting of Admiral William D. Leahy, President Franklin D. Roosevelt's chief of staff; Admiral Ernest J. King, Chief of Naval Operations and Commander in Chief, U.S. Fleet; General George C. Marshall, Chief of Staff, U.S. Army; and General Henry H. Arnold,

---

[1] United States Strategic Bombing Survey (USSBS) (Pacific), Naval Analysis Division, *Interrogations of Japanese Officials,* 2 vols. (Washington, 1946) (hereafter cited as USSBS, *Interrogations*), II, 356.

[2] USSBS (Pacific), Naval Analysis Division, *The Campaigns of the Pacific War* (Washington, 1946) (hereafter cited as USSBS *Campaigns*), p. 220; USSBS, Chairman's Office, *Japan's Struggle to End the War* (Washington, 1946) pp. 2–3; Robert J. Butow, *Japan's Decision to Surrender* (Stanford, Calif., Stanford University Press, 1945), pp. 26–29, *et passim.*

[3] Msg, JCS to MacArthur and Nimitz, 5171 and 989, 12 Mar 44, CM–OUT 5137.

Commanding General, U.S. Army Air Forces—was responsible, under the President and in conjunction with its British counterpart, for the strategic direction of World War II. On 12 March it ordered Admiral Chester W. Nimitz, Commander in Chief, U.S. Pacific Fleet and Pacific Ocean Areas, to occupy the southern Marianas beginning 15 June next. The objective as stated was "to secure control of sea communications through the Central Pacific by isolating and neutralizing the Carolines and by the establishment of sea and air bases for operations against Japanese sea routes and long range air attacks against the Japanese home land."

The 12 March directive was the product of a slow if not always steady growth, emerging only after a long and sometimes bitter conflict of strategic ideas, military interests, and personalities. A leading issue of this conflict was what can best be called the "Central Pacific concept" of American strategy in a war against Japan.

Prewar Origins of the Central Pacific Concept

Shortly after the termination of World War I, when Japan's pretensions in the western Pacific and the Far East were becoming steadily more apparent, American strategic planners set to work to examine possible ways and means of defeating the Japanese Empire in the event of war between the two nations. From these deliberations emerged a series of plans, dating from 1924 through 1938, entitled the ORANGE plans.[4] The product of joint

Army-Navy effort, these were issued by the Joint Army and Navy Board, the predecessor to the Joint Chiefs of Staff.

Although the several plans varied in detail, certain assumptions remained fairly constant. The basic concept of the war against Japan, as expressed by the Joint Board in 1929, was that it would be "primarily naval in character throughout, unless large Army forces are employed in major land operations in the Western Pacific, directed toward the isolation and exhaustion of Japan, through control of her vital sea communications and through aggressive operations against her armed forces and her economic life."[5] To conduct such a war, the U.S. Fleet must first move west from Hawaii and establish an advanced naval base in the Philippines, preferably at Manila Bay if it could be held. Such an advance would be either a direct movement or a step-by-step process involving seizure and occupation of key Japanese Mandated Islands in the Marshalls and Carolines, depending upon the nature and extent of the enemy resistance. From a naval base in the Philippines, it was presumed that Japanese trade routes through the South China Sea could be cut and Japan's economic life throttled. American forces might also move north to establish still more bases in the Ryukyus and other islands neighboring Japan, from which American naval control could be exercised over Japanese home waters and American aircraft could harass the homeland itself.

---

[4] JB 325, Ser. 228, 15 Aug 24, sub: Joint Army and Navy Basic War Plan, ORANGE; Ser. 280, 14 Jun 28–11 Jan 29; Ser. 546, 9 May 35; Ser. 570, 19 May 36; Ser. 618, 28 Feb 38. For further discussion of prewar strategic plans, see Louis

Morton, Strategy and Command: Turning the Tide, 1941–1943, a forthcoming volume in the UNITED STATES ARMY IN WORLD WAR II series.

[5] JB 325, Ser. 280, 14 Jun 28–11 Jan 29, sub: Joint Army and Navy Basic War Plan, ORANGE -Estimate of the Situation, p. 39.

The plans assumed it would be essential to establish subsidiary U.S. bases in the Japanese Mandates, especially in the Marshalls, for the purpose of protecting the line of communications between the Philippines and the continental United States. It was generally agreed that bases in the Marshalls, and probably in the Carolines, would have to be occupied by U.S. forces either in offensive operations in advance of a fleet approach to the Philippines or as a defensive measure to protect the line of communications of American forces operating in the western Pacific. The Marianas figured only incidentally in the scheme, since they lay north of the main route of advance from Hawaii to the Philippines. Thus first emerged the Central Pacific concept of strategy.

The ORANGE plans were based on the assumption that the United States alone would be engaged in a war with Japan. With the outbreak of war in Europe in 1939, and with the gradual strengthening of bonds between the United States and the anti-Axis nations, especially Great Britain, this assumption no longer held. It became necessary to agree to some combined strategic measures in anticipation of the day when the United States might actively enter the war against the Axis.

As a consequence, British and American military staff representatives met in Washington in early 1941 to discuss possible strategy should the United States become a belligerent.[6] In their final report, ABC-1,[7] the representatives agreed first that

"should the United States be compelled to resort to war," both nations would consider the Atlantic and European area to be "the decisive theater," since Germany was the predominant member of the Axis Powers. Thus was enunciated the doctrine of "beat Germany first" that prevailed until the surrender of Germany on 8 May 1945. Until the Germans were defeated, Allied strategy in the Far East would be primarily defensive. American and British forces would defend Hong Kong, the Philippines, and the Netherlands Indies and hold Malaya, Singapore, and Java against Japanese attack. Within this defensive pattern, the U.S. Navy was assigned the specific offensive mission of capturing positions in the Marshalls and preparing to establish control over the entire Caroline and Marshall Islands area.[8] Thus was restated the main principle of the ORANGE plans: hold the Philippines, if possible, and gain control over the islands and waters of the Central Pacific west of Hawaii.

In April 1941 the U.S. Joint Board set about bringing its own plans up to date in the light of these American-British Conversations. The new strategic plan, entitled RAINBOW 5, merely restated the decisions of ABC-1 and assigned more specific tasks to the U.S. forces. Germany was to be beaten first; the Philippines were to be held as long as possible; the U.S. Fleet was to prepare to capture positions in the Marshalls and the Carolines.[9] Thus, once

---

[6] ABC-1, 27 Mar 41, in *Pearl Harbor Attack: Hearings before the Joint Committee on the Investigation of the Pearl Harbor Attack* (Washington, 1946) (hereafter cited as *Pearl Harbor Hearings*), Part 15, pp. 1487–1550.

[7] ABC stands for American-British Conversations.

[8] *Pearl Harbor Hearings,* Part 15, pp. 1511–12, 1516, 1518–19.

[9] *Ibid.,* Part 18, pp. 2885, 2889–90, 2894, 2919, 2916. RAINBOW 5 was approved by the Secretaries of War and Navy, and although never formally approved by the President, it was in fact the war plan that went into effect on 7 December 1941.

again, the role of the Central Pacific in the forthcoming war against Japan was affirmed.

War in the Pacific: First Year

The rapid succession of Japanese victories after Japan's attack on Pearl Harbor made it impossible for the United States and her allies to put into immediate execution any of the prewar plans. Guam fell to the invaders, followed by Hong Kong, Singapore, Manila, and the Philippine Islands. In short order the United States and Great Britain were stripped of all the usable advanced bases they once possessed. The Netherlands Indies, Malaya, and Burma were overrun and the Bismarck Archipelago–New Guinea–Solomons area was invaded. By May of 1942 the Japanese were well ensconced in a far-flung system of mutually supporting bases including the Kurils, the Marianas, the Marshalls, the Carolines, the Palaus, and Rabaul (in New Britain), with outposts in the Gilberts, the Solomons, and New Guinea.

Flushed with victory, the Japanese high command decided to ride its good fortune to the limit and push on to Port Moresby, New Guinea—the very threshold of Australia; to New Caledonia, Fiji, and Samoa, astride the sea lanes between Australia and the United States; and to Midway and the western Aleutians. The first plan was frustrated by the Allied naval victory in the Coral Sea in early May 1942, while the second died aborning. The Japanese gained a tenuous foothold in the Aleutians, but in attempting to seize Midway they suffered their first decisive defeat of the war at the hands of the U.S. Pacific Fleet in the great naval and air battle of 3–4 June 1942.[10] The time had come for Allied counteraction.

The United States, which had assumed major responsibility for the war in the Pacific, had laid the groundwork for future offensive operations against the enemy. On 30 March 1942 the Joint Chiefs of Staff, with the approval of President Roosevelt, organized the Pacific theater into two commands—the Southwest Pacific Area (SWPA) and the Pacific Ocean Areas (POA). The former fell to the command of General Douglas MacArthur, with headquarters in Australia, and included Australia, New Guinea, the Bismarck Archipelago, the Solomons, the Netherlands Indies (except Sumatra), the Philippines, and adjacent waters.[11] The Pacific Ocean Areas was to be commanded by Admiral Nimitz, whose headquarters was at Pearl Harbor and who was concurrently Commander in Chief, U.S. Pacific Fleet. This theater included virtually the entire remainder of the Pacific Ocean. Within its boundaries lay the Hawaiian Islands, Midway, Wake, the Gilberts, the Marshalls, the Carolines, the Palaus, the Marianas, the Bonins, the Ryukyus, Formosa (Taiwan), and the Japanese home islands.[12] Because of the immensity of the theater, it was subdivided into three areas, North, Central, and South Pacific. Nimitz directly commanded the first two, but as-

---

[10] See Samuel Eliot Morison, *History of United States Naval Operations in World War II*, Vol. IV, *Coral Sea, Midway and Submarine Actions, May 1942–August 1942* (Boston, Little, Brown and Company, 1949).

[11] Memo, Marshall and King for President, 30 Mar 42, no sub, with two inclosures, Directive to CINCPOA and Directive to the Supreme Commander, SWPA, ABC 323.31 POA (1–29–42), 1–B.

[12] Excluded from POA were the waters off the west coast of South America.

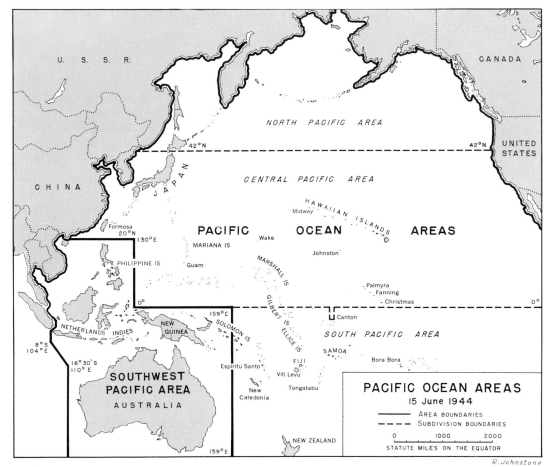

MAP 1

signed the third to a subordinate commander who from October 1942 to June
1944 was Admiral William F. Halsey, Jr.[13]

The first task facing MacArthur and
Nimitz after the Japanese fleet had been
turned back at Midway was to render more
secure the line of communications between

the United States and Australia. On 2
July 1942 the Joint Chiefs of Staff ordered
their Pacific commanders to advance
through the Solomons and New Guinea
and seize the Japanese stronghold of Rabaul. On 1 August 1942 the area under
MacArthur's control was reduced slightly
by moving his eastward boundary line
from 160°E to 159°E from the equator
southward. This in effect took the lower
Solomon Islands including Tulagi, Guadalcanal, Florida, the Russells, Malaita, and

[13] Fleet Admiral William F. Halsey, USN, and
Lieutenant Commander J. Bryan, III, USNR,
Admiral Halsey's Story (New York and London,
Whittlesey House, McGraw-Hill Book Company,
Inc., 1947).

San Cristobal out of MacArthur's jurisdiction. (*Map 1*) There followed the lengthy and exhausting Guadalcanal and Papua Campaigns. By January of 1943 the line of communications was safe, even though Rabaul remained in enemy hands.[14]

The Japanese were at last on the defensive; the losses at Pearl Harbor were more than replaced by the naval repair and construction program. Allied military planners could now direct their attention to devising ways and means of taking up the offensive, and it is not surprising that their thoughts turned once again to the prewar plans for the Pacific.

Revival of the Central Pacific Concept

The Casablanca Conference

In January 1943 President Roosevelt and the U.S. Joint Chiefs of Staff met with Prime Minister Winston S. Churchill and the British Chiefs of Staff at Casablanca, French Morocco. There, the American and British Chiefs, known collectively as the Combined Chiefs of Staff, mapped out as best they could the main lines of global strategy for the coming year.[15] In the midst of prolonged and sometimes acrimonious discussion concerning forthcoming operations in Europe and the Mediterranean, proposed offensives in Burma, and aid to China, Admiral King stepped forth to assume the role that he was to fill for the next two years—that of the leading advocate of a greater effort in the Pacific and more specifically of a Central Pacific thrust against the Japanese.

King addressed himself primarily to the problem of where to go after Rabaul was captured—an operation that was optimistically assumed to be already well advanced with the campaigns in Guadalcanal and Papua drawing to a successful close. He adhered to the concept of the ORANGE plans and urged that the first main Allied objective in the Pacific be the Philippines, since they lay athwart the line of communications between Japan and the oil-rich East Indies and since their occupation by Allied forces would permit that line to be cut. The best route to this objective, he claimed, lay through the Central Pacific. Such a drive would involve "establishing a base in the northwestern Marshalls and then proceeding to Truk and the Marianas." "The Marianas" he added, "are the key of the situation be-

---

[14] See John Miller, jr., *Guadalcanal: The First Offensive* (Washington, 1949), and Samuel Milner, *Victory in Papua* (Washington, 1957), both in UNITED STATES ARMY IN WORLD WAR II series; Samuel Eliot Morison, *History of United States Naval Operations in World War II,* Vol. IV, *Coral Sea, Midway and Submarine Actions,* and Vol. V, *The Struggle for Guadalcanal, August 1942–February 1943* (Boston, Little, Brown and Company, 1949); Maj. John L. Zimmerman, USMCR, *The Guadalcanal Campaign,* Historical Division, Division of Public Information, Headquarters, U.S. Marine Corps (Washington, 1949); Wesley Frank Craven and James Lea Cate, eds., *The Army Air Forces in World War II,* Vol. IV, *The Pacific: Guadalcanal to Saipan, August 1942 to July 1944* (hereafter cited as Craven and Cate, *AAF IV*) (Chicago, The University of Chicago Press, 1950).

[15] For excellent discussions of the Casablanca Conference, see Lt. Grace P. Hayes, USN, The War Against Japan, Part I, Ch. X, MS, JCS Hist Sec; John Miller, jr., "The Casablanca Conference and Pacific Strategy," *Military Affairs,* XIII (Winter, 1949); Fleet Admiral Ernest J. King and Walter M. Whitehill, *Fleet Admiral King, A Naval Record* (New York, W. W. Norton & Company, 1952), Ch. XXXIII; Maurice Matloff, *Strategic Planning for Coalition Warfare: 1943–1944,* UNITED STATES ARMY IN WORLD WAR II (Washington, 1959).

cause of their location on the Japanese line of communication."[16]

An important addition was thus introduced into the ORANGE concept of the war in the Pacific. The Marianas, which had received little attention from the Joint Board in its prewar plans, now emerged as a major objective in the mind of Admiral King. The other participants at the Casablanca meeting were too concerned about more immediate problems to pay much attention to King's remarks about the Marianas, but the conferees did endorse planning for a drive through the Central Pacific in 1943.

On 17 January the U.S. Joint Staff Planners, a subcommittee of the Joint Chiefs of Staff, presented a fourfold program for the forthcoming year's operations in the Pacific: (1) seizure of the Solomons, of eastern New Guinea as far as Lae and Salamaua, and of the New Britain–New Ireland area; (2) seizure of Kiska and Agattu in the Aleutians; (3) after the fall of Rabaul, seizure and occupation of the Gilberts, the Marshalls, and the Carolines through Truk, and extension of the occupation of New Guinea to the border of Netherlands New Guinea; and (4) operations in Burma designed to keep China in the war and increase the employment of China-based aircraft against Japanese shipping.[17]

Most of this program was acceptable to the Combined Chiefs, although they stipulated that the advance in the Central Pacific should not be allowed to prejudice the recapture of Burma. The final agreement at Casablanca authorized plans to be made for a campaign in the Aleutians, an advance northwest from Samoa along the Solomons–New Britain–New Ireland–New Guinea axis to protect the line of communications between the United States and Australia, diversionary attacks against the Malay Barrier, and a Central Pacific advance west against the Truk–Guam line.[18]

TRIDENT Conference

In May of 1943 the President and the Prime Minister with their Combined Chiefs of Staff convened again, this time in Washington at the TRIDENT Conference.[19] Most of the discussion again centered around questions concerning the Mediterranean theater and Burma and China, but during the course of the meeting, the Combined Chiefs reaffirmed their determination to get on with the war in the Central Pacific.[20]

On 14 May the American representatives circulated to the Combined Chiefs a paper drawn up by the various subcommittees of the Joint Chiefs, entitled Strategic Plan for the Defeat of Japan.[21] This paper was more of an estimate than a plan,

---

[16] Min, 56th mtg CCS, 14 Jan 43.

[17] CCS 153 (Rev.), 17 Jan 43, title: Situation To Be Created in Eastern Theater (Pacific and Burma) in 1943.

[18] CCS 170/2, 23 Jan 43, title: Final Rpt to President and Prime Minister Summarizing Decisions by CCS in Casablanca Conf.

[19] For a more detailed discussion of the TRIDENT conference, see Philip A. Crowl and Edmund G. Love, *Seizure of the Gilberts and Marshalls,* UNITED STATES ARMY IN WORLD WAR II (Washington, 1955), pp. 12–17; Matloff, *Strategic Planning for Coalition Warfare, 1943–1944;* Hayes, The War Against Japan, Sec. IV, Part II, Ch. XIII.

[20] See Charles F. Romanus and Riley Sunderland, *Stilwell's Mission to China,* UNITED STATES ARMY IN WORLD WAR II (Washington, 1953), pp. 327–33.

[21] CCS 220, 14 May 43; Min, 86th mtg JCS, 20 May 43; JSSC 40/2, 3 Apr 43; JPS 67/4, 28

but it did articulate more clearly than before the main strategic principles endorsed by the highest U.S. planners for the war in the Pacific in 1943–44. It was assumed that to bring about the unconditional surrender of Japan it would first be necessary for the Allies to secure a foothold in China in order to make best use of the enormous Chinese manpower and to provide air bases from which to bomb the Japanese mainland. China could be entered by three routes: through Burma, through the Strait of Malacca and the South China Sea to Hong Kong from the west, and across the Pacific through the Celebes Sea to Hong Kong from the east. The British, with American and Chinese aid, should be held responsible for operations along the first two routes. The United States would assume major responsibility for the third.

Next came the question of how American forces could best get to the Celebes Sea and Hong Kong from positions held by the United States. The American planners proposed a two-pronged drive by U.S. forces, one westward from Hawaii through the Central Pacific, the other west and north along the Solomons–Bismarck–New Guinea line in General MacArthur's Southwest Pacific Area. The two thrusts were to merge in the Philippines–South China Sea area and join in the descent upon Hong Kong. In determining priorities as between the two drives, it was declared that the main effort in the westward advance should be made through the Central Pacific and a subsidiary role assigned to the South and Southwest Pacific.

Once again Admiral King took the floor to press the argument in favor of the Central Pacific drive and more particularly to champion his favorite project, the invasion of the Marianas. For years, he said, officers at the Naval War College in Newport had been studying the problem of supporting or recovering the Philippines as the *sine qua non* of defeating Japan. Their conclusions all pointed to the route straight through the Pacific from the Hawaiian Islands as the best approach. The Marianas, he insisted, were the key to the western Pacific. A major offensive there, he claimed, would seriously jeopardize Japanese lines of communications, most probably force the Japanese Fleet into a decisive naval engagement, and provide bases from which to bomb the Japanese home islands.[22]

In its final session at TRIDENT the Combined Chiefs of Staff, although not committing themselves on the question of the Marianas, agreed to American recommendations for a two-pronged attack across the Pacific. Specifically, they listed the following strategic objectives in the Pacific for 1943–44:

1. Conducting air operations in and from China,

2. Ejection of the Japanese from the Aleutians,

3. Seizure of the Marshall and the Caroline Islands,

4. Seizure of the Solomons, the Bismarck Archipelago, and Japanese-held New Guinea, and

---

Apr 43; JCS 287/1, 8 May 43. All these bear the title Strategic Plan for the Defeat of Japan or a similar one. The subordinate committees of the JCS included the Joint War Plans Committee (JWPC), the Joint Strategic Survey Committee (JSSC), and the Joint Staff Planners (JPS). For more detailed discussion of the paper Strategic Plan for the Defeat of Japan, see Crowl and Love, *Gilberts and Marshalls,* pp. 12–17.

---

[22] Min, 92d mtg CCS, 21 May 43; King and Whitehill, *Fleet Admiral King,* pp. 437–38, 444.

5. Intensification of operations against enemy lines of communication.

Two months later the Joint Chiefs of Staff decided to modify the plans for launching the Central Pacific drive. A direct assault on the Marshalls from Hawaii, they reasoned, would require more shipping and troops than were immediately available in the Central Pacific and might necessitate draining General MacArthur's Southwest Pacific Area of some of its resources. Also, it would be well to have better aerial photographs of the Marshalls before attempting the dangerous amphibious assault on these Japanese strongholds about which almost nothing was known. Air bases from which photographic missions could be flown should therefore be built close to the Marshalls. Largely for these reasons the Joint Chiefs, on 20 July, ordered Nimitz to capture Tarawa, in the Gilberts, and Nauru as a preliminary to going into the Marshalls themselves. The target date selected was 15 November 1943.[23]

In August the Combined Chiefs, meeting at Quebec for the QUADRANT Conference, accepted the revision as well as a schedule of operations proposed by the American representatives for the period after the capture of the Marshalls. For the Central Pacific this included the capture of Ponape, Woleai, and Truk in the Carolines, the development of Truk as a major fleet base, and the seizure of Yap and the Palaus. At Admiral King's suggestion, an invasion of the Marianas was included in this program as a possible alternative to the Palaus or as a concurrent operation.[24]

A few days after this decision was made Admiral Nimitz suggested one further change in the plan for initiating the Central Pacific drive. He proposed substituting Makin in the Gilberts for Nauru because Makin could more easily be assaulted and because it was closer to the Marshalls. The proposal was accepted, and Nimitz was authorized to seize Tarawa, Makin, and Apamama in the Gilberts.[25] On 20 November 1943 simultaneous amphibious landings were launched against Makin and Tarawa by elements of the 27th Infantry Division and the 2d Marine Division, respectively. Within four days both atolls were captured, following which Apamama was occupied.[26] The Central Pacific drive was under way.

General MacArthur's Strategy

Meanwhile, halfway around the world at his headquarters in Brisbane, General MacArthur was developing strategic plans that were not always consonant with the ideas prevailing among high echelon plan-

---

[23] Min, 97th mtg JCS, 20 Jul 43; JCS 386/2, 20 Jul 43, title: Strategy in the Pacific; Rad, JCS to CINCPAC, 20 Jul 43, CM–IN 14465. See also Crowl and Love, *Gilberts and Marshalls*, pp. 18–25.

[24] JCS 446, 5 Aug 43, title: Specific Opns in the Pacific and Far East, 1943–44; Min, 101st mtg JCS, 7 Aug 43; CCS 301/3, 27 Aug 43, title: Specific Opns in the Pacific and Far East; CCS 319/5, 24 Aug 43, title: Final Rpt to President and Prime Minister.

[25] Msg, Nimitz to JCS, 260439, 26 Sep 43; Memo, Roberts for Handy, 27 Sep 43, Sub: Substitution of Makin for Nauru in Operation GALVANIC, ABC 384 Pacific (28 Jun 43); Memo, U.S. CofS for COMINCH, 27 Sep 43, same sub; OPD Exec 2, Item 1b.

[26] See Crowl and Love, *Gilberts and Marshalls;* Historical Division, War Department, *The Capture of Makin,* AMERICAN FORCES IN ACTION (Washington, 1946); Captain James R. Stockman, USMC, *The Battle for Tarawa,* Historical Division, Division of Public Information, Headquarters, U.S. Marine Corps (Washington, 1947).

ners in Washington. MacArthur, having left the Philippines in early 1942, was determined to return as quickly and with as strong a force as possible. He was also determined that the major role in this undertaking should be assigned to the forces under his command and that the main approach to the Philippines should be made through his own Southwest Pacific theater.

In early 1943 MacArthur's immediate concern was with current operations leading up to the eventual capture of Rabaul.[27] At the same time, his staff was preparing a long-range plan (RENO I) for a return to the Philippines. As first set forth in February 1943, this plan called for the progressive seizure in New Guinea of Hansa Bay, Hollandia, Geelvink Bay, and the Vogelkop Peninsula. With the north coast of New Guinea under control, Southwest Pacific forces would then advance north to Halmahera or to the Celebes before the final jump into the southern Philippines.[28]

This schedule of operations expressed perfectly MacArthur's fundamental strategic ideas. The Philippines could best be approached by a series of amphibious jumps along the entire northern coast of New Guinea, each so distanced as to permit full cover by land-based aviation. A similar move into Halmahera or to the Celebes would bring him to the threshold of the Philippines. Then, with his eastern flank secured by previous capture of the Palaus and his western flank possibly protected by the occupation of islands in the Arafura Sea, he would be fully prepared to make good his promise to return.

Preoccupied as he was with his own theater, MacArthur could only view with alarm the growing pressure for an advance through the Central Pacific. The Joint Chiefs of Staff and the Combined Chiefs of Staff notwithstanding, he strongly opposed an invasion of the Marshall Islands. Even after the Combined Chiefs had approved and authorized the Marshalls operation, he radioed General Marshall:

From a broad strategic viewpoint I am convinced that the best course of offensive action in the Pacific is a movement from Australia through New Guinea to Mindanao. This movement can be supported by land based aircraft which is utterly essential and will immediately cut the enemy lines from Japan to his conquered territory to the southward. By contrast a movement through the mandated islands will be a series of amphibious attacks with the support of carrier based aircraft against objectives defended by Naval units and ground troops supported by land based aviation. Midway stands as an example of the hazards of such operations. Moreover no vital strategic objective is reached until the series of amphibious frontal attacks succeed in reaching Mindanao. The factors upon which the old Orange plan were based have been greatly altered by the hostile conquest of Malaya and the Netherlands East Indies and by the availability of Australia as a base . . . .[29]

This protest may have helped persuade the Joint Chiefs to postpone the Marshalls operation until the Gilberts were taken,[30] but it did nothing to sway the majority of Washington planners from their determination to attack through the Central Pacific. Two months later, in August at the

---

[27] See John Miller, jr., *CARTWHEEL: The Reduction of Rabaul*, UNITED STATES ARMY IN WORLD WAR II (Washington, 1959).

[28] See Robert Ross Smith, *The Approach to the Philippines*, UNITED STATES ARMY IN WORLD WAR II (Washington, 1953), pp. 3–4.

[29] Rad, MacArthur to Marshall, C3303, 20 Jun 43, CM–IN 13149.

[30] See Crowl and Love, *Gilberts and Marshalls*, pp. 18–21.

Quebec meeting of the Combined Chiefs of Staff (QUADRANT), it was decided, against General MacArthur's previous advice, to bypass Rabaul.[31] These decisions on the part of higher authority did nothing to dissuade the Southwest Pacific commander from continuing his opposition to an extension of the Central Pacific drive. Specifically, he was strongly set against an invasion of the Marianas.[32]

Enter the Army Air Forces

In the autumn of 1943 a new factor entered into the strategic picture of the war against Japan—a factor that was to have an important bearing on the decision to invade the Marianas. The Army Air Forces announced the imminent appearance of a very long range bomber—the B-29.

An experimental model of the plane was first flown in September 1942, but it took about another year to iron out the "bugs" and make arrangements for quantity production. From the point of view of strategic bombing, the outstanding characteristic of this four-engine plane was that with a bomb load of four tons it had an estimated range of approximately 3,500 miles. In effect, once the B-29 was produced in sufficient quantity, mass bombing raids could be conducted from friendly air bases against enemy targets located as much as 1,750 miles away, although for optimum efficiency and safety a 1,500-mile radius was usually used as a basis for calculation.[33]

As 1943 drew to a close, it became apparent that the B-29's would not be off the production line in sufficient number in time to play a significant role in the preinvasion bombardment of Europe, and that in any case the B-17's and B-24's already assigned to the European theater were adequate for the job there.[34] The question then arose as to how the B-29's could best be employed against Japan. To which of the various theaters of operations in the Pacific and Far East should the bulk of the bombers be assigned? Three possibilities suggested themselves: Australia, China, and the Marianas.

From the Southwest Pacific came urgent representations by Lt. Gen. George C. Kenney of the Fifth Air Force that first priority in the allocation of the new bombers be assigned to his command. He argued that the best way of using the B-29's against Japan was to knock out the pe-

---

[31] JCS 446; Min, 101st mtg JCS; CCS 301/3; and CCS 319/5. All cited n. 24. MacArthur's opposition to bypassing Rabaul was strongly put in a radio to Marshall, C4183, 23 Jul 43, CM-IN 16149.

[32] General MacArthur reiterated his opposition to the invasion of the Marianas as late as 1955. He stated, "The 'Central Pacific Concept' . . . lost its validity when it was abandoned in favor of a 'Europe First' policy as the Japanese actually struck the Philippines. That was the time which presented the golden opportunity, both in strategy and logic, for a Central Pacific drive by our combined fleets aimed at engaging and destroying Japan's naval power on the Pacific . . . . Having missed this initial opportunity, the belated Central Pacific drive toward the Marianas in July [*sic*] 1944 could at best produce local tactical successes without bringing to bear any decisive influence upon the course of the war." Ltr, MacArthur to Maj Gen A. C. Smith, Chief of Mil Hist, Dept of the Army, 7 Jan 55, OCMH.

[33] For an excellent treatment of the development of the B-29, see Wesley Frank Craven and James Lea Cate, eds., *The Army Air Forces in World War II*, Vol. V, *The Pacific: Matterhorn to Nagasaki, June 1944 to August 1945* (hereafter cited as Craven and Cate, *AAF V*) (Chicago, The University of Chicago Press, 1953), Ch. I.

[34] H. H. Arnold, General of the Air Force, *Global Mission* (New York, Harper & Brothers, 1949), p. 477.

troleum industry in the Netherlands Indies from bases in Australia. In Washington, however, the Air Forces chief, General Arnold, and his staff had other ideas, and Kenney's suggestion was rejected.[35]

At the Quebec conference of August 1943 General Arnold presented to the Combined Chiefs his "Air Plan for the Defeat of Japan."[36] Arnold estimated that by October 1944 ten B–29 groups of twenty-eight planes each might be available for employment against Japan. It was assumed that by that time no Pacific island within fifteen hundred miles of the Japanese main island of Honshu would have been captured. Therefore he proposed to build a chain of airfields north and south of Changsha in China, all of which would be within the required range of most of Japan's war industries. Since the Air Forces high command refused to believe either that a port on the east coast of China could be captured in time to supply these operations or that the Burma Road could be opened, it concluded that logistical support of any airfield built in China must come from India, flown over the Hump in B–24's.[37]

Air Forces planners were none too happy about basing their new bombers in China, partly because of the logistical difficulties involved and partly because they were skeptical of the ability of the Chinese to hold the fields against the Japanese.[38] Hence, after the conclusion of the Quebec

conference, they urged that the Marianas be seized and that D Day for the operation be advanced to mid-1944 by neutralizing and bypassing intervening Pacific islands.[39] The Air Forces planners argued strongly that "plans for the acceleration of the defeat of Japan would place emphasis upon the seizure of the Marianas at the earliest possible date, with the establishment of heavy bomber bases as the primary mission."[40] The Marianas, it will be recalled, were about 1,270 miles from Tokyo, well within the estimated optimum 1,500-mile cruising radius of the B–29's.

Cairo Conference

At last Admiral King had a powerful ally in his persistent campaign for an invasion of the Marianas. At the meeting of the President and Prime Minister with the Combined Chiefs in Cairo in December 1943 (SEXTANT), the joint Navy-Air Forces efforts bore fruit. Among the operations submitted to and approved by President Roosevelt and Prime Minister Churchill was the "seizure of Guam and the Japanese Marianas," tentatively set for 1 October 1944.

This operation was to follow the capture of important objectives in the Marshalls in January, Ponape in the Carolines in May, and Truk in July. Meanwhile, General MacArthur was scheduled to seize Kavieng on New Ireland, Manus Island in the Admiralties, and Hansa Bay on the northeast coast of New Guinea, and then

[35] Craven and Cate, *AAF V,* pp. 12, 316; George C. Kenney, *General Kenney Reports, A Personal History of the Pacific War* (New York, Duell, Sloan and Pearce, 1949), pp. 378, 419, 426.
[36] CCS 323, 20 Aug 43, title: Air Plan for the Defeat of Japan.
[37] Craven and Cate, *AAF V,* pp. 17–18.
[38] Arnold, *Global Mission,* p. 477.

[39] Craven and Cate, *AAF V,* p. 19.
[40] JPS 288, 4 Oct 43, sub: Plans for Defeat of Japan Within 12 Months After Defeat of Germany, CCS 381, Japan (8–25–42), Sec. 7.

move on to the tip of Vogelkop Peninsula by August 1944.[41]

The Combined Chiefs chose this occasion to again endorse the Central Pacific route as part of a two-pronged drive to Japan. In presenting their "Overall Plan for the Defeat of Japan," they stated that their ultimate aim was "to obtain objectives from which we can conduct intensive air bombardment and establish a sea and air blockade against Japan, and from which to invade Japan proper if this should prove necessary." This would necessitate one advance along the New Guinea – Netherlands Indies – Philippines axis and another through the Central Pacific in time for a major assault in the area of Formosa–Luzon–China by the spring of 1945. The two lines of advance were to be "mutually supporting," but should there be conflicts, "due weight should be accorded to the fact that operations in the Central Pacific promise at this time a more rapid advance toward Japan and her vital lines of communication; the earlier acquisition of strategic air bases closer to the Japanese homeland; and, of greatest importance, are more likely to precipitate a decisive engagement with the Japanese Fleet."[42] Here in a capsule was the rationale of the Central Pacific concept of strategy.

Scheduling Operations

Upon receiving word of these latest decisions of the Combined Chiefs of Staff, Admiral Nimitz set about preparing a schedule for forthcoming operations in the Central Pacific. A preliminary draft of his campaign plan, GRANITE, was finished by 27 December. It tentatively outlined operations as follows:[43]

Capture of	*Date*
Kwajalein	31 January 1944
Kavieng (and air attack on Truk)	20 March 1944
Manus	20 April 1944
Eniwetok	1 May 1944
Mortlock (Nomoi Is.)	1 July 1944
Truk	15 August 1944
Saipan, Tinian, and Guam	15 November 1944

On 13 January, Nimitz issued another GRANITE plan revising his original somewhat.[44] Operations to seize Mortlock Island and Truk were scheduled for 1 August. The possibility of bypassing Truk was considered, and it was suggested that if Truk could be bypassed, the Palaus should be invaded by Central Pacific forces on 1 August. The Marianas could then be invaded by 1 November since capture of the Palaus, it was assumed, would be a less costly and time-consuming venture than assaulting the Japanese stronghold on Truk. In any case, both the original plan and the revision looked to the Marianas as the culmination of the 1944 campaign.

A curious turn of events in Pacific planning now took place. In order better to co-ordinate future operations in the two Pacific theaters, a meeting of representatives of the Southwest Pacific and the Pacific Ocean Areas was convened at Pearl

---

[41] CCS 397 (Rev.), 3 Dec 43, title: Specific Opns for Defeat of Japan.
[42] CCS 417, 2 Dec 43, title: Overall Plan for Defeat of Japan.

[43] CINCPOA Campaign Plan GRANITE, 27 Dec 43.
[44] CINCPOA Campaign Plan GRANITE, 13 Jan 44.

Harbor in the last days of January 1944. Present, among others, were Admiral Nimitz, and from his staff, Rear Adm. Charles H. McMorris, Rear Adm. Forrest P. Sherman, and Vice Adm. John H. Towers, Commander, Air Force Pacific. From the Southwest Pacific came Maj. Gen. Richard K. Sutherland, MacArthur's chief of staff; General Kenney, Commander, Allied Air Forces, Southwest Pacific Area; and Vice Adm. Thomas C. Kinkaid, Commander, Allied Naval Forces, Southwest Pacific Area.[45]

Admiral Nimitz presented his revised GRANITE plan for the consideration of the conferees. Immediately, and from all sides, objections were voiced to the proposal to invade the Marianas. General Sutherland advocated pooling all available resources in the Pacific and concentrating upon operations in MacArthur's theater. "If Central Pacific will move against Palau as the next operation after the Marshalls," he argued, "and make available to Southwest Pacific Area the amphibious force now contemplated for Truk, we can take all of New Guinea, the Kai and Tanimbars, and Halmahera in time to join you in amphibious movement to Mindanao this year." General Kenney spoke of bombing Japan by B–29's based on the Marianas as "just a stunt." Admiral Kinkaid remarked that "any talk of the Marianas for a base leaves me entirely cold."[46]

Even Nimitz' own staff members showed themselves to be less than enthusiastic over the Marianas, although Nimitz himself favored the project. Admiral McMorris doubted if long-range bombing from the Marianas would cause the capitulation of Japan. Admiral Sherman admitted that operations in the Marianas would be extremely costly and that when captured the harbors would be of limited usefulness to the Navy.

When word of these proceedings reached Admiral King, he read them "with indignant dismay." In a stern message to Nimitz he pointed out, "The idea of rolling up the Japanese along the New Guinea coast, through Halmahera and Mindanao, and up through the Philippines to Luzon, as our major strategic concept, to the exclusion of clearing our Central Pacific line of communications to the Philippines, is to me absurd. Further, it is not in accordance with the decisions of the Joint Chiefs of Staff." Assuming correctly that Nimitz agreed with his own strategic ideas, he continued, "I'm afraid . . . that you have not . . . maintained these views sufficiently positively vis-a-vis the officers from the South and Southwest Pacific."[47] Admiral King was not one to stand idly by while theater staffs undermined his favorite and long-nourished war plan almost at the very moment of its fruition.

Acceleration of Operations

On 31 January Central Pacific forces attacked Kwajalein Atoll in the central Marshalls and, after a four-day fight by the 7th Infantry Division and the 4th Marine Division, secured the objective. At the same time, Majuro in the eastern Mar-

[45] Min, Pacific Conf, 27–28 Jan 44, OPD 334.8, Case 125; Memo, Col William L. Ritchie for Handy, 4 Feb 44, sub: Brief of Pacific Conf, Held at Pearl Harbor 27–28 Jan 44, same file; Hayes, The War Against Japan, Sec. IV, Part II, Ch. XXI, pp. 6–8; Kenney, *General Kenney Reports*, pp. 347–49.

[46] Min, Pacific Conf, and Memo, Ritchie for Handy, cited n. 45.

[47] Memo, King for Nimitz, Ser. 00409, 8 Feb 44, COMINCH file.

shalls was occupied without a battle.[48] The conquest of these important positions had been relatively easy, and the reserve troops intended for the operation had not been committed. Nimitz could thus speed up his plan for moving into the western Marshalls, and accordingly he launched, on order, an amphibious assault against Eniwetok on 17 February, two months ahead of schedule. At the same time he delivered a carrier strike against Truk.[49]

Eniwetok fell in six days before the combined assault of the 22d Marines and the 106th Regimental Combat Team of the 27th Infantry Division. On 17–18 February (Tokyo time) Rear Adm. Marc A. Mitscher's Fast Carrier Force struck the once mighty Japanese bastion at Truk, destroying at least seventy planes on the ground and in the air and about 200,000 tons of merchant shipping in the harbor.[50] The defenses of Truk were so weak as to lend strong support to the idea that it might be bypassed altogether.

Shortly after the successful conclusion of these operations in the Central Pacific, General MacArthur found opportunity to step up his own schedule. The most recently approved plans called for the Southwest Pacific Area commander to conduct simultaneous invasions of Kavieng on New Ireland and Manus in the Admiralties on 1 April.[51] Then, on 23 February, an incident took place that persuaded MacArthur that he could safely accelerate at least part of this plan. Planes from the Southwest Pacific flying over the Admiralties on that date reported no evidence of the enemy. The general decided to act at once. He dispatched elements of the 1st Cavalry Division to Los Negros to conduct a reconnaissance in force and, when initial resistance was discovered to be light, sent the rest of the division in to capture the entire Admiralties group.[52]

Washington Planning Conferences February–March 1944

In the light of these events, the time had obviously come for the Washington planners to reconsider their schedule of operations for both Pacific theaters for the rest of 1944.

Most planners by this time agreed that the primary objective for the next phase of the war against Japan was to establish a lodgment somewhere in the "strategic triangle" represented by Luzon, Formosa, and the neighboring China coast. From there it was believed that communications between the Japanese homeland and the Netherlands Indies could be completely cut off, bases for the very long range bombers could be set up within effective range of the enemy's industrial centers, and forward bases could be established for the ultimate invasion of Japan, if that operation should prove necessary.

---

[48] See Crowl and Love, *Gilberts and Marshalls,* pp. 302–04; Lt. Col. Robert D. Heinl, Jr., USMC, and Lt. Col. John A. Crown, USMC, *The Marshalls: Increasing the Tempo,* Historical Branch, G–3 Division, Headquarters, U.S. Marine Corps (Washington, 1954).

[49] Rad, CINCPOA to COMINCH, 022212, 2 Feb 44, CM–IN 1855; Min, 143d mtg JCS, 3 Feb 43; Rad, CINCPOA to COMINCH, 150749/2, 15 Feb 44, CM–IN 10592.

[50] See Samuel Eliot Morison, *History of United States Naval Operations in World War II,* Vol. VII, *Aleutians, Gilberts and Marshalls, June 1942 –April 1944* (Boston, Little, Brown and Company, 1951), Ch. XVIII.

[51] Msg, JCS to CINCSWPA, 23150/Z, Jan 44, CM–IN 15765, and to CINCPOA, 231515/Z, Jan 44, CM–IN 15699.

[52] See Miller, *CARTWHEEL: The Reduction of Rabaul.*

Beyond this point agreement ceased. The arguments that ensued were many and various, but they can be resolved into two main issues. First, which was the better route of approach to the strategic triangle, the Central Pacific route through the mandated islands or the Southwest Pacific route along the coast of New Guinea to Mindanao? Second, which of the two theaters would be given priority in the allocation of resources, especially those troops, ships, and aircraft that had until now been assigned to the South Pacific, a command that had practically completed its mission and was about to become a rear area?

Early in February Admiral Sherman from Nimitz' staff and General Sutherland, MacArthur's chief of staff, appeared in Washington to represent their respective commanders in the discussions that the Joint Chiefs of Staff and their subordinate committees were to hold. Sutherland argued that RENO and GRANITE plans were "relatively weak and slow of progress." As a substitution, he proposed "an advance along the general axis, New Guinea–Mindanao, with combined forces." Truk, he believed, could be bypassed and, with "the capture of Truk thus obviated, amphibious forces can be combined for an advance along the northern coast of New Guinea." This, he claimed, would enable United States forces to enter Mindanao as early as 1 December 1944. For such a drive, naval forces could be based at Manus Island. He did not propose to limit the freedom of action of the Pacific Fleet. Admiral Nimitz and General MacArthur could operate by co-operation. But, he added, the "Southwest Pacific Area needs certain naval forces for direct support of its operations. It is General MacArthur's

hope that Admiral Halsey will be assigned as Commander, Allied Naval Forces, because of his ability, rank, prestige, and experience."[53]

From General MacArthur himself came representations of the same nature. To General Marshall he radioed:

There are now large forces available in the Pacific which with the accretions scheduled for the current year would permit the execution of an offensive which would place us in the Philippines in December if the forces were employed in effective combination. However, under the plan of campaign that has been prepared in Washington, the forces will be employed in two weak thrusts which can not attain the major strategic objective until several months later . . . .[54]

In the same message MacArthur insisted that the forces of the South Pacific should remain under his command. These forces, he argued, had been engaged in operations within his own theater since their advance from Guadalcanal. He could not continue to operate effectively without them. "I must state," he added, "that any reduction in the forces presently engaged in the Southwest Pacific by actual withdrawal of forces of any category would be incomprehensible."[55]

At the same meeting of the Joint Chiefs of Staff addressed by General Sutherland, Admiral Sherman attempted to explain Nimitz' Plan GRANITE. The plan, he pointed out, differed from that proposed by General MacArthur in that it "envisages occupation of Luzon at the same time that an attack is made in the south [Mindanao] and is predicated upon the occupation of Eniwetok about 1 May, the

---

[53] Min, 145th mtg JCS, 8 Feb 44.
[54] Msg, MacArthur to CofS, C1217, 2 Feb 44, CM–IN 1443.
[55] Ibid.

Carolines about 1 August, and the Marianas, or such other point as might be selected as the next objective, by the end of the year."[56]

MacArthur's chief antagonist in this strategic debate was neither Sherman nor Nimitz, but, as usual, Admiral King. King vigorously opposed handing MacArthur the naval forces of the South Pacific. MacArthur already had the Seventh Fleet under his command, King argued. The South Pacific forces were operating in a separate area and were "primarily concerned in such circumstances with the probability of enemy forces from the Pacific Ocean Areas threatening the operations of both the South and Southwest Pacific." King could see no sound reason for placing them under MacArthur.[57] He called attention to the decision of the Combined Chiefs of Staff at Cairo (SEXTANT) that the advance in the Pacific should be along two axes and that in case of conflicts between the two, "due weight should be accorded to the fact that operations in the Central Pacific promise at this time a more rapid advance toward Japan and her vital line of communications."[58] "General MacArthur," said King, "has apparently not accepted this decision and desires a commitment to an advance along a single axis. I do not think that this is a propitious time to change our agreed strategy."[59]

At this point in the argument, General Marshall suggested that, in the light of developments since the Cairo conference, the time had come for the Joint Chiefs to issue a new directive to both Pacific commanders. Specifically, Marshall recommended that the Joint Strategic Survey Committee, which consisted of Vice Adm. Russell Willson (Navy), Lt. Gen. Stanley D. Embick (Army), and Maj. Gen. Muir S. Fairchild (Army Air Forces), be directed to study the matter anew and report its views as to what geographic objectives should be seized, the order of their seizure, and what axis of advance appeared to offer the best chance for victory in the Pacific.[60] Admiral King immediately concurred.[61]

To the disappointment of the advocates of the Southwest Pacific concept of strategy, the Joint Strategic Survey Committee came forth with a statement clearly favoring King's and Nimitz' strategic plan.[62] The committee, repeating its earlier convictions, stated that the Joint Chiefs of Staff "should resolve the present situation as between these two plans by deciding and directing that the primary effort against Japan will be made through the Central Pacific, with operations in the Southwest Pacific cooperating with and supporting that effort." The primary objective, said the committee, was the Formosa–Luzon–China triangle, and that objective "would seem to be more effectively supported by the Central Pacific concept than by the concept of the Southwest Pacific. The former leads most directly and most promptly to the vital Formosa, Luzon, China coast area. The latter after reaching Mindanao will require further ex-

[56] Min, 145th mtg JCS, 8 Feb 44.

[57] Memo, King for CofS, 8 Feb 44, sub: CINCSWPAC Despatch C121702 Feb 44, OPD 381, Case 301.

[58] CCS 417, cited n. 42.

[59] Memo cited n. 57.

[60] Memo, CofS for King, 10 Feb 44, OPD 381, Case 301.

[61] Memo, King for Marshall, 11 Feb 44, sub: 1944 Opns in Pacific Theater, OPD 381, Case 301.

[62] Apparently this report was written mostly by Admiral Willson. General Embick, the Army representative, however, was in general accord. Memo, Gen T. T. Handy, no addressee, 19 Feb 44, OPD 381, Case 301.

tensive operations before reaching that vital area."[63]

The Joint Strategic Survey Committee report not only disappointed the representatives of the Southwest Pacific but also failed to satisfy General Marshall. He did not feel that the committee had sufficiently explored the problem of allotting resources between the two theaters or the question of how best to employ the great Allied superiority in land-based air.[64] He wanted other subcommittees of the Joint Chiefs, specifically the Joint Staff Planners and the Joint Logistics Committee, to study the matter further.[65] In reply to these proposals, Admiral King, while agreeing in principle that further long-range studies would be beneficial, expressed his fear that any more delays in committee might kill the momentum of the drive now under way in the Pacific.[66]

With Admiral King pressing for immediate action either in the direction of Truk or straight for the Marianas or the Palaus, General MacArthur on 5 March came forward with a proposal to accelerate operations in his own theater. He advised the Joint Chiefs of Staff to omit the Hansa Bay operation scheduled for about 22 April and to move instead to Hollandia, some three hundred miles up the coast of New Guinea. To accomplish this, he proposed to use not only the forces of the South and Southwest Pacific Areas but also Central Pacific aircraft carriers and other shipping tentatively earmarked to support the Kavieng-Manus operation.[67]

These suggestions were in keeping with General MacArthur's latest RENO plan, which reached Washington within a few days. It proposed a four-phase program: first, a continued advance along the north coast of New Guinea through Hollandia to Geelvink Bay; second, establishment of air bases in the Arafura Sea area for strategic bombing in the Netherlands Indies and to support subsequent operations into the Vogelkop and Halmahera; third, seizure of the western tip of the Vogelkop and Halmahera; and fourth, occupation of Mindanao, southernmost of the Philippines, and the establishment of bases there for an attack upon the Formosa–Luzon–China coast area.[68]

Admiral Nimitz, who had meanwhile been summoned to Washington, was quick to note that these proposals, if accepted, would have the effect of slowing up operations in his own theater. To the Joint Chiefs he argued that a retention by MacArthur of forces from the Central Pacific after the capture of Kavieng and Manus would result in "stopping the Central Pacific Campaign, losing its momentum, deferring movement into the MARIANAS until the approach of the typhoon season, and by allowing the enemy additional time to strengthen his defenses in the CAROLINES and MARIANAS would jeopardize our ability to reach the LUZON–

[63] JCS 713, 16 Feb 44, title: Strategy in the Pacific.

[64] Memo, CofS for Leahy and King, 24 Feb 44, OPD 381, Case 301.

[65] Memo, Marshall for COMINCH and CNO, 1 Mar 44, sub: Your Memo of 24 Feb on Proposed Directive to CINCPOA and Memo of 27 Feb on JCS 713, OPD 381, Case 297.

[66] Memo, King for CofS, 1 Mar 44, OPD 381, Case 297.

[67] Msg, MacArthur to JCS, C2473, 5 Mar 44, CM–IN 3318.

[68] RENO IV, Outline Plan for Operations of the Southwest Pacific Area to Include the Reoccupation of the Southern Philippines, 6 Mar 44, CNO (WPD) file, Env 68, Case 184, NR&H.

FORMOSA–CHINA area in early 1945 as now planned."[69]

On the affirmative side, Nimitz suggested two alternative schedules for the remainder of 1944. The first contemplated an invasion of Truk on 15 June, the southern Marianas on 1 September, and the Palaus on 15 November. The second proposed bypassing Truk and going into the southern Marianas on 15 June, Woleai on 15 July, Yap on 1 September, and the Palaus on 1 November. On reconsideration, Nimitz decided that, if the second schedule were accepted, the capture of Yap could be deferred until the Palaus had been taken and that a fleet harbor could be established in Ulithi. This would advance the target date for the Palaus to 1 October.[70]

In the end, the Joint Chiefs of Staff accepted neither MacArthur's nor Nimitz' schedules *in toto*. Nor did they accept without change the final conclusion of the Joint Strategic Survey Committee that to seize the desired objective in the Formosa-Luzon-China coast area, "a fundamental strategic prerequisite is our control of the Marianas, Carolines, Palau [Pacific] Ocean area."[71] At the insistence of General Marshall, Mindanao was added to the vital intermediate objectives that United States forces must capture before proceeding on to the strategic triangle.[72]

Thus the directive that the Joint Chiefs of Staff issued to General MacArthur and Admiral Nimitz on 12 March represented in a sense a compromise between the Central Pacific and the Southwest Pacific concepts of strategy. It declared "that the most feasible approach to the Formosa-Luzon-China area is by way of Marianas –Carolines–Palau–Mindanao area, and that the control of the Marianas–Carolines –Palau area is essential to the projection of our forces into the former area, and their subsequent effective employment therefrom." Specifically, the Joint Chiefs ordered:

1. Cancellation of the Kavieng operation and the complete isolation of the Rabaul–Kavieng area with the minimum commitment of forces.

2. Early completion of the occupation of Manus and its development as an air and fleet base.

3. Occupation of Hollandia by MacArthur, target date 15 April 1944.

4. Establishment of control of the Marianas–Carolines–Palau area by Nimitz' forces by neutralizing Truk; by occupying the southern Marianas, target date 15 June 1944; and by occupying the Palaus, target date 15 September 1944.

5. Occupation of Mindanao by MacArthur's forces supported by the Pacific fleet, target date 15 November 1944.

6. Occupation of Formosa, target date 15 February 1945, or occupation of Luzon if necessary, target date 15 February 1945.[73]

With this directive in hand, Admiral Nimitz and his subordinates could at last

---

[69] Memo, CINCPAC, no addressee, 7 Mar 44, sub: Sequence and Timing of Opns, Central Pacific Campaign, with JCS Info Memo 200, same date, CCS 381 POA (6–10–43), Sec. 2.

[70] Memo, Nimitz for King, 8 Mar 44, sub: Sequence and Timing of Opns, Central Pacific Campaign, CCS 381 POA (6–10–43), Sec. 2.

[71] JCS 713/3, 11 Mar 44, sub: Future Opns in the Pacific.

[72] Marshall's penciled notes on Draft Directive [JCS to MacArthur and Nimitz, 12 Mar 44], OPD 381, Case 301.

[73] Msg, JCS to MacArthur and Richardson for Nimitz, 12 Mar 44, CM–OUT 5137.

prepare their tactical plans in detail. The southern Marianas would be assaulted and the target date was to be 15 June. The largest amphibious operation yet to be undertaken in the Pacific was about to get under way.

CHAPTER II

The Marianas

In History

The islands thus chosen as the next point of American amphibious assault in the Central Pacific had had a long and not altogether happy experience as minor pawns in the international rivalries of great powers. Magellan discovered them in 1521 in the course of his famous first voyage around the world. Struck by the sailing powers of the native boats and by the similarity of their rigging to that of the small craft that abounded in his own Mediterranean, the navigator labeled his discoveries, "Islas de los Velas Latinas" (Islands of the Lateen Sails). Other members of the expedition were more impressed by the natives' pilfering habits and accordingly called them "Islas de los Ladrones" (Islands of the Thieves), a name that remained in popular usage well into the twentieth century, even though it had long since been officially abandoned. Late in the seventeenth century the islands were officially renamed "Las Marianas" in honor of Maria Anna of Austria, wife of Philip IV and Queen of Spain, who took a personal interest in converting their inhabitants to the Church of Rome.[1]

The original native population of the Marianas, the Chamorros, were a hardy race, probably of Polynesian origin, but not hardy enough to withstand the encroachments of western civilization as represented by Spanish traders and missionaries. In spite of mass baptisms by the latter, native resentment toward the rigid rule of the priesthood increased until finally, in the 1690's, armed revolution broke out in the islands. The result was inevitable; the Spaniards with their superior weapons and organization overcame the rebels, killed large numbers and forced most of the remainder to flee. The center of the trouble was on Guam, and from there many of the remaining Chamorros fled to the northern Marianas, where they were relentlessly pursued and persecuted. Others finally escaped south to the Carolines to become intermingled with the Kanaka population of those islands.

Spanish control, which had become progressively weaker during the nineteenth century, was finally severed completely in 1898–99. Imperial Germany was the first of the Western Powers to challenge Span-

---

[1] Historical data presented here are derived from the following sources: R. W. Robson, comp., *The Pacific Islands Year Book, 1942* (Sydney, Australia, Pacific Publications, Limited, 1942); R. W. Robson, comp., *The Pacific Islands Hand-* *book, 1944* (New York, The Macmillan Company, 1946); Laura Thompson, *Guam and Its People* (Princeton, N.J., Princeton University Press, 1947); OCNO Div of Naval Intel, ONI 99 Strategic Study of Guam, 1 Feb 44 (hereafter cited as ONI 99).

ish hegemony in Micronesia.[2] In August 1885 the Germans hoisted their flag over Yap in the western Carolines and laid claim to much of the surrounding territory. After violent Spanish protest, the dispute was submitted to papal arbitration and Spain's sovereign rights were confirmed, although Germany obtained important commercial concessions at the same time. Negotiations for transfer between the two countries continued in the 1890's, and in 1899 Spain ceded all of her possessions in the Carolines, the Marshalls, and the Marianas to the German Empire for the sum of about $4,000,000. Meanwhile, a small American naval expeditionary force had seized Apra Harbor on Guam, and at the termination of the Spanish-American war that island was ceded to the United States.

Another radical change in the disposition of the entire Central Pacific area occurred as the result of World War I. Japan, having emerged successfully from her recent war against Russia and being anxious to expand her commercial and military influence throughout the Orient and its adjacent waters, was quick to seize the opportunity of a European war to realize her own imperialist ambitions. As one of the Allied Powers, Japan contributed her share to the ultimate downfall of the German Empire by seizing the Carolines, the Marshalls, the Palaus, and the Marianas (except, of course, Guam) in the first year of the war. Then, under the Treaty of Versailles, all former German possessions north of the equator were mandated to Japan, although they theoretically

still remained under League of Nations authority. During the 1920's and 1930's the Japanese proceeded vigorously to colonize these new holdings and to exploit their economic resources for the benefit of Japanese economy. After 1935, when Japan withdrew from the League of Nations, no further effort was made to give even lip service to the idea that the islands were mandated territories. They became, to all intents and purposes, outright possessions.[3]

Meanwhile, the United States had occupied Guam and had converted it into a minor naval base. By an executive order of President William McKinley dated 23 December 1898, the island was placed under control of the Navy Department, a naval officer was commissioned as governor of Guam, and the same officer was appointed by the Secretary of the Navy as commandant of the naval station, which encompassed the entire island. Progress in constructing a naval base of respectable proportions was slow and halting. In 1939 the Hepburn Board reported to Congress that the area should and could be developed into a major naval base, but the necessary appropriations failed to pass.

The Japanese Invasion of Guam

At the time of the outbreak of war between the United States and Japan, the American garrison on Guam consisted of 153 marines and 271 U.S. Navy personnel, supported by a force of 308 Guamanians. The garrison had no artillery or fixed defenses and, in addition to its small arms, possessed only a few .30-caliber and .50-caliber machine guns. The local naval surface force consisted of three small pa-

---

[2] Micronesia is the name applied to the islands of the western Pacific Ocean including the Marianas, the Carolines, the Marshalls, and the Gilberts.

[3] See Ch. IV, below.

trol craft and an old oiler. One of the patrol craft, the USS *Penguin*, mounted two 3-inch antiaircraft guns and the oiler boasted two .50-caliber antiaircraft machine guns.[4]

Japanese designs against this tiny force and the outpost that it garrisoned began to materialize well before the attack on Pearl Harbor. As early as the middle of October 1941, the *18th Air Unit*, a small force of reconnaissance seaplanes based in the Marianas, began conducting a reconnaissance of Guam and during the following November flew frequent secret photo reconnaissance missions over the island at altitudes of 3,000 meters or higher.[5] At the same time, small Japanese vessels began patrolling the waters around the island, mostly at night, and in early December succeeded in landing several native Guamanians friendly to their cause.

Japanese plans for an amphibious invasion of Guam were complete by 8 November. On that date Maj. Gen. Tomitara Hori, who commanded the *South Seas Detachment*, a unit of about 5,500 Army troops, received his orders. He was to assemble his forces in the Bonins in November and wait there until definite word of the first Japanese air attack against the United States had been received. Then, naval air units based on Saipan were to fly to Guam and attack U.S. ships and installations. Meanwhile, Army troop transports with a naval escort were to proceed from the Bonins to Guam, where landing operations would commence in the early morning of 10 December. In addition to the Army troops assigned, the Navy was to contribute a special landing force of about 400 men drawn from the *5th Defense Force* stationed on Saipan.[6]

The planes assigned to softening up the target came to about twenty in number, including the *18th Air Unit*, which had been busy on reconnaissance missions over the island since October. At 0525 on 8 December word came to the airmen waiting on Saipan that the Greater East Asia War had begun. The message read, "Begin attack on Guam immediately."[7] The shooting war in the Marianas had started. It would not formally end for another two years and nine months.

Within three hours of receiving this command, Japanese planes bore down on Guam and bombed the American oiler *Barnes* in the harbor. Next they turned their attention to the patrol boat *Penguin*, which was attempting to escape to the open sea, and finally they dumped their remaining bombs over shore targets. *Penguin* was sunk and *Barnes* damaged to

---

[4] Capt G. J. McMillin, USN, to CNO, 11 Sep 45, sub: Surrender at Guam to the Japanese; ONI 99, p. 2; JICPOA Bull 52-44, 15 Apr 44, Guam, p. 6; Historical Division, War Department, *Guam: Operations of the 77th Division (21 July–10 August 1944)*, AMERICAN FORCES IN ACTION (Washington, 1946) (hereafter cited as AFAS, *Guam*) p. 17; Samuel Eliot Morison, *History of United States Naval Operations in World War II*, Vol. III, *The Rising Sun in the Pacific, 1931–April 1942* (Boston, Little, Brown and Company, 1948), pp. 32–34, 184–86.

[5] *18th Air Unit* Combat Rpt, G Opn, WDC 161418; Land Forces, Vol. 2, NA 11665, WDC 161013. Both these documents are now located in the National Archives, Washington. WDC numbers are the Washington Document Center accession numbers; NA numbers are the National Archives accession numbers.

[6] Japanese Studies in World War II, 55, Operations in the Central Pacific, pp. 1–6, copy in OCMH; CINCPAC-CINCPOA, 12060, Handwritten Account of the Civil and Military Situation on Guam from the Japanese Occupation Unit February 1944, dated November 1943 and January 1944, GHQ FEC, G-2 Hist Sec, Doc. 56871.

[7] *18th Air Unit* Combat Rpt, G Opn, WDC 161418.

the extent that she had to be abandoned. A second flight appeared over the island at 1330 the same afternoon, the planes concentrating their attack on the still unsunk *Barnes* and the cable and wireless stations ashore.

The following day, Japanese aircraft again made morning and afternoon raids. Two bombs struck the Marine barracks, and many other hits were scored. The Japanese airmen reported that fire from the ground was very light and that they had spotted no artillery emplacements and no mines in any of the harbors or bays— only a machine gun position in the northern suburbs of Agana. (*See Map V.*)

While Guam burned under the bombs of its attackers during the first two days of the war, the troop-laden assault vessels and their escorts were on the way down from the north. At 0900 on 4 December, the main elements of the convoy, carrying the 5,500 Army troops, moved out of Hahajima and headed toward Rota, where they were joined by the ships carrying the small naval detachment from Saipan. From Rota the force advanced in separate groups to Guam, where all arrived during the first hour of 10 December. Landing operations commenced at 0230. The main force of the Army troops landed on the west coast between Facpi Point and Merizo, intending to drive northward along the coast to Agat. This plan miscarried when it was discovered that there was no adequate road from the beachhead to Agat, and the troops had to re-embark and land again at Facpi Point. The maneuver proved superfluous since by the time the new landing was completed the American garrison had already surrendered to the smaller naval unit.

The naval detachment landed about two miles north of Agana. As it advanced toward the city, it flushed the machine gun emplacement, reported by planes the night before, about one kilometer from the city itself. The main body of the U.S. marines had taken positions at the Marine rifle range on Orote Peninsula, and only about eighty Guamanians and a few Americans were in Agana when the Japanese arrived. These few put up a stiff fight and twice at Agana Plaza drove the invaders back with rifle and machine gun fire before finally being overcome. After the skirmish on the plaza, the Japanese went on to occupy the naval hospital and the wireless station, and the naval repair station at Piti. Finally, at 0545, the island governor, Capt. C. J. McMillin, USN, realized that resistance was useless and commenced negotiations for surrender. Soon after, the American ensign was run down from Government House and replaced by the Imperial flag of Japan. The Japanese had completed the occupation of the Marianas chain.[8]

Description of the Islands

The Marianas are a chain of volcanic islands running in an approximately north–south direction from $20° 32'$ N, $144° 54'$ E to $13° 15'$ N, $144° 43'$ E. From Farallon de Pajaros in the north to Guam in the south, the chain numbers fifteen islands in all. Guam has an area of over 200 square miles but about two thirds of the chain is little more than mountainous rocks and of practically no military value.

[8] McMillin, Surrender at Guam to the Japanese; Morison, *Rising Sun in the Pacific,* pp. 184–86.

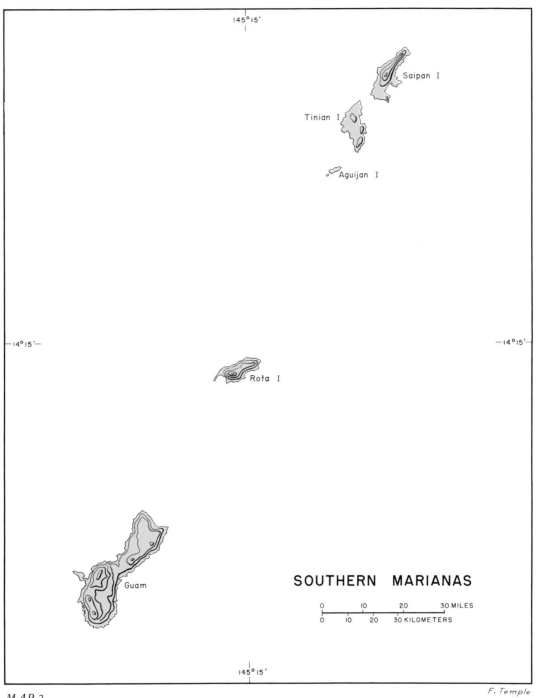

145°15'

Saipan I

Tinian I

Aguijan I

—14°15'—

—14°15'—

Rota I

Guam

SOUTHERN MARIANAS

| 0 | 10 | 20 | 30 MILES |

| 0 | 10 | 20 | 30 KILOMETERS |

145°15'

MAP 2

F. Temple

The four largest islands and those having the chief military utility are all in the southern half of the chain. These, from north to south, are Saipan, Tinian, Rota, and Guam. (*Map 2*) Of these, Rota was eliminated by the U.S. planners as a feasible target because of the inaccessibility of most of its coast line, its inadequate harbor facilities, and its general inferiority to the other three islands as a naval and air base for future operations against Japan.

Saipan, Tinian, and Guam lay directly athwart or on the near flank of the advance of Central Pacific forces from their westernmost base at Eniwetok to almost any part of Japanese-held territory that might become the object of future amphibious operations—the Philippines, Formosa, the Volcano Islands, the Ryukyus, and Japan proper. Saipan lies about a thousand nautical miles west of Eniwetok and over 3,200 miles from Pearl Harbor. Northwest, Tokyo is only about 1,260 miles distant, and Manila Bay is 1,500 miles almost due west. Tinian is just three miles south of Saipan; Guam, approximately another hundred miles in a southerly direction.

The main geographic factors that planners of the operation had to take into consideration were climate, the location of beaches and the approaches thereto, topography of the terrain inland from the beaches, the nature of the vegetation as it would affect military operations, harbor facilities, the location and size of towns and cities, and the location of roads, railroads, and other transportation facilities. The necessary information was gleaned from a variety of sources—prewar surveys and hydrographic charts, aerial and submarine reconnaissance missions executed during the war, and enemy documents captured in earlier operations.

The first aerial photographs of Saipan and Tinian were taken on 22 and 23 February 1944 by planes flown from Marc Mitscher's fast carrier force (Task Force 58). At that time, a total of twenty-five sorties at various heights and angles was flown, but because of cloud formations only a partial coverage of the islands was obtained.[9] These were supplemented by full photographic coverage provided by a flight of five Navy PB4Y's, escorted by Army bombers, that took off from Eniwetok on 18 April for a round trip of more than two thousand miles and thirteen hours in the air. A second mission flown by a similar group of planes on 25 April also photographed Guam.[10] Guam was covered again on 7 May by six Navy photographic "Liberators," and the northern islands as well as Guam were rephotographed on 29 May.[11]

In addition, the submarine USS *Greenling* made a series of sorties around all three islands between 2 and 29 April and obtained excellent photographs, which were made available to the expeditionary troops. The submarine's photographs were chiefly remarkable for their accuracy of detail on the beach approaches.[12]

Between 15 January and 10 May, Joint Intelligence Center, Pacific Ocean Areas (JICPOA), issued a total of eight infor-

---

[9] Hq Expeditionary Troops, Task Force 56 Report on FORAGER (hereafter cited as TF 56 Rpt FORAGER), Incl D, G-2 Rpt on FORAGER, p. 2; App. C, pp. 1-2.

[10] CINCPAC-CINCPOA Opns in POA—Apr 44, pars. 37-39.

[11] CINCPAC-CINCPOA Opns in POA—May 44, pars. 49-50; TF 56 Rpt FORAGER, Incl D, p. 2. All of these Navy photographic missions were escorted by Army B-24's of the Seventh Air Force flown out of the Marshalls. Craven and Cate, *AAF IV*, pp. 684-87.

[12] CINCPAC-CINCPOA Opns in POA—May 44, pars. 49-50.

mation bulletins covering the proposed island targets.[13] In addition, the Office of Naval Intelligence (ONI) made available a monograph on the geography of the Palaus and the Marianas that had been prepared in the spring of 1942.[14] More detailed was another ONI bulletin on Guam that was an exhaustive, although somewhat obsolete, study based chiefly on a monograph completed by Marine Corps Schools in Quantico as early as 1937 and the notes and personal recollections of a naval officer, Comdr. R. F. Armknecht (CEC) (USN), who had left the island only a month before the Japanese captured it.[15] Other materials, including diagrams of tides, sunlight and moonlight tables, and captured Japanese charts, completed the list of information on the Marianas upon which plans for the landings had to be based.[16]

Some of this proved to be inaccurate in detail. The number of enemy installations and the size and disposition of troops were generally underestimated. Many terrain features were erroneously depicted in the maps made on the basis of photographic intelligence. On the whole, however, a fairly good general understanding of the nature of the targets could be gleaned from the various sources.

Climatic conditions vary little as between the sister islands of Saipan and Tinian in the north and Guam in the south. The year can be conveniently divided into two seasons: the dry or winter monsoon season from November through March, and the wet or summer monsoon season from April through October. During most of the dry period the prevailing wind is from north and east with an average velocity of ten to fifteen knots. By June the wind usually shifts from east to south and by August and September the southwestern monsoon frequently occurs. Thus, if landings on the western beaches were to be considered, it was clear that they should be made before August in order to be certain of a lee shore.

Average cloud cover is nearly 70 percent for most of the year, which added to the problem of achieving adequate aerial observation and aerial reconnaissance. Generally, however, weather conditions offered no serious obstacle to military operations. The climate is mild and healthful. Mean temperature on Saipan varies between a January maximum and minimum of 81° F. and 72° F., respectively, and June values of 85° F. and 75° F. Guam, being a hundred miles closer to the equator, is somewhat warmer and more humid but not enough so to make any significant difference. The summer months constitute the rainy season, during which the total precipitation is from 80 to 86 inches. Most rain falls in the form of showers, lasting from only a few minutes to two hours, but there are occasional steady, light rains. August is the wettest month—an additional reason for concluding any proposed military operations before the end of July. Typhoons occur in the area, but not with as much regularity or intensity as elsewhere in the Pacific. This is a region of typhoon genesis and storms are usually not

[13] JICPOA Bull 7-44, Mariana Islands, 15 Jan 44; Bull 29-44, Weather Survey for Carolines and Marianas, 26 Feb 44; Bull 31-44, Carolines and Marianas, Part I, Tides and Currents, Part II, Daylight and Dark, 4 Mar 44; Bull 34-44, Saipan, Tinian, and Rota, 10 Mar 44; Bull 52-44, Guam (2 vols.), 15 Apr 44; Bull 66-44, Saipan (Target Survey), 10 May 44; Bull 67-44, Tinian (Target Survey), 10 May 44; Bull 73-44, Saipan, Tinian, and Rota, 10 May 44.
[14] ONI 29, Palau, Mariana Islands, 11 May 42.
[15] ONI 99, p. vii.
[16] TF 56 Rpt FORAGER, Incl D, App. B.

fully developed. About once every two years disturbances of the typhoon type hit the islands or pass near enough to cause violent winds and heavy rainfall, but even so the storm diameter is generally comparatively small.[17]

None of the three islands offered ideal beach conditions for landing assault troops. On Saipan the land on the western side slopes rather gently up from the shore line, but the beaches themselves could be reached only with difficulty because of fringing and barrier reefs that extend for most of the island's length. (*See Map I.*) A small gap existed in the reef just off the town of Charan Kanoa and a dredged channel led into Tanapag Harbor, but for most of the area the coral barrier presented a serious impediment to the landing of troops boated in small craft. The north end and east side of the island have deep water close inshore and are free of reefs except for a fringing one around Magicienne Bay on the east coast. However, the beaches were generally narrow and the shores steep, thus making landing operations and movement inshore extremely hazardous. The same conditions prevailed for the most part on the southern end.

Harborage facilities ranged from poor to mediocre. Tanapag Harbor, the principal anchorage area, was the only one that provided even partial protection from all winds, and against heavy seas from the west the reef barrier on the seaward side offered little real safety to ships at anchor within. Vessels could anchor off Garapan and find some shelter from easterly winds and sea, but it was no more than an open roadstead, and landing and unloading would be impossible during strong westerly winds. The only shelter against northerly and westerly winds was at Magicienne Bay on the southeast coast. However, the bay was deep and open to winds and seas from the southeast.[18]

Tinian was even better equipped topographically to resist an amphibious landing. The main obstacle to invasion was an almost unbroken barrier of abrupt cliffs close to the water line and ranging from a few feet to over a hundred feet in height. Although the cliffs were not unscalable, especially along the northern and western shores, there was very little landing space at the water's edge for small craft, and the flow of supplies inland from such narrow beaches would be seriously handicapped. The cliffs were broken at various spots in the neighborhood of Tinian Harbor and again on the northwest coast and along the northeastern shore line, but none of these locations offered ideal landing conditions.[19] (*See Map III.*)

Guam, like the other islands of the Marianas, presented to would-be invaders the combined hazards of reefs and shore-line cliffs. The northern half of the island was virtually inaccessible to amphibious troops because of the reef, the surf, and the sheer cliffs rising from the beaches. Although there were some possible landing points on the southeast and southern coasts, the most practicable beaches were south of Orote Peninsula and north of the naval station at Piti, both on the southwest coast. These were obstructed by barrier reefs and, in the north, by low-level cliffs, but were at least negotiable by amphibian craft and

---

[17] JICPOA Bull 29–44, Detailed Weather—Guam, pp. 1–3; Detailed Weather—Saipan and Tinian, pp. 1–3; Comdr Fifth Fleet Opn Plan Central 10–44, 12 May 44, App. I, Weather Summary.

[18] JICPOA Bull 73–44, pp. 6, 11; Bull 34–44, p. 24; Bull 7–44, pp. 53–56.

[19] JICPOA Bull 7–44, pp. 43–49; Bull 34–44, p. 34; Bull 73–44, p. 20.

vehicles. The only good harbor was at Port Apra, north of Orote Peninsula. The port was protected by the peninsula proper, by Cabras Island on the north, and by a breakwater extending from the island, and was considered safe from wind and sea from almost any direction except during the typhoon season.[20]

Although terrain features inland from the shore line on each of the islands were in some ways unique, the similarities were more marked than the differences. The most distinct characteristics of all the Marianas, at least to seasoned troops, were to be their novelty and variety. Heretofore, practically all operations of American forces in the Pacific had been confined to tropical jungle or to coral atolls where maneuver was limited either by the denseness of the vegetation or by the smallness of the area to be seized. Now American troops were to find themselves maneuvering over moderately large land masses with highly varied topography and vegetation. They would have to fight their way through mangrove swamps and fields of lashing sword grass and sugar cane; through fairly sizable towns where the enemy might have to be routed by house-to-house fighting; and, finally and worst of all, up and down precipitous volcanic mountains pocked with caves and creased with endless ridges, escarpments, and other natural concealments that the enemy could be expected to exploit to the fullest.

The dominating physical feature of Saipan is Mount Tapotchau, which rises to an elevation of 1,554 feet near the center of the island.[21] Between this summit and Mount Marpi, located at the north end of

the island and having an elevation of 832 feet, there is a ridge over seven miles long with peaks ranging between 720 and 934 feet. To the west of this ridge there is a fairly level coastal area in the region of Tanapag Harbor, but to the east the slope ends abruptly in steep coastal cliffs. South and southeast of Tapotchau, the backbone ridge slopes off into the plateau forming Kagman Peninsula on the eastern and the southern third of the island. In the southern area Mount Kagman, on the east, and Mount Nafutan, on the southern peninsula of the same name, form conspicuous headlands. Approximately 70 percent of the island's 85 square miles was under sugar cultivation at the time of the invasion. Cane can present a serious obstacle to troops, impeding movement by foot, limiting fields of fire, and offering excellent concealment for the defenders. Another obstacle to attacking troops, especially from west coast beaches, was an extensive marsh that was inland from the town of Charan Kanoa and centered on freshwater Lake Susupe. Saipan is better than fourteen miles along its north–south axis and about six miles across at its widest point.[22]

Tinian is somewhat smaller, being about 10.5 miles in length and 5.5 miles in width at its widest point. Its terrain is also considerably less difficult for military operations than is that of its sister island. It is basically a broad elevated limestone plateau, the highest point of which is Mount Lasso (564 feet) in the north-central part. Most of the southern end of the island is of rolling hills and flatlands except for the southernmost tip, which is marked by precipitous cliffs and ravines. At the time

[20] JICPOA Bull 7–44, pp. 9–12; Bull 52–44, pp. 44–51.

[21] Unless otherwise stated, the elevations in the text of this volume are in feet.

[22] JICPOA Bull 7–44, pp. 53–54; Bull 73–44, p. 6.

of the invasion about 90 percent was in sugar cane and the remainder, along the rocky slopes between the broad terraces and along the coasts, was covered with dense vegetation.[23]

Guam, the largest of the Marianas, is 32 miles long and from 4 to 8 miles wide, with a total surface of over 200 square miles. The northern half is a large coral limestone plateau sloping upward from the lowlands in the middle of the island between the town of Agana on the west coast and Port Pago on the east. It is broken in the south by Mount Barrigada and in the east-central section by Mount Santa Rosa, which rises to an elevation of 870 feet. The southern half of the island is characterized by broken mountain country. Inland from Apra Harbor on the west coast below Agana lie the mountain peaks of Chachao, Alutom, and Tenjo, all above a thousand feet in elevation. South of these peaks and opposite Agat Bay, the ridge slopes down to a 400-foot saddle and then rises again at the southern end of the island to elevations of over 1,200 feet. On the westward side the range slopes steeply to low foothills and narrow belts of lowlands. On the east the slopes are more gradual, ending in a plateau about 400 feet high stretching to the coastal highlands, which rise in steep bluffs from a narrow coastal flat. Five streams pierce the plateau in their eastward course. The highlands of the southern half of Guam are largely volcanic rock except for Orote Peninsula and Cabras Island on the west coast and the east coastal regions, all of which consist of coral limestone. Most of southern Guam, volcanic in origin, was covered with breast-high sword grass, and sparse scrub growth. In the coral limestone regions were found weeds, trailing vines, and tropical vegetation thick enough to make even roads impassible if not cleared continuously. In addition to these undesirable features, the coastal areas abounded in marshes and lowlands that were usually cultivated as rice paddies and that were either deep in mud or covered with cogon grass and weeds reaching heights of fifteen to twenty feet. In short, Guam even more than the other islands of the Marianas contained a superabundance of terrain difficulties to harass and impede the progress of attacking troops.[24]

---

[23] JICPOA Bull 73–44, p. 20.

[24] JICPOA Bull 7–44, pp. 8–10; AFAS, *Guam*, pp. 14–15.

PART TWO

SAIPAN

CHAPTER III

Planning the Invasion

Organization and Composition
of the Attack Force

For the Marianas, as in the case of all operations in the Pacific outside of General MacArthur's jurisdiction, Admiral Nimitz retained over-all command of the campaign. Under him in the chain of command was Vice Adm. Raymond A. Spruance, commander of the Fifth Fleet, and under him Vice Adm. Richmond Kelly Turner, who was to command the Joint Expeditionary Force (Task Force 51), was charged with the actual job of taking the islands. Turner wore a second hat. Until 15 July 1944, he was also in command of the Northern Attack Force (Task Force 52), which was made up of all the amphibious elements assigned to the attack on Saipan and Tinian, and which was one of the two component parts of Task Force 51. Its equivalent for Guam was designated Southern Attack Force (Task Force 53) and was commanded by Rear Adm. Richard L. Conolly. Vice Adm. Marc A. Mitscher's Fast Carrier Task Force (Task Force 58) and Vice Adm. Charles A. Lockwood's Submarine Force, Pacific Fleet (Task Force 17), were assigned supporting missions according to their appropriate capacities. The former operated as part of the Fifth Fleet and the latter directly under Admiral Nimitz. (*Chart 1*)

Tactical command of all troops ashore for the Marianas operation devolved upon Lt. Gen. Holland M. Smith, USMC. General Smith was perhaps as well grounded in the fundamentals of amphibious techniques as any general officer in either the Army or the Marine Corps at that time. In 1941 and 1942 he had supervised the training of the 1st Infantry Division and the 1st Marine Division in basic landing problems on the U.S. east coast. At that time amphibious warfare was still something of a novelty, and United States forces were generally innocent of the fundamentals of launching an assault of seaborne troops against a hostile shore.

For at least two decades before the outbreak of World War II, it is true, the Marine Corps had slowly been piecing together a workable body of amphibious doctrine, and after 1934, in conjunction with the U.S. Navy, it had conducted yearly landing exercises, chiefly on the island of Culebra, Puerto Rico. These had been valuable, indeed indispensable, experiments. They were in no small measure responsible for the ability of American troops to invade the beaches of Africa, Europe, and countless Pacific islands.

Not until after the fall of France did the United States commence to prepare in earnest for large-scale amphibious landings. In February of 1941 General Smith and

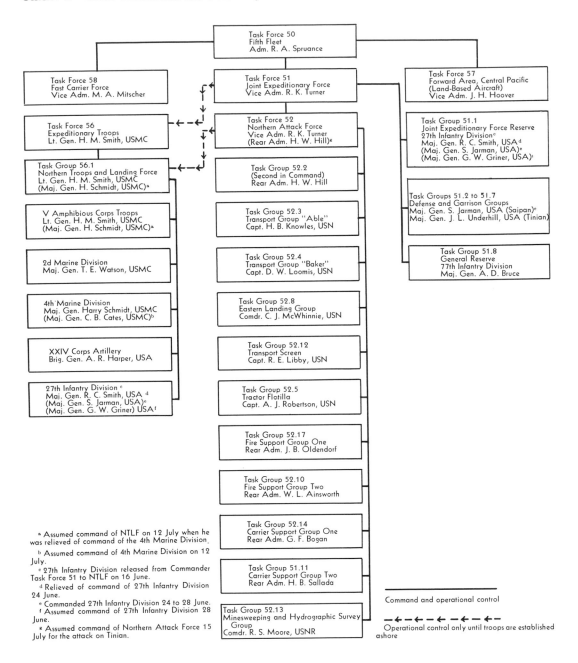

ᵃ Assumed command of NTLF on 12 July when he was relieved of command of the 4th Marine Division.

ᵇ Assumed command of 4th Marine Division on 12 July.

ᶜ 27th Infantry Division released from Commander Task Force 51 to NTLF on 16 June.

ᵈ Relieved of command of 27th Infantry Division 24 June.

ᵉ Commanded 27th Infantry Division 24 to 28 June.

ᶠ Assumed command of 27th Infantry Division 28 June.

ᵍ Assumed command of Northern Attack Force 15 July for the attack on Tinian.

Command and operational control

Operational control only until troops are established ashore his staff planned and oversaw a joint Army-Marine Corps practice landing in the Culebra area. In June of the same year the first full two-division landing exercise was conducted at New River, North Carolina, under their supervision. Another was held on a somewhat smaller scale off Lynn Haven Roads, Virginia, in January of 1942. Two months later, General Smith was ordered to duty as Commander, Amphibious Corps, Atlantic Fleet, an amphibious training command, and later in the year he served in much the same capacity as Commanding General, Amphibious Corps, Pacific Fleet. In September 1943 he and his staff left San Diego for the Central Pacific, where Smith was to be commander of the V Amphibious Corps.[1] As such, he commanded the expeditionary troops that captured Tarawa and Makin in the Gilbert Islands and Kwajalein and Eniwetok in the Marshalls.[2] Now his task was even greater.

Holland Smith's designation for this operation was Commanding General, Expeditionary Troops (Task Force 56). He was directly responsible to Admiral Turner until the amphibious phase was completed. Like Turner, he was to play a dual role. As Commander, Northern Troops and Landing Force (Task Group 56.1), he personally exercised tactical control of all troops ashore during the capture of Saipan. He was relieved on 12 July 1944 from this command (but not from command

of Expeditionary Troops) by Maj. Gen. Harry Schmidt, USMC, who thereafter performed the same role during the seizure of Tinian. Their counterpart on Guam was Maj. Gen. Roy S. Geiger, USMC, the commanding general of III Amphibious Corps and of Southern Troops and Landing Force (Task Group 56.2). Although in this capacity Geiger and Smith held parallel commands, the former was subordinate to the latter as Commanding General, Expeditionary Troops.[3]

The command relationships among General Smith, his naval superiors, and his Marine and Army subordinates, although resembling in complexity the hierarchy of saints, can be reduced to fairly simple terms. In effect Admiral Spruance enjoyed, by delegation from Admiral Nimitz, supreme command of the operation. He retained operational command throughout and upon him devolved the responsibility of determining when the capture and occupation phase of each island had been completed. Tactical command during the amphibious phases of the operation was placed in the hands of Admiral Turner, who exercised it directly at Saipan and through Rear Adm. Harry W. Hill on Tinian and Admiral Conolly on Guam.

The completion of the amphibious phase was determined in each instance by the landing force commander—whenever he decided that the situation warranted it, he was to establish his command ashore. Thereafter, all tactical decisions regarding the disposition of troops would be made by him. On Saipan the landing force commander was Holland Smith, on Tinian Harry Schmidt, and on Guam Roy S. Geiger. On all three islands, however, "overall

---

[1] Holland M. Smith, "The Development of Amphibious Tactics in the U.S. Navy," U.S. Marine Corps *Gazette* (October, 1946), pp. 45–48, 53–55; Holland M. Smith, *Coral and Brass* (New York, Charles Scribner's Sons, 1949), Chs. IV, V, VI. Jeter A. Isely and Philip A. Crowl, *The U.S. Marines and Amphibious War* (Princeton, N.J., Princeton University Press, 1951), Chs. II, III.

[2] See Crowl and Love, *Gilberts and Marshalls.*

[3] TF 56 Rpt FORAGER, pp. 7–8.

Top Naval Commanders in the Marianas Campaign. *From the left: Vice Adm. Raymond A. Spruance, commander of the U.S. Fifth Fleet; Fleet Admiral Ernest J. King, Chief of Naval Operations and Commander in Chief, U.S. Navy; and Admiral Chester A. Nimitz, Commander in Chief, U.S. Pacific Fleet and Pacific Ocean Areas.*

troop command" was retained by General Smith as Commander, Expeditionary Troops.[4]

There were 105,859 assault troops assigned to capture the three islands; 66,779 were allocated to Saipan and Tinian and the remaining 39,080 to Guam. The bulk of the force was made up of two reinforced Army divisions, three reinforced Marine divisions, and a provisional Marine brigade consisting of two regimental combat teams.[5]

The landing on Saipan was to be made by the 2d and 4th Marine Divisions, with the 27th Infantry Division in reserve.[6] All three of these organizations had seen previous action in the Pacific. The 2d Marine Division was activated in San Diego on 1 February 1941. One regiment (2d Marines) took part in the initial attack on Guadalcanal on 7 August 1942, and the remaining two entered that campaign in

---

[4] *Ibid.,* Incl A, Opn Plan 3–44, Annex I, Change 1, 5 May 44.

[5] Commander Joint Expeditionary Force, Marianas (Task Force 51), Report of Amphibious Op-

erations for the Capture of the Marianas Islands (Forager Operation), 25 Aug 44 (hereafter cited as TF 51 Opn Rpt Marianas), p. 6.

[6] See Appendix A, below, for breakdown of troops assigned to Northern Troops and Landing Force.

November and January. The division had also fought the bloody battle of Tarawa, losing over 3,000 casualties there.[7] An independent Marine unit, the 1st Battalion, 29th Marines, which was formed in the spring of 1944 around cadres of 2d Marine Division veterans of Guadalcanal and Tarawa, was attached to the 2d Division for the Saipan operation.[8] In the Marianas, the division was commanded by Maj. Gen. Thomas E. Watson, USMC, who had previously led the Marine and Army regimental combat teams that captured Eniwetok in the Marshalls.

The 4th Marine Division was not form-

[7] Richard W. Johnston, *Follow Me!: The Story of the Second Marine Division in World War II* (New York, Random House, 1948), pp. 7–156.
[8] Bevan G. Cass, ed., *History of the Sixth Marine Division* (Washington, 1948), p. 11.

VICE ADM. RICHMOND KELLY TURNER

ally activated until 16 August 1943, but it was by no means totally unseasoned. In early February 1944 it had captured Roi and Namur Islands in Kwajalein Atoll while troops of the 7th Infantry Division were taking nearby Kwajalein Island in the central Marshalls.[9] The 4th was to be commanded at Saipan by General Schmidt, who had been the division's commander since it was first formed. When General Schmidt relieved Holland Smith of command of the Northern Troops and Landing Force after Saipan was officially declared secure, he in turn was succeeded in command of the 4th Marine Division by Maj. Gen. Clifton B. Cates, a veteran of Guadalcanal and an alumnus of the 1st Marine Division.[10]

The 27th Infantry Division was a National Guard unit of New York State when it was called into federal service in October 1940. Its three regiments, the 105th, 106th, and 165th, had had their headquarters at Troy, Albany, and New York City, respectively.[11] It was the first combat division to leave the United States for Pacific duty and by the war's end had spent a longer time overseas than any National Guard division in the United States Army. In March 1942 advance echelons arrived in Hawaii and for the next year and a half the division served as base defense force, first for the outer islands and then on Oahu after the 25th Division was sent to

[9] Carl W. Proehl, ed., *The Fourth Marine Division in World War II* (Washington, 1946), pp. 16–33; Crowl and Love, *Gilberts and Marshalls*, pp. 304–08.
[10] Proehl, *Fourth Marine Division*, pp. 2–4.
[11] When the division was triangularized in 1942 its fourth regiment, the 108th Infantry, was transferred to the 40th Division. Edmund G. Love, *The 27th Infantry Division in World War II* (Washington, Infantry Journal Press, 1949), pp. 1–2.

LT. GEN. HOLLAND M. SMITH

Guadalcanal. In November 1943 the 165th Infantry, reinforced by the 3d Battalion, 105th Infantry plus organic artillery, engineer, and service units, invaded and captured Makin simultaneously with the 2d Marine Division's assault on Tarawa. Three months later two battalions (1st and 3d) of the 106th Infantry, plus an independent Marine regiment,[12] took Eniwetok Atoll. Thus, of the entire 27th Division only the 1st and 2d Battalions, 105th Infantry, and 2d Battalion, 106th, which secured Majuro Atoll without battle, were unseasoned in atoll warfare.[13]

Maj. Gen. Ralph C. Smith joined the 27th Division as commanding general in November 1942. His previous wartime duty had been with the Military Intelligence Division (G-2) of the War Department General Staff and with the 76th Infantry Division at Fort George G. Meade.[14] His primary job for the next year was to supervise training of the division for forthcoming operations. His own initiation into Pacific warfare came at Makin, where he exercised tactical command over the reinforced 165th Infantry Regiment.

Aside from the three reinforced infantry divisions, the largest single unit attached to Northern Troops and Landing Force for the Marianas operation was the XXIV Corps Artillery (Army). The organization was formally activated on 25 March 1944 and consisted of two battalions each of 155-mm. howitzers and 155-mm. guns. The nucleus of this new organization consisted of coastal artillery and field artillery battalions orginally assigned to the defense of Oahu. One battalion (145th) had participated in the Kwajalein Island landing, but the rest were new to combat.[15] For the Marianas Campaign the corps artillery was commanded by Brig. Gen. Arthur M. Harper, a field artilleryman since 1920. Between the commencement of the war and his assignment to XXIV Corps, he had served as artillery officer of I Corps, of the 30th Infantry Division, and as commanding general of III Corps Artillery.[16]

---

[12] The 22d Marines. This unit later was incorporated into the 1st Marine Provisional Brigade, which fought on Guam. The brigade was subsequently expanded to the 6th Marine Division, which saw action on Okinawa.

[13] Love, *The 27th Infantry Division*, pp. 18–111; Hq 27th Inf Div, Hist of 27th Inf Div From Induction, 15 Oct 40, to Date, 20 Mar 45, pp. 1–3.

[14] General Officers, Service Biographies, DRB AGO, Misc 201.

[15] XXIV Corps Arty Final Rpt on FORAGER Opn, Phases I and III, S-3 Rpt, pp. 1–2.

[16] General Officers, Service Biographies, DRB AGO, Misc 201.

Tactical Planning

Headquarters, V Amphibious Corps, was first alerted to its forthcoming responsibilities in the Marianas on 15 January 1944, when it received Admiral Nimitz' Campaign Plan GRANITE setting forth the concept and outlining a tentative schedule of operations for the Central Pacific area for the year 1944.[17] Operation FORAGER, involving the seizure, occupation, and defense of Saipan, Tinian, and Guam, was included as the final phase of this program.

The first two months of 1944 witnessed an unexpected speed-up in Pacific operations. By 17 February, as already noted, Kwajalein Atoll had been seized, a successful landing had been made on Eniwetok, and, most important, a fast carrier strike against Truk had revealed the alleged impregnability of that once-powerful base to be a myth.

On 13 March, therefore, Nimitz assigned highest priority to the Marianas operation. A week later he issued his Joint Staff Study for FORAGER to all major commanders as a guide for advanced planning. The study indicated that V Amphibious Corps, including the 2d and 4th Marine Divisions, would be mounted in the Hawaiian area for the initial assault on the beaches of Saipan with the 27th Infantry Division in reserve. The III Amphibious Corps, consisting of the 3d Marine Division and the 1st Provisional Marine Brigade, was to be mounted in the Guadalcanal area for an invasion of Guam. The 77th Infantry Division was to be alerted in the Hawaiian area for possible movement to the Mari-

MAJ. GEN. RALPH C. SMITH

anas twenty days after the initial landing on Saipan. The probable target day (D Day) for Saipan was set as 15 June. The date for the invasion of Guam (W Day) was tentatively established as 18 June.[18]

On 12 April General Holland Smith divided his V Amphibious Corps staff into two separate components. One, initially known as the Red Staff, later functioned as Northern Troops and Landing Force (Task Group 56.1) for the capture of Saipan and Tinian. The other portion, first known as Blue Staff, later served as Headquarters Expeditionary Troops (Task Force 56).[19] General Smith's two staffs were heavily augmented by U.S. Army per-

---

[17] See above, p. 13. Planning for the Guam and Tinian phase of FORAGER, although undertaken concurrently with that for Saipan, is discussed in detail in Chapters XIII and XV.

[18] TF 56 Rpt FORAGER, Incl C, G–3 Rpt, pp. 1–2; Commander in Chief Pacific Ocean Areas, FORAGER Joint Staff Study.

[19] Headquarters Northern Troops and Landing Force Report, Marianas, Phase I (Saipan) (hereafter cited as NTLF Rpt Marianas, Phase I), Incl E, G–3 Rpt, p. 1.

sonnel. On the Northern Troops and Landing Force Staff, the assistant chiefs of
staff for both intelligence (G–2) and supply (G–4) were Army officers—Lt. Col.
Thomas R. Yancey and Lt. Col. Joseph C.
Anderson.

There were disadvantages to this cellu-
lar fission, however unavoidable it may
have been. First, there was a decided shortage of trained personnel, especially of special staff sections, officer assistants and
trained clerks, draftsmen, and stenograph-
ers; and second, a shortage of headquarters and corps troops already existed in V
Amphibious Corps.[20] "In effect," as one
commentator put it, "you have here an
army and a corps trying to operate with
a staff too small for a corps." [21]

All echelons prepared their plans simultaneously, and the normal time sequence
of planning from highest echelon down,
with each subordinate basing his own plan
on that of his immediate superior, was seldom achieved. For example, Headquarters
Expeditionary Troops (Task Force 56)
Operation Plan 3–44 was issued on 26
April, whereas the next higher echelon, Admiral Turner's Headquarters Northern Attack Force (Task Force 52) did not issue
its plan until 21 May.[22] Again, it was not
until 12 May that Admiral Spruance, who
was superior to both Turner and Smith,
came out with his operation plan for the
Fifth Fleet.[23]

Northern Troops and Landing Force
Headquarters Operation Plan 3–44 of 1
May summarized all previous plans from
higher echelons and governed the tactical
order of all troops in the proposed landings
on Saipan.[24] The 4th Marine Division (reinforced) was to land on Blue and Yellow
Beaches, extending from the town of
Charan Kanoa south almost to Agingan
Point. Its first objective was to be a line
inland from the beaches about 2,000 yards
at the north and tapering down to the
water's edge at the southern end. Then,
on order, the division was to advance rapidly and seize Aslito airfield and the surrounding terrain. (*Map I.*)

The 2d Marine Division was to land simultaneously to the north of Charan Kanoa
on Green and Red Beaches, seize the first
commanding ground inland, and then advance rapidly and capture Mount Tapotchau and Mount Tipo Pale and the adjacent ground. The XXIV Corps Artillery
was to land on order on beaches to be
designated and to execute missions as assigned.

North of the 2d Marine Division's
beaches, in the vicinity of Tanapag Harbor, a naval force consisting of transport
divisions carrying reserve regiments from
the 2d and 4th Marine Divisions would
conduct a diversionary demonstration to
last from a half hour before sunrise to an
hour after the main landing.

Finally, the 1st Battalion, 2d Marines,
was detached from its parent organization
to perform a separate mission. Originally,
the battalion was to land from destroyer
transports (APD's) on Magicienne Bay on
the southeast side of the island the night
before the main landing on the west coast.

---

[20] *Ibid.*, p. 2.
[21] C&GS School, Ft. Leavenworth, Kans., Second Command Class, Recent Operations, FORAGER
(Marianas), Annex C, p. 2.
[22] Northern Attack Force (TF 52) Attack Order
A11–44, 21 May 44. As Commander, Expeditionary Forces (TF 51), Turner issued his Operation
Plan A10–44 on 6 May 1944.
[23] Comdr Fifth Fleet Opn Plan Central 10–44,
12 May 44; TF 56 Rpt FORAGER, Incl B, G–5
Rpt, p. 5.

---

[24] NTLF Opn Plan 3–44 (FORAGER), 1 May 44.

It would then move rapidly inland, attempt to seize Mount Tapotchau before daylight and hold on until relieved by the main elements of the 2d Marine Division. Later, on 7 May, this order was changed, and the battalion was to be prepared to land on Magicienne Bay or perhaps other beaches after the main landing had been effected and then move west and north to attack enemy positions from the rear.[25] Eventually, the whole scheme was canceled as impractical and involving excessive risks.

The final decision was in all probability the soundest one. To have committed a single battalion armed with nothing heavier than 60-mm. mortars against the formidable defenses the Japanese had set up around Magicienne Bay would in all likelihood have proved disastrous. As events turned out, it took the entire 2d Marine Division ten days to reach Mount Tapotchau's summit.[26]

At headquarters of the 27th Division the problem of planning for landings on Saipan was seriously complicated because there was no certainty as to how the division would be employed. It was the corps reserve and might be committed on Saipan only in part or piecemeal, might be reserved for later action on Tinian and Guam, or might not be used at all. In short, there were a large number and wide variety of possibilities, and operations officers had to plan accordingly. Hence, Ralph Smith's G–3 (operations) section

found it necessary to prepare a total of twenty-one complete plans for tactical employment of the division. A few of these were discarded as higher headquarters made progress in outlining the details of their own plans. By the time the troops sailed from Hawaii it appeared that, if used on Saipan at all, the division would probably be employed in one of three ways and, accordingly, three preferred plans were devised. The first contemplated a landing of two regiments (105th and 165th) on beaches at Magicienne Bay and a rapid advance northwest across the island to capture the seaplane base at Flores Point. The second envisaged a landing by the same two regiments on the beaches north of Charan Kanoa, on the left of the 2d Marine Division, followed by a northward thrust to Garapan Village. If either of these were executed, the third regiment (106th Infantry) would act as floating reserve. Plan number three called for the two assault regiments to go ashore at Tanapag Harbor and prepare to move southward to join forces with the 2d Marine Division. In this case, the 106th Regimental Combat Team (RCT) was to seize Maniagassa Island off Tanapag and support the main assault.[27] A final plan was made only after the division had sailed from Hawaii. On its arrival at Kwajalein the 106th Infantry was attached to the Southern Landing Force and ordered to prepare plans for a landing on Guam.[28]

In actual fact, all of the plans had to be abandoned early in the battle for Saipan. Although it cannot be said that all the laborious preparations by the 27th Division were entirely wasted, it is true that

---

[25] *Ibid.*, Change 1, 7 May 44.

[26] These conclusions are based on a concurrence of opinion of several planning and intelligence officers in the 2d Marine Division and the V Amphibious Corps. See Major Carl W. Hoffman, USMC, *Saipan: The Beginning of the End,* Historical Division, Headquarters, U.S. Marine Corps (Washington, 1950), p. 28.

[27] Hq 27th Inf Div Opn Plans I, II, III.

[28] Hq 106th Inf FORAGER Opn Rpt, p. 2.

neither the division nor the corps head-quarters had on hand a detailed plan that exactly fitted the situation as it had developed by the time the division was committed.

Preliminary naval and aerial bombard-ment of the Marianas was planned along lines by then well established in the Central Pacific theater. Landings at Tarawa and in the Marshalls left little doubt of the necessity for heavy preliminary pounding of the beaches from both the air and the sea if excessive American casualties were to be avoided.[29]

For Saipan, an impressive armada of ships and planes was allocated to do the job. A total of fifty-five ships was original-ly scheduled to deliver fire against the main island: 7 fast battleships from Marc Mitscher's fast carrier force, 4 old battle-ships, 2 heavy cruisers, 3 light cruisers, 15 destroyers, and 24 LCI gunboats (LCI (G)'s). Simultaneously with this bombard-ment, the smaller island of Tinian was to be subjected to similar fire from an additional 33 ships, including 3 old battle-ships, 4 heavy cruisers, 2 light cruisers, 7 destroyers, and 24 LCI (G)'s.[30]

Two days before the scheduled landing, fast battleships and destroyers of Task Force 58 were to bombard Saipan and Tinian, destroy aircraft, put airfields out of commission, destroy coast defense and antiaircraft batteries, burn off cane fields in the landing area, deliver antipersonnel fire, and, finally, cover mine-sweeping oper-ations off the western shore line. Next day, old battleships and smaller fire support ships of Turner's Task Force 52 were scheduled to deliver counterbattery fire,

area bombardment, and interdiction fire, commencing at daybreak and continuing throughout the day. Their primary mission was to destroy as many coast defense guns, antiaircraft batteries, artillery weapons, and other enemy defenses and personnel as possible. Ships were directed to remain well beyond the range of enemy shore bat-teries on that day, which meant in effect that their fire would be delivered at ranges in excess of 10,000 yards.[31] They were instructed to pay particular attention to gun positions at Magicienne Bay and to the beach defenses and installations on the selected landing beaches on the west coast. Also, they were to cover mine-sweeping op-erations and beach reconnaissance by the underwater demolition teams, whose job it was to inspect the beaches and ap-proaches thereto for mines, underwater obstacles, and explosives. Simultaneously, ships of Admiral Conolly's Task Force 53 were to work over neighboring Tinian in much the same manner, although these vessels were to conserve most (80 percent) of their ammunition allowance for preas-sault bombardment of Guam.[32]

For D Day (15 June) on Saipan the schedule of fires was to be stepped up sharply, with particular attention to be paid to the landing beaches. Counterbat-tery fire was to commence at dawn and to cover known and suspected positions of enemy coast defense guns and antiaircraft, dual-purpose, and field artillery batteries both on Saipan and on Tinian. Ships were to be in position to bombard beach de-fenses and possible flanking positions, with close-range fire to commence at the low-

---

[29] See Crowl and Love, *Gilberts and Marshalls.*
[30] NTLF Opn Plan 3-44 (FORAGER), 1 May 44, Annex Charlie, pp. 1-2.

[31] TF 56 Rpt FORAGER, Rpt on Naval Gunfire Support, p. 10.
[32] *Ibid.,* pp. 2-4; TF 52 Attack Order A11-44, 21 May 44, Annex C, pp. 3-9.

water line and extend 400 yards inland. Area bombardment of secondary defenses such as supply installations, barracks, and bivouac areas was to be continued, as was supporting bombardment of Tinian by Task Force 53. Shortly before the scheduled landing hour (H Hour) on Saipan, close supporting fires were to be delivered against the Charan Kanoa beaches and in the Tanapag Harbor area, the latter being in support of the demonstration landing and therefore on a smaller scale. All naval gunfire, except for counterbattery fire necessary to the protection of ships and landing craft, was to cease for a half hour (between H minus 90 and H minus 60) to permit a low-altitude aerial strike on the beaches, and then resume for the hour before the landing. For the hour remaining before the troops were scheduled to touch shore, battleships, cruisers, and destroyers were directed to move in to close range and bombard the selected landing beaches and adjacent installations.[33]

Then, just before the scheduled landing hour, when the assault troops were assembled in the leading waves of amphibian tractors, twenty-four LCI gunboats, equipped with rockets and 20-mm. and 40-mm. guns, were to move slowly forward toward the beach in line-abreast formation, just ahead of the first wave of amphibian tanks. As the LCI's reached the line where the heavier fire support ships lay to, they were directed to open fire on the beach areas with their 40-mm. guns. Those off the northern beaches (Green and Red) were to stop dead in the water at this line, let the leading waves pass through them, and continue to fire as long as safety to the landing craft permitted. No rockets

were to be fired by the northern group of gun boats since the reef in this area would keep them out of effective range of the beach (1,100 yards). At the southern beaches (Blue and Yellow), LCI(G)'s were ordered to proceed at a distance two hundred yards ahead of the first landing craft until they reached a line 1,000 yards off the beach, then fire their rockets and 40-mm. guns as long as safety allowed.[34]

Just as impressive as the plans for preparatory naval fire were those for prelanding aerial bombardment. Mitscher's Task Force 58 had made its first strike against the islands of Guam, Rota, Tinian, and Saipan on 23 February,[35] and thereafter on the occasions when aerial reconnaissance missions were flown across the islands[36] some bombs were released, although with dubious results. According to the original plans, however, not until two days before the scheduled landing on Saipan would a heavy and prolonged aerial bombardment of that island and Tinian be undertaken. The fast carriers of Mitscher's force, working in conjunction with escort carriers under command of Admiral Turner, would undertake this task.[37] One D minus 2 (13 June) planes from the fast carrier force were to make fighter sweeps on airfields on both Saipan and Tinian to destroy enemy aircraft. On the same day thirty-three planes would deliver counterbattery fire against guns firing on the mine sweepers. Combat air patrol and antisubmarine patrol missions were to be flown simultaneously. The next day a more intensive pro-

---

[33] CTF 52 Attack Order A11-44, App. 6A to Annex C.

[34] *Ibid.*, App. 6A to Annex C, p. 2; App. 5 to Annex J, p. 14.

[35] CINCPAC-CINCPOA Opns in POA, Feb 44.

[36] See below, pp. 50-51.

[37] CTF 51 Opn Plan A10-44, Annex F; CTF 56 Opn Plan 3-44, Incl A to TF 56 Rpt FORAGER, Annex D; CTF 56.1 Opn Plan 3-44, Annex D.

gram of destruction was to be undertaken. Inland coast defense and dual-purpose and antiaircraft guns were to be bombed heavily. Cane fields not already burned were to be fired. Other priority targets were inland defense installations and structures, the buildings around Aslito airfield, and communications and transportation facilities on the west coast of Saipan including small craft, radio stations, observation towers, railroad and road junctions, and vehicles. The same day six smoke planes were to provide protection for underwater demolition teams operating close offshore, if necessary. Also, vertical photographs were to be made of all beaches from Tanapag Harbor to Agingan Point.

On 15 June, in addition to continuing most of the above duties, a heavy half-hour aerial attack on both islands was to be carried out and to be terminated only one hour before the scheduled landings. During this period naval gunfire was to be lifted so that planes could fly in low for precision bombing and rocketing of enemy installations. A total of 60 fighters, 51 dive bombers, and 54 torpedo bombers were to take part in this final preliminary saturation attack. Thereafter, until the carriers were withdrawn, the carrier-based planes would act as aerial observers for land-based artillery make photographic sorties, lay smoke on request, and provide deep and close support for the troops ashore.

For the critical movement of assault troops from ship to shore the plans followed, with some variation, the pattern used so successfully in the Marshalls operation.[38] Astern of the LCI gunboats, amphibian tanks (LVT(A)'s) would con-

stitute the bulk of the leading wave. They mounted either 75-mm. howitzers or 37-mm. guns plus machine guns, and their first job was to lead the waves of assault amphibian tractors (LVT's) from the reef's edge to the shore line. The LVT(A)'s would provide the only close fire support for the assault troops during the critical few minutes between the time that naval gunfire and aerial bombardment were compelled to lift and the time that the infantrymen actually hit the beach's edge. Moreover, for the Saipan landing the mission of the amphibian tanks was not to cease at the shore line. On the 4th Marine Division beaches, the tanks of the 708th Amphibian Tank Battalion (Army) were to push inland approximately 1,500 yards to the first objective line and set up a perimeter defense closely supported by infantry in the amphibian tractors.[39] To the northward, in the 2d Marine Division's zone of action, the 2d Armored Amphibian Battalion (Marine) was ordered to move four companies of its amphibian tanks inland only about three hundred yards to the tractor control line and there cover the debarkation of assault troops from its LVT(A)'s. Thereafter, most of the amphibian tanks were to remain under cover and engage targets as far inland as 1,500 yards, but only on call from the infantry.[40] Thus, LVT(A)'s were scheduled to proceed beyond the beaches' edge and to act, to all intents and purposes, as land tanks until such time as heavier tanks could be brought ashore. This was an innovation in amphibious techniques and one that, as

---

[38] See Crowl and Love, *Gilberts and Marshalls,* pp. 172–82.

[39] NTLF Rpt Marianas, Phase I, Incl H, LVT Rpt, Rpt of 708th Armd Amph Tank Bn, 5 Jul 44, p. 3.

[40] *Ibid.,* Incl G, Rpt of 2d Armd Amph Bn, 1 Jul 44, p. 1.

events developed, proved to be of dubious merit.[41]

Training and Rehearsals

With the conclusion of the Marshalls operation, it became apparent that the future promised a shift in the Central Pacific Area from atoll warfare to operations on larger land areas that were both mountainous and jungle-covered. Hence, even before the official warning orders came down from corps headquarters, all three divisions assigned to Northern Troops and Landing Force had commenced training their troops to meet the particular conditions that the forthcoming campaign would impose.

The 27th Division, stationed on Oahu, made an early study of the methods of burning sugar cane and the movement of foot troops through freshly burned fields. Groups from all of the infantry regiments conducted exercises in methods of burning fields, cutting passage through them, and the movement of large and small numbers of troops through standing and freshly burned cane.

The division also concentrated heavily on training its men in combined tank-infantry operations. All infantry companies engaged in field exercises involving the use of tanks in direct support, a particularly important exercise for the Army division since its tank battalions were not organic but were specifically attached to the infantry for the Marianas operation. Other specialized training included intense education in amphibious communications procedures. The 295th Joint Assault Signal Company (JASCO) was attached to the division sufficiently far in advance to allow for thorough familiarization of the infantry

battalions with the functions and abilities of the various JASCO teams.

All units were instructed in the proper organization and plan of fires for a night perimeter defense. A period of five weeks was devoted to the study and practice of methods of loading 105-mm. howitzers in amphibian trucks (DUKW's). Combat engineers were instructed in the use of flame throwers and demolitions for the reduction of fortified positions. The 27th Cavalry Reconnaissance Troop conducted rubber boat training with emphasis on beach reconnaissance, hydrographic studies, and night landings.[42]

The 2d Marine Division boasted excellent training facilities in the vicinity of its "Camp Tarawa" on the main island of Hawaii. It too held special exercises in the techniques of fighting through sugar cane. Also, the jungle and mountainous terrain on Hawaii approximated the type that the division would meet on Saipan and was ideal for the simulation of realistic combat conditions.[43]

The 4th Marine Division fared less well. Its camp site on Maui was new, its living and training facilities were incomplete. Hence, camp construction and training had to be carried out simultaneously—a situation that, though common enough in the Pacific, was never desirable. Nevertheless, by instituting emergency measures for the acquisition of suitable land and through co-operation with the Navy and Army authorities, "a fairly satisfactory schedule of individual, unit and combined training was completed," according to the division's commanding officer.[44]

[41] See below, pp. 85–87.

[42] 27th Inf Div Rpt FORAGER, G–3 Combat Rpt, pp. 1–5.

[43] 2d Marine Div SAR, Phase I, FORAGER, p. 1.

[44] 4th Marine Div Opns Rpt Saipan, p. 6.

The chief training problem facing XXIV Corps Artillery was that of converting two coast artillery battalions into field artillery battalions. The XXIV Corps Artillery was not activated as a unit until the end of March 1944. At that time the 225th Field Artillery Group was alerted to take part in the Marianas operation and relieved of its defensive mission on Oahu. Two of its field artillery battalions were detached, and the 32d Coast Artillery Battalion and 2d Battalion, 55th Coast Artillery, were attached. As finally organized, the XXIV Corps Artillery was made up of one 155-mm. howitzer group of two battalions and one 155-mm. gun group of two battalions drawn from available field artillery personnel and supplemented by coast artillery personnel. Because of its infancy as an organization and the lack of combat experience of most of its personnel, adequate training for the unit was urgent.

Coast artillery officers were immediately given an intensive education in basic field artillery methods, and a similar program for enlisted personnel followed. Demonstrations held by field artillery batteries and battalions were followed by four field exercises per week. On 1 May two batteries of the 53d Field Artillery Battalion were loaded on an LST and taken to Maui to experiment with methods of loading 155-mm. guns and to obtain training in unloading across sandy beaches. Experiments were also conducted in loading the 155's on the smaller LCT's (landing craft, tank).

Because of the shortness of time and its relative lack of basic training, XXIV Corps Artillery did not participate in the final grand rehearsal. Instead, the two-month intensive training period culminated in a corps artillery field exercise held during the rehearsal period.[45]

On 14 May ships carrying the two Marine divisions with their full loads of equipment rendezvoused in the area of Maalea Bay, Hawaii, for final rehearsals before shoving off to Saipan. LVT's and other amphibious craft were launched; the assault battalions practiced ship-to-shore movements; shore party team personnel and beach parties were landed with their communications equipment; artillery was beached and dragged ashore. On 16 and 17 May each of the divisions made a co-ordinated landing on the island of Maui and battle conditions were simulated as far as was practicable. However, in view of the fact that the island was populated, ship and aerial bombardment had to be "constructive" only. Moreover, the landing beaches were separated and maneuver area ashore was extremely limited, preventing rehearsal of co-ordinated movements inland and any extensive deployment of troops once they had reached the shore line. As an exercise in ship-to-shore movement the rehearsal was useful, but it failed to give the troops an adequate foretaste of the problems involved in consolidating a beachhead once they had landed.[46]

Finally, on 19 May, a simulated landing was made jointly by the two Marine divisions on the nearby island of Kahoolawe. This time troops approached the shore under actual cover of naval and aerial fire. On reaching a line 300 yards from the beaches they turned back, but in every other respect the exercise was a full-dress

---

[45] XXIV Corps Arty Final Rpt on FORAGER Opn, Phases I and III, S-3 Rpt, pp. 1-3.
[46] 2d Marine Div SAR, Phase I, FORAGER, Sec. III, pp. 1-2; 4th Marine Div Opns Rpt Saipan, Incl A, pp. 7-8.

rehearsal of the plans for the forthcoming landing on Saipan, with units, positions, intervals, distances, and other details as prescribed in the operation plans. This was followed immediately by a second exercise in which air and naval gunfire did not take part. Then troops were re-embarked in the vessels in which they were scheduled to sail overseas and returned to their respective rehabilitation areas.[47]

The only incident that had marred last-minute training was the loss of three deck-loaded LCT's over the sides of the LST's that were carrying them to the rehearsals. This resulted in twenty-nine casualties to the 2d Marine Division. Moreover, two of these LCT's had been specially equipped with 4.2-inch mortars. Plans called for their employment on Saipan as support ships to supplement the rocket-firing LCI's in the last minutes between the lifting of heavy ships' fire and the landing of troops. Their loss during rehearsals prevented the equipment from being tested until a later operation and deprived the assault troops of that much additional naval support.[48]

From 18 to 24 May the 27th Division (minus its artillery), fully loaded on three transport divisions, conducted similar rehearsals. The exercise emphasized the technique of debarking and landing a large number of troops with a limited number of boats, a situation thought likely to occur if reserve troops had to be landed at all on Saipan. Ship-to-shore communication was established although, as in the case of the two Marine divisions, no supplies were un-loaded since all ships had already been assault loaded for the actual landing.[49]

Loading and Embarkation

The task of carrying three reinforced divisions and almost seven thousand corps and garrison troops with all their supplies and equipment over a distance of 3,200 miles from Hawaii to Saipan was the heaviest yet imposed upon the Navy in the Pacific war. To accomplish it, Admiral Nimitz assembled a flotilla of 110 naval transport vessels of all varieties—37 troop transports (APA's and AP's), 11 cargo ships (AKA's and AK's), 5 LSD's (landing ships, dock), 47 LST's, and 10 APD's.[50]

In addition, a whole division of Liberty ships had to be organized to transport the 106th Regimental Combat Team because of the scarcity of Navy troop transports in the area.[51]

All together, a total of 74,986.6 measurement tons of cargo representing 7,845,194 cubic feet was loaded. By comparison, during the invasion of Kwajalein in January 1944, only 49,283 tons were carried in the assault shipping.[52] Nimitz' operation plan provided that assault and garrison forces should be allowed 32 days of Class I supplies (rations), 20 days of Class II (organizational and individual equipment), 20 days of Class III (fuels and lubricants), 20 days of Class IV (miscellaneous), and

---

[47] *Ibid.*

[48] 2d Marine Div SAR, Phase I, Forager, Sec. III, p. 1; United States Army Forces Central Pacific Area (USAFICPA), Participation in the Marianas Operation, Jun–Sep 44, Vol. I, p. 58.

[49] 27th Inf Div Rpt Forager, G–3 Combat Rpt, p. 5.

[50] Commander in Chief, U.S. Fleet, Amphibious Operations, Invasion of the Marianas, June to August 1944 (Washington, 1944) (COMINCH P–007), V–1.

[51] TF 56 Rpt Forager, Incl G, TQM Rpt, p. 7.

[52] COMINCH P–007, V–4; TF 56 Rpt Forager, Incl G, TQM Rpt, p. 3.

7 (CINCPOA) units of fire for ground weapons and 10 for antiaircraft weapons.[53]

Staging areas for the three divisions were widely separated and not all were conveniently located. Ships assigned to the 2d Marine Division loaded at Hilo on the main island of Hawaii, those of the 4th Marine Division at Kahului, Maui, and those of the 27th Division at Oahu. The ports of Kahului and Hilo were ill suited to loading the two Marine divisions efficiently. The piers at each could berth only four ships alongside the dock at one time. There were not enough dock cranes, stevedore equipment, and warehouses. There were no dock lighting facilities, and it was difficult for LST's to beach properly.[54] Also, Hilo was some sixty miles away from the 2d Marine Division's Camp Tarawa, which complicated the problem of loading both troops and equipment.[55]

Standard combat unit loading procedures were followed as a rule, but shipping shortages sometimes made this impossible.[56] This was especially true of supplies and equipment belonging to V Amphibious Corps troops, XXIV Corps Artillery, and garrison troops. The last available AP in the Pacific (USS *G. F. Elliott*), two AK's

(USS *Hercules* and USS *Jupiter*), and two LST's were assigned to lift these units, but the shipping space was inadequate. Excess personnel (approximately 4,000) were distributed among the transports carrying the two Marine divisions. As a result most of these units, especially the XXIV Corps Artillery, were separated from their cargo. In other words these particular units were "convoy unit loaded"—which was highly undesirable from the point of view of tactical disposition.[57]

Even after parceling out more than half of its attached troops to the ships carrying the Marine divisions, V Amphibious Corps still did not have enough room aboard its own vessels. It was impossible to combat load its cargo. To have tried to vertically load each of the twenty-five units carrying cargo on the corps ships would have meant leaving from 25 to 35 percent of the cargo behind. The upshot was that a top priority was assigned to corps artillery and the corps signal battalion, and the remainder of the units' equipment was stowed wherever it could be fitted in.[58]

As early as 1 May 1944, Holland Smith's headquarters had ordered 25 to 50 percent of all supplies and two to five units of fire to be palletized.[59] The object was to per-

---

[53] CINCPAC-CINCPOA Opn Plan 3-44, Annex C; TF 56 Rpt FORAGER, Annex E, G-4 Rpt, pp. 4-5; for CINCPOA units of fire, see Appendix B, below.

[54] TF 56 Rpt FORAGER, Annex G, TQM Rpt, pp. 13-16.

[55] 2d Marine Div SAR, Phase I, FORAGER, Sec. II, p. 1.

[56] Combat unit loading is defined as the method "in which certain units, selected because of their probable employment to meet tactical situations immediately upon landing, are completely loaded in a single transport with at least their essential combat equipment, transportation, and supplies available for immediate debarkation with the troops." (Office of Naval Operations, Division of Fleet Training, Landing Operations Doctrine United States Navy, 1938 (FTP 167), p. 211.)

This means, in effect, that materials most urgently needed will be stowed near the top of ships' holds and immediately under hatch covers. Lower priority supplies will be stowed lower in the holds and away from the hatch covers where they cannot be unloaded without first removing everything between.

[57] Convoy unit loading is defined as the method in which "the troops with their equipment and supplies are loaded in transports of the same convoy, but not necessarily in the same vessel." FTP 167, p. 211.

[58] TF 56 Rpt FORAGER, Incl G, TQM Rpt, pp. 6-7.

[59] V Phib Corps Order 3-44, 1 May 44, par. (g). Pallets are wooden, sledlike structures to which supplies can be lashed.

mit rapid transfer from the beach to inland dumps by using tractors to drag the pallets instead of resorting to the older method of trucking loose supplies inland employing manpower to load the trucks. From the outset, the two Marine divisions were lukewarm toward the project, and in the end loaded only a few pallets. The 27th Infantry Division, however, had had several months' experience in handling palletized cargo and was enthusiastic about this technique for loading and unloading supplies.[60] The division not only complied with corps orders, but went beyond it and palletized between 80 and 90 percent of all supplies.[61]

One reason for the Marine divisions' failure to follow suit was inexperienced labor and a shortage of equipment. The 4th Marine Division reported that it could procure only enough material to palletize 10 to 15 percent of all supplies and that the job was done so poorly that some pallets broke down during handling.[62] In the end, the division decided that palletization of supplies at least for the initial stages of the assault was not worth the trouble. The marines argued that palletized supplies took up too much space aboard ship, were difficult to transfer from one type of landing craft to another, and required too much extra equipment. Furthermore, it was contended that pallets were not practical where dumps were located more than 500 yards inland and where reefs were encountered.[63]

Neither corps headquarters nor the 27th Division agreed. Holland Smith's transport quartermaster maintained that the "reasons for palletization overbalance the negative effects," and cited as the primary benefits the rapid unloading of landing craft at the beaches and the release of large working parties formerly engaged in transferring cargo from landing craft to trucks.[64] The 27th Division headquarters was so enthusiastic about the process that it diverted from training one and sometimes two companies of infantry in addition to a platoon of engineers for a period of six weeks just to palletize supplies.[65]

Amphibian tanks and tractors, the all-important vehicles of assault, were as usual transported aboard LST's. Each LST carried seventeen LVT's, loaded in two rows of eight with the odd one secured on the ramp. By loading LVT's in this manner, about fifteen feet of clear space remained on the after portion of the LST tank deck, and emergency supplies were "preloaded" thereon. In addition to the amphibian vehicles, each LST carried more than 300 marines from Hawaii to Eniwetok. There, they received fifty to seventy-five more from transports to fill the complement of the assault waves. A serious LST shortage almost occurred when six were destroyed by fire at Pearl Harbor on 21 May. However, LST's originally assigned to the garrison force were used as substitutes, and loading and embarking was only delayed twenty-four hours.[66]

One impediment to well-planned and well-co-ordinated combat loading was that

[60] TF 56 Rpt FORAGER, Incl G, TQM Rpt, p. 15.

[61] 27th Inf Div Rpt FORAGER, G–4 Rpt, Supply Phase of FORAGER Opn, Incl 3, p. 1.

[62] 4th Marine Div Opns Rpt Saipan, Annex D, Supply and Evacuation, p. 6.

[63] Ibid., Annex E, p. 23.

[64] TF 56 Rpt FORAGER, Annex G, TQM Rpt, p. 33.

[65] 27th Inf Div Rpt FORAGER, G–4 Rpt, Supply Phase of FORAGER Opn, p. 3.

[66] TF 56 Rpt FORAGER, Incl G, TQM Rpt, pp. 10, 17.

troop transport quartermasters too often received insufficient or inaccurate information on the characteristics of the ships assigned to them. Precise data on the location, size, and shape of ships' holds, the number and location of hatches and winches and other equipment, plus myriad other details concerning ship structure are essential to proper combat loading. This was not always forthcoming. New ships arrived at the very last moment, and there was little or no time available to obtain correct ships' characteristics.[67] For two AP's (USS *Storm King* and USS *John Land*) assigned to the 4th Marine Division, no characteristics were obtainable before actual loading. The division's supply section had been instructed to assume that these vessels' characteristics were similar to those of another AP, USS *LaSalle*. Upon arrival of the ships, it was discovered there was no such resemblance, that the new ships were not entirely suitable for combat loading, and that the winchmen were inexperienced and too few in number to cope with the problems at hand. Hence, many valuable items of equipment, especially twenty-five $2\frac{1}{2}$-ton cargo trucks, had to be left behind.[68]

In spite of these and kindred difficulties, the three divisions met Admiral Turner's loading schedu'. By 14 May both the Marine divisions were aboard their transports and ready to depart for rehearsals, completely loaded except for a few last-minute items. By 18 May the 27th Division was also set to go.[69]

After a brief period of rehabilitation following rehearsals, all units of Northern Troops and Landing Force once again boarded their ships and prepared to set sail for the final ordeal. The slower LST's carrying assault elements of the two Marine divisions sortied from Pearl Harbor on 25 May. On 29 and 30 May two groups of naval transports followed. All ships carrying the assault troops rendezvoused at Eniwetok, where last-minute intelligence data was disseminated and additional troops assigned to the initial landing waves were transferred from transports to LST's. By 11 June the last of the attack transports had weighed anchor in Eniwetok lagoon and the mighty convoy, split into four separate groups, was steaming westward through hostile waters toward still more hostile shores.[70] Well to the rear came the transport and tractor (LST) groups carrying the reserve troops, the 27th Infantry Division. These had sailed from Pearl Harbor between 25 May and 1 June and had rendezvoused at Kwajalein. There, the 106th Regimental Combat Team was informed that it would undoubtedly be detached to the Southern Attack Force for the invasion of Guam. Otherwise, the voyage for all units was uneventful.[71]

The Prospects Ahead: Intelligence of the Enemy

While still at anchor in Eniwetok, the intelligence section of Headquarters, Expeditionary Troops (Task Force 56), received a final batch of aerial photographs

[67] *Ibid.,* Incl G, TQM Rpt, p. 17.
[68] 4th Marine Div Opns Rpt Saipan, Annex D, p. 3.
[69] TF 56 Rpt FORAGER, Incl G, TQM Rpt, p. 16, and Incl JJ; 27th Inf Div Rpt FORAGER, G-3 Rpt, p. 5.

[70] 2d Marine Div SAR, Phase I, FORAGER, Sec. IV, pp. 1-2; 4th Marine Div Opns Rpt Saipan, p. 12.
[71] 27th Inf Div Rpt FORAGER, G-3 Rpt, p. 6; 27th Inf Div Arty Rpt FORAGER, p. 6.

of Saipan and the southern Marianas. These had been made on 28 May for Saipan and on 29 May and 7 June for Guam. They were disseminated to the two Marine divisions before their departure from Eniwetok on 11 June, although the initial assault elements aboard the LST's had left before the new information could reach them. Hence, the leading waves of troops would make their landings on the basis of information of the enemy situation as derived from photographic sorties flown on 18 April.[72]

A final G–2 "Summary of the Enemy Situation" was prepared by Holland Smith's intelligence section on 13 June and represents the last-minute estimate of enemy potentialities in the Marianas before the actual landing.[73] This document predicted that the Japanese had on Saipan alone from 15,000 to 17,600 troops, with an additional 10,150 to 10,750 on nearby Tinian. Of the total, 9,100 to 11,000 were thought to be ground combat troops located on Saipan. The rest of the garrison, it was believed, was made up of air base personnel, maintenance and construction personnel (including Koreans), and a home guard. This represented a considerable increase over an estimate made a month earlier (9 May), which put the total number of enemy troops on Saipan at 9,000 to 10,000 and on Tinian at 7,500 to 8,500.[74]

Saipan had three airfields in varying stages of preparedness. Aslito Naval Air Station in the south was 3,600 feet in length and believed to be fully operational; an emergency landing strip 3,280 feet in length had been sited in the area of Charan

Kanoa; and at Marpi Point a large airfield (4,300 feet) was still under construction and was considered to be nonoperational. In addition, a major seaplane base at Flores Point in Tanapag Harbor was thought to be fully operational.

The latest estimate of air strength on Saipan before the carriers' strikes was a total of 152 aircraft. However, on 11 and 12 June 140 aircraft were destroyed on Saipan, Tinian, and Guam, and since no aerial opposition was encountered at Saipan on 13 June, Japanese aerial resistance from Saipan was thought unlikely.[75]

The newest photographs of Saipan revealed several significant increases in the number of gun installations since 18 April, when the last photographic sortie had been flown. The most notable of these were an increase of 32 percent in the number of heavy antiaircraft guns, 28 percent in medium antiaircraft guns, and 37 percent in machine guns.[76]

The following table indicates the number and type of enemy installations estimated to be emplaced on Saipan as of 29 May 1944:

Blockhouses	1
Possible blockhouses	1
Coast defense guns	13
Possible coast defense guns	2
Dual-mount dual-purpose guns	5
Single-mount dual-purpose guns	11
Single-mount heavy AA	49
Possible single-mount heavy AA	9
Single-mount heavy AA emplacements	5
Single-mount medium AA	134
Possible single-mount medium AA	8
Single-mount medium AA emplacements	1
Covered artillery emplacements	3
Pillboxes	37
Possible pillboxes	4
Machine guns (20-mm. or under) AA	264
Possible machine guns (20-mm. or under) AA	6
Machine gun emplacements	4
Empty emplacements	23

[72] TF 56 Rpt FORAGER, Incl D, G–2 Rpt, p. 2.
[73] Ibid., Annex F, pp. 1–15.
[74] NTLF Rpt Marianas, Phase I, G–2 Rpt, App. A, G–2 V Phib Corps Special Study of Enemy Strength in the Southern Marianas, 9 May 44.
[75] TF 56 Rpt FORAGER, Incl D, G–2 Rpt, Annex F, p. 1.
[76] Ibid., pp. 5–6.

According to intelligence estimates, the preferred landing beaches off Charan Kanoa were defended by a well-developed system of trenches, tank traps, pillboxes, and machine guns. It was assumed that infantry elements on the island would be assigned chiefly to the defense of this area. The absence of extensive field fortifications and the presence of heavy-caliber weapons between Garapan and Flores Point suggested to intelligence officers that the defense of that area would be primarily the responsibility of artillery and antiaircraft elements of whatever guard forces, special landing forces, and antiaircraft units that were stationed on the island. Intelligence officers also believed that the machine guns around Aslito field, at the southern end of Charan Kanoa strip, and on the eastern end of Marpi Point would probably be manned by similar elements and by air base defense antiaircraft personnel.

Intelligence also led the officers to believe that the enemy probably had a tank detachment or at least an amphibious tank unit on Saipan. This, plus other factors, suggested that the Japanese contemplated a strong defense at the shore line combined with a mobile defense in the area behind the preferred landing beaches.[77]

The last assumption was essentially correct, even if some of the detailed estimates as to the number of enemy troops and installations proved to be well under the mark. At any rate, nothing in the last-minute intelligence surveys indicated that a basic change in the preferred landing plans was necessary. The die was cast. Under mild skies and through gently rolling seas the advance groups of troop-laden ships moved in slow procession toward the battleground.

---

[77] *Ibid.,* p. 7.

CHAPTER IV

The Enemy

Prewar Japanese Activities
in the Marianas

At the termination of World War I Japan, as one of the Allied powers, was awarded a Class C mandate over all of the islands and atolls north of the equator that had formerly been in the possession of the German Empire. These included the Marshalls, the Carolines, the Palaus, and the Marianas except for Guam. Under the terms of Article 22 of the Covenant of the League of Nations, Japan agreed to refrain from "the establishment of fortifications or military and naval bases" in her newly acquired territories. Eleven years later Japan gave the required two years notice of her intention to withdraw from the League and did so officially on 27 March 1935.[1]

Whether or not the Japanese made any active effort to fortify or garrison the mandates before 1933 remains in doubt, although their policy of excluding foreign visitors from these scattered islands inevitably raised suspicions in the minds of interested westerners as to what was going on behind the silken curtain. In any event after her withdrawal from the League and before the outbreak of hostilities it is certain that Japan embarked on a program of military construction in the area. This was done in spite of the fact that Japan's secession from the League was a unilateral act and in international law did not relieve her of accepted obligations under the League Covenant.[2]

From 1934 to 15 November 1940, the Japanese Government is known to have appropriated at least 14,456,800 yen ($3,939,478) for construction in the Marianas alone.[3] For the year beginning 15 No-

---

[1] Denys P. Myers, *Handbook of the League of Nations* (Boston and New York, World Peace Foundation, 1935), p. 378; International Military Tribunal for the Far East (IMTFE), International Prosecution Section (IPS) Doc. 6527, p. 13. The proceedings of the IMTFE and attached documents are filed in the Law Library, Office of the Judge Advocate General, Department of the Navy.

[2] IMTFE Proceedings, pp. 39, 43, 205–16, 408–15; Earl S. Pomeroy, *Pacific Outpost: American Strategy in Guam and Micronesia* (Stanford, Calif., Stanford University Press, 1951).

It should be noted that Japan was under no obligation to the United States not to fortify the mandated islands. The United States was not a signatory to the League Covenant. By the Five Power Treaty signed at Washington in 1922, Japan agreed with the United States and Great Britain to maintain the *status quo* in regard to fortifications and naval bases in certain of her island possessions, but the Pacific mandates were not included in the agreement. See Harold and Margaret Sprout, *Toward a New Order of Sea Power* (Princeton, N.J., Princeton University Press, 1940), Chs. X, XIII, and App. B.

[3] For this chapter, dollar value of the yen has been obtained by averaging the dollar value of the yen for the years 1934–40. Figures for all conversions from yen to dollars have been taken from *Japan Statistical Yearbook: 1949* (Nihon Statistical Association, 1949), p. 612.

vember 1940, a minimum of 121,189,666 yen ($28,406,858) was appropriated for construction in the Marianas, Carolines, and Marshalls, of which 15,605,885 yen ($3,658,019) was allocated to the Marianas. Of the total of over thirty million yen ($7,032,000) spent in the Marianas, about 60 percent was assigned to Saipan, 25 percent to Tinian, and 15 percent to Pagan. About 40 percent of the Saipan appropriation was for air installations, the remainder being allocated to fortifications, barracks, storage buildings, offices, water supply facilities, ammunition storage facilities, and communications stations. Practically all of the money allocated to Tinian and Pagan was earmarked for airfield construction.[4]

In 1934 work began on Aslito airfield, located near the southern end of Saipan. Aslito was the principal Japanese air base in the Marianas, and its capture and development was to be the main objective of the American forces that invaded the Marianas in 1944. In addition to Aslito, a seaplane base in Tanapag Harbor, Saipan, was completed in 1935. Five years later nearby Tinian could boast an airfield costing about 7.5 million yen ($1,758,000).

Although various Japanese spokesmen after the close of World War II pretended that these airfields and other building activities in the mandates were undertaken for peaceful purposes, the pretense was a flimsy one. A close examination of appropriations made by the Japanese Government for construction in the Marianas in 1940 and 1941 clearly indicates that Japan had launched an active program of military fortification of the mandates well before the actual outbreak of hostilities. In November of 1940 a sizable appropriation was made for the construction of "lighthouses" throughout the mandated islands. Each "lighthouse" came equipped with barracks, ammunition storage facilities, a command post, and a lookout station. Actually, of course, these were naval lookout stations.

On Saipan, construction was fairly extensive. Twelve "lighthouses" were constructed at a cost of 1,333,333 yen ($312,533). In February 1941, 100,000 yen ($23,440) was set aside to build four gun positions of reinforced concrete, to be completed by the end of July. During 1941 almost 700,000 yen ($164,080) was devoted to the construction of the Saipan branch of the *4th Fleet Naval Stores Department,* including ammunition storage sheds with a floor area of 800 square meters. Also during 1941, almost 800,000 yen ($187,520) was earmarked for construction of communications facilities, including receiving and sending stations, radio direction finders, and barracks for the personnel to man them. In September 1941, 1,500,000 yen ($351,600) was devoted to building military barracks, baths and latrines, kitchens, infirmaries, storehouses, workshops, torpedo storage sheds, garages, and air raid shelters. The order authorizing this expenditure specifically stated that these structures were intended for the use of a base force and a defense force, both of which under Japanese naval organization were acknowledged combat units.[5]

---

[4] Unless otherwise noted, the sources of information on Japan's prewar fortifications in the mandates are: Special Forces, Early Series, Vols. 9 and 10, in U.S. National Archives, World War II Seized Enemy Records, Record Group 242, NA 12226 and NA 12255, WDC 160867 and WDC 161009.

[5] For similar details on Japanese prewar military preparations in the Marshalls, see Crowl and Love, *Gilberts and Marshalls,* Chapter IV.

There is other evidence to prove that in the year or two before Pearl Harbor Japan was making active preparations to use the mandates, including the Marianas, as military and naval bases, contrary to the terms of the League Covenant.

On 15 November 1939 the *4th Fleet* of the Imperial Japanese Navy was organized and placed in charge of garrisons and fortifications in the mandates.[6] This fleet, which was primarily a base defense unit rather than the more orthodox type of naval combat unit, established its headquarters at Truk. For administrative and defense purposes, the mandates were divided into four sectors—East Carolines, West Carolines, Marshalls, and Marianas, with sector headquarters at Truk, the Palaus, Kwajalein, and Saipan, respectively. Each sector was controlled by a base force subordinate to the *4th Fleet*, and each base force commanded subordinate shore and surface units within its own sector.

Shortly after the creation of the *4th Fleet*, the *5th Special Base Force* was activated in Japan and assigned the duty of preparing for the fortification and defense of the Marianas. Attached to it were the *5th Communications Unit* and the *5th Defense Force*, the latter unit comprising the bulk of the combat personnel located in this area before the outbreak of war with the United States. These troops arrived in the Marianas in December of 1940. Not long afterward their strength was augmented by a detachment each of the *4th Fleet Naval Stores Department* and the *4th Naval Air Depot*, both located on Saipan.[7]

The mission of the *5th Special Base Force* from December 1940 to 31 May 1941 was to defend its assigned areas and speed up preparations for combat in the event of a war. The subordinate *5th Defense Force* engaged in construction of gun positions, road building, harbor improvement, and sundry other duties aimed at enhancing the security of Saipan. During the succeeding period, from 1 June through 30 November, an additional mission was assigned to the *5th Special Base Force*— that of "planning and preparation for the Guam invasion operation." No additional evidence need be adduced to show that well before the Pearl Harbor attack, Japan had committed herself unequivocally to a policy of fortifying the Marianas for offensive as well as defensive purposes.

From Pearl Harbor to Invasion

For the first two years after the Pearl Harbor attack, the fighting war between Japan and the United States remained far from the shores of Saipan and her sister islands except, of course, for the Japanese invasion of Guam. The Marianas during this period served the Japanese chiefly as supply and staging bases for troops, ships, and planes engaged in battle well to the east and south, and the strength of combat naval shore units in the area remained low. The *5th Special Base Force* on Saipan ranged from a low of 919 military troops and 220 civilians in May 1943 to a total of 1,437 men in February of the following year. The *54th Naval Guard Force* on Guam had 302 men in September 1942, and in early 1944 received an additional 425 recruits. In September 1943 the *Yoko-*

---

[6] USSBS (Pacific), Naval Analysis Division, *The Reduction of Truk* (Washington, 1947), p. 2.

[7] Base Forces and Defense Forces, Early Series, Vols. 9 and 10, NA 12245 and NA 12229, WDC 106869 and WDC 160867; Special Forces, Early

Series, Vols. 9 and 10, NA 12226 and NA 12255, WDC 160867 and WDC 161009.

suka 1st Special Naval Landing Force, numbering about 1,500 men, arrived on Saipan, but in the following January was reduced by about a third when detachments were sent to the Rabaul area.[8]

Considering the magnitude of the Empire's troop commitments elsewhere, the garrison assigned to the Marianas can be considered no more than a token force.[9] This is not at all surprising. The Marianas were a rear area. Simple military logic dictated that the Japanese concentrate their efforts in the Rabaul–New Guinea area to the south and build up the defenses of the Gilberts and Marshalls to the east. There was not enough money, manpower, or matériel to build strong fortifications and defenses on every one of Japan's myriad island possessions, and those farther away from the direct line of American advance had to suffer neglect. Not until the Marshall Islands finally fell to the Americans did the position of the Marianas become dangerous enough to justify urgent measures in their defense.

Reinforcement of the Marianas

By February 1944 the Marianas garrisons could predict that their time had

come. Tarawa and Makin in the Gilberts had been captured by U.S. forces in November 1943. Kwajalein Atoll in the Marshalls fell in early February 1944, and Eniwetok, less than a thousand nautical miles from Saipan, in mid-February.[10] Also in mid-February, Admiral Mitscher's Fast Carrier Task Force (Task Force 58) executed a two-day raid against Truk, thus opening the way to the complete neutralization of that formidable bastion.[11] Following the Truk raid, Mitscher moved on to the Marianas and on 22–23 February administered to those islands their baptism of fire.[12] The rear area had obviously become a forward area.

As the first step in recognition of the approaching threat to the Marianas, Carolines, and Palaus, the Japanese high command reorganized the command structure in the Central Pacific. For the first two years of the war, the *4th Fleet* had commanded all Japanese garrisons in the mandates and was itself directly responsible to the *Combined Fleet.* By March of 1944 the *4th Fleet* had lost effective control of its remaining garrisons in the Marshalls and had been further weakened by Mitscher's February raids on Truk and the Marianas. On 10 March 1944 a new headquarters was placed between the *Combined Fleet* and the *4th Fleet* and given control of all Navy and Army forces in the mandates and in the Bonin Islands to the north. This was the *Central Pacific Area Fleet,* commanded by Vice Adm. Chuichi Nagumo, who had led the attack on Pearl Harbor. Thereafter, *4th Fleet* control was confined to naval garrisons in Truk and the

---

[8] JICPOA Trans 4071, Monthly Personnel Totals for Units Under the Jurisdiction of the *4th Fleet,* September 1942–July 1943; CINCPAC-CINCPOA Trans 11601, *5th Special Base Force* (Saipan), Situation Rpt, dated 12 Feb 44; CINCPAC-CINCPOA Trans 12060, account of the civil and military situation on Guam from the Japanese occupation until February 1944; Tabular Records of Special Landing Forces, NA 11651, WDC 161406.

[9] For example, in January of 1944 the number of Japanese Army personnel in the Marshalls, on Wake, and on Kusaie numbered 13,721. This does not include the numerous naval personnel stationed in the same area whose exact numerical strength is not known. See Crowl and Love, *Gilberts and Marshalls,* p. 210.

[10] Crowl and Love, *Gilberts and Marshalls.*

[11] Morison, *Aleutians, Gilberts and Marshalls,* Ch. XVIII.

[12] See below, p. 71.

eastern Carolines, though it was theoretically exercised over the lost garrisons in the Marshalls. Naval garrisons in the Marianas, Bonins, and western Carolines (Palau Sector) fell under the direct control of the *Central Pacific Area Fleet*. Also, this new headquarters, in theory at least, commanded all Army forces in the mandates and the Bonins, commanding through *Headquarters, 31st Army*. In fact, Army troops remained practically independent of the naval command, and to all intents and purposes *31st Army* had exclusive tactical and administrative control over all Army personnel in the area. Speaking of the *Central Pacific Area Fleet* headquarters, a Japanese naval commander captured on Saipan said, "It is a purely administrative command and has no tactical significance. . . . in actual fact it never got beyond the stage of paper organization."[13]

Failure to establish clear-cut command relationships between the Army and Navy was characteristic of Japanese military organization in the Central Pacific. In the Marianas, as elsewhere, it had serious consequences. From the very beginning there was friction between Army and Navy from the highest headquarters to the lowest ranks. In early March, about the time the *Central Pacific Area Fleet* was officially placed in over-all command, a furious administrative squabble arose between that headquarters and the *31st Army*, the latter objecting to being subordinate to the Navy. The final decision, reached on 15 March, took the form of a compromise between the two headquarters. It was agreed that the command of each separate island was to rest with the senior Army or Navy officer present. It was also agreed orally between the Commander in Chief, *Central Pacific Area Fleet,* and the Commanding General, *31st Army*, that neither would assume complete responsibility, thus apparently leaving the area without a supreme command.[14]

The failure to carry out the principle of a unified command was to prove seriously detrimental to the efficiency of future Japanese operations in the Central Pacific. The resultant confusion was further compounded because of the high degree of mutual interdependence that necessarily existed between Army and Navy units. For example, all of the air strength in the Central Pacific was naval, under command of the *Central Pacific Area Fleet*. However, many of the air installations were serviced by Army units. Similarly, although the Army was only partially dependent on the Navy for surface transport, Army convoys had to be escorted by Navy ships.[15]

More significant than the administrative changes reorganizing the structure of command in the Central Pacific was the rapid acceleration of troop movements into the area following the fall of the Marshalls and the strike against Truk. By May 1944 the Japanese had five divisions, six independent brigades, and five independent regiments in the *31st Army* area, supported by innumerable smaller units ranging in size

---

[13] NTLF Rpt Marianas, Phase I, G-2 Rpt, p. 98. The organization of the *Central Pacific Area Fleet* is shown in *Central Pacific Area Fleet* Orders, NA 11810, WDC 150941.

[14] CINCPAC-CINCPOA Trans 12058, Excerpts Taken From a Staff Diary of the *31st Army* Headquarters, 25 February–31 March 1944, in CINCPAC-CINCPOA Trans, Vol. 3, pp. 99–148.

[15] Japanese Studies in World War II, 72, History of the Army Section, Imperial General Headquarters, 1941–1945, pp. 94–95, OCMH; CINCPAC-CINCPOA Trans 10145, *31st Army* Staff, table showing passengers and cargo of the *Natsu 2 Convoy*, dated 18 Mar 44, in CINCPAC-CINCPOA Trans, Vol. 3, pp. 79–98.

from tank and antiaircraft artillery regiments down to independent machine cannon companies. About one third of the Army personnel in the Central Pacific was concentrated in the Marianas, including two divisions, two independent brigades, and two independent regiments.[16] The two divisions sent to the Marianas were the *29th* and the *43d*. The *29th* was transferred from Manchuria to Saipan in February, later moving to Guam. The *43d*, organized in June 1943, moved from Japan to Saipan in late May 1944.[17]

In addition, the Japanese organized sundry independent Army units for service in the Central Pacific Area. Units of battalion size and smaller were detached from their parent divisions and reorganized into eight expeditionary units, three of which were sent to the Marianas. The *1st Expeditionary Unit*, consisting of four infantry battalions and two artillery battalions, was allocated to Saipan; the *5th Expeditionary Unit*, of two infantry battalions and one artillery battalion, was moved to Pagan; and the *6th Expeditionary Unit*, made up of six infantry battalions and two artillery battalions, was sent to Guam.[18]

In May, after most of the expeditionary units had reached their destinations, Army Section, Imperial General Headquarters, ordered a reorganization of the expeditionary units into independent mixed brigades and independent mixed regiments. In the Marianas the *1st Expeditionary Unit* (Saipan) became the *47th Independent Mixed Brigade*, the *5th Expeditionary Unit* (Pa-

gan) became the *9th Independent Mixed Regiment*, and the *6th Expeditionary Unit* (Guam) was divided into the *48th Independent Mixed Brigade* and the *10th Independent Mixed Regiment*.[19]

The Navy, too, began to increase its strength in the Marianas shortly after the fall of the Marshalls. The *55th* and *65th Naval Guard Forces* were established on Saipan and Tinian, respectively, and several antiaircraft artillery units were also dispatched to the area. A large variety of small administrative offices were established to handle the greatly increased volume of supplies and troop movements, and labor units for construction work and loading and unloading ships were added to the garrisons. Finally, air strength was poured into the Marianas during the period as local airfields were developed and war came closer, so that many naval airmen and maintenance men swelled the number of naval air personnel in the islands.

This accelerated movement of troops into the Marianas was not allowed to go uncontested by the ever-advancing American forces. From the very beginning of the Japanese attempt to reinforce the islands, submarines of the U.S. Pacific Fleet began to take their toll. American submariners played an important role in the capture of the Marianas; in fact it can be said that the American campaign actually began in February with the first submarine attacks on Japanese troop convoys bound for Saipan.

The first of the major Japanese troop movements involved the transfer of the *29th Division*, which left Ujina, Japan,

---

[16] Japanese Studies in World War II, 55, Operations in the Central Pacific, pp. 17–19, 36–38, OCMH.

[17] MID WD, Order of Battle of the Japanese Armed Forces, 1 March 1945, pp. 99–100; Japanese Studies in World War II, 72, pp. 92–93.

[18] Japanese Studies in World War II, 55, p. 17.

[19] CINCPAC-CINCPOA Trans 16035, chart indicating change in organization of old units (undated), rev. trans by Hq NTLF in the field, 23 Jul 44.

on 26 February aboard three troop transports. Late in the afternoon of the 29th
the convoy was attacked by American submarines. One transport (*Sakito Maru*),
laden with 3,080 troops was torpedoed and
sunk. Only 1,688 were rescued. The survivors (members of the *18th Infantry Regiment*) landed on Saipan with almost no
equipment. According to one report, "All
their weapons were lost except seven rifles,
one grenade thrower, two light machine
guns and 150 bayonets."[20]

The next large convoy to sail for the
Marianas left Yokohama on 12 March and
carried the *1st, 5th,* and *6th Expeditionary
Units*. The convoy was attacked by American submarines and, although no Army
troops were lost, a naval transport (*Ko-
kuyo Maru*) carrying 1,029 reinforcements
for the *54th Naval Guard Force* on Guam
was torpedoed and sunk.[21]

In April two more convoys left Japan
for the Marianas, and although the first
was attacked by submarines and two of its
ships sunk, all troops were rescued and put
ashore safely on Saipan.[22] The last two
convoys to reach the Marianas, however,
arrived with the units seriously depleted
and without their equipment. The first of
these departed Yokohama on 5 May and
reached Saipan on the 14th. None of the
troops carried aboard were originally intended for the Marianas, but when two of
the transports were torpedoed the survivors
were landed on Saipan. Fifteen hundred
of these, members of the *9th Expeditionary
Unit* bound for Yap, remained on Saipan
until the American invasion. About six
hundred were reorganized as a battalion of
the *47th Independent Mixed Brigade,* but
the rest remained on Saipan as ill-equipped
stragglers. Other survivors of the same ill-
fated convoy belonged to the *15th Infantry
Regiment,* destined for the Palaus. They
formed another straggler group on Saipan,
where the American invasion caught
them still awaiting transportation to the
Palaus.[23]

The last major troop movement to the
Marianas, and certainly one of the most
significant, was the transfer of the *43d Division* from Japan to Saipan. Arriving only
a few weeks before the American invasion,
the division was to play a leading role in
the defense of the island, and its commander, Lt. Gen. Yoshitsugu Saito, would
assume effective control of the Saipan
defenses. For transportation purposes the
division was divided into two echelons, the
first of which made its way safely through
to Saipan sometime in May. The second
was not so fortunate. On 30 May a convoy
of seven transports carrying more than
7,000 troops of the *43d Division* sailed
from Tateyama and headed south. It was
subjected to almost continous submarine
attack, and within three days five of the
seven transports were sunk. The two remaining vessels picked up the survivors and

---

[20] CINCPAC-CINCPOA Trans 12058.

[21] CINCPAC-CINCPOA, Trans 10145, pp. 79–
98; CINCPAC-CINCPOA Trans 12058, pp. 34–
36; CINCPAC-CINCPOA Trans 9767, Situation
Rpt, *4th Special Shipping Engineer Company*
(Saipan), dated Apr 44.

[22] CINCPAC-CINCPOA Trans 10931, a file of
orders and tables showing troop movements and
locations of units in the Central Pacific Area. The
Joint Army-Navy Assessment Committee, *Japanese
Naval and Merchant Shipping Losses During
World War II By All Causes* (Washington, 1947)
(hereafter cited as JANAC, *Japanese Shipping
Losses*).

[23] CINCPAC-CINCPOA Trans 10931;
CINCPAC-CINCPOA Trans 9485, Army Section
Order 982 (1 Apr 44); CINCPAC-CINCPOA
Trans 10959, Extracts From an Account of the
Sinking of the *Hiyori Maru;* CINCPAC-
CINCPOA Trans 9883, File of Shipping Orders,
Shipping Operation Order 283 (7 Apr 44).

steamed the rest of the way to Saipan.[24]

About 80 percent of the troops of this convoy were saved and landed on Saipan, but they arrived as hapless survivors without weapons or equipment. The *118th Infantry Regiment* lost about 850 men, and the survivors had virtually no resemblance to the organized fighting team that had left Japan. So little time was left before the American invasion that the regiment could not be reorganized and re-equipped sufficiently to raise its combat efficiency much above nil.[25]

All together, from January to early June 1944, the Japanese dispatched about 45,000 Army troops to the Marianas. Of these about 40,000 were allotted to Saipan, Guam, and Tinian; the remainder to Pagan and Rota. At least 12,000 of these troops were aboard torpedoed vessels, and about 3,600 died as a result of the sinkings. While many of the survivors were successfully reorganized, rehabilitated, and re-equipped, about half, perhaps four or five thousand, became stragglers on Saipan, equipped and armed only with their resolution to die for the Emperor. Thus, well before the initial American strikes against Saipan from surface ships and aircraft, U.S. submarines had seriously disrupted Japan's major effort to reinforce the Marianas against the imminent threat of invasion.

Military Construction in 1944

Along with their hasty and not altogether successful effort to enlarge the garrisons of the Marianas, the Japanese in early 1944 undertook an ambitious program of building up the islands' fortifi-

cations and defenses. First priority was assigned to airfield construction. At the beginning of the war Saipan had an airfield (Aslito) and a seaplane base and Tinian had an airfield. All three appear to have been operational. The situation remained unchanged as late as mid-1943, when the Imperial Navy commenced a new program of airfield construction in the Marianas and Carolines, planning to increase the operational airfields from one to two on Saipan and from one to three on Tinian. In addition, the program called for two new fields on Guam, and one each on Pagan and Rota, where none had existed before. By February 1944 Aslito airfield was being enlarged, and two more fields on Saipan were under construction. The Saipan seaplane base, constructed in 1935, was in full operation. On Tinian, the Ushi Point field was in operation, and another field was under construction. On Guam, Sumay airfield was almost completed, and three other fields and a seaplane base were under way or in the planning stage.[26]

In March plans were developed for an even more rapid build-up of airfield facilities. *Combined Fleet* and *Central Pacific Area Fleet* each issued orders outlining an ambitious policy of airfield construction. The *Combined Fleet* order provided that three independent complexes of bases were to be rapidly completed in the Marianas–Truk area and in the Palau–Yap area.[27] The *Central Pacific Area Fleet* order de-

---

[24] USSBS, *Interrogations* I, 212; CINCPAC-CINCPOA Trans 10931, p. 40.

[25] CINCPAC-CINCPOA Trans 10931, p. 40.

[26] JICPOA Trans 5577, *11th Air Fleet* Secret Bull 37, data tables for surface craft assigned or attached to the *11th Air Fleet;* Japanese Studies in World War II, 60, The AGO Operation, 1944, p. 11, OCMH; CINCPAC-CINCPOA Trans 10092, *Advance Expeditionary Unit, 13th Division,* intelligence record dated 29 February 1944.

[27] CINCPAC-CINCPOA Trans 9497, *Combined Fleet* Secret Order 20 (19 Mar 44), Construction of Air Bases in the Central Pacific Area.

fined construction policy as: "To build rapidly a large number of bases so as to make possible the immediate development of great aerial strength." In the Marianas, the bases were first to be built on a rough and ready basis and then gradually brought to a finished state as conditions permitted. Each field was to be integrated into the land defenses; machine gun positions for plane-mounted guns were to be built near plane shelters, and air force personnel were to be organized for ground combat.[28]

These plans were intended to result in fourteen airfields and two seaplane bases: Saipan, three airfields and a seaplane base; Tinian, four airfields; Guam, four airfields and a seaplane base; Pagan, two airfields; Rota, one airfield. Each airfield was to be capable of handling forty-eight planes, except for the Marpi Point field on Saipan, which would handle twenty-four, and the Charan Kanoa strip, also on Saipan, which was for emergency use only. The entire network of bases would be sufficient for six hundred planes of various types.[29]

Although the *Combined Fleet* order specified that normal air facilities were to be completed by April, the estimate proved much too optimistic. When the American landing forces came upon the scene in June, much of the construction was still unfinished. On Saipan, Aslito airfield was, of course, operational, as was the Charan Kanoa emergency airstrip, but the Marpi Point field was still unfinished and non-operational. Guam had two operational

strips and two still unfinished. Tinian, the air center of the Marianas, had three fields finished and one to go. Rota and Pagan each boasted a surfaced runway. All together, of the fourteen fields planned, nine had been completed and were capable of handling at the most a total of four hundred planes rather than the originally planned six hundred.[30]

While the Imperial Navy was hurriedly attempting to build up air strength in the Marianas, *31st Army* was making similar plans for ground fortifications. The précis of the *31st Army* defense plan gives a general outline of the Army fortification program:

While deploying the troops the defensive constructions must be strengthened and general preparations for the annihilation of the enemy landing on the beaches must be completed, including the protection of our air bases. The field positions must be completed within one month after the arrival of troops and within three months the positions must be strengthened by constructing permanent fortifications in the most important points.[31]

The hope that this schedule could reach completion before the American landings, if ever seriously held, proved a vain one. The *43d Division* did not arrive on Saipan until early June, a matter of days before the invasion. The *7th* and *16th Independent Engineer Regiments,* which were responsible for most of the "permanent fortifications," arrived in April, only two months before the invasion. The job, even under ideal conditions, would have been difficult, and conditions were far from ideal. Troops arrived in a haphazard fashion, often depleted in number and missing

---

[28] CINCPAC-CINCPOA Trans 9498, *Central Pacific Area Force* Secret Order 2 (21 Mar 44), Construction of Air Bases in the Marianas and Carolines.

[29] *Ibid.;* CINCPAC-CINCPOA Trans 9692, *Central Pacific Area Fleet* Secret Order 30–8 (20 Apr 44), New Nomenclature for Air Bases.

[30] TF 56 Rpt FORAGER, G–2 Rpt, App. F, pp. 1–4.

[31] Japanese Studies in World War II, 55, pp. 19–20.

their arms and equipment. Moreover, American submarine warfare accounted for the loss of more than mere manpower. Essential building matériel went to the bottom of the sea along with the men. A report, dated 31 May, from the chief of staff of the *31st Army* gives a clear survey of the difficulties facing the Japanese in their hurried effort to construct adequate fortifications on Saipan and the other islands in the Marianas:

> We cannot strengthen the fortifications appreciably now unless we can get materials suitable for permanent construction. Specifically, unless the units are supplied with cement, steel reinforcements for cement, barbed wire, lumber, etc., which cannot be obtained in these islands, no matter how many soldiers there are they can do nothing in regard to fortifications but sit around with their arms folded, and the situation is unbearable.
>
> I would like this matter of supply of construction materials dealt with immediately.[32]

Japanese Doctrine for Island Defense

The failure on the part of the Japanese to meet their time schedule in reinforcing the Marianas' physical defenses had an important effect on the tactical doctrine to which they adhered throughout the campaign. It was one of the factors that compelled them to rely more heavily on beach defenses than would logically have been called for by the size and physiographic features of these particular islands.

In the Gilberts and Marshalls, Japanese defensive doctrine stressed defense at the beaches. At Tarawa, Makin, Kwajalein,

and Eniwetok the fortifications were concentrated on a thin line along the shores with little defense in depth.[33] By concentrating the majority of their positions on the beaches proper, and with the aid of fringing coral reefs and offshore obstacles, the Japanese hoped to annihilate the Americans before they could gain a foothold ashore. If the U.S. troops did succeed in establishing a beachhead, doctrine called for a counterattack to push them back into the sea.

This doctrine of island defense was based to a great extent on purely geographical and terrain considerations. The Gilberts and Marshalls are composed of widely scattered coral atolls, each in turn composed of many small islets. Although the Japanese usually selected the larger of the islets for their bases, these still had very little area and were generally elongated in shape. Defense in depth was impractical not only because there was little depth to defend but also because what little there was usually contained an airstrip that had to be left free of obstacles if it was to land and dispatch planes. Moreover, the flat terrain of the atolls provided no natural features such as hills and caves that could be exploited to set up an adequate defense in depth.

The Marianas are much different. They are volcanic islands, not coral atolls. They are generally much larger in size, have considerable elevation, and the terrain is rugged and mountainous, providing favorable opportunities for defense in depth. Yet, in spite of this the Japanese continued to place great emphasis on defending the shore lines of Saipan, Tinian, and Guam

---

[32] Report on the Defenses of the Various Islands, from CofS *31st Army* to CofS *Central Pacific Area Fleet,* Trans 116 of Japanese Document by Hq NTLF, 11 Jul 44, copy in archives of Hist Br G–3, Hq U.S. Marine Corps.

[33] See Crowl and Love, *Gilberts and Marshalls,* Chs. IV, XIII.

to the consequent neglect of fortifications and gun positions in the interior.

The continued reliance on beach defenses is illustrated in the defense plan for Saipan drawn up by the *1st Expeditionary Unit:*

Tactical Command Doctrine

A. Objective

It is expected that the enemy will be destroyed on the beaches through a policy of tactical command based on aggressiveness, determination, and initiative. . . .

When the enemy elements are attempting to land: The main fire-power will be directed at the enemy landing forces prior to their arrival on the beach. Taking advantage of the confusion, the enemy will be rapidly destroyed by counter attacks, mounted from all sectors wherever the opportunity presents itself.

Should the enemy succeed in gaining a foothold on the beach, intense fire will be concentrated and determined counter-attacks launched with the aid of reserves and tanks. Although the advantages of surprise will be lost, the enemy landing forces can be dealt with by further attacks after night fall.[34]

Later in the war and under conditions similar to those obtaining in the Marianas, the Japanese abandoned or modified their earlier doctrine and concentrated heavily on defenses in depth. When the U.S. Marines landed on Iwo Jima, they found a well-prepared network of defenses in depth as well as fortifications commanding the shore line.[35] At Okinawa the landing beaches on the west coast were left practically undefended, and the main Japanese forces had retired before the invasion to the southern part of the island, where they holed in along the Shuri line with its elaborate system of caves and underground installations.[36]

Why, then, did the Japanese as late as June 1944 cling to the older concept, which though valid enough for atoll warfare was clearly not so suitable for the type of fighting that would inevitably develop in the mountainous terrain of the Marianas? The failure to adjust tactical doctrine to changing conditions of terrain can probably be attributed in part to the highly aggressive spirit of the Japanese military mind. Generally, the Japanese preferred to sally forth sword in hand against the enemy rather than bide their time in prepared positions. As noted in the U.S. Army handbook on the subject of Japanese tactics:

No matter what the situation, a Japanese commander's first reaction to it is to act aggressively to maintain the traditions of his army. . . . Even when the Japanese commander assumes the defensive, he will, so far as possible, carry out that defense by using the most aggressive tactics that the situation permits.[37]

In the case of the Marianas, there was an even more compelling consideration that forced the Japanese to rely most heavily on their beach defenses. There was simply not enough time to complete the fortification program. The *31st Army* program for defense had made provision for falling back upon prepared "strategic inland positions"

---

[34] CINCPAC-CINCPOA Trans 8946, *1st Expeditionary Unit* Defense Plan for Saipan Island, dated 10 May 44.

[35] Isely and Crowl, *The U.S. Marines and Amphibious War,* Ch. X.; Lt. Col. Whitman S. Bartley, USMC, *Iwo Jima: Amphibious Epic,* Historical Branch, G-3 Division, Headquarters U.S. Marine Corps (Washington, 1954), pp. 5-18.

[36] Roy E. Appleman, James M. Burns, Russell A. Gugeler, and John Stevens, *Okinawa: The Last Battle,* UNITED STATES ARMY IN WORLD WAR II (Washington, 1948).

[37] TM-E 30-480, Handbook on Japanese Military Forces, Ch. VII, Japanese Tactics, 1 Jun 45, p. 2.

in the event that an enemy landing force was not thrust back into the sea. That plan reads, in part:

> First priority in construction will be given to improvised positions designed to frustrate enemy landings on the beaches . . . and to temporary protective measures designed to minimize our losses in personnel and materials. Later, these constructions will be rapidly supplemented and strengthened by extending the positions in depth, converting actually the island into an invulnerable fortress.[38]

The speed-up of the U.S. invasion plans, coupled with the loss of valuable building materials to the U.S. submarines, made the fulfillment of the second part of this plan impossible.

In line with the doctrine of defense at the beaches, the *31st Army* planned to cover all segments of the shore line "where the enemy could land without difficulty" with independent strongpoints several hundred meters or one kilometer apart. Each strongpoint would be manned by an infantry company or a heavy weapons platoon. Patterns of fire were to be arranged so that each strongpoint could provide flanking fire on its neighbors' fronts, and areas not otherwise provided for were to be covered by machine guns and mortars.[39] In this manner, whole companies would be deployed along the beaches.

Behind the coastal positions, at a distance depending on terrain, was to be constructed a second line that would cover any partial collapse of the coastal positions and serve as a starting point for counterattacks by reserve units. The second line was to be organized on the same principle as the coastal positions. The *31st Army* plan emphasized the construction of dum-

my positions between strongpoints and between the coastal positions and the second line. These positions were to deceive the enemy and divert his fire. They were to be especially thick on those stretches of the shore line where enemy landings were less likely because of natural obstacles, and where only small forces or lookouts might be stationed.

Since the artillery was to fire antiboat missions, many pieces were to be emplaced in the coastal positions and the second lines, as well as farther to the rear. Antiaircraft artillery was to be located in positions where it could lend support to ground actions as well as fulfill its primary function. Finally, the plan made rather vague provision for final strongpoints to the rear of the second lines, providing that "if time allows the rear positions . . . must be strongly built and also completely equipped for the counter-attack."[40] Actually, time did not allow the Japanese to provide for such positions.

Enemy Troop Strength and Dispositions on Saipan

Command of all Army troops in the Marianas rested with the *31st Army* under Lt. Gen. Hideyoshi Obata, who had headquarters on Saipan.[41] When the American forces landed on 15 June, Obata was in the Palau Islands and consequently exercised no tactical command during the campaign. His headquarters on Saipan, consisting of about 1,100 officers and men, was largely administrative in function and had little tactical significance. The largest single Army unit on the island at the time

---

[38] Japanese Studies in World War II, 55, p. 25.
[39] *Ibid.*, pp. 26–32.

[40] *Ibid.*, p. 29.
[41] See below, App. C, Japanese Order of Battle on Saipan.

of the landing was the *43d Division,* commanded by General Saito. It was Saito who actually exercised tactical command until his death a few days before the close of the battle. The division consisted of three infantry regiments, the *118th, 135th,* and *136th,* plus a signal company, a transport company, an ordnance company, a field hospital, and an "intendance duty unit" responsible for quartermaster and finance functions. All together, the division numbered about 12,939 officers and men.[42]

Next in size among Army units was the *47th Independent Mixed Brigade,* commanded by Col. Yoshiro Oka. The brigade had four organic battalions, but one, the *315th,* was on Pagan. The three others, the *316th, 317th,* and *318th Independent Infantry Battalions,* were on Saipan. An engineer unit and an artillery unit, the latter consisting of one battery of eight field guns and two batteries of seven howitzers each, also belonged to the brigade. Total strength of the brigade on Saipan at the time of the landing was about 2,600.

To this nucleus was attached a host of smaller units including many that had originally been destined for other islands but had been stranded on Saipan as a result of shipping damage inflicted by American submarines. The most important of these were the *3d Independent Mountain Artillery Regiment* consisting of two battalions, each with twelve 75-mm. mountain guns; the *16th Shipping Engineers Regiment;* the *7th Independent Engineer Regiment;* the *9th Tank Regiment* with thirty-six medium and twelve light tanks; and the *25th Antiaircraft Artillery Regiment.* Total strength of Japanese Army troops on Sai-

pan on the eve of the American invasion was about 25,469.

To this number must be added about 6,160 naval personnel. Among the naval units present on the island were the *Headquarters, Central Pacific Area Fleet,* under Admiral Nagumo and the *Headquarters, 5th Base Force,* under Rear Adm. Takahisa Tsujimura. The latter unit had been in command of the Marianas since before Pearl Harbor, but with the arrival of Army troops in 1944 it assumed a less important role in the defense of Saipan, though it continued to command naval shore forces and surface units within the Marianas. The largest single element of the naval forces was the *55th Naval Guard Force,* about 2,000 officers and men, which was chiefly responsible for manning coast defense guns. The only other large naval unit was the *Yokosuka 1st Special Naval Landing Force,* consisting mainly of a headquarters, three rifle companies, a machine gun platoon, and a gun section.

For purposes of ground defense, Saipan was divided into four parts. (*Map 3*) The first was the Northern Sector, that portion of the island north of a line beginning at Flores Point on the west coast and extending to the east coast in a southeasterly direction. The most important troop unit located here was the *135th Infantry Regiment,* less one battalion.

The second division was the Navy Sector, which was bounded on the north by the Northern Sector, on the west by the shore line from Flores Point to a point just below Garapan, thence on the south by a line to a point just southwest of Mount Tapotchau's summit, and on the east by a line from this point up the axis of the island to the center of the Northern Sector's boundary. The *5th Base Force* controlled

---

[42] Sources for this data on the Japanese Order of Battle are given in Appendix C.

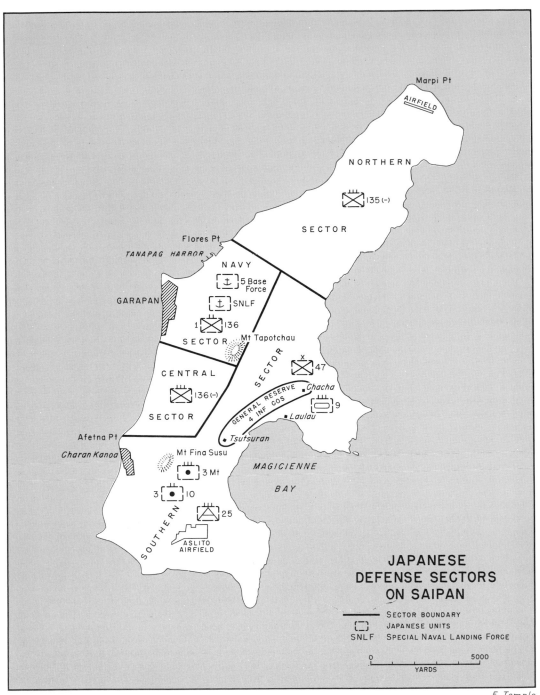

MAP 3

JAPANESE
DEFENSE SECTORS
ON SAIPAN

Sector boundary
Japanese units
SNLF Special Naval Landing Force

0   5000
YARDS

F. Temple

the Navy Sector, but the beach defenses were actually manned by a battalion of the *136th Infantry Regiment.*

The Central Sector lay directly south of the Navy Sector. Its shore line extended from a point below Garapan to Afetna Point. Inland, to the east, it was bounded by an extension of the Navy Sector's boundary down the central axis of the island to a point directly east of Afetna Point. Here the boundary turned west to Afetna, enclosing the sector from the south. Responsibility for the defense of the Central Sector rested with the commanding officer of the *136th Infantry Regiment.* His regiment was reduced to the *2d Battalion* reinforced by one company of the *3d,* since the *1st Battalion* was assigned to the Navy Sector and the remaining two companies of the *3d Battalion* were in *43d Division* reserve.

The fourth defense area was the Southern Sector, whose shore line extended along the west coast from Afetna Point, around the entire south coast, and up the east coast beyond Kagman Peninsula to the boundary line of the Northern Sector. This sector, commanded by the commanding officer of the *47th Independent Mixed Brigade,* encompassed about half of the island, and probably contained the same proportion of the island's troops. Here were concentrated all the reserve troops as well as the forty-eight tanks, the main artillery batteries, and the antiaircraft units clustered around Aslito airfield.[43]

Within each of these sectors, the disposition of troops was generally in accordance with the doctrine of concentrating on defeating the enemy at the shore line. For example, a *136th Infantry Regiment* operations order dated 25 May makes the following disposition of the regiment's forces in the Central Sector, which included most of the shore line upon which the 2d Marine Division was to make its landing:[44]

> Front Line (Beaches)
> > *4th Company*
> > *5th Company*
> > *6th Company* (less 1/3)
> > *8th Company* (less 1/3)
> > *2d Infantry Gun Company*
> Sector Reserves
> > 1/3 *6th Company*
> > 1/3 *8th Company*

The commitment to beach defense of such a large portion of troops of the *136th Regiment* with the consequent neglect of reserve power was entirely consistent with prevailing Japanese tactical doctrine.

Reserves for the island were located in the area just north of Magicienne Bay and included two companies of the *3d Battalion, 136th Infantry Regiment,* with two companies of the *3d Battalion, 9th Independent Mixed Brigade,* attached. The *16th Shipping Engineers Regiment* (less detachments) and the main body of the

---

[43] Map, Sectors for Units Defending Saipan, reproduced from overlay attached to captured Japanese Northern Marianas Group Operations Order A–4, reproduced in NTLF Rpt Marianas, Phase I, G–2 Rpt, pp. 8–9; *136th Infantry Regiment* Operation Order 12, 0800, 25 May, copy in Field Diary, *2d Artillery Battery, 136th Infantry Regiment,* 1–31 May 1944 (NA 21961). The di-

version of the *1st Battalion, 136th Regiment,* to the Navy Sector, a last-minute change that does not appear in American sources, is indicated by a *136th Infantry Regiment* Order, 2000, 29 May 44, signed by the regimental commander, Col. Yukimatsu Ogawa, and found in Field Diary, *1st Infantry Gun Company, 136th Infantry Regiment,* 1–31 May 1944, entry for 29 May (NA 22286).

[44] *136th Infantry Regiment* Operation Order 7, 1300, 25 May 44, Field Diary, *2d Artillery Battery, 136th Infantry Regiment,* 1–31 May 44 (NA 21961).

9th Tank Regiment were also in this area. In case of landings in the Garapan–Tanapag sector, the tanks were to assemble in the mountains two miles east of Garapan and there prepare to counterattack. If landings took place in the Magicienne Bay or Charan Kanoa area, the tanks were to assemble about one-half mile north of Aslito airfield's west end and prepare for operations against either area, or both.[45]

Most of the Army mobile artillery, organized as the *3d Independent Mountain Artillery Regiment* and the *47th Independent Mixed Brigade Artillery Unit,* was located along the ridge overlooking the Charan Kanoa beaches to the north and south of Mount Fina Susu. From these positions the guns were to fire missions on the east and west coasts. Japanese artillery preparations on Saipan were careful and elaborate, preliminary sightings having been made on important points such as breaks in the reefs. However, these preliminary sightings seem to have been conducted independently by separate pieces of batteries, and no common survey control was established. As a result, the Japanese were unable to mass fires by tying in batteries or battalions, and the Japanese artillery dissipated itself in local un-coordinated missions.[46] Another defect in Japanese artillery on Saipan arose from the lack of prime movers. All of the field artillery was mobile, but there were neither horses nor trucks on the island and the pieces therefore had to be moved by hand, if at all.

In addition to the Army's mobile artillery, Saipan could boast an elaborate system of naval coast defense and dual-purpose batteries. The Japanese Navy's scheme of artillery fire was intended to cover almost every square inch of both Saipan and neighboring Tinian, large sweeps of the adjacent sea, and nearly all of the air overhead. According to the Navy's plan, coast defense guns (12, 14, and 15-cm's.) were to be lined up along the west coast of Saipan from Agingan Point to Tanapag in a series of seven batteries covering the entire approach from the west with interlocking sectors of fire. A second concentration of Navy coast defense guns, in five batteries, was to be emplaced on Nafutan Point and the shores of Magicienne Bay, covering the sea approaches to Saipan from the south and southeast. A battery of 4-cm. guns on Marpi Point emplaced to fire to the north would complete the picture. Two batteries of 12-cm. dual-purpose guns were to cover the Aslito airfield; two more of the same size were to cover the center of island; an 8-cm. battery, the Tanapag area; and a battery of 12-cm's., Marpi Point.[47] Not all of these emplacements were completed at the time of the American landings, but most of the Navy's coast and aerial defense program was in working order by mid-June of 1944.

Army antiaircraft batteries on Saipan were spread from Mutcho Point to Aslito airfield, mostly along the ridges and hills overlooking the west beaches. The air over the entire southern portion of the island was covered by the guns of the *25th Antiaircraft Artillery Regiment's 1st, 2d,* and *6th Batteries.* The central portion of Saipan was covered by the *43d Independent*

---

[45] NTLF Rpt Marianas, Phase I, G–2 Rpt, pp. 8, 76.

[46] CINCPAC-CINCPOA Trans 9604, Battle Plan of Artillery Unit of the *1st Expeditionary Unit.*

[47] CINCPAC-CINCPOA Trans 12252, Disposition of Navy Dual-Purpose and Coastal Defense Batteries on Saipan and Tinian, dated 15 May 44. Reprinted in CINCPAC-CINCPOA Trans, Vol. 8, p. 9.

Antiaircraft Company and the *45th Field Machine Cannon Company*.[48] In general, however, a shortage of ammunition handicapped the antiaircraft artillery. Maximum allowance for antiaircraft weapons on Saipan was three units of fire, but in fact the *25th Antiaircraft Artillery Regiment* and its two attached companies probably did not have as much as one unit of fire (4,800 rounds) on hand. Antiaircraft ammunition was in short supply not only in the Marianas but in all other *31st Army* areas as well.[49]

Japanese Expectations

Immediately after the February strike against Truk by Marc Mitscher's fast carrier task force, the Japanese reached a state of near panic in their apprehensions of an imminent American attack against the Marianas. Preparations for moving the *31st Army* headquarters to the Marianas had already begun when U.S. forces seized the Marshalls and Eniwetok, and the headquarters staff was scheduled to leave Tokyo for Saipan when Mitscher's follow-up strike on the Marianas took the Japanese by surprise. This strike occurred on 22–23 February, and on the following day General Tojo himself suddenly ordered the staff to depart at once. On 3 March *31st Army* issued an emergency plan for the defense of the archipelago, which at that time was virtually defenseless. On 4 March civil government was abolished on Guam, and shortly afterward martial law was established throughout the islands. In early March the Japanese actually feared an invasion of the Marianas by the end of the month, as indicated by the following excerpt from the *31st Army* staff diary: "The central command was very much concerned over the enemy attacks. After the enemy striking force hit the Marianas Sector on the 22d and 23d of February, thereby revealing our lack of defenses, they were afraid of an enemy invasion in March."[50] The sinking of *Sakito Maru*, which was carrying the *18th Infantry Regiment* to Saipan, only increased the alarm. For a while *31st Army* headquarters planned to divert the *8th Expeditionary Unit*, bound for Truk, to the Marianas, but this plan was not carried through. By late March the apprehension over an immediate invasion had somewhat abated, and Army troops were being used to build airfields.[51]

Then at the end of March Mitscher raided the Palaus, and on 22 April MacArthur captured Hollandia in Netherlands New Guinea. The Japanese pulse once again beat faster. The Japanese Navy and Army high command differed somewhat in their estimates of the situation. The raid on the Palaus, the capture of Hollandia, and, finally, the operations around Biak in May led the naval high command to anticipate that the next American attack would come in the Palaus or Carolines rather than as far north as the Marianas.[52] On 3 May Admiral Soeumu Toyoda assumed command of the *Combined Fleet* and received a directive from Imperial GHQ outlining

---

[48] CINCPAC-CINCPOA Trans 12251, order for change in location of Army antiaircraft batteries on Saipan, dated 10 May 44.

[49] CINCPAC-CINCPOA Trans 9698, *31st Army* table showing immediate supply of ammunition necessary for antiaircraft guns and antiaircraft machine cannon.

[50] CINCPAC-CINCPOA Trans 12058, Excerpts Taken From a Staff Diary of the *31st Army* Headquarters, 25 February–31 March 1944, p. 32.

[51] *Ibid.*, pp. 5, 14–17, 32, 45.

[52] USSBS, *Campaigns*, pp. 3–9, 204–15.

the *A Operation* (also known as the *A-GO Operation*), which called for the surface striking force and land-based air units to be prepared for a decisive engagement with the U.S. fleet by the end of May, presumably in the Palau–Carolines area.

Army officers in Imperial GHQ at the same time seem to have taken more seriously the possibility of an early invasion of the Marianas. On the assumption that the main objective would be the Philippines, they concluded that the Americans might advance along the north coast of New Guinea or into the Carolines and Marianas. It was also estimated that "there is a great possibility that both of the operations will be commenced simultaneously." [53]

Whatever may have been their belief in regard to an ultimate invasion of the Marianas, it is clear that the Japanese did not expect a full-scale attack against Saipan by mid-June. As late as 8 June, *31st Army* headquarters issued an order for the transfer of troops from Saipan to other islands in the archipelago, which, had it been carried out, would have reduced the Saipan garrison by 2,500 men.[54] An even more striking indication that the Japanese were caught off guard by the rapidity of the American approach comes from an order issued by Admiral Nagumo on 14 June, the day before the first American troops hit the beaches on Saipan, that reads, in

part, "It is a certainty that he [the enemy] will land in the Marianas Group either this month or next." [55]

The conclusion, then, is inescapable that the Japanese were simply not prepared for the American landings on Saipan when they came. In the short time intervening between the American capture of the Marshalls and the invasion of Saipan, the Japanese found it physically impossible with the means at hand to build up the defenses of the Marianas to a point where they might successfully resist a landing by U.S. forces. In their race against time the Japanese were further handicapped by the deadly efficiency of American submarines, which by now had extended the radius of their operations well to the west of the Marianas perimeter. Finally, U.S. forces achieved a measure of surprise by attacking Saipan before they were expected, thus adding the element of shock to the already preponderant strength they were able to bring to bear against this vital point in Japan's inner defensive perimeter.

Prepared or not, the Japanese forces on Saipan were by no means feeble. The more than 30,000 troops on the island were backed by forty-eight tanks and an elaborate, if incomplete, network of artillery positions and reinforced by their determination to die if necessary for the Emperor. They could be expected to put up a fierce battle.

---

[53] Japanese Studies in World War II, 72, p. 123.
[54] CINCPAC-CINCPOA Trans 9645, *31st Army* Operation Order 369–72 (Jun 44, Saipan).

[55] NTLF Rpt Marianas, Phase I, G–2 Rpt, 12 Aug 44, p. 5.

CHAPTER V

Invasion

Softening the Target:
Pre-D-Day Bombardment

On 6 June, while the convoys carrying the attack troops headed westward for their staging bases in the Marshalls, Marc Mitscher's Task Force 58 weighed anchor and slipped out of Majuro for waters east of the Marianas. For this operation Admiral Mitscher had gathered together a total of seven carriers, eight light carriers, seven fast battleships, three heavy cruisers, ten light cruisers, and fifty-two destroyers.[1] Their missions were to prevent Japanese aircraft from interfering with the capture of Saipan, Tinian, and Guam; to protect the expeditionary force and the troops ashore from attack by enemy surface vessels; and, commencing on D minus 3 (12 June), to destroy aircraft and air facilities in the Marianas. Finally, on 13 June when it was presumed that Japanese aircraft operating from fields in the Marianas would be eliminated, Task Force 58 was directed to destroy all other types of Japanese defenses both by aerial bombardment and by ships' fire from its supporting vessels.[2]

This was to be the culmination of an accelerated program of aerial neutralization of the Marianas. Mitscher's fast carriers

had raided the islands on 22–23 February, and a few bombs had been dropped in April on both Saipan and Guam by B–24's of the Seventh Air Force escorting Navy photographic planes over those islands.[3] For almost three months Army heavy bombers and Navy and Marine Corps fighters and dive bombers had steadily pounded Truk, the western Carolines, the Palaus, and Marcus and Wake Islands. After the destructive carrier strike against Truk on 17 February, primary responsibility for neutralizing that base as well as sister islands in the Carolines fell to planes of the Seventh Air Force, stationed in the Marshalls, and the Thirteenth Air Force, based at Empress Augusta Bay, Bougainville Island, and later (early May) in the Admiralities. The neutralization plan had called for almost daily attacks, since Japanese runways could otherwise have been quickly repaired to accommodate replacement planes flown down through the chain of mandated islands. As the target day for Saipan approached, B–24 raids against Truk were stepped up sharply and other possible danger points in the Carolines were hit proportionately.[4] Meanwhile, late in May Mitscher's Task Group 58.6 had conducted a successful raid on Marcus and Wake Islands to eliminate the possibility of

---

[1] CINCPAC-CINCPOA Opns in POA—Jun 44, Annex A, p. 28.
[2] *Ibid.*, p. 22.

[3] See Craven and Cate, *AAF IV*, pp. 684–87.
[4] *Ibid.*, pp. 677–88.

intervention from that direction in the forthcoming Marianas operation.[5] Thus, with all possible routes of enemy aerial interception from the south, east, and northeast successfully interdicted, Task Force 58 was assured a relatively free hand to deal with Japanese airpower based on the Marianas themselves.

The original plan for the preinvasion bombing of the Marianas called for the first Task Force 58 carrier strike to be launched at dawn of 12 June, three days before the scheduled landing. Because of unexpectedly good weather conditions en route, the escorting destroyers were fueled more rapidly than had been anticipated, and the entire force arrived at points within fighter range of its targets earlier than planned. This bit of good fortune induced Admiral Mitscher to request permission to launch his first fighter sweep on the afternoon of 11 June rather than wait until the following morning. His main reason was that all previous carrier attacks by Task Force 58 had been launched at dawn and that an alteration in the pattern would surprise the enemy and be that much more effective. Admiral Spruance approved, and at 1300 on the 11th the first planes took off from the carriers, which at that time were approximately 192 miles northeast of Guam and 225 miles southeast of Saipan and Tinian. The results were altogether gratifying. Of the 225 planes launched in this initial fighter sweep, only twelve were lost. By contrast, the enemy suffered heavily. Estimates as to Japanese aircraft put

out of operation either through destruction or serious damage ran from 147 to 215.[6]

Ashore on Saipan a Japanese soldier, member of the *9th Tank Regiment*, wrote of the strike in his diary:

At a little after 1300, I was awakened by the air raid alarm and immediately led all men into the trench. Scores of enemy Grumman fighters began strafing and bombing Aslito airfield and Garapan. For about two hours, the enemy planes ran amuck and finally left leisurely amidst the unparallelledly inaccurate antiaircraft fire. All we could do was watch helplessly. At night we went to extinguish the mountain fires which had been caused by gun fire. They were finally brought completely under control.[7]

In spite of the magnitude of the attack, the Japanese command on Saipan apparently did not realize on the 11th that this was the prologue to a full-size invasion. At 1600 on that date *43d Division* headquarters ordered the construction of a new road between the Marpi Point and Aslito airfields. The north–south highway already in use ran along the west coast adjacent to the ocean shore, and General Saito felt that in "the event of a battle occurring at the shore, there would be a great danger of the direction of the battle being hindered by an immediate interruption of communications."[8] The new road was to be inland from the coast line and follow the comparatively well-concealed foot of the mountains. Nothing could illustrate more graphically the Japanese failure to grasp

---

[5] Lt. (j.g.) A. O. Van Wyen and Lt. (j.g.) W. G. Land, Office, DCNO, Naval Air Operations in the Marianas: 11–20 June 1944, pp. B-10–B-17, copy in Records and Research Sec, Hist Br G-3, Hq USMC.

[6] *Ibid.,* pp. D-1–D-4, D-6; Comdr Fifth Fleet to COMINCH, Initial Rpt on Opn to Capture the Marianas, 13 Jul 44.

[7] CINCPAC-CINCPOA Trans 10238, Extracts From the Diary of Matsuya Tokuzo, *9th Tank Regiment.*

[8] CINCPAC-CINCPOA Trans 9378, *43d Division* Operation Orders, pp. 27, 28, 29 (Saipan, Jun 44).

the fact that the 11 June bombing was not merely another hit-and-run strike but the beginning of an invasion. If it had suspected an immediate invasion, the Army command on Saipan would not have diverted to a long-range project when men and matériel that could and should have been devoted to emergency fortifications.

Though there was a wide discrepancy in the estimates of damage inflicted on the Japanese during the attack of 11 June, there was no doubt that the enemy's power of aerial resistance in the Marianas had been considerably reduced. At no time thereafter were Japanese land-based aircraft more than a minor nuisance to American operations. According to Admiral Nimitz, "Control of the air had been effected by the original fighter sweep on 11 June." [9]

For the next three days (12–14 June) all four of Mitscher's task groups flew scheduled strikes over Saipan, Tinian, Guam, Rota, and Pagan with the object of continuing the destruction of enemy aircraft, rendering airfields at least temporarily useless, destroying coastal defense and antiaircraft batteries, and burning cane fields south of Mutcho Point on Saipan to prepare for forthcoming troop landings. In addition, last-minute photographic missions were flown over all three of the larger islands. During this period another fifty planes were reported destroyed with an additional sixty-six put out of operation. The task groups were less successful in bombing enemy airfields. Few runways on these or any other outlying bases were surfaced with concrete, macadam, or steel strip since the comparatively light weight of Japanese aircraft made such expenditure

of time and material unnecessary, and it proved almost impossible to render the earthen airfields permanently unserviceable by moderate bombing attacks.[10]

The effectiveness of preliminary aerial bombardment of coastal defense and antiaircraft artillery is difficult to assess. Pilots reported direct hits on gun positions on all three islands, but the accuracy of these reports could not be precisely measured. The mere fact that enemy guns remained silent after a strike was no indication that they had been destroyed or even seriously damaged since the Japanese might have been holding their fire in order to save ammunition or avoid detection. Indeed, one dive bomber squadron leader after a run on Tinian admitted, "The odds of a dive bomber hitting a target the size of a gun are astronomical even under ideal conditions." He concluded that, on the basis of photographs and observations, shrapnel and blast resulting from the bombing caused the chief damage to enemy installations, knocking out the control posts and damaging some of the guns.[11]

On 12 June Admiral Mitscher's carrier pilots came into an unexpected windfall in the form of two Japanese convoys trying to escape the area. One of these, composed of about twenty vessels and located about 125 miles west of Pagan on a northerly course, was immediately bombed and strafed heavily.[12] Nine merchant ships, with a total tonnage of almost 30,000 tons, along with their escort vessels including one large torpedo boat, three submarine chasers, and a converted net tender, were

---

[9] CINCPAC-CINCPOA Opns in POA—Jun 44, Annex A, p. 30.

[10] Van Wyen and Land, Naval Air Operations in the Marianas, pp. C-2–C-5.

[11] *Ibid.,* p. C-5.

[12] CINCPAC-CINCPOA Opns in POA—Jun 44, pp. 30–31.

sunk.[13] On the same day, other carrier planes hit two cargo vessels just off the northwest coast of Saipan, sinking one and damaging the other so badly that it had to be beached. Still another was sunk while being repaired in Tanapag Harbor.[14] On 13 June a convoy fleeing south of the west coast of Guam was struck by planes of Rear Adm. Joseph G. Clark's Task Group 58.1. One high-speed transport was definitely sunk and other shipping was reported set on fire.[15]

Also on 13 June, while the carrier planes continued their bombing and strafing missions against the islands, the fast battleships and certain designated destroyers were detached from escort and screening duties and assigned the mission of initiating naval shore bombardment of Saipan and Tinian and covering mine-sweeping operations. Seven fast battleships and eleven destroyers were detached and formed into a separate bombardment group under command of

Vice Adm. William A. Lee, Jr. From 1040 until about 1725 they pounded the west coast of Saipan and Tinian. Meanwhile, ten fast mine sweepers probed the waters off the west coast of Saipan from distances of about six to two miles offshore. They found no moored contact or acoustics mines and received no fire from the beach. That night the battleships withdrew, but five destroyers remained in the area to deliver harassing fire.[16]

The results of the first day's naval gunfire were doubtful. At the close of the day's bombardment, headquarters of the *31st Army* reported that although the city streets in Garapan and Charan Kanoa had been almost destroyed, personnel losses had been relatively slight.[17] In spite of naval reports of considerable damage done to shore installations, General Holland Smith's naval gunfire officers remained skeptical. In their opinion, the effectiveness of the firing by these ships of Mitscher's task force had been limited because of severe handicaps. With one exception, the fast battleships had received no continuous training in shore bombardment as had most of the old battleships. This type of firing, which required slow, patient adjustments on specific targets, was quite different from that normally experienced in surface engagements and called for specialized training. Also, air spotters off the fast battleships had neither experience nor training in locating ground targets. Finally, because none of the ships was allowed to move closer than 10,000 yards (five nautical

---

[13] JANAC, *Japanese Shipping Losses,* pp. 12, 60–61. Naval pilots mistook this torpedo boat, the *Otori,* for a destroyer and so reported it. (Van Wyen and 'Land, Naval Air Operations in the Marianas, p. C–27.) The error is understandable since the *Otori,* though less than half the size of a destroyer, resembled it somewhat in silhouette. Otherwise, American damage claims for this action erred on the side of modesty. Postwar studies indicated a total of fourteen ships sunk, whereas the official American Navy claim came only to ten. Van Wyen and Land, Naval Operations in the Marianas, p. C–27; JANAC, *Japanese Shipping Losses,* pp. 12, 60.

[14] JANAC, *Japanese Shipping Losses,* pp. 60–61; Japanese Studies in World War II, 97, *A-GO* Operations Log, pp. 13–14, OCMH. The Joint Army-Navy Assessment Committee claimed that one of these, the *Keiyo Maru,* was sunk. Japanese sources examined since the war indicate that it was only badly damaged and was subsequently beached on Saipan.

[15] JANAC, *Japanese Shipping Losses,* p. 12; Van Wyen and Land, Naval Air Operations in the Marianas, p. C–13; CINCPAC-CINCPOA Opns in POA—Jun 44, Annex A, p. 31.

[16] CINCPAC-CINCPOA Opns in POA—Jun 44, Annex A, pp. 34–35, and Table XII, App. 1.

[17] CINCPAC-CINCPOA Item 9983–85, translation of captured Japanese document, *SONAE* Staff Msg 1011.

DESTRUCTION AT CHARAN KANOA

miles) from the shore for fear of mines, accurate fire against anything but large buildings and other such obvious targets was virtually impossible.[18]

Nevertheless, to the Japanese on the island the bombardment of the 13th, and especially that of the naval vessels, was a terrifying experience. One soldier described it thus:

At 0500 there was a fierce enemy air attack. I have at last come to the place where I will die. I am pleased to think that I will die calmly in true samurai style. Naval gunfire supported this attack which was too terrible for words. I feel now like a full-fledged warrior. Towards evening the firing died down

but at night naval gunfire continued as before. About 1700 communications with battalion headquarters were cut off.[19]

Another eyewitness, a Japanese naval officer, noted: "The shells began to fall closer and closer to the airfield. It was frightful. The workers were all rather depressed." [20] The same officer reported that shortly after the naval shelling started he ordered his lookouts, his fire-fighting unit, and his workers to withdraw to caves in the hills. He himself remained behind with a junior officer and a "superior petty officer." "On the veranda of the destroyed

---

[18] TF 56 Rpt FORAGER, Incl G, Sec. 2, Rpt on Naval Gunfire Support, p. 10; NTLF Rpt Marianas, Phase I, Incl I, Sec. 3, Naval Gunfire Rpt, p. 5.

[19] CINCPAC-CINCPOA Trans 10051, Extracts From the Diary of an Unidentified Japanese Soldier.

[20] CINCPAC-CINCPOA Translations and Interrogations, Vol. 29, Trans B-1938, Diary of a Naval Officer, June–July 1944.

workers' quarters," he notes, "we who had stayed behind bolstered our spirits with five bottles of beer."[21]

Early on the morning of 14 June, Rear Adm. Jesse B. Oldendorf arrived off the coast of Saipan with the two bombardment groups that would carry the main burden of naval gunfire support both before and during the seizure of the island. This force consisted of seven old battleships, eleven cruisers, twenty-six destroyers, and a few destroyer transports and fast mine sweepers.[22] The battleships had all been commissioned between 1915 and 1921.[23] Four of them, *California, Pennsylvania, Maryland,* and *Tennessee,* were survivors of the attack on Pearl Harbor.[24] All had undergone the rigorous training program for shore bombardment set up by V Amphibious Corps at Kahoolawe Island in the Hawaiian Islands.

These ships were able to move into closer range than had the fast battleships in the previous day's bombardment. Mine sweepers had reported the area to the seaward of two miles from the shore line free of mines and were steadily moving in closer to the reef line. Better results were reported from this day's activities, and many installations were believed to have been directly hit, in spite of the facts that the time allowed for

deliberate pinpoint fire was too short and that air spotters again revealed their lack of training in distinguishing important land targets.

There is evidence that this preinvasion bombardment was especially effective against prepared gun positions of antiaircraft units, which were for the most part fixed. Two prisoners of war taken on 29 June reported that their antiaircraft unit, the *1st Battery, 25th AAA Regiment,* had been annihilated before D Day in the Magicienne Bay area.[25] The Japanese naval officer quoted above noted in his diary, "Practically all our antiaircraft gun and machine gun positions were destroyed by bombing and shelling on the 13th, 14th, and 15th." [26]

In other respects, however, the American preliminary bombardment was far from perfect. A Japanese artillery instructor, assigned to Saipan as an observer, managed to radio the following report on the effects of the shelling:

Beach positions withstood four days of bombardment. Those observation posts and gun emplacements that were protected by splinter-proof shelters were able to withstand the bombardment. Dummy positions proved very effective. During bombardment, both day and night, movement to alternate positions was very difficult. Communication lines were cut frequently, and the need for repairs and messengers was great.[27]

During this naval bombardment of the 14th, two of the supporting ships were hit by fire from the shore. The destroyer *Braine,* while bombarding Tinian, took a 4.7-inch shell that caused three deaths and

---

[21] The consumption of five bottles of beer by three men is not as harmless as it would appear at first glance. Japanese beer is stronger than the standard Western brew and normally comes in bottles holding a little more than a quart. Also, Japanese are notoriously poor drinkers, with consumption and sobriety levels far below Western standards. This particular naval officer may have been an exception, for, as noted below, he resorted to stronger stuff on D Day.

[22] CINCPAC-CINCPOA Opns in POA—Jun 44, Annex A, Table IV, App. 1.

[23] *Jane's Fighting Ships, 1944-45* (New York, The Macmillan Company, 1947), pp. 438–46.

[24] Morison, *Rising Sun in the Pacific,* pp. 106–08, 111–13, 117–19.

[25] NTLF Rpt Marianas, Phase I, G–2 Rpt, 12 Aug 44, p. 86.

[26] CINCPAC-CINCPOA Trans B–1938.

[27] CINCPAC-CINCPOA Trans 15282, Tactical Lessons Learned on Saipan, by Captain Shimamura, *Combined Fleet,* Aug 44.

DUMMY SEARCHLIGHT PLATFORM ON EAST COAST OF SAIPAN. *False positions such as this effectively diverted some air and sea bombardment from genuine defense positions.*

numerous injuries. The battleship *California* was struck by a small caliber artillery shell; one man was killed, nine were wounded, and the ship's fire control system was damaged.[28]

Also on the 14th, three naval underwater demolition teams reconnoitered the landing beaches of Saipan as well as other parts of the shore line. Each team consisted of about sixteen officers and eighty men, all naval personnel except for one Army and one Marine liaison officer per team. The men were dispatched from destroyer transports in small boats to the edge of the reef whence they swam close into the shore line in full daylight under the protection of ships' fire. No obstacles were reported and hence no demolition work was necessary. The teams performed their work under considerable fire from the beach, but even so only two men were killed and fifteen wounded—a low figure considering the inherent danger of the operation and the fact that promised air support failed to materialize and ships' fire was generally too far inland to provide much protection.[29]

One result of the underwater demolition activities was to alert the Japanese on Sai-

[28] TF 51 Opn Rpt Marianas, Incl A, p. 5; CO USS *California*, Rev Rpt of Participation in Saipan Opns, 7 Jul 44, p. 9.

[29] TF 51 Opn Rpt Marianas, Incl G, pp. 2–3.

JAPANESE TYPE 96 25-MM. MACHINE CANNON. *U.S. marines repaired this damaged twin-mount weapon fitted with speed ring sights and promptly put it to use against the enemy.*

pan as to the probable place and time of the forthcoming landing. At 0800 a *31st Army* message stated: "The enemy at about 0730 was making reconnaissance of reef with small boats. It is judged that the enemy will land here." Later in the day another message from the same headquarters reported:

Since early this morning the enemy small vessels have been planting markers and searching for tank passages on the reef. Because as far as one can see there are no transports, the landing will have to be after tonight or dawn tomorrow. The enemy bombardment is being carried out on coastal areas in anticipation of a landing.[30]

D-Day Bombardment and Ship-to-Shore Movement

On the night of 14–15 June most of the support ships retired, leaving a handful to continue harassing fire along the coast line. Meanwhile the Western Landing Group, commanded by Admiral Hill and consisting mostly of transports and LST's carrying the 2d and 4th Marine Divisions, was slowly approaching the island from the east. As dark fell the marines could observe fires burning ashore and the glow of star

---

[30] CINCPAC-CINCPOA Trans 9983–85, *31st Army* Msg File, Msgs 1012, 1015.

shells fired by the naval ships left in the area. Shortly after 0500 the gigantic convoy moved into the transport area off the west coast of Saipan. In the early dawn, Mount Tapotchau lay silhouetted in the east. Streaks of fire from the armada of naval support ships colored the sky and the shore was blurred in a haze of smoke and dust. As the light improved, the town of Charan Kanoa became visible. To the north lay Garapan, the capital city. In its harbor, called Tanapag, lay several Japanese ships, beached, half-sunken, and smoking.

Naval bombardment commenced about 0530. Heavy close support ships were ordered not to approach closer than 1,500 yards from the reef. Destroyers were permitted to move in as far as 1,000 yards. Two old battleships, two cruisers, and seven destroyers were assigned the duty of last-minute preparation of the landing beaches themselves.[31] At dawn these ships took station and shortly thereafter the two battleships commenced main battery fire at the beach defenses; less than an hour later the two cruisers opened up with their 12-inch guns.

In spite of the apparent intensity of this barrage, the Japanese high command was not overly impressed—at least not officially. From *31st Army* headquarters came the report: "They did not carry out large scale shelling and bombing against the positions on the landing beach just prior to landing. When they came to the landing, even though we received fierce bombing and shelling, our basic positions were completely sound." [32]

But to other less exalted defenders of the island, the shelling appeared more formidable. One member of the *9th Tank Regiment* observed fairly effective results from the shelling of the Magicienne Bay area. A naval supply warehouse was hit, causing a considerable number of casualties, and a nearby ammunition dump was set off. "There was no way," he reported, "of coping with the explosions. We could do nothing but wait for them to stop." [33] Somewhere in the same vicinity, the Japanese naval officer mentioned above took to the bottle again to calm his nerves against the shock of the shelling. "I quietly opened the quart I brought along," he noted in his diary, "and took my first 'shot' from it. There is something undescribable about a shot of liquor during a bombardment." [34]

At 0545 the word was passed throughout the American task forces that H Hour, the moment at which the first troops were supposed to land, would be 0830, as scheduled. Guns and winches were manned; boats were lowered into the water from the transports.

Shortly after 0700 the thirty-four LST's carrying the Marine assault battalions moved into position and dropped anchor about half a mile off the line of departure. The line, the starting point from which the assault landing craft would take off, was located 4,250 yards offshore. Bow doors swung open; ramps lowered, and hundreds of amphibian tractors and amphibian tanks crawled into the water and commenced to circle. In all, 719 of these craft would be employed in the operation.

Astern of the assault landing ships lay twelve other LST's carrying light artillery,

[31] CINCPAC-CINCPOA Opns in POA—Jun 44, Plate XV, App. A.
[32] CINCPAC-CINCPOA Trans 9983–85, *31st Army* Msg File, Msg 1027.

[33] CINCPAC-CINCPOA Trans 10238.
[34] CINCPAC-CINCPOA Trans B–1938.

most of which would be landed in DUKW's. Still further seaward of each division's beach lay two dock landing ships embarked with heavier landing craft (LCM's) that would take ashore the tanks and heavy artillery as soon as enough beachhead had been secured by the infantry.[35] About 18,000 yards offshore the larger troop transports swung at anchor. Aboard were reserve troops, headquarters troops, shore party teams, heavy artillery, trucks, tractors, bulldozers, and sundry equipment and supplies.

Meanwhile, north of the main transport area, marines of the 2d Regimental Combat Team (2d Marine Division) and the 1st Battalion, 29th Marines, were conducting a diversionary demonstration off the town of Garapan. Boats were lowered, troops embarked, standard waves were formed and went in as far as 5,000 yards off the beach. There they circled for ten minutes without receiving any fire and then returned to their mother ships.

Off the main landing beaches, all ships' fire ceased at 0700 to allow a thirty-minute strike by carrier planes. Fifty fighters, 51 scout bombers, and 54 torpedo bombers conducted an area bombing attack along the beaches with the primary aim of demoralizing the enemy rather than knocking out particular installations. As soon as this strike lifted, the naval ships assigned to close support took up the course once again and continued to hit the beaches with heavy guns until the first wave of troops was only 1,000 yards from the shore line and with 5-inch guns until the

troops had progressed to within 300 yards.[36]

The line of departure was marked by four naval patrol craft (PC's), each anchored and flying flags designating the number and color of the beaches opposite them. At 0750, H Hour was postponed to 0840 because of a delay in launching the amphibian tractors. Small control craft escorted the leading waves toward the line of departure. A few minutes after 0800 the control craft hoisted their Wave-1 flags and twenty-four LCI gunboats crossed the line of departure, firing their automatic weapons as they went. About five minutes later wave flags were run down from the signal yardarms of the anchored patrol craft and the first wave of amphibian tanks and tractors crossed the line of departure. Following waves—three for the northern beaches and four for the southern—were spaced at intervals of from two to eight minutes. The run into the beach would take a few minutes less than half an hour at maximum LVT(A) speed of 4.5 knots. About 1,600 yards from shore the gunboats on the northern beaches stopped engines and lay to just short of the reef but kept up their fire as the first wave passed through them. On the southern beaches, where the reef was closer to the shore, the LCI(G)'s moved in to 400 yards and let loose salvos of 4.5-inch rockets in a last-minute saturation of the beach. As the leading troops came within 300 yards of the shore, all naval gunfire ceased except in the area around Afetna Point, which lay between the two divisions' beaches. A last-

---

[35] LCM—landing craft mechanized—a shallow draft vessel, fifty feet long, equipped with a bow ramp and primarily designed to carry a tank or motor vehicles directly onto the beach.

[36] This account of D-Day preliminary bombardment is taken from the following sources: CINCPAC-CINCPOA Opns in POA—Jun 44, Annex A, pp. 41–47; TF 56 Rpt FORAGER, Incl G, Sec. 2, pp. 40–41; 2d Marine Div SAR FORAGER, Phase I, Sec. V.

AMPHIBIAN TRACTORS IN LINE ABREAST FORMATION *churn toward Saipan's beaches.*

minute strafing attack by seventy-two carrier-based planes commenced when the leading waves were 800 yards from the shore line, continued until the first troops were within 100 yards of the beaches, then shifted to 100 yards inland until the first landings were made.

The formation of the assault waves differed between the two Marine divisions. North of Afetna Point, the 2d Marine Division was landing with four battalion landing teams abreast. From north to south (left to right) the 6th Marines headed for Red Beaches 2 and 3; the 8th Marines for Green Beaches 1 and 2, immediately in front of the Charan Kanoa airstrip. South of Afetna Point, the 4th Marine Division proceeded toward Blue and Yellow Beaches with the 23d Regimental Combat Team on the left and the 25th on the right. (*Map 4*)

In the 2d Marine Division's zone the first wave consisted of eight separated lines of six amphibian tractors, each in line-abreast formation. Between each line of six

LVT's was echeloned one platoon of amphibian tanks (LVT(A)(4)'s) mounting 75-mm. howitzers. The succeeding three waves consisted of LVT's alone in line-abreast. The amphtracks (LVT's) were crewed by the Marine's 2d Amphibian Tractor Battalion and the Army's 715th Amphibian Tractor Battalion. The amphibian tanks, seventy in number, belonged to the Marine's 2d Armored Amphibian Battalion.[37]

The 4th Marine Division's landing plan differed. The first wave consisted exclusively of sixty-eight amphibian tanks, formed abreast and manned by the Army's 708th Amphibian Tank Battalion. Most of these were old style LVT(A)(1)'s with only a 37-mm. gun on the bow, but sixteen of them were LVT(A)(4)'s carrying 75-mm. howitzers. Astern in four successive waves

[37] Army and Marine Corps nomenclature for these vehicles differed. In the Marine Corps they were designated "armored amphibians"; in the Army, "amphibian tanks." The latter usage will be followed in this volume. LVT's were sometimes called amtracs or amphtracks.

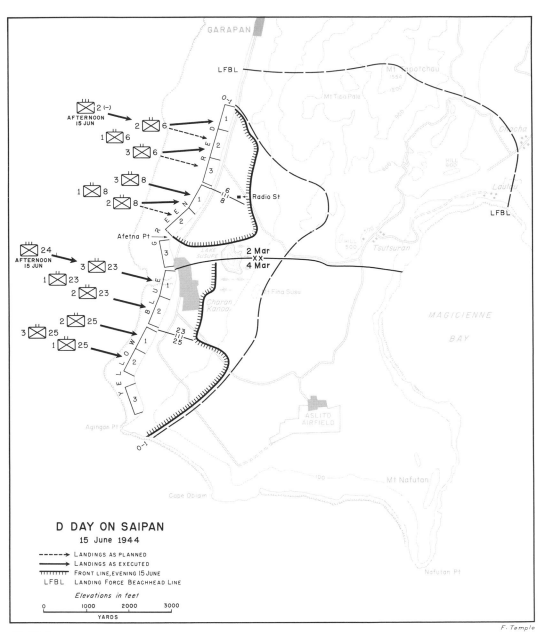

D DAY ON SAIPAN
15 June 1944

- - - -> LANDINGS AS PLANNED
———→ LANDINGS AS EXECUTED
ΙΙΙΙΙΙ FRONT LINE, EVENING 15 JUNE
LFBL   LANDING FORCE BEACHHEAD LINE

Elevations in feet

0   1000   2000   3000
              YARDS

F. Temple

MAP 4

came the assault troops boated in amphibian tractors of the Marine 10th Amphibian Tractor Battalion (less Company A, plus Company C, 11th Amphibian Tractor Battalion) and the Army 773d Amphibian Tractor Battalion.[38]

From the line of departure to the reef the first waves moved in good order and met only moderate enemy gunfire. Once across the reef, however, the picture changed. All along the line the Japanese opened up with automatic weapons, anti-boat guns, and artillery and mortar barrages against the first wave. These increased in intensity as the second, third, and fourth waves climbed over the reef. In the 2d Marine Division's zone, three amphibian tanks and four tractors were knocked out of action between the reef and the beach.[39] Surf in the area ran as high as twelve to fifteen feet, too high for amphtracks to operate with any great degree of safety. Nevertheless, only two capsized as a result of the swells. About 98 percent of all the tractors got ashore safely.

Once across the reef, the wave formation in the 2d Division area broke down completely. Because of their superior speed, many of the tractors commenced to overtake their supporting amphibian tanks and to compress them from echelon almost into column formation. Some tractors crossed in front of the tanks thus masking their fire.[40]

Even more serious, the Navy guide boat led the leading waves off course. This has been variously attributed to compass error, a strong drift of current to the northward, and the fact that extremely heavy fire was coming at the boats on the right flank from the area around Afetna Point. Whatever the reason, the entire right flank of the leading waves veered to the left, thus causing a northerly shift along the entire line and considerable crowding in the center. The 2d Battalion, 8th Marines, which was scheduled to land on Green Beach 2, went ashore instead on Green 1, where it became badly intermixed with the 3d Battalion of the same regiment. The two assault battalions of the 6th Marines landed about 400 yards north of their assigned beaches, Red 2 and 3.[41]

The first assault waves of the 8th Marines landed on the Green Beaches at approximately 0843; the last were being landed by 0900. On the Red Beaches the first assault wave landed at 0840, the last at 0908.

To the south, in the area of the 4th Marine Division, the ship-to-shore movement was proceeding somewhat more smoothly. Here, the sixty-eight amphibian tanks of the Army's 708th Amphibian Tank Battalion constituted the entire first wave. All commenced to fire 75-mm. howitzers or 37-mm. guns about 400 yards from the shore after mounting the reef. From each beach came answering fire of all types including mortar, small arms, and artillery. Japanese artillery markers—small flags on bamboo sticks that were apparently a part

---

[38] This account of the organization of the ship-to-shore movement is derived from the following sources: TF 51 Opn Rpt Marianas, Incl C, pp. 2–3. COMINCH P–007, Ch. IV, p. 6, Diagrammatic Chart Showing Organization of Boat Waves, Saipan. NTLF Rpt Marianas, Phase I, Incl E, G–3 Rpt, pp. 13–14. *Ibid.,* Incl H, LVT Rpt, with the following inclosures: Incl A, Rpt of 2d Amph Trac Bn, pp. 5–7; Incl B, Rpt of 5th Amph Trac Bn, pp. 2–3; Incl C, Rpt of 10th Amph Trac Bn, pp. 1, 4; Incl E, Rpt of 715th Amph Trac Bn, pp. 1–3; Incl F, Rpt of 773d Amph Trac Bn, p. 5; Incl G, Rpt of 2d Armd Amph Tk Bn, pp. 1–2; and Incl H, Rpt of 708th Amph Tk Bn, pp. 1–2. 2d Marine Div SAR, Phase I, FORAGER, Part I, Sec. V, p. 1. 4th Marine Div Opns Rpt Saipan, Annex C, pp. 1–9.

[39] NTLF Rpt Marianas, Phase I, Incl H, LVT Rpt; Incl A, Rpt of 2d Amph Trac Bn, p. 7; Incl E, Rpt of 715th Amph Trac Bn, p. 3; Incl G, Rpt of 2d Armd Amph Bn, p. 1.

[40] *Ibid.,* Annex G, Rpt of 2d Armd Amph Bn, p. 1.

[41] Hoffman, *Saipan,* p. 50.

CONGESTION ON 2D MARINE DIVISION BEACH, *the result of the right-flank battalion landing north of its assigned area. Note disabled LVT(A)(4) at upper right.*

of the enemy's prearranged fire plan and for unknown reasons had not been removed by underwater demolition teams on the previous day—were scattered along the reef. Of the sixty-eight tanks in the first wave all but three arrived safely. One burned, one was swamped on the reef, and one received a direct hit from an antitank weapon firing from the shore at about twenty-five yards range.[42]

Astern of the tanks came the amphibian tractors of the Marine 10th Amphibian Tractor Battalion and the Army 773d Amphibian Tractor Battalion in four waves, spaced from two to six minutes apart. Of the 196 troop-carrying tractors, only two failed to land their cargo; one was hit by a shell on the reef and the other

[42] 1st Lt. Russell A. Gugeler, FA, 1st I and H Sv, Army Amphibian Tractor and Tank Battalions in the Battle of Saipan, 15 June–9 July 1944, 20 Jan 45, pp. 6–7, MS in OCMH. These figures differ from those given in the official action report of the 708th Amphibian Tank Battalion, which

states that two of its tanks were overturned and three lost due to maintenance difficulties. The report mentions no direct hits. (NTLF Rpt Marianas, Phase I, Incl H to Incl Y, p. 1). The former figures are accepted as more accurate because the author of that account gives a detailed description of the LVT(A) casualties in the battalion as well as the names and actions of the personnel involved.

developed mechanical difficulties. Between 0843 and 0907 all of the leading waves with about 8,000 marines embarked were ashore.[43]

Breakdown of the Landing Plan

From the outset, two factors marred the smooth execution of the landing plan. The first was the wide gap that had developed between the right battalion (2d Battalion, 8th Marines) of the 2d Marine Division and the left battalion (3d Battalion, 23d Marines) of the 4th Marine Division. The landing plan had provided for a gap between the two divisions. Troops were not to land on Afetna Point itself because of the reasonable fear that the enemy would have placed his heaviest concentration of artillery there to guard the only channel through the reef to the pier at Charan Kanoa.[44] However, the distance between the two divisions was more than double that envisaged because the 2d Battalion, 8th Marines, landed north of its assigned beach. Almost three days would elapse before firm contact between the divisions was established.

Perhaps more serious was the breakdown of the scheme to employ amphibian tanks and tractors to carry the assault inland from the water's edge. The basic plan for the landing on Saipan prescribed a blitz assault, continuous from shipboard inland to the first high ground. In the 2d Marine Division's zone of action the four companies of amphibian tanks were to proceed inland about three hundred yards to the tractor control line, cover the debarkation of the assault troops from their tractors, and support their advance to the first objective line, which lay about 1,500 yards inland.[45] Tractors of the first wave were to accompany the LVT(A)'s to the tractor control line and there debark their troops. The succeeding three waves were supposed to discharge their troops on the beach.[46]

In the zone of the 4th Marine Division, the initial wave—amphibian tanks—was to lead the next two waves—tractors—all the way to the first objective line, which was located on the first high ground a mile inland. There, the tanks would deploy and support the troops as they debarked and moved forward. The fourth and fifth waves were to be discharged at the beach and mop-up areas bypassed by the leading waves.[47]

None of these plans succeeded completely, and for the most part the scheme of employing amphibian tanks as land tanks and amphibian tractors as overland troop-carrying vehicles must be marked off as a failure. The LVT(A)'s had neither the armor nor the armament to withstand the terrible pounding from enemy artillery and supporting weapons that could be expected during this phase of the assault. Moreover,

---

[43] NTLF Rpt Marianas, Phase I, Incl H, LVT Rpt; Incl C, Rpt of 10th Amph Trac Bn, p. 4; Incl F, Rpt of 773d Amph Trac Bn, p. 5.

[44] Information from Maj. Carl Hoffman, USMC, who commanded the right flank company (Company G) of the 8th Marines, to the author, 30 March 1950.

[45] NTLF Rpt Marianas, Phase I, Incl H, LVT Rpt; Incl G, Rpt of 2d Armd Amph Bn, p. 1. The tractor control line should not be confused with the transfer control line, which was on the seaward side of the reef and marked the point at which troops and supplies would be transferred from small craft (LCVP's) to amphibian tractors.

[46] NTLF Rpt Marianas, Phase I, Incl B, Rpt of 5th Amph Trac Bn, p. 5.

[47] 4th Marine Div Opns Rpt Saipan, Annex H, 23d RCT Rpt, p. 29; Annex J, 25th RCT Rpt, p. 3.

the LVT(A)'s were underpowered and were stopped by sand, trenches, holes, trees, and other minor obstacles, most of which a land tank could have negotiated with ease.[48] Once the tractors were out of the water, their hulls were exposed and they became easy targets for enemy fire, which their armor was too light to resist. On shore they were clumsy and slow. It proved far healthier for troops to extricate themselves from these death traps as fast as possible and find shelter in whatever natural protection the terrain and the vegetation offered.

On the 2d Marine Division's beaches the situation rapidly became chaotic. Trees, trenches, and shell holes stopped some of the tanks of the 2d Armored Amphibian Battalion before they could even cross the beach. Between the beach and the tractor control line, twenty-eight LVT(A)'s, more than one-third the total number, were disabled. Only a few points of ingress from the beach inland could be discovered, and while the amphibian tanks were maneuvering up and down trying to locate the points they became almost hopelessly intermixed with the tractors of the first and succeeding waves. Up to the tractor control line infantry troops were able to maintain close contact with the tanks, but the eighteen LVT(A)'s that went beyond that point got little infantry support. Tanks fired indiscriminately among troops and tractors and in general merely added to the confusion instead of aiding the battalions they were supposed to support.[49]

Congestion was particularly bad in the area of Green Beach 1, where the two battalions of the 8th Marines were trying to land at the same time because the right flank of the first wave had veered to the left. These troops were all embarked in the amphibian tractors of the 715th Amphibian Tractor Battalion. Directly ahead of them was a heavily wooded bank constituting an almost impassable barrier for tanks and tractors alike. The marines forthwith abandoned their tractors and took cover behind the embankment. Within five minutes after the first wave touched shore, the second wave arrived and landed a little to its right. By the time the third and fourth waves had landed, the men on foot were being squeezed between the tractors to their rear and the Japanese to the front. All together, only two tractors were able to get beyond the beach, one making its way as far as the radio tower 700 yards inland. Two days later, the driver wandered back to the beach but was too shell-shocked to be able to remember how he had got that far or what had happened when he got there.[50]

On the southern beaches, the 708th Amphibian Tank Battalion fared a little better. Of the sixty-eight tanks in the first wave, about half reached Fina Susu ridge by ten o'clock.[51] Contrary to expectations, progress through the town of Charan Kanoa was fairly easy, and by 0915 thirteen tanks of Company B, assigned to this sector, had arrived at the objective. South of them the going was more difficult. The tanks

---

[48] NTLF Rpt Marianas, Phase I, Incl H, LVT Rpt; Incl G, Rpt of 2d Armd Amph Trac Bn, pp. 8–9; Incl H, Rpt of 708th Amph Tk Bn, pp. 6–7.

[49] *Ibid.*, Incl G, Rpt of 2d Armd Amph Trac Bn, pp. 1–2; 6th RCT 2d Marine Div SAR, Phase I, FORAGER, Incl A, p. 1.

[50] Gugeler, Army Amph Trac and Tk Bns at Saipan, p. 22.

[51] *Ibid.*, p. 10. Gugeler states that thirty-three tanks reached the O–1 line, most of them by 1000. According to the action report of the battalion itself, forty tanks were on the O–1 line by 1000. NTLF Rpt Marianas, Phase I, Incl H, LVT Rpt; Incl H, Rpt of 708th Amph Tk Bn, p. 3.

that landed below Charan Kanoa had to fight swampy ground, tank trenches, heavy artillery, a burning gas dump, and a steep railroad embankment before attaining the ridge. Nineteen made it. Those on the extreme right had the most difficulty. Swinging south, three tanks reached the tip of Agingan Point about a thousand yards south of the lowest landing beach. They braved it out against fairly heavy Japanese mortar and artillery fire, but when American naval shells commenced to drop in the area they discreetly withdrew.[52] Agingan Point would have to wait another day for capture.

Meanwhile, back on the beaches most of the troops were deserting their amphibian tractors for the dubious safety of traveling on foot and belly. The 23d Marines, which landed in and just south of Charan Kanoa, made fair progress inland. Fifteen LVT's of the second wave were able to carry their troops through the town itself and on to the ridge behind. On the beach immediately below, thirty-three tractors got as far as a railroad embankment about 400 yards inland before the infantry commanders ordered their troops to debark.[53]

On the southern (Yellow) beaches, where the fighting was fiercest, no such progress was made. One company of the 773d Amphibian Tractor Battalion got as far as a railroad spur about 700 yards inland, but the rest unloaded their troops as rapidly as possible and shoved off back to the transfer line beyond the reef. In spite of the hasty withdrawal of most of the first group of LVT's, the shore line soon was

thick with tractors as succeeding waves telescoped onto the beach. It was small wonder. After a full hour's fighting the 1st Battalion, 25th Marines, had succeeded in pushing just twelve yards in from the beach, and the 2d Battalion's progress was only a little better.[54] The tractor plan failed most signally here. The infantryman was on his own.

Expanding the Beachead

Action of the 2d Marine Division

On the Red Beaches to the north, the two assault battalions of the 6th Marines met fierce enemy fire immediately upon landing. The failure of most of the amphibian tanks and tractors to proceed any considerable distance inland and the rain of enemy shells caused unexpected congestion and confusion on the beaches.[55] The command posts of both battalions received direct hits that seriously injured battalion commanders and most of their staffs. The regimental commander, Col. James P. Risely, USMC, came ashore at 1000 and established his command post practically at the water's edge. Forty minutes later the regimental reserve (1st Battalion, 6th Marines) commenced to land and prepare to support the assault elements.

By 1105 the front line had advanced only 400 yards inland. The 3d Battalion, on the right, was suffering especially heavy casual-

[52] Gugeler, Army Amph Trac and Tk Bns at Saipan, pp. 10–11.
[53] NTLF Rpt Marianas, Phase I, Incl H, LVT Rpt; Incl C, Rpt of 10th Amph Trac Bn, p. 4.

[54] 4th Marine Div Opns Rpt Saipan, Annex J, 25th RCT Rpt, p. 3.
[55] The following account of D-Day activity in the 2d Marine Division's zone of action is derived from: 2d Marine Div SAR, Phase I, FORAGER, Sec. V, pp. 1–5; 6th RCT 2d Marine Div SAR, Phase I, FORAGER, Incl A, pp. 1–2; 1st Bn 20th Marine SAR Saipan, Incl A, p. 1; Hoffman, Saipan, pp. 51–55.

EARLY WAVE ON THE BEACH, *protected by embankment. Black rods in foreground are portable radio antennas. Note disabled amtracks.*

ties, and the 1st Battalion was therefore ordered to pass through the 3d. Weak points began to appear all along the line. More serious, a dangerous gap developed between the right flank of the 6th Marines and the left flank of the 8th Marines when the 6th Marines landed some 400 yards north of its assigned beaches. In spite of the fact that Companies K and L of the 6th Regiment were ordered to establish physical contact, a gap of 300 yards still existed, although covered by fire.

Around noon the 6th Regiment's casualties had mounted to an estimated 35 percent. An hour later three Japanese tanks counterattacked in the area in front of the command post. Two of the tanks were knocked out by bazookas before penetrating the front line, but the third managed to push through to within seventy-five yards of the command post before being disabled by a bazooka rocket fired from the post itself. During the morning and early afternoon the regiment had no supporting weapons ashore other than those carried as organizational—bazookas, antitank grenades, and 37-mm. guns. Meanwhile, however, some tanks had commenced to land. Shortly after 0900 a pilot tank was disembarked at the reef's edge to explore the best passage through the reef. By 1020 it had searched out a path to Green Beach

1, although it was under heavy fire all the way. Once on the beach, enemy fire forced the crew to abandon the tank, but a reef route was marked and by 1300 the first of the 2d Division's tanks had landed on Green 1 and moved northward to support the 6th Marines. By midafternoon those tanks assigned to the 8th Marines had successfully landed and were in operation.

Southward, on the Green Beaches, the chief problems facing the 8th Marines were confusion and congestion. The right flank battalion (the 2d) had landed from 700 to 1,000 yards north of its assigned beaches. As a result, the two assault battalions of the 8th Marines and part of one battalion of the 6th Marines all found themselves in the same beach area. To add to the confusion, the commanders of the two assault battalions of the 8th Marines were both wounded early in the action and had to be evacuated. The 2d Battalion, 8th Marines, had the most difficult job—to attack south along the beach toward Afetna Point. The object was not only to remove the menace of antiboat weapons located in that area but also to secure the single reef channel off Charan Kanoa and permit the early entry of tank-carrying landing craft, which could not negotiate the reef itself. According to their prescribed scheme of maneuver, one company (Company G) moved south along the beach and the other two (E and F) fanned out to the southeast. Company G was heavily armed with shotguns in addition to its normal weapons. These short-range guns with wide dispersion patterns were allotted to Company G chiefly as insurance against its firing into the lines of the 4th Marine Division toward which it was advancing. Progress was slow —the beach itself was thickly covered with

pillboxes, and enemy riflemen situated east of the Charan Kanoa airstrip made the most of the flat, open terrain to harass the company's left flank as it inched southward. At 0950 the 1st Battalion, in regimental reserve, was ordered to land. Company B was attached to the 2d Battalion to support Company G's attack toward Afetna Point. Companies A and C were committed between the 2d and 3d Battalions.

Later in the afternoon, the 1st Battalion, 29th Marines, was landed and also attached to the 8th Marines on the Green Beaches. Because of a shortage of amphibian tractors, the battalion was unable to boat up properly and hence landed in considerable disorder. Company B, 29th Marines, was ordered to proceed at once to fill a gap between Companies E and G of the 8th Marines. However, its knowledge of the terrain was inaccurate and it was furnished no guides, so the company ended up about 600 yards north of its assigned position. The gap between the two right companies of the 2d Battalion, 8th Marines, still remained unfilled, and Company A, 29th Marines, was ordered at 1730 to take that position. The approach of darkness and a heavy barrage of enemy artillery pinned these troops down before they could arrive at their destination.[56]

Meanwhile, the 2d Marines, which had participated in the demonstration off Tanapag, was beginning to come ashore on Red Beach 2. By 1800 the 3d Battalion had landed and was attached to the 6th Marines, taking station before nightfall on the division left flank. By nightfall one company from the 2d Battalion, 2d Marines,

---

[56] 1st Bn 29th Marines SAR Saipan, Incl A, p. 1.

MARINES DIGGING FOXHOLES, *checking weapons, and keeping a steady watch.*

in addition to the regimental commander and the advance echelon of his command post, was also ashore. The rest of the regiment was ordered to return to the area of the control vessel on the line of departure and remained boated throughout the night, to be landed by midmorning of the following day.[57]

By noon of D Day Red Beach 3 was sufficiently clear to permit shore parties to land. The first team came ashore at 1300, and supplies began to flow over the two central beaches. Two more shore parties landed before the end of the day. Late in the day the two 75-mm. pack howitzer battalions of the 10th Marines were ashore

and in position to support the infantry. The 1st Battalion landed by 1403 and supported the 6th Marines; the 2d Battalion was ashore at 1730 and in position to support the 8th Marines. Before dark the 2d Marine Division's commander, General Watson, had established his command post on Red Beach 2. By this time the division was digging in for the night and consolidating its positions against counterattack. Amphibian tanks and tractors had set up a defensive net against possible counteramphibious attacks from the sea. Division casualties were estimated to amount to 1,575—238 killed, 1,022 wounded, and 315 missing in action.[58]

---

[57] 2d Marines 2d Marine Div SAR, Phase I, FORAGER, p. 2.

[58] 2d Marine Div SAR, Phase I, FORAGER, Sec. V, p. 5.

D-DAY COMMAND POST, *a captured Japanese gun position in the Red Beach area.*

Action of the 4th Marine Division

South of Afetna Point, the 4th Marine Division was having it own share of problems.[59] To be sure, opposition in the town of Charan Kanoa was comparatively light. Japanese riflemen sniped away as troops and tractors moved through the rubble of the town, but they caused small damage. The 3d Battalion, 23d Marines, reached the first objective line with phenomenal speed. On its right flank, however, the 2d Bat-

talion of the same regiment was not so lucky. Troops debarked from their tractors unevenly and there was no semblance of a continuous line. Fighting degenerated into a series of small unit actions, and not until midafternoon was tactical control regained by the battalion commander. The farther south, the worse the situation became. After a full hour, the 25th Marines had penetrated only twelve yards in from the beach. From its right flank the 1st Battalion caught the heaviest load of fire from pillboxes and mortars on Agingan Point. Amphibian tanks, bombs, and naval shells were unable to abate this nuisance for the remainder of the day, and at nightfall the 1st Battalion, 25th Marines, had to dig in with its right flank exposed.

[59] This account of operations in the 4th Marine Division's zone is derived from the following sources: 4th Marine Div Opns Rpt Saipan, pp. 13–15; Annex C, Opns, pp. 9–12; Annex H, 23d RCT Rpt, pp. 30–35; Annex I, 24th RCT Rpt, p. 18; Annex J, 25th RCT Rpt, pp. 3–4; Annex K, Rpt of 4th Tk Bn, p. 3; Hoffman, *Saipan,* pp. 134–53.

Tanks of the 4th Marine Division began to come ashore about two hours after the initial landing. Their progress from ship to shore was seriously impeded since the channel off Afetna Point was still interdicted by enemy fire, thus making it necessary in most cases for tanks to debark from landing craft at the reef and attempt to negotiate the lagoon under their own power. Mounting seas during the afternoon increased the hazards of the trip. Of the sixty tanks of the 4th Tank Battalion, twenty-one failed to reach the 4th Marine Division's beaches. One sank with the LCM on which it was boarded, another settled into a pothole off the reef, others were unable to locate landing craft to take them ashore or had their wiring systems fouled en route. Finally, six medium tanks were misdirected to Green Beach 2, a 2d Division beach. Of these, five were immobilized in deep water inside the lagoon and the sixth was appropriated by the 2d Division and failed to reach its parent organization until several days later. The only decisive tank action on the southern beaches occurred on the extreme right flank. There, the 1st Platoon of Company A helped to break up a counterattack that, if successful, would have driven the 1st Battalion, 25th Marines, back into the sea.[60]

In the matter of artillery, the 4th Marine Division was more fortunate than the 2d Division. Whereas the latter got only two battalions of 75-mm. pack howitzers ashore on D Day, the entire 14th Regiment, consisting of two 75-mm. pack howitzer battalions and three 105-mm. howitzer battalions, was landed by 1630 to support the 4th Marine Division.[61] Shortly thereafter the reserve regiment, the 24th Marines, landed and proceeded to an area about 800 yards south of Charan Kanoa.[62]

At 1930 General Schmidt, commander of the 4th Division, came ashore. His command post was a series of foxholes about fifty yards from the beach and very poorly protected from enemy light artillery, which was firing from the high ground about 1,500 yards away. General Schmidt later recalled, "Needless to say the command post during that time did not function very well. It was the hottest spot I was in during the war, not even excepting Iwo Jima."[63]

By the time the division commander had landed, the division's left flank had been pulled back to conform to the configuration of the remainder of the line. The 2d and 3d Battalions, 23d Marines, were both ordered to withdraw to positions roughly 800 yards west of the first objective line on the reverse slope of Fina Susu ridge. The movement was executed under cover of darkness—a difficult operation but one carried out successfully and without alerting the enemy. After the withdrawal was completed, the 1st Battalion relieved the 3d, and the latter assembled in what was

---

[60] This account of 4th Marine Division tank action on D Day is derived from: 4th Marine Div Opns Rpt Saipan, Annex K, Rpt of 4th Tk Bn, pp. 2–3; Hoffman, *Saipan,* pp. 143–48.

[61] 4th Marine Div Opns Rpt Saipan, p. 14. At the time of the Marianas Campaign, the Marine Corps artillery regiment was ordinarily composed of only four battalions, two of 75-mm. pack howitzers and two of 105-mm. howitzers. At Saipan, V Amphibious Corps attached an extra 105-mm. battalion to the 4th Marine Division and a 155-mm. howitzer battalion to the 2d Division.

[62] 4th Marine Div Opns Rpt Saipan, Annex 1, 24th RCT Rpt, p. 18.

[63] Comments by General Schmidt on draft copy of this volume, OCMH.

euphemistically called a "rear area" to protect the left flank.[64]

Summary of the Situation at Nightfall

By darkness of the first day it could be concluded that the landing was a success, even though only about two thirds of the area within the first objective line was under the marines' control. In spite of the failure of the initial plan to carry some of the assault waves 1,500 yards inland aboard amphibian tractors, the troops had established a beachhead approximately 10,000 yards in length and over 1,000 yards in depth in most places. Two divisions were ashore with almost all their reserves. Seven battalions of artillery had landed, as had most of the two tank battalions. Both division command posts were ashore by the time the troops had dug in for the night. The most serious weaknesses in the Marine position were on its flanks. Afetna Point, between the two divisions, was still in enemy hands. So was Agingan Point on the right flank, and the 6th Marines' hold on the extreme left was precarious.

As for the Japanese, they had exacted a heavy toll—how heavy cannot be accurately stated because of the inadequacy of casualty figures for D Day. The American landings had been made against what the enemy considered his strongest point and at a time when his garrison there was four battalions overstrength. He had registered the landing area, using flags on the reef for registration markers, and as successive waves landed artillery and mortar fire in-creased in intensity. The Japanese had massed at least sixteen 105-mm. howitzers and thirty 75-mm. field pieces on the first high ground and the reverse slope thereof about 1.5 miles southeast of Charan Kanoa. Directly east of the airstrip they had emplaced a 150-mm. howitzer battery of four weapons with a similar battery south of it. All of these weapons were well sited, and they were responsible for a tremendous amount of fire on the landing beaches.[65]

Although the enemy realized that the diversionary maneuver off Tanapag was a ruse, he did retain one infantry regiment (the *135th*) in that area instead of committing it, as was intended, to the south of Garapan. At no time on D Day did the Japanese employ infantry in any great strength. They relied almost entirely on artillery, heavy weapons, and scattered tank attacks.

In the opinion of Holland Smith's operations officer, the "most critical stage of the battle for Saipan was the fight for the beachhead: for the security of the landing beaches, for sufficient area into which troops and heavy equipment could be brought, and for the ability to render logistical support to those forces once landed." [66] This, to be sure, could be said of any amphibious landing where strong opposition is encountered. On Saipan, it was six days before the beachhead could be considered completely secured, but it was the first day's action that was crucial. The most critical stage of "the most critical stage" was past.

---

[64] 4th Marine Div Opns Rpt Saipan, Annex H, 23d RCT Rpt, p. 34.

[65] TF 56 Rpt FORAGER, Incl D, G–2 Rpt, pp. 12–13.

[66] *Ibid.,* G–3 Rpt, p. 5.

CHAPTER VI

Capture of Aslito Airfield

Counterattack
Night of 15–16 June

Nightfall brought little hope of respite to the battle-weary marines on Saipan as they dug in on their narrow strip of beachhead with the Philippine Sea at their backs and a vengeful and still potent enemy lurking in the dark ahead. All had been alerted to the strong possibility of a night counterattack. Few doubted that it would come—the only questions being where, when, and in what force.

In fact, by midafternoon of the 15th the Japanese high command on Saipan had already issued orders to drive the Americans back into the sea before daylight next day. To Tokyo, *31st Army* radioed optimistically, "The Army this evening will make a night attack with all its forces and expects to annihilate the enemy at one swoop." [1] To the troops, the order went out, "Each unit will consolidate strategically important points and will carry out counterattacks with reserve forces and tanks against the enemy landing units and will demolish the enemy during the night at the water's edge." [2]

First to feel the effects of these measures was the 6th Marines, 2d Division, which held the left flank of the beachhead. [3] About 2000, a large force of Japanese infantry, supported by tanks, bore down from the north along the coastal road. [4] With flags flying, swords waving, and a bugle sounding the Japanese fell upon the marines' outposts. Unhappily, the 2d Marine Division had been able to land none of its 105-mm. howitzer battalions during the day so the regiment under attack had only one battalion of 75-mm. pack howitzers to support it. However, naval star shells fired from American destroyers lying close off the coast silhouetted the attackers as they approached, and the first attack was stopped by the withering fire of machine guns and rifles, assisted by naval 5-inch guns.

A second, though smaller counterattack developed in the same area around 0300 on the 16th. It, too, failed to penetrate the marines' lines. Finally, just before daylight another organized force of infantry and tanks rolled down the road from Garapan. Again, the Japanese were repulsed, this time with the help of five American me-

[1] *SONAE* 1030, CINCPAC-CINCPOA Item 9983, p. 5.
[2] NTLF Rpt Marianas, Phase I, Incl D, G–2 Rpt, p. 9.

[3] The account of the night's action in the 2d Marine Division zone is taken from: 2d Marine Div SAR, Phase I, FORAGER, Sec. VI, p. 1; 6th Marines SAR Saipan, pp. 3–4; Hoffman, *Saipan,* pp. 71–72.
[4] The exact timing of the beginning of the main counterthrust is not precisely known since the reports vary. The time stated here is derived from the 6th Marines SAR Saipan, page 3.

dium tanks. By dawn the full measure of the enemy's failure was revealed. About 700 Japanese lay dead just to the north of the 6th Marines flank.

In the zone of the 4th Marine Division, enemy countermeasures on the night of 15–16 June were less well organized and less powerful. Also, the 4th Division had all three of its 105-mm. howitzer battalions ashore by nightfall and was in a better position to resist.[5] On the southern beaches, small groups of enemy soldiers, one shielded by a spearhead of civilians, hit once at 0330 and again an hour later. Both thrusts failed, with much of the credit for the successful defense going to a battalion of 105-mm. howitzers.

The most vulnerable spot in the 4th Marine Division's zone of action, of course, lay on the exposed left flank, where the 23d Marines had not yet tied in with the 2d Division to the north. All through the night Japanese artillery fire swept the beaches in this area from one end to the other. From dusk to dawn small groups of the enemy managed to filter through front-line units only to be wiped out in the rear areas by either infantry or shore party personnel. Among the latter were the 311th Port Company and the 539th Port Company. These were attached to the 4th Marine Division and were the first Army units to be put ashore on Saipan. Finally, at 0530, about 200 Japanese launched an organized attack. Through the gap it came, apparently aimed at the pier at Charan Kanoa. It too was stopped. Only a few individual enemy soldiers reached the beaches, where they were disposed of by members of the shore parties.

One important factor that contributed to the marines' success in warding off these early morning counterattacks was the bright illumination provided by the Navy. The battleship *California,* assisted by two destroyers, cruised off the west coast of Saipan all night firing star shells to light up danger spots from which surprise attacks might be launched. That they were highly successful was later confirmed by *31st Army* headquarters itself, "The enemy is under cover of warships nearby the coast; as soon as the night attack units go forward, the enemy points out targets by using the large star shells which practically turn night into day. Thus the maneuvering of units is extremely difficult." [6]

In spite of precarious holds on both the extreme flanks and the gap in the middle between the two divisions, the marines therefore succeeded in maintaining their positions and thwarting all major efforts to drive them back into the sea. Those few Japanese who managed to infiltrate behind the lines were wiped out without causing any considerable damage. The enemy plan of maneuver had relied in the main on repelling the American assault troops at the beach by counterattacks with artillery and tanks in support. As dawn broke on the morning of 16th June, the miscarriage of the Japanese first basic defense plan was more than evident.

Consolidating the Beachhead
16 June

Daylight brought to the grateful marines hugging the beaches a respite at least from

---

[5] The account of the night's action in the 4th Marine Division zone is taken from: 4th Marine Div Opns Rpt Saipan, p. 16; 23d Marines SAR Saipan, p. 35; 25th Marines Final Rpt Saipan Opn, pp. 16–17; Hoffman, *Saipan,* pp. 73–74.

[6] *31st Army* Msg File, Msg 1038.

the fearful dread of night counterattacks and infiltration. But immediate and pressing duties lay ahead. No more than a half of the designated beachhead (west of the O–1 line) was under their control. (*See Map 4.*) Afetna Point had not been secured, which meant that a gap of about 800 yards lay between the two divisions. The tip of Agingan Point, the southwest extremity of the island, still remained in enemy hands. Finally, an unknown number of Japanese could be presumed to be still lurking behind the lines, ready to ambush the unwary and harass the attacking troops from the rear.

On the left (north) flank, the 6th Marines held fast and consolidated the positions won the day before. South of the 6th, the 8th Marines made rapid progress in its zone of action. Afetna Point offered little resistance, and the few Japanese left there after the previous night's counterattack were quickly mopped up. By 0950 the right flank company of the 2d Marine Division had reached Charan Kanoa pier and about two hours later established contact with the left flank of the 4th Marine Division.[7]

The heaviest fighting of the day took place in the zone of the 4th Marine Division, especially on its right flank. Orders called for the capture of all ground lying west of the O–1 line along Fina Susu ridge by nightfall, but the assault was held up until 1230 while lines were rearranged. On the division right, the 25th Marines encountered considerable opposition from machine guns, mountain guns, and the antiaircraft weapons guarding the western approaches to Aslito field. By the end of

the day's fighting the 25th had overrun Agingan Point and accounted for five machine guns, two mountain guns, and approximately sixty Japanese combatants. Meanwhile, the left and center regiments, the 23d and 24th, moved abreast of the 25th Marines and by 1730, when the fighting was called off, the lines of the 4th Marine Division rested generally along the Fina Susu ridge line.[8]

On the same day, to the north of the main area of fighting, additional elements of infantry and artillery were being landed on the beaches controlled by the 2d Marine Division. By 1000 of the 16th those men of the 2d Battalion, 2d Marines, that had not come ashore on D Day were landed and took positions on the division left.[9] Around 1600 the 1st Battalion, 2d Marines, which had originally been scheduled to invade Magicienne Bay,[10] was landed, minus its heavy weapons, on the 2d Marine Division's beaches. The heavy weapons were subsequently dropped by parachute from carrier torpedo planes, but because the planes flew at a low altitude the equipment was almost completely destroyed.[11]

At the same time that the remaining infantry elements of the 2d Marine Division were being dispatched shoreward, the two 105-mm. battalions of the 10th Marines were also going into position in the area.[12] About 1600 the 4th Battalion landed just north of Afetna Point and set up its batteries to support the 8th Marines, while an

---

[7] 8th Marines SAR FORAGER, 20 Jul 44, pp. 1–2; 6th Marines SAR Saipan, 18 Jul 44, pp. 4–5; Hoffman, *Saipan,* pp. 79–80.

[8] 4th Marine Div Opns Rpt Saipan, Annex H, 23d RCT Rpt, pp. 35–36; Annex I, 24th RCT Rpt, p. 18; Annex J, 25th RCT Rpt, p. 17; Hoffman, *Saipan,* pp. 81–83.

[9] 2d Marine Div SAR, Phase I, FORAGER, p. 2.

[10] See above, pp. 40–41.

[11] Hoffman, *Saipan,* pp. 80–81.

[12] The two 75-mm. pack howitzer battalions had landed on D Day.

hour later the 3d Battalion came ashore on Red Beach 3 behind the 6th Marines.[13]

At 1515 on the 16th, General Harper, USA, commanding the XXIV Corps Artillery, left the flagship *Cambria* and an hour later arrived on Blue Beach 2 just south of Charan Kanoa. There, he set up his command post about a hundred yards inland from the southern edge of Blue Beach 2, and before dark advance parties of the 149th and 420th Field Artillery Groups, the 225th and 531st Field Artillery Battalions, and elements of his staff reported to him there. No corps artillery equipment came ashore on 16 June, and the advance elements spent an uneasy night dug-in in a partially destroyed enemy gasoline dump.[14]

Night of 16–17 June

General Saito's failure to "drive the enemy back into the sea" the first night after the landing did not discourage him from making a second try. During the afternoon of the 16th he ordered the *136th Infantry Regiment* and the *9th Tank Regiment* to launch a co-ordinated attack at 1700 toward the radio station that now lay behind the lines of the 6th Marines. Another, through un-co-ordinated, attack was to be carried out by the *Yokosuka Special Naval Landing Force* from the direction of Garapan.[15]

The scheduled hour came and passed, but the units assigned to the task were apparently too disorganized to carry it out

on time. Meanwhile, the marines were able to prepare their night positions undisturbed except by artillery and mortar fire.

About 0330 the Japanese struck— chiefly against the 6th Marines. No less than thirty-seven Japanese tanks were involved, and perhaps a thousand infantrymen. They approached the American lines through a ravine that cut westward through the mountains toward the radio station. The tanks came in groups of four and five, each with a few riflemen aboard. Each group of riflemen carried at least one light machine gun. When they came within range, they were met by a furious barrage of fire from the marines' artillery, machine guns, mortars, bazookas, and rifles. Within an hour, a good percentage of the tanks had been either destroyed or incapacitated. Although the escorting infantrymen kept up the fight until about 0700, their efforts were fruitless. By the end of the battle the Japanese had lost at least twenty-four and possibly more of their tanks and an uncounted number of infantrymen. Saito's second counterattack was a total failure.

Change of Plans

The initial plan for the capture of the Marianas had set 18 June as the tentative date (W Day) for the landing on Guam, which was to constitute Phase II of the FORAGER operation. On the night of 15 June, after it appeared that the marines could hold their narrow beachhead on Saipan, Admiral Spruance confirmed this date, and preparations were set under way for an immediate invasion of Guam. But before daybreak of the 16th, Spruance received new information that caused him to reverse his own decision.

[13] 10th Marines SAR, 22 Jul 44, pp. 2–3.

[14] XXIV Corps Arty Final Rpt on FORAGER Opn, Phases I and III, S–3 Rpt, p. 5.

[15] The account of this attack is from: NTLF Rpt Marianas, Phase I, G–2 Rpt, pp. 77–78, 85; *31st Army* Msg File, Msg 1039; 6th Marines SAR Saipan, p. 4; Hoffman, *Saipan,* pp. 86–91.

At 1900 on the evening of 15 June, the U.S. submarine *Flying Fish* sighted a Japanese task force of battleships, cruisers, destroyers, and aircraft carriers making its way eastward through San Bernardino Strait in the central Philippines. Four hours later another submarine, *Seahorse,* reported another enemy task force about two hundred miles east of Leyte Gulf steaming in a northwesterly direction.[16] It was clear that the Japanese Fleet was preparing to do battle and that the U.S. Fifth Fleet would be called upon to take the necessary countermeasures.

The next morning Admiral Spruance, in the light of these developments, postponed indefinitely the date for the invasion of Guam and joined Admiral Turner aboard *Rocky Mount* off the coast of Saipan. Together, Turner and Spruance decided that unloading should continue at Saipan through 17 June, that as many transports as possible would be retired during the night and that only those urgently required would be returned to the transport area on the morning of the 18th. The old battleships, cruisers, and destroyers of the Saipan bombardment group would cover Saipan from the westward, and Admiral Conolly's force would be withdrawn well to the eastward out of any presumable danger from enemy naval attack. Certain cruiser and destroyer units heretofore attached to Admiral Turner's Joint Expeditionary Force were to be detached and directed to join Admiral Mitscher, who would carry the brunt of the attack against the approaching enemy fleet. Patrol planes based in the Marshalls were to be dis-

patched forthwith and would prepare to make night radar searches as far as 600 miles west of Saipan. Finally, Admiral Mitscher was ordered to discontinue all support aircraft operations over Saipan and restrict his carrier air operations on 17 June to searches and morning and afternoon neutralization strikes on Guam and Rota. Thus were begun the preparations for the Battle of the Philippine Sea.

First Landings of the 27th Infantry Division

The imminence of a full-scale naval battle also demanded an immediate decision regarding the disposition of the troops of the 27th Division, which had been assigned to corps reserve. The division had sailed from Oahu in three separate transport divisions under command of Rear Adm. William H. P. Blandy and was scheduled to reach Saipan the day after the main landings. On 15 June, while still en route to the objective, the 106th Regimental Combat Team (RCT) was detached from the division and ordered to join Admiral Conolly's Southern Attack Force as the reserve force for the Guam invasion, which at that time was still scheduled to take place on 18 June. Shortly before noon of the 16th, when the ships carrying the other two regiments were still about thirty miles from Saipan, General Ralph Smith, aboard the transport *Fremont,* was notified by radio that the division, less the 106th RCT, was to land as soon as practicable over the beaches held by the 4th Marine Division. The general himself was ordered to report to *Cambria,* flagship of Admiral Hill and headquarters of Brig. Gen. Graves B. Ers-

---

[16] Comdr Fifth Fleet, Initial Rpt on Opn to Capture the Marianas, 13 Jul 44, p. 3.

kine, USMC, chief of staff to Holland Smith.[17]

Aboard *Cambria*, General Ralph Smith received his orders to land his division artillery as soon as possible to support the 4th Marine Division. The 165th Regiment was to land immediately and move to the right flank of the 4th Marine Division, to which it would be attached. The 105th Regiment would follow. The 106th was to remain afloat as reserve for the Southern Landing Force for the Guam operation, which by now had been postponed indefinitely. As soon as the 105th Regiment and other elements of the division were ashore they were to unite with the 165th and relieve the 4th Marine Division on the right zone, which included Aslito airfield.

General Ralph Smith returned to his own flagship about 1930, where the assistant division commander, Brig. Gen. Ogden J. Ross, and the 165th Regiment commander, Col. Gerard W. Kelley, were anxiously awaiting him. Kelley had already instructed his executive officer, Lt. Col. Joseph T. Hart, to land the regimental combat team over Blue Beach 1 immediately south of the Charan Kanoa pier. Ross and Kelley were then ordered to go ashore, establish contact with the 4th Marine Division, and to make whatever arrangements were practicable during the night.

The two officers, accompanied by a small advance group, left *Fremont* about 2100. The coxswain of their small boat lost

his way, and, after much fumbling in the dark and many futile inquiries among other landing craft in the area, the party finally located a guide boat to steer them through the channel to Blue Beach 2, where they waded ashore about 0130. (*Map II.*)

In spite of the darkness and confusion on the beach, they succeeded in locating the command post of the 23d Marines about 300 yards south of the point where they had landed. General Ross raised 4th Marine Division headquarters by telephone and was informed that the 165th Regiment was expected to move to the right flank of the line and jump off at 0730. By this time it was 0330 and the Army troops were scattered along the beach over a three-mile area. General Ross and Colonel Kelley immediately set forth to locate the command post of the 4th Marine Division. There, Kelley was ordered by the division chief of staff to pass through the lines held by the 3d Battalion, 24th Marines, and relieve on his left elements of the 25th Marines. Jump-off hour for the attack toward Aslito field was confirmed as being 0730.

Meanwhile, Colonel Kelley had established telephone contact with his executive officer, who reported that the 1st and 2d Battalions of the 165th Infantry had landed.[18] After getting his orders, Kelley joined the two battalions and moved them south along the road running down the beach from Charan Kanoa. Just before dawn they took positions along the railroad embankment paralleling and east of the coastal highway and about 1,000 yards behind the line of departure. As the first

---

[17] The account of the landing of the 165th Regiment is derived from: Ralph C. Smith to CG USAF Central Pacific Area, Preliminary Rpt on Opns of 27th Div at Saipan, 15–24 Jun 44 (11 Jul 44), Annex I, Notes on Opns of 27th Div at Saipan (hereafter cited as Ralph Smith, Notes, Saipan), pp. 1–2; Brig Gen Ogden J. Ross, Summary of Opns by 27th Div, 16 Jun–10 Jul (13 Jul 44), pp. 1–2; 165th RCT Rpt of Saipan Action, 14 Jul 44, pp. 1–2.

[18] The 3d Battalion, 165th RCT, remained afloat during the night. Part of the landing team stayed aboard ship because of the scarcity of landing craft; the remainder spent the night aboard landing craft, unable to locate the Charan Kanoa channel. 3d Bn 165th RCT Jnl, 16 Jun 44.

glimpses of light appeared in the eastern sky before them, they prepared to jump off in support of the 4th Marine Division.

During these same early morning hours, three of the 27th Division's four artillery battalions were also moving toward shore. The 105th Field Artillery Battalion landed at Blue Bleach 1 at 0515 and by 1055 was in position and ready to fire in support of the 165th Regiment. The other two field artillery battalions (the 106th and the 249th) came ashore somewhat later but were registered and ready to fire by about the same time. The fourth battalion, the 104th Field Artillery Battalion, remained afloat and detached from division artillery.[19]

D Plus 2: 17 June

165th Infantry

The immediate objective assigned to the 165th Infantry, which was attached to the 4th Marine Division, was Aslito airfield and as much of the surrounding area as could be secured in a day's fighting. Before that could be accomplished, the regiment would have to take the small village that lay on the boundary line between its two battalions, pass through a series of densely planted cane fields, and seize the ridge that ran in a southwesterly direction along most of the regimental front and that commanded the western approaches to the airfield. The ridge at its highest points was about 180 feet. The distance between the line of departure and the westernmost point of the airfield along the regiment's line of advance was roughly 1,500 yards.

Colonel Kelley placed his 1st Battalion on the right, his 2d on the left. Maj. James H. Mahoney, commanding the 1st Battalion, disposed B Company on the left, and A Company on the right just inshore of the southern coast of the island. Lt. Col. John F. McDonough put his E Company on the right and G Company on the left, tying in with the 25th Marines.[20]

The 1st Battalion crossed the line of departure at 0735, the 2d about fifteen minutes later.[21] Company A, on the right, immediately ran into a fire fight. Three Japanese pillboxes located just inland from the beach opened fire on the advancing troops and were not eliminated until an amphibian tank had been called in to assist and engineers were brought up to place shaped charges and scorch out the enemy inside with flame throwers.

Along the rest of the regimental line the troops ran into no difficulty until they approached the small settlement that lay on the boundary line between the two battalions. As B Company tried to skirt south of the village, it came under simultaneous fire from the direction of the village itself and from the ridge to the eastward. 1st Lt. Jose Gil, B Company's commander, called for an air strike at 0955, but five minutes later canceled the request in favor of artillery fire from the 14th Marines.[22]

For the next two hours the whole line was more or less immobilized. It had become apparent that the ridge line in front was strongly held by the enemy. The ridge istelf was covered by sparse undergrowth and the approaches to it were all across open cane fields. The cane offered some

---

[19] 27th Inf Div Arty Rpt FORAGER Opn, p. 7.

[20] Unless otherwise noted, this account of the action of the 165th Infantry is derived from: 27th Inf Div G–3 Jnl; 165th RCT Rpt of Action Saipan, pp. 2–3; 165th RCT Jnl; 1st Bn 165th RCT Jnl; 2d Bn 165th RCT Jnl; Edmund G. Love, The Battle for Saipan, pp. 43–83, MS in OCMH.

[21] 165th RCT Jnl, 17 Jun 44, Msg 13.

[22] 1st Bn 165th RCT Jnl, 17 Jun 44, Msgs 23, 25.

NARROW-GAUGE RAILROAD NEAR CHARAN KANOA. *Infantrymen of the 1st and 2d Battalions wait for the jump-off signal, 17 June.*

cover from enemy observation as long as the terrain was level, but entrenched as they were on the hill above these fields, the Japanese could follow every movement made by the Americans approaching below them.[23]

By noon Colonel Kelley had more troops available. The 3d Battalion, part of which had remained aboard its transport while the other part spent the night offshore in small boats, was finally landed and assembled during the morning.[24] Company I was ordered to report to the 1st Battalion commander to act as reserve in place of C Company, which was now to be committed to the support of Company B.

At 1150 the 1st Battalion moved off again in the attack with A Company on the right, B on the left, and C to the rear of B. At 1230 the 2d Battalion jumped off following a fifteen-minute artillery preparation.[25] Immediately, the 1st Battalion came under a concentration of mortar and machine gun fire from the high hill that marked the southern extremity of the ridge line. For the next hour and fifteen minutes this position was pounded by the field pieces of the 105th and 249th Field Artillery Battalions as well as by naval gunfire. At 1414 the attack was resumed.[26]

[23] Love, Battle for Saipan, pp. 52–53.
[24] 3d Bn 165th RCT Jnl, 17 Jun 44.

[25] 1st Bn 165th RCT Jnl, 17 Jun 44, Msg 32; 2d Bn 165th RCT Jnl, 16 Jun 44, Msg 39.
[26] 1st Bn 165th RCT Jnl, 17 Jun 44, Msgs 39, 41, 46, 52, 53, 54, 55.

SOLDIERS WATCH DESTRUCTION OF A PILLBOX, *the last of three that had slowed their advance toward Aslito airfield on 17 June.*

By 1535 Company A had gained the crest after losing three men killed and four wounded.[27] About an hour later it was joined by two platoons of B Company, but the third platoon got involved in a fire fight in the cane fields below and failed to reach the summit during the rest of the day.[28]

Meanwhile, a gap had developed between Companies B and E, and the 1st Battalion commander ordered Capt. Paul Ryan to pull his C Company around to the left of B. Ryan was ordered to make a reconnaissance to determine whether he could move to the right behind A Company and up the ridge by the same route

it had taken. Once on the ridge, it was supposed that he could move his company directly to the left and take position on the left of Company B. Ryan made the crest with about half of his second platoon, but the rest of his company failed to reach the objective.[29]

While Company A and most of Company B on top of the hill were digging in and Company C was attempting to reinforce them by various routes, the Japanese again struck. Starting about 1725, the enemy managed to work his way between B Company and the 2d Battalion and commenced to pound the hill with mortars and dual-purpose guns from the southern tip

---

[27] *Ibid.*, Msg 66.
[28] *Ibid.*, Msg 73; Love, Battle for Saipan, pp. 63–66.

[29] Love, Battle for Saipan, pp. 72–74.

REINFORCEMENTS MOVING INLAND. *Men of the 3d Battalion, 165th Infantry, landed on 17 June and proceeded directly to assigned areas.*

of the airfield.[30] After about half an hour of this, both Lieutenant Gil and Capt. Laurence J. O'Brien, commander of Company A, decided to move off the hill.[31]

Captain O'Brien moved over to his extreme left and ordered his platoons to withdraw by leapfrogging. The 3d Platoon was to pull back behind the 2d while the latter covered, and then the 2d was to pull back below the ridge while the 1st covered. The 1st Platoon eventually withdrew down the hill while O'Brien himself covered its movement. The company commander was the last man down over the cliff.

Meanwhile, Captain Ryan, commanding Company C, decided to move off to the left to reinforce B Company and hold at least part of the hill if possible. His attitude was reflected by one of his men, Pfc. Cleve

E. Senor: "I fought all day for this ridge," Senor is reported to have said, "and by God I'll help hold it." Both Senor and Captain Ryan were killed in the attempt, and the C Company platoon joined Company A in its withdrawal to the beach.[32]

Captain O'Brien led most of the withdrawing battalion back along the southern beach for a distance of about 1,400 yards, then cut inland where he met guides from battalion headquarters. Shortly after 2000 he reached the command post with elements of all three companies and dug in for the night practically at the line of departure from which the companies had attacked in the morning. Except for scattered elements that remained dug in along the approaches to the ridge, progress in the 1st Battalion's zone of action had been

---

[30] 1st Bn 165th RCT Jnl, 17 Jun 44, Msg 79.
[31] *Ibid.,* Msgs 80, 81.

[32] Love, Battle for Saipan, pp. 75–77.

nil.[33] Casualties for the day's fighting in the battalion were reported as 9 killed and 21 wounded.[34]

The 2d Battalion had been more successful. After the 1230 jump-off, E Company, on the battalion right, was immediately hit by an enemy artillery barrage that killed three men and wounded four others. Except for the 1st Platoon, the whole company retired to the extreme west edge of the village that lay on the battalion boundary line and for the next hour reorganized its scattered elements and evacuated its wounded. The 1st Platoon, however, instead of withdrawing when the artillery barrage hit, rushed forward in an effort to take concealment in the heavy cane at the foot of the ridge line. From there it began to move on to the ridge itself, but after the leading squad was cut off by Japanese fire, the rest of the platoon halted.

Capt. Bernard E. Ryan, the company commander, had been with the forward elements of the 1st Platoon when his company was hit and was already in the cane field making a reconnaissance forward.[35] With two of his men, he made his way through the cane and up to the top of the ridge. For thirty minutes they waited in vain for the rest of the platoon to come up, and when it finally appeared that they were isolated, Ryan decided to conduct a reconnaissance. For three hours this officer and his two men wandered around the hilltop observing the enemy from a distance

sometimes of only thirty yards. He ordered one of his men, S. Sgt. Laurence I. Kemp, to carry the information gained back to the company executive officer. Kemp, equally fearful of friendly and enemy fire along the return route, solved his dilemma by tying a white hankerchief to the barrel of his rifle, executing a right shoulder arms, and marching safely down the hill in full view of both the enemy and his own troops.

Upon receiving Kemp's information the battalion commander immediately requested reinforcements. Colonel Kelley released F Company, which was then moved into the line to the left of E. Both companies jumped off at 1610 behind a screen of heavy mortar, small arms, and automatic weapons fire.[36] Within thirty minutes they reached the ridge line about two hundred yards west of Aslito field and began to dig in.[37]

On the extreme left of the battalion front, Capt. Paul J. Chasmar's G Company met with little difficulty. By 1416, less than two hours after the jump-off, the company had reached the ridge line and commenced to dig in.[38] Chasmar sent two patrols onto the airfield. They investigated the installations along the west side of the field and up to the south edge of the stretch without running into opposition. About 1530 temporary contact was established on the left with the 25th Marines, which had by this time penetrated into the building area north of the airfield proper.[39]

Thus, by the end of 17 June the 2d Battalion had succeeded in pushing about

[33] Ibid., p. 79.

[34] 27th Inf Div G-1 Periodic Rpt 1.

[35] Ryan was the brother of Capt. Paul Ryan, C Company commander, who was killed later in the afternoon while trying to hold a portion of this same ridge. Because of Paul Ryan's death, men of the 27th unofficially named the position Ryan's Ridge.

[36] 2d Bn 165th RCT Jnl, 17 Jun 44, Msg 51.

[37] Ibid., Msg 53; Love, Battle for Saipan, pp. 57-60.

[38] 2d Bn 165th RCT Jnl, 17 Jun 44, Msg 46.

[39] Love, Battle for Saipan, p. 60; Hoffman, Saipan, p. 95.

1,300 yards from the line of departure, was firmly dug in just two hundred yards short of Aslito airfield, and was in a good position to attack the field the following morning. In the day's fighting the battalion had lost six killed and thirty-six wounded.[40] It failed to attack the airfield on the 17th only because of regimental orders to the contrary. Colonel Kelley decided that in view of the difficulty encountered by his 1st Battalion on the right flank, it would be unwise for the 2d Battalion to push forward any farther. From its positions on top of the ridge line commanding Aslito, the 2d Battalion "had an excellent field of fire against any possible counterattack," so the regimental commander ordered it to hold there for the night and to resume the attack against the airfield the next day.[41]

4th Marine Division

To the left of Colonel Kelley's regiment the 25th Marines jumped off at approximately the same time in columns of battalions. Against light resistance the regiment pushed rapidly ahead to its O–2 line. Because of the marines' more rapid progress, a gap developed between them and the 2d Battalion, 165th Regiment, that was filled by two companies of marines. By midafternoon the companies had searched the building area north of the airfield proper and sent patrols onto the field itself. When Colonel Kelley's determination not to attack the airfield until the 18th became known to the 25th Marines, its 3d Battalion was shifted to the north side of the airfield, facing south, and as it dug in for the night

there was no contact between the marines and the Army unit.[42]

In the center of the 4th Marine Division's line, progress was more difficult. The 24th Marines jumped off on time about 0730. In spite of continuous fire from antiaircraft guns located east of the airfield, the right flank battalion reached the foot of the ridge line quickly and by noon commenced the ascent. By 1630 the battalion commander reported that his men were digging in on the O–2 line. In the center and to the left enemy resistance was even stronger, and after reaching the approaches to the ridge by late afternoon, the marines withdrew a full 600 yards before digging in for the night.[43]

To the 23d Marines on the division's left flank fell the hardest fighting in the 4th Marine Division zone for the 17th. On the right, the 2d Battalion made fairly rapid progress against light opposition, but on the left, the 1st Battalion was not so fortunate. Having once cleared Fina Susu ridge, the marines started to advance across the open ground to the eastward but were quickly pinned down by heavy mortar and enfilade machine gun fire from their left front. After retiring to the ridge line to reorganize, the battalion pushed off again at 1500 after a ten-minute artillery fire. Again the attack was stopped. Meanwhile, the 2d Battalion on the right had been pushing steadily forward and contact was lost between the two battalions. Even more serious was the 600-yard gap on the left between the 23d Marines and the right flank of the 2d Marine Division. From this

---

[40] 27th Inf Div G–1 Periodic Rpt 1.
[41] 165th RCT Rpt of Action Saipan, p. 3.

[42] 4th Marine Div Opns Rpt Saipan, Annex J, 25th RCT Rpt, p. 4; Hoffman, *Saipan,* p. 95.
[43] 4th Marine Div Opns Rpt Saipan, Annex I, 24th RCT Rpt, pp. 18–19; Hoffman, *Saipan,* pp. 95–96.

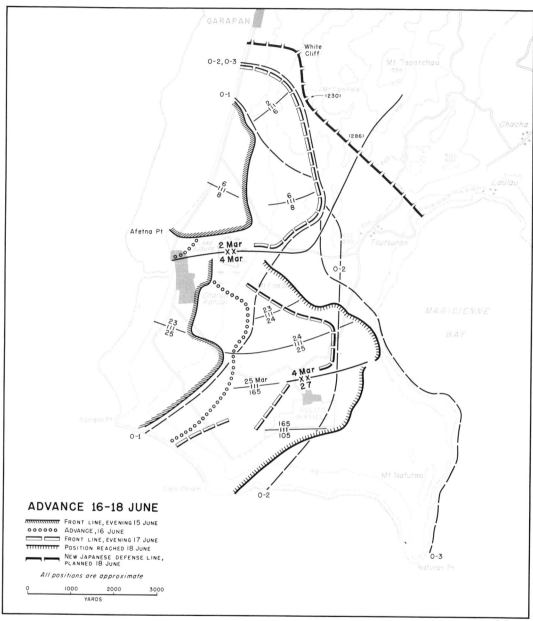

ADVANCE 16–18 JUNE

	FRONT LINE, EVENING 15 JUNE
	ADVANCE, 16 JUNE
	FRONT LINE, EVENING 17 JUNE
	POSITION REACHED 18 JUNE
	NEW JAPANESE DEFENSE LINE, PLANNED 18 JUNE

All positions are approximate

0   1000   2000   3000
                YARDS

MAP 5   F. Temple

area came most of the enemy fire, and the failure of the two Marine divisions to close this gap early in the day seriously endan-

gered the flanks of both.

As night approached it became apparent that, with the advance of the 2d Battalion

105TH INFANTRYMEN WADING IN FROM THE REEF *on 17 June.*

and the delay of the 1st, the right flank was extended and the left retarded so that it was impossible to close the gap with the units then on line. Consequently, the 3d Battalion, 23d Marines, was ordered to tie in the flanks of the two. Later, the 3d Battalion, 24th Marines, was attached to the 23d Regiment and under cover of darkness was moved into position to relieve the 3d Battalion, 23d Marines, tie in, and defend the gap between the two leading battalions. But between the two Marine divisions as they dug in for the night, the wide gap in the area around Lake Susupe still remained unclosed.[44]

2d Marine Division

In the zone of the 2d Marine Division, the day's plan called for an attack by the 2d and 6th Regimental Combat Teams to the northeast, while the 8th Marines, on the division right, was to drive due east toward the O–1 line.[45] (*Map 5*) The jump-off hour was originally scheduled for 0730 but was subsequently changed by General Holland Smith's headquarters to 0930. Word of the change, however, failed to reach division headquarters in time, so the troops crossed the line of departure according to the original schedule, following a 90-minute intensive preparation by aerial bombardment, naval gunfire, and artillery shelling.

On the extreme right, the marines of the 2d Division met with the same problems that were besetting the left flank of the 4th Division, and more besides. The 1st Battalion, 29th Marines, attached to the 8th Marines, had first to slosh its way

[44] 4th Marine Div Opns Rpt Saipan, Annex H, 23d RCT Rpt, pp. 36–37; Hoffman, *Saipan,* p. 96.

[45] The following account of action in the 2d Marine Division zone is from: 2d Marine Div SAR, Phase I, FORAGER, Sec. VI, p. 4; Hoffman, *Saipan,* pp. 92–93.

through the sniper-infested swamp that ran about 1,000 yards north of Lake Susupe.[46] Directly east of the swamp was a coconut grove from which periodically came enemy mortar fire, described in the division action report as "bothersome." Northeast of the coconut grove was a high hill on which the Japanese were entrenched in caves, and beyond this on a sharp nose was a series of heavily manned positions.

Throughout the day the 1st Battalion, 29th Marines, was unable to seize the coconut grove and in fighting for it the battalion commander, Lt. Col. Guy E. Tannyhill, was wounded and had to be evacuated. By late afternoon the battalion, with the help of four tanks of the 2d Marine Tank Battalion, succeeded in taking the hill to the north of the grove where it dug in for the night. Meanwhile, the other two assault battalions of the 8th Marines had reached their objective line with little difficulty and were tied in for the night with the 6th Marines on their left.

The 6th Marines had jumped off on schedule at 0730 and soon after 0900 had reached its objective line, encountering little resistance on the way. Further progress was held up because of the danger of overextending its lines as a result of the relatively slow progress of the 8th Marines on the right.

The 2d Marines, on the division left, regulating its advance by that of the regiment to its right, moved forward at 0945 in a column of battalions. By 1020 the leading battalion had advanced four hundred yards against light resistance. By 1800

the regiment had reached its objective line, which was coincident with the Force Beachhead Line[47] in its zone and lay only a thousand yards from the southern outskirts of the town of Garapan.

Landing Reinforcements

At 0605 on the 17th, Col. Leonard A. Bishop received orders to land his 105th Regimental Combat Team as soon as boats were available.[48] By 0845 the 1st Battalion was loaded and headed for the beach; the other two followed during the morning.[49] However, because of low tide and the heavy congestion in and around the Charan Kanoa channel, the troops had to be landed piecemeal. Not until late afternoon were all of the infantrymen ashore. That evening the 2d Battalion was attached to the 4th Marine Division as reserve, and the 1st Battalion was attached to the 165th Infantry and moved to an assembly area just west of Aslito field. Also, the 27th Division Reconnaissance Troop landed and commenced to establish an observation post area running from Agingan Point about 1,500 yards along the southern shore. The rest of the 105th Regiment remained in bivouac in the area of Yellow Beach 3 during the night.[50]

The slowness with which the 105th Regiment was landed brought one later embarrassment to that unit. In view of the bottleneck at the Charan Kanoa channel, orders were issued shortly after noon to stop unloading equipment through the channel until the congestion had been

---

[46] The swampy ground around Lake Susupe was much more extensive than it had appeared on the map used by U.S. planners. See map of Saipan Island reproduced from captured Japanese maps by ACofS G–2 NTLF, 26 Jun 44.

[47] The Force Beachhead Line is the line that fixes the inshore limits of a beachhead.

[48] 105th RCT Jnl, 17 Jun 44, Msg 4.

[49] *Ibid., passim.*

[50] *Ibid.,* Msgs 60, 61, 67; 105th RCT Opn Rpt FORAGER, pp. 4–5.

cleared up.[51] This caught most of the regiment's organizational equipment still aboard the transport *Cavalier*. That night *Cavalier,* along with most of the other transports, retired eastward after an air raid warning. Meanwhile, the Japanese fleet was reported to be moving toward Saipan. In the light of these circumstances, *Cavalier* was ordered to stay out of the danger zone and did not return until 25 June to continue unloading.[52] As General Ralph Smith later testified:

> The 105th Infantry was thus placed under great handicap in operating as a regimental unit. It had very little communication equipment or personnel ashore, either radio or telephone. It had almost no staff facilities or blackout shelter such as regimental headquarters is compelled to use if orders arrive after dark.[53]

North of the 27th Division's beaches other important elements were coming ashore on the 17th. General Holland Smith left *Rocky Mount* in midafternoon and at 1530 set up the Northern Troops and Landing Force command post at Charan Kanoa. General Harper, corps artillery commander, moved his command post to a point about 200 yards inland from Yellow Beach 2, and advance parties of the 532d Field Artillery Battalion got ashore.[54]

Night of 17–18 June

Compared to the first night on Saipan, that of the 17th was quiet for the American troops in their foxholes. Only in the zone of the 2d Marine Division did the Japanese exert themselves. Around midnight, they attempted to breach the Marine lines near the boundary between the 6th and 8th Regiments. About fifteen or twenty Japanese overran two machine guns, but the attack was shortly stopped. For a brief time the enemy penetration destroyed contact between the two regiments, but the gap was quickly filled and the lines were restored.[55]

A more serious enemy threat occurred on the morning of the 18th in the form of an attempted counteramphibious landing. A month before the American landings, *31st Army* had established a force consisting of the *1st Battalion, 18th Infantry,* to be held in readiness for amphibious attacks on either Saipan or Tinian in the event the Americans were able to establish a beachhead.[56] About 0430 on the 18th this group sortied from Tanapag Harbor in thirty-five small boats to put the plan into effect. The Japanese failed. LCI gunboats intercepted the boats and, with the help of Marine artillery, destroyed most of the landing party and turned back the rest.[57]

This uninterrupted series of reverses sustained by the Japanese on Saipan merely reinforced their determination to hold the island at all costs. On the 17th the chief of the Army General Staff in Tokyo attempted to bolster the spirits of the defenders in a message to *31st Army* headquarters: "Because the fate of the Japanese Empire depends on the result of your operation, inspire the spirit of the officers and men and to the very end continue to destroy the enemy gallantly and persistent-

---

[51] 27th Inf Div G–4 Jnl, 17 Jun 44.
[52] USS *Cavalier,* Action Rpt Saipan–Tinian, 28 Aug 44, p. 3.
[53] Ralph Smith, Notes, Saipan, p. 3.
[54] NTLF Rpt Marianas, Phase I, p. 12; XXIV Corps Arty Final Rpt on FORAGER Opn, Phases I and III, S–3 Rpt, pp. 5–6.

[55] Hoffman, *Saipan,* pp. 99–100.
[56] JICPOA Trans 8905, *SONAE* Operation Order 44 (14 May 44) *31st Army* Order.
[57] NTLF Rpt Marianas, Phase I, Incl D, G–2 Rpt, p. 14.

ly; thus alleviate the anxiety of our Emperor."

To which the Chief of Staff, *31st Army*, responded: "Have received your honorable Imperial words and we are grateful for boundless magnanimity of the Imperial favor. By becoming the bulwark of the Pacific with 10,000 deaths we hope to requite the Imperial favor."[58]

D Plus 3: 18 June

27th Division

General Holland Smith's orders for 18 June called for all three divisions under his command to seize the O–3 line within their respective zones of action. For the 4th Marine Division and the 27th Division this meant that the end of the day should see them resting on the eastern coast of Saipan from a point opposite Mount Nafutan up the shore line about 5,000 yards in a northerly direction to a point about one third up Magicienne Bay. From there the objective line for the 4th Marine Division bent back in a northwesterly direction to correspond with the advance of the 2d Marine Division, which was not intended to cover so much territory. The boundary between the 4th Marine Division and the 27th Infantry Division ran eastward to Magicienne Bay, skirting Aslito field to the north. Army troops were to capture the field itself.[59] (*See Map II.*)

For action on the 18th, the 27th Division had under its command only the 165th Regiment and the 1st and 3d Battalions of the 105th. The 2d Battalion, 105th Regiment, remained in corps reserve in an area to the rear of the 4th Marine Division, and

the 106th Infantry was still at sea. In spite of the fact that as early as 0758 the Marine division had notified General Ralph Smith that control of the 165th Regimental Combat Team was passing to Col. Kelley,[60] the regimental commander remained uncertain as to his own exact status. He later reported:

I was unable to determine (by telephone conversation with Hq 4th Marine Div) whether I was still attached to the 4th Marine Division or had passed to the command of CG 27th Div. . . . Shortly after this, Major General Ralph Smith visited my CP and advised me that I should receive notice of my release from the Marines and reversion to the 27th Division. I did receive notice from the 27th Division but never received such orders from 4th Marine Division Headquarters.[61]

This confusion, however, though indicative of poor liaison, was to have no significant effect on the action of the units involved.

Jump-off hour for the two Marine divisions was to be 1000; for the Army division it was 1200.[62] The immediate concern of Colonel Kelley, however, was to recapture the ridge southwest of Aslito that his 1st Battalion had given up the previous day. Accordingly, at 0605, he ordered Maj. Dennis D. Claire to move the 3d Battalion into the line on the right in order to launch a co-ordinated attack with the 1st Battalion at 0730.[63] The 165th Infantry jumped off on schedule after a half-hour naval and artillery preparation along the whole front. The 1st and 3d Battalions with four tanks preceding them stormed up the ridges while the 2d Bat-

---

[58] *31st Army* Msg File, Msgs 115 and 1046.
[59] NTLF Opn Order 6–44, 17 Jun 44.
[60] 27th Inf Div G–3 Jnl, 18 Jun 44, Msg 16.
[61] 165th RCT Rpt Saipan, p. 3.
[62] NTLF Opn Order 6–44.
[63] 3d Bn 165th RCT Jnl, 18 Jun 44, Msg 3.

talion on the edge of the airfield held its lines until the other units on its right came abreast. A few minutes after 1000 the ridge that had caused so much trouble the preceding day was secured against very light opposition and with negligible casualties to the assaulting units.[64]

Meanwhile, at 0800, Colonel Kelley authorized his 2d Battalion to cross Aslito airfield.[65] Beginning about 0900, Captain Chasmar, commanding G Company, ordered his men across the airfield along the north side. Capt. Francis P. Leonard, in command of F Company, followed suit shortly after, although he kept his company echeloned to the right rear in order to keep physical contact with E Company, which in turn was in contact with the 1st Battalion. Chasmar reported that he had crossed the airfield at 1000. Sixteen minutes later, Aslito was announced as secured.[66] That afternoon when General Ralph Smith arrived at the regimental command post the airfield was officially renamed Conroy Field in honor of Col. Gardiner J. Conroy, former regimental commander of the 165th, who had been killed at Makin.[67] Later, it was renamed Iseley (sic) Field in honor of a naval aviator, Comdr. Robert H. Isely, who had been shot down over Saipan.[68]

Up until 1000 the troops that had overrun the airstrip had met no opposition. Only one Japanese was discovered on the whole installation, and he was found hiding between the double doors of the control tower. All of the Aslito garrison still alive had retired to Nafutan peninsula.[69]

Upon reaching the eastern end of the airstrip, Captain Chasmar stopped to build up his line because he had been having considerable trouble during the morning trying to cover his frontage. He had tried unsuccessfully to make contact with the marines on the left who were now veering off to the northeast and in his move across the airport had temporarily lost contact on the right with F Company. At the same time, F Company was itself developing large gaps between platoons. By 1100 the whole 2d Battalion advance was stopped while the battalion commander waited for his companies to close up. For the next two hours the forward line remained stationary along the eastern boundary of the airfield. Unfortunately, the terrain in which G and F Companies had taken up positions was overlooked by the high ground of Nafutan ridge, and the men had hardly begun to dig in when they came under fire from dual-purpose guns located in that sector. The fire lasted for about two hours until friendly artillery was brought to bear on the Japanese positions, which were temporarily silenced.[70]

With the airfield secure in the hands of the 2d Battalion, 165th Regiment, and the ridge west and southwest of it occupied by the 1st and 3d Battalions, General Ralph Smith rearranged his units to launch the main attack at noon as ordered. Into his right flank he ordered the 1st and 3d Battalions, 105th Regimental Combat Team, which had landed the day before and so far had seen no action on Saipan. On the extreme right the 3d Battalion,

---

[64] 165th RCT Jnl, 18 Jun 44, Msgs 45, 54.

[65] *Ibid.*, Msg 16.

[66] *Ibid.*, Msg 56; Love, *Battle for Saipan,* pp. 86–87.

[67] 165th RCT Jnl, 18 Jun 44, Msg 76. See Crowl and Love, *Gilberts and Marshalls,* pp. 96–97.

[68] Hoffman, *Saipan,* p. 104n.

[69] Love, *Battle for Saipan,* p. 87.

[70] 2d Bn 165th RCT Jnl, 18 Jun 44; Love, *Battle for Saipan,* pp. 87–88.

ASLITO FIELD BECOMES CONROY FIELD. *General Ralph Smith (left) congratulating Col. Gerard W. Kelley at ceremonies renaming the airfield following its capture. Brig. Gen. Ogden Ross, at right, looks on.*

105th, completed the relief of the 3d Battalion, 165th, at 1245, three quarters of an hour late.[71] The 3d Battalion, 165th, then went into reserve. About the same time, the 1st Battalion, 105th, relieved the 1st Battalion, 165th. The latter was then shifted to the left flank of the division line to close the gap between the 4th Marine Division and the 2d Battalion, 165th, which was occupying the airfield.[72] From right to left, then, the new division line consisted of Companies L, I, C, and A,

105th Infantry, and Companies F, G, B, and C, 165th Infantry, with the remaining infantry companies in reserve in their respective battalion zones.

As the afternoon wore on it developed that, as on the previous day, progress on the extreme right of the division front was the slowest, and again the chief obstacle was terrain. In the area inland from the southern coast the ground was a series of jagged coral pinnacles that jutted up from the water's edge to a height of about 90 feet. Between these peaks were a heavy undergrowth of vines, densely planted small trees, and high grass. Against these odds, but luckily not against the added encum-

[71] 3d Bn 165th RCT Jnl, 18 Jun 44, Msgs 34, 35.

[72] 1st Bn 165th RCT Jnl, 18 Jun 44, Msgs 41, 43, 44, 45, 57.

brance of Japanese opposition, Company L on the extreme right advanced a mere 200 yards from the line of departure by nightfall, and I Company's progress was only a little better.[73] The situation on the left of the 105th Regimental line was somewhat more promising. In spite of artillery fire from Nafutan Point, Lt. Col. William J. O'Brien, 1st Battalion commander, succeeded by 1400 in pushing forward to a line running southwest from the southeast corner of the airfield.[74]

While the 105th Regiment was having more than a little difficulty getting started on the division right flank, the 165th on the left was faring better. By 1700 the entire regimental line had almost reached Magicienne Bay, having met only light opposition. The original intention had been to proceed on to the water's edge, but the heavy undergrowth and coral outcroppings persuaded the regimental commander to pull back to the high ground west of the shore line for the night. About 1700 the commanding officer of the 3d Battalion, 25th Marines, who was on the right flank of the 4th Marine Division line, reported the imminence of a Japanese counterattack between the 24th and 25th Marines. In view of the necessity of the latter's pulling north to pour in reinforcements against this threat, the lines of the 165th were shifted left about 600 yards to establish contact with the marines for the night.[75]

4th Marine Division

North of the 27th Division zone, the 4th Marine Division attacked toward the east coast with three regiments abreast: the 25th Marines on the right, 24th Marines in the center, and 23d Marines on the left.[76] The right half of the objective line for this day's action was to be on the coast of Magicienne Bay, and from there it bent back to the northwest to meet the more slowly progressing 2d Marine Division.

The 25th Marines jumped off on schedule at 1000. Opposition was light, and by 1330 the regiment had reached the beaches on Magicienne Bay well in advance of the 165th Infantry on its right. The occupation of these beaches on the east coast completed the initial drive of the division across Saipan. The island now, at this point at least, was cut in two. One battalion of the 25th Regiment was left behind to mop up the southern extremity of a heavily defended cliff line that had been bypassed by the 24th Marines on its left.

The latter regiment had had a little difficulty organizing its lines before the jump-off and consequently was delayed forty-five minutes in the attack. Nevertheless, in the face of "moderate to heavy" machine gun and rifle fire, it had succeeded by 1400 in pushing forward to a point only 300 yards west of Magicienne Bay. Then, about 1615, two Japanese tanks suddenly appeared in the zone of the 2d Battalion, causing considerable anxiety and about fifteen American casualties before they were chased away by bazookas and artillery. By nightfall the elements of the 24th on the right had reached the O–3 line, part of which rested on the coast, and the unit was well tied in with the regiments on its right and left.

---

[73] Love, Battle for Saipan, pp. 89–90.

[74] 105th RCT Jnl, 18 Jun 44, Msg 35.

[75] 165th RCT Jnl, 18 Jun 44, Msgs 93, 99, 100, 109.

[76] This account of 18 June action of the 4th Marine Division is derived from: 23d RCT Rpt, pp. 37–38; 24th RCT Rpt, p. 19; 25th RCT Rpt, pp. 4–5; Hoffman, *Saipan*, pp. 102–04.

EXAMINING AN ENEMY GUN. *This Japanese Type 10 120-mm. gun was one of several captured when Aslito airfield was overrun.*

As was the case of the 165th Infantry, the 23d Marines on the extreme left of the 4th Division line had to capture its line of departure before the scheduled jump-off hour. At 0730 the 3d Battalion, 24th Marines (attached to the 23d), passed through the 1st Battalion, 23d, with orders to seize the line of departure before the main attack, which was scheduled for 0900. The battalion never made it—not that day at least. Intense mortar and enfilade machine gun fire from the left flank stopped the men after an advance of about 200 yards. On the right the 2d Battalion, 23d, made about the same gain before it too was pinned down. At 1300 the attack

was resumed and after fierce fighting against stubborn Japanese resistance the troops advanced about 300 yards. By 1715 the regiment had established a line some 400 yards east of Lake Susupe. Progress on the left flank of the 4th Marine Division had been far less than anticipated. It was becoming apparent that the main line of Japanese resistance would be in the area north and east of Lake Susupe and not in the southern sector of the island.

2d Marine Division

The left flank of the corps line remained almost stationary during the 18th. As the

2d Marine Division's commander explained it, "At this stage, the frontage occupied by the Division was such that its lines could not be further lengthened without dangerously thinning and overextending them."[77] The strong pocket of resistance encountered by the 4th Division near the division boundary line formed a hostile salient into the beachhead and forced both divisions to maintain abnormally long lines in the sector. The inability of the 4th Division to make substantial progress on its left flank in turn prevented the 2d Division from risking further extension of its own lines.

Only the 8th Marines saw significant fighting on the 18th. The enemy-infested coconut grove on the regiment's right that had proved so bothersome the previous day was assaulted and captured. Here, a large number of Japanese dead were found. Before the 18th the enemy had systematically removed its dead before the advance of the attacking forces, but by now, with the American beachhead firmly established and Aslito airfield overrun, Japanese commanders on Saipan had more urgent matters on their minds.[78]

The Japanese Situation

By the night of 18 June, the Japanese high command in Tokyo as well as its subordinates on Saipan were at last compelled to confess that the situation was critical. The island had been cut in two and the southern part, including the main airfield, was for all practical purposes in American hands. True, remnants of Japanese units,

including most of the Aslito garrison, were still holed up on Nafutan peninsula and along the southern shore west of it, but they were cut off from the main body of troops and incapable of anything more serious than harassing attacks against the American lines. (*See Map 5.*)

In the face of unrelenting pressure from their attackers, the Japanese on the 18th began withdrawing to a defense line extending across the island in a southeasterly direction from a point just below Garapan via the south slopes of Mount Tapotchau to Magicienne Bay. To be more exact, the new "line of security" drawn up by *31st Army* headquarters on the night of the 18th was to run from below Garapan east to White Cliff, then south to Hill 230 (meters) and southeast through Hill 286 (meters) to a point on Magicienne Bay about a mile west of the village of Laulau.[79]

The line roughly paralleled the O–4, or fourth phase line of the American attackers, and was the first of two last-ditch defense lines scratched across the island in a vain attempt to stabilize the battle during the retreat to the north. If the Americans could be brought to a standstill, the Japanese hoped to prolong the battle and eventually win out with the aid of rein-

---

[77] 2d Marine Div SAR, Phase I, FORAGER, Sec. VI, p. 6.

[78] Hoffman, *Saipan*, p. 102.

[79] CINCPAC-CINCPOA Item 9983–85, p. 10, *31st Army* CofS, Msg 1060. The map of Saipan prepared before the operation by American troops, on which the maps in this volume are essentially based, is by necessity not very accurate—particularly from the point of view of terrain configuration and spot elevation data.

The troops also used a captured Japanese map of the island. The heights on this map, which is more accurate as to relief features, are in meters. Elevations in meters derived from the Japanese map are shown on the maps of this volume in parentheses.

forcements. To Tokyo, *31st Army* headquarters radioed its plans:

Situation evening of 18 June:
The Army is consolidating its battle lines
and has decided to prepare for a showdown
fight. It is concentrating the [*43d Division*]
in the area E of Tapotchau. The remaining
units [two infantry battalions of the *135th
Inf*, about one composite battalion, and one
naval unit], are concentrating in the area E
of Garapan. This is the beginning of our
showdown fight.[80]

In reply, Imperial General Headquarters
ordered Maj. Gen. Keiji Iketa to hold on
to the beaches still in his possession, wait
for reinforcements over those beaches, and
"hinder the establishment of enemy airfields."[81] Iketa reported that he would
carry out these orders, that Aslito airfield
would be neutralized by infiltration patrols "because our artillery is destroyed,"

and that the Banaderu (Marpi Point) airfield would be repaired and defended "to
the last." "We vow," he concluded, "that
we will live up to expectations."[82] Stabilize the battle, keep beaches open for
reinforcements, recover and preserve the
use of the Marpi Point airfield, and deny
to the Americans the use of Aslito—these
four objectives were now the cornerstones
of Japanese tactics on Saipan.

And from the Emperor himself came
words of solemn warning and ominous
prescience: "Although the front line officers are fighting splendidly, if Saipan is
lost, air raids on Tokyo will take place
often, therefore you absolutely must hold
Saipan."[83]

Five months later American B–29 bombers taking off from Saipan for Tokyo would
confirm the Emperor's worst fears.

---

[80] *31st Army* Msg File, Msg 1050.
[81] *Ibid.*, Msg 150.

[82] *Ibid.*, Msg 1054.
[83] *Ibid.*, Msg 152.

CHAPTER VII

Supporting Arms and Operations

Battle of the Philippine Sea

While the marines and soldiers of the V Amphibious Corps were still pushing toward the east coast of Saipan, Admiral Spruance received news that was to prove even more significant than that of the capture of Aslito field. Beginning on 15 June, American submarines patrolling the waters east of the Philippine Islands sent in a series of reports on enemy ship movements that seemed to indicate strongly that the Japanese were massing a fleet and were sending it to the rescue of the beleaguered defenders of Saipan.

Spruance, like all other high-ranking U.S. naval commanders in the Pacific, had hoped that an invasion of the Marianas would bring the enemy fleet out fighting. That hope now seemed likely to be fulfilled.

The Japanese Navy, like the American, had long been imbued with Alfred Thayer Mahan's doctrine that the *sine qua non* of victory in naval warfare is the destruction of the enemy fleet. In their own national history, the Japanese had only to look back as far as 1905 for historical warrant for this assumption. In that year, Admiral Heigachiro Togo had met and almost annihilated the Russian Fleet at the Battle of Tsushima, thus paving the way to Japan's victory in the Russo-Japanese War

and a long-coveted place in the international sun.

In the early stages of World War II the Japanese sought to put this doctrine to test, but always fell short of complete success. In spite of the tremendous damage done to it at Pearl Harbor, the U.S. Fleet survived and recovered with remarkable rapidity. Important sea battles were won by the Japanese in the Solomons, but none of them were conclusive. At Midway the tables were turned when U.S. carrier planes repelled an attempted invasion and administered a sound drubbing to the Japanese naval forces supporting it.

By late 1943 the high command of the Imperial Navy felt that conditions were ripe for a decisive fleet engagement. Twice in the autumn of that year Admiral Mineichi Koga, Commander in Chief, *Combined Fleet,* sallied forth from Truk in an effort to engage the U.S. Central Pacific Fleet. Both times he failed to discover his adversary. In the end he retired to Truk and allowed most of his carrier air strength to be diverted to the Rabaul area, where two thirds of it was lost.[1] In the spring of 1944, as American forces threatened to

---

[1] Thomas Wilds, "The Admiral Who Lost His Fleet," *United States Naval Institute Proceedings,* Vol. 77, No. 11, Whole No. 585 (November, 1951), pp. 1175–81; Crowl and Love, *Gilberts and Marshalls,* Ch. IV; Morison, *Aleutians, Gilberts and Marshalls,* Ch. IX.

press farther into western Pacific waters, the Japanese prepared another plan, *Operation A-GO,* in the hope of forcing a major fleet engagement.

On 3 May 1944 Admiral Toyoda, Koga's successor as Commander in Chief, *Combined Fleet,* issued the general order for *Operation A-GO.* It was assumed that the next major thrust of the U.S. Fleet would be into waters around the Palaus, in the western Carolines, and that there it could be met and bested by the Japanese. Thought was given to the possibility that the Americans might move first against the Marianas rather than Palaus, but the consensus among high Japanese naval circles favored the latter alternative. Probably wishful thinking entered the picture here, for it was obviously to the advantage of the Japanese to concentrate their naval forces in the more southerly waters. The *1st Mobile Fleet,* commanded by Admiral Jisaburo Ozawa, was soon to be moved to Tawi Tawi in the Sulu Archipelago, and it was to this force that major responsibility for carrying out *Operation A-GO* was assigned. The Japanese were already suffering a shortage of both fuel and tankers, and should Ozawa extend the range of his operations as far north as the Marianas he would take considerable logistical risks.[2]

Before *A-GO* could be executed, an American thrust in another quarter caused Toyoda to change his plans. On 27 May General MacArthur's forces invaded the island of Biak in the Geelvink Bay area of New Guinea and placed the Japanese admiral in a dilemma. If Biak were lost to the invaders, the success of *A-GO* could

easily be jeopardized by American aircraft based on that island. On the other hand, to reinforce Biak would entail at least a temporary dispersion of forces, and of course the first principle upon which *A-GO* was based was that of concentration of force. Faced with this choice, the Japanese decided to accept the risks of dispersion and to dispatch some of their ships and planes to the Biak area in an effort to drive the Americans off. This decision was reflected in a new plan of operations known as *KON.*[3]

Three times within eleven days Japanese naval forces sailed forth for Biak with troop reinforcements. The first of the expeditions turned back on 3 June, having lost the element of surprise on being sighted by American submarines and planes. The second was struck by B–25's and suffered one destroyer sunk and three others damaged before the entire task force was chased away by American warships. The third, which included the superbattleships *Yamato* and *Musashi,* the light cruiser *Noshiro,* and six destroyers, all detached from the *1st Mobile Fleet,* was abruptly called off on 12 June when Admiral Toyoda received definite word that Admiral Spruance's forces were attacking the Marianas.

Thus, the American soldiers on Biak were saved from further naval harassment by the timely appearance of Central Pacific forces off the Marianas. By the same token, the invasion of Biak by Southwest Pacific forces was to prove a boon to Admiral

---

[2] Information on *Operation A-GO* is derived from: Japanese Studies in World War II, 60 and 97; USSBS, *Campaigns,* pp. 213–72; USSBS, *Interrogations,* II, 316.

[3] Information concerning *KON* and its effects is derived from: Smith, *Approach to the Philippines,* Ch. XV; Samuel Eliot Morison, *History of United States Naval Operations in World War II,* Vol. VIII, *New Guinea and the Marianas, March 1944–August 1944* (Boston, Little, Brown and Company, 1953), pp. 119–33.

Spruance. Japanese plans for *A-GO* relied heavily on the support of naval land-based planes of the *1st Air Fleet* stationed in the Marianas, Carolines, and Palaus, but one third to one half of all these planes were sent to Sorong and other bases in western New Guinea in response to the invasion of Biak. There, large numbers of pilots fell prey to malaria, and most of the aircraft were lost either to U.S. action or to bad weather. By the time the U.S. Fifth Fleet showed up to meet the challenge of *A-GO*, the land-based aircraft available to Toyoda had been sizably reduced in number.

On 11 June the Japanese admiral received word of Mitscher's carrier strike against Saipan and immediately suspended the *KON* operation, ordering the task force bound for Biak to join forces with the main body of Ozawa's *1st Mobile Fleet*. Ozawa himself sortied from Tawi Tawi two days later, and on the morning of the 15th *Operation A-GO* was activated. Contrary to earlier Japanese expectations, the Americans had chosen to attack the Marianas rather than the western Carolines. Hence the scene of the impending "decisive fleet engagement" could only lie somewhere in the Philippine Sea—that vast stretch of ocean between the Philippines and the Marianas.[4]

On the evening of 15 June Ozawa's fleet had completed its progress from Tawi Tawi up the Visayan Sea and through San Bernadino Strait into the Philippine Sea. On the next afternoon it was joined by the *KON* force that had been diverted from Biak. Both fleets were sighted by American submarines, and it was apparent that the Japanese were heading in a northeasterly direction toward the Marianas.

All together, Ozawa had mustered 5 carriers, 4 light carriers, 5 battleships, 11 heavy cruisers, 2 light cruisers, 28 destroyers, and 430 carrier-based combat aircraft. He was outnumbered by the Americans in every respect except in heavy cruisers. Spruance had at his disposal 7 carriers, 8 light carriers, 7 battleships, 8 heavy cruisers, 13 light cruisers, 69 destroyers, and 891 carrier-based planes.[5] The mammoth American fleet was divided into four carrier task groups under Admiral Mitscher, Commander, Task Force 58. Mitscher was in tactical command, but his major tactical decisions had to be approved by Spruance as Commander, Fifth Fleet.

By the morning of 18 June all four American carrier groups had rendezvoused and were steaming in a southwesterly direction toward the approaching enemy. Spruance had ordered: "Action against the enemy must be pushed vigorously by all hands to ensure complete destruction of his fleet," but had added the precautionary note, "Task Force 58 must cover Saipan and our forces engaged in that operation."[6] That night Admiral Mitscher learned the full meaning of this qualification when his superior ordered him to change course to the east and maintain it

---

[4] The following account of the Battle of the Philippine Sea is derived from CINCPAC-CINCPOA Opns in POA—Jun 44, Annex A, Part VII; Morison, *New Guinea and the Marianas*, Chs. XIV–XVI.

The Philippine Sea was so named as the result of a recommendation made by Admiral Nimitz in 1944, at the time of operations against the Marianas. The name was officially approved by the U.S. Board on Geographic Names in March 1945. The Philippine Sea applies to that area limited on the north by Japan, on the east by the Bonins and the Marianas, on the south by the Carolines, and on the west by the Philippines, Formosa, and the Ryukyu Islands.

[5] Figures are from Morison, *New Guinea and the Marianas*, p. 233.
[6] *Ibid.*, pp. 243, 250.

until daylight. Mitscher protested but was overruled. Admiral Spruance was fearful that Ozawa might attempt an end run under cover of darkness and put the Japanese fleet between him and Saipan. The Fifth Fleet commander was unwilling to jeopardize the landing operations even if it meant a delay in closing with the enemy fleet. Actually, no such end run was contemplated by the Japanese commander, but Spruance had no way of knowing that at the time.

On the morning of the 19th, after the American carriers had turned west again, Ozawa's planes, which were lighter and less well armed and therefore capable of greater range than their American rivals, delivered the first blow. In four separate raids lasting for almost five hours Japanese planes roared over the horizon in a futile effort to knock out Mitscher's mighty fleet. Out of all the American surface vessels present, only one was hit—the battleship *South Dakota,* which lost 27 men killed and 23 wounded, but was not seriously damaged. For the rest, the raids were broken up and the raiders destroyed or turned back by the combined might of American ships' fire and planes, chiefly the latter. Later that afternoon American strikes on Guam and Rota, which had been ordered for the morning, were resumed. By evening the "Great Marianas Turkey Shoot" was over with disastrous results to the Japanese. Out of 430 carrier planes, Ozawa lost 330. Some went down under the fire of American ships and planes; others were destroyed on Guam and Rota; and still others were counted as operational casualties. Against this, only twenty-four American planes were shot down and six lost operationally. The same day, two Japanese carriers, *Shokaku* and *Taiho* (Admiral

Ozawa's flagship) were sunk by American submarines operating well to the south of Mitscher's fleet.

That night Ozawa changed course to the northwest hoping to put distance between himself and the American fleet and to allow himself opportunity to refuel. Mitscher held to a westerly course in the belief that it would bring him across the track of his enemy. However, he could not send out night air patrols because none of his carrier aircraft were equipped with search radar,[7] and not until late the following afternoon was aerial contact finally made with the Japanese fleet, which was now heading in the general direction of Okinawa. Mitscher immediately launched a twilight air attack that succeeded in destroying about 65 of Ozawa's remaining 100 aircraft, sinking the carrier *Hiyo,* hitting another carrier and a battleship, and damaging two fleet oilers to the extent that they had to be scuttled. American plane losses came to 100, mostly incurred through crashes when the returning planes tried to land on their carriers after dark. Personnel casualties were not so heavy, coming to only 49.

Thus ended the Battle of the Philippine Sea. Mitscher would have detached his battleships, cruisers, and destroyers to pursue and destroy the fleeing enemy, but Spruance refused to break up the fleet. It would have made no difference anyway since Ozawa was by now too far away to be overhauled.

Despite the escape of six carriers and their escorts, the Imperial Navy had suffered a severe blow—one from which it never recovered. In the opinion of Samuel Eliot Morison, the Battle of the Philippine

---

[7] Ltr, Admiral Spruance to Maj Gen A. C. Smith, 28 Feb 55, OCMH.

Sea "decided the Marianas campaign by giving the United States Navy command of the surrounding waters and air. Thus, the Japanese land forces on Saipan, Tinian, and Guam were doomed, no matter how bravely and doggedly they fought."[8]

There can be no doubt of the decisive influence of the sea battle on the ultimate outcome of the land campaigns in the Marianas. On the other hand, the immediate effects were not altogether beneficial from the point of view of the troops fighting ashore on Saipan. On first getting word of the approach of the Japanese Fleet, Admiral Spruance had detached from Admiral Turner's attack force five heavy cruisers, three light cruisers, and twenty-one destroyers to supplement Task Force 58.[9] This left Turner without adequate fire support for his transport shipping, which was still in the process of unloading at Saipan. Consequently, most of the transports retired well to the eastward of Saipan on the night of 17 June and remained away from the Saipan area until the Battle of the Philippine Sea was over.[10] The withdrawal of these transports naturally interrupted unloading and imposed additional strains on the already overburdened logistical program on Saipan.

Logistics

No aspect of an amphibious landing against a hostile shore presents more complex problems than that of transporting supplies from ship to shore and allocating them at the proper time and place and in the proper amounts to the troops that need

them. Similarly, no phase of an amphibious operation is so likely to become disorganized and even disorderly. Ordinarily, the assault landing craft and vehicles move from ship to shore in scheduled wave formations and in a fairly methodical fashion. Once ashore the troops deploy and eventually move inland according to prearranged plan. Supplies, on the other hand, cannot move off the beach under their own power. More often than not they are dumped at the water's edge in a haphazard fashion by landing craft whose naval crews are primarily interested in putting out to sea again. The supplies stay at the shore line until shore parties can segregate them in some order on the beaches or until mechanical transportation comes ashore to haul them in to inland dumps. To the casual observer at least, the pile up and congestion of supplies at the shore line during the first phase of a normal amphibious assault presents a picture of total chaos.

To be sure, in a well-conducted amphibious operation the chaos is often more apparent than real, but even under the best conditions the problem of ship-to-shore supply is a complicated one and not easy of solution. At Saipan it was further complicated by local circumstances, which were formidable, although not unique. On the first day unloading was hampered by heavy artillery and mortar fire on the beaches that did not cease altogether until three days later. Hydrographic conditions were unfavorable to a steady movement of supplies and equipment in to the beaches. The uncertain naval situation made it necessary for the transports to retire to seaward each of the first three nights. Finally, for the next five days and nights most of the transports stayed at sea awaiting the

---

[8] Morison, *New Guinea and the Marianas*, p. 318.

[9] *Ibid.*, p. 242.

[10] TF 52 Opns Rpt Marianas, Incl A, pp. 6–7.

outcome of the Battle of the Philippine Sea.[11]

Enemy harassment of the beaches and the unfavorable hydrographic conditions offshore were of course felt most seriously by the two Marine divisions during the first two days of the operation. Sporadically, enemy fire caused all unloading work to be suspended as shore parties took cover. The beaches on the flanks of the landing area were completely inaccessible to boats of any kind. LST's and LCT's could ground on the abutting reef, but supplies from that point to shore had either to be man-handled or transferred to LVT's and DUKW's. Some landing craft could reach shore at the interior beaches by way of the narrow channel off Charan Kanoa, but at low tide its use was restricted to those of the most shallow draft, and at all times it was congested because both assault divisions were using it.[12]

Inevitably, too, along the six thousand yards of beach there was some mix-up of supplies in spite of the elaborate organization to supervise the unloading of the transports and the movement of supplies to the troop units to which they were allocated. In accordance with standard amphibious doctrine, this task was shared by naval beach parties and ground force shore parties. The beach parties supervised the unloading of the transports and the progress of landing craft and vehicles to the shore line. Also, they marked channels and controlled traffic in the lagoon. In command of these operations was a force master who had under him two transport group beachmasters, one for each Marine

division, each of whom in turn commanded two transport division beachmasters, one for each assault regiment. All of these naval officers were landed as soon as satisfactory lateral communications had been established, and each was provided with a communication team of one officer, five radiomen, and five signalmen.[13]

Paired with the naval beachmasters and working in close co-ordination with them were the Marine and Army shore party commanders whose job it was to control traffic on the beaches themselves, receive the supplies as they were landed, and distribute them to the appropriate troop units. Each Marine division was authorized a shore party of 98 officers and 2,781 enlisted men. The 2d Marine Division based its shore party organization on the pioneer battalion of its engineer regiment. Nine teams were organized under three shore party group headquarters. The organization of the 4th Marine Division's shore party differed somewhat in that two shore party groups were set up, each with three teams. These were drawn from personnel of the 121st Naval Construction Battalion as well as from the pioneer battalion of the division engineering regiment.[14] Each of the three Army regiments had its own shore party battalion—the 152d Engineers for the 165th Infantry, the 34th Engineers for the 105th, and the 1341st Engineers of the 1165th Engineer Group for the 106th Infantry.[15]

Notwithstanding this system of interlocking and parallel controls, the first two days of the operation frequently saw supplies of the 2d Marine Division being

---

[11] COMINCH P–007, Ch. 5, p. 7.
[12] 4th Marine Div Opns Rpt Saipan, Annex D, pp. 8–9; 2d Marine Div SAR, Phase I, FORAGER, Part II, p. 32.

[13] TF 51 Opns Rpt Marianas, Incl C, pp. 5–6.
[14] NTLF Rpt Marianas, Phase I, Incl J, Engr and Shore Party Rpt, p. 2.
[15] 27th Inf Div G–4 Rpt, pp. 12, 17.

SHORE PARTIES UNLOADING SUPPLIES ON BLUE BEACH 1

dumped on the beaches of the 4th Division and vice versa. When the 27th Division began to land the situation rapidly deteriorated. On the night of 16 June the 165th Infantry commenced to come ashore over Blue Beach 1 in the zone of the 4th Marine Division. Next day the 105th Infantry followed. Few, if any, preliminary plans had been made by higher headquarters to cover the details of landing the reserve division, and the division itself, in its initial planning, had made no provision for a landing in this particular area.[16] Hence, the process of getting the troops and supplies ashore inevitably became a makeshift proposition. Col. Charles Ferris, Division G–4, set up an on-the-spot system of controls, but was unable to persuade either the Navy beachmaster or the senior shore party commander at corps headquarters to agree to routing cargo to any single beach

or to order the transports' boats to report to a single control craft in the channel so that an accurate record could be kept of items discharged. The result was that the 27th Division's supplies were landed over several beaches, and the Army troops had to scramble and forage to get what they needed.[17]

On 18 June all ships carrying troops and supplies of the 27th Division retired eastward of the island to await the outcome of the Battle of the Philippine Sea. To add to the division's difficulties, the 152d Engineers, which had been assigned as the shore party for the 165th Infantry, was detached and assigned to corps, leaving only the 34th Engineers to perform shore party functions for the two Army regiments that landed. By the morning of the 19th the supply situation within the division had become critical. True, there was

---

[16] See above, p. 41.

[17] 27th Inf Div G–4 Rpt, p. 17.

CATERPILLAR TRACTOR PULLING AMMUNITION PALLETS FROM AN LCM

enough food and water on hand for immediate needs, but only by dint of borrowing K rations from Marine dumps and capturing the water cisterns on Aslito field. The quantities of Class II, III, and IV (organization equipment, fuel and lubricants, miscellaneous equipment) supplies on hand were almost negligible. Small arms ammunition would last four days, but there were only about 600 rounds of 155-mm. ammunition available for each battalion and 1,200 rounds per battalion of 105-mm. ammunition, most of the latter borrowed from the Marines. Of the division's vehicles, there were on shore only three 2-1/2-ton cargo trucks, twenty-three 3/4-ton weapon carriers, and forty-nine DUKW's. Not until 20 June did the ships carrying the troops of the 106th

Regiment return to Saipan, and not until the 27th were the division's supplies and equipment fully unloaded.[18]

The 27th Division was not alone in suffering an interruption to the flow of its supplies and equipment because of the Battle of the Philippine Sea. The hasty withdrawal of the naval transports on the 18th made an orderly discharge of any cargo over the proper beaches impossible. Priorities were assigned to rations, ammunition, and fuels, and other items had to be neglected. Moreover, in order to dispatch the cargo ships with all possible speed out of the danger area, it was necessary to permit them to unload over the beach that was the handiest. Thus, it was

---

[18] *Ibid.,* pp. 18–19.

PONTOON CAUSEWAY AND BARGE IN CHARAN KANOA HARBOR

impossible to prevent a division's supplies from being scattered among all the dumps.[19] The only advantage enjoyed by the two Marine divisions in this respect lay in the three full days they had had to unload their cargo before the general exodus of naval shipping, but this was at least partly offset by the fact that for most of the time their landing beaches were under fire.

Meanwhile, during the period when most of the transports were cruising east of Saipan, shore parties were furiously at work improving the beach approaches and eliminating obstacles to a more rapid delivery of supplies across the reef. Twelve ponton

sections had been hauled to Saipan lashed to the sides of LST's, and others came later, side-carried by ships of the first garrison echelon. By 18 June naval Seabees had floated three of these and commenced construction of a causeway pier off Charan Kanoa, which was increased in length as fast as additional sections could be obtained from LST's on their return from retirement to sea.[20] Next day the 34th Engineer Battalion opened up Yellow Beach 3 just north of Agingan Point by blowing two channels through the reef to permit small boats to discharge on the shore during high tide. The battalion also rigged up a crane on an overhanging point off the beach to enable it to unload matériel di-

[19] NTLF Rpt Marianas, Phase I, Incl F, G–4 Rpt, Part II, p. 5; Incl J, p. 5.

[20] COMINCH P–007, Ch. 5, p. 15.

rectly from landing craft into trucks waiting on a level above the beach itself. On 21 June the 1341st Engineer Battalion removed all the mines from White Beach 1 below Agingan Point and prepared access roads from the beach. Naval underwater demolition teams searched for antiboat mines and blew landing slips in the offshore reef for LST's and LCT's.[21]

One factor that eased the 27th Division's unloading problems was that a large percentage of its supplies had been palletized before embarkation from Oahu. Unlike the two Marine divisions, which were skeptical of the process, the 27th Division had responded enthusiastically to General Holland Smith's administrative order that 25 to 50 percent of all supplies and two to five units of fire be palletized. In fact, the Army division had palletized almost 90 percent of all its supplies and had reason to be grateful for its own forehandedness.[22] Securing the matériel to wooden pallets permitted a more rapid unloading of landing craft at the beaches, released working parties that otherwise would have been engaged in the arduous labor of transferring cargo from landing craft into trucks, and reduced the number of men at the landing beaches in positions exposed to enemy fire. In the opinion of Holland Smith, "These advantages were clearly manifest at Saipan when palletized supplies of the 27th Division were handled as against unpalletized supplies of the 2d and 4th Marine Divisions."[23]

Not all of the logistical difficulties that beset the fighting troops were due to unloading difficulties. Some shortages can be traced back to the point of embarkation and are attributable to insufficient shipping. This was particularly true in the case of motor transportation. There was simply not enough space aboard the transports assigned to the operation to stow all of the vehicles of the three infantry divisions and of the XXIV Corps Artillery. General Smith's headquarters cut the table of organization and equipment allowances, and his own allowances were reduced again because of inadequate shipping space. In the end, out of all motor transport vehicles allowed by corps, only 94 percent of the ambulances, 83 percent of the trucks, 71 percent of the trailers, and 75 percent of the tractors could be embarked from Oahu.[24] Although these cuts were distributed more or less equally among all the units involved, the 27th Division suffered somewhat less than the others, being able to carry with it 86 percent of its trucks, 99 percent of its trailers, and 99 percent of its tractors.[25] However, this advantage was more than offset when, after arrival on Saipan, corps headquarters commandeered thirty-three of the Army division's 2-1/2-ton trucks and refused to return them even as late as 6 July.[26]

As a partial compensation for the shortages in standard types of motor transportation, a substantial number of DUKW's was provided for the Saipan operation—more than had hitherto been used in the Central Pacific. All together, 185 of these

---

[21] 27th Inf Div G–4 Rpt, p. 19; NTLF Rpt Marianas, Phase I, Incl J, p. 5.
[22] See above, pp. 48–49.
[23] Quoted in COMINCH P–007, Ch. 5, p. 11.

[24] NTLF Rpt Marianas, Phase I, Incl F, G–4; Incl A, Annex A, p. 1.
[25] Ibid. The following table gives the distribution of motor transportation among the three divisions:

Division	Trucks	Trailers	Tractors
2d Marine	437	222	16
4th Marine	558	201	40
27th Infantry	624	196	122

[26] 27th Inf Div G–4 Rpt, pp. 20–23.

vehicles were embarked. Each infantry division had a DUKW company attached, as did XXIV Corps Artillery.[27] The DUKW's initial function was to land the artillery. This had entailed some modification both of the DUKW's bodies and of the 105-mm. howitzer wheels. After the landing phase, the amphibian trucks were used continually throughout the campaign, chiefly for hauling ammunition from shipboard or supply dumps to artillery emplacements and as prime movers for 105-mm. howitzers. In the opinion of General Holland Smith's G-4 officer, Colonel Anderson, GSC, "the DUKW was the outstanding single type of equipment employed in this operation." [28]

Later, as the fight in the central and northern part of Saipan progressed, one other serious supply shortage manifested itself. The heavy demand for artillery support and close-in infantry support by 81-mm. and 60-mm. mortars created an unexpected drain on the mortar ammunition supply. Previous experience in the Central Pacific had seemed to indicate that a total of seven units of fire would be sufficient for Saipan, but this proved to be too low an estimate, and on the basis of experience in the Marianas ten units was recommended for future operations.[29] The initial fault in not loading enough ammunition aboard the assault ships was compounded by the fact that resupply ships were frequently not vertically loaded, thus making it difficult for the troops to get their ammunition ashore when they needed it. Also, the first ammunition resupply ship was late in arriving in the area, and many of these vessels withdrew at night because of threatened air attacks, thus making a build-up of reserves impossible.[30]

The extent to which these shortages and delays, avoidable and unavoidable, affected the course of the battle on Saipan cannot definitely be determined. The shortages and delays were real enough, but the fact that they were reported in such detail by supply officers and others might be taken to be as much in evidence of the wealth of matériel to which Americans in combat were accustomed as of any real privation suffered on Saipan. The records show no single instance wherein any infantry or artillery unit had to cease fire for want of ammunition or became completely immobilized for lack of transportation. On the other hand, it can be assumed that any defects in a supply system automatically impede the progress of ground troops. It is highly probable that had more supplies been on hand and had they reached the front lines in a more expeditious fashion, the combat troops would have been able to move against the enemy with greater force and speed.

Postlanding Naval Gunfire Support

On Saipan, as elsewhere in the island warfare typical of the Pacific, one of the most effective weapons in support of the infantry proved to be ships' fire. Naval vessels ranging in size from LCI gunboats to old battleships, and mounting guns of calibers from 20-mm. to 14 inches, cruised the

---

[27] 1st Amphibian Truck Company for the 2d Marine Division; 2d Amphibian Truck Company for the 4th Marine Division; Provisional DUKW Company (from Quartermaster Company) for the 27th Division; 477th Amphibian Truck Company for XXIV Corps Artillery.

[28] NTLF Rpt Marianas, Phase I, Incl F; Incl B, p. 1.

[29] For the Pacific Ocean Areas unit of fire, see Appendix B.

[30] NTLF Rpt Marianas, Phase I, Incl F, Part II, p. 7.

coasts of the island prepared at all times to support the troops on call, lay down preparatory fire, illuminate the night with star shells, and perform a host of other duties. True, the configuration and terrain of Saipan imposed some natural limitations on the fullest exploitation of this support. Naval guns have a flat trajectory and the mountains and hills of the volcanic island often masked fire from the sea. Also, the reefs fringing many parts of the island kept the larger vessels from approaching within optimum range for direct fire at some targets. On the other hand, many of the enemy's guns and installations were emplaced in defilade in valleys that ran perpendicular to the shore line on the east and west coasts, and against these naval gunfire could be particularly effective. The caves along the shore line offered ideal hiding places for enemy troops and were also ideal targets for ships firing from the sea, especially for the vessels of more shallow draft.[31]

In general, two types of controls were set up to permit the co-ordination between troops and ships so necessary to efficient operations of this sort.[32] For close support missions it was customary each day to assign a certain number of vessels to each infantry battalion in the assault—usually two or three destroyers. During the entire course of the operation 2 old battleships, 2 heavy cruisers, 3 light cruisers, and 39 destroyers delivered call fires at various times. Attached to each battalion was a shore fire control party consisting of naval and ground force personnel furnished by the 1st, 2d, and 295th Joint Assault Signal Companies, which were attached, respectively, to the 4th Marine Division, the 2d Marine Division, and the 27th Infantry Division. These parties were in direct radio communication with their supporting ships and from their positions on shore would request fire missions and spot the results.

This system of control was generally employed for two types of missions. First were the close support missions fired sometimes within fifty yards of friendly troops. Destroyers' five-inch guns were usually used for this purpose, and the bulk of all five-inch ammunition (139,691 rounds) was consumed in this fashion. How effective it was is doubtful. Admiral Turner's final opinion was, "Field Artillery is much better qualified for this type of fire by reason of its greater accuracy and smaller burst patterns."[33] The second type of mission usually controlled by shore fire control parties was night illumination. Star shells were fired on request of the infantrymen to prevent infiltration, to help stop counterattacks, and to keep enemy activity to their immediate front under surveillance. Unfortunately, there were not enough of these projectiles on hand to satisfy the wants of the troops, and after the first night a quota of six per hour per ship had to be imposed except during emergencies.

Except for these two types of missions, request for all other sorts of ships' fire on ground targets originated from the naval gunfire officer of the Northern Troops and Landing Force. His headquarters was set up ashore near those of the corps air officer and the corps artillery officer and the three worked in close co-ordination so as to avoid duplication of effort and waste of ammunition.

---

[31] TF 52 Opns Rpt Marianas, Incl F, p. 13.

[32] This account of naval gunfire is derived chiefly from NTLF Rpt Marianas, Phase I, Incl I, Sec. 3, and TF 52 Opns Rpt Marianas, Incl F.

[33] TF 52 Opns Rpt Marianas, Incl F, p. 13.

Under the naval gunfire officer's supervision, all deep support fire missions were arranged, including preparation fires, deliberate and methodical destruction fires, counterbattery, harassing, and interdiction fires, and fires on targets of opportunity. Since these missions were not controlled by shore fire control parties, it was considered necessary to fix definite safety limits and to specify safe lines of fire. Preparation fires were not brought closer than 1,500 yards from the nearest friendly troops. Deliberate and moderate destruction fires, fires on targets of opportunity, and counterbattery, harassing, and interdiction fires were usually confined to areas 2,500 yards from the front line. On the whole these various missions were executed far more effectively than were close support fires, and it was in this field that naval gunfire won its laurels at Saipan. Other chores ably performed by the support ships were the guarding of Saipan against amphibious reinforcements from Tinian, neutralization of the airfields at Marpi Point and Ushi Point, Tinian, and destruction of enemy cave positions along the seacoast that were inaccessible to anything but the 40-mm. fire of LCI gunboats.

The testimony of prisoners of war captured on Saipan leaves no doubt of the impression made on the Japanese by American naval gunfire. Maj. Takashi Hiragushi, *43d Division* intelligence officer,[34] testified, "the most feared of . . . [American] weapons was the naval shelling which managed to reach the obscure mountain caves where . . . CP's were located." [35] A captured Japanese lieutenant

declared that the greatest single factor in the American success was naval gunfire. When asked how he distinguished between naval gunfire and land-based artillery, he laughed and said that it was not difficult when one was on the receiving end. Everyone in the hills "holed up" and waited when a man-of-war started to fire.[36] Other Japanese prisoners of war, when interrogated on the matter, were in almost unanimous agreement. Perhaps the highest testimonial of the efficacy of this particular weapon came from General Saito himself when he wrote on 27 June, "If there just were no naval gunfire, we feel with determination that we could fight it out with the enemy in a decisive battle." [37]

Close Air Support

Once the assault troops had landed on Saipan and established their beachhead, the role of aircraft for the remainder of the operation was twofold. First, and most important, it was to keep the battlefield isolated from the inroads of enemy air and surface craft. Second, it was to support the advance of the ground troops in somewhat the same manner as naval gunfire and artillery.

After the Battle of the Philippine Sea no serious threat of enemy air intervention remained, and except for occasional nuisance raids the troops on Saipan could enjoy virtual immunity from that quarter. Thereafter, the planes of Mitscher's Task Force 58 were employed on occasional troop support missions, while Admiral Turner's escort carriers provided the aircraft for combat air patrols and antisubmarine patrols.[38] Once Aslito airfield was captured

---

[34] He was mistakenly identified as Maj. Kiyoshi Yoshida, *31st Army* intelligence officer.
[35] NTLF Rpt Marianas, Phase I, Incl I, Sec. 3, p. 19.

[36] *Ibid.,* p. 20.
[37] CINCPAC-CINCPOA Item 9983–85, p. 25.
[38] TF 51 Opns Rpt Marianas, Incl I, p. 4.

and put into operation, these duties were shared by P-47's of the 19th and 73d Fighter Squadrons, Seventh Air Force.[39]

Whether in deep support or close support, the planes assigned to assist the ground forces flew three types of missions —bombing, rocketing, and strafing. Of these, the first was the least effective in knocking out comparatively small targets such as gun installations. After the initial softening up of the landing beaches, bombing missions were ordinarily employed against enemy troop concentrations, supply dumps, and buildings. The first extensive use of aircraft rockets in the Central Pacific was on Saipan. The rockets proved to be the most valuable weapon for support aircraft, in spite of the fact that there was insufficient training in its use and that no delay fuzes were available. The most common technique for close support missions was strafing, which was not only effective against the enemy but safer for friendly troops.[40]

Troop requests for close air support were radioed by air liaison parties attached to each regiment and battalion. The requests were filtered through division and corps headquarters, each of which had the opportunity of rejecting them before final decision was made by the Commander, Support Aircraft, Capt. Richard F. Whitehead, USN, who was aboard Admiral Turner's flagship. Once a strike was ordered, it would be controlled either by Captain Whitehead himself, by the support aircraft commander on Holland Smith's staff, by the air co-ordinator (who was a group or squadron leader from one of the participating carriers and was on station

over the island at all times during daylight hours), or by the flight leader assigned to the particular mission.

Air liaison parties on the ground had no direct radio communication with the planes and were therefore unable to coach the pilots into their targets. Targets were designated in a variety of ways. Sometimes the infantry marked them with white phosphorus mortar shells. At others, planes flew dummy runs and waited to execute their missions until battalion air liaison parties notified the Commander, Support Aircraft, who in turn notified the flight leader if the runs were made on the correct area. Fluorescent panels were used to mark the front lines of the troops.[41]

The highly centralized system of close air support control used at Saipan had the advantage of reducing to a minimum the danger of duplication of missions and of planes bombing and strafing within friendly lines. On the other hand, it was time consuming to a degree that was highly unsatisfactory to the troops. The time lag between requests for and execution of an air strike was sometimes more than an hour and seldom less than a half hour.[42]

One reason for the delay was the difficulty of co-ordinating air with the other supporting arms. No single co-ordinating agency had been established before the invasion of Saipan. This created no especially difficult problem when it came to co-ordinating air and naval gunfire, since by mutual agreement naval gunfire was lifted in certain areas when requested by the Commander, Support Aircraft, and air attacks were stopped on the request of firing ships. On the other hand, the co-ordination

[39] AAF Hist Div, Army Air Forces in the Marianas Campaign, pp. 15-26, MS, OCMH.
[40] TF 51 Opns Rpt Marianas, Incl I, p. 11.
[41] Ibid., pp. 9-10.
[42] 4th Marine Div Opns Rpt Saipan, Incl H, pp. 97-103.

of air and artillery presented a more difficult problem because of the higher ordinates of artillery pieces, their rapid rate of fire, and the lack of central control for the four separate artillery units.[43] For these and other reasons, close air support was the least satisfactory of the three supporting arms.

Artillery

Artillery support was of course provided by the three divisions' organic pieces, as well as by the twenty-four 155-mm. guns and twenty-four 155-mm. howitzers of XXIV Corps Artillery, which was commanded by General Harper. Corps artillery commenced to land and go into position on 18 June, and by 22 June all four battalions were ashore and firing.[44] The two 155-mm. howitzer battalions and one of the gun battalions were emplaced 1,500 to 2,000 yards south of Charan Kanoa on the low, flat, plain adjacent to Yellow Beaches, while the other gun battalion was emplaced on the higher ground just southwest of Aslito airfield. Initially, all battalions faced north on Saipan except for Battery B, 531st Field Artillery Battalion, which was positioned to fire on Tinian.[45] On 27 June the front lines had advanced to an extent calling for a forward displacement of the heavy battalions of the corps, and by the 28th all had been displaced to positions northeast of Magicienne Bay. On 7 July the 225th Field Artillery Battalion displaced again, this time to the northeastern edge of Kagman Peninsula. In addition to supporting

the troops on Saipan, XXIV Corps Artillery had the job of guarding the back door to Tinian. Observation posts overlooking the southern island were manned twenty-four hours a day, and various harassing and destructive missions were fired on Tinian airfields and other targets on that island throughout the Saipan operation.[46]

For the most part corps artillery was assigned the job of delivering deep support fires for the advancing troops, and a minimum safety band of 1,500 yards in front of the infantry was established. The division's batteries engaged in night harassing fires, preparation fires in advance of the daily infantry jump-offs, fires on targets of opportunity, and call fires at the request of the troops.[47] On several occasions division artillery fired rolling barrages. Close liaison was maintained between corps and each division artillery headquarters by liaison officers numbering as many as three per division. A similar system was maintained by the divisions themselves. Each light artillery battalion had a command liaison officer with its supported infantry regiment, and usually the Marine and Army artillery units exchanged liaison officers to co-ordinate fires near division boundaries. Primary means of communication was by wire, although this was not altogether satisfactory because the large number of tracked vehicles used on Saipan made maintenance of wire lines difficult. As a substitute, all corps liaison officers were provided with truck-mounted radios.[48]

---

[43] TF 51 Opns Rpt Marianas, p. 10.

[44] XXIV Corps Arty Final Rpt on FORAGER Opn, Phases I and III, S–3 Rpt, p. 6.

[45] Hq Central Pacific Base Comd, Target Saipan: A Story of XXIV Corps Artillery, p. 6.

[46] XXIV Corps Arty Final Rpt on FORAGER Opn, Phases I and III, S–3 Rpt, pp. 7–8. See below, Ch. XIII.

[47] Ibid., passim; 27th Inf Div Arty Rpt FORAGER Opn, Sec. II.

[48] XXIV Corps Arty Final Rpt on FORAGER Opn, S–3 Rpt, p. 16; 27th Inf Div Arty Rpt FORAGER Opn, Annex A, p. 4.

NORTH CENTRAL SAIPAN *from the crest of Mt. Tapotchau to the northern tip of the island. Northern end of Death Valley is visible at right center.*

All together, the four artillery units were to fire about 291,500 rounds before the end of the battle for Saipan. Of these, 37,730 can be attributed to the corps artillery.[49] In spite of this considerable volume of fire, there were certain limiting factors to the optimum employment of artillery. Chief among these was terrain. After the major portion of southern Saipan had been secured and the main American attack reoriented to the north, General Holland Smith disposed almost all of his field artillery to support the northward thrust. True, one battery of 155-mm. guns (later increased to three) was pointed to the south against Tinian, but all the remaining pieces were ordered to direct their fire against the Mount Tapotchau–Death Valley–Kagman Peninsula line and beyond.

The terrain in this central part of Saipan presented several problems to the gunners. XXIV Corps Artillery was assigned the

---

[49] The estimate is derived from Hoffman, *Saipan*, p. 250; corps figures are from XXIV Corps Arty Final Rpt on FORAGER Opn, S–3 Rpt, p. 8.

general mission of deep support, which meant that most of its targets were located in the northern half of the island. Since Mount Tapotchau lay athwart the line of sight between ground observers and these targets, corps artillerymen had to rely entirely on air spotters. Six L–4 liaison planes were assigned for this purpose, and by the end of the operation each of the pilots and his accompanying air observer had put in approximately a hundred hours in the air over enemy territory.[50]

A more serious problem faced the artillerymen of the three divisions whose mission was to fire in close support of the advancing troops. In the center of the island, just east of Mount Tapotchau, lay Death Valley, which ran north and south along the axis of the attack. Since most of the enemy's guns and mortars in this area were sighted into the valley from the hills and cliffs on either side, they could not easily be reached by American artillery firing from the south. This was one reason for the slow progress made by infantrymen up the center corridor of the island. Furthermore, since the troops on the right and left pushed on more rapidly than those in the center, the front line became more and more bent back in the middle. The unevenness of the line made the adjustment of artillery fire all the more difficult.

Nevertheless, in spite of the fact that Saipan was far from an artilleryman's paradise, the main body of Holland Smith's troops during the attack to the north did at least have continuous artillery support. Not so those troops of the 27th Division that were left to clean out the Japanese who were holed up on Nafutan Point, the southeastern tip of the island. Except for tanks, naval gunfire, and, later, antiaircraft guns, the infantrymen assigned to this mission would have to depend entirely on their own weapons.

---

[50] Hq Central Pacific Base Command, Target Saipan, p. 6.

The Capture of Nafutan Point

By the end of 18 June the 4th Marine Division had penetrated to Magicienne Bay and cut the island of Saipan in two. General Holland Smith's plans for the next phase of the operation called for a change of direction of the main attack from east to north across the breadth of the island. Specifically, this meant that the 2d Marine Division would hold and consolidate its positions on the extreme left flank south of Garapan and would constitute the pivot of a wheeling movement. The outer end of the wheel's spoke would be the right flank of the 4th Marine Division resting on Magicienne Bay. When the turn had been completed the two divisions would be abreast and ready to launch their northerly drive against the main enemy defense line, which now stretched across the island in a southeasterly direction from the outskirts of Garapan to Magicienne Bay.

Meanwhile, Nafutan Point and the approaches to it along the south coast of Saipan remained occupied by Japanese troops that had to be cleared out before Aslito field could be considered entirely safe from counterattack and infiltration.

Nafutan Point is a short peninsula—a southward extension of the east coast of Saipan. Dominating most of the peninsula is a high cragged ridge running in a north–south direction not far inland from the east coast. This is Mount Nafutan, whose highest point is about 407 feet. Its northern and western faces are almost sheer cliffs. About 400 yards west of the northern part of Nafutan mountain lies a ridge about 300 feet in height. Although the lowlands in the western portion of the peninsula and in the valley between Mount Nafutan and Ridge 300 were mostly under cultivation, the hilly and mountainous areas in the east were generally covered with thick underbrush. (*See Map II.*)

Compressed into this area by the advance of the American troops was a motley crowd of Japanese military personnel mixed with civilians. All together, the military contingent numbered about 1,050. Included were survivors of the *317th Independent Infantry Battalion, 47th Independent Mixed Brigade;* naval personnel who had manned the coastal defense guns located near the southern tip of the peninsula; antiaircraft and service troops that had been swept out of Aslito field; and probably stragglers from many other units. The men were under no single command, at least in the strict sense of that word, but the highest ranking officer seems to have been a Captain Sasaki, who commanded the *317th Independent Infantry Battalion.*[1]

The job of disposing of these people and securing Nafutan Point was initially assigned to the two regiments of the 27th

---

[1] See below, p. 159.

Agingan Pt   Cape Obian   Aslito Airfield   Mt Nafutan

WHITE BEACH 1

WHITE BEACH 2

SEAWARD CLIFF LINE, NAFUTAN PENINSULA

Infantry Division that were ashore by the 18th of June. Holland Smith's headquarters assumed that the task could be completed in a short time, and that it would be little more than a mopping-up operation. The assumption proved to be optimistic in the extreme. Not until 27 June was the southeastern extremity of Saipan completely cleared of the recalcitrant, if disorganized, enemy troops holed up in that vicinity.

Action of 19 June

Holland Smith's orders for the 19th directed the 27th Infantry Division to "complete missions assigned" in the previous day's order, which meant in effect that the division was to push to the east coast of Saipan along its entire front including all of Nafutan Point. Jump-off

hour was set by division orders at 0730.[2] In position along the front line from right to left (south to north) were the 3d and 1st Battalions, 105th Infantry, and the 2d and 1st Battalions, 165th. The latter regiment had on the preceding day almost reached Magicienne Bay, but the line of the 105th bent back sharply to the westward to a position on Saipan's south coast only 700 yards east of Cape Obiam.

On the extreme right, the 3d Battalion, 105th Regiment, met no opposition to speak of. During the day not an enemy shot was fired except for a few random rounds of artillery that were lobbed into the battalion's area from Nafutan Point. Nevertheless, the rugged terrain along the southern coast made progress difficult, and

---

[2] NTLF Opn Order 7-44, 19 Jun 44; 27th Inf Div G-3 Jnl, 19 Jun 44, Msg 5.

by nightfall the battalion had advanced only about 1,800 yards in its zone.[3]

To its left and well ahead, the 1st Battalion, 105th, jumped off at 0730, as scheduled, with Company A on the right, B on the left. After three hours of unopposed progress, the battalion came up against the first of the series of ridges that flank Mount Nafutan to the northwest. In spite of considerable enemy small arms and automatic weapons fire, both companies reached the top of the ridge without trouble, but as they went over the crest to a stretch of level ground with clear fields of fire they were pinned down by heavy fire from five separate pillboxes to their immediate front. The pillboxes were located near the boundary line between the two advance companies, and the company commanders drew their units into a semicircle around the area and poured fire into it. After an hour and a half of futile effort to place shaped charges against the pillboxes, both companies pulled back to a line below the ridge out of range of enemy fire.[4]

On being informed of the situation, regiment ordered the 1st Battalion to re-form, move to the left, and try to outflank the enemy by an attack from the north, rather than by a frontal assault. As a prelude to the attack, naval planes were to deliver a fifteen-minute air strike, which was to be followed by a half hour's concentrated division artillery fire.[5]

Promptly at 1610 the battalion jumped off and almost immediately ran into trouble. B Company, on the left, had to climb the ridge some distance back from the enemy positions in order to execute the flanking movement. Once on top, it was to attack south. However, in getting onto the ridge, the men were held up by an exploding artillery dump and had to take a circuitous route. No sooner had they reached the top of the ridge than the Japanese opened fire with dual-purpose guns. By this time it was 1730, well on toward darkness.

Company A, meanwhile, had not been able even to get into position to attack. Before it could swing into line on the right flank of Company B, it too came under fire from the enemy positions and the men jumped for cover. One soldier (Pvt. Thomas C. Baker) succeeded in knocking out one of the enemy's pillboxes with a bazooka, but even so the company made no substantial progress. Shortly after 1800, Colonel O'Brien halted the attack, and the whole battalion retired to the line of departure for the night. There, Company C replaced Company B.[6]

To the north, the 165th Infantry was faring somewhat better. The previous evening the regiment had stopped short of the shore line, and its first task was to complete its penetration to the sea. Ahead was a steep slope that ran down to a line of cliffs at the water's edge, there to drop fifty to sixty yards straight down to the ocean. The slope was a coral formation studded with sharp rocks and pocketed with holes, deep canyons, crevasses, and caves. The whole area was heavily overgrown with a tangle of vines, small trees, and bushes. The only feasible means of approach to the shore line was by way of a series of parallel paths running eastward through the undergrowth.[7]

[3] Love, Battle for Saipan, p. 108; 105th RCT Jnl, 19 Jun 44, Msg 62.
[4] Love, Battle for Saipan, pp. 101–06.
[5] 27th Inf Div G–3 Jnl, 19 Jun 44, Msg 48.
[6] Love, Battle for Saipan, pp. 107–08.
[7] Ibid., pp. 96–97.

27TH DIVISION TROOPS AT CLIFF EDGE, NAFUTAN PENINSULA

The regiment jumped off on schedule at 0730 with the 2d Battalion on the right (south), 1st on the left (north).[8] Only A Company on the extreme left had any serious trouble. An advance platoon ran into a Japanese machine gun position and was fired upon from ambush and held up for over two hours. By 1300 lead elements of both battalions had picked their way cautiously to the ocean's edge.[9] The only apparent enemy opposition remaining in the area was in a small pocket along the boundary line between the Army regiment and the 4th Marine Division. During the afternoon appeals were sent out over a public address system in an attempt to persuade this isolated remnant of enemy troops to surrender, but the action met with no success. Before the troops dug in for the night, the 1st Battalion, on the left, was relieved by the 3d, which had been in reserve during the day.[10]

At the close of operations on the 19th, two battalions of the 165th Infantry were drawn up in defensive positions along the southern coast of Magicienne Bay. The 1st and 2d Battalions had completed the process of cutting off the enemy on Nafutan Point from the rest of the island. However, the leftward swing of the 1st Battalion,

[8] 1st Bn 165th RCT Jnl, 19 Jun 44, Msg 7.
[9] 165th RCT Jnl, 19 Jun 44, Msg 63.

[10] 1st Bn 165th RCT Jnl, 19 Jun 44, Msgs 23, 47, 64.

INFANTRYMAN AT THE BASE OF CLIFF, NAFUTAN PENINSULA

105th Infantry, and the slow advance of the 3d Battalion, 105th, along the southern shore, had resulted in a large gap in the middle of that regiment's line. In order to fill the gap and protect Aslito airfield, Colonel Kelley ordered the 1st Battalion, 165th, to move back to the airfield and dig in.[11]

Along the 27th Division front the night was quiet except for two widely separated actions. On the south coast, a group of twenty to thirty civilians stumbled into the perimeter of Company L, 105th Infantry, and were all killed. In the Magicienne Bay area, about an hour after dark, some twenty Japanese launched a counterattack against the right flank of B Company, 165th Infantry, but the attack was broken up within half an hour.[12]

Action of 20 June

The morning of 20 June brought about a change in the 27th Division's plans and a reorientation of the attack against Nafutan Point. General Ralph Smith, after reviewing the difficulties encountered the preceding day by the 1st Battalion, 105th Infantry, in its attempt to assault Nafutan Ridge frontally from the west, decided that the direction of the attack should be changed from eastward to southward. He

---

[11] *Ibid.*, Msg 62.

[12] Love, Battle for Saipan, p. 110.

attached the 1st Battalion, 105th, to the 165th Infantry and then at 0800 called a conference of the unit commanders most concerned with the new plan of attack. In attendance, besides General Smith, were his operations officer, Lt. Col. Frederic H. Sheldon; Colonel Kelley, commanding officer of the 165th Infantry; and the three battalion commanders of that regiment, as well as Colonel O'Brien who commanded the 1st Battalion, 105th.[13]

As a result of the conference, General Smith issued his Field Message No. 1, which called for a co-ordinated attack by the 165th Infantry, with the 1st Battalion, 105th, attached, southward along the main axis of Nafutan Point, to commence at 1000. The day's objective was a line drawn across the peninsula about halfway between the line of departure and the southern tip.[14] The 3d Battalion, 105th, in the meanwhile would continue to advance eastward along the southern coast until it could close lines with the rest of the division in a tightening noose around Nafutan.[15]

For the main attack down the peninsula, the line-up of units from right to left (west to east) was: Companies C and A of the 105th Infantry and Companies I, K, F, and G of the 165th. The terrain to the front of the three battalions varied. Immediately ahead of the right flank of the 1st Battalion, 105th, the ground was fairly smooth with no serious obstacles. On its left the land sloped upward abruptly to a cane-covered plain in Company I's zone. Between the two levels, at the line of departure, a short ramplike piece of ground

served as an approach to the higher plain from the west, but as one proceeded farther southward the ramp became progressively steeper and finally developed into sheer cliff. Originally, A Company was deployed across this ramp from top to bottom with Company C tied in on the flat land to its right. As the advance progressed it would be necessary for Company A to keep edging more and more to the right until eventually it would end up on the level ground at the foot of the ridge. This necessarily would make effective contact with Company I on the left impossible. Thus it was that the action of the 1st Battalion, 105th, was to all intents and purposes independent of that of the 165th on its left.

Immediately in front of K and F Companies, 165th Infantry, there was nothing but open cane field sloping gently down to the bay on the left. Ahead of Company G, however, was a rubble of coral topped with the thick undergrowth that lined Magicienne Bay. Approximately 800 yards ahead of the line of departure the ground in front of the 165th sloped upward to a hill. On the left of the 3d Battalion zone the incline was gradual, but on the right of the 2d Battalion the slope gave way to an abrupt cliff—the face of Mount Nafutan itself.[16]

Although the original jump-off hour had been set at 1000, General Smith found it necessary to postpone it to 1115 and later to 1200 in order to permit the 1st Battalion, 165th, to relieve the other two battalions, which were still in position along Magicienne Bay north of the line of departure.[17] At 1145 division artillery laid down a concentrated fire along the whole front, particularly along the hill that

---

[13] 165th RCT Jnl, 20 Jun 44, Msgs 3, 6, 13, 14; 165th RCT Rpt of Action Saipan, p. 5.

[14] 165th RCT Jnl, 20 Jun 44, Msg 14. Also, see attached overlay in 27th Inf Div G-3 Jnl.

[15] 105th RCT Jnl, 20 Jun 44, Msg 12.

[16] Love, Battle for Saipan, pp. 114–15.

[17] 27th Inf Div G-3 Jnl, 20 Jun 44, Msgs 9, 17.

crossed the 165th's line of advance. Then Company C, 88th Chemical Battalion, which had been brought up to lend general support to the attack, fired its 4.2-inch chemical mortars and set up a smoke screen. Six tanks from the 766th Tank Battalion supported the 3d Battalion, 165th, in the center of the regimental line. Promptly at 1200 the troops jumped off.[18]

On the right of the regimental line the 1st Battalion, 105th Infantry, almost immediately came under machine gun fire from its left front and flank, while the right flank received some fire from a heavy flat-trajectory weapon. The whole line stopped, and C Company on the right dug in. Colonel O'Brien, the battalion commander, came up in an effort to locate the source of enemy fire and finally determined that it came from a small group of buildings almost on the battalion boundary line. Company A immediately put automatic weapons fire into this whole area. This seemed to stop the fire, and Colonel O'Brien went out to make a reconnaissance. He had moved over into the buildings when snipers began opening up on him from various houses. O'Brien immediately ordered all the buildings burned down. For the next hour the battalion was held up while the settlement was burned to the ground, tanks, self-propelled mounts, antitank guns, and flame throwers joining in the arson.

Upon completion of this task, the 1st Battalion, 105th, pushed forward again and for the rest of the afternoon ran into no trouble except occasional small arms fire. Contact with Company I on the left

was lost during the burning of the settlement and was not regained for the rest of the afternoon, chiefly because of the gradually rising ridge that now separated the two battalions. When the 1st Battalion dug in at nightfall, it had advanced about 500 yards.[19]

In the zone of the 3d Battalion, 165th Infantry, Company I, led by three tanks, fell under enemy fire almost immediately and remained stationary for about an hour and a half. Its tanks proved to be more of a hindrance than a help since they drew enemy artillery fire into the area of advance but could not be controlled by the infantry because of radio failure. On the left, Companies K and F were faring considerably better, and at 1405 Company K reported that it was 400 yards ahead of I Company and out of contact.[20] Meanwhile, on the extreme left of the regimental line G Company was stopped by a nest of Japanese hidden in the underbrush near the ocean shore and made no further advance. With both flanks of the line retarded, the two battalion commanders ordered their reserve Companies, E and L, to take positions on the extreme left and right, respectively. These moves were completed about 1630, and the regiment prepared to continue the advance.[21]

Heavy mortar fire was laid down, and both battalions jumped off in a continuance of the attack. On the regimental right progress was slow since the entire 3d Battalion had to contend with the heavy undergrowth and was moving up hill. On the left, E Company commenced to receive considerable fire from the hills north of

[18] 165th RCT Jnl, 20 Jun 44, Msgs 45, 47, 48, 50, 51; 105th RCT Jnl, 20 Jun 44, Msg 23; Roy E. Appleman, Army Tanks in the Battle for Saipan, p. 18, MS in OCMH.

[19] Love, Battle for Saipan, pp. 124–26.
[20] 3d Bn 165th RCT Jnl, 20 Jun 44, Msg 38.
[21] 2d Bn 165th RCT Jnl, 20 Jun 44, Msg 28; 3d Bn 165th RCT Jnl, 20 Jun 44, Msg 49.

Mount Nafutan and was pinned down. By 1730 no further progress seemed possible before nightfall, and all units were ordered to dig in for the night. Company E withdrew about a hundred yards before doing so.[22] Casualties had been relatively light, the 105th suffering only one man killed and five wounded; the 165th, six killed, twenty-one wounded, and one missing in action.[23]

Meanwhile, the 3d Battalion, 105th Infantry, which was still under control of its parent regiment, had been pushing eastward along the southern shore. Little infantry opposition was encountered by either of the two assault companies, although they did receive scattered artillery fire at different times during the day. By nightfall the battalion had reached a point only a hundred yards short of tying in with the attack coming down Nafutan peninsula from the north. The division line, therefore, presented an almost solid front that hemmed the southern defenders of the island into an ever-tightening pocket.[24]

During 20 June the 106th Infantry Regiment landed on Saipan and was assigned as corps reserve.[25] As soon as the regiment was ashore the 2d Battalion, 105th Infantry, was released to the control of the 27th Division, and General Ralph Smith immediately ordered it to assemble in division reserve at the southwest corner of Aslito airfield.[26]

Along the division's front line that night there was little activity except in the center in the zone of the 3d Battalion, 165th Infantry. Shortly before 2200 enemy guns

began opening up not more than 150 yards to the direct front. The fire was point blank and was aimed at both the 3d Battalion zone and the area held by the 1st Battalion, 105th Infantry. In the zone of the former, the Japanese guns overshot their mark and no damage was done, but during the barrage some rounds fell on A Company, 105th, killing one man and wounding three.[27]

Action of 21 June

Plans for 21 June called for a continuance of the attack to the south on Nafutan Ridge. At a conference held at the 27th Division command post at 2200 on 20 June, the plan was reaffirmed, but with some changes. At Colonel Kelley's request, General Ralph Smith ordered the fresh 2d Battalion, 105th Infantry, to relieve the 2d Battalion, 165th, on the left of the line as early as possible the next morning. The attack was to jump off at 0930 after a thirty-minute artillery preparation. Upon reaching the first phase line, where the 3d Battalion, 165th Infantry, was to be pinched out, control of the attack southward was to be assumed by Colonel Bishop of the 105th Infantry. Field Order Number 45, 27th Infantry Division, which contained these plans, was issued at 0615, 21 June.[28] By 0900 the 2d Battalion, 105th, had relieved the 2d Battalion, 165th, on the left of the line.[29] As the action opened, then, on the morning of 21 June, the 27th Division units on the line from right to left (west to east) were: Companies L, I, C, and A, 105th Infantry; Companies

---

[22] Love, Battle for Saipan, pp. 122–24.
[23] 27th Inf Div G–1 Periodic Rpt 4.
[24] Love, Battle for Saipan, p. 126.
[25] 106th RCT Jnl, 20 Jun 44, Msg 11.
[26] 27th Inf Div G–3 Jnl, 20 Jun 44, Msg 42.

[27] Love, Battle for Saipan, p. 128.
[28] 27th Inf Div FO 45, 21 Jun 44.
[29] 165th RCT Jnl, 21 Jun 44, Msg 21.

INFANTRYMAN MILKING AN ISLAND GOAT *in Nafutan area, 20 June.*

L, and K, 165th; and Companies G and F, 105th.

On the extreme right, the 3d Battalion of the 105th, still pushing its way eastward along the southern coast of Saipan, met serious enemy opposition for the first time. Shortly before noon the right platoon of Company I, operating along the seashore, crossed the face of a cave in the ridge and a Japanese machine gun opened up, placing enfilade fire all along the platoon line. The advance stopped at once. On request of the company commander, division dispatched a platoon of tanks from those that had come ashore with the 106th infantry. In the meantime, Lt. Col. Edward T. Bradt, battalion commander, sent forward a self-propelled mount from the Cannon Company. The vehicle sprayed the area with fire but failed to get close enough to the cave to deliver direct fire into its mouth. Shortly after 1500 the tanks arrived and immediately knocked out the position with their machine guns and 37-mm's. The battalion line then remained stationary while a loud speaker was sent forward from division headquarters in an unsuccessful attempt to persuade the remaining Japanese troops and/or civilians to come out of the cave. Shortly before 1700 the battalion line pushed forward to a point about 600 yards from the morning line of departure and dug in for the night. Contact with the 1st Battalion, 105th, on the left had been lost during the day's movement, and a small gap remained between the two battalions.[30]

---

[30] Love, Battle for Saipan, p. 154.

In the zone of the 1st Battalion, 105th, Company A on the battalion left lost ground even before the drive got under way. At daylight, when it became evident from the sound of firing on its left that the enemy had entrenched himself firmly to the front, Capt. Louis F. Ackerman ordered his men to move back about a hundred yards to a less exposed position. A further backward movement to adjust its lines to those of the unit on its left brought Company A a full 200 yards behind the positions where it had dug in the night before.

After jumping off at 0930, the 1st Battalion, 105th, moved forward slowly without opposition. The advance was delayed to permit cane fields to be burned to the company's front, and even two hours after the jump-off Company A had not yet reached the place where it had bivouacked the night before. Finally, at 1255, when Company A had advanced about a hundred yards ahead of the line where it had spent the previous night, it was hit by a heavy mortar concentration coupled with sweeping small arms and automatic weapons fire. This caught the advancing troops in open terrain without cover. Ackerman immediately radioed battalion headquarters for tanks and ordered his men back into the foxholes of the night before.

On the right of the battalion line, Company C had guided its advance on Ackerman's company. Most of the men in this part of the line had better protection than did A Company, so when the mortar barrage hit, 1st Lt. Bernard A. Tougow, in command of C, kept his men on the line. Within a few minutes after A pulled back, Colonel O'Brien, battalion commander, arrived at the C Company command post with three tanks, which immediately went to work to break up a small Japanese counterattack. The tanks then moved over to the left to meet Captain Ackerman, who had put in the request for their assistance.

O'Brien organized a co-ordinated attack along the whole front of his battalion and supported it by the tanks, which he placed in front of Company A. Shortly before 1500 the assault moved off after a brief artillery preparation. The tanks, which were buttoned up, moved out ahead of the line of infantrymen for a few minutes, then veered to the left and finally reversed their course and headed back toward the American line firing as they came. Colonel O'Brien's frantic efforts to contact the tankers by radio failed, and he finally ran out in the midst of this fire to meet them. Crawling up on the turret of the first tank he met, he banged on it with his pistol butt. The tank then contacted the other two by radio and the firing stopped momentarily. O'Brien turned the vehicles around and then took up a position atop the lead tank's turret and ordered the advance to proceed.

The whole battalion jumped off in a rapid push that carried it across the open ground. Throughout the movement most of the men advanced at a dogtrot behind the tanks, keeping up a steady fire to the front. O'Brien continued to ride the tank turret of the lead tank, giving directions to the men inside with his pistol butt and waving the infantrymen forward. During the advance A Company lost two men killed and three wounded. Company C on the right suffered no casualties.[31]

In the center of the division line, Companies L and K of the 165th Infantry jumped off on schedule at 0930. They had

[31] *Ibid.*, pp. 147–50; 105th RCT Jnl, 21 Jun 44, Msgs 19, 21, 27.

made some progress by 1255, when they were held up by a heavy concentration of mortar fire, most of which landed in the L Company area. Within the space of a few minutes one man was killed and eleven were seriously wounded; then the barrage ceased as abruptly as it had begun. By that time all of the 3d Battalion was badly disorganized and made no further advance during the afternoon. This left L Company of the 165th some 500 yards to the left rear of Company A, which had advanced rapidly during the afternoon with the aid of the tanks under Colonel O'Brien's personal direction.

To fill the gap, O'Brien ordered in the 1st Platoon of his reserve Company B. The platoon leader sent out a patrol that reported that a number of Japanese had taken up position with a machine gun at the crest of the ridge between the two battalions and that the only way firm contact could be established was by knocking out the position. O'Brien then ordered the platoon to face the ridge, deploy, and assault it frontally from the west. After a short mortar concentration the platoon attacked at 1615, but was immediately pinned down by enemy fire that killed two men and wounded three others. Shortly afterward, O'Brien received an urgent radio message indicating that Company L was being fired on from the direction of the 1st Platoon, Company B. The assault on the west face of the ridge was promptly called off and the gap along the battalion line remained unclosed for the night.[32]

The most serious difficulties of the day's fighting for Nafutan came on the extreme left of the division line. Here, the unblooded 2d Battalion, 105th Infantry, was

inserted in the line with Company G on its right and Company F on its left close to the ocean shore, while the reserve company took position north of the front line along the eastern coast.

The terrain to the immediate front was extremely difficult. The most prominent feature was the nose of Mount Nafutan, a sheer cliff splitting the battalion front like the bow of a ship. The cliff was not more than thirty feet high, but the approach to it was up a steep slope through the stubble of a cane field that offered no cover.

The battalion jumped off on schedule at 0930. On the right, Company G was immediately hit by enemy small arms, machine gun, and mortar fire. One source of the fire was soon found to be a machine gun located on the top of the cliff. Capt. Frank Olander, company commander, ordered one squad to assault the cliff itself, but the men had no sooner reached the top of the cliff than they were recalled because of their precarious and isolated situation. A second squad was sent to the top, but the underbrush was so thick that the men failed to spot the critical machine gun. Another platoon that had meanwhile attempted to infiltrate around to the right of the nose of Mount Nafutan was soon pinned down by the enemy fire from the top. The squad on top of the cliff was then called back, and the company commander made his way to the battalion command post to request more aid.

Lt. Col. Leslie M. Jensen, the battalion commander, immediately ordered two self-propelled mounts from the 165th Infantry Cannon Company (the 105th Cannon Company was not yet ashore) to carry rations and water to the isolated men around the base of the cliff. He then called division artillery for help but was advised that a

---

[32] Love, Battle for Saipan, pp. 145–46, 151–52.

concentration on the nose of the ridge or near any part of Jensen's front line was inadvisable because of the advanced positions of the rest of the American line. Eventually, however, it was agreed that one battery of 105-mm. howitzers could be sent forward to fire point-blank against the cliff. Olander was instructed to withdraw his men under cover of this fire. The decision was reached at 1535, and Battery B, 104th Field Artillery Battalion, was ordered to the front lines at once.[33]

For the next hour, under Olander's instructions, Company G attempted no further movement. Then, under cover of the artillery barrage the entire company drew back to positions to the rear of that morning's line of departure.[34]

On the extreme left, close to the ocean shore, Capt. Earl White, commanding Company F, 105th Infantry, sent his 2d Platoon south through the scrub fringing the shore line with instructions to search for a route that would lead them onto Mount Nafutan from the rear. At 1700, after an afternoon of extremely difficult work through the coral and underbrush, the platoon finally gained the top of Mount Nafutan. During this period, White had kept mortar fire on the Japanese positions on top of the ridge that were holding back the rest of his company. Sometime during the afternoon the Japanese appear to have picked up their guns and moved out. When the 2d Platoon arrived on top of the ridge at 1700 the men found it unoccupied, but within a few minutes of the arrival of the platoon the company commander ordered it to return to its starting point. Upon the return of the platoon, White ordered Com-

pany F to pull back behind the line of departure where there was better cover and where Company G had already dug in.[35]

Thus, by the close of the fighting on 21 June, troops of the 27th Division had made insignificant progress on either flank of its attack down Nafutan Point, but had made a slight dent in the center.[36] The intermediate objective line about halfway down the peninsula from the original line of departure of 20 June was still from five hundred to a thousand yards away. The nose of Mount Nafutan, which had been reached by elements of Companies F and G, 105th Infantry, had been relinquished and the mountain itself still had to be scaled before the southeastern tip of the island could be secured. Casualties for the day's fighting on Nafutan came to seven killed and fifty-seven wounded in action.[37]

Change of Plan: Relief of the 165th Infantry on Nafutan Point

By 21 June the two Marine divisions had completed their pivoting movement to the north, and General Holland Smith prepared to launch a full-scale attack against the Japanese main line of resistance in that area. To do so, he would need the bulk of the 27th Division as corps reserve and, accordingly, he decided to reduce the number of troops committed to Nafutan Point and to remove most of the men to the reserve area behind the Marine front lines to the north. His opinion that these troops would no longer be needed on Nafutan was reinforced by a report from 27th Division

---

[33] 165th RCT Jnl, 21 Jun 44, Msg 121.
[34] Love, Battle for Saipan, pp. 137–45.

[35] Ibid., pp. 136–37.
[36] See attached Hq 27th Inf Div Situation Overlay to Accompany G–3 Periodic Rpt 4, Saipan, 1/20,000, 211600 Jun 44.
[37] 27th Inf Div G–1 Periodic Rpt 5.

headquarters stating that the only enemy left in that area consisted of 300 to 500 service personnel from the remnants of naval air units originally stationed on Aslito, plus a larger number of civilians.[38]

Hence, on 21 June Holland Smith issued his operations Order Number 9–44, which was received at 27th Division Headquarters at 1215 that day.[39] The 27th Infantry Division (less one infantry battalion and one light tank platoon) was to assemble northwest of Aslito airfield in corps reserve. Division artillery was to pass to control of the XXIV Corps Artillery. One infantry battalion (undesignated) of the division was ordered to remain in the garrison area, that is, Nafutan peninsula. "It will mop up remaining enemy detachments, maintain anti-sniper patrols . . . and protect installations within its zone of action with particular attention to ASLITO Airfield."

The slow progress that his division had made on the afternoon of the 21st, however, convinced General Ralph Smith that more than a single battalion would be necessary to clean up the point. Accordingly, at 1435, his headquarters notified Col. Robert Hogaboom, USMC, G–3 of Northern Troops and Landing Force, that at least two battalions would be needed for the next day's operations in that area.[40] At 1700 General Ralph Smith called General Holland Smith and recommended that all of the 105th Regimental Combat Team be left in the Nafutan Point area. General Holland Smith agreed to this but stipulated that only two of the 105th's battalions be used there. The other would be held in

reserve ready for use elsewhere if necessary.[41]

This modification of Operations Order Number 9–44 was contained in a mail brief issued by General Holland Smith that arrived at 27th Infantry Division headquarters at 0830 on 22 June. In the words of the message, "1 RCT will continue mission in Garrison Area [Nafutan] of cleaning up remaining resistance & patrolling area."[42] The order did not designate specifically which regimental combat team was intended, although the previous day's conversation had clearly indicated that the 105th was to be used for the mission.

At 2000, 21 June, after his conversation with General Holland Smith but before receiving the mail brief modifying the latter's original orders, General Ralph Smith issued his Field Order Number 45–A, which contained the following instruction to the 105th Infantry:

RCT 105 *will hold present front line* facing NAFUTAN PT, with two Battalions on the line and one Battalion in Regimental Reserve. It will relieve elements of RCT 165 now on the present front line by 0630 22 June. The Battalion in reserve will not be committed to action without authority from the Division Commander. Reorganization of the present front line to be effected *not later than 1100 22 June and offensive operations against the enemy continued.* Reserve Battalion will maintain anti-sniper patrols in the vicinity of ASLITO AIRFIELD.[43]

The wording of this paragraph and the fact that it was issued at all to the 105th Infantry by 27th Division's commanding general was soon to become a major bone of contention between Generals Holland

---

[38] 27th Inf Div G–2 Periodic Rpt 5, 21 Jun 44.
[39] NTLF Opn Order 9–44, 21 Jun 44; 27th Inf Div G–3 Jnl, 21 Jun 44, Msg 34.
[40] 27th Inf Div G–3 Jnl, 21 Jun 44, Msg 43.

[41] *Ibid.*, Entry 65.
[42] 27th Inf Div G–3 Jnl, 22 Jun 44, Msg 14.
[43] 27th Inf Div G–3 Rpt, Battle for Saipan, FO 45, Able, 2000, 21 Jun 44. Author's italics.

Smith and Ralph Smith and was one of the alleged reasons for the latter's being subsequently relieved of his command.

Action of 22 June

22 June was spent reorganizing the front lines facing Nafutan Point.[44] On the right General Ralph Smith ordered the 3d Battalion, 105th Infantry, to hold its line and spread out to the left to relieve the 1st Battalion of the same regiment, which was to revert to corps reserve. On the left, the 2d Battalion, 105th, was to hold its line facing Mount Nafutan and move to the right to relieve the 3d Battalion, 165th Infantry. On the right, the 3d Battalion accomplished its assigned relief mission, but on the left the 2d Battalion ran into trouble.

During the preceding night it had become evident that the Japanese were preparing positions on the nose of Mount Nafutan, and Captain Olander, G Company commander, requested permission to pull his men back to less exposed positions. Permission was granted, but before the move could be executed the enemy on Mount Nafutan opened fire with machine guns, small arms, and mortars, killing seven men and wounding twenty-one.

Companies G and F immediately pulled back a considerable distance to the rear for reorganization, leaving E Company to

prevent any breakthrough. Company G, which had been badly hit on the 21st as well as on the morning of the 22d, took more than two hours to reorganize. By 0946 Captain Olander was ready to move again, but by this time his company had four officers and only seventy-two enlisted men, less than half of its original strength. With these few soldiers he was expected to take over a zone then held by a full battalion. The reorganization had taken place some 400 yards behind the position of the night before and the men now marched another 600 yards to the original line of departure from which the attack had jumped off on 20 June. From this point the company commander moved his men up to relieve the 3d Battalion, 165th, at 1025.[45] Because his company was understrength, Olander had to place his men some twenty yards apart in the skirmish line.

The 2d Battalion, 105th, spent the rest of the afternoon reorganizing its line, and made no further advance. By nightfall, in fact, there was a net loss of ground on the 2d Battalion front.

Meanwhile, about 1515 General Ralph Smith visited headquarters of Northern Troops and Landing Force to consult with the corps commander about plans for the immediate future. General Holland Smith expressed his concern regarding the slowness of the advance on Nafutan Point. He said that "he did not wish to be unreasonable but that Colonel Bishop [Commanding Officer, 105th Infantry] must not be permitted to delay. If he couldn't do it, to send somebody who could."[46] In response, General Ralph Smith "pointed out difficult terrain and Jap positions in caves and said

---

[44] The following narrative of the Nafutan Point action from 22 to 28 June is derived mostly from information gained by Capt. Edmund G. Love and set forth in his manuscript, Battle for Saipan. During most of this period only one battalion was engaged at Nafutan, the 2d Battalion, 105th Infantry. All of the records of the battalion were destroyed by fire on 7 July, and the records of higher echelons contain very little detailed information concerning activity in the area. See Love, Battle for Saipan, p. 162ff.

[45] 3d Bn 165th RCT Jnl, 22 Jun 44, Msg 14.
[46] Ralph Smith, Notes, Saipan, p. 9.

rapid advance was impracticable if undue losses were to be avoided and if Japs were to be really cleaned out. [He] said that continuing pressure would be applied and that [he] thought the point could be cleaned in a couple of days more."[47]

Shortly after this meeting, General Ralph Smith went to see General Erskine, Holland Smith's chief of staff. General Erskine apprised him of the corps plan to pass the 27th Division between the two Marine divisions on the northern front. As to Nafutan Point, Erskine expressed his belief that one battalion could finish up the job there.[48]

As a result of these afternoon conferences, General Ralph Smith returned to the division command post and drew up Field Order Number 46, which was issued at 2100. In part, the order read: "2d Battalion, 105th Infantry (1 Platoon Light Tanks attached) [will] continue operations to mop-up remaining enemy detachments in NAFUTAN POINT area. On completion of this mission, [it will] revert to Corps control as Corps Reserve."[49]

An hour later Holland Smith issued Operations Order Number 10–44, which was received at 27th Division command post at 2330.[50] In reference to Nafutan Point this order read: "2d Battalion, 105th Infantry (with one light tank platoon attached) [will] continue operations at daylight to mop up remaining enemy detachments in NAFUTAN POINT area. Upon completion this mission [it will] revert to Corps control as Corps reserve."

Although there was no serious discrep-

ancy between these two sets of orders, General Holland Smith was becoming alarmed over the fact that the battalion on Nafutan Point was getting orders from two different sources. Next day he warned General Ralph Smith: "2d Battalion, 105th by my operations order 10–44 not under your tactical control and should not be included in your tactical orders. Please take steps to rectify."[51]

Later in the operation, in requesting the relief of General Ralph Smith, General Holland Smith alleged that Field Order 46 "contravened the NT and LF order by issuing tactical orders to the 2d Battalion, 105th Infantry, to continue operations to mop up enemy resistance in NAFUTAN POINT area. The 2d Battalion, 105th Infantry, by NT and LF Order No. 10–44, had been removed from the tactical control of the 27th Infantry Division."[52]

Stalemate on Nafutan
23–24 June

As a result of these new orders the job of finishing off Nafutan peninsula was left to a single rifle battalion supported by one platoon of six light tanks. The battalion was to have no assistance from artillery except for whatever fire support might be provided by naval ships operating in the area. The front line currently held by the American troops ran along the northern base of the peninsula for a distance of roughly 2,500 yards. The terrain was mountainous, full of cliffs, crevices, and caves. Yet, it must be added that, because of the shape of the peninsula, any continuous forward advance of the attacking

---

[47] *Ibid.*
[48] *Ibid.*, p. 11.
[49] 27th Inf Div FO 46, 2100, 22 Jun 44, in 27th Inf Div G–3 Rpt.
[50] NTLF Opn Order 10–44, 2200, 22 Jun 44; 27th Inf Div G–3 Jnl, 22 Jun 44, Entry 78.

[51] NTLF G–3 Jnl, 23 Jun 44, Msg 231411.
[52] CG Expeditionary Troops to CO TF 51, 24 Jun 44, Buckner Board Rpt, p. 2 and Exhibit D.

troops would automatically reduce the length of the front and thereby shorten the line. In effect, the troops were moving down an inverted isosceles triangle from base to apex. An advance of a thousand yards along the axis of the attack would reduce the front from approximately 2,500 yards to approximately 1,000 yards.

Nevertheless, General Ralph Smith was sufficiently alarmed at the wide dispersion of the troops left along the front line on Nafutan to warn General Holland Smith of the possible consequences. "I want to draw your attention," he wrote on 23 June, "that it is within the enemy's capabilities at NAFUTAN Point to infiltrate small bodies of men through our lines at night and execute considerable damage to the planes and supplies at Conroy [that is, Aslito or Isely] field." He added that the Seabees and Air Forces troops working on the field should be alerted and would have to provide their own local security against enemy groups that might infiltrate through the lines of the 2d Battalion, 105th Infantry.[53]

General Holland Smith had withdrawn the bulk of the troops previously committed to Nafutan because they were more urgently needed in the north and because his intelligence reports indicated that the number of Japanese remaining on the point was small and probably ill-equipped. Two days earlier the intelligence sections of both the 27th Division and the 105th Infantry had estimated that only from three to five hundred enemy service personnel remained bottled up in that area, and no revision of that estimate had been made since.[54] Actu-

ally, as later events were to prove, the number was much larger, but as of the 23d no responsible authority had issued any report to indicate that this was so.

The change in orders now necessitated another shuffling of the line. Lt. Col. Leslie Jensen, commanding officer of the 2d Battalion, 105th, ordered E Company to march to the right and relieve the 3d Battalion, 105th. Company G was shifted to the right so that part of the company was below the 300-foot ridge line west of Mount Nafutan and part was on the north slope of the ridge. This reorganization was completed at 1230, and the company was ordered to attack at 1400. Company F, which on the morning of 23 June was still in position before the nose of Mount Nafutan, was ready to attack at 0800, but, before the attack could be launched, was withdrawn and reorganized. Colonel Jensen then waited until he saw how far his other two companies would stretch before ordering F back into the line. Thus, in spite of Holland Smith's orders to "continue operations at daylight," the 2d Battalion spent the entire morning trying to readjust its lines to stretch clear across Nafutan Point. When this readjustment was completed, the three companies were in position in a broken line with Company E on the right, G in the center, and F on the left.[55]

On the right (west) flank, one platoon of Company E managed to push through the coral fringing the beach for a distance of about 300 yards without any opposition. However, at the day's end this advance platoon was pulled back to its starting position because Capt. Clinton F. Smith, the company commander, had not been

<hr>

[53] Ralph Smith to CG NTLF, 23 Jun 44, Buckner Board Rpt, Exhibit VVV.
[54] 105th Inf FO 30, 1200, 21 Jun 44; 27th Inf Div G-2 Periodic Rpts 5, 6, 7.

[55] Unless otherwise noted, the account of the actions of the 2d Battalion, 105th Infantry, is derived from Love, Battle for Saipan, pages 175-98.

able to establish contact with G Company on his left and was fearful of infiltration.

Meanwhile Company G moved up to the top of Ridge 300. There it came under fire from at least four machine gun positions to its left (east). Captain Olander ordered his men not to return fire for fear of endangering the men of F Company, who were presumably operating in the general area from which the enemy was firing. Efforts to bring up the three light tanks attached to the unit failed because of the precipitous coral terrain, and finally the company commander ordered his men to withdraw to the bivouac area of the night before.

In the zone of Company F, the 2d Platoon reached the top of Mount Nafutan by skirting it to the left through the brush just inland of the east coast and coming up to it from the rear. The men met no opposition en route. The 1st Platoon was ordered to move up the valley between Ridge 300 and Mount Nafutan. For about an hour it proceeded without any opposition, but suddenly the whole column came under fire from a machine gun on the right in the direction of Ridge 300. Three tanks were called up and for better than half an hour these vehicles sprayed the hills on both sides of the valley. Nevertheless, at 1700 Captain White, the company commander, called the platoon back out of the valley and ordered it to dig in along the morning's line of departure. Meanwhile, the 3d Platoon had moved along the inside, east of Ridge 300, with no opposition until about 1500. There it halted and waited for the rest of the company to move abreast. When this failed to happen, it too withdrew to dig in for the night with the rest of F Company.

Thus at the close of the day the 2d Battalion, except for one platoon atop Mount Nafutan, had withdrawn to approximately the same positions it had occupied at the beginning of the day's advance. The battalion was dug in in four widely separated perimeters with no contact between them. The perimeter of E Company on the right was about 1,000 yards from that of G in the center; G, in turn, was about 800 yards from the Company F positions, while one platoon of F was in an inaccessible position another 800 yards to the left front.

As before, General Holland Smith's orders for 24 June called for the 2d Battalion, 105th Infantry, to "continue operations at daylight to mop up remaining enemy detachments in NAFUTAN POINT area."[56] However, not until 0800 did the battalion actually commence moving. The interim was spent trying to readjust the overextended lines of the battalion and trying to establish at least a semblance of contact between the various units.

On the extreme right flank, two platoons of Company E, against almost no opposition, reflushed the area they had traversed the day before and by nightfall reached a point about 100 yards beyond that previously gained. The 3d Platoon of this company, on the left, ran into more difficulty. During the early part of the morning the unit had moved to the left and re-established contact with G Company. By 1000, without running into any Japanese, it had reached the point of its furthest advance of the day before. Shortly thereafter the leading squad was hit by heavy small arms and machine gun fire from its left rear and was forced to take cover in a group of small houses. Mean-

---

[56] NTLF Opn Order 11–44, 23 Jun 44.

while, the other two squads to the rear laid mortars on the suspected source of enemy fire, but failed to knock it out. Then, about 1500, a force of from fifty to seventy-five Japanese rose up out of the ground and launched a counterattack through the gap that had developed between E and G Companies. With this, all further progress ceased, and shortly after dark the entire platoon moved back to the company perimeter of the night before.

G Company in the center was late in moving out. Captain Olander waited until Company E on his right had made contact and until F on his left had been reorganized. He then further delayed his jump-off until the arrival of the three light tanks he had requested. Moving off about 1130 Company G quickly recovered the ground it had taken the previous day, and then it again ran into machine gun fire. A tank was brought forward, succeeded in locating one of the enemy guns, and in a few minutes silenced it with 37-mm. fire. Shortly after this the Japanese counterattack on the right developed, and although G Company was not hit, it remained stationary for two hours.

At approximately 1630 Olander once again ordered his company to advance. Four enemy machine gun positions in the immediate front were taken out by tank guns. The reduction of these positions put the company ahead of the units on the right and left, and Captain Olander swung his men to the left in an attempt to take out a group of machine guns that were holding back the advance of Company F. This move was effected in spite of approaching darkness, and within a few minutes after making the turn G Company surprised a pocket of about fifty Japanese and wiped them out within ten minutes.

In the ensuing darkness, however, all organization within the company broke down. Olander lost contact with his platoon leaders, and the latter pulled their men back to the bivouac area of the night before.

The action of Company F on the left was in general a repetition of that of the previous day. The 2d Platoon, which had spent the night on Mount Nafutan, was ordered to build up a skirmish line and comb the nose of the ridge until the 1st Platoon could move up on its right. However the latter unit, while en route to the top of Mount Nafutan, ran into scattered rifle fire and stopped in its tracks. Meanwhile, on the company's right, the 3d Platoon was held up by a Japanese machine gun. A self-propelled mount from the 105th Cannon Company knocked this position out, but retired before disposing of a second machine gun, which had wounded one of its crew. The platoon leader then sent out a squad to get the weapon, but a third gun opened up and pinned the squad down. By this time night was approaching and, as no further progress seemed likely, Captain White ordered his entire company including the platoon on top of Mount Nafutan to withdraw to the G Company perimeter of the night before.

At nightfall then, the 2d Battalion, 105th Infantry, occupied positions in practically the same area in which it had dug in the previous night, except that the platoon atop Mount Nafutan had been recalled. At 1818 control of the battalion had passed to the Army Garrison Force.[57]

---

[57] Memo, Col Geoffrey M. O'Connell for Gen Richardson, 12 Jul 44, sub: Opns of 2d Bn, 105th Inf, Saipan, on Nafutan Point, Buckner Board Rpt, Exhibit WW.

Since Maj. Gen. Sanderford Jarman, USA, the island commander, had taken command of the 27th Division during the day, command of the forces on Nafutan Point passed to the control of Col. Geoffrey M. O'Connell, General Jarman's chief of staff.

Nafutan Secured
25–28 June

Colonel O'Connell's first step to expedite the capture of Nafutan was to assign two batteries of 90-mm. antiaircraft guns and four 40-mm. guns to support the advancing infantry. The 90-mm. guns were to fire from their fixed positions on Aslito field, and the 40-mm.'s were ordered to move into forward positions in direct support. Because of the mountainous terrain and the impossibility of bringing direct fire against most of the Japanese positions, the 90-mm. guns were ordered to fire air bursts into the tree tops, approximately twelve feet above ground level. In the opinion of Colonel O'Connell, "The high muzzle velocity of these weapons, their rapid rate of fire and the flexibility obtainable by raising and lowering the height of burst made them particularly effective for support in this type of terrain." [58] The 40-mm.'s were used for direct fire and were to prove remarkably accurate in hitting cave entrances as small as four or five feet in diameter from an average range of 2,000 yards.[59]

O'Connell's plan for the infantry differed somewhat from that previously employed. Company E was ordered to leave its 3d Platoon in the area adjacent to the penin-sula's west coast at the point where the company had bivouacked the two preceding days. The other two platoons were to move to the left, establish firm physical contact with G Company, build up a skirmish line, and move south along the west slope of Ridge 300. Company G was to form a line on E Company's left flank and advance in co-ordination with that unit. F Company was to deploy two platoons across the mouth of the valley between Ridge 300 and Mount Nafutan, while the third platoon moved along the east slope of the ridge in co-ordination with the other two companies.[60]

By 1030 of 25 June, the 1st and 2d Platoons of E Company had swung left and established contact with Company G. About 1130, after an advance of nearly 150 yards, the leading squad of the 1st Platoon on the right ran into a fusillade of fire and was pinned down. Tanks were called up but became entangled in the undergrowth and rocks and could be of no assistance. At 1600 the company commander ordered both platoons to retire about forty yards behind their farthest point of advance and tie in with Company G and spend the night.

Company G had little or no opposition during the day, but its advance was slow because it was held up by the halting forward movement of the units on both flanks and because the tanks had extreme difficulty in maneuvering over the terrain. About noon the company reached the gun position it had knocked out during the late afternoon of the preceding day, and after a heavy fire by antiaircraft guns, moved on through it. The position contained four

---

[58] O'Connell, Opns in Nafutan Point Area, Saipan, 2 Jul 44, Buckner Board Rpt, Exhibit XX, p. 3.
[59] Ibid.; see also, Memo cited n. 57.

[60] The following account, unless otherwise noted, is derived from Love, Battle for Saipan pp. 199–215.

SKIRMISH LINE *on west slope of Ridge 300. Note man with bazooka at extreme right.*

heavy machine guns and two 50-mm. mortars. The company advanced another twenty-five yards but was then held up because of the dense growth of scrub brush. Captain Olander worked his tanks into position and for two hours sprayed this area with machine gun fire and canister. Just as he was about to continue the advance, the tanks notified him that it was 1600 and they were about to withdraw. This notice plus the fact that Company E was making no further progress induced Olander to pull his men back to the demolished enemy strongpoint and dig in there for the night.

Meanwhile, Company F was undergoing a repetition of the trouble it had encountered the day before. Shortly after jumping off, the 3d Platoon on the right discovered that the Japanese had mined the only available tank route and engineers were called up to abate the nuisance. Two tanks were then called up and succeeded in destroying two machine guns that lay athwart the line of advance. Immediately, another gun opened up. A squad went forward to take out this position but was pinned down by machine gun fire and a shower of grenades. Further tank action was delayed when radio communications between the tanks and infantry gave out, and not until 1500 was the platoon leader able to direct his tanks into the area of resistance. Finally, the two tanks succeeded in bringing their guns to bear against the position, and shortly after 1500 the whole platoon pushed forward and into the Japanese line. Here they found six heavy machine guns, several mortars, a wrecked dual-purpose gun, and all types of grenades and ammunition, together with the dead bodies of over a hundred Japanese. The platoon dug in for the night. The other two platoons of Company F had remained stationary during the day guarding the northern approach to the valley between Mount Nafutan and Ridge 300.

June 25 marked the climax of the campaign for the capture of Nafutan Point. During the day the 2d Battalion knocked out and overran the main defensive line of Japanese positions on top of Ridge 300. These positions controlled the approach to the point, and it was from Ridge 300 that the advance of the whole line had been held up since 22 June.

Plans for 26 June were the same as on the previous day except that the 1st and 2d Platoons of Company F were to leave the northern mouth of the valley and take position on the left flank of the battalion line. At 0645 concentrated mortar fire was directed along the whole front, and at 0750 both batteries of 90-mm. antiaircraft guns fired a ten-minute concentration. Promptly at 0800 all three companies jumped off.

On the right, Company E moved slowly forward, fighting the terrain and the underbrush. By 1400, when it was some fifty yards ahead of its farthest point of advance of the previous day, a machine gun opened up directly in front of the 2d Platoon. A self-propelled mount came forward but could not bring its gun to bear against the enemy position. Finally, the enemy gun was taken out by a BAR belonging to Company G, whose right flank was moving along an elevation to the left of E Company and was therefore in a better position to fire on the enemy in front of the latter unit. That company resumed its advance and for the next 200 yards met no opposition. At 1600 Captain Smith was notified that the other two companies were pulling back to approximately the same

positions they had held the night before, so he did likewise.

Company G made more rapid progress. After cleaning out the position to the front of E Company, Captain Olander's men pressed ahead. At 1600 their tanks left to return to their maintenance pool for the night, but the company commander elected to go on without them. Within half an hour his men had arrived at the southern edge of Ridge 300.

It was on the left flank in the zone of Company F that the greatest progress was registered on the 26th. With three platoons abreast, and without benefit of tank support, the company pushed steadily forward without meeting any enemy fire. By 1700 it had reached the southern end of Mount Nafutan, a thousand yards from the tip of the peninsula. There, the men began to receive small arms fire and came to a halt. At 1830 F and E Companies withdrew all the way back to the area in which G had spent the previous night. This withdrawal was made because both company commanders felt that their positions on the top of the high rocky points of Mount Nafutan and Ridge 300 were too exposed to provide satisfactory spots to dig in and establish perimeters.

The battalion dug in in four perimeters on the night of 26 June. The three rifle companies, less E Company's 3d Platoon but reinforced by elements of H Company, dug in on Ridge 300. The 3d Platoon of E Company still occupied the old bivouac area near the west coast of the peninsula. The whole area between the 2d Battalion positions on Ridge 300 and the sea to the east was unoccupied by American troops and serious gaps appeared on the right of the line.

Americans Rescuing Baby From Nafutan Cave

Shortly after midnight of 26 June, a body of Japanese estimated at 500 sneaked through the 2d Battalion's outposts. Their destination was Hill 500, formerly the site of headquarters of the *47th Independent Mixed Brigade*, but now occupied by the 25th Marines in Northern Troops and Landing Force reserve. One small force hit the rear command post of the 2d Battalion, 105th Infantry, and in the darkness was driven off with a loss of twenty-seven dead in return for four Americans killed and twenty wounded.[61] Otherwise the infiltration was undetected.

This desperate Japanese move was led by Captain Sasaki, commanding officer of the *317th Independent Infantry Battalion, 47th Independent Mixed Brigade*. The troops composing the force consisted of those remnants of his own command that had escaped to Nafutan plus scattered Army and Navy men from other units, including the service and antiaircraft troops formerly stationed on Aslito.

Sasaki's order read in part:

26 June 1944

1. The enemy situation is the same as you have been informed.

2. The Battalion will carry out an attack at midnight tonight. After causing confusion at the airfield, we will advance to Brigade Headquarters in the Field.

3. . . . Units will assemble at 1930 in areas to be designated separately. You must carry out the attack from the designated places.

4. Casualties will remain in their present positions and defend Nafutan Mount. Those who cannot participate in combat must commit suicide.

5. We will carry the maximum of weapons and supplies.

6. The pass word for tonight will be "Shichi Sei Hokoku" [Seven lives for one's country].[62]

The word "battalion" as applied here is a courtesy title only. The force was a conglomerate mixture of all kinds of troops, of which the remnants of Sasaki's battalion formed only the nucleus.

About 0230 Sasaki's force hit Aslito field and splattered the area with machine gun and small arms fire before moving on toward Hill 500, where it apparently expected to find the command post of the *47th Independent Mixed Brigade*. Arriving at its destination around 0530, one part of the force found instead that the hill was occupied by the 25th Marines, who instantly gave battle with small arms and hand grenades.

Simultaneously, another group of Japanese fell upon the 14th Marine Artillery Regiment in positions between Hill 500 and Aslito. Here another hot fight ensued, the Marine artillerymen killing 143 Japanese at the cost to themselves of 33 killed and wounded.[63] Still another segment hit the command post of the 104th Field Artillery Battalion, where 15 to 20 of them were killed. The 25th Marines mopped up the remaining stragglers the next morning, and with that Sasaki's breakthrough was finished.[64]

On the morning of 27 June all three companies of the 2d Battalion, 105th Infantry, formed a skirmish line and swept to the end of the peninsula with no trouble. Not a live Japanese was encountered, and at 1840 Nafutan Point was declared secure.[65] Two hundred dead Japanese, mostly soldiers, were found in five of the caves

---

[61] *Ibid.*, p. 216.

[62] NTLF Rpt Marianas, Phase I, Incl D, G-2 Rpt, p. 34.

[63] *Ibid;* TF 51 Opn Rpt Marianas, Incl A, p. 10.

[64] NTLF Rpt Marianas, Phase I, Incl D, G-2 Rpt, p. 34; TF 51 Opn Rpt Marianas, Incl A, p. 10; 27th Inf Div G-2 Jnl, 28 Jun 44, Msg 19.

[65] 27th Inf Div G-2 Jnl, 27 Jun 44, Msg 64.

on Mount Nafutan, and later another 350 dead enemy soldiers were counted in the area of the operation of the 2d Battalion, 105th Infantry.[66] These figures, plus the estimated 500 that had participated in the breakthrough, bring the total estimate of enemy combat personnel in the area to about 1,050, considerably above the original estimate of 300 to 500 that had been agreed upon by the 105th Infantry, the 27th Infantry Division, and Northern Troops and Landing Force.

Also captured on Nafutan Point on 28 June were four 6-inch guns of British manufacture and three 14-cm. guns manufactured in 1925 at the Yokosuka Naval Arsenal. All were in the vicinity of the radar station on the point but had not yet been emplaced. One of the 14-cm. guns was slightly damaged; one 6-inch gun was badly damaged, two were slightly damaged, and one was almost intact.[67]

Nafutan Point had taken a long time to capture, probably longer than was necessary. General Holland Smith and his staff were bitterly disappointed, not to say outraged, by the slow progress made by the 2d Battalion, 105th Infantry. They complained frequently about "1000 Americans being held up by a handful of Japs."[68]

The number of enemy troops isolated on Nafutan Point was actually considerably more than a handful, and probably totaled about 1,050. Also, the effective strength of the 2d Battalion, 105th Infantry, as of 27 June, was down to 556 officers and men according to Colonel O'Connell, USA, who

commanded the unit during the last stage of the capture of Nafutan.[69]

In addition, the terrain that the American soldiers faced was far from suitable for rapid assault. As described in the battalion report, "The terrain consisted of steep ridges, deep gulches with cliffs, ground broken with coral pinnacles, and thick jungle type underbrush which impeded progress and made observation impossible." [70] Also, for the first three days of the assault, the battalion had no artillery support, and after that only the 40-mm. and the 90-mm. antiaircraft guns that Colonel O'Connell brought down when he took over command, plus naval gunfire from three destroyers.

The low estimate of the number of Japanese troops in the area that was entertained by corps headquarters was derived from an intelligence report emanating from the 27th Division itself. As of 21 June, the division had estimated the number of remaining Japanese on Nafutan to be between two and three hundred.[71] Since no change in this figure had been made, General Holland Smith's staff had some reason to assume that only a "handful" remained. Also, the bare figure of 1,050 enemy troops cited above offers no real picture of the combat efficiency of the Japanese left on the peninsula. These were, it must be remembered, stragglers who had made a disorderly retreat before the onslaught of the American push across Aslito field. They were disorganized, short of supplies, and in some cases unarmed.

Against these people, the American drive

---

[66] O'Connell, Opns in Nafutan Point Area, Saipan, 2 Jul 44, Buckner Board Rpt, Exhibit XX, pp. 2–3.

[67] Ibid.

[68] O'Connell Rpt, Buckner Board Rpt, Exhibit WW; Testimony of Maj Norvel H. Moore, USA, Exhibit BBB.

[69] Buckner Board Rpt, Exhibit WW.

[70] 2d Bn 105th Inf Narrative of Events, Saipan, p. 3.

[71] 27th Inf Div G–2 Periodic Rpt 5, 21 Jun 44.

was halting and slow. There was some justification for Holland Smith's lack of confidence in the leadership of the regiment, and later of the battalion, committed to cleaning up Nafutan. The attack of the infantry companies was frequently un-coordinated; units repeatedly withdrew from advanced positions to their previous nights' bivouacs; they repeatedly yielded ground they had gained. Whatever the extenuating circumstances, these facts could not fail to raise doubts about the aggressiveness and combat efficiency of the unit assigned to the mission.

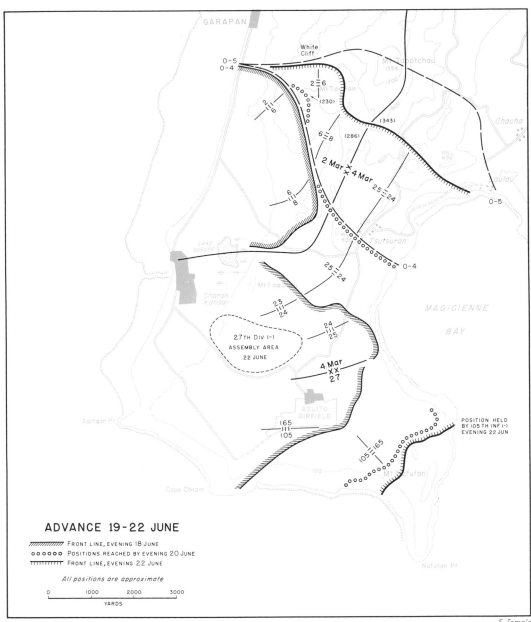

GARAPAN

White
Cliff

Mt Tapotchau
1554

0-5
0-4

2≡6 Mt Tipo Pale
(230)

2≡6

(343)

6≡8 (286)

HILL
600

Chacha

2 Mar × 4 Mar
× 25≡24

aulau

6≡8

0-5

LAKE
SUSUPE

5 Tsutsuran

0-4

Charan Kanoa

Mt Fina

25≡24

MAGICIENNE

BAY

23 ⫼ 24

24 ⫼ 25

27TH DIV (−)
ASSEMBLY AREA
22 JUNE

Agingan Pt

4 Mar
××
27

ASLITO
AIRFIELD

POSITION HELD
BY 105 TH INF (−)
EVENING 22 JUN

165 ⫼ 105

105 ≡ 165

Mt Nafutan

Cape Obiam

ADVANCE 19-22 JUNE

///////// FRONT LINE, EVENING 18 JUNE

ooooooo POSITIONS REACHED BY EVENING 20 JUNE

|||||||| FRONT LINE, EVENING 22 JUNE

Nafutan Pt

All positions are approximate

0   1000   2000   3000

YARDS

F. Temple

MAP 6

CHAPTER IX

The Fight for Central Saipan—I

Preparations for the Drive to the North

While elements of the 27th Division were slowly inching their way down Nafutan Point, the two Marine divisions prepared to launch the drive against the main line of Japanese defenses, which stretched across the waist of the island from just below Garapan to the northwest corner of Magicienne Bay.[1] (*Map 6*) The 2d Marine Division in the north had little more to do than consolidate the lines it already held, send out patrols, and mop up small isolated pockets of enemy troops still lurking within its sector. The 4th Marine Division, before it could be in a position to attack, would have to reorient the direction of its drive from east to north and then push forward (northward) about a thousand yards to tie its left flank in with the right flank of the 2d Division. When this was accomplished the two Marine divisions would be drawn up abreast on what was designated the O–4 line, which ran roughly parallel and a little to the south of the Japanese main line of defense.[2]

During the period in which the 4th Marine Division was pivoting to the left, the only serious fighting occurred around Hill 500, on 20 June. This 500-foot eminence just west of the village of Tsutsuuran had once been the site of the command post of Colonel Oka, commander of the *47th Independent Mixed Brigade*, who had since left it for a safer location to the northward. Hill 500 fell within the zone of the 25th Marines, which attacked it in column of battalions.

Following an advance preparation of rockets, artillery, heavy weapons, and mortars, the lead battalion moved forward about 1030 under cover of smoke. By noon it had seized the hill, and it spent the rest of the day mopping up the network of caves that ran through the area. All together, the marines suffered forty-nine casualties and accounted for forty-four enemy dead. The hill had been well organized for defense but not strongly manned.[3]

That same day the 8th Marines, which constituted the 2d Marine Division's right (south) flank, made a forward advance against no opposition to tie in with the left flank of the 4th Division. There was little other activity in the 2d Division's zone of action.[4] By nightfall of the 20th the marines rested securely on the designated O–4 line ready to jump off on order for the big drive northward. They spent June

---

[1] See above, pp. 116–17.

[2] See NTLF Opn Order 8–44, 19 Jun 44, Annex A, and Japanese Situation Map, 19 Jun 44, Incl to Ch. VI.

[3] 25th RCT 4th Marine Div Rpt, p. 5; Hoffman, *Saipan,* p. 115.

[4] Hoffman, *Saipan,* p. 114.

HILL 500. *Marines in foreground await signal to advance on the hill.*

21st resting and sending out patrols. Men of the 4th Division moved as far as 1,500 yards to their front without meeting any organized enemy resistance.[5]

Landing the 106th Infantry

Before leaving Hawaii, the 106th Infantry Regiment had been assigned as reserve for the 27th Division with the probable mission of landing on Saipan. On arrival at Kwajalein, Col. Russell G. Ayers, the regimental commander, was informed that his unit would be attached to the Southern Landing Force, destined for Guam. The regiment was to land in the rear of the 1st Provisional Marine Brigade and to capture Orote Peninsula on that island.[6] On 16 June, however, because of the imminent

engagement with the approaching Japanese fleet, Admiral Spruance indefinitely postponed the landing on Guam,[7] and on the 18th the transports carrying the 106th Infantry were detached from Admiral Conolly's Southern Attack Force and ordered to Saipan.[8]

On the evening of the 18th General Holland Smith requested that the 106th be landed "in order to maintain the continuity of the offensive," but Admiral Turner was reluctant to comply because to do so would inevitably delay the Guam attack until another reserve force for that landing could be brought up from the Hawaiian area. Nevertheless, Smith continued to press his case, and at last Turner con-

---

[5] *Ibid.*, p. 120.

[6] 106th (Reinf) RCT Narrative Rpt, FORAGER Opn, 29 May–14 Aug 44, pp. 1–2.

[7] See above, p. 121.

[8] 106th RCT Rpt FORAGER, p. 2. The other landing troops originally assigned to Guam were subsequently returned to Eniwetok. TF 53 Rpt of Amph Opns for Capture of Guam, 10 Aug 44, pp. 5–6.

MARINES ON THE CREST OF HILL 500 *mop up network of caves.*

curred and ordered the 106th Infantry to commence landing early on the morning of 20 June.[9]

The regiment landed on order and except for its attached artillery was assigned to Northern Troops and Landing Force reserve. Next day Colonel Ayers directed all of his units to initiate reconnaissance in the zones of action of both Marine divisions. In conducting this reconnaissance, one group from the Antitank Company was ambushed and suffered four casualties, the first to occur in the regiment.

The rest of the day the 1st Battalion patrolled Susupe swamp with the mission of clearing Japanese stragglers from the vicinity of corps headquarters and a nearby Marine hospital. For this purpose the battalion was attached to the 2d Marine Division under whose control it remained until the morning of 23 June. During this period the battalion killed eighteen Japanese in the swamp and took two prisoners of war.[10]

Japanese Situation on the Eve of the Northern Attack

While the marines pivoted on the 2d Marine Division's left flank below Garapan, the Japanese too were pivoting on almost the same point. By the 19th they were in position along a new "line of security" that ran from below Garapan, east to White Cliff, south to Hill 230, and then southeast through Hill 286 to Magicienne Bay.[11] General Saito disposed his troops in new sectors divided by Mount Tapotchau. On the extreme right (west) of the Japanese flank the town of Garapan was occupied

---

[9] Comdr Amph Forces, Ser. 000156, 4 Sep 44, Incl A; 106th RCT Rpt FORAGER, p. 2.

[10] 106th RCT Jnl FORAGER, p. 4.
[11] See above, p. 116.

JAPANESE TYPE 93 13.2-MM. MACHINE
GUN. *This dual-purpose gun was captured at Saipan.*

by naval units, chiefly the *Yokosuka 1st
Special Naval Landing Force.* To their left,
the *135th Infantry* held the area between
Garapan and the west slopes of Mount
Tapotchau. The *118th Infantry,* a straggler unit, was to hold the area southeast
of Tapotchau and be prepared to check
enemy landings from Magicienne Bay. Kagman Peninsula was to be held by those
remnants of the *47th Independent Mixed
Brigade* that had not already been destroyed or isolated on Nafutan Point. The
9th Expeditionary Unit, another straggler
force, was placed under command of the
47th Independent Mixed Brigade and assigned to defend the shore north of Kagman Peninsula. In general reserve was the
136th Infantry, which had been ordered to
assemble at Chacha at sunset on the 19th.
The *9th Tank Regiment* had a dual

mission—to co-operate with the *118th Regiment,* and to check any advances along
the coast or against the beaches of Magicienne Bay.[12]

Even this late in the campaign, the
Japanese expected either a landing on
Magicienne Bay or a tank attack up the
bay coast. Their fear of American tanks
was especially acute, as a report from *31st
Army* headquarters attests: "The changes
in the battle up until today have been the
results of naval gunfire and bombing but
from now on the main thing will be to
gain unfailing victory in antitank warfare.
Our army has new ideas concerning this
point and we hope this is not a miscalculation." [13]

The stubborn determination of the Japanese to continue their resistance is all the
more remarkable in view of their losses to
date. As of 19 June approximately three
and a half of the *43d Division's* original
eight battalions had been destroyed. Only
one of five artillery battalions remained.
The *47th Independent Mixed Brigade* had
been all but eliminated as an organized
fighting unit. Two and a half battalions of
infantry belonging to other units were
destroyed, only one composite battalion
remaining. Sixty percent of the *9th Tank
Regiment* was destroyed, as were most of
the *7th* and *11th Independent Engineers.*[14]
On the eve of the American attack to the
north the personnel losses of Japanese line
units were reported to be not lower than
50 percent.[15]

In terms of artillery and tanks, the Japanese were just as badly off and as hope-

---

[12] Japanese Studies in World War II, 55, map
facing p. 79.
[13] *31st Army* Msg File, Msg 1059; CINCPAC-
CINCPOA Trans 9983–85.
[14] *31st Army* Msg File, Msg 1060.
[15] *Ibid.,* Msg 1071.

PURPLEHEART RIDGE

DEATH VALLEY

JAPANESE FIELD OF FIRE *from Mt. Tapotchau.*

lessly outnumbered. All that remained to them on 20 June after six days of fighting were eleven 75-mm. field pieces, twenty-seven tanks, three operational antiaircraft guns, and nine machine cannon.[16]

But though the Japanese on Saipan were weak in manpower and short of weapons and equipment, they lacked nothing of the traditional spirit that had driven and was to drive so many of their countrymen to glorious if futile death on the battlefield. On the eve of the battle one tanker doubt-

less spoke for most of his compatriots when he inscribed in his diary:

The fierce attacks of the enemy only increase our hostility. Every man is waiting for the assault with all weapons for close quarters fighting in readiness. We are waiting with 'Molotov cocktails' and hand grenades ready for the word to rush forward recklessly into the enemy ranks with our swords in hands. The only thing that worries me is what will happen to Japan after we die.[17]

22 June: The Jump-off

General Holland Smith's orders for 22 June called for an attack to the north by

---

[16] Corrected figures are derived from *31st Army* *Msg File*, Msgs 1060, 1064, 1068. These figures do not include the equipment in the hands of straggler elements on Nafutan Point.

[17] CINCPAC-CINCPOA Trans 10238, extracts from the diary of Matsuya Tokuzo.

the two Marine divisions in line abreast, the 2d Division on the left, the 4th on the right. The jump-off hour was to be 0600, the objective line (O–5) to run through Laulau village on Kagman Peninsula on the right, Mount Tapotchau in the center, and a point on the west coast of the island about 1,000 yards south of Garapan on the left.[18]

In view of the fact that this northward push would automatically extend the lines of the two Marine divisions, especially as the 4th Division was required to spread eastward on Kagman Peninsula, the corps commander alerted the 27th Division to the fact that it might soon be committed to the northern line. The Army division, which was then in corps reserve, was ordered to reconnoiter routes to both of the Marine divisions' zones of action. 27th Division Artillery was passed to the control of General Harper's XXIV Corps Artillery to deliver close and deep support missions in advance of the marines. All together, the troops on the northern line would have eighteen battalions of artillery to support their drive on the morning of 22 June.[19]

On the right of the 4th Marine Division zone in the area inland from Magicienne Bay, the 24th Marines jumped off on schedule, made rapid progress against light opposition, and by 1330 reached an intermediate objective line that had been established by the division commander about 2,000 yards in front of its line of departure.[20]

To its left, the 25th Marines found the going more difficult. The regiment jumped off on schedule in column of battalions,

and within half an hour the lead battalion was attacked by a force of Japanese troops accompanied by a tank. Ninety of the enemy were killed and the tank was destroyed. For the rest of the morning the regiment encountered light resistance, but just south of the intermediate objective line received severe machine gun fire, a situation that was aggravated by an exploding Japanese ammunition dump. This slowed progress so that by the day's end the 25th Marines were still short of the day's objective, although the regiment had made an advance of about 2,000 yards.[21]

Meanwhile, the 23d Marines, which had been in division reserve, was committed between the two assault regiments shortly after noon. Fighting against light enemy resistance but over stubborn terrain, the 23d Regiment, too, fell just short of reaching the day's objective by the time it dug in for the night.[22]

The 2d Marine Division had the more difficult task of gaining the approaches to Mount Tapotchau and of pushing to the top of Mount Tipo Pale. General Watson, the division commander, placed all three of his regiments in line abreast, the 8th, 6th, and 2d Marines from right to left. As the official Marine Corps historian described the scene, "Looking to the north of the 6th and 8th Marines' lines, a nightmare of sheer cliffs and precipitous hills could be observed, separated in crisscross fashion by deep gashes . . . . Dense foliage which cloaked the region often limited visibility to a few feet." [23]

Both assault battalions of the 8th Marines made fair progress against little

---

[18] NTLF Opn Order 9–44, 21 Jun 44.
[19] NTLF Rpt Marianas, Phase I, Incl E, G–3 Periodic Rpt 8.
[20] 4th Marine Div Opns Rpt Saipan, Annex I, 24th RCT Rpt, p. 20.

[21] *Ibid.,* Annex J, p. 6; Hoffman, *Saipan,* p. 127.
[22] 4th Marine Div Opns Rpt Saipan, Annex H, 23d RCT Rpt, p. 40.
[23] Hoffman, *Saipan,* p. 128.

opposition during the morning even though their axis of attack was cut by deep ravines, cliffs, and transverse ridges. As they neared the top of the first ridge line, they lost contact, and about noon the reserve battalion had to be committed in the center. An hour later forward movement stopped as mortar fire began to fall heavily all along the line. Enemy machine guns located on a hill to the right in the zone of the 25th Marines commenced to lay enfilade fire along the right flank of the 8th Marines. The summit of Mount Tapotchau still lay about 1,200 yards (as the crow flies) ahead, but no further progress could be made that day, and the regiment dug in for the night.[24]

In the center the 6th Marines was initially held back by the slow progress of the division's right flank. Shortly after noon the advance toward Tipo Pale got under way, only to come up against several pockets of Japanese machine guns, which stopped the lead elements on the slopes of the mountain. After a futile attempt to get at these positions by a flanking movement, the marines bypassed them altogether, and by 1400 the lead battalion had pushed to the top of Tipo Pale.[25]

The advance to the top of Tipo Pale marked the farthest and most significant progress in the zone of the 2d Marine Division. This eminence was about 1,000 feet in height and lay about 1,200 yards southwest of Tapotchau's summit.[26] Its capture was essential to cover any approach to the western slope of Tapotchau.

No forward movement was made on the extreme left of the 2d Division's zone. The 2d Marine Regimental Combat Team occupied the O–5 line south of Garapan for several days, and since the whole forward maneuver of the two divisions pivoted on this regiment it was forced to remain stationary until the other regiments pulled abreast.[27]

Meanwhile, preparations were proceeding apace to move the 27th Infantry Division into the main line of attack. On the evening of 21 June General Holland Smith had ordered the division to conduct reconnaissance to the north over the road net that led to the 2d and 4th Marine Division areas.[28] By late afternoon of the 22d all three battalions of the 165th Infantry had completed the reconnaissance as ordered by Colonel Kelley.[29] That evening Colonel Ayers took the commanders of the 2d and 3d Battalions, 106th Infantry, with him on a road reconnaissance and before dark had reached a point where his regiment would leave the road system and move cross country in the direction of the front held by the 4th Marine Division.[30]

About 1600 that afternoon General Ralph Smith visited the headquarters of General Erskine, chief of staff to General Holland Smith, where he first received definite information that his division would be fed into the Marine front line the following day. The plan was for the Army division to relieve the left flank elements of the 4th Marine Division so as to permit that

---

[24] 8th Marines 2d Marine Div SAR Forager, p. 4.
[25] 6th Marines 2d Marine Div SAR Forager, p. 7.
[26] See Map of Saipan reproduced from captured Japanese map by ACofS G–2 NTLF, 26 Jun 44.

[27] 2d Marines 2d Marine Div SAR Forager, p. 4.
[28] NTLF Opn Order 9–44, 21 Jun 44.
[29] 165th RCT Jnl, 22 Jun 44, Msg 15; 2d Bn 165th RCT Jnl, 22 Jun 44, Msg 7; 3d Bn 165th RCT Jnl, 22 Jun 44, Msg 19.
[30] Testimony of Col Ayers, Buckner Board Rpt, Exhibit CCC, p. 2.

unit to move eastward to cover Kagman Peninsula. This would put the 27th Division in the center of a three division front and at the entrance to the valley that lay between Mount Tapotchau and its hill system on the left (west) and a series of hills and ridges on the right (east) that ran north from Magicienne Bay.[31] Jump-off hour for the next morning was set at 1000.

As soon as this decision was reached, General Ralph Smith called Brig. Gen. Redmond F. Kernan, Jr., and ordered the division artillery to begin reconnaissance for positions from which to support the division attack next morning. Smith then left for his own command post where he met with Colonels Kelley and Ayers, commanders of the two regiments that would go into action next day. General Smith assigned Ayers' 106th Infantry to the left of the division line and Kelley's 165th to the right. Zones of approach to the line of departure were assigned to each of the regimental commanders, who in turn were to work out their routes of approach within their zones.

Ayers and Kelley returned to their own command posts shortly after 1800 and began briefing their battalion commanders.[32] In the 106th Regiment the 3d Battalion, under Lt. Col. Harold I. Mizony, was designated the assault battalion. It was to be followed in column by the 2d, under Maj. Almerin C. O'Hara, and the 1st, under Lt. Col. Winslow Cornett.[33] Colonel Kelley designated his 2d Bat-

talion, under Lt. Col. John F. McDonough, as the lead battalion during the approach. The 2d was to be followed by the 1st, under Major Mahoney, and the 3d, under Major Claire. Upon relieving the marines, the 165th was to take up the line with its 2d Battalion on the left and its 1st on the right.[34]

Orders from division headquarters confirming these decisions were issued at 2100.[35] The line of departure for the two Army regiments was to be the "line held by the 4th Marine Division within the [27th] Division zone of action." Two and a half hours later General Holland Smith's headquarters issued substantially the same order.[36] In this case, the line of departure was designated as the "front lines at King Hour [1000]," which was essentially no different from that specified by Ralph Smith.

23 June: Into Death Valley

Promptly at 0530, just as day was breaking, both regiments began to move toward the front lines.[37] (*Map 7*) In the 106th Infantry zone Colonel Mizony's 3d Battalion led off with Company L in the lead, followed by K, then battalion headquarters, and finally I Company.[38] Colonel McDonough's 2d Battalion, 165th, took the lead in that regiment. About 0620 the head of McDonough's column cut into Mizony's column just behind L Company, thus splitting the 3d Battalion, 106th Infantry,

---

[31] Information concerning this conference and General Ralph Smith's actions on 22 June is derived from Ralph Smith, Notes, Buckner Board Rpt, Exhibit M, pp. 10–13.

[32] 106th RCT Jnl, 22 Jun 44, p. 32.

[33] 106th Inf FO 8, 0100, 23 Jun 44.

[34] Col Kelley, Rpt of Action Saipan Island, 165th Inf, 16–27 Jun 44, Buckner Board Rpt, Exhibit N, p. 6.

[35] 27th Inf Div FO 46, 222100, Jun 44.

[36] NTLF Opn Order 10–44, 22 Jun 44.

[37] 3d Bn 106th RCT Jnl, 23 Jun 44, p. 8; 1st Bn 165th RCT Jnl, 23 Jun 44, Msg 2.

[38] 3d Bn 106th RCT Jnl, 23 Jun 44, p. 8.

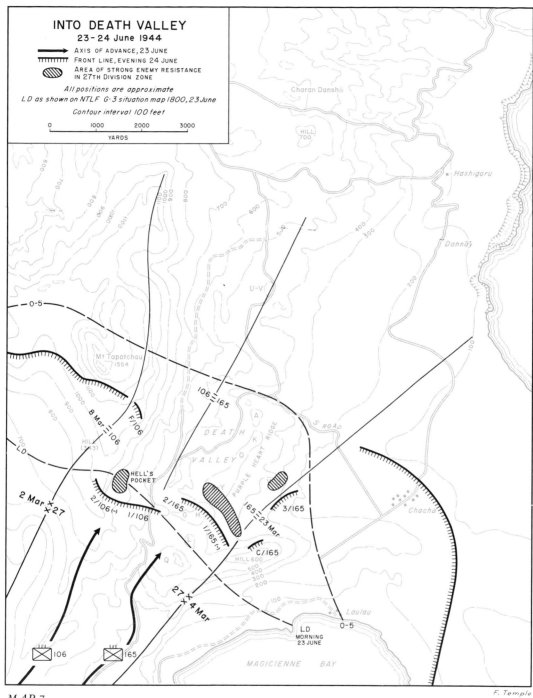

INTO DEATH VALLEY
23–24 June 1944

➤ AXIS OF ADVANCE, 23 JUNE
� FRONT LINE, EVENING 24 JUNE
▨ AREA OF STRONG ENEMY RESISTANCE
IN 27TH DIVISION ZONE

All positions are approximate
LD as shown on NTLF G-3 situation map 1800, 23 June

Contour interval 100 feet

0   1000   2000   3000
YARDS

Charan Danshii

HILL 700

Hashigoru

Donnay

U-V

0-5

Mt Tapotchau 1554

106 165

S ROAD

F/106

DEATH VALLEY

8 Mar 106

HILL (163)

LD

A

K

PURPLE HEART RIDGE

HELL'S POCKET

2 Mar X 27

2/106 (-)   1/106

2/165

G   H

1/165 (-)

165 23 Mar

3/165

Chacha

C/165

HILL 600

500
400
300
200

Q

27 X 4 Mar

100

Laulau   0-5

LD
MORNING
23 JUNE

106   165

MAGICIENNE   BAY

MAP 7

F. Temple

at that point.[39] The two regimental commanders conferred but nothing could be done to unscramble the units until they reached a clearing that would permit the 165th to move eastward and the 106th to proceed north toward its assigned zone of action. At this point of divergence an officer control station was set up to sort out the vehicles and units of the two regiments and direct each to its proper destination. All together, this delayed Companies K and I, 106th Infantry, upwards of an hour, though Company K was due to move into the assault at the line of departure at 1000. Company L, 106th, on the other hand, was ahead of the traffic jam and was able to push on unhindered.[40]

The two assault battalions of the 165th Infantry relieved the 24th Marines at 1000 on schedule.[41] Company L, 106th Infantry, completed the relief in its zone at 0930. Only Company K of the 106th was late, but its tardiness was to hold up the entire division attack. Not until 1055, or almost an hour after the scheduled jump-off time, was Company K in line, and not until then could the 3d Battalion jump off in the attack.[42]

When the men of the 106th Infantry got into the line, they were surprised to discover that some of the marines whom they were to relieve had fallen back two or three hundred yards from positions held the day before.[43] Company K of the 25th Marines

had pulled back to its right rear on the previous evening to tie in the night defense.[44] This caused some consternation at 106th headquarters because the regimental commander was under the mistaken impression that the line of departure for the morning's attack was the forward line of the previous day's advance as indicated on his overlay, rather than the "front lines at King Hour" as stated in the operation order. Actually, of course, this withdrawal on the part of the Marine company eased Colonel Ayers' immediate problem by reducing the distance his already tardy troops would have to cover before reaching the line of departure. It did, however, create a gap between the 106th and the 165th on his right that would have to be covered before the two units could move forward abreast.

The positions the 27th Division was ordered to assault had, since 19 June, been held by the *118th Infantry Regiment*, which as of that date was made responsible for the entire Japanese line of defense from the east slope of Mount Tapotchau to Magicienne Bay.[45] The Japanese regiment had been torpedoed en route from Japan to Saipan less than three weeks earlier and had arrived on the island minus about 850 of its troops and almost completely stripped of its weapons and equipment.[46] Total troop strength of the regiment on its arrival on Saipan was estimated to be about 2,600.[47] The Japanese command had had neither time nor opportunity to re-equip the survivors and reorganize them into a first-class fighting unit. The degree of attrition suffered by the regiment since

---

[39] *Ibid.* This movement to the line of departure is described in Colonel Kelley, Rpt of Action Saipan, Buckner Board Rpt, Exhibit N, and Ayers Testimony, Buckner Board Rpt, Exhibit CCC.

[40] 27th Inf Div G-3 Jnl, 23 Jun 44, Msg 34.

[41] 1st Bn 165th RCT Jnl, 23 Jun 44, Msg 4; 2d Bn 165th RCT Jnl, 23 Jun 44, Msg 3.

[42] 106th RCT Jnl, 23 Jun 44, Msgs 110, 118.

[43] Ayers Testimony, Buckner Board Rpt, Exhibit CCC, p. 3.

[44] Hoffman, *Saipan,* p. 134.

[45] See above, pp. 116–17.

[46] See above, p. 60.

[47] See App. A.

the American invasion is unknown but it cannot have escaped damage from the terrible pounding from air, sea, and land to which the island had been subjected since 12 June.

Before the 27th Division was committed, the *136th Infantry Regiment, 43d Division,* which had previously been in reserve around Chacha village was ordered to move out to Hill 286 (meters), Hill 343 (meters), "and the hills E[ast] of there."[48] Hill 286 was in the zone of action of the 2d Marine Division, but Hill 343, the "hills East," and the valley in between were directly athwart the line of advance of the 27th Infantry Division.

Initially, the *136th* had been one of the Saipan garrison's best fighting forces, being at full strength and fully equipped at the time of the landing. However, the regiment had taken a frightful beating in the first days of the invasion. Manning the Central Sector facing Red and Green Beaches, it had borne the brunt of some of the hardest fighting on Saipan. Although not literally decimated, its combat strength had been severely weakened. Two men of the regiment who had been captured on 25 June testified that its *2d Battalion* had been depleted approximately 67 percent on the first day of the landing, that the remnants of the *2d* and *3d Battalions* were combined as a single battalion, and that the total strength of the regiment was less than 1,000.[49]

But whatever losses in manpower and equipment the Japanese in this sector may have suffered, they still had one enormous advantage. That was terrain.

The soldiers of the 27th Division were soon to dub the area "Death Valley."[50] The "valley" is really a terracelike depression on the eastern slope of the sprawling mountain mass that fills most of central Saipan and culminates in the towering peak of Mount Tapotchau. The floor of the valley, less than 1,000 yards in width, is dominated along its entire length by the rugged slopes of Mount Tapotchau on the west and a series of hills, the highest about 150 feet above the valley floor, on the east. This eastern hill system was to be called "Purple Heart Ridge" by the soldiers who fought there. Death Valley, then, was a sort of trough into which the men of the 27th Division were to advance. The valley itself was almost devoid of cover except for a line of trees near the southern end and for three or four small groups of farm buildings surrounded by trees. The cliff on the left was for the most part bare, but above the cliff was wooded ground. The hills on the right were tree-covered. A narrow road—little more than a cowpath— ran up the valley a short distance then branched off, the left branch skirting the cliffs of Mount Tapotchau, the right heading toward the north face of Hill Able and then cutting to the east.

Obviously, this terrain was ideally suited for defense against any attack through the valley, and the Japanese made the most of

---

[48] CINCPAC-CINCPOA Trans 10531, excerpts from a notebook of field orders, 14 Jun to Jul 44.
[49] NTLF Rpt Marianas, Phase I, Annex D, G–2 Rpt, p. 85.

[50] This description of Death Valley is derived from: Brig Gen Ogden J. Ross, Summary of Opns by 27th Inf Div, 13 Jul 44, Buckner Board Rpt, Exhibit RR, p. 4; Col Albert K. Stebbins, Jr., Narrative Account of Opns of 27th Inf, 14 Jul 44, Buckner Board Rpt, Exhibit TT, p. 3; Sworn Statement of General Ralph Smith, Buckner Board Rpt, Exhibit AAA, p. 4; Love, *The 27th Infantry Division in World War II,* pp. 228–29.

MT. TAPOTCHAU DOMINATING DEATH VALLEY, *where 27th Division troops fought from 28 through 30 June.*

it. In the words of Col. Albert K. Stebbins, Jr., 27th Division chief of staff:

The cliffs and hillsides were pocketed with small caves and large caves. The wooded area was rough, filled with boulders, and excellent for defensive operations. Bands of fire were laid by the enemy thru the underbrush and in such manner as to make it most difficult to discover their locations: Well-placed, hostile guns fired only when lines passed and striking our forces in the rear disrupted the attack.[51]

The Japanese had at their disposal all kinds of automatic weapons, light and heavy mortars, and some 75-mm. mountain

guns. These were well concealed, usually in caves whose mouths were covered with brush. Troops approaching through the valley could get at the positions only by direct shots from tanks or self-propelled guns. It was impossible to reach them with artillery, at least during the initial stages of the attack, because the axis of the caves was at right angles to the line of fire of the artillery.

"Cannon to right of them, Cannon to left of them." Not so much cannon perhaps, but enough other fire to make this seem to the men caught in the middle a true replica of Tennyson's "Valley of Death."

[51] Stebbins, Account of 27th Inf Opns, Buckner Board Rpt, Exhibit TT, p. 3.

TREE LINE IN DEATH VALLEY, *where elements of the 2d Battalion, 165th, were pinned down on 23 June.*

The units of the 27th Division lined up from right to left (east to west) as follows:

165–C: 1st Lt. Edward L. Cloyd, Jr.
165–A: Capt. Laurence J. O'Brien
165–G: Capt. Paul J. Chasmar
165–F: Capt. Francis P. Leonard
106–K: Capt. William T. Heminway
106–L: Capt. Charles N. Hallden

The regimental boundary line coincided with the road that ran through Death Valley.

On the division right the first obstacle to be overcome by the 1st Battalion, 165th, was Hill Love, lying roughly on the border line between Companies A and C. This eminence rose about 700 feet above sea level, was tree-covered, and was infested with Japanese. A patrol from A Company met heavy machine gun and rifle fire that killed the patrol leader and wounded one other man. It was then decided that the two companies would circle the hill and meet at its northern base. Company C on the right jumped off at 1015 and by 1400 had succeeded in working its way around the hill to the northern face. Here, the men were pinned down by heavy fire to their front and made no further advance. During the course of the afternoon the company suffered three men killed and fourteen wounded. A platoon of tanks from the 762d Provisional Tank Battalion was brought forward in an effort to reduce the

DRIVEN TO CONCEALMENT BY THE INTENSITY OF ENEMY FIRE *in Death Valley on 23 June, 27th Division soldiers worked their way into a small wooded area.*

enemy positions. One of these, commanded by 1st Lt. Louis W. Fleck, was set on fire with a "Molotov Cocktail." All the tankers but one were killed as they emerged from the turret.[52] The men of Company C who witnessed the incident were helpless to avert it because by now marines had pushed ahead directly into their line of fire and the battalion commander had ordered them not to fire.

Meanwhile, Company A had also reached the northern face of Hill Love. It too could make no further progress. At 1630 the tanks withdrew for the night and

the two companies dug in. Company B was brought in and completed the encirclement of the promontory by digging in on the south face.[53]

The 2d Battalion, 165th Infantry, also had considerable trouble during the afternoon. After reaching the tree line that lay about 300 yards to their front, both of McDonough's companies remained stationary for two hours, waiting for Company K, 106th Infantry, to work its way up on the left. General Ralph Smith finally ordered McDonough to advance without regard to

---

[52] Appleman, *Army Tanks in the Battle for Saipan,* pp. 34–37.

[53] Love, *Battle for Saipan,* pp. 240, 245; Kelley Testimony, Buckner Board Rpt, Exhibit PP, pp. 2–3.

what was going on in the 106th area and instructed Colonel Kelley to commit his reserve if necessary.[54] Regiment therefore ordered an attack for 1315.[55] Company E was brought up and ordered to deploy one platoon on the regimental left to maintain contact with K Company of the 106th and the other on the right to maintain contact with the 1st Battalion, 165th.[56]

As soon as McDonough's battalion moved out from the line of trees it was greeted by a hail of small arms, machine gun, and heavy weapons fire from the cliff line on its left. A similar concentration of fire from Purple Heart Ridge on the right soon followed and the advance platoons of Company F were badly hit in the cross fire. Under cover of a smoke screen laid down by the chemical battalion, the men eventually pulled back to the tree line from which they had started. Company G, witnessing the results of F Company's advance also withdrew to the tree line and remained there for the rest of the day.[57]

In the zone of the 106th Infantry on the division left the action can be characterized as two separate battles since K and L Companies had no physical contact during most of the day. Company K on the right pushed off at 1055. Shortly thereafter the leading scout of the advance platoon was struck by machine gun fire. The rest of the company hit the ground and was immediately subjected to mortar fire. The company commander, Captain Heminway, ordered his men to move forward by infiltration. This movement began about 1300, and by 1500 the company had worked its way into a small wooded area

that provided some cover against the enemy weapons. There it waited for L Company on its left to come up, and since the latter unit did not pull abreast until 1615 both decided to dig in there for the night.[58]

Company L had arrived on the line in sufficient time to push the attack at 1000 but had been held up by K Company's tardiness in relieving the marines in its zone. On Captain Hallden's left was the cliff of Mount Tapotchau and on his right a series of ravines. About 400 yards ahead, the cliff line receded to form a little cove in the mountain wall that the soldiers dubbed "Hell's Pocket." In the midst of this cove was a lone rock that rose a hundred feet and was covered with ivy. Caves in the rock and in the cliff walls that surrounded it provided ideal spots for Japanese machine guns.[59]

Company L advanced about fifty yards from its line of departure, and Japanese mortar fire began to fall in the area. Hallden pushed his men on, moving along the base of the cliff, which formed the west wall of Hell's Pocket. As the troops probed deeper into the pocket an enemy mortar shell set off a Japanese ammunition dump and the flying debris kept the men pinned down for over an hour. Self-propelled mounts were brought forward in an effort to knock out the cave positions of the Japanese but the vehicles were too exposed to fire from above to accomplish much. Finally, a platoon of medium tanks came in to support the infantry.[60]

By this time the gap between K and L Companies had grown wider so Hallden

---

[54] 165th RCT Jnl, 23 Jun 44, Msg 29.
[55] Ibid., Msg 13.
[56] 27th Inf Div G-3 Jnl, 23 Jun 44, Msg 89.
[57] Love, Battle for Saipan pp. 237–53.

[58] Ibid., pp. 253–55.
[59] Love, The 27th Infantry Division in World World War II, p. 231.
[60] 106th RCT Jnl FORAGER, 23 Jun 44, Msg 193.

shifted to the right rear out of Hell's Pocket and by 1530 had re-established contact with Company K on the valley floor where both companies dug in for the night. Company I, which had been in reserve most of the afternoon, was brought up and dug in on the rear of this position.[61] Progress for the day in the zone of the 106th was about 100 yards.

Throughout the day the 106th Regiment experienced considerable difficulty in maintaining contact with the 2d Marine Division on its left. The corps order had stipulated that the burden of contact was from right to left.[62] Responsibility for contact therefore rested with L Company, 106th, but the marines were moving along the top of the cliff at whose base the Army troops were located, and physical contact was impossible. As Company L moved to the right to tie in with Company K, even visual contact was lost. At 1703 division headquarters ordered Colonel Ayers to gain contact with the marines on his left "with sufficient force to maintain it,"[63] and half an hour later Ayers ordered the 2d Battalion, 106th, to cover the gap.[64] On the theory that it would be easier to maintain contact between two companies of the Army division than between Marine and Army units, Company F was ordered to move to the top of the cliff and tie in with the marines while G Company moved forward to positions below the cliff and established contact on the left of L Company. This move was not completed until 1910, and both companies had to build up a defensive line under cover of darkness.[65]

Later that night, Company F's 1st Platoon, which was hugging the cliff overlooking the edge of Hell's Pocket, was attacked by a party of about fifteen Japanese who made their way through the perimeter before being discovered. In the intense hand-to-hand fight that ensued, bayonets, grenades, knives, and fists came into play. The Japanese killed two men of the platoon and wounded two others before being destroyed or routed.[66]

Progress in the zone of the 27th Division on 23 June had been disappointing, especially in the area assigned to the 106th Infantry. During the afternoon General Holland Smith expressed his alarm over the situation in a conversation with General Jarman, the island commander and the senior Army officer on Saipan. In General Jarman's words:

General Smith, CG of the V Phib Corps, called me to his quarters and indicated that he was very much concerned about the situation which he was presented with in regard to the 27th Div. He outlined to me the many things that had happened with respect to the failure of the 27th Div to advance. He indicated that this division had suffered scarcely no [sic] casualties and in his opinion he didn't think they would fight. . . . He stated that if it was not an Army division and there would be a great cry set up more or less of a political nature, he would immediately relieve the division commander and assign someone else.[67]

Next morning, General Holland Smith registered his displeasure in a stern dispatch to General Ralph Smith himself:

COMMANDING GENERAL IS HIGHLY DISPLEASED WITH THE FAILURE OF THE 27TH DIVISION ON JUNE TWENTY THIRD TO LAUNCH ITS ATTACK AS ORDERED AT KING HOUR AND THE LACK OF OFFENSIVE ACTION DISPLAYED BY THE DIVISION IN ITS FAILURE TO ADVANCE

---

[61] Love, Battle for Saipan, pp. 255–58.

[62] NTLF Opn Order 10–44, 22 Jun 44.

[63] 27th Inf Div G–3 Jnl, 23 Jun 44, Msg 126.

[64] Ibid., Msg 134.

[65] 2d Bn 106th RCT Jnl, 23 Jun 44, Msg 85; 106th RCT Jnl, 23 Jun 44, Msg 201; Hoffman, Saipan, p. 137.

[66] Love, Battle for Saipan, p. 262.

[67] Buckner Board Rpt, Exhibit J.

AND SEIZE OBJECTIVE O-5 WHEN OP-
POSED ONLY BY SMALL ARMS AND MORTAR
FIRE X THE FAILURE OF THE 27TH TO AD-
VANCE IN ITS ZONE OF ACTION RESULTED IN
THE HALTING OF ATTACKS BY THE 4TH AND
2D MARINE DIVISIONS ON THE FLANKS OF
THE 27TH IN ORDER TO PREVENT DANGEROUS
EXPOSURE OF THEIR INTERIOR FLANKS X
IT IS DIRECTED THAT IMMEDIATE STEPS BE
TAKEN TO CAUSE THE 27TH DIVISION TO AD-
VANCE AND SEIZE OBJECTIVES AS ORDERED
X.[68]

There can be no doubt of the truth of
General Holland Smith's charges that the
27th Division had been late in the jump-
off, that its advance had been slow, and that
it had held up progress of the two Marine
divisions on its flanks. It is apparent, however, that he underestimated the stubborn-
ness of the Japanese defenses in the area
by dismissing the opposition in the zone
of the 27th Division as being "only by
small arms and mortar fire."

When subsequently queried on this
point, Colonel Ayers, commanding officer
of the 106th Infantry, was of the firm belief that if he had tried to advance rapidly
across the open ground in front of him
his regiment "would have disappeared." [69]
General Ralph Smith agreed. He later testified that, after visiting the front lines
shortly after noon, he was "satisfied that
Col. Ayers was making every effort possible
to advance in the valley, and considered
that any further pushing of troops in that
zone would only lead to increased casualties, without accomplishing adequate results." [70]

On the other hand, General Jarman
testified that in his conversations with
General Ralph Smith on the afternoon of

23 June the division commander had been
far from satisfied with the conduct of his
troops. In General Jarman's words:

I talked to General Smith and explained
the situation as I saw it and that I felt from
reports from the Corps Commander that his
division was not carrying its full share. He
immediately replied that such was true; that
he was in no way satisfied with what his
regimental commanders had done during the
day and that he had been with them and
had pointed out to them the situation. He
further indicated to me that he was going to
be present tomorrow, 24 June with his division when it made its jump-off and he
would personally see to it that the division
went forward . . . . He appreciated the situation and thanked me for coming to see
him and stated that if he didn't take his
division forward tomorrow he should be relieved.[71]

The First Night in Death Valley

At 1925, just as darkness fell, the Japanese launched a six-tank attack down the
road that ran the length of Death Valley and marked the boundary between
Mizony's and McDonough's positions.[72]
Not until the column had almost reached
the American outposts was it discovered,
and by then the lead tank was too close to
be fired upon from either side of the road
without endangering the men on the other.
The other five tanks, however, were taken
under fire by both battalions with every
weapon available. Bazookas, antitank guns,
grenade launchers, and artillery went into
action, and all five tanks were knocked out.
The lead tank proceeded on through the
lines and circled back, firing constantly.
One shell landed in a Japanese ammunition dump located in the midst of the 3d

[68] *Ibid.*, Exhibit G.
[69] *Ibid.*, Ayers Testimony, Exhibit CCC, p. 5.
[70] *Ibid.*, Ralph Smith, Sworn Statement, Exhibit
AAA, p. 5.

[71] *Ibid.*, Exhibit J.
[72] 106th RCT Jnl, 23 Jun 44, Msg 202.

MARINES EMERGING FROM PURPLE HEART RIDGE COMPLEX

Battalion, 106th's, lines and set it afire. The tank then turned east and was finally knocked out in the zone of the 23d Marines.[73]

Meanwhile, the ammunition dump in the middle of the 3d Battalion, 106th, was going off in all directions. Simultaneously, the Japanese on Mount Tapotchau began to throw mortar shells and machine gun fire into the area. Company L suffered sixteen men wounded within the space of an hour. The position of the entire 3d Battalion was now untenable. 1st Lt. George T. Johnson of I Company ordered his men to disperse as soon as the dump started to explode. He later assembled them across the road to the rear of the 165th line and dug in there for the rest of the night. The other two infantry companies withdrew about 100 yards behind the conflagration, thus canceling altogether the small gain made by the battalion during the day's action.[74]

23 June: Marines on the Flanks

On the right of the 27th Division, the 4th Marine Division attacked with two regiments abreast, 24th on the right and 23d on the left. The 24th Marines pushed

---

[73] Love, Battle for Saipan, pp. 264–65.

[74] Ibid., pp. 266–67.

rapidly ahead along the shore of Magicienne Bay and by midafternoon had
reached the O–5 line at one point just east
of the village of Laulau.[75] On the left the
23d Marines made somewhat slower progress, partly because its advance was held
back by the 165th Infantry. Within a short
time after the jump-off, one battalion
seized the top of Hill 600, which though
lightly manned by the enemy was admir-
ably suited for defense and took thirty
minutes of close fighting to capture. There,
the battalion was ordered to hold, pending
the advance of the Army troops on the left,
but since the 1st Battalion, 165th, was held
up, the marines spent the rest of the afternoon in a stationary position, firing and
pitching grenades at the Japanese who still
occupied in force the northern face of the
hill.[76] That night a group of enemy tanks
launched an attack against Hill 600 but
was repulsed with the loss of three of its
five vehicles.[77]

On the other side of Death Valley, the
8th Marines jumped off on schedule except
on the right flank, which was held up by
the late arrival of the 106th Infantry. To
fill the gap between these units, the reserve
battalion was ordered into position to protect the right flank and the three battalions
in the assault moved forward. By midafternoon the right battalion seized the cliff that
dominated the only feasible route to the
top of Mount Tapotchau. On the regimental left, the marines ran into a nest
of about thirty Japanese riflemen and six
heavy machine guns, which held up their
progress for the rest of the day.

Soon after the 6th Marines in the center
of the 2d Division's line launched its attack, the right flank battalion was pinched
out by the reduced frontage. On the left,
the regiment made no advance during the
day because it was already so far forward
that any further move would have caused
too much of a contact strain. The same
was true of the 2d Marines on the division
left flank. Not until the center of the corps
line made more significant progress would
it be safe for the elements on the left to
move ahead.[78]

24 June: Action of the 27th Division

General Holland Smith's order for June
24th called for a continuation of the attack with three divisions abreast in the
same order as before, commencing at 0800.
Corps artillery was assigned to general support and ordered to reinforce the fires of
divisional artillery.[79] In the zone of the
27th Division, its own organic artillery
would fire a ten-minute preparation before
the jump-off and thereafter support the
attack on call.[80]

165th Infantry Attack Against
Purple Heart Ridge

At 0705 corps reminded 27th Division
that the slope on the right side of Purple
Heart Ridge was in the zone of action of
the 165th Infantry, which would capture
it with the help of fire from the 4th Marine
Division on its right.[81] This meant in effect that the 106th Infantry alone would

[75] 4th Marine Div Opns Rpt Saipan, Annex I,
24th RCT Rpt, p. 20.
[76] *Ibid.*, Annex H, 23d RCT Rpt, pp. 40–42;
Hoffman, *Saipan,* p. 136.
[77] 4th Marine Div Opns Rpt Saipan, Annex H,
23d RCT Rpt, p. 41; Hoffman, *Saipan,* p. 140.

[78] 2d Marine Div SAR, Phase I, FORAGER, Sec.
VI, pp. 10–11; Hoffman, *Saipan,* pp. 137–39.
[79] NTLF Opn Order 11–44, 2100 23 Jun 44.
[80] 27th Inf Div FO 47, 232100, Jun 44, 27th Inf
Div G–3 Jnl, Incl.
[81] 27th Inf Div G–3 Jnl, 24 Jun 44, Msg 8.

be responsible for the frontal attack up Death Valley. Simultaneously, the 2d Battalion, 165th, would attack along the crest of Purple Heart Ridge itself and the 1st Battalion, 165th, would move up on the right (east) of the ridge.

Purple Heart Ridge was in reality a series of hills connected by a ridge line running in a northerly direction. From south to north these hills were designated Queen, Love, George-How, Xray-Yoke, Oboe, King, and Able.[82] Hill Queen had already been overrun by the 4th Marine Division in its advance eastward toward Kagman Peninsula. Hill Love had been surrounded by the 1st Battalion, 165th Infantry, which had dug in the night before around its base.[83]

There were obvious tactical advantages to an early capture of this ridge line or any considerable part of it. It overlooked Death Valley from the east just as the higher cliffs around Mount Tapotchau did from the west. The commanders were becoming aware that any movement north through the valley could be easily interdicted by fire from the elevations on either side. If the lower of the two walls of the corridor—Purple Heart Ridge—could be seized, then fire could be brought directly to bear against the caves that dotted the west cliffs from which such effective fire

was being trained on the troops trying to advance through the valley below.

At 0800 the two assault battalions of the 165th Infantry jumped off on schedule[84] in the same order they were in at the end of the previous day's fighting: On the front line from right to left were Cloyd's Company C, O'Brien's Company A, Chasmar's Company G, and Leonard's Company F. In reserve for the 1st Battalion was Gil's B Company; for the 2d Battalion, Ryan's E Company. The regimental plan called for Company C on the right flank to swing well to the right and then northeast into the zone of the 23d Marines. There it would wait until the rest of the battalion came abreast. Company B was to come up from behind Hill Love on A Company's left, execute a turning movement, and then attack eastward across A's front in order to enfilade the enemy positions to the north of Hill Love.[85]

Within a little more than an hour after the jump-off, Company C had moved to the right and gained physical contact with the marines.[86] Lieutenant Cloyd stopped his advance on the northern nose of Hill 600 to await the approach of the rest of the battalion on his left. He made no further progress that day.[87]

On the battalion left, Companies A and B ran into immediate trouble. As A pushed off from Hill Love toward the same positions that had caused so much trouble the day before, it came under heavy fire from small arms and machine guns. Company B then moved up to the left and, as planned,

[82] According to standard usage in the Central Pacific, the maps used in the Marianas were overlaid with a grid. Each large square of the grid measured 1000 by 1000 yards and was given a numerical designation. These were in turn subdivided into twenty-five smaller squares of 200 square yards, each given a letter designation according to the phonetic alphabet then in use. Thus, Hill Love derived its name from the fact that it was located in small square "L" of large square "175." The squares, both large and small, were called "target areas."

[83] See above, p. 176.

[84] 27th Inf Div G-3 Jnl, 24 Jun 44, Msg 16.

[85] Love, Battle for Saipan, p. 277.

[86] 27th Inf Div G-3 Jnl, 24 Jun 44, Msg 22.

[87] Unless otherwise indicated, the following account of the actions of the 165th Infantry is derived from Love, Battle for Saipan, pp. 276–87, 310–15.

tried to execute a turning movement to the right across A Company's front. Company B, too, met a fusillade of fire and finally withdrew after losing twelve wounded, two mortally. It was only 0930, but the 1st Battalion attempted no further movement until midafternoon.

Colonel Kelley then decided to commit his 3d Battalion to the right of the line. The 3d was to move to the right, following the same route used by Company C and, upon reaching the latter's positions on the left flank of the Marine lines, pass through and launch an attack that would carry it to the top of Hill King, almost at the northern edge of Purple Heart Ridge. While this was taking place, B Company was to circle the pocket of resistance north of Hill Love and build up a line facing the pocket from the north. Thereafter, the 1st Battalion was to mop up this area of resistance and retire into regimental reserve. The change of plans was agreed upon at 0904, and orders were accordingly issued at 1015.[88] The 3d Battalion completed its move by 1335, and by that time Company B had encircled the pocket and was facing south ready to attack.

Meanwhile, the 2d Battalion, 165th Infantry, moved off on schedule in an effort to take the ridge by a direct assault from the southwest. The night before, the battalion had occupied positions about three hundred yards to the north and west of Hill Love. G Company moved off with Company F following, echeloned to the left rear. By 1000 the lead platoon had reached the southern face of Hill Xray-Yoke, about the midpoint of the ridge. Here the men found a steep gulch directly across the

path of advance. In order to get up on the hill itself, they would have to climb down the near cliff, cross the bottom of the canyon, and scale the cliff on the other side. As the first platoon attempted this feat of acrobatics it came under rifle fire from the hill ahead and was stopped in its tracks. Company G made no further progress that day.

F Company to the left rear had also run into trouble. As it came abreast of G, Company F spread out to the left where the gully in front of Hill Xray-Yoke was not quite so precipitous. Here the terrain was friendlier, but the enemy was not, and heavy mortar and machine gun fire kept the bulk of the company pinned down for two hours. Around 1130 Captain Leonard sent a patrol out to his left toward a small house located on the floor of Death Valley. His purpose was to protect his flank from a possible attack from that direction. Of the twenty men dispatched on this mission six were wounded and one was killed by machine gun fire before the patrol was withdrawn. F Company, too, now held its lines for the remainder of the day. At nightfall the whole battalion dug in just below the gulch. The day's action represented an advance of about 150 yards.

While the stalemate was developing on the left flank of the regimental line, stubborn resistance continued on the extreme right. The 3d Battalion had swung right behind the ridge and passed through Company C at 1335.[89] Shortly after 1600 Capt. Howard Betts, who commanded Company K, made a frontal assault in column of platoons up Hill Xray-Yoke from the east. The lead platoon reached the tree line well up the hill without much trouble, but just

---

[88] 1st Bn 165th RCT Jnl, 24 Jun 44, Msg 13; 3d Bn 165th RCT Jnl, 24 Jun 44, Msg 10.

[89] 3d Bn 165th RCT Jnl, 24 Jun 44.

as it started into the undergrowth, Japanese machine guns opened fire from the left front, traversing the length of Betts' line and wounding two men. The platoon took to earth and was pinned there by a continuous grazing fire for almost two hours. Betts immediately swung his second platoon into line on the right, but after about fifty yards further advance up the hill, it too ran into machine gun fire and was stopped. By this time darkness was coming on, and Company K was pulled down the hill to tie in with I Company for the night. Meanwhile, the 1st Battalion's effort to mop up the pocket of resistance north of Hill Love had failed, and that unit, with the exception of Company C, dug in around the same positions it had occupied the night before.

106th Infantry: Into Death Valley Again

The units, from right to left, on the front line facing the mouth of Death Valley on the morning of 24 June were: Company K, 106th Infantry, Captain Heminway; Company L, 106th Infantry, Captain Hallden; and Company G, 106th Infantry, Capt. David B. Tarrant. Company F of the 106th was still on top of the cliff, and, since its movement was geared to that of the 2d Marine Division, its actions must be considered as separate from those of the rest of the 106th Regiment.

The 3d Battalion jumped off on time, but immediately encountered such heavy mortar fire that many of the men fell back to the line of departure and in some cases behind it.[90] By 0945 the front-line troops had advanced from 50 to 100 yards into the valley, but there was no sign of any abatement of enemy fire, especially from the cliffs of Tapotchau. Division headquarters was severely disappointed, and at 1012 General Ralph Smith radioed Colonel Ayers: "Advance of 50 yards in 1-1/2 hours is most unsatisfactory. Start moving at once." [91]

In response to this pressure, Company K, supported by a platoon of medium tanks of Company B, 762d Tank Battalion, immediately pushed forward into the valley. Captain Heminway had two platoons abreast, the 1st on the right, the 3d on the left. He left the 2d Platoon at the entrance to the valley to deliver covering fire to his front. He also set up his machine guns on the high ground beside the valley road and had some support from M Company's heavy weapons. Heminway's men advanced in a long, thin skirmish line, moving rapidly toward the center of the valley. They had pushed forward fifty yards without event when the entire cliff on the left of the valley seemed to open up. The company broke into a run toward a fold in the ground that offered some cover. Here the company commander stopped to reorganize his line. Just as he got up to wave his men forward again he was shot in the head and killed. This paralyzed the entire line until 1st Lt. Jefferson Noakes, the company executive officer, could come forward and take command.[92]

Meanwhile, the platoon of tanks attached to Company K had been roaming around the floor of the valley trying to silence the Japanese fire from the cliff. One of the tanks, commanded by the platoon leader, 2d Lt. Richard Hitchner, received

---

[90] 106th RCT Jnl, 24 Jun 44, Msg 230.

[91] *Ibid.*, Msg 243.
[92] Love, Battle for Saipan, pp. 294–95.

TANK-INFANTRY CO-OPERATION. *Medium tank leading men of Company* K, *106th Infantry, into Death Valley on 24 June.*

two hits from enemy shells, was knocked out, and had to be abandoned.[93] Around 1100 another tank was hit, and the whole platoon withdrew.

At this juncture 3d Battalion called the company headquarters and announced that a smoke screen would be laid down and that under its cover the men of Company K were to withdraw from their exposed positions. Some of the men did withdraw under the smoke, but one platoon failed to get the word and remained holed up until two tanks that had been supporting L Company went over and covered its withdrawal.[94]

Meanwhile, Company I, under Lieutenant Johnson, had been ordered into the line between the other two companies of the

3d Battalion. Reporting at 1015,[95] Johnson was told to move two platoons out into the valley in column, swing left until he made contact with L Company's right flank, and then deploy his men to the right to close the gap that existed between Companies L and K. Immediately upon entering the pass into the valley, both platoons were subjected to brutal fire from the cliffs on the left and stayed pinned down for better than two hours. The men lay on an open slope without any means of protection, unable even to lift their heads to fire back. Seven were killed and thirteen wounded. A little before 1200, as the men still lay out on the open ground, three Japanese tanks came down the valley road from the north firing in all directions. Just as they were about to overrun the area

---

[93] Appleman, Army Tanks in the Battle for Saipan, pp. 44–46.
[94] Love, Battle for Saipan, pp. 296–98.

[95] 106th RCT Jnl, 24 Jun 44, Msg 245.

occupied by Company I, all three were knocked out by antitank guns from both sides of the valley.

Meanwhile, Lieutenant Johnson was frantically trying to get at the source of the enemy fire that was proving so deadly to his unit. He had the antitank guns of battalion headquarters open up on the face of the western cliff with canister and set up all of M Company's heavy machine guns to deliver covering fire in that direction. His 3d Platoon, which was just at the entrance to the valley, took up positions and delivered supporting small arms fire all along the face of Mount Tapotchau. Johnson himself took his company headquarters and moved along the edge of the trees to the left in an effort to get at the Japanese position in front of Company L. As this group moved to the left through the undergrowth, it too was pinned down by mortar fire and discovered the woods to be full of enemy riflemen between the valley road and L Company's right flank. Johnson was wounded.

It was at this point that the battalion commander ordered K and I Companies to withdraw under cover of smoke. In the latter unit's zone, the screen was neither effective nor of long enough duration, and only a handful of Johnson's men could get out. Finally, about 1225, Colonel Mizony brought every weapon he had to bear on the Japanese positions along the cliff and in Hell's Pocket. Under cover of this fire the remainder of Company I was able to crawl and scramble back to the cover of the trees.[96] Casualties in the 3d Battalion, 106th, alone, for the day had amounted to 14 killed and 109 wounded.[97]

Meanwhile, the 1st Battalion, 106th Infantry, had been ordered up to relieve the 3d Battalion. The relief was accomplished at 1515.[98] Upon assuming its position in the line the 1st Battalion was ordered to dig in for the night since it was considered too late in the day to launch further attacks into the valley.[99]

While the 3d Battalion had been enengaged in trying to push out into the valley, Company G, on the left flank, had advanced no more than two hundred yards during the day. The unit had not itself encountered much enemy fire, but when Company L ran into so much trouble during the morning, Captain Tarrant held his line firm rather than push out ahead of the unit on his right.[100]

The attempt of the 106th Infantry to push up Death Valley by frontal assault had failed again. In the words of Colonel Ayers, "We were thrown right back on to the original line of departure."[101]

Once again corps headquarters ordered the 27th Division to renew the attack into the valley next morning with the "main effort on the left."[102] General Ralph Smith, however, now decided that any further headlong rush up the valley would only result in increased casualties, and ordered his division to make the main effort on the right.[103] Beginning on the morning of the 25th, the 2d Battalion, 106th Infantry, would take up positions along the entrance to the valley and contain the Japanese there while the 165th Infantry

[96] Love, Battle for Saipan, pp. 301–04.
[97] 106th RCT Jnl, 24 Jun 44, Msg 308.

[98] Ibid., Msgs 261, 285.
[99] Love, Battle for Saipan, p. 304.
[100] Ibid.
[101] Ayers Testimony, Buckner Board Rpt, Exhibit CCC, p. 6.
[102] NTLF Opn Order 12–44, 1800, 24 Jun 44.
[103] 27th Inf Div FO 48, 141800 Jun 44, 27th Inf Div G–3 Jnl, Incl.

and the other two battalions of the 106th would circle around the east (right) flank and come out into the valley at its northern end to the rear of the Japanese positions. This, it was hoped, would put the Army division abreast of the two Marine divisions, and the encircled Japanese in Death Valley could then be mopped up at leisure.[104]

There is no evidence that this discrepancy between corps and division orders was ever noted at the time. In any case, before he could put this plan into execution, General Ralph Smith was relieved of his command, and it was left to his successor, General Jarman, to solve the problem of Death Valley.[105]

24 June: Action on the Flanks

On the right of the corps line, the 4th Marine Division was ordered to press eastward across Kagman Peninsula and secure that area before reorienting its drive toward the north of the island. The division jumped off on schedule at 0800, the 24th Marines on the right, the 23d on the left. The 24th Regiment moved out rapidly along the coast to Kagman Peninsula against "moderate" resistance. By the end of the day the 24th Marines had advanced about 1,200 yards.

On its left the 23d Marines was initially held up by a pocket of resistance on the slopes of Hill 600 that marked the boundary line between the Marine division and the Army division. About noon the Marine regiment detoured the pocket and commenced to swing around the arc toward Kagman Peninsula, pivoting on the 24th

Marines on its right. As the 23d Regiment accelerated its swing, the gap between it and the 165th Infantry increased and toward late afternoon amounted to from 800 to 1,000 yards. By 1630 Chacha village was overrun and the advance halted for the night since the gap on the left precluded any further progress. The 1st Battalion, 23d Marines, in division reserve, was ordered to occupy Hill 600 and assist its parent regiment in patrolling the gap. Opposition in the 4th Division's zone on the 24th was characterized as "moderate" and "light," although total casualties came to 380, including killed, wounded, and missing in action.[106]

To the west (left) of Death Valley the 2d Marine Division was drawn up abreast, from right to left, 8th Marines (with the 1st Battalion, 29th Marines, attached), 6th Marines, and 2d Marines. On the right flank the 1st Battalion, 29th Marines, was struggling along the cliff overlooking Death Valley. The ground was "a tangle of tree ferns and aerial tree-roots overgrown with a matting of vines. This formation led up to a ridge, access to which required an almost vertical climb."[107] By nightfall the battalion had succeeded in climbing the ridge, which connected with and was within machine gun range of the summit of Mount Tapotchau. The battalion's advance for the day was about 800 yards.[108]

During this movement of the 1st Battalion, 29th Marines, Company F of the 106th Infantry was virtually an integral

---

[104] Ralph Smith, Notes, Buckner Board Rpt, Exhibit M, p. 15.

[105] See below p. 203.

[106] 4th Marine Div Opns Rpt Saipan, pp. 24–25; NTLF Rpt Marianas, Phase I, Incl C, G–1 Rpt, App. 1, Casualty Rpt; Hoffman, *Saipan*, pp. 145–46.

[107] 2d Marine Div SAR, Phase I, FORAGER, Sec. VI, p. 12.

[108] *Ibid.*, p. 13.

part of the Marine battalion and had been ordered by its own battalion headquarters to gear its movements to those of the marines.[109] About 1230, F Company came to a halt when the marines on its left engaged in a fire fight. The company's right flank rested along the edge of the cliff overlooking Death Valley just opposite the north rim of Hell's Pocket. The terrain to the right consisted of a down-sloping nose of ground that broke off abruptly in the cliffs that scaled down the valley. Capt. Roderick V. Le Mieux, the company commander, ordered a patrol to probe down this nose and investigate the source of enemy rifle fire coming from that direction. The patrol soon flushed a covey of Japanese and a full-scale fire fight developed. The patrol leader, finding himself outnumbered, returned for more men. With the larger group he again went down the nose and succeeded in driving the enemy back down the hill.[110]

Meanwhile, Captain Le Mieux had moved ahead a short distance and observed a Japanese artillery piece in a cave in the side of the cliff about 500 yards to his front. The Japanese were playing a hide and seek game with the piece, running it out of the cliff to fire at the line of trees along the south edge of the valley below, then quickly dragging it back under cover. Le Mieux observed about a hundred of the enemy in the vicinity of this position as well as a large ammunition dump. He ordered up heavy weapons from Company H, which succeeded in catching the gun out of the cave and destroying it. In addition they blew up the ammunition dump, killing

about thirty Japanese. Shortly thereafter an enemy patrol was discovered advancing toward the heavy weapons outpost. Rifle fire and grenades quickly dispersed the Japanese, but not before Captain Le Mieux received a serious fragmentation wound and had to be replaced by 1st Lt. Herbert N. Slate, the company executive officer. A few minutes later the company was ordered to pull back to the left and to tighten up the lines before digging in for the night.

In the center, the 8th Marines advanced with no particular difficulty, maintaining contact with units on both of its flanks. The battalion on the regimental left, on the other hand, after advancing a short distance, encountered heavy enemy resistance in an area honeycombed with caves and irregular coral limestone formations covered with trees and undergrowth. This was the same pocket that had retarded the battalion on the previous day. Contact with the 6th Marines on the left was temporarily broken. Shortly after noon the pocket was cleaned out and contact was restored with the regiment on the left. The advance continued until late afternoon and by the time the 8th Marines dug in for the night it had registered a day's gain of about 700 yards.[111]

The advance of the 6th Marines in the division center was not so rapid, especially on the right flank where it faced cliffs and thickly wooded ravines and encountered strong enemy positions in natural cave formations. By evening the regiment had progressed from about 900 yards on the left to 500 to 600 yards on the right. The regimental lines had become too extended

---

[109] 2d Bn 106th RCT Jnl, 24 Jun 44, Msg 96.
[110] This account of F Company's activities is derived from Love, Battle for Saipan, pages 306–08.

[111] 2d Marine Div SAR, Phase I, FORAGER, Sec. VI, p. 12; Hoffman, *Saipan*, p. 143.

IN HELL'S POCKET AREA

for safety, and an additional company was committed to the line.[112]

On the division left the 2d Marines jumped off at 0800. On its right, progress was slow against heavy fire from a hill, just southeast of Garapan, that the marines did not occupy until 1500. Shortly thereafter the Japanese counterattacked the hill, which from their side (north) was virtually a cliff. Firing with muzzles depressed against the enemy below, the marines easily repulsed the attack and dug in for the night along the ridge overlooking "Radio Road," which ran at right angles to the line of advance. Meanwhile, the battalion on the left had quickly advanced 500 yards

along the beach into the southern outskirts of Garapan itself. Around 1625, as these men were preparing their defenses along the flatlands bordering the sea, seven enemy tanks unaccompanied by infantrymen suddenly moved out from Garapan against them. Marine tanks and 75-mm. half-tracks were rushed in and quickly broke up the attack, destroying six of the Japanese vehicles and routing the seventh. The 2d Marines had now reached the O–6 line and would again have to hold up until the units on its right came abreast. Casualties for the entire 2d Division on the 24th amounted to 31 killed, 165 wounded, and one missing in action.[113]

---

[112] 2d Marine Div SAR, Phase I, FORAGER, Sec. VI, p. 13.

[113] *Ibid.;* Hoffman, *Saipan*, pp. 141–42.

Garapan Pier   Mutcho Pt   Hill occupied by 2d Marines

INLAND OF GARAPAN HARBOR *from hill position southeast of the town, 24 June.*

After two days of fighting on a three divisional front, the attack of Holland Smith's corps against the center of the Japanese main line of resistance had stalled. On the right, the 4th Marine Division had overrun most of Kagman Peninsula, an area that presented no particular terrain problems but that still contained plenty of live Japanese, judging from the casualties suffered there by the marines. On the left, the 2d Marine Division had fought its way into the outskirts of Garapan and up the craggy approaches to Mount Tapotchau, although it would take another day to reach the summit of the mountain. In the corps center, the 165th Infantry on the

27th Division's right had captured Hill Love, but had made no further advance along the hill system called Purple Heart Ridge. Progress of the 106th Infantry into Death Valley had been negligible. Thus, in the center—the 27th Division zone—the corps line bent back as much as 1,500 yards. Total reported casualties in the 4th Marine Division for the two days were 812; for the 2d Marine Division, 333; for the 27th Infantry Division, 277.[114]

[114] 27th Infantry Division casualty figures are from 27th Inf Div G–1 Periodic Rpts; 2d Marine Division casualty figures are from 2d Marine Div SAR Phase I, FORAGER, Sec. VI; 4th Marine Division casualty figures are from NTLF Rpt Marianas, Phase I, Incl C, G–1 Rpt.

CHAPTER X

Smith Versus Smith

Relief of Major General Ralph C. Smith

By 24 June General Holland Smith had made up his mind that the "all-round poor performance" of the 27th Division could only be remedied by a drastic shake-up in its command structure.[1] Accordingly, he decided to ask for the relief of General Ralph Smith.

He first visited Admiral Turner, who agreed with him, and together the two officers boarded the flagship *Indianapolis* to consult with Admiral Spruance. As a result of this discussion, Admiral Spruance "authorized and directed" that General Ralph Smith be relieved by General Jarman, the island commander. It was understood that Jarman would take over only until such time as another general officer could be dispatched from Hawaii to command the division. In Spruance's words, "No other action appeared adequate to accomplish the purpose."[2]

The bill of particulars presented by General Holland Smith against General Ralph Smith broke down into two general charges: (1) that on two separate occasions the Army commander had issued orders to units not under his command and had contravened orders of the corps commander; and (2) that on the morning of 23 June the 27th Division had been late in launching its attack and had thereafter retarded the progress of the Marine divisions on the flanks.[3]

On the first point, the corps commander charged that the "27th Infantry Division Field Order No. 45[4] contravened the NTLF Operation Order Number 9-44 by ordering the 105th Infantry to hold its present positions, although the 105th Infantry had been removed from the tactical control of the Division Commander," and that the 27th Division "Field Order No. 46 again contravened the NTLF order by issuing tactical orders to the 2d Battalion, 105th Infantry to continue operations to mop up enemy resistance in NAFUTAN POINT Area," although that battalion "by NTLF Operation Order No. 10-44 had been removed from the tactical control of the 27th Infantry Division."[5]

On the second point, it was alleged that on the morning of 23 June, the "27th Infantry Division was from 77 minutes to two hours late in launching its attack, although the major elements of this division did not

---

[1] The words are General Holland Smith's. See Smith, *Coral and Brass*, p. 171.

[2] Ltr, Comdr Fifth Fleet to CINCPAC-CINCPOA, 29 Jun 44, Ser. 00025, Buckner Board Rpt, Exhibit C.

[3] Ltr, CTF 56 to CTF 51, 24 Jun 44, Ser. 00055-3, Buckner Board Rpt, Exhibit D.

[4] He meant Field Order Number 45-A.

[5] Ltr, CTF 56 to CTF 51, 24 Jun 44, Ser. 00055-3, Buckner Board Rpt, Exhibit D.

have to move more than about three miles to execute the order." [6] In a report to Admiral Turner written three days later, General Holland Smith revised this figure downward to "55 minutes to two hours" and added that the "lack of coordination in the attack" resulting from the 27th Division's late arrival and "the slow advance of the Division against small arms and mortar fire uncovered the flanks of the 4th and 2d Marine Divisions to such extent that it was necessary to slow down and eventually halt these units and thereby retard otherwise favorable offensive operations which were in progress." [7]

Interservice Controversy

It is doubtful whether the relief of General Ralph Smith brought about any marked change one way or the other in the "aggressiveness" of the 27th Division about which General Holland Smith was so concerned.[8] There is no doubt, however, that it precipitated an interservice controversy of alarming proportions—a controversy that seriously jeopardized harmonious relations at all levels among the Army and the Navy and the Marine Corps in the Pacific.

The first signs of strain appeared naturally enough on Saipan itself, where soldiers and marines still had to fight shoulder to shoulder for more than two weeks to secure the island. Army officers were quick to resent the slur on their service implied by the relief of General Ralph Smith, and by the end of the battle

relationships between top Army officers and Holland Smith's staff had reached the breaking point. Various Army officers who had contact of one sort or another with that staff reported that the Marine officers at headquarters made little effort to disguise their feeling that the 27th Division was an inferior organization. In the opinion of one of the Army officers, "the Commanding General and Staff of the NTLF held the units of the 27th Division in little esteem, actually a position bordering on scorn." [9]

The reaction on the part of the ranking Army officers present on Saipan was a determination never to serve under General Holland Smith again if they could help it. Gen. Ralph Smith urged Lt. Gen. Robert C. Richardson that "no Army combat troops should ever again be permitted to serve under the command of Marine Lieutenant General Holland M. Smith." [10] General Kernan, who commanded the 27th Division Artillery, agreed.[11] Maj. Gen. George W. Griner, who took over command of the Army division on 26 June, quarreled so bitterly with the corps commander that he came away from Saipan with the "firm conviction that he [Holland Smith] is so prejudiced against the

---

[6] *Ibid.*

[7] Ltr, CG NTLF to CTF 51, 27 Jun 44, Ser. 00063–3, with Incl A, Buckner Board Rpt, Exhibit E.

[8] See below, Chs. XI, XIII.

[9] Ltr, Maj Stephen J. McCormick, SC, to CG Army Garrison Force, Saipan, 2 Sep 44, sub: Reflections on 27th Inf Div, in Hq AFMIDPAC, Correspondence Incident to Relief of Maj Gen Ralph C. Smith, 27th Division (hereafter cited as AFMIDPAC Corresp, Ralph Smith) bound photostatic copy in OCMH. See also Brig Gen Edgar B. Colladay, USA, Memo for Island Comdr Saipan, 5 Sep 44; Lt Col P. B. Stiness, GSC, Memo for CG Army Garrison Force, APO 244, 4 Sep 44, both in corresp cited above.

[10] Maj Gen Ralph C. Smith, Recommendation to CG USAFICPA, 28 Aug 44, in AFMIDPAC Corresp, Ralph Smith.

[11] Ltr, Kernan to Richardson, 16 Aug 44, in AFMIDPAC Corresp, Ralph Smith.

Army that no Army Division serving under his command alongside of Marine Divisions can expect that their deeds will receive fair and honest evaluation." [12]

When, less than a week after the conclusion of organized hostilities on Saipan, the island was visited by General Richardson, the commanding general of all Army forces in the Pacific Ocean Areas, the dispute waxed even hotter. While on the island, Richardson reviewed the Army troops and presented decorations—all without the previous knowledge or consent of Holland Smith.[13] The corps commander was quick to resent these actions, which he considered to be a breach of military etiquette and an unwarranted infringement on his own authority. On his part, General Richardson is reported to have said angrily to the Marine general, "I want you to know you can not push the Army around the way you have been doing." [14] At this juncture Admirals Spruance and Turner jumped into the fight and complained strongly to Admiral Nimitz of the irregularity of Richardson's actions on Saipan, and especially his berating of Holland Smith.[15]

General Richardson's visit to Saipan was in fact incident to a more general inquiry into the relief of Ralph Smith, which Richardson had called at his headquarters back on Oahu. On 4 July, five days before the conclusion of the battle for Saipan,

Maj. Gen. Sanderford Jarman, *talking with Admiral Spruance, June 1944.*

Richardson had appointed a board of inquiry to examine the facts involved.[16] The board was headed by Lt. Gen. Simon B. Buckner, Jr., and consisted, in addition to the chairman, of four Army officers, Maj. Gen. John R. Hodge, Brig. Gen. Henry B. Holmes, Jr., Brig. Gen. Roy E. Blount, and Lt. Col. Charles A. Selby. It convened first on 7 July and continued until the 26th, hearing the testimony of Army officers and examining those official reports from Army files that were available to it.[17]

After examining all the available evidence—which was admitted to be limited

---

[12] Ltr, Griner to CG USAFPOA, 11 Oct 44, in AFMIDPAC Corresp, Ralph Smith.

[13] One account of this visit is given by General Holland Smith in *Coral and Brass,* pages 176–78.

[14] CG Fleet Marine Force, Pacific, Rpt of Visit of Lt Gen Robert C. Richardson, Jr., 18 Jul 44, filed in RS Hist Br G–3, Hq USMC.

[15] Ltr, Comdr V Phib Force to CINCPAC, 16 Jul 44, with COMCENPAC 1st Ind, 18 Jul 44, sub: Rpt of Unwarranted Assumption of Comd Authority by Gen Richardson, filed in RS Hist Br G–3, Hq USMC.

[16] Rad, Richardson to WDCSA, 4 Jul 44, in AFMIDPAC Corresp, Ralph Smith.

[17] Buckner Board Rpt, Ralph Smith Personal File.

LT. GEN. HOLLAND M. SMITH

because only personnel and records of the U.S. Army Forces, Central Pacific Area, could be examined—the "Buckner Board" arrived at four conclusions:

1. that General Holland Smith had full authority to relieve General Ralph Smith;

2. that the orders effecting the change of command were properly issued;

3. that General Holland Smith "was not fully informed regarding conditions in the zone of the 27th Infantry Division," when he asked for the relief of General Ralph Smith; and

4. that the relief of General Ralph Smith "was not justified by the facts." [18]

In reaching these conclusions, the Buckner Board reasoned that the situation facing

the 27th Division at the entrance to Death Valley was far more serious than General Holland Smith had imagined. "The bulk of the 27th Division," the board reported, "was opposed by the enemy's main defensive position on a difficult piece of terrain, naturally adapted to defense, artificially strengthened, well manned and heavily covered by fire." General Holland Smith, it concluded, "was not aware of the strength of this position and expected the 27th Division to overrun it rapidly . . . . The delay incident to this situation was mistaken by Lt. Gen. Holland M. Smith as an indication that the 27th Division was lacking in aggressiveness and that its commander was inefficient . . . ."[19] Furthermore, the board argued, there was no evidence that General Ralph Smith attempted to "contravene" orders during the clean-up on Nafutan Point.

These findings, coming as they did from an all-Army board of inquiry by no means ended the controversy. Holland Smith wrote to Admiral Nimitz to the effect that the Buckner Board's conclusions were unwarranted, and added, "I was and am convinced that the 27th Division was not accomplishing even the combat results to be expected from an organization which had had adequate opportunity for training." [20] Admiral Turner, resenting the board's implied criticism that he had been overzealous in "pressing Lt. Gen. Holland M. Smith . . . to expedite the conquest of Saipan so as to free the fleet for another operation," [21] also demurred from the findings of the board. He at no time had brought pressure to bear on Holland

[18] *Ibid.*, p. 10.

[19] *Ibid.*, p. 3.
[20] CG Fleet Marine Force, Pacific, to CINCPAC 29 Aug 44, Proceedings of the Buckner Board, RS Hist Br G–3, Hq USMC.
[21] Buckner Board Rpt, p. 3.

Smith, he asserted, and he was confident that no part of the Marine general's action against Ralph Smith "was based on either personal or service prejudice or jealousy." [22]

When the detailed report of the proceedings of the Buckner Board reached Washington, General Marshall's chief advisers tended to take a "plague on both your houses" attitude. Maj. Gen. Thomas T. Handy, Assistant Chief of Staff, advised Marshall that Holland Smith had some cause for complaining of the 27th Division's lack of aggressiveness in the attack into Death Valley; that "Holland Smith's fitness for this command is open to question" because of his deep-seated prejudice against the Army; and that "bad blood had developed between the Marines and the Army on Saipan" to such a degree that it endangered future operations in the theater. "In my opinion," he concluded, "it would be desireable that both Smiths be ordered out of the Pacific Ocean Area. While I do not believe we should make definite recommendation to the Navy for the relief of Holland Smith, I think that positive action should be taken to get Ralph Smith out of the area. His presence undoubtedly tends to aggravate a bad situation between the Services." [23]

Lt. Gen. Joseph T. McNarney, Deputy Chief of Staff, was of much the same mind

LT. GEN. ROBERT C. RICHARDSON, JR.

as General Handy. After examining the Buckner Board Report, he concluded that the staff work of Holland Smith's V Amphibious Corps was below acceptable standards; that there was reasonably good tactical direction on the part of Ralph Smith; and that Ralph Smith failed to exact the performance expected from a well-trained division, as evidenced by poor leadership on the part of some regimental and battalion commanders, undue hesitancy to bypass snipers "with a tendency to alibi because of lack of reserves to mop up," poor march discipline, and lack of reconnaisance.[24]

On 22 November General Marshall expressed to Admiral King his deep concern over the fact that "relationships between

_____

[22] Comdr V Phib Force to CINCPAC, 18 Aug 44, RS Hist Br G–3, Hq USMC.

[23] Memo, Handy for CofS, 16 Aug 44, atchd to Buckner Board Rpt. This recommendation was acted upon favorably. Ralph Smith was relieved of his command of the 98th Infantry Division, which was on garrison duty in the Hawaiian Islands. He was later transferred to the European Theater of Operations. Holland Smith, while relieved of his command of V Amphibious Corps, was elevated to the command of the newly organized Fleet Marine Force, Pacific.

[24] Memo, McNarney for Handy, 19 Aug 44. atchd to Buckner Board Rpt.

the Marines and the Army forces on Saipan had deteriorated beyond mere healthy rivalry. To avert future controversies of the same sort, General Marshall suggested that he and Admiral King send identical telegrams to Richardson and Nimitz adjuring them "to take suitable steps to promptly eradicate any tendency toward . . . disharmony among the components of our forces." Marshall also suggested that both commanders should conduct an immediate investigation into the Saipan affair with an eye to preventing the recurrence of any such imbroglio in the future.[25] To this Admiral King replied that in his mind the findings of the Buckner Board were unilateral and suspect, and that the record improperly included intemperate attacks on the personal character and professional competence of General Holland Smith. He could not concur in any further investigations in which General Richardson was to be a party because he felt that that officer had already done enough damage by his "investigational activities during his visit to Saipan" and by convening the Buckner Board.[26] There the matter was dropped as far as official action was concerned.

The American public, however, was not to be permitted any early respite from the heated journalistic dispute that followed Ralph Smith's relief. First among the newspapers to air the matter was the Hearst press. Various affiliates of that syndicate pointed editorially to two lessons from the battle for Saipan. First, it was claimed that

Marine Corps casualties were excessive, especially in contrast to those in MacArthur's theater. Second, divided command was a mistake. The Hearst papers' conclusion was that "the supreme command in the Pacific should, of course, be logically and efficiently entrusted to General Douglas MacArthur."[27]

Another powerful syndicate, the Henry Luce publications, took the other side. *Time* and *Life* magazines both carried articles favoring Holland Smith's side of the controversy, the former concluding, "when field commanders hesitate to remove subordinates for fear of interservice contention, battles and lives will be needlessly lost."[28]

More than four years after the event, the issue was reopened publicly when General Holland Smith published part of his wartime memoirs in the *Saturday Evening Post*.[29] He was answered by Capt. Edmund G. Love, the official historian of the 27th Infantry Division, in a rebuttal that was printed in part in the *Saturday Evening Post,* and in full in the *Infantry Journal*.[30] The capstone of this particular literary controversy was inserted when General Holland Smith published his memoirs in book form in 1949, and Captain Love in the same year came out with the

---

[25] Memo, Marshall for King, 22 Nov 44, WDCSA 000.7 and draft of proposed telegram to Richardson from Marshall (a similar telegram to be sent by King to Nimitz).

[26] Memo, COMINCH for Marshall, 23 Nov 44, sub: Article in *Time* Magazine, 12 Sep 44, WDCSA 000.7.

[27] San Francisco *Examiner,* July 6, 1944, p. 5. See also New York *Journal American,* July 17–18, 1944.

[28] *Time,* September 18, 1944, pp. 26–27. See also *Life,* August 28, 1944, pp. 33–42.

[29] General Holland M. Smith and Percy Finch, "Howlin' Mad's Own Story," a book condensation in three parts, *Saturday Evening Post,* November 6, 13, 20, 1948.

[30] Edmund G. Love, Official Historian of the 27th Division, "The Army Says Holland Smith Is Wrong," *Saturday Evening Post,* November 13, 1948, pp. 33, 65; Edmund G. Love, "Smith *versus* Smith," *Infantry Journal,* LXIII (November, 1948), 3–13.

official history of the 27th Division in World War II.[31]

Conclusions

To resolve the controversy of Smith versus Smith conclusively and to the satisfaction of all is probably impossible. But a dispassionate re-examination of the salient facts of the case as presented in the foregoing chapters may serve at least to clarify the issue and to point to some satisfactory conclusions.

The first charge against Ralph Smith dealt with his alleged usurpation of authority and contravention of orders in handling the troops of the 27th Division that were left to finish the capture of Nafutan Point. In order to examine this charge it will be necessary first to recapitulate some of the events that took place on 21 and 22 June.

It will be remembered that on the morning of 21 June Holland Smith issued Operations Order Number 9–44, which directed that the bulk of the 27th Infantry Division be removed from the front lines on Nafutan peninsula and be assembled northwest of Aslito field in corps reserve. In Paragraph 3(d) of this operations order, one infantry battalion (undesignated) of the division was ordered to remain on Nafutan peninsula, where it would "mop up remaining enemy detachments, maintain anti-sniper patrols . . . and protect installations within its zone of action with particular attention to ASLITO Airfield." [32]

After an afternoon in which his troops made little progress on Nafutan, Ralph

MAJ. GEN. RALPH C. SMITH

Smith called Holland Smith and persuaded him that at least two battalions would be needed to mop up the enemy in that area. Accordingly, the corps commander modified his initial order in a mail brief that arrived at 27th Division headquarters at 0830 on 22 June. This message read, "1 RCT will continue mission in Garrison Area [Nafutan] of cleaning up remaining resistance and patrolling area . . . ." [33] Like the initial order, this mail brief did not specifically designate the unit intended for the mission, although it was understood from previous conversations that the 105th Infantry would be given the job.

At 2000, 21 June, after his conversation with General Holland Smith but before receiving the mail brief modifying Operations Order Number 9–44, General Ralph Smith

---

[31] Smith, *Coral and Brass;* Love, *The 27th Infantry Division in World War II.*

[32] NTLF Opn Order 9–44, 21 Jun 44; 27th Inf Div G–3 Jnl, 21 Jun 44, Msg 34.

[33] 27th Inf Div G–3 Jnl, 22 Jun 44, Msg 14.

issued his Field Order Number 45–A. This order, insofar as it applied to the 105th Infantry, read:

RCT 105 will *hold present front line* facing NAFUTAN POINT, with two Battalions on the line and one Battalion in Regimental Reserve. It will relieve elements of RCT 165 now on the present front line by 0630 22 June. The Battalion in reserve will not be committed to action without authority from the Division Commander. Reorganization of the present front line to be effected *not later than 1100 22 June and offensive operations against the enemy continued.* Reserve Battalion will maintain anti-sniper patrols in vicinity of ASLITO AIRFIELD.[34]

In asking for the relief of Ralph Smith, Holland Smith claimed that in issuing this field order, the 27th Division commander had committed two offenses simultaneously. He had usurped authority of his immediate superior by issuing formal orders to a unit no longer under his control, and he had contravened his superior's orders by instructing that unit to "hold" rather than to fight offensively. Holland Smith argued that his corps Operation Order Number 9–44, as modified by the mail brief, placed the entire 27th Division in reserve status and removed the 105th Infantry from tactical control of the 27th Infantry Division. Hence, Ralph Smith had no right at all to issue orders to the 105th. Furthermore, Holland Smith claimed, his own order directed the 105th Infantry "to conduct offensive operations to mop up enemy units in the NAFUTAN POINT area."[35] Ralph Smith's Field Order Number 45–A, on the other hand, in-

structed the 105th Infantry "to hold its present positions" rather than to conduct offensive operations. This, according to Holland Smith, was a clear contravention of orders.

Both Army and Marine Corps regulations concerning the composition of combat orders tend to support Holland Smith's argument on the question of where control of the 105th Infantry lay on the night of 21 June. Furthermore, they account in part for his own conviction that tactical control over the 105th had been clearly removed from the 27th Division and had been placed under his own headquarters by his Field Order Number 9–44. These regulations state that Paragraph 3 of a field order "assigns definite missions to each of the several elements of the [issuing] command charged with execution of the tactical details for carrying out the decision of the commander or the assigned mission."[36] Since the "one Infantry Battalion, 27th Infantry Division (to be designated)," was assigned a specific mission in Paragraph 3(d) of Holland Smith's Field Order Number 9–44 and since the entire 105th Infantry was shortly thereafter substituted for this one battalion, it seemed clear to members of Holland Smith's staff that the unit would execute its mop-up task as an immediate subordinate of Holland Smith's headquarters.[37]

General Ralph Smith, on the other hand, was just as clear in his mind that the unit left on Nafutan was still under his own command. Speaking of his telephone conversation with General Holland Smith, he later recollected, "Nothing was mentioned

---

[34] 27th Inf Div G-3 Rpt, Battle for Saipan, Field Directive 45, Able, 2000, 21 Jun 44. Italics are the author's. Where the order used abbreviations, the words have been spelled out.

[35] Ltr, CTF 56 to CTF 51, 24 Jun 44, Buckner Board Rpt, App. D.

[36] War Dept FM 101-5, 19 Aug 40, p. 43. This manual was in effect in 1944 and governed both Army and Marine Corps procedures.

[37] Hoffman, *Saipan,* p. 122n.

in his conversation about having the regiment [105th] operate under NTLF control." [38] He continued that, in his opinion, his Field Order Number 45–A was neither a usurpation nor a contravention of orders. No written confirmation of the mission to be assigned to the 105th Infantry arrived until 0830, 22 June, much too late to have permitted issuing any instructions for that day's operation. The 105th Infantry was to take over with two battalions a front line covered the previous day by four battalions. "It seemed elementary military common-sense to have these two battalions first take over the front from the units being relieved." Hence, in the absence of any further orders from higher headquarters, at 2000 on the night of the 21st Ralph Smith had ordered the 105th to "hold present front line," relieve elements of the 165th Infantry, and jump off not later than 1100 the following morning. "The 105th Infantry was thus directed to resume offensive operations as soon as the lines were adjusted, thus to carry out the plan recommended by me and approved by General Holland Smith."[39]

Two facts stand out in support of General Ralph Smith's contention. In the first place, Corps Order Number 9–44 did not specifically and expressly detach the 105th Infantry from the 27th Division and attach it to corps. Secondly, neither Corps Order Number 9–44 nor the subsequent mail brief mentioned the regiment by name, nor is there any record that either was sent to the command post of that regiment. Presumably, had General Ralph Smith not issued his Field Order Number

45–A, the 105th Infantry would have been without orders for 22 June.[40]

On the afternoon of 22 June, General Holland Smith decided that a single battalion would be sufficient to clean up Nafutan Point. His chief of staff, General Erskine, personally communicated this decision to General Ralph Smith. That evening, the 27th Division commander drew up his Field Order Number 46, which he issued at 2100. In part, the order read: "2d Battalion, 105th Infantry (1 Platoon Light Tanks attached) [will] continue operations to mop-up remaining enemy detachments in NAFUTAN POINT area. On completion of this mission, [it will] revert to Corps control as Corps Reserve." [41]

Just one hour later, Holland Smith issued his Operations Order Number 10–44, which was not received at 27th Division headquarters until 2330.[42] This order read in part: "2d Battalion 105th Infantry (with one light tank platoon attached) [will] continue operations at daylight to mop up remaining enemy detachments in NAFUTAN POINT area. Upon completion this mission [it will] revert to Corps control as Corps reserve."

In requesting the relief of Ralph Smith, Holland Smith alleged that the Army general's Field Order Number 46 contravened Corps Order Number 10–44 "by issuing tactical orders to the 2d Battalion, 105th Infantry, to continue operations to mop up enemy resistance in NAFUTAN POINT area. The 2d Battalion, 105th Infantry, by NT and LF Order No. 10–44, had been

---

[38] Ralph Smith, Notes, Saipan, Buckner Board Rpt, Exhibit M, p. 7.
[39] Ibid.

[40] The 105th RCT Journal for 21 and 22 June 1944 contains no record of the receipt of Corps Order Number 9–44.
[41] 27th Inf Div FO 46, 2100, 22 Jun 44, in 27th Inf Div G–3 Rpt, Battle for Saipan.
[42] NTLF Opn Order 10–44, 2200, 22 Jun 44; 27th Inf Div G–3 Jnl, 22 Jun 44, Entry 78.

removed from the tactical control of the 27th Infantry Division." [43]

Actually, of course, the only difference between Ralph Smith's Field Order Number 46 and Holland Smith's Order Number 10–44 in respect to the 2d Battalion, 105th Infantry, is that the latter included the words "at daylight" and the former omitted them. Otherwise, they are identical in all essential points. Later, Ralph Smith testified that in his conversations with General Holland Smith up to date no mention had been made of any question of control of the 105th Infantry nor had he been given any indication that that unit was no longer under direct control of the 27th Division.[44] His belief that the 2d Battalion, 105th, was still under his tactical control was reinforced by the wording of Corps Order Number 10–44 itself. The fact that the order stipulated that "upon completion this mission" the battalion was to "revert to Corps control as Corps reserve" would seem to indicate strongly that until its mission was completed, the unit was not under corps control but still under the division.

The fact is that the orders from Holland Smith's headquarters were never clear as to where command authority over the troops on Nafutan Point did lie. Ralph Smith had to issue some orders, or none would have reached the front-line troops in time. There was no important difference between the commands that he issued and those that later came down from corps headquarters. There is no indication that any "contravention" of orders was intended or effected. At best, this charge appears to have been a rather flimsy legal peg upon which to hang a justification for Ralph Smith's relief.

The second charge was more serious. It concerned the tardiness of the 27th Division in jumping off into Death Valley on the morning of 23 June, the alleged poor co-ordination of the division in the attack, and its slow advance against "small arms and mortar fire," which slowed down the whole corps attack. Connected with this charge was Holland Smith's opinion, as later expressed, that the Army division was guilty of "all-round poor performance." [45] Here was undoubtedly the core of Holland Smith's complaint against the 27th Infantry Division and its commander, and it is on these allegations that the case between him and Ralph Smith must be decided.

The details of the fighting at the entrance to Death Valley on 23 and 24 June have already been presented.[46] Out of this complex of events, several conclusions emerge. On the one hand, it appears clear that Holland Smith and his staff underestimated both the formidability of the terrain and extent of enemy opposition that faced the 27th Division in Death Valley on the days in question.

The terrain facing the 27th Division was most difficult. Two parallel ridges on the division flanks dominated its zone of action, and flanking fire from well-concealed enemy positions on the slopes interdicted the valley between the ridges. Before the division could accomplish its mission the enemy occupying these dominant terrain features had to be eliminated.

---

[43] CG Expeditionary Troops to CO TF 51, 24 Jun 44, Buckner Board Rpt, Annex D, p. 2.
[44] Ralph Smith, Notes, p. 11, Buckner Board Rpt, Exhibit M.

[45] CG NTLF to CTF 51, 27 Jun 44, Buckner Board Rpt, Incl B; Smith, *Coral and Brass*, p. 171.
[46] See above, Ch. IX.

The conditions obtaining in the left part of the division zone precluded the possibility of maneuver, and an attack along the east slopes of Mount Tapotchau would have to be a frontal assault. Because of extremely rugged terrain, flanking enemy fire from Purple Heart Ridge, and the difficulty of co-ordination with the Marines on the left, any such frontal attack would necessarily be costly.

In the right part of the division zone the terrain was less rugged, and, more important, there was a possibility of a flanking maneuver east of Purple Heart Ridge. This was clearly the more promising area for the main attack by the Army division. Yet even as late as the evening of 24 June after two days of heavy and generally fruitless fighting on the part of the 27th Division, corps headquarters still ordered the main effort to continue on the left.[47]

On the other hand, there is no doubt that the 106th Infantry Regiment of the 27th Division was late in jumping off in the attack on the morning of 23 June— even though not so late as Holland Smith

charged. On the 23d and again on the 24th, the Army troops attacking Death Valley were slow and faltering in their advance. According to the testimony of General Jarman, who took over the division from Ralph Smith, the unit leaders of the 106th Infantry were hesitant and apparently confused. Although the Army troops in Death Valley sustained fairly heavy casualties, the two Marine divisions on the flanks suffered greater ones. Yet the marines made considerable advances while the 165th Infantry registered only small gains —the 106th Infantry almost none at all.

No matter what the extenuating circumstances were—and there were several—the conclusion seems inescapable that Holland Smith had good reason to be disappointed with the performance of the 27th Infantry Division on the two days in question. Whether the action he took to remedy the situation was a wise one, however, remains doubtful. Certainly the relief of Ralph Smith appears to have done nothing to speed the capture of Death Valley. Six more days of bitter fighting remained before that object was to be achieved.

---

[47] See above, p. 186.

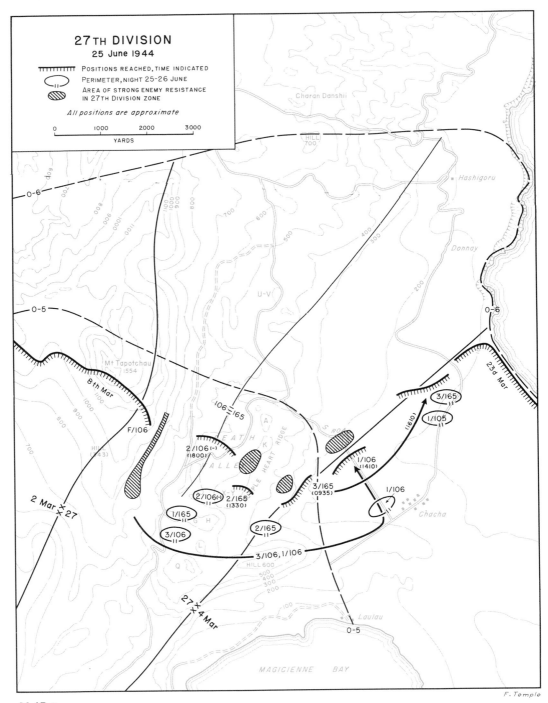

27TH DIVISION
25 June 1944

ㅠㅠㅠㅠㅠ Positions reached, time indicated
⬯ Perimeter, night 25-26 June
▨ Area of strong enemy resistance
in 27th Division zone

All positions are approximate

0   1000   2000   3000
YARDS

F. Temple

MAP 8

CHAPTER XI

The Fight for Central Saipan—II

With General Ralph Smith's relief effected, General Jarman received orders to take over command of the 27th Division. He reported to division headquarters in the middle of the afternoon of 24 June and discovered that General Ralph Smith was at the front inspecting troops. Late that afternoon General Smith returned to the command post and remained there in consultation with General Jarman until about 0100 the next morning. The plan agreed upon for 25 June was essentially the one General Smith had already devised. Rather than continue the frontal assault on Death Valley with all three battalions of the 106th Infantry, it was decided that one battalion would be left at the mouth of the valley to contain the Japanese while the other two would circle to the right (eastward), then turn northwest and establish contact with the 2d Marine Division north of the Japanese positions that had held up the 27th Division's advance through the valley.[1] Early on the morning of the 25th, while the two generals were still together, General Smith received his orders to report not later than 0530 that day for air transportation back to Pearl Harbor.[2]

25 June

General Jarman issued his orders for the 25th soon after his long conversation with General Ralph Smith. He directed the 165th Infantry to continue its advance and seize the O–5 line in its zone, including all of Purple Heart Ridge. Jump-off hour was to be 0730. One battalion was to mop up the Japanese on Hill Xray-Yoke and in the gulch to the south of it while the other two were to move up the ridge itself. Starting at 0600 the 1st and 3d Battalions, 106th Infantry, were to move by covered route in the rear of the 165th, then advance to the northwest, cross the northern entrance of the valley, and establish contact with the 2d Marine Division. The 2d Battalion, 106th, was ordered to remain in its current position at the southern end of Death Valley, conduct mop-up operations, and "assist in containing and eliminating enemy positions" within the valley. Division artillery was to fire a fifteen-minute preparation.[3] XXIV Corps Artillery would be in general support and was ordered to place the mass of its fires in the zone of the 27th Division.[4] (*Map 8*)

---

[1] Jarman, Memo for Record, 24 Jun 44, Buckner Board Rpt, Exhibit J; Ralph Smith Notes, Buckner Board Rpt, Exhibit M, p. 16.

[2] CG NTLF to Ralph Smith, 25 Jun 44, Ser. 2445, Buckner Board Rpt, Exhibit O.

[3] 27th Inf Div FO 46, 242100 Jun 44, Incl to 27th Inf Div G–3 Jnl.

[4] NTLF Opn Order 12–44, 24 Jun 44.

Attack on Purple Heart Ridge

Early on the morning of the 25th, Colonel Kelley issued orders to his three battalions to move northeast up Purple Heart Ridge. The 2d Battalion, 165th, was to attack Hill Xray-Yoke frontally from its position at the foot of the hill and then move on to Hills Oboe and King beyond. The 3d Battalion was to move up on the right of the 2d Battalion so that the two could jump off together at 0730. The 1st Battalion was to mop up all enemy resistance behind the two assault battalions and follow them northward.[5] Had these orders been carried out and had the 1st Battalion, 106th, succeeded in tying in with the right flank of the 165th as planned, the assault on Purple Heart Ridge would have been conducted as a co-ordinated movement with three battalions abreast and one in support. As it turned out, the fighting degenerated into separate and un-co-ordinated actions by each of the four battalions involved.

The 1st Battalion, 165th, moved off on schedule from the base of Hill Love and after a short fire fight cleared the last vestige of the enemy from the area to the north. The battalion combed the area in its immediate zone without incident and then retired to its bivouac area of the two previous nights without taking any further part in the day's attack on Purple Heart Ridge.[6]

The immediate task of the 2d Battalion, 165th, was to take Hill Xray-Yoke, which Company K had unsuccessfully attacked the previous day. Company F had bivouacked the night before southwest of the gulch below the hill. Instead of attempting

another frontal attack from that direction, Captain Leonard conducted a wide detour and came upon Hill Xray-Yoke from a southeasterly direction. Company G, after investigating the gulch itself, moved directly up the face of the hill from the south.[7] Company F arrived at the eastern foot of Hill Xray-Yoke about 0930[8] and commenced to move up the slope in column of platoons, led by 1st Lt. Ford Martin. Captain Leonard, meanwhile, had joined the battalion commander, Colonel McDonough, who was conducting a separate reconnaissance for the purpose of locating a site to establish an observation post. McDonough was desperately trying to close the gap between his own troops and the Marine line to the northeast. Just two hundred yards to the east he could observe a road so congested with American troops and vehicles that it reminded him of Times Square on New Year's Eve. "It was a machine gunner's dream," he later recalled, "but not one shot was being fired at it from the ridge to my front and this ridge showed *no* signs of life." [9]

As McDonough's party reached the top of the hill, just before the main body of the company was approaching it, a machine gun opened up and felled the entire group.[10] McDonough was wounded, as were Captain Leonard, Lieutenant Martin, and five enlisted men of F Company. 1st Lt. Henry W. Morrow, also of F Company, was killed.[11] Captain Leonard later died

---

[5] 165th RCT Jnl, 25 Jun 44, Msgs 1, 2.
[6] Love, Battle for Saipan, pp. 321–22.

[7] Unless otherwise noted, this account of the action of the 2d Battalion, 165th, is derived from Love, Battle for Saipan, pages 323–30.
[8] 27th Inf Div G–3 Jnl, 25 Jun 44, Msg 38.
[9] Comment USNG, McDonough, Incl to Ltr, Brig Gen Gerard W. Kelley, to General A. C. Smith, n.d., OCMH.
[10] 2d Bn 165th RCT Jnl, 25 Jun 44, Msg 9.
[11] 165th RCT Jnl, 25 Jun 44, Msgs 51, 62.

of his wounds, and McDonough had to be replaced as battalion commander by Maj. Gregory Brusseau. Company F was so stripped of its officer personnel that later in the day 1st Lt. Joseph Trummel had to be transferred from G Company to take over command.[12]

Enemy mortars joined the machine gun, first to pin down and then to scatter the troops of Company F as they approached the summit of the hill. In the absence of any officers on the spot, 1st Sgt. Edward Heikens took command of the company, collected the men, built a firm line, and reorganized the company front about halfway up the hill. There the men remained until late afternoon, when they were ordered down the hill to dig in for the night.[13]

Meanwhile, Company G had reached the top of Hill Xray-Yoke from the south and was pushing out along the ridge that ran north from it. As it reached the point where McDonough and his party had been hit, firing broke out all along the front and Captain Chasmar halted his advance. The new battalion commander, Major Brusseau, ordered Chasmar to hold fast and then requested tanks and self-propelled

mounts.[14] However, the approach to the position was too precipitous and rocky to permit the vehicles to be brought forward, and when F Company withdrew Company G also pulled back down the hill and dug in with battalion for the night.

Somewhat to the east and north of Hill Xray-Yoke lay another elevation, a sort of tongue jutting eastward from the main line of Purple Heart Ridge. This was labeled Hill Victor and lay within the zone of the 3d Battalion, 165th Infantry.[15] Before jump-off hour on the 25th, Captain Betts of Company K had sent patrols along the west side of the promontory only to have them pinned down by fire from the top. Therefore he decided to move around the east side of the hill in an effort to take it from the north. Accordingly, K Company moved out at 0730 in column of platoons, 2d Platoon in the lead. Immediately, the whole line came under heavy rifle and machine gun fire from the top of Hill Victor and from caves in the sides of the cliffs. The company was pinned down, as was I Company on its right, and no further effort was made to reach the top of the hill.

By midmorning it had become apparent that the 3d Battalion, 165th, was not making any progress toward reaching the top of Purple Heart Ridge. Colonel Kelley therefore decided to leave that job to the 2d Battalion and to send the 3d off to the right to establish contact with the 4th Marine Division north of Chacha. The idea was for the 3d Battalion to extend the right flank of the 106th Infantry, which was supposed to be moving north through the valley east of Purple Heart Ridge in order

---

[12] *Ibid.*, Msg 78.

[13] As a commentary on the difficulties of terrain appreciation in this area of Saipan, it might be noted that throughout the action described above, battalion, regiment, and division headquarters were under the mistaken belief that the attack was being conducted not against Hill Xray-Yoke, but against Hill Able some 600 yards to the north (see 27th Inf Div G-3 Jnl, Msgs 27, 28, 67). This mistake derived from the erroneous reports of Captain Chasmar of G Company, who believed himself to be well north of where he actually was. It was his report that he had reached the top of Hill Able that partly induced McDonough and his party to go exploring around Hill Xray-Yoke for an observation post. See Love, Battle for Saipan, pp. 379–80.

[14] 2d Bn 165th RCT Jnl, 25 Jun 44, Msg 10.

[15] Unless otherwise noted, the account of the action of the 3d Battalion, 165th, is derived from Love, Battle for Saipan, pages 330–36.

to seal off the Japanese in Death Valley from the north.

At 1445 the 3d Battalion, 165th, moved off toward the north.[16] The advance was rapid, since there was no opposition. Within a short time the battalion had established contact with the marines along a line northwest of Chacha, and by nightfall was digging in on the left flank of the 4th Marine Division.[17] To the rear, forming a perimeter, was the 1st Battalion, 106th, which had been attached to the 165th in the morning.

While the 165th Infantry was making unsuccessful efforts to work its way to the top of Purple Heart Ridge, the 1st and 3d Battalions of the 106th had moved off from the lower end of Death Valley in the circling movement that was intended eventually to bring them into contact with the 2d Marine Division north of the main pocket of Japanese resistance. The plan, which had been conceived by General Ralph Smith and concurred in by General Jarman and Colonel Ayers, was for the two battalions to move up the valley to the east of Purple Heart Ridge behind the 165th Infantry, then cut northwest along the road that ran north of Hill Able and establish a new line across the northern opening of Death Valley. Instead of carrying out this plan, which would have involved cutting across open country, the two battalion commanders, with the approval of Colonel Ayers, chose to stick to the roads. The reason given was that the inside route was too rough to permit the passage of vehicles and heavy weapons. The decision resulted in the troops of the two battalions moving in a wide circle east-

ward onto Kagman Plain into the zone of action of the 4th Marine Division.[18]

Colonel Ayers had ordered the 1st Battalion to make this move at 0600, but the troops were delayed for an hour and fifty minutes while the 2d Battalion, 106th Infantry, extended its lines eastward in order to cover the position formerly held by the 1st Battalion and seal off the whole lower end of Death Valley. At 0750 the 1st Battalion, commanded by Colonel Cornett, moved off, followed ten minutes later by the 3d Battalion under Colonel Mizony.[19] When Colonel Cornett reached the point where he was supposed to turn off the road he was following and cut overland into the valley east of Purple Heart Ridge, guides from the 165th Infantry informed him that the valley route would be impassable to vehicles and that heavy fighting was going on in the area through which his battalion was supposed to pass.[20] Cornett then decided to continue eastward along the road until it crossed a road (called S Road) that ran northwest past Hill Able into Death Valley. He then intended to follow S Road to his assigned positions.

Pursuing this course, the 1st Battalion reached the road junction, turned left, and had proceeded up S Road for about 400 yards when its lead vehicles drew fire. There, about 1130, Cornett built up a skirmish line 200 yards on either side of the road, with A Company on the right and B on the left.[21] Immediately upon

---

[16] 3d Bn 165th RCT Jnl, 25 Jun 44, Msg 43.
[17] 27th Inf Div G-3 Jnl, 25 Jun 44, Msgs 71, 81.

[18] Jarman, Memo for Record, 24 Jun 44, Buckner Board Rpt, Exhibit J; Gen Ross, Summary of Opns by 27th Inf Div, Buckner Board Rpt, Exhibit RR, p. 4.
[19] 106th RCT Jnl, 25 Jun 44, p. 57.
[20] Love, Battle for Saipan, p. 337. Unless otherwise noted, account of the action of the 2d and 3d Battalions, 106th Infantry, is derived from Love, Battle for Saipan, pages 337–45.
[21] 106th RCT Jnl, 25 Jun 44, Msg 348.

jumping off from this position, the battalion began to receive heavy fire from small arms, automatic weapons, and mortars situated in the hills to its front. Within twenty minutes Company A on the right had succeeded in reaching this high ground, although at the cost of twenty-one casualties, including the company commander, 1st Lt. Robert C. McCoy, who was wounded. On reaching the high ground, Company A remained immobile for the next two hours, waiting for B Company on its left to come up. By 1410 Company B pulled abreast, and the battalion occupied a line across S Road about 400 yards from where it had jumped off shortly before noon.[22] No further progress was made during the day. The enemy, from his positions in the defiles of Purple Heart Ridge, was able to cover the whole area with continuous machine gun and mortar fire. Finally, at 1615, Colonel Ayers ordered Colonel Cornett to withdraw his troops to the road junction from which they had begun their movement northwest toward Death Valley.[23] This was accomplished by 1840, and the 1st Battalion bivouacked at the junction for the night. The 3d Battalion, 106th, meanwhile, had made no progress during the day beyond the same road junction. It had arrived there in the wake of the 3d Battalion, 165th, by 1155 and reported that it was being held up by congestion caused by the 23d Marines.[24] Thereafter, it made no move and finally, late in the afternoon, pulled back to the point from which it had started in the morning at the south end of Death Valley.[25]

That night General Jarman, highly displeased with the failure of the 106th Infantry to comply with its orders to skirt the eastern slope of Purple Heart Ridge or to make any significant progress along the wider route that it had taken, asked Colonel Ayers for an explanation. In the division commander's words, "He [Ayers] had no excuse and could offer no explanation of anything he did during the day. He stated he felt sure he could get his regiment in hand and forward the next morning (26 June). I told him he had one more chance and if he did not handle his regiment I would relieve him."[26]

Attack up Death Valley

The part of General Jarman's plan that had called for an encirclement of Death Valley by skirting Purple Heart Ridge to the east had failed. Collaterally, on 25 June the 2d Battalion, 106th Infantry, was to execute a holding attack across the mouth of the valley, contain the enemy there, and apply whatever pressure was feasible from that direction. General Jarman hoped to make better use of his artillery than had been previously possible, and early in the morning ordered the commanding officer of Battery A, 106th Field Artillery, to conduct a reconnaissance along the southern end of Purple Heart Ridge with a view to moving one battery of 155-mm. howitzers to positions from which they could fire directly into the cliffs that walled the valley on the left.[27]

By 0800 the 2d Battalion had taken its position across the lower end of the valley and by 0830 was ready to move off with

---

[22] *Ibid.*, Msg 366.

[23] *Ibid.*, p. 65, and Msg 400.

[24] *Ibid.*, Msg 350.

[25] 27th Inf Div G–3 Jnl, 25 Jun 44, Msg 77.

[26] Jarman, Memo for Record, 24 Jun 44, Buckner Board Rpt, Exhibit J.

[27] 27th Inf Div G–3 Jnl, 25 Jun 44, Msg 24.

LOWER END OF DEATH VALLEY, 25 June. Elements of 106th Infantry are waiting for signal to attack.

Company E on the right, G on the left. (Company F was still on top of the cliff, tied in with the 2d Marine Division.) Because of the breadth of the front, all three rifle platoons of each company had to be committed to the line.[28]

Though the men moved forward cautiously, the constant fire from the cliffs on the left precluded any real progress during the morning. General Jarman now, for the first time since the beginning of the attack on Death Valley, decided to bring direct artillery fire to bear against the cliffs on the left. At 1400 he ordered the 106th Field Artillery Battalion to move two bat-

teries of artillery into position to fire point-blank at the cliff line just north of Hell's Pocket. The artillery battalion commander was directed to co-ordinate his fire with the movement of the 2d Battalion, 106th, and to deliver at least a half hour's preparation before the infantry jumped off again in the assault. General Jarman also attached one platoon of medium tanks from Company B of the 762d Tank Battalion to the infantry. He ordered Major O'Hara, commanding officer of the 2d Battalion, 106th, to launch his afternoon attack up the right side of Death Valley along Purple Heart Ridge using Companies E and G, drive all the way up the corridor, and establish contact with Company F, 106th, on the left and with the 165th Infantry on

[28] 2d Bn 106th RCT Jnl, 25 Jun 44, Msg 27. Unless otherwise noted, the account of this action of 2d Battalion, 106th Infantry, is derived from Love, Battle for Saipan, pages 347–66.

the right. The time of attack was set for 1600.[29] This drive, if successful, would bypass and seal up the remaining enemy in Hell's Pocket and the left side of Death Valley and would bring the 27th Division abreast of the Marine divisions on either side.

At 1630 the attack jumped off following the artillery preparation, which was deemed "very satisfactory." [30] Further artillery fire had to be called off because of complaints from the marines on Mount Tapotchau that fragments were falling within their lines.[31] The medium tanks moved into the valley ahead of the infantry but were out of contact with the troops for the rest of the afternoon and operated independently, firing at will against targets of opportunity.[32]

Capt. David Waterson's E Company took the lead and was followed on its right rear by Company G, which was commanded by Captain Tarrant.[33] The 3d Platoon of Company G was held in reserve at the battalion command post to prevent any possible attempt on the part of the enemy to break out of the valley to the south. Once again heavy fire from both sides of the valley greeted the men. The 3d Platoon of Company E managed to reach the battalion's intermediate objective —a line of trees running across the valley about 800 yards from the line of departure —but was quickly forced to withdraw to the cover of another tree line about 200

yards to the rear. The 2d Platoon, Company E, after being scattered by enemy fire, retreated all the way back to the line of departure, while the 1st Platoon never left it.

Initially, Company G met with more success. Most of the men of this unit reached the tree line, which was the intermediate objective, and Captain Tarrant started to organize his defense, but a barrage from the side of Mount Tapotchau persuaded him to pull back into a gully about twenty-five yards to his rear. Tarrant tried to attract the attention of the tank platoon that was moving through the valley but neither smoke pots nor flares succeeded in bringing aid from the tanks. In the gathering dusk G Company, too, moved back to the first tree line where the 3d Platoon of Company E had taken cover. There, under cover of night, the men commenced to dig in, but at midnight the two company commanders conferred and decided to pull back to the line of departure. Their wounded were uncared for, their ammunition, water, and rations were low, and they were out of radio contact with battalion.

The march back was full of horrors. Flares lighted the valley about every five minutes, silhouetting the retreating troops and occasionally revealing foxholes full of Japanese—who luckily did not fire. Many of the wounded fainted and had to be carried by their comrades; some of them died en route. Finally, about 0300, both companies straggled into tree line at the south edge of the valley that had marked their line of departure of the morning before.[34] Once again the attempt to force Death Valley from the south had failed.

---

[29] 27th Inf Div G-3 Jnl, 25 Jun 44, Msg 69; 2d Bn 106th RCT Jnl, 25 Jun 44, Msg 161.

[30] 27th Div Arty Unit Rpt 9, 25 Jun 44, Incl to 27th Inf Div G-3 Jnl, 25 Jun 44.

[31] 106th RCT Jnl, 25 Jun 44, Msg 394.

[32] Appleman, Army Tanks in the Battle for Saipan, pp. 47–48.

[33] 27th Inf Div G-3 Jnl, 25 Jun 44, Msg 84.

[34] This account is derived from Love, Battle for Saipan, pages 353–65.

Kagman Peninsula Secured

In the zone of the 4th Marine Division the major accomplishment of the day was the final occupation of the whole of Kagman Peninsula. This served not only to reduce the corps front by about 3,000 yards, but also to clear the way for the construction of an auxiliary airfield on Kagman Plain.

The division jump-off, which was scheduled at 0730, was from forty minutes to an hour late, but thereafter the advance was rapid. The 24th Marines on the right met little or no enemy resistance and by 1015 had secured Kagman Hill on the southeastern extremity of the peninsula. The rest of the day was spent patrolling the area and investigating caves along the coast. On the left, the 23d Marines ran into occasional sniper fire and was harassed by an enemy field piece located on Purple Heart Ridge but nevertheless managed to reach the O–6 line on the east coast by 1533. Thus Kagman Peninsula was completely blanketed and sealed off, and the 4th Marine Division for the first time in four days was permitted to relax.[35]

Seizure of Mount Tapotchau

Honors for the capture of the summit of Tapotchau, the highest point of the island, were shared by the 2d Battalion, 8th Marines, and the 1st Battalion, 29th Marines.[36] The 2d Battalion, 8th Marines,

---

[35] 4th Marine Div Opns Rpt Saipan, Annex H, 23d RCT Rpt, pp. 41–42; Annex I, 24th RCT Rpt, p. 21.

[36] The following account of the actions of the 2d Marine Division is derived from: 2d Marine Div SAR, Phase I, FORAGER, Sec. VI, p. 14; and Hoffman, *Saipan*, pp. 151–55.

pushed off at 0730 and advanced rapidly against little resistance along the cliff line overlooking Death Valley until it found itself, three hours later, at the base of a sheer 50-foot cliff, just beyond which was the peak of the mountain itself. Patrols scaled the cliff, worked their way almost to the crest of the mountain, and returned shortly after noon with the information that the small plateau that constituted the summit of Tapotchau was unoccupied. On receiving this information, the 1st Battalion of the 29th Marines, on the left, gradually worked its way to the right along the route that had been followed by the patrols and by late afternoon had established itself on the mountain top. During the operation enemy fire was not severe, but that night a force of Japanese counterattacked and had to be repulsed. Eighteen enemy dead were counted the next morning. During this period Company F, 106th Infantry, moved forward with the 2d Battalion, 8th Marines, guarding its right rear flank.

On the western slopes of Tapotchau the other two battalions of the 8th Marines made little progress against the multitude of machine gun nests in the network of crevices and ravines that crisscrossed that side of the mountain. The heaviest fighting occurred on the right flank of the 6th Marines, where for the third successive day the attack was held up by the Japanese strongpoint north of Mount Tipo Pale.

On the left of the 6th Marines' zone the lines had been extended as far as was feasible, and no further advance was possible until the difficulty on the right had been cleared up. On the western coast and on the high ground overlooking Garapan the 2d Marines, too, remained immobile, waiting for the elements on its right to come abreast.

In terms of yardage gained the 2d Marine Division had made little progress on 25 June, but the capture of Tapotchau's peak yielded it control of Saipan's key terrain feature. In the words of the official Marine Corps historian, "From this point forward, the Marines would look down on the Japanese, who heretofore had enjoyed the advantages of superior ground observation. In addition the Marines could now fight downhill for a while. The change would be appreciated." [37]

The Plight of the Japanese

By the end of 25 June it was obvious to the Japanese high command on Saipan that the situation was desperate almost (but not quite) to the point of hopelessness. A telegram from *31st Army* headquarters to the *29th Division* on Guam stated that the ten-day battle had reduced the strength of the line forces to the following approximate levels: [38]

Unit	Approximate Strength
118th Infantry Regiment	300
135th Infantry Regiment (exclusive of the *1st Battalion,* which was on Tinian)	350
136th Infantry Regiment	300
47th Independent Mixed Brigade	100
7th Independent Engineers	70
3d Independent Mountain Artillery Regiment	(no weapons in firing condition)
9th Tank Regiment	3 tanks

In addition to the losses, the message added, "reserve units (companies and platoons), hospital units, equipment, maintenance and supply units, etc. are either completely wiped out or reduced to the point where no fighting strength can be expected of them."

With the failure of the defense effort along the line south of Tapotchau the Japanese, in spite of occasional lapses of wishful thinking, realized full well that the island could not be held. In a lengthy telegram, probably of 25 June, *31st Army* headquarters said as much and analyzed some of the reasons for its failure:

The fight on Saipan as things stand now is progressing one-sidedly since, along with the tremendous power of his barrages, the enemy holds control of sea and air. In daytime even the deployment of units is very difficult, and at night the enemy can make out our movements with ease by using illumination shells. Moreover, our communications are becoming disrupted, and liaison is becoming increasingly difficult. Due to our serious lack of weapons and equipment, activity and control is hindered considerably. Moreover, we are menaced by brazenly low-flying planes, and the enemy blasts at us from all sides with fierce naval and artillery cross-fire. As a result even if we remove units from the front lines and send them to the rear their fighting strength is cut down every day. Also the enemy attacks with fierce concentration of bombs and artillery. Step by step he comes toward us and concentrates his fire on us as we withdraw, so that wherever we go we're quickly surrounded by fire. [39]

Continuing, the message noted two difficulties peculiar to the Saipan campaign. The first was the confusion caused by the presence on the island of so many straggler units, the waifs cast up by American submarine attacks. The second was the ever-growing shortage of water. There had been little enough at the beginning of the campaign, and the American bombardment had closed many of the sources of supply.

The prospect was dim: "The attack of the enemy proceeds ceaselessly day and

---

[37] Hoffman, *Saipan,* p. 153.
[38] *31st Army* Msg File, Msg 1102.
[39] *Ibid.,* Msg 1101.

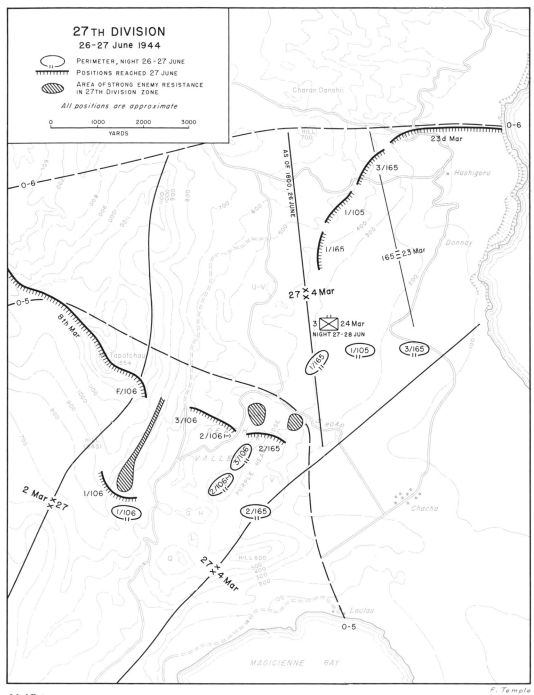

27TH DIVISION
26-27 June 1944

⬭ PERIMETER, NIGHT 26-27 JUNE
⊤⊤⊤⊤⊤⊤ POSITIONS REACHED 27 JUNE
▨ AREA OF STRONG ENEMY RESISTANCE
IN 27TH DIVISION ZONE

All positions are approximate

0   1000   2000   3000
YARDS

Charan Danshii

HILL 700

O-6

23d Mar

3/165

Hashigoru

1/105

O-6

1/165

165 ⊨ 23 Mar

Donnay

U-V

27 ×× 4 Mar
××

O-5

8th Mar

3 ⊠ 24 Mar
NIGHT 27-28 JUN

Tapotchau
1554

1/165

1/105

3/165

F/106

3/106

2/106 (-)

2/165

HILL
(843)

3/106

VALLEY

2/106(-)

1/106

PURPLE HEART RIDGE

Chacha

2 Mar × 27
×

1/106

G H

V

2/165

Q

L

27 × 4 Mar
×

HILL 600
500
400
300
200

100

Laulau

O-5

F. Temple

MAP 9

MAGICIENNE BAY

night and as they advance with the aid of terrific bombardments it becomes apparent that the northern part of the island for the above mentioned reasons of (1) water, (2) food, (3) supply, and (4) terrain, cannot be held with our skeleton strength of 520."

Yet in spite of the admitted futility of resistance, resistance continued. Surrender, the only practical thing to do in such a situation by Western standards, was out of the question for the Japanese. The order of the day read, ". . . the positions are to be defended to the bitter end, and unless he has other orders every soldier must stand his ground." [40]

Grasping at straws, General Saito on 24 June had ordered an infantry company from Tinian to conduct a landing operation on the coast of Saipan, east of Chacha.[41] On the night of 25 June eleven barges departed Sunharon (Tinian) harbor for Saipan. The destroyer *Bancroft* intercepted and dispersed them. One of the barges was reported sunk; the rest scurried back to Tinian Town. Still later, in the early morning hours of 26 June, several troop-laden barges came out of Tanapag Harbor, destination unknown. Two LCI (G)'s on patrol opened fire, sank one of the barges, and damaged another.[42] Thus ended Saito's immediate prospects of aid from counterlandings.

26 June

Action of the 27th Division

With the failure of the 106th Infantry to accomplish its mission on the 25th, Gen-

eral Jarman proposed a new scheme of maneuver for that regiment on the 26th. His plan called for the 3d Battalion to push along the inside (western) slope of Purple Heart Ridge, build up a line there, and, if possible, push on to the regimental objective line at the north end of Death Valley. The 2d Battalion, after reorganizing, was to follow the 3d, then swing left across the valley and move on to the regimental objective. The 1st Battalion would be in regimental reserve. Later (at 0920) Colonel Ayers ordered the 1st Battalion to move out on the left of the valley and clean out Hell's Pocket, which was still infested with Japanese.[43] At the same time the 2d Battalion, 165th, was to continue the attack against Purple Heart Ridge from the southeast.[44] (*Map 9*)

The 3d Battalion, 106th, jumped off at 0600 in column of companies with Company L in the lead, followed by I, M, and K.[45] By 1020 the leading elements of Company L had reached the top of Hill Oboe without encountering significant resistance and had started down into the saddle between Oboe and Hill King to the north.[46] Company I followed immediately behind. As Company L advanced toward Hill King a machine gun opened up, and the heavy weapons company was called up to train its mortars and machine guns on the suspected source of fire. At 1245, under cover of this protection, Company L moved forward, but within ten minutes the lead platoon had six men killed and seventeen wounded.[47] The advance halted,

<hr />

[40] NTLF Rpt Marianas, Phase I, Incl D, G-2 Rpt, p. 104.
[41] *31st Army* Msg File, Msg 1093.
[42] TF 51 Opn Rpt Marianas, Incl A, p. 9.

[43] 106th RCT Jnl, 26 Jun 44, p. 70; 106th Inf Narrative Rpt FORAGER, p. 9.
[44] Unless otherwise noted, the account of the actions of the 27th Division on 26 June is derived from Love, Battle for Saipan, pages 375-96.
[45] 27th Inf Div G-3 Jnl, 26 Jun 44, Msg 6.
[46] 3d Bn 106th RCT Jnl, 26 Jun 44, Msg 16.
[47] 27th Inf Div G-3 Jnl, 26 Jun 44, Msg 44.

BAZOOKA TEAM PREPARING TO FIRE *a 2.36-inch rocket launcher during mopping-up operations along the ridge line.*

then the company was withdrawn. By the time Captain Hallden had worked his way back to Hill Oboe and reorganized his company, it was in a highly demoralized condition. The 1st Platoon was down to twelve men, as was the 2d Platoon, which had been hard hit during the explosion of the enemy ammunition dump on 23 June. Company I was sent in to relieve Company L. It enjoyed no more success than its predecessor and retired to Hill Oboe to dig in with the battalion for the night.

The 2d Battalion, 106th, had stayed behind the 3d during the day and made no effort to work its way out into the valley. It dug in on Hill Xray-Yoke for the night.

While the 106th Infantry was moving along the inside of Purple Heart Ridge, the 2d Battalion, 165th, had begun to mop up on the outside (east) of the ridge line. Major Brusseau had ordered Company G to fan out and clean up Hills Xray-Yoke, Oboe, and Victor. Upon completion of this mission Company G was to move on north to Hill Able. Meanwhile, Company E was to push patrols to the base of Hill Victor and then proceed up S Road to the point where it cut into Death Valley.[48]

The 1st Platoon, Company G, took over Hill Xray-Yoke without opposition. By 0840 Captain Chasmar's 3d Platoon was atop Hill Victor without much trouble, but thereafter the Japanese began to show some fight. The enemy had taken refuge

[48] Love, Battle for Saipan, p. 379.

in ledges and caves just below the crest of the hill and from there commenced lobbing hand grenades up into the line of the Americans on top. Some thought was given to getting at these positions by tying charges onto ropes and letting them swing down into the protected strongpoints, but rather than attempt this device, Chasmar withdrew the lead platoon to the ground below and called up self-propelled mounts (M7's) to fire into the ledges where the enemy was entrenched. The M7's failed to accomplish the mission and had to retreat when the Japanese began dropping mortar shells on them. Three tanks were then brought forward, but to no avail. As a last resort Captain Chasmar sent up some M8 self-propelled mounts. These vehicles were equipped with 75-mm. rather than 105-mm. howitzers and had smaller openings at the top, thus offering better protection to the gunners from fire from above. For half an hour the M8's plugged away at the sides of the cliffs, forcing many of the enemy into the open where they could be picked off by riflemen.

At 1500 the 3d Platoon ventured to the top of the hill again, followed an hour later by the 2d Platoon. Machine gun fire from the west along the main line of Purple Heart Ridge held down their advance however, and since darkness was approaching they were recalled down the hill to dig in for the night.[49]

Meanwhile, E Company had worked its way under scattered fire up S Road, along the route taken the day before by the 1st Battalion, 106th Infantry. It had reached the point of the previous day's farthest advance and had begun to dig in when the Japanese on the hills to the left opened

with machine guns and mortars. Inasmuch as the company was in an isolated position almost a thousand yards from the rest of the battalion, the new commander, 1st Lt. John J. Raleigh, took his men back to join the rest of the battalion for the night.[50]

Purple Heart Ridge was beginning to crack under the combined assault of the 2d Battalion, 165th, and the 3d Battalion, 106th Infantry. Meanwhile, on the other side of Death Valley, Colonel Cornett's 1st Battalion, 106th, was vainly trying to clear out Hell's Pocket. The battalion moved off at 1245 following a thirty-minute preparation by the Cannon Company but was quickly pinned down by fire from the pocket.[51] Company C alone lost three men killed, and twenty-two wounded including Capt. Robert T. Bates, the company commander, who was replaced by 1st Lt. Andrew B. Campbell. Within the next hour the 104th Field Artillery put 360 rounds of 105-mm. howitzer fire into the pocket. It was to no avail. The battalion still encountered heavy fire from the walls of the pocket and from the high rock in the center, so Cornett retired his men to the line of departure where they dug in for the night.[52]

Sometime after ten o'clock on the morning of 26 June General Kernan, division artillery commander, in company with Colonel Sheldon, the operations officer, made a trip up to the southern edge of Death Valley. There they found that the 2d Battalion had made no advance out of the assembly area, where it was mingled with the rear elements of the 3d Battalion.

[49] *Ibid.,* pp. 388–91.

[50] *Ibid.,* p. 392.

[51] 27th Inf Div G-3 Jnl, 26 Jun 44, Msgs 39, 51, 53.

[52] Love, Battle for Saipan, pp. 393–94.

They reported that "the battalions were standing still and there was no reason why they should not move forward." The 106th Infantry, they concluded, was in a demoralized state. On the basis of this report, which confirmed his previous dissatisfaction with this regiment's conduct, General Jarman relieved Colonel Ayers of his command and assigned Colonel Stebbins, the division chief of staff, as commander.[53]

Action of the Marines

Having completed its occupation of Kagman Peninsula, the 4th Marine Division was ordered on the 26th to mop up the area, outpost the coast line of Magicienne Bay, and then assemble in the vicinity of the beaches along the northern coast of the bay in corps reserve. The marines encountered no enemy opposition except from small groups of snipers in the vicinity of Chacha and in the caves along the coast, although Japanese artillery occasionally opened up from the unsecured portions of Purple Heart Ridge. Before the division could properly assemble in corps reserve plans were changed, and it was ordered to take over the right of the line again next morning.[54]

In the zone of the 2d Marine Division the most important event of the day was the bypassing of the pocket north of Mount Tipo Pale by the 2d Battalion, 6th Marines. One company passed to the right, another to the left, while the third was left behind to reduce the pocket.

The 8th Marines registered only small gains in the Mount Tapotchau area. In the regimental center the 3d Battalion, 8th Marines, and the 1st Battalion, 29th Marines, moved forward slowly through nightmarish terrain, receiving heavy mortar and machine gun fire as they went. The 2d Battalion, 8th Marines, and Company F, 106th Infantry, remained stationary on the right flank, holding back to deny enemy approaches from that direction. No great yardage was gained in this area, but the positions on the heights of Tapotchau were consolidated and the regimental line was straightened out. On the division left the 2d Marines again remained immobile except for patrols, who reported that there was no Japanese activity to the immediate front.[55]

27 June

Death Valley Broached

The first permanent inroads into Death Valley were made on 27 June. Up to that date the only significant progress in the zone of the 27th Division had been in the hills that made up the lower part of Purple Heart Ridge. Death Valley itself had defied capture; the Japanese from their commanding positions in the cliffs on the left and the northern part of Purple Heart Ridge on the right were able to interdict any movement along the floor of the valley itself.

General Jarman's plan for 27 June called for a reorientation of the direction of the attack. For this purpose he had four battalions under his control—all of the 106th Infantry plus the 2d Battalion, 165th, which had been detached from its parent regiment the night before when the 165th

[53] Jarman, Memo for Record, 24 Jun 44, Buckner Board Rpt, Exhibit J; 27th Inf Div Special Order 118, 26 Jun 44, Incl to 27th Inf Div G-3 Jnl.
[54] 4th Marine Div Opns Rpt Saipan, p. 27.

[55] 2d Marine Div SAR, Phase I, FORAGER, Sec. VI, p. 15.

Regiment was attached to the 4th Marine Division.[56] The 2d Battalion, 165th, was ordered to continue mopping-up operations against Purple Heart Ridge, working from the eastern slopes. Meanwhile, the 3d Battalion, 106th, was to move north along the ridge until it reached Hill King, then pivot left and attack west across the valley toward Mount Tapotchau. Once a corridor had been driven across the valley, the battalion was to pivot again, this time to the right, and move off toward the northern end of the valley. Before this drive was completed the 2d Battalion, 106th, was to take positions on the right flank of the 3d. In the meantime the 1st Battalion, 106th, in an independent movement, would renew its attempt to clean out Hell's Pocket.[57]

The 3d Battalion, 106th, jumped off for Hill King at 0620, with Company I on the right, K on the left.[58] Almost immediately machine gun fire opened up, killing one man and wounding seven, and the battalion was ordered back to Hill Oboe, which had been the line of departure. Division then ordered twenty-five-minute artillery preparation, to commence at 1020, but the position of the American troops on Purple Heart Ridge was so hard to ascertain that the artillerymen held fire for more than half an hour.[59]

Following the artillery preparation, which was completed by 1120, the attack

moved off again with Company L on the left in place of Company K, whose strength was now down to about that of one platoon. This time there was no opposition. The battalion moved up Hill King through a litter of enemy dead, and not a shot was fired. As Company I moved over the crest of the hill and down its northern slope, it surprised a large party of Japanese hiding among the rocks and grass. After a brief exchange of rifle fire and hand grenades, the Americans withdrew to the reverse slope and mortar fire was requested. This lasted only a few minutes, after which the attackers were able to push down the north slope of the hill without trouble.

With Hill King secured, the 3d Battalion, 106th Infantry, could now push off to the west across Death Valley according to plan. The attack jumped off at 1150, Company L on the left and I on the right.[60] The terrain to the battalion front was a steep slope down into the valley proper. The descent would be made through thick, high tufts of grass for most of the way, and then through cane fields into a low ridge line that cut across the valley at that juncture. Directly to the battalion front, about a thousand yards away, were the cliffs of Mount Tapotchau.

Immediately upon reaching the floor of the valley, the men of the 3d Battalion began to receive machine gun and mortar fire from Hill Able behind them and from the cliff sides of Tapotchau to their front. Among others wounded was 1st Lt. Robert M. Smith, who had taken command of Company I only that morning. This left the company without officers except for one platoon commander, whose unit had become separated from the rest of the

---

[56] 27th Inf Div Fld Msg 1(a), 26 Jun 44, Incl to 27th Inf Div G-3 Jnl.

[57] Love, Battle for Saipan, pp. 400-401, 403, 428.

[58] 27th Inf Div G-3 Jnl, 27 Jun 44, Msg 24. Unless otherwise noted, the account of the action of the 3d Battalion, 106th Infantry, is derived from Love, Battle for Saipan, pages 401-03, 406-15.

[59] 27th Inf Div G-3 Jnl, 27 Jun 44, Msgs 33, 39.

[60] 106th RCT Jnl, 27 Jun 44, Msg 545.

company. In the hiatus thus created, Captain Hallden of Company L incorporated the scattered remnants of I Company with his own unit and took command of both.

Meanwhile, Company K had been ordered into the line on L Company's left, with the mission of securing the tree line that ran across the valley at this point and of establishing physical contact with Company F, 106th Infantry, which was still on the cliff top just below the summit of Mount Tapotchau. No sooner was Company K abreast of L Company than it, too, came under heavy fire that by now was general throughout the valley floor.

Nevertheless, the 3d Battalion succeeded in cutting across the valley and was sending out patrols to establish contact with Company F on the cliff in front by 1545.[61] By this time all three companies were badly in need of ammunition. They had no supplies of water or rations, and parts of each company had been cut off from the main body of the battalion. Colonel Mizony placed Captain Hallden in charge of the remnants of all three companies and dispatched a platoon of light tanks, not only to lay fire on both sides of the valley but to supply the infantry with rations, water, and ammunition.[62] The tanks accomplished their mission before dark, and the 3d Battalion dug in along the low ridge line that traversed Death Valley west of Hill Able. There it was joined by the 2d Battalion, which had come up behind, and the two battalions prepared to attack to the north the next morning.

Meanwhile at 1120, following a delayed artillery preparation, Company G, 165th Infantry, pushed up the eastern slope of Hill King, which 3d Battalion, 106th Infantry, was attacking from the other side.[63] Within three hours G Company had reached the summit of the hill and was driving down its forward slope toward Hill Able to the north. Hill Able was more an outsized rock than a hill. The south face toward which Captain Chasmar's company was moving was a sheer cliff about fifty feet high, crosscut by a series of ledges. The right (east) face of the hill was steeply terraced and the west side was another sheer cliff. The top was a rounded knob covered with dense undergrowth and was heavily defended, judging from the intense fire that began to pour down on the heads of the advancing troops.

About 1600, before it reached the foot of the hill, Company G was attacked by a party of Japanese moving down through the corridor between Hills King and Able. The enemy movement was undetected until the Japanese were within a few yards of Chasmar's positions. A severe hand-to-hand fight ensued, resulting in seven American casualties and thirty-five enemy killed. By this time it was too late to warrant a continuation of the attack against Hill Able, and G Company moved back to Hill King to dig in with the battalion for the night. Before the men could prepare their foxholes, however, a heavy barrage of mortar and machine gun fire fell on the area, killing five and wounding nineteen. Among the latter was Major Brusseau, the 2d Battalion commander,

[61] 27th Inf Div G-3 Jnl, 27 Jun 44, Msg 71.
[62] Appleman, Army Tanks in the Battle for Saipan, pp. 51-53.

[63] 27th Inf Div G-3 Jnl, 27 Jun 44, Msg 39; Love, Battle for Saipan, pp. 419-27. Unless otherwise noted, this account of the actions of the 2d Battalion, 165th Infantry, is derived from the latter source.

who later died of his wounds. He was replaced by Capt. James A. Dooley,[64] who was in turn later relieved by Major Claire. Claire's command of the 3d Battalion, 165th, was taken over by his executive officer, Maj. Martin Foery. At the conclusion of the fire G Company, 165th Infantry, withdrew past Hill Oboe and back to Hill Xray-Yoke for the night, where it was joined by Company E. The latter had spent the day unsuccessfully trying to move up S Road to the point where it entered Death Valley. Scattered rifle fire, coupled with heavy mortar and machine gun fire from a hill that commanded the road, had thwarted the effort to break into Death Valley by this route.

During the afternoon General Jarman had still been skeptical of the staying power of the 106th Infantry and had instructed the executive officer of that regiment to get word to all units that "they" must hold and under no case fall back." [65] Now, with the drive across Death Valley successfully completed, Jarman was relieved and gratified. To the commanders of the 2d and 3d Battalions he dispatched the message: "Congratulations on a day's work well done. I have the utmost confidence in our continued success in a vigorous push against the remaining enemy. Keep up the good work." [66]

In the meantime, the 1st Battalion, 106th Infantry, was taking the first effective step of the campaign toward mopping up Hell's Pocket at the southwest end of the valley. To accomplish this mission, Colonel Cornett planned to use Company C to contain the Japanese at the mouth of the pocket while the other two rifle companies climbed the cliff to the left in order to approach the enemy's positions from above and the rear.[67]

Company A took the lead in the enveloping movement, slowly groped its way to the top of the cliff, and commenced circling the rim around Hell's Pocket. Soon the lead platoon stumbled upon a deep crater, almost fifty yards wide, that turned out to be a nest of live and very active Japanese. Grenades and rifle fire failed to silence the position. Mortars were then dragged up the cliff to accomplish the job, after which the infantrymen moved on through and past the crater. Twenty dead Japanese were found in the area, as well as two machine guns and three fully operative American Browning automatic rifles.[68] Company B, meanwhile, was held up behind A Company until the latter had cleaned out the crater. During this wait the battalion executive officer, Maj. John Nichols, who was in charge of the cliff-top operation, came forward and relieved 1st Lt. Frank J. Pryor of command of the company replacing him with 1st Lt. Charles Warge. The new company commander immediately began to deploy his unit to the left, and by the time the crater was cleaned out he was abreast of Company A. Both companies then formed a skirmish line and moved forward another hundred yards north along the edge of the pocket without flushing any more Japanese. There, Major Nichols ordered the advance halted and both companies pulled 500 yards to the left of the cliff line where they dug in for the night.

---

[64] 27th Inf Div G–3 Jnl, 27 Jun 44, Msg 107.
[65] Ibid., Msg 87.
[66] 106th RCT Opns Rpt FORAGER, p. 11.

[67] Ibid. Unless otherwise noted, the account of the action of 1st Battalion, 106th Infantry, is derived from Love, Battle for Saipan, pages 428–34.
[68] 106th RCT Opns Rpt FORAGER, p. 11.

Action on the Flanks

On the right flank of the three-division front, the 4th Marine Division was ordered to continue northward and seize all of the O–6 line within its zone.[69] For this operation the division had under its control a total of nine battalions—the 23d and 24th Marines and the 165th Infantry (less 2d Battalion) with the 1st Battalion, 105th Infantry, attached.

On the right, the 23d Marines made rapid progress against only occasional small arms fire from the villages of Hashigoru and Donnay and by 1640 had reached its objective. The advance would have been even more rapid but for dense underbrush and the ragged cliff line along the coast that called for cautious movement and thorough investigation.[70]

On the left of the 23d Marines, the 165th Infantry jumped off at 0730 on schedule with the 3d Battalion on the right, in direct contact with the left flank of the 23d Marines, and the 1st Battalion, 105th Infantry, on the left, followed about 600 yards to the rear by the 1st Battalion, 165th.[71] The advance was rapid, especially on the right flank where the 3d Battalion, 165th, met little resistance. Toward late afternoon the 1st Battalion, 105th, encountered some heavy enemy fire from positions along the road that ran west of the village of Hashigoru. Colonel Kelley ordered the battalion commander to bypass the positions, which he did.

Meanwhile the 1st Battalion, 165th, which was moving up on the left rear flank of the regimental line, had lost all contact with the 2d Battalion, 165th, which was still held up among the hills of Purple Heart Ridge. On Colonel Kelley's recommendation the 3d Battalion, 24th Marines, was brought up and committed to fill the gap. Action in the regimental zone was broken off about 1700, and all three battalions of the 165th Infantry dug in for the night in positions that bent back on the left to retain contact with the 106th Infantry.

The 2d Marine Division's advance on the 27th was much slower than that of its sister division because of continued terrain difficulties around Tapotchau and heavy Japanese resistance in the center. During the morning the marines completed the occupation of the entire main crest of Mount Tapotchau and started down its northern slope.[72] In the division center the lines had been tightened sufficiently by noon to permit one badly battered battalion of the 6th Marines to be pinched out and retired to reserve status. Later that afternoon the battalion on the 6th Marines' right ran into heavy resistance from the ridge line north of Tipo Pale and was stopped in its tracks, causing the remainder of the regiment to hold back too, although the opposition on the regimental left had been comparatively light. On the extreme left flank the 2d Marines was again compelled to stand still on the outskirts of Garapan until the rest of the division pulled abreast. It spent the day consolidating its positions and sending out patrols.

---

[69] NTLF Opn Order 14–44, 26 Jun 44.

[70] 4th Marine Div Opns Rpt Saipan, Annex H, 23d Marines Rpt, p. 44.

[71] 165th RCT Jnl, 27 Jun 44, Msg 29; 165th RCT Rpt of Action Saipan, p. 6. Unless otherwise noted, this account of the action of the 165th Infantry is derived from the latter source.

---

[72] 2d Marine Div SAR, Phase I, FORAGER, Sec. VI, p. 16; Hoffman, *Saipan*, pp. 171–73.

Japanese Reactions

June 27th marked another turning point for the Japanese in their stubborn, futile battle to save Saipan from the invaders. On that day General Saito established a final line of resistance where a last stand would be made. This was the third such battle line to be laid down. The first had been the shore line; the second, the mid-island defense line; and now a third was to be held across the island from Tanapag on the west coast, through Hill 221 (meters) and Tarahoho to the east coast, cutting across the base of the island's northern tip. (See Map I.)

The withdrawal was to be gradual. What remained of the mid-island defense line would be held until the new line could be established. This policy of conducting a delaying action until a new line could be built up was explained by *31st Army* headquarters to Tokyo: "The Defense Force, along with the firmest possible defense of its present defense line and its activities toward annihilation of the enemy, is at present setting up with a line between Tanapag–Hill 221–Tarahoho as the final line of resistance." [73]

General Saito still clung to the small hope that a renewed Japanese air attack might alter the situation and save Saipan and the Marianas for the Empire. In a telegram to the assistant chief of staff in Tokyo, to the Minister of War, and to the *29th Division* on Guam, he painted a gloomy picture of the future of Japanese forces on Saipan, but closed with a hopeful reference to the Marpi Point airfield, which was still in his hands:

The pressing need of the moment is that the mistake be not made of allowing this important experience in the defense of Saipan to be put to no practical end, and, the soldiers here be robbed of the fruits of victory after having fought so bravely. . . . Especially, the Banadero [Marpi Point] airport has not been completed, but in case the necessity arises, it can be used, and the Saipan defense forces trust that they can hold out until the first 10 days of the month [July], awaiting its completion. [74]

In another message to Guam, the Japanese general made a more specific plea for air reinforcements to be sent to Tinian:

The attacking force of the enemy has the appearance of becoming less intense from now on. Even though the Banadero airport has not yet been completed, we are endeavoring to finish it, so that it may be an air base in the Marianas which we can use. However, for the present it is an impossibility.

Because the enemy planes which have appeared in the air are only carrier borne bombers and recco planes, the situation is such that our large fighter formations could seize good opportunity for daylight sinking of enemy destroyers, etc.

However as the fate of the Empire will be decided in this one section, we trust that you will decide to send fighters to Tinian. [75]

28 June

Action of the 27th Division

The key to the battle in the zone of the 27th Division on 28 June was the fight for Hill Able, the northernmost promontory of Purple Heart Ridge, and the failure of the 2d Battalion, 165th Infantry, to capture this hill brought progress through Death Valley to a standstill once more. After the heavy pounding that had been taken by G Company on the preceding night, the whole battalion had pulled back from Hill King, past Hill Oboe, and had dug in atop

<hr>

[73] *31st Army* Msg File, Msg 1120.

[74] *Ibid.*, Msg 1121.
[75] *Ibid.*, Msg 1122.

Hill Xray-Yoke in almost the same place where it had spent the previous two nights. On learning of this, General Jarman expressly ordered, "No [future] withdrawal will be made for the night for the purpose of consolidation." [76]

Major Claire had been transferred the night before from the 3d Battalion, 165th, to take over command of the 2d Battalion after Major Brusseau had been mortally wounded. Claire's plan for the 28th called for G Company again to make the assault along the ridge. F Company was to circle the low ground on the east side and come up between Hills King and Able. Company E was to be maintained as battalion reserve.[77] (*Map 10*)

Company G jumped off promptly at 0630 and pushed rapidly over Hill Oboe. On reaching Hill King the men discovered that the enemy had either reoccupied the hill during the night or had remained well concealed from the American troops who had "captured" it the previous day. At any rate, the Japanese suddenly came to life with machine guns and rifles and the advance of Company G was stopped. Around noon, self-propelled mounts were brought forward and after an hour's fire from these vehicles enemy fire ceased. Company G moved forward again and encountered no trouble until the men went over the crest of the hill. There, the whole line was greeted by a shower of grenades and machine gun fire from the east slope, which had not been touched by the self-propelled mounts.

For half an hour there was a furious fire fight, but the Americans did not advance. At 1330 Captain Chasmar called battalion headquarters to report his casualties, which numbered about twenty.[78] He was ordered to pull back to Hill Oboe until mortar fire could be brought to bear upon the enemy line. At Oboe he stopped to reorganize, but enemy mortar shells falling into his lines caused complete confusion. Major Claire ordered one platoon of Company E to move up and take over Hill Oboe. Company G was withdrawn to Hill Xray-Yoke, where it dug in in the bivouac area of the night before. There it was joined by Company F, which had met with no more success in trying to assault Hill King from the east.

The setback suffered by the 2d Battalion, 165th Infantry, on the 28th was to govern, retard, and finally frustrate the effort of the 2d and 3d Battalions of the 106th to break out of Death Valley. So long as the Japanese held Hill Able they could interdict the entire northern half of the valley and pour devastating fire on any troop movements through the area.

The attack order of the two battalions of the 106th Infantry called for them to jump off at 0630 on 28 June, following a fifteen-minute artillery preparation, and to capture the O-6 line, which lay about 3,000 yards to the north.[79] Between them and their objective lay a series of low ridge lines, the first one of which crossed the valley about 400 yards to their front.

The advance moved off on schedule with the 2d Battalion on the right and the 3d on the left, and by 0930 the men had reached

---

[76] 27th Inf Div FO 51, 27 Jun 44, Incl to 27th Inf Div G-3 Jnl, 27 Jun 44.

[77] Unless otherwise noted, the account of the action of the 2d Battalion, 165th Infantry, is derived from Love, Battle for Saipan, pages 456-63.

---

[78] 2d Bn 165th RCT Jnl, 28 Jun 44, Msg 30.

[79] 27th Inf Div FO 51, 27 Jun 44, and 106th Inf FO 10, 27 Jun 44, Incls to 27th Inf Div G-3 Jnl, 28 Jun 44.

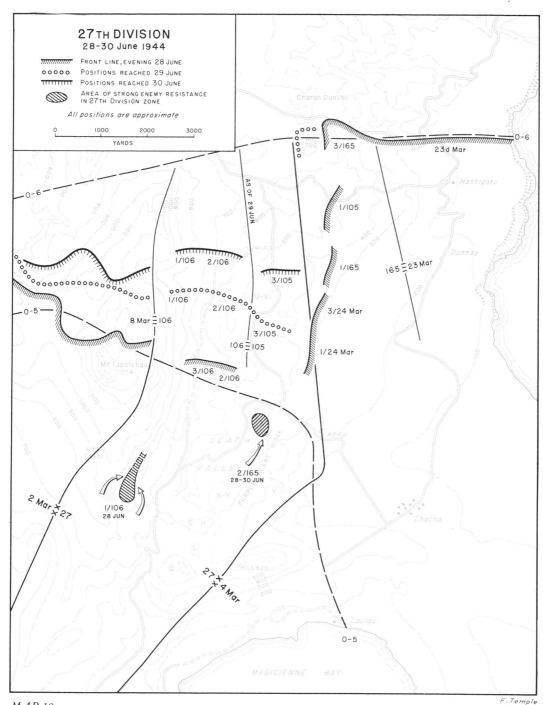

Charan Danshii

3/165
23d Mar
0-6

Hashigaru

1/105

0-6

1/165

Donnay

1/106 2/106

3/105

165 ≡ 23 Mar

1/106
2/106

3/24 Mar

0-5

8 Mar ≡ 106

3/105

106 ≡ 105

1/24 Mar

Mt Tapotchau

3/106 2/106

DEATH

ROAD

2/165
28-30 JUN

2 Mar ✕ 27

1/106
28 JUN

Chacha

27 ✕ 4 Mar

HILL 600

Laulau

0-5

MAGICIENNE   BAY

MAP 10

F. Temple

the first ridge line.[80] There they were ordered to dig in to await supplies that were to be brought forward in self-propelled mounts. Almost as soon as the vehicles appeared and began to unload, the enemy, who had been more or less quiescent for over an hour, opened up from Hill Able with intense fire. The self-propelled mounts promptly dropped their supplies and scurried for cover,[81] and the infantry commanders had to send out carrying parties to pick up the supplies. The men who went back to recover the hastily jettisoned supplies were caught in heavy enemy mortar fire that was being directed at the Cannon Company vehicles. Within the space of a few minutes seven men were killed and twenty-two wounded, mostly from Companies I and K. Among those killed was 2d Lt. Robert J. Bonner, commander of Company I. He was the fourth commander to have led that unit in three days and his death left only one officer, 2d Lt. Spencer M. Pitts, in the company. The 3d Battalion was now virtually decimated. A count of heads revealed that there were only a hundred riflemen left in it as of 1010.[82]

Following this debacle, Company F, 106th Infantry, which previously had been ordered from Mount Tapotchau to join its parent regiment after serving for five days with the 2d Marine Division, moved down into the valley and took up positions in a small group of trees just behind Company E.[83] There the men

were soon joined by remnants from Companies I and K as well as by the headquarters of both the 2d and 3d Battalions, which by 1315 had displaced forward.

Suddenly, two Japanese tanks moved into view over the brow of a small hill just 200 yards north of the crowded grove. The lead tank opened up on the trees with machine guns and its 40-mm. turret gun. Enemy fire continued for ten minutes before a single American shot was fired in return. Casualties were frightful. In the 2d and 3d Battalions of the 106th Infantry, twelve were killed or mortally wounded, and sixty-one others were wounded. Among those killed were Colonel Mizony, commander of the 3d Battalion, 1st Lt. John T. McGregor, commanding officer of Company M, and Captain Tarrant of G Company. As the suddenness and intensity of the tank attack seemed to indicate a more general one, Major O'Hara, the senior officer present, ordered both battalions to dig in immediately. During the next hour a strong defensive position was constructed on the ridge, and artillery fire was directed on the whole area to the front. All plans for further forward movement during the day were abandoned, and the two battalions remained where they were for the night.

While this stalemate was developing in Death Valley proper, the 1st Battalion, 106th Infantry, was completing its task, started the day before, of eliminating enemy resistance in Hell's Pocket. Instead of holding at the south end of the area on the 28th, Company C moved straight across the mouth of the pocket, while Companies A and B mopped up along the cliffs above. Company A, which was given the job of skirting the cliff edge on the rim of the pocket, encountered the most difficulty.

---

[80] 27th Inf Div G-3 Jnl, 28 Jun 44, Msg 22. Unless otherwise noted, this account of the actions of the 2d and 3d Battalions, 106th Infantry, is derived from Love, Battle for Saipan, pages 440-56.
[81] 106th RCT Jnl, 28 Jun 44, Msg 621. In this message the supply vehicles are misnamed "tanks."
[82] 106th RCT Jnl, 28 Jun 44, Msg 609.
[83] Ibid., p. 99.

Enemy mortar and rifle fire harassed the men throughout the morning, causing several casualties. Major Nichols, the battalion executive officer, was mortally wounded. By midafternoon the Japanese guns that were molesting the area were cleared out with the aid of heavy machine guns and mortars. Meanwhile, Company C managed by late afternoon to push all the way across the pocket and move up the left edge of the valley before being called back to the southern entrance of the valley to bivouac with the rest of the battalion. By nightfall there were still a few Japanese soldiers holed up in Hell's Pocket, but all organized resistance there had finally been eliminated.

At 1030 on 28 June, command of the 27th Infantry Division passed from General Jarman to General Griner, who had formerly commanded the 98th Infantry Division in Hawaii.[84] He had received his orders as soon as word of General Ralph Smith's relief had reached the headquarters of General Richardson, Commanding General, United States Army Forces in the Central Pacific Area. General Jarman had taken over command of the division only on an interim basis since he had other previously assigned duties as island commander.

Among the problems facing General Griner was the disposition of the 3d Battalion, 106th Infantry, which in its present state could not be expected to continue on the front line. Accordingly, early in the evening of 28 June General Griner ordered the 1st Battalion, 106th Infantry, to relieve the 3d and establish contact with the 2d Marine Division on the left.[85] The 3d Battalion, 105th Infantry, which had seen

MAJ. GEN. GEORGE W. GRINER, *who assumed command of the 27th Infantry Division on Saipan, 28 June 1944.*

no action since its withdrawal from Nafutan Point was ordered into the right of the division line with the responsibility of seizing Hill Able. The 2d Battalion, 165th Infantry, which for the past three days had been attached to the 106th Infantry, was now attached to the 105th to assist it.[86] With these shifts in the line ordered, the new division commander prepared to complete the capture of Death Valley and Purple Heart Ridge.

Action on the Flanks

In view of the success of the 4th Marine Division in overrunning Kagman Peninsula and in securing most of the O–6 line in its

---

[84] 27th Inf Div G–3 Jnl, 28 Jun 44, Msg 32.
[85] 106th RCT Jnl, 28 Jun 44, p. 106.

[86] 27th Inf Div FO 52, 28 Jun 44, Incl to 27th Inf Div G–3 Jnl, 28 Jun 44.

zone of action, Holland Smith—on the 28th—ordered it to "hold present positions until further orders" and to assist the advance of the 27th Infantry Division by supporting fires from the east.[87] The 24th Marines and the 165th Infantry (less 2d Battalion), which was still attached to it, were ordered to establish one battalion apiece on the division boundary and support the 27th Division in its movement along Purple Heart Ridge and Death Valley.

On the extreme right, the 23d Marines held its positions on the O–6 line and continued to mop up the rear area and the caves that studded the coast line.[88] The 24th Marines remained in division reserve except for the 3d Battalion, which maintained its position on the boundary line between the 165th Infantry and the 27th Division. Late in the afternoon the 1st Battalion, 24th Marines, was brought up to fill the gap that still existed between the two divisions, but was unable to establish contact with the 27th Division on the left before dark.[89]

The only significant advance in the Kagman Peninsula area on the 28th was in the zone of the 165th Infantry. There the 3d Battalion, which was in position along the regimental boundary on the left flank of the 23d Marines, jumped off at 0630 and within an hour had progressed to the O–6 line, about 440 yards forward. From there it moved west toward Hill 700, a dominating terrain feature on the division boundary.[90] While consolidating positions

in that area, Capt. Joseph P. Stampher, commander of Company L, was wounded and was replaced by 1st Lt. George R. Weigand.[91]

Meanwhile, the 1st Battalion, 105th Infantry, was following to the left rear of the 3d Battalion, 165th. Moving along the tortuous mountain trails that lay in its zone, the battalion cleaned out the area that marked the boundary between the 4th Marine Division and the 27th Infantry Division.[92]

Earlier in the morning Colonel Kelley, commanding officer of the 165th Infantry, was struck by a fragment of a mortar shell and had to be evacuated. The regiment was turned over to Colonel Hart, its former executive officer, who commanded it for the rest of the operation.[93]

In the 2d Marine Division's zone, the movement toward the O–6 line was again slowed down by the broken terrain and by the Japanese, who were exploiting it to the utmost. In the zone of the 8th Marines on the division right the day's objective was a series of four small hills, nicknamed "the Pimples," across the front.[94] On the regimental right, the marines advanced with relatively little difficulty around the east cliffs of Mount Tapotchau before redeploying on the northern slope. About 1300 they came to a steep ravine that could be traversed only by a slow descent down a narrow crevice leading to the bottom. This took the remainder of the day. On the higher ground to the immediate

---

[87] 4th Marine Div Opns Rpt Saipan, p. 28.

[88] *Ibid.*, Annex H, 23d Marines Rpt, p. 44.

[89] *Ibid.*, Annex I, 24th Marines Rpt, p. 22.

[90] 165th RCT Jnl, 28 Jun 44, Msgs 8, 22; 4th Marine Div Opns Rpt Saipan, p. 128; 165th RCT Rpt of Action Saipan, p. 9.

[91] 165th RCT Jnl, 28 Jun 44, Msg 41.

[92] *Ibid.*, Msgs 33, 40; 165th RCT Unit Rpt 11, 28 Jun 44.

[93] 165th RCT Rpt of Action Saipan, p. 10.

[94] This account of the action of the 2d Marine Division is derived from: 2d Marine Div SAR, Phase I, FORAGER, Sec. VI, pp. 15–16; Hoffman, *Saipan*, pp. 174–75.

left, the marines made more rapid progress against moderate resistance and succeeded in pushing ahead of the units on either flank. Two battalions of the 8th Marines were held up throughout the day by mortar and heavy machine gun fire and at 1600, when the fighting was called off, were still short of the Pimples.

In the division center, the 6th Marines continued to slug away at the low ridge line north of Tipo Pale against heavy enemy opposition. Medium tanks and light flame throwers were brought forward in an effort to dislodge the Japanese, but it proved to be an infantry-engineer task since the tanks could not depress their weapons sufficiently to reach the fortified positions that lay between the regiment and the hills to the front. At the day's end the advance amounted only to 150 to 200 yards, although one company finally succeeded in wiping out the bypassed enemy pocket that had been occupying Tipo Pale for the past four days.

South of Garapan the 2d Marines again held in place, fearing a forward movement would force them to break contact with the units on its right. Close air support by American planes accounted for the only casualties on the 28th suffered by the marines in this area. In one air strike against Garapan, three misdirected rockets fell within the lines of the 1st Battalion, 2d Marines, causing twenty-seven casualties.

29 June

Action of the 27th Division

June 29th was a day of mixed blessings for the 27th Infantry Division. On the one hand, it was the first day since the beginning of the assault into Death Valley that the Army troops were able to make sufficient inroads to establish contact with the marines on at least one of their flanks. On the other hand, at the day's end, the tally showed another failure to seize Hill Able.

With the 3d Battalion, 106th Infantry, almost depleted, General Griner had decided to replace it with the 1st Battalion, 106th, which had heretofore been occupied with the task of cleaning out Hell's Pocket. Company C of the 1st Battalion was to guard the mouth of the pocket, but the rest of the battalion was ordered into the left of the division line with the specific admonition, "It is of utmost importance that you gain contact with the 8th Marines today before dark."[95]

The 2d Battalion, 106th Infantry, was already in position in the center of the line across Death Valley at the beginning of the day's fighting. The 3d Battalion, 105th Infantry, was ordered into the right to complete the cordon that, it was hoped, would squeeze the remaining life out of the enemy in the valley. To the right rear the 2d Battalion, 165th, now attached to the 105th Infantry, was ordered to finish capturing Purple Heart Ridge by overrunning Hill Able.

The two advance battalions of the 106th Infantry jumped off on schedule but were at first held up by fire from what appeared to be dug-in tanks and machine guns located along S Road north of Hill Able.[96] The 2d Battalion requested artillery fire but was denied it because the area in question was too close to the boundary line of the 2d Battalion, 165th Infantry, the

[95] 106th RCT Jnl, 29 Jun 44, Msg 679; 27th Inf Div FO 52, 28 Jun 44, Incl to 27th Inf Div G–3 Jnl, 28 Jun 44.
[96] 27th Inf Div G–3 Jnl, 29 Jun 44, Msgs 17, 27, 28, 34.

battalion that was supposed to be working up Hill Able from the south.[97]

To add to the delay, friendly artillery fire began to fall on the front lines of the 3d Battalion, 105th Infantry, and it had to reorganize before it could jump off.[98] Finally, Company K got lost and was involved in an extracurricular fire fight before reaching the right flank of the front line in Death Valley to which it was assigned.[99]

Company K had moved out of the battalion assembly area around 0700 and had skirted the inside (west) slope of Purple Heart Ridge until it reached Hill King. There, one of the guides furnished by the 106th Infantry informed Capt. Alexander C. Bouchard, the company commander, that Hill King was cleared and offered an easy route to the battalion line of departure. Unfortunately, Hill King had been lost to the enemy two days before and had not been recovered. As K Company began to climb to the top it came under severe enemy rifle fire, which was soon followed by an American artillery barrage designed to clear the hill of Japanese troops in advance of the attack of Company E, 165th Infantry, which was coming up from a different direction. Nineteen of Bouchard's men were immediately wounded, and the rest scattered. Company E then assaulted the hill and, with some help from K Company, cleared the remaining Japanese, most of them hidden in foxholes.[100] This eliminated Hill King as a source of trouble, but Company K had to stop and reorganize before advancing to its line of departure. Not until about 1300 was it able to take position on the right of Company I and close the line across Death Valley.[101]

Finally, about 1400, all three battalions —the 1st and 2d of the 106th, and the 3d of the 105th—jumped off in line abreast toward the northern end of Death Valley.[102] Within less than twenty minutes the 106th Infantry had advanced 400 yards; the 105th was only a little behind. By 1445 another 300 yards had been gained. By the end of the day the 106th had scored a total gain of 900–1,000 yards, while the 3d Battalion, 105th, had moved ahead about 600 yards.[103] By 1530 the men of 1st Battalion, 106th, had visual contact with the 2d Marine Division on the northern slopes of Mount Tapotchau on their left.[104]

At last the long-broken link was restored. At last General Holland Smith, corps commander, could find good words to say for the 27th Division. Viewing its progress through Death Valley on the 29th from the vantage point of Mount Tapotchau, he "expressly complimented" the division's performance to General Griner, its new commander.[105]

No such good fortune attended the efforts of the 2d Battalion, 165th Infantry, on the division right flank. After recapturing Hill King, Company E moved off at 1335 toward Hill Able.[106] A shower of hand grenades greeted the men who tried to scale the steep southern slope. Com-

[97] 106th RCT Jnl, 29 Jun 44, Msg 700.

[98] 27th Inf Div G–3 Jnl, 29 Jun 44, Msgs 12, 13; 105th RCT Jnl, 29 Jun 44, Msg 2.

[99] 105th RCT Jnl, 29 Jun 44, Msgs 5, 6.

[100] Love, Battle for Saipan, pp. 473–74.

[101] 105th RCT Jnl, 29 Jun 44, Msgs 13, 14; 105th RCT S–3 Dispatch Summary, 29 Jun 44, Incl to 27th Inf Div G–3 Jnl, 29 Jun 44.

[102] 27th Inf Div G–3 Jnl, 29 Jun 44, Msg 50; 105th RCT Jnl, 29 Jun 44, Msg 1410.

[103] 27th Inf Div G–3 Jnl, 29 Jun 44, Msg 50; 106th RCT Jnl, 29 Jun 44, Msgs 729, 733; 27th Inf Div G–3 Periodic Rpt 13.

[104] 27th Inf Div G–3 Jnl, 29 Jun 44, Msg 59.

[105] 27th Inf Div Fld Msg 2, 29 Jun 44, Incl to 27th Inf Div G–3 Jnl, 29 Jun 44.

[106] 105th RCT Jnl, 1335, 29 Jun 44.

TRUCK-MOUNTED ROCKET LAUNCHERS FIRING *at hills north of 8th Marines position on 29 June.*

pany E withdrew. Meanwhile, Company F on the right was making slow progress in a move to come up Hill Able from the east. Continuous mortar fire from the hill impeded its movement, and one shell wounded Lieutenant Trummel, the company commander. By late afternoon the company had worked its way into a position just east of Hill Able, but by that time the hour was too late to warrant an attack.[107]

Action on the Flanks

The 4th Marine Division again spent the day patrolling and consolidating its posi-

tions while waiting for the 27th Infantry to reach the O–6 line and establish contact on its left flank.[108] The 23d Marines sent out patrols as far as 1,200 yards to the front, capturing small groups of unarmed Japanese.[109] To the left rear of the division zone, elements of the 24th Marines received fairly heavy machine gun and mortar fire from enemy groups that had apparently filtered in to escape the pressure of the 27th Division.[110] The 3d Battalion, 165th Infantry, continued to improve its positions by consolidating on Hill 700 on the left flank of the division zone and on

---

[107] Love, Battle for Saipan, pp. 480–85.

[108] 4th Marine Div Opns Rpt Saipan, p. 29.
[109] *Ibid.,* Annex H, 23d Marines Rpt, p. 44.
[110] *Ibid.,* Annex I, 24th Marines Rpt, p. 22.

Charan Danshii ridge to the north. In so doing, the battalion fell under considerable artillery and mortar fire from enemy positions on its left front in the zone of the 27th Division. Around 1400 the fire reached such intensity that the battalion withdrew from Charan Danshii and dug in for the night on Hill 700.[111] Colonel Hart informed the Marine division headquarters that in order to hold Hill 700 he would have to move the 3d Battalion about 300 yards to the west, leaving about the same distance between his troops and the 23d Marines. To fill this gap, some eighty men of the 1st Battalion, 165th, were sent into the front lines, their own previous positions being taken over by elements of the 3d Battalion, 24th Marines.[112]

On the corps left the 2d Marine Division again made slow progress against rugged terrain and determined enemy resistance. On the division right the 8th Marines struggled through dense jungle until about noon, when it was stopped by heavy fire from the Pimples to the north. Two well-placed rocket concentrations were put on these hills with excellent coverage of the area, but before the regiment could move forward sufficiently to undertake its assault it was too late to justify an attack, and the hills remained uncaptured for another day.[113]

In the center, a readjustment of the lines of the 6th Marines took so long that the attack did not jump off until about noon and made little progress during the rest of the day. Once again, too, the 2d

Marines below Garapan were forced to wait for the rest of the division to come into line. Their day was not spent in idleness, however. A group of Japanese of about platoon size had dug in on a small hill some 500 yards ahead of the Marine lines in such a manner as to defy extermination by artillery or mortars. In order to entice the enemy out of his underground caves and passageways, the 2d Marines simulated an infantry attack on the morning of 29 June. Following a heavy artillery preparation, the marines opened with small arms and machine guns as though preparing for an assault, then ceased their machine gun fire but continued with small arms to heighten the illusion of an infantry attack. At this the Japanese emerged to man their machine guns and automatic weapons, whereupon they were immediately wiped out by American artillery and mortars. Thus, the way was cleared for a relatively easy entry into Garapan once the 2d Division's lines had been sufficiently straightened to justify the movement.

30 June

Death Valley: Capture and Breakthrough

The last day of June witnessed the end of the long and bitter struggle of the 27th Division to capture Death Valley and Purple Heart Ridge. As General Schmidt, USMC, later testified, "No one had any tougher job to do." [114] General Griner's orders for the day read that operations to reduce Hill Able would "be concluded" by the 2d Battalion, 165th Infantry.[115] The

[111] 165th RCT Unit Rpt 12, 29 Jun 44; 165th RCT Jnl, 29 Jun 44, Msgs 37, 39.

[112] 165th RCT Jnl, 29 Jun 44, Msgs 28, 29.

[113] This account of the action of the 2d Marine Division is from: 2d Marine Div SAR, Phase I, FORAGER, Sec. VI, p. 18; Hoffman, *Saipan*, pp. 182–83.

[114] Ltr, Gen Schmidt, USMC (Ret.), to Gen A. C. Smith, 10 Jan 55 (Incl), OCMH.

[115] 27th Inf Div Fld Msg 2, 29 Jun 44, Incl to 27th Inf Div G–3 Jnl.

orders were complied with. Jumping off at 0715, the battalion launched its attack, with Company F assaulting the hill from the east (right), G from the west. Company E remained back on Hill King to lend fire support.[116] Opposition was light and by 0940 the hill was reported secured. For the rest of the day the battalion dug in and consolidated its positions.[117]

Meanwhile, the troops in the valley below sustained the momentum of the previous day. Since Colonel Bradt's 3d Battalion, 105th Infantry, had lagged behind the 106th on the 29th, the main effort was to be in his zone, on the right of the division line.

Bradt's battalion, accompanied by nine tanks, jumped off promptly at 0715 following a fifteen-minute artillery preparation.[118] After about two hours of fairly easy going the battalion came under fire from Hill Uncle-Victor, located about 1,400 yards north of Hill Able. "It appears," reported Bradt, "to be another Hill Able." [119] Colonel Stebbins then proposed to place an artillery barrage in the area, but could not safely do so until the tanks that were operating at the foot of the hill withdrew, so the attack on the division right came to a temporary standstill. Around noon the artillery preparation was completed, and Colonel Bradt's troops moved up onto the troublesome hill and declared it secured.[120]

Meanwhile, at two points on the division boundary contact was at last established between the 27th Infantry Division and the 4th Marine Division. Soon after 1000 a patrol sent out from the 3d Battalion,

105th, made contact with a party of marines at a point about 600 yards northeast of Hill Able.[121] Two hours later a platoon of the 27th Reconnaissance Troop that had in the morning been fed into the right of the division line for that express purpose, established contact with the 1st Battalion, 24th Marines, just northeast of Hill Able.[122] At long last the 4th Marine Division was in a position to move forward without fear of exposure on its left flank.

In the center of the 27th Division's line, 106th's 2d Battalion made fairly steady progress throughout the day against light opposition, but on the left its 1st Battalion discovered to its sorrow that the cliffs of Mount Tapotchau were still not entirely cleared of the enemy. Mortar and machine gun fire sporadically harassed the battalion as it tried to keep pace with the rest of the division in its move to and through the northern end of Death Valley.

Late in the afternoon, 2d Lt. Ralph W. Hill of the 1st Platoon, Company B, located at least one of the positions in the cliffs that had been causing the battalion so much trouble. Taking two enlisted men with him, and against the advice of his company commander, he reconnoitered the cliff line and discovered a machine gun position on a tiny ledge about thirty feet up the side of the cliff. The party was soon detected by the Japanese. Hill was shot and then all three Americans were wounded by the explosion of a hand grenade. The two enlisted men retreated but came back later to find their platoon leader, undaunted by his serious wounds, still firing at the enemy position, which was forthwith silenced. Whether this action was decisive or not is unknown, but by the

---

[116] 27th Inf Div G-3 Jnl, 30 Jun 44, Msgs 7, 15.
[117] *Ibid.*, Msgs 21, 24.
[118] *Ibid.*, Msg 7.
[119] *Ibid.*, Msg 17.
[120] *Ibid.*, Msg 46.

[121] *Ibid.*, Msg 41.
[122] *Ibid.*, Msg 54.

next morning the cliff was clear of Japanese, and it was assumed that they had come down from the caves and withdrawn to the north during the night.[123]

All together, the advance of the 27th Division's line on 30 June was about 400 yards.[124] By the day's end, physical contact had been established on both the right and the left with the two Marine divisions.[125] Death Valley had been left behind.

Action on the Flanks

Once more the 4th Marine Division on Kagman Peninsula spent the day resting, patrolling, and consolidating its lines. Along the coast the 23d Marines pushed its patrols as deep as 800 yards north of the O-6 line but, aside from capturing a few civilians, made no contact with the enemy. With the advance of the 27th Division, the 1st Battalion, 24th Marines, which was the southernmost Marine unit disposed along the division boundary line, was pinched out. Throughout the day little enemy artillery and mortar fire was received, although small arms fire from pockets of resistance located in the 27th Division's zone continued to cause some casualties.[126]

On the left of the 27th Division, the 2d Marine Division continued its slow progress through the wooded hills and ravines north of Tapotchau. The 2d Battalion, 8th Marines, captured one of the Pimples, and a medium tank platoon from the Army's 762d Tank Battalion came up in the late

afternoon to lay fire on the remaining hills similarly nicknamed. In the division center, the 6th Marines gained little ground but was able to straighten its lines, while on the left the 2d Marines again waited on the outskirts of Garapan for the rest of the corps line to come abreast.[127]

Central Saipan: Sum-up

With the closing of the gaps on either side of the 27th Division's line, the battle for central Saipan can be said to have come to a successful end. The cost had been high and the progress painfully slow.

Total American casualties came to an estimated 3,987.[128] Of these, the 4th Marine Division suffered 1,506; the 2d Marine Division, 1,016; the 27th Infantry Division, 1,465. The Army division was especially hard hit among its line officers. The 165th Infantry lost its commander, Colonel Kelley, who was wounded in action. Colonel McDonough, commander of the 2d Battalion, 165th, was wounded and evacuated; his successor, Major Brusseau was wounded and later died; and Colonel Mizony of the 3d Battalion, 106th, was killed in action. In addition, a total of twenty-two company commanders of the 165th and 106th Regiments were either killed or wounded in action during the period.

---

[123] This action is described in Love, Battle For Saipan, pages 606–08.

[124] 27th Inf Div G–3 Jnl, 30 Jun 44, Msg 94; Love, Battle for Saipan, p. 600.

[125] 27th Inf Div G–3 Jnl, 30 Jun 44, Msgs 32, 41, 54.

[126] 4th Marine Div Opns Rpt Saipan, pp. 29–30.

[127] 2d Marine Div SAR, Phase I, FORAGER, pp. 19–20; Hoffman, *Saipan*, pp. 183–84.

[128] NTLF Rpt Marianas, Phase I, Incl C, G–1 Rpt, App. 1; 27th Inf Div G–1 Periodic Rpts 7 through 14. Casualty figures for the 27th Division are derived from the second source cited, since NTLF figures for the Army division are obviously incomplete. In computing 27th Division casualties for central Saipan for the period 23–26 June, the figures for the 105th Infantry have been deducted from the total division casualties, since that regiment was either in reserve or fighting on Nafutan Point during the period.

In the center of the corps line, it had taken the 27th Division eight days to advance 3,000 yards. In the same time the 2d Marine Division had advanced 2,600 yards on its right and 1,500 yards on its left where any further forward movement was unfeasible until the rest of the line came abreast. Only on the corps right, in the zone of the 4th Marine Division, had the troops advanced rapidly. By the close of 30 June this division, with its Army attachments, had pushed about 4,400 yards east to the tip of Kagman Peninsula and about 5,000 yards northwest from its original line of departure of June 23d. Undoubtedly, it would have gone farther had it not been held back by the relatively slow advance in the center of the corps line.

This bald account of the yardage gained is by no means a true measure either of the difficulties of the fighting or of the results achieved. Unlike the 4th Marine Division, the other two divisions faced extremely difficult terrain, which the Japanese, in spite of their dwindling strength, exploited to the utmost. The main drive of the 27th was up the long axis of a valley flanked on both sides by fortified hills, cliffs, and mountains. That of the 2d Marine Division was across the largest and most precipitous mountain mass on the island. Against any but a completely prostrated enemy, the assault could only have been slow and painstaking.

Whatever the cost of the drive, the results were decisive. Mount Tipo Pale and Mount Tapotchau were captured; Death Valley, Purple Heart Ridge, and Kagman Peninsula occupied. The main line of resistance set up by the Japanese after their withdrawal from the beachhead was broached and overrun.

CHAPTER XII

The Capture of Northern Saipan

Drive to Tanapag

1–2 July

With Death Valley cleared, Holland Smith was at last in a position to push his forces rapidly ahead and seal off the Japanese remaining in the northern neck of Saipan. On 1 July he established the next corps objective at a line (O–7) that cut across the base of this neck in an arc, at a distance from about 1,000 yards on the right to 6,000 yards on the left from the respective flanks of the corps front. Between line O–7 and the corps front, as of 1 July, lay the hill mass (Hills 221 and 112 meters)[1] on which the Japanese had chosen to anchor their last defensive position across the island. The attack was to be made with the three divisions abreast in the same order as before, the main effort again to be in the center, in the zone of the 27th Division.[2] (*Map 11*)

In the earlier phases of the fighting on Saipan, General Holland Smith had noted a tendency on the part of his infantry commanders to neglect the abundant artillery support available to them, and to rely too heavily on their own weapons. Too frequently, he believed, the front-line troops

had failed to call for massed artillery fires before jumping off in attack. Moreover, even when artillery concentrations had been properly called for, they were often not followed promptly by tanks and infantry, and thus the whole effect of the artillery preparation was wasted.[3] To correct this situation the corps commander specifically ordered:

Massed artillery fires will be employed to support infantry attacks whenever practicable. Infantry will closely follow artillery concentrations and attack ruthlessly when the artillery lifts. Absence of tanks is no excuse for failure of infantry to press home the attack.[4]

Even before the order calling for a quick thrust to Tanapag had been issued, the corps line had been pushed forward and straightened in preparation for the drive. In the center the 27th Division, on 1 July, registered a gain of about 400 yards on the right and 600 on the left against moderate opposition.[5] On the right, the 4th Marine Division maintained its positions and sent patrols as far out as 1,500 yards in front of its line without establishing contact with the enemy.[6] It was clear that the

---

[1] American troops called Hill 221 "Radar Hill." On the American map, Hill 112 was located just southeast of Tarahoho.

[2] NTLF Opn Order 19–44, 1 Jul 44.

[3] NTLF Dispatch 011806 to 2d Marine Div, 4th Marine Div, 27th Inf Div, Incl to 27th Inf Div G–3 Jnl.

[4] NTLF Opn Order 19–44, 1 Jul 44.

[5] 27th Inf Div G–3 Periodic Rpt 15, 1 Jul 44.

[6] 4th Marine Div Opns Rpt Saipan, Annex H, 23d RCT Rpt, p. 45; *Ibid.*, Annex I, 24th RCT Rpt, p. 62.

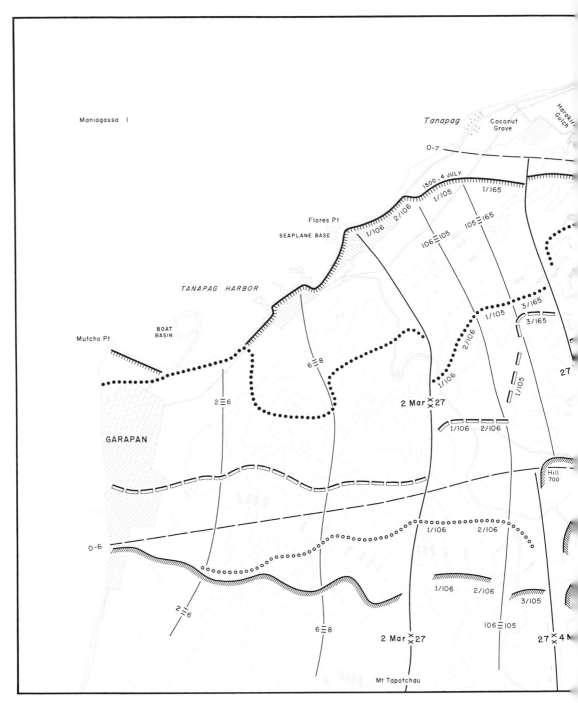

MAP 11

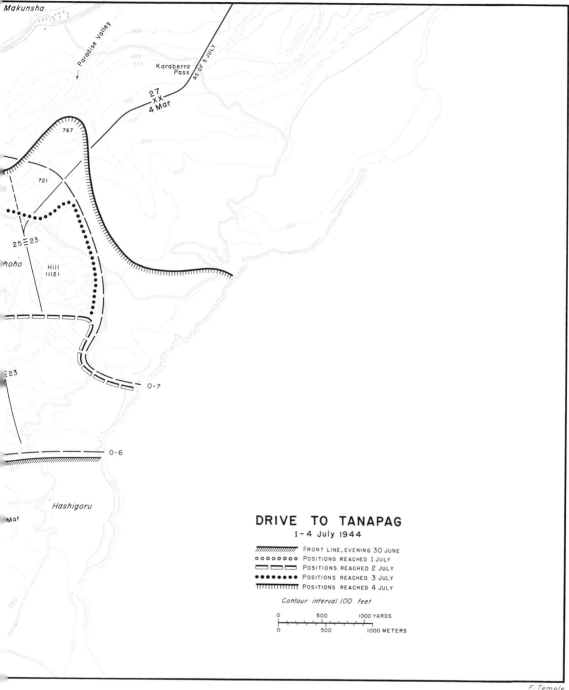

Makunsha

Paradise Valley

Karaberra
Pass

AS OF 5 JULY

27
XX
4 Mar

767

721

25 ⊟ 23

hoho

Hill
(112)

⊟23

0-7

0-6

Hashigoru

Mar

DRIVE TO TANAPAG
1–4 July 1944

⫻⫻⫻⫻⫻⫻⫻	FRONT LINE, EVENING 30 JUNE
ooooooo	POSITIONS REACHED 1 JULY
▭ ▭ ▭	POSITIONS REACHED 2 JULY
●●●●●●●	POSITIONS REACHED 3 JULY
⫳⫳⫳⫳⫳⫳⫳	POSITIONS REACHED 4 JULY

Contour interval 100 feet

0   500   1000 YARDS

0   500   1000 METERS

F. Temple

Japanese were retreating to the north. Early on 1 July members of the 27th Division had seen a small body of Japanese lugging ammunition up one of the roads that led out of Death Valley. All morning long, a 4th Marine Division observation post atop Hill 700 reported, the Japanese had been retreating in groups of three or four, carrying their packs and equipment with them.[7]

While these events were taking place on the right and in the center of the line, the 2d Marine Division gained more yardage than on any other day since the landing. The strong line of resistance through Mount Tapotchau had been smashed. Over terrain that was far better suited to the employment of tanks than the cliffs and defiles of Tapotchau, the 8th Marines advanced 800 yards. On its left, the 6th Marines kept pace in spite of having to overcome several pockets of heavy resistance, and on the extreme left the 2d Marines continued to patrol south of Garapan in preparation for the long-awaited push into the city itself, which was scheduled for 2 July.[8]

On 2 July, the 4th Marine Division, which had spent most of its time during the past days resting and patrolling, plunged ahead for about 1,500 yards in its zone. Resistance was so light that the assault battalion of the 24th Marines suffered only one man wounded during the day.[9]

On the 4th Division's immediate left, the 3d Battalion, 165th Infantry, which had now been returned to the control of its

parent division, maintained the same pace. By 1400 Major Foery's men had pushed ahead about 1,700 yards,[10] leaving behind at about the same distance to their left rear the 3d Battalion, 105th Infantry. This unit was held back by intense rifle and machine gun fire, leaving a deep re-entrant between the 3d Battalion, 165th, on its right and the 106th Infantry on its left. The latter had succeeded in advancing about 1,000 yards after clearing out five enemy tanks emplaced as pillboxes. To close the gap, General Griner late in the afternoon ordered the 1st Battalion, 105th Infantry, which had been in regimental reserve, to make a wide end run around the regiment's left flank, bypass the enemy strongpoint that was holding up the 3d Battalion, 105th, and establish contact with the left flank of the 3d Battalion, 165th.[11] This the 1st Battalion did by 1800.[12]

In the zone of the 2d Marine Division, the two regiments on the right made good progress (800–1,200 yards) during the day in spite of rough terrain and the fact that the 8th Marines was temporarily disorganized when friendly artillery fire fell into its lines causing forty-five casualties. On the division left flank the 2d Marines, after its prolonged wait before Garapan, was at last ordered to enter the city. As it did so, the devastating effect of the many days of artillery bombardment and naval shelling was revealed on all sides. Garapan was little more than a mass of rubble, and though there was some hostile rifle fire, the 2d Marines quickly occupied the center of

---

[7] NTLF Rpt Marianas, Phase I, Incl D, G–2 Rpt, pp. 43–44.
[8] 2d Marine Div SAR, Phase I, FORAGER, Sec. VI, pp. 20–21.
[9] 4th Marine Div Opns Rpt Saipan, Annex H, 23d RCT Rpt, p. 45; *Ibid.*, Annex I, 24th RCT Rpt, p. 22; Hoffman, *Saipan*, p. 193.

[10] 165th RCT Jnl, 2 Jul 44, Msg 58.
[11] 27th Inf Div G–3 Jnl, 2 Jul 44, Msg 62.
[12] 105th RCT Opns Rpt FORAGER, p. 8; 106th RCT Opns Rpt FORAGER, p. 18; 27th Inf Div G–3 Periodic Rpt 16, 2 Jul 44.

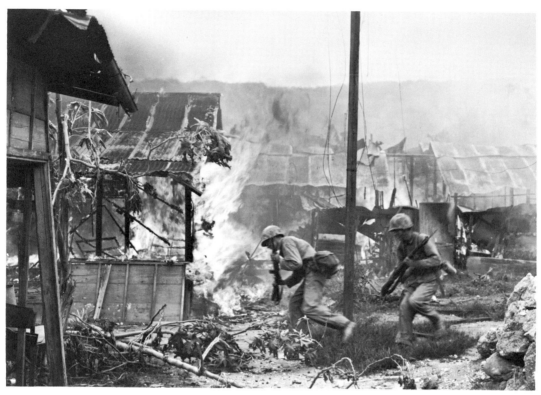

MARINES DASH THROUGH BLAZING GARAPAN, *2 July.*

the town with the help of tanks and armored amphibians. To the immediate east the Japanese, entrenched on a hill overlooking the city, caused considerable trouble, but by nightfall enemy resistance had subsided, and the regiment dug in about 700 yards from its morning line of departure.[13]

Under the mounting pressure of the American attack, the Japanese on the night of 2 July once more fell back to new positions. Six days earlier General Saito had decided to make his last stand along a line running from north of Garapan through Radar Hill and Hill 112 (meters) on to the coast.[14] Now those troops able to do so were to retire to the new line. It was high time. Many of them had been so pressed for provisions that they were eating field grass and tree bark.[15]

3–4 July

The axis of the drive to Tanapag Harbor now took a more northwesterly direction, with the main effort still in the center in the zone of the 27th Division. The Japanese were retreating rapidly and in a piecemeal manner. Saito's plans for an orderly withdrawal to the north were obviously

---

[13] 2d Marine Div SAR, Phase I, FORAGER, Sec. VI, p. 22; Hoffman, *Saipan*, pp. 186–87.

[14] Japanese Studies in World War II, 55.
[15] *Ibid.*

INFANTRYMEN OBSERVE HILL 767 *before approaching. Note abandoned Japanese 37-mm. gun in foreground.*

breaking down in the face of the gathering momentum of the attacking troops.

On the morning of 3 July the attack on the right got off to a slow start as a result of confusion shared by the 4th Marine Division and the 1st Battalion, 165th, as to the intentions of each. The Army unit was prepared to jump off on schedule at 0800, but held back because an air strike in front of the Marine division's lines prohibited forward movement. After the strike the soldiers continued to hold, waiting for the marines to go forward. The latter made no move on the false assumption that the 1st Battalion, 165th, was waiting for the unit on its left to come abreast. This misunder-

standing continued until 1100, when the Marine division and the Army battalion jumped off together.[16]

The 4th Marine Division attacked in columns of battalions, with the 3d Battalion, 23d Marines, 3d Battalion, 25th Marines, and 1st Battalion, 24th Marines, in the assault from right to left. After a few hours of fairly unimpeded movement, the battalion on the right was pinned down by heavy machine gun, mortar, and rifle fire from well-concealed positions in caves and wooded recesses on Hill 721 and on a nose

[16] 165th RCT Record of Opns FORAGER, Sec. IV, S–3 Rpt, p. 7; 27th Inf Div G–3 Jnl, 3 Jul 44, Msgs 11123, 11127; Hoffman, *Saipan,* p. 202.

abutting south from it that the marines were later to dub "Fourth of July Hill." Several attempts were made to penetrate the position by both frontal assault and envelopment, but each time the troops were so badly shot up that they were forced to retire. The approaches were heavily mined, and neither tanks nor self-propelled mounts could come in close. Finally, at 1715, after three hours of continuous fighting, the battalion pulled back 300 yards to safe positions and let the artillery take over. All night long howitzers of the 14th Marines pounded the strongpoint and kept it neutralized.[17]

Daylight of 4 July revealed that the Japanese had either withdrawn during the night or been eliminated by the intense artillery fire, and by 1135 both Fourth of July Hill and Hill 721 were in American hands. Within another hour a battalion of the 23d Marines had moved 800 yards to the northeast and had taken Hill 767 without opposition.[18] Meanwhile, the other two regiments of the 4th Marine Division had kept abreast. The 25th tied in with the 23d around Hill 767 on the night of 4 July, by which time most of the 24th Marines had been relieved by the 165th Infantry.[19]

In the zone of the 27th Division, the 3d Battalion of the 165th kept abreast of the marines on 3 July without meeting more than sporadic fire from the Japanese.[20] To its left the 1st Battalion, 105th, moved even faster against negligible opposition and by 1410 reached its objective for the day—the high ground 2,000 yards east of Tanapag Harbor overlooking the plains of Tanapag.[21]

The 106th Infantry on the division left jumped off on schedule and also reached the high ground north of Tanapag by late afternoon. Earlier in the morning the 1st Battalion had found a pocket of Japanese close to the division boundary line, but these men were quickly silenced by tanks and self-propelled mounts. Thereafter opposition was light. Meanwhile, to the rear of the front line the 3d Battalion was mopping up a bypassed enemy position in the cliffs north of Tapotchau. While one company of the 8th Marines tried to get at the Japanese-infested caves from above, Company K, 106th, contained the enemy from the plain below. After this maneuver failed to produce results, artillery was called upon to lay down a concentration. This too accomplished nothing, and at nightfall the strongpoint was still in enemy hands.[22]

In the early morning hours of 4 July a large group of Japanese, trying to escape to the north to join General Saito, stumbled into the command post of the 165th Infantry. After a brisk fire fight, twenty-seven of the enemy were killed including a number of officers, one of whom proved to be Colonel Ogawa, commanding officer of the *136th Infantry Regiment*.[23]

On his body Ogawa carried Saito's withdrawal order of 2 July. Ogawa himself had ordered the remnants of his own regiment, now bypassed by the Americans, to commence their withdrawal at 2200 on the

---

[17] 4th Marine Div Opns Rpt Saipan, Annex H, 23d RCT Rpt, pp. 45–46.

[18] *Ibid.*, p. 46.

[19] 4th Marine Div Opns Rpt Saipan, Annex I, 24th RCT Rpt, p. 23; *Ibid.*, Annex J, 25th RCT Rpt, pp. 7–8; Hoffman, *Saipan*, pp. 203–06.

[20] 165th RCT Record of Opns FORAGER, Sec. IV, S–3 Rpt, p. 7.

[21] 105th RCT Opns Rpt FORAGER, pp. 8–9.

[22] 106th RCT Opns Rpt FORAGER, Sec. I, pp. 18–19.

[23] 165th RCT Record of Opns FORAGER, Sec. IV, G–3 Rpt, p. 7; NTLF Rpt Marianas, Phase I, Incl D, G–2 Rpt, p. 49.

night of the 3d. When he was killed, Ogawa was bound for his new command post, which he hoped to locate on a cliff about 500 meters east of Hill 221.[24] Ogawa was not merely in command of a decimated regiment, but of the entire Japanese left and thus one of the few key men remaining among the Japanese defenders. His death was a heavy blow to the already stunned and reeling enemy, but the circumstances of his death indicate that an even greater misfortune had befallen the Japanese. It is more than likely that many if not most of the units under Ogawa's command behind the American lines never reached their assigned positions to the north. Thus the Japanese left flank, toward which the main drive of the American forces was now oriented, lay weakened, exposed, and almost leaderless.

The Fourth of July was to see the culmination of the 27th Division's thrust to Tanapag Plain. On the right the 1st Battalion, 165th, jumped off at 0730 on schedule and, meeting almost no opposition, quickly pushed forward to the last low ridge line overlooking the Flores Point seaplane base. A heavy downpour, the first daylight rainfall of any severity since the landing on Saipan, mired the tanks, but it made little difference since there were no targets at which they could fire. The rest of the regiment failed to keep pace so, from 1030 until midafternoon when new orders were issued changing the direction of the attack, the men of the 1st Battalion rested atop the ridge and took pot shots at the Japanese milling in the coastal valley below.[25]

In the center of the division line, the 1st Battalion, 105th, made rapid progress to a position just beyond the same ridge line, where it found a strongpoint manned by about three hundred enemy soldiers, with some machine guns. A called artillery barrage scattered the Japanese, and by 1600 most of the battalion had succeeded in reaching the beach.[26] On the left, the two assault battalions of the 106th had an easier time in spite of the heavy undergrowth through which they had to push. By 1430 they made their way into the Flores Point seaplane base, where they were joined in mopping-up operations by the 8th Marines. To their rear the 3d Battalion, 106th, spent most of the day finishing off the troublesome caves that had occupied it on the 3d. First, flame thrower teams went forward to destroy the ring of enemy machine gun positions that had been protecting the largest cave. Next, a public address system was brought up and interpreters broadcast pleas to the main body of Japanese to surrender. When this failed, the infantry resumed the attack and reduced the position. It yielded one wounded Japanese and fifty dead plus an unknown number sealed up in the smaller caves adjacent to the main position. It was the last Japanese strongpoint remaining on the slopes below Tapotchau.[27]

In the zone of the 2d Marine Division, by nightfall of 3 July the 6th Marines was still held up on the ridge line about 1,000

---

[24] In Japanese terrain designation, this was Hill 205 (meters). NTLF Rpt Marianas, Phase I, Incl D, G–2 Rpt, map, pp. 50–51; CINCPAC-CINCPOA Trans 10531, excerpts from a notebook of field orders, 14 Jun–3 Jul.

[25] 165th RCT Record of Opns FORAGER, Sec. IV, G–3 Rpt, p. 7; Love, Battle for Saipan pp. 670–72, 680.

[26] 105th RCT Opns Rpt FORAGER, p. 9; 27th Inf Div G–3 Periodic Rpt 18.

[27] 106th RCT Opns Rpt FORAGER, p. 20.

TROOPS SEARCHING OUT THE ENEMY *in the Tapotchau cliff area on 4 July.*

yards from the ocean shore, but the 2d Marines had finished mopping up Garapan and had pocketed the small enemy garrison remaining on the tip of Mutcho Point. Next day, both regiments reached the shore line.[28]

During most of the day the Japanese, under relentless pressure from the attackers, had been retreating steadily toward Saito's last headquarters, the rallying point for the final desperate counterattack that would come two days later. The Japanese commander had set up his command post in the valley running south from the village of Makunsha—appropriately enough labeled "Paradise Valley" by the Americans and "Hell Valley" by the Japanese.[29] A captured Japanese officer was later to describe in moving terms the miserable situation in which Saito and his staff found themselves:

This area is generally called the Valley of Hell and we felt that this was an unpleasant hint and suggestion concerning our future.

The intelligence which managed to reach me at this last place was all depressing.

On 4 July, an enemy unit appeared on the other side of the valley and fired at us with heavy automatic weapons. At that time I felt we were entirely surrounded and had lost all hope.

---

[28] 2d Marine Div SAR, Phase I, FORAGER, Sec. VI, p. 23; Hoffman, *Saipan,* pp. 198–207.

[29] NTLF Rpt Marianas, Phase I, Incl D, G–2 Rpt, pp. 51–52.

General Saito was feeling very poorly because for several days he had neither eaten nor slept well and was overstrained. He was wearing a long beard and was a pitiful sight.

That morning that very valley received intense bombardment (I don't know whether it was naval gunfire or pursuing fire from artillery, but it was the second most intense bombardment I had been in). It was so fierce that I thought maybe the cave where the headquarters was would be buried. At this time the staff and Lt. Gen Saito received shrapnel wounds.

I felt that the final hour was drawing near.[30]

Change of Direction

As it became apparent that the drive to Tanapag Harbor could be successfully concluded on the 4th, General Holland Smith prepared plans for the last phase of the Saipan campaign. The direction of the drive would change to the northeast— toward Marpi Point and the remaining Japanese airfield, which bore the same name. Most of the 2d Marine Division, which had by now been pinched out, was assigned to corps reserve. The final assault was to be conducted with the 4th Marine Division on the right, 27th Infantry Division on the left. To allow time for the necessary shifts, jump-off hour was set at noon, 5 July.[31] General Griner was ordered to relieve the two left battalions of the 4th Marine Division. The division boundary line would now cut down the northern end of the island slightly west of the middle. Griner decided to commit the 165th Infantry on the right, the 105th on the left, the 106th going into reserve.[32]

Late in the afternoon he ordered the 2d and 3d Battalions, 165th, to relieve the marines in that portion of the line now assigned to the Army division. In effecting this relief, contact with the 1st Battalion, 165th, on the regimental left was lost, so Griner ordered Colonel Bradt's 3d Battalion, 105th, to fill the gap. Unfortunately, Bradt's orders were garbled in transmission and he moved to the left rather than to the right of the 1st Battalion, 165th. By this time night had fallen, and before the error could be rectified almost a hundred Japanese were able to infiltrate through the gap and harass the front-line troops throughout the night. The attacks were sporadic, however, and by morning the gap had been filled, and the enemy repulsed or destroyed.[33] (*Map III.*)

5 July

4th Marine Division

On the right half of the corps line, General Schmidt placed the 25th Marines on the right and the 24th on the left, and ordered the 23d to clean up the area between the designated line of departure and the division's night positions before the division jumped off. The division launched its drive about 1330, an hour and a half late. The delay was largely because the 25th Marines, after being relieved by Army units in midmorning, had to move laterally about 2,500 yards to take position on the right of the line. Once they jumped off, the marines drove forward against very little resistance and by 1630 reached their objec-

---

[30] *Ibid.,* App. G, pp. 2–3.
[31] NTLF Opn Order 22–44, 4 Jul 44.
[32] 27th Inf Div G–3 Jnl, 4 Jul 44, Msg 46.

[33] 165th RCT Record of Opns FORAGER, p. 9; Love, Battle for Saipan, pp. 693–703.

tive for the day, the O–8a line, which was about 1,200 yards from the line of departure.[34]

The rapid and almost uncontested progress was indicative of the total collapse of General Saito's plans for establishing a final defense line across the entire northern neck of Saipan. The 4th Marine Division had overrun the whole left flank of the proposed line. The *136th Infantry Regiment* should have contested this ground, but whatever remained of that unit was scattered and isolated behind the American lines, mostly in the area around Radar Hill.[35] With the collapse of the enemy left, all that remained under Saito's control was the Navy sector and a thin slice of the *135th Infantry*'s area. These were in the zone of the 27th Division. Even there, the defense was disorganized and confused. Japanese officers captured on the 5th revealed that their "front line units were mixed up, the communications were badly disorganized, . . . there was little or no organized resistance at the present time, no organized supply plan and very little artillery, if any, remaining."[36] Yet to the Japanese military mind, disorganization, lack of supplies, and lack of communications was no excuse for an abatement of effort. What the enemy lacked in the ordinary sinews of war he made up in determination. As the 27th Division began to probe into Saito's last shattered defense line, the degree of that determination was made manifest.

27th Division

The newly designated line of departure for the 27th Division ran east from the beach just north of the village of Tanapag to a point just south of Hill 767. Facing this line from right to left were the 2d Battalion, 165th Infantry, 3d Battalion, 165th, 3d Battalion, 105th, and 2d Battalion, 105th. The terrain over which the division was to move was of two kinds. On the left in the zone of action of the 105th Infantry, the ground was a low, slightly rolling, coastal plain. The most important landmark on the plain was a large coconut grove about 600 yards east of Tanapag village. The main coastal road ran along the beach and was paralleled by a small cane railroad. Just above Tanapag, at Road Junction 2, the coastal road was joined by a cross-island highway. Just to the east of the coconut grove, the highway made a U-shaped turn and from the north leg of the U, at Road Junction 64, another, smaller, road branched off, wound in a southeasterly direction through a canyon fifty to sixty feet deep, and came out into the hills below Hill 721, one of the two high points on the ridge that rose up from the plain in the center of the island. The canyon, winding uncertainly between steep, cave-studded cliffs on either side, was soon to be called "Harakiri Gulch" by the men of the 27th. The floor of the gulch, never more than fifty yards wide, was covered with sparse undergrowth dotted with trees. In length, it ran about 400 yards.[37] Lying athwart the main line of advance, the canyon was an ideal defensive position. From the west mouth of the gulch, running all way to the sea, was a

---

[34] 4th Marine Div Opns Rpt Saipan, Annex I, 24th RCT Rpt, p. 63; *Ibid.,* Annex J, 25th RCT Rpt, p. 8.
[35] NTLF Rpt Marianas, Phase I, Incl D, G–2 Rpt, pp. 53–55, 93.
[36] *Ibid.,* p. 54.

[37] Love, Battle for Saipan, pp. 715–16.

HARAKIRI GULCH. *27th Division soldiers patrolling road following capture of this strongpoint on 7 July.*

deep dry gully that also provided ideal cover for enemy movement.[38]

K Company of the 165th Infantry drew first blood in the two-day fight for Harakiri Gulch. Soon after the jump-off, an advance patrol climbed down the south face of the canyon but received such inhospitable treatment from the Japanese below that the men climbed right back up again, dragging their wounded with them. Shortly thereafter two tanks started down into the gulch via the road to the west. Within a

few minutes both were disabled by Japanese who darted out from the ditches and placed mines on them. Three more tanks from the same platoon appeared over the edge of the precipice in an attempt to rescue those below. After an hour and a half of maneuvering and firing, one of the stricken vehicles was recovered; the other had to be abandoned.[39] For the rest of the afternoon Company K made repeated stabs into the gulch, but each failed. Self-propelled mounts were sent down the road to search the caves on the north side with

[38] Historical Division, War Department, AMERICAN FORCES IN ACTION, *Small Unit Actions* (Washington, 1946) (hereafter cited as AFAS, *Small Unit Actions*), p. 74, map on p. 99.

[39] Appleman, Army Tanks in the Battle for Saipan, pp. 76–80.

point-blank fire from their 75-mm. and 105-mm. howitzers, but the infantrymen who followed found the going still too rough, and Captain Betts withdrew the company from the gulch and called for artillery. Along the southern rim the entire 3d Battalion, 165th, dug in for the night, tying in on the right with the 2d Battalion, 165th, which had seen no significant action during the day.[40]

On the left of the 3d Battalion, 165th, Company L of the 105th was stopped in its tracks by fire from the opposite side of Harakiri Gulch and made no effort to force an entry into the canyon. To its left Company K, 105th, tried to work its way into the coconut grove, but fire from the uplands on the right interdicted the area, mortally wounding Captain Bouchard. The new company commander, 1st Lt. Roger P. Peyre, then withdrew south of the grove. The 2d Battalion, 105th, had spent the day working its way slowly along the shore line and the coastal plain north of Tanapag. It had mopped up a series of small pillboxes, most of them abandoned, and had discovered a live mine field directly in the path of its advance. By the end of the day it had not quite reached its scheduled line of departure, although the men had moved almost 800 yards through ground not previously reconnoitered.[41]

6 July

4th Marine Division

Holland Smith's orders for 6 July called for the 27th Division to jump off at 0700 in an effort to bring its line abreast of the marines on the right by 0900. Assuming this would be accomplished on time, the 4th Marine Division was to launch its attack at 0900, and the two divisions would continue to move abreast in a northeasterly direction toward the tip of the island, sweeping the remaining Japanese before them.[42] An hour or two after the 27th Division had jumped off it became apparent to the corps commander that it was going to be impossible for it to keep pace with the marines. Consequently, at 0900 General Smith changed his plans and assigned new missions. The 27th Division was to reorient the direction of its attack from northeast to north, thus assuming responsibility for about 2,600 yards of coastal strip from just above Tanapag to just above Makunsha, as well as for the first high ground immediately inland from the beaches, Harakiri Gulch, and Paradise Valley. The entire remainder of the island northeast of this sector was to be taken over by the 4th Marine Division. Once the right flank of the Army division reached its objective on the west coast just above Makunsha, it would be pinched out.[43]

To take over his newly expanded front, General Schmidt put all three of his Marine regiments into the line—25th, 24th, and 23d Marines from right to left. Accompanied by thirteen tanks, the 25th Marines made fairly rapid progress north along the east coast of the island, mopping up isolated Japanese troops and civilians in the many caves and cliffs that bordered the ocean. In this work the 25th was assisted by naval vessels, whose flat trajectory fire was ideally suited to the coastal targets. By midafternoon Mount Petosu-

---

[40] Love, Battle for Saipan, pp. 717–23.
[41] Ibid., pp. 728–35.

[42] NTLF Opn Order 23–44, 5 Jul 44.
[43] NTLF Rpt Marianas, Phase I, Incl E, G–3 Rpt, G–3 Periodic Rpt 22.

kara was occupied, and the two assault battalions dug in for the night on either side of that elevation. Just before dark a group of from seven to eight hundred civilians came into the lines of the 25th and surrendered. Meanwhile, to the rear, the reserve battalion in mopping up a by-passed hill flushed a sizable covey of Japanese soldiers and killed sixty-one in a brief but lively fire fight.[44]

In the division center, the 24th Marines registered a day's gain of 1,400 to 1,800 yards against sporadic resistance.[45]

On the left, the 23d Marines encountered considerably more difficulty. Having been in reserve in the morning when it received its orders, the unit had to march some 4,300 yards before reaching its line of departure. Jumping off at 1415, it soon came upon the cliff line that rimmed Paradise Valley on the east. Here, the regiment came under enemy fire from caves well concealed by dense underbrush. As the marines pushed down the slopes into the valley, hidden enemy machine guns and knee mortars opened up from the rear. With only an hour of daylight remaining, the regimental commander decided it was impossible to continue the attack, and at 1730 pulled his men back to establish defensive positions for the night on the high ground. There, the 23d Marines tied in with portions of the 27th Division but was entirely out of contact with the 24th Marines on the right.[46]

The Battle for Tanapag Plain

On the morning of 6 July the 27th Infantry Division was still on the near side of Harakiri Gulch and still short of its line of departure on the plain north of Tanapag village. On the line from right to left were Major Claire's 2d Battalion, 165th Infantry, Major Mahoney's 1st Battalion, 165th,[47] Colonel Bradt's 3d Battalion, 105th, and Maj. Edward McCarthy's 2d Battalion, 105th. The plan for the day, as revised by General Smith's order of 0900, called for the 2d Battalion, 165th, to push toward the coast above Makunsha by way of Paradise Valley. On its left the 1st Battalion, 165th, and the 3d Battalion, 105th, were to rout the enemy still entrenched in Harakiri Gulch and then proceed northward. Finally, to the 2d Battalion, 105th, was given the job of pushing up the coastal plain to a point just south of Makunsha.[48]

On the right the division made no progress in the effort to push through Paradise Valley. Capt. William J. Smith, commanding Company F, 165th Infantry, tried to force his way into the valley by the trail that ran along its floor, but the hail of fire that greeted this effort discouraged him and he withdrew his men. After a futile effort to rout the enemy with tanks and

---

[44] 4th Marine Div Opns Rpt Saipan, Annex J, 25th RCT Rpt, p. 9; Hoffman, *Saipan*, pp. 220–21.

[45] 4th Marine Div Opns Rpt Saipan, Annex I, 24th RCT Rpt, p. 24; Hoffman, *Saipan*, p. 219.

[46] 4th Marine Div Opns Rpt Saipan, Annex H, 23d RCT Rpt, p. 47; Hoffman, *Saipan*, pp. 218–19.

[47] This unit had taken over the positions occupied on the 5th by the 3d Battalion, 165th Infantry.

[48] The account of action of the 27th Infantry Division on 6 July, unless otherwise noted, is derived from Love, Battle for Saipan, pages 738–838, and AFAS, *Small Unit Actions*, pages 69–118. These accounts were written largely from interviews conducted shortly after the action by Captain Love, the historian assigned to the division. The official records are sparse to the point of being almost useless. This is particularly true of the records of the 105th Infantry, most of which were destroyed by fire.

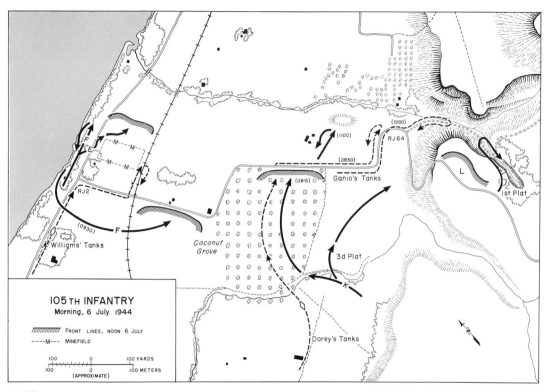

MAP 12

self-propelled mounts, the whole battalion fell back to the western base of Hill 767 and dug in for the night.

The attack on Harakiri Gulch met with no more success. Jumping off about noon the 1st Battalion, 165th Infantry, attempted, as had the 3d Battalion the day before, to assault the canyon frontally, moving perpendicularly to its axis. In the course of this effort the men of Company A witnessed an incident that was to give the name to the area. Following an intense ten-minute mortar preparation, the company proceeded slowly into the valley and was greeted by a series of explosions that forced the lead platoon to duck for cover. When the fireworks had abated about fif-

teen minutes later, the men investigated a group of straw shacks located on the sides of the gulch in the path of their advance. In each of these they found groups of three or four Japanese soldiers who had committed suicide by pressing hand grenades to their abdomens. All together, about sixty of the enemy were discovered to have ended their lives in this fashion. Nevertheless, fire from the gulch below continued intermittently throughout the afternoon, and by evening Major Mahoney's battalion abandoned all thought of further advance and dug in again on the rim overlooking the gorge.

On the western flank of the gulch, the 3d Battalion, 105th Infantry, was equally unsuccessful. (*Map 12*) In this area, most of the burden of combat fell on Capt. Robert J. Spaulding's Company L. During the morning Spaulding made two separate attempts to get across the gulch. He ordered his 1st Platoon, on the right, to crawl down into a small tributary draw that branched off from the main gulch in a southwesterly direction. The platoon was to work down the draw to its mouth and there set up machine guns that could cover enemy positions on the floor of the gulch and fire into the caves on the opposite side. Under cover of this support, Spaulding proposed to send his 2d Platoon over the near walls of the canyon, across the floor of the gulch, and up the opposite side. He also had at his disposal a skeleton platoon of four light tanks that he intended to send up the gulch along the trail that entered it from the east.

Company L moved off to the attack at 0700. The 1st Platoon crawled up over the ridge and down into the tributary ravine without drawing fire. Moving stealthily in single file along this narrow corridor, the platoon escaped detection and reached the corridor's mouth. There, the men set up two light machine guns and began firing at the caves in the face of the opposite wall, only to be greeted by return fire from the disabled American tank that had been left in the gulch the day before and was now in the hands of the Japanese. Meanwhile, the four light tanks had arrived, and Spaulding ordered them to work up the trail that ran through the middle of the gulch. An infantryman, Pfc. James R. Boyles, volunteered to accompany the buttoned up lead tank to guide it, but he was soon killed and thereafter no direct communication could be maintained between tanks and infantrymen. To add to the con-

fusion, three enemy soldiers then jumped out of the bushes and clapped a magnetic mine onto the side of the third tank in line, disabling it. Eventually the crew from the crippled tank was evacuated, and the tank platoon commander, 2d Lt. Gino Ganio, was able at last to get well up into the gulch and spray the walls on the north side. Nevertheless, by this time (noon) Company L had withdrawn again to the rim of the gorge, and no further effort to breach the canyon was made on the 6th.

Meanwhile, Company K, 105th Infantry, commanded by Lieutenant Peyre, was having its own troubles in the area of the coconut grove in the valley below and to the west of the mouth of Harakiri Gulch. Jumping off on schedule at 0700, Peyre's men moved along a deep gully that circled the south edge of the grove, making use of the cover and concealment it offered. Once they emerged from the ditch, however, they were taken under fire by Japanese machine guns located near the center of the grove, and the whole company was pinned down. At this juncture a platoon of five light tanks commanded by 1st Lt. Willis K. Dorey hove into view and within ten minutes cleared the way for the infantrymen to move into the grove. For about an hour the men of Company K worked their way among the stock piles of enemy supplies that abounded in the area and by 0815 reached the north edge of the grove, facing the open ground beyond the cross-island road.

Once his troops arrived at this objective, Lieutenant Peyre ordered Dorey's tanks to move along the road until they reached positions from which they could put effective fire on the cliffs to the right front. So long as the tanks were firing the infantrymen were able to move about the grove at will, but whenever the tankers ceased fire the Japanese in the cliffs opened up again. Unfortunately too, at this point, tank-infantry communications failed, and Peyre could neither reach Dorey by radio nor attract his attention with hand signals. Consequently the tank commander merely kept patrolling the road, laying down a blanket of fire on the cliffs, until about 1000 when the tanks ran out of ammunition and had to retire.

Peyre dug in as well as he was able to await the tankers' return. A hundred yards ahead of him in the open terrain north of the grove was a small knoll on which were located three enemy machine gun positions. To interdict these as well as the remaining guns on the cliffs to his right, Company K's commander brought his own machine guns to the north edge of the grove and prepared to launch an attack against the knoll.

When the tanks returned at 1030, Lieutenants Peyre and Dorey conferred and laid their plans. The right platoon of Company K would move ahead to capture the knoll under cover of fire from the left platoon. Dorey, with his tanks, would again proceed up the cross-island road, take the trail that led into Harakiri Gulch, and neutralize the enemy fire in the cliffs.

The lead platoon jumped off about 1045 and was immediately met by a deadly hail of small arms and machine gun fire that forced the men to take to the earth. Lieutenant Peyre, seeing his right platoon stalled, ordered his left platoon to try for the rise. Just as these men were venturing out of the coconut grove, the Japanese counterattacked down the cliffs and along the paths that led to a gully just behind the rise of ground that was the American objective. Total chaos ensued as a result

of a tremendous explosion that sent bodies and limbs of the leading Japanese into the air in all directions. Apparently, one of the enemy had stepped on the horn of an embedded sea mine, thus setting off a series of mines scattered over the area. Whatever the cause of the explosion, it created havoc among the Japanese and abruptly stopped the counterattack. In the American lines the results were not so serious, and although a few men were wounded by flying debris, the effect of the concussion was short-lived.

Meanwhile, orders had come down for Company G, 105th Infantry, to relieve Company K in the coconut grove. After receiving General Smith's orders indicating that the 27th Division would change the direction of its attack from northeast to north toward the coast line, General Griner had decided to shift the emphasis of his division attack from the left to the right of his line. Hence, to bolster the efforts of the 3d Battalion, 105th, against Harakiri Gulch, he ordered Company G to relieve Company K so that the latter could move out of the coastal plain and into the reserve area behind its parent unit. For the rest of the afternoon the area along the coast would be assigned entirely to the 1st and 2d Battalions, 105th Infantry.

It was the second of these battalions, commanded by Major McCarthy, that had been responsible for the area immediately abutting the seacoast during the morning. As day broke McCarthy had Companies E and F drawn up in a tight perimeter around Road Junction 2. Directly ahead athwart his line of advance, was the mine field, discovered the day before, that ran from the coastal road to the railroad and that was about 250 yards in depth. It consisted of about 150 Japanese general pur-

WAITING TO MOVE UP *north of the coconut grove on 3 July.*

pose bombs set in the ground in four rows, noses up. Only about a hundred had been fuzed.[49] Immediately beyond the mine field was the gully that ran down to the sea from the western mouth of Harakiri Gulch. To the right (east) of McCarthy's bivouac area was a wide expanse of open, slightly rolling ground, which was covered by small arms and automatic weapons fire from the cliffs still farther to the east.

The 2d Battalion's commander decided to move his men along the narrow strip of beach between the road and the lagoon in order to avoid the mine field. To eliminate the series of pillboxes strung along the

shore in this area, he called for a rolling artillery barrage in advance of the infantry. Company F was to take the lead, to be followed by E Company, which would fan out to the right once the far edge of the mine field was passed.

Promptly at 0700 Company F jumped off and within a few minutes had reached the northern limit of the mine field. At this point it received a heavy burst of machine gun and small arms fire from its direct front. McCarthy at once tried to put in a call for tanks and self-propelled mounts, but discovered that his radio communications were out; he then sent a runner to order up the vehicles. This involved a trip all the way back to Tanapag.

---

[49] 27th Inf Div G–2 Periodic Rpt 20, 6 Jul 44.

Meanwhile, the men of Company E had managed to crawl to the right along the north edge of the mine field and to deploy in a three-platoon front along a line running east of the coastal road. About 0900 Major McCarthy decided to withdraw Company F from its cramped positions between the road and the beach and send it around to the right of Company E to close the gap between the 2d and 3d Battalions. This move took about an hour. Also, Company A of the 102d Engineer Combat Battalion was brought forward to deactivate the mine field.

At 1000 five medium tanks commanded by 1st Lt. Dudley A. Williams of the 762d Tank Battalion put in their appearance at Road Junction 2. Rather than send them down the road, which he believed was almost certainly mined, McCarthy ordered them to proceed single file along the railroad track to the right. The lead tank unfortunately snarled its tread in the steel rails and became immobilized. While an effort was being made to clear a path through the mine field so that the second tank could be worked around the first, the enemy opened fire, scoring direct hits on both tanks. Lieutenant Williams hooked cables to the two vehicles and hauled them loose of the tracks and clear of the area before any more damage was done.

By this time it was apparent that the chief source of enemy fire came from the gully in front of the mine field, and Company E sent out a squad to rush the gully and knock out the machine gun position that seemed to be causing most of the trouble. The squad leader got as far as the gully and located the position in question, but was wounded and had to withdraw before he could eliminate it.

By midafternoon the entire 2d Battalion, 105th Infantry, appeared to have bogged down. Companies E and F were facing the gully just north of the mine field and Company G was still at the north edge of the coconut grove. Anxious to get on with the day's business, General Griner at 1520 ordered the regimental commander, Colonel Bishop, to commit his reserve, the 1st Battalion, 105th, commanded by Colonel O'Brien. Bishop objected to committing his reserves at such a late hour and argued that an attack would not give sufficient time before dark for the front-line troops to prepare a proper perimeter defense.[50] His objection was overruled. On Griner's orders, O'Brien's unit was to be inserted on the right flank of the 2d Battalion, 105th, and from that point was to drive north to Makunsha village on the shore before nightfall.[51]

Even before this move could be executed, relief to the men immediately in front of the enemy-infested gully came from a different quarter. About 1530 Lieutenant Dorey, after refueling and resupplying, arrived on the scene with two other tanks in addition to his own. Observing that the infantry was apparently completely immobilized, he drove straight into the troublesome gully pushing the enemy before him and slaughtering them with canister and machine guns. For half an hour he kept this up, killing about 150 Japanese in the gully and literally paving with dead bodies the way for a renewed advance of the 2d Battalion. In the course of this action, Japanese soldiers, armed with magnetic mines, attacked one of the

---

[50] Ltr, Bishop to Gen A. C. Smith, 25 Feb 55, OCMH.
[51] 27th Inf Div G–3 Jnl, 6 Jul 44, Msg 36.

light tanks and it lost its track. In spite of his valiant efforts, Dorey was unable to rescue either the damaged tank or its crew.[52]

Meanwhile, back at the regimental command post, Colonel Bishop was outlining his plans for the final move up the coast to Makunsha. As directed by the division commander, O'Brien's 1st Battalion was to move into line between the other two battalions of the 105th. To make room for this maneuver, Company F was to move back around the rear of Company E to the left of the regimental line where it would again take up a position between the railroad track and the beach. Company G, commanded by Captain Olander and still in the coconut grove, was to be attached to the 3d Battalion and swing on its right flank across the western mouth of Harakiri Gulch in order to bottle up the enemy there. Such a movement would presumably protect the rear of the 1st Battalion, and the next morning the rest of the 3d Battalion could mop up the enemy isolated in the gulch.

Pursuant to these instructions, Colonel O'Brien brought his battalion into line, with Company B on the right, A on the left, and C echeloned to the right rear. His apprehension over the role assigned to his men was apparent to Captain Ackerman, A Company commander, who later testified: "Obie was nervous and restless, as usual. He drew a picture for us and told Dick [Capt. Richard F. Ryan, of Company B] and I that no matter what else happened, we were to keep going. 'Its the old end run all over again. Whenever they got a job nobody else can do, we have to do

it. Sooner or later we're going to get caught and this may be it.'"[53]

The 1st Battalion was in line by approximately 1645, following F Company's shift to the division left flank along the beach. Between that time and 1715 both battalions resupplied and organized their lines. At 1715 the 105th Infantry moved off in a co-ordinated attack.[54] (*Map 13*)

On the left of the line, the 2d Battalion had little difficulty moving ahead in the wake of the devastation caused by Lieutenant Dorey's tanks. Although Company F delayed slightly to investigate a series of Japanese pillboxes along the beach, by 1800 the whole battalion had advanced about 600 yards. At that point it built up its perimeter for the night. O'Brien's battalion ran into more trouble. On reaching the gully, Company A encountered a nest of fifteen to twenty Japanese. Some were wounded and some were still trying to hide from Dorey's tank fire by hugging the walls of the trench on the near side. Ackerman's men waded in with bayonets and knives and after a 20-minute hand-to-hand fight, cleaned out the pocket. Once across the gully, Company A rushed headlong some 500 yards in spite of increasingly heavy machine gun fire from the cliffs to the right. This fire was falling even more heavily on Company B and succeeded, among other things, in killing the company commander, Captain Ryan, who was replaced by 1st Lt. Hugh P. King. Meanwhile, on the battalion right rear, Company C was faced with the same machine guns emplaced on the knoll north of the coconut grove that had previously stopped both K Company, 165th, and G Company, 105th. For the rest of the day and even

---

[52] Appleman, Army Tanks in the Battle for Saipan, pp. 91–92.

[53] Quoted in Love, Battle for Saipan, p. 810.
[54] 105th RCT Jnl, 6 Jul 44, p. 72.

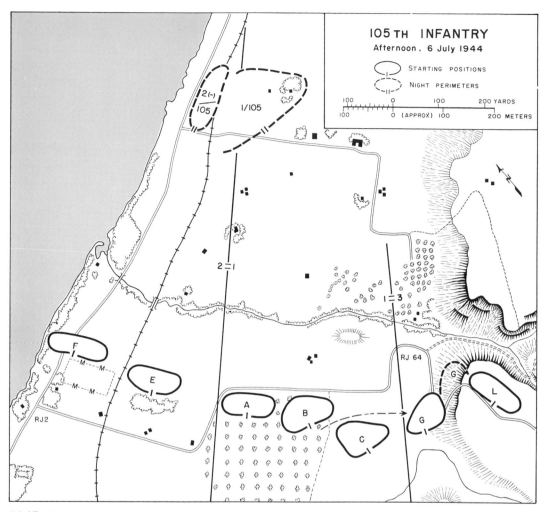

MAP 13

after dark, Company C battled to take out these positions. Not until a self-propelled mount was finally brought in to wipe them out was the entire company able to rejoin the rest of the battalion in its night perimeter.

Meanwhile, immediately to the right Captain Olander of Company G, 105th, was trying to carry out his mission of sealing up the western mouth of Harakiri Gulch. Working its way along the road that led into the gulch the lead platoon, just before dark, stumbled onto a nest of Japanese. A brisk hand-to-hand fight ensued, with inconclusive results, and, in view of the lateness of the hour, the company commander ordered all of his men to pull back west along the road to the point from which they had started. There Captain Olander called Colonel Bradt, to whose battalion he was now attached, and admitted his inability to build up a line across the mouth of the gulch. He was given permission to dig in on the high ground overlooking Road Junction 64, from which point he hoped to be able to interdict movement from the gulch with machine gun fire.

By nightfall then, the 1st and 2d Battalions, 105th (less Company G), were digging in in positions about 900 yards northeast of Road Junction 2. On the left, Companies E and F bivouacked in a tight perimeter between the road and the railroad. The narrow corridor between the road and the beach was outposted by two men armed with carbines and with express orders to report any signs of enemy movement along the beach. Inside the perimeter were stationed the mortars of both rifle companies as well as the mortars and machine guns of the heavy weapons company. In placing his heavy weapons and machine guns, Major McCarthy assumed that before nightfall the 1st Battalion would have reached its objective north of his perimeter. Hence, without neglecting the northern approaches to his position altogether, he concentrated his defenses on the eastern side.

Meanwhile, Colonel O'Brien's 1st Battalion had come abreast. Rather than push on to the beach ahead of the 2d Battalion as originally planned, O'Brien, after consultation with McCarthy, decided to tie in for the night to the right of the 2d Battalion. His perimeter was drawn up in the shape of an arc whose terminal points rested on the railroad just east of the right side of the 2d Battalion's perimeter. This arrangement meant that two whole platoons of the 2d Battalion were now in-

side the final perimeter. More important, O'Brien's perimeter screened one of the 2d Battalion's antitank guns as well as all of Company H's heavy machine guns, which had been emplaced so as to protect the eastern leg of McCarthy's original perimeter. Thus, by hedging in the 2d Battalion from the east, O'Brien in effect subtracted from the combined fire power of the two-battalion perimeter.

Even more significant was the fact that between the 1st Battalion, 105th, and Company G, 105th (attached to the 3d Battalion), lay a gap of about 500 yards. However, the ground was open and O'Brien took the precaution of placing all of his antitank guns in such a position as to bear directly on the gap. By the time all these arrangements were completed it was well after dark. The morning, it was hoped, would bring the 105th Infantry to its objective line at the shore and an end to its labors.

7 July

Banzai Attack

About an hour after dark, an American soldier patrolling the road in the vicinity of the command post of the 3d Battalion, 105th Infantry, came upon a lone, armed, Japanese lying asleep. He forthwith took him prisoner and sent him back to headquarters for interrogation. The Japanese proved to be a "leading seaman" of the *55th Guard Force,* and his testimony, reluctantly given, was sufficient cause for deep alarm. An all-out attack by the entire remaining Japanese force on the island, he said, had been ordered for the night of 6–7 July. Word was immediately sent out to all major units of the division as well as to

Holland Smith's headquarters to prepare for the worst.[55]

In the front line below Makunsha, Colonel O'Brien and Major McCarthy went into conference on receiving this information. Both were worried about the gap that extended some 500 yards southeastward to the night positions of Company G, 105th Infantry. O'Brien called the regimental command post and asked for reinforcements to fill the gap but was told that none were available. Colonel Jensen, the regimental executive, in turn called for help from division headquarters. He too received a negative answer. The two battalion commanders would have to make out with what they had on hand.[56]

The Japanese counterattack that was now mounting had in fact been ordered early on the morning of the 6th. At 0600 General Saito had issued his final proclamation:

MESSAGE TO OFFICERS AND MEN
DEFENDING SAIPAN

I am addressing the officers and men of the Imperial Army on Saipan.

For more than twenty days since the American Devils attacked, the officers, men, and civilian employees of the Imperial Army and Navy on this island have fought well and bravely. Everywhere they have demonstrated the honor and glory of the Imperial Forces. I expected that every man would do his duty.

Heaven has not given us an opportunity. We have not been able to utilize fully the terrain. We have fought in unison up to the present time but now we have no materials with which to fight and our artillery for attack has been completely destroyed. Our comrades have fallen one after another. Despite the bitterness of defeat, we pledge, "Seven lives to repay our country."

The barbarous attack of the enemy is being continued. Even though the enemy has occupied only a corner of Saipan, we are dying without avail under the violent shelling and bombing. Whether we attack or whether we stay where we are, there is only death. However, in death there is life. We must utilize this opportunity to exalt true Japanese manhood. I will advance with those who remain to deliver still another blow to the American Devils, and leave my bones on Saipan as a bulwark of the Pacific.

As it says in the "SENJINKUM" [Battle Ethics], "I will never suffer the disgrace of being taken alive," and "I will offer up the courage of my soul and calmly rejoice in living by the eternal principle."

Here I pray with you for the eternal life of the Emperor and the welfare of the country and I advance to seek out the enemy.

Follow me![57]

Actually, General Saito was too feeble and sick to lead the charge in person. Shortly after issuing his final order he committed suicide. A captured Japanese officer who was with the general almost until the end described what probably took place: "Cleaning off a spot on the rock himself, Saito sat down. Facing the misty EAST saying 'TENNO HEIKA! BANZAI! [Long live the Emperor] . . . he drew his own blood first with his own sword and then his adjutant shot him in the head with a pistol." [58]

The exact number of Japanese to participate in the attack is unknown. A count taken later on the authorization of General Griner revealed 4,311 enemy dead in the area covered by the attackers, although undoubtedly some of these had been killed by naval gunfire or artillery before the banzai charge got under way.[59] A captured in-

---

[55] 27th Inf Div G-3 Jnl, 6 Jul 44, Msg 57; 27th Inf Div G-2 Periodic Rpt 21, 7 Jul 44.
[56] Love, Battle for Saipan, pp. 858-59.

[57] NTLF Rpt Marianas, Phase I, Incl D, G-2 Rpt, pp. 57-58.
[58] Ibid., App. G, p. 3.
[59] Buckner Bd Rpt, Exhibit FFF, Ltr, CG 27th Inf Div to CG NTLF, 16 Jul 44.

telligence officer of the *43d Division* at first estimated that the total Japanese force came to no more than 1,500, but later revised this upward to 3,000.[60] Another prisoner of war, a Korean laborer, also gave 3,000 as the approximate number,[61] and this is probably as acceptable an estimate as any.[62]

The truth is that even the Japanese commanders themselves had no very clear picture of the number of men left under them. The attacking force was drawn from almost every conceivable unit on the island, forming a composite group of stragglers. Specific identifications made among Japanese dead included the *118th, 135th,* and *136th Infantry Regiments, 43d Division* headquarters and *43d Field Hospital, 3d Independent Mountain Artillery Regiment, 16th Shipping Engineer Regiment,* and sundry naval units including combat, maintenance, and labor personnel. Many of the Japanese were poorly armed with rusty rifles and some merely carried poles

to which crude knives and bayonets were attached.[63]

Poorly armed or not, the impact of this horde was overwhelming. In the words of Major McCarthy, one of the few officers to survive it, "It was like the movie stampede staged in the old wild west movies. We were the cameraman. These Japs just kept coming and coming and didn't stop. It didn't make any difference if you shot one, five more would take his place. We would be in the foxholes looking up, as I said, just like those cameramen used to be. The Japs ran right over us." [64]

About 0400 on 7 July the main body of the desperate attackers started south from Makunsha between the shore line and the base of the cliffs bordering Tanapag plain. Although there is no evidence that the movement was organized, the mounting flood sluiced out along three principal channels. The main group charged down the railroad track, hitting the American perimeter below Makunsha; another attacked positions of the 3d Battalion, 105th, at Harakiri Gulch; the attackers facing the gap between these two American positions continued through unopposed.[65]

Shortly before 0500 the full force of the attack struck the perimeter of the 1st and 2d Battalions, 105th Infantry, and in twenty-five minutes of fierce close-quarter fighting the American positions were overrun. During the first moments of impact Colonel O'Brien again made himself conspicuous by his fortitude. With a pistol in each hand he joined battle with the

---

[60] *Ibid.*, Annex H, p. 7; Hq FEC, Mil Hist Sec Special Staff, to Chief of Mil Hist, 5 Jun 52, Incl, Comments by Maj. Takashi Hiragushi. Major Hiragushi, was taken prisoner after the counterattack of 7 July. For reasons unknown he assumed the name of Maj. Kiyoshi Yoshida, the *31st Army* intelligence officer, who had been killed in action. The NTLF G-2 Report refers to this officer as Yoshida. His true identity was not revealed until after the war.

[61] NTLF Rpt Marianas, Phase I, Incl D, G-2 Rpt, p. 96.

[62] General Holland Smith's final estimate lay between 1,500 and 3,000 (Smith, *Coral and Brass*, p. 195). General Griner believed the number was not less than 3,000 and probably more (CG 27th Inf Div to CG NTLF, 16 Jul 44, Buckner Board Rpt, Exhibit FFF). A special board, appointed by Admiral Spruance to survey the circumstances surrounding the counterattack, estimated the number of enemy involved to lie between 2,500 and 3,000 (Comdr Fifth Fleet, Rpt of Japanese Counterattack at Saipan on 7 Jul 44, 19 Jul 44).

[63] NTLF Rpt Marianas, Phase I, Incl D, G-2 Rpt, pp. 59-60.

[64] Quoted in Love, Battle for Saipan, pp. 870-71.

[65] Unless otherwise noted, the account of the banzai charge is derived from Love, Battle for Saipan, pages 871-92.

deluge, firing until his magazines were empty. Then, though seriously wounded, he manned a .50-caliber machine gun and kept firing until killed.[66] With him went a good percentage of the officers and men of both battalions.

The tide rolled on, and before it stumbled most of the survivors of the perimeter. Among those left behind was Sgt. Thomas A. Baker of Company A. Although severely wounded, he refused to let himself be carried back with the retreat. Preferring certain death to further risking the lives of his comrades he demanded to be left, armed only with a loaded pistol. When his body was later discovered the gun was empty and around him lay eight dead Japanese.[67]

Meanwhile, the left flank of the enemy had swiftly penetrated the gap. One group of Japanese spread out to attack the 3d Battalion, 105th, but from their dominating positions on the high ground above Harakiri Gulch the men of the 3d Battalion were able to repulse the attack and hold their positions intact.[68] Another group hit the 3d Battalion, 10th Marines (Artillery), which had set up its guns the day before about 500 yards southwest of Tanapag village. Only one of the batteries (H) was in a position to fire and it succeeded, among other things, in knocking out a Japanese tank before the men were forced to retreat pell-mell, leaving the breechblocks and firing locks in their howitzers. The marines of Battery I, after expending all of their small arms ammunition, removed the firing locks from their howitzers and fell back south along the railroad track to the positions of Battery G, where the two units held fast until relieved that afternoon by the 106th Infantry.[69]

Meanwhile, the 27th Division artillery was pouring as many shells into the enemy as could safely be done without endangering the retreating American troops. Between 0515 and 0615 the three light battalions expended a total of 2,666 rounds in the zone of action of the 105th Infantry. This represented an average of more than forty rounds a minute.[70]

By the time the men of the two advanced battalions had retreated as far as the northern edge of Tanapag village, they ran into the van of the left prong of the Japanese force, which had come through the gap, past the positions of the 10th Marines, and then gone on to the command post of the 105th Infantry, where the attack was finally stopped. At this point, two officers, Captain White of Company F and Lieutenant King of Company B, rallied the retreating men and brought some organization out of the confusion. They were able to persuade most of the troops to take cover in Tanapag village. While directing this diversion, King was killed. Meanwhile Major McCarthy, the 2d Battalion commander, had come up, and with the help of other surviving officers and noncommissioned officers he was able to organize a perimeter within Tanapag village by about 0800, three hours after the initial attack had been made.[71]

---

[66] For this and other notable demonstrations of bravery on Saipan, O'Brien was posthumously awarded the Medal of Honor (WDGO 35, 9 May 1945).

[67] For this action, Baker was posthumously awarded the Medal of Honor (WDGO 35, 9 May 1945).

[68] 105th RCT Opns Rpt FORAGER, p. 10.

[69] Hoffman, *Saipan,* pp. 224–25.

[70] 27th Inf Div G–3 Periodic Rpt 21, 7 Jul 44, p. 2.

[71] This account is derived from Love, Battle for Saipan, pages 876–932.

MARINES EXAMINING DESTROYED ENEMY TANK, *which was knocked out by a battery from the 10th Marines during the Japanese banzai attack.*

For the next four hours the beleaguered men fought a bitter house-to-house battle with the Japanese that had surrounded and were infiltrating the village. The Americans were out of communication with the command posts to the rear, short of ammunition and water, and had no means of evacuating or properly caring for their wounded. Shortly after 1100 McCarthy tried to lead a small force back to the regimental command post to bring up help for the wounded. Just as he got under way, his group was hit by two concentrations of American artillery and those men who were able to do so stampeded into the water and swam for the reefs. Some of these returned to establish another small perimeter below Tanapag, where they remained out of touch with the main body of their regiment's troops in the village itself and the command post, which was still farther to the rear.

Finally, shortly after noon, the first sign of relief appeared in the form of a platoon of medium tanks that rolled down the road from the direction of the command post. The vehicles fired indiscriminately at areas that might be presumed to contain enemy troops, but because there were no communications between the tanks and the infantry there could be no co-ordinated effort to route the enemy or rescue the surrounded troops. Finally, McCarthy was able to get to the lead tank, and climbing in himself, lead a group of about thirty-five of his men back down the road, reaching the regimental command post by about 1500. Under his persuasion a convoy of trucks and DUKW's, loaded with medical supplies and ammunition, was dispatched toward Tanapag village. Some of the vehicles were knocked out en route, but three got through and returned fully loaded with wounded. Still later, a group of LVT's of the 773d Amphibian Tractor Battalion was sent by water to rescue some of the men still fighting on the beach or stranded on the reefs. Others had already swum out and had been picked up by naval landing craft to be carried to destroyers waiting outside the reef. About 2200 the last survivor left the perimeters in Tanapag village and below. All together, out of the 1st and 2d Battalions, 105th Infantry (less Company G), 406 officers and men were killed and 512 wounded.[72]

American Countermeasures

Back at 27th Division and corps headquarters, word of the Japanese banzai charge was gradually filtering through. In response to the news, General Griner at 0920 ordered Colonel Stebbins to commit his 106th Regiment into the line and attack northeast astride the railroad track.[73] About the same time corps attached the 3d Battalion, 6th Marines, to the 27th Division, and at 1050 the battalion was ordered to mop up an enemy force, reported to be 100 strong, in the Tanapag area.[74] At 1100 Griner requested that some Marine tanks be released to the division from corps control, but this was refused.[75] According to the 27th Division commander, "headquarters did not accept my version of the importance of the action

then in progress." [76] However, not long afterward, Holland Smith did order the two Marine divisions to release 1,000 rounds of 105-mm. howitzer ammunition to the Army division, which by now was running short.[77]

By 1000 Colonel Stebbins had the 106th Infantry in line with the 1st Battalion on the left and the 2d Battalion on the right of the railroad track.[78] They moved forward slowly. The 1st Battalion met little opposition, but O'Hara's men on the right encountered a considerable number of Japanese still alive and firing.[79] By 1540 Company F had recaptured two of the Marine batteries, the first one with the help of some of the Marine artillerymen who had remained in the vicinity after being driven off their guns.[80] A short while later the 1st Battalion reported that it had recaptured the abandoned guns of Battery H of the 3d Battalion, 10th Marines.[81] By 1600 the 106th Infantry was still 200 to 300 yards short of positions of the 105th Infantry, which it was supposed to relieve. Colonel Stebbins nevertheless decided to dig in where he was, although against the advice of one of his battalion commanders. Stebbins was concerned lest there be too many bypassed enemy to his rear.[82] This left the division commander with no alternative but to evacuate the remainder of his isolated troops by water.

Meanwhile, on the division right the 165th Infantry was touched only lightly by

---

[72] For this day's action, the 105th Infantry (less 3d Battalion and Company G) was awarded the Distinguished Unit Citation (Department of the Army, GO 49, 14 July 1948).

[73] 106th RCT Jnl, 7 Jul 44, Msg 1072.

[74] 27th Inf Div G-3 Jnl, 7 Jul 44, Msgs 28, 37.

[75] Ibid., Msg 39.

[76] George W. Griner, Certificate, 12 Jul 44, Buckner Board Rpt, Exhibit ZZ.

[77] 27th Inf Div G-3 Jnl, 7 Jul 44, Msg 46.

[78] Ibid., Msg 32.

[79] 106th RCT Opns Rpt FORAGER, p. 23.

[80] 106th RCT Jnl, 7 Jul 44, Msgs 1089, 1107.

[81] Ibid., Msg 1108.

[82] George W. Griner, Certificate, 12 Jul 44, Buckner Board Rpt, Exhibit ZZ.

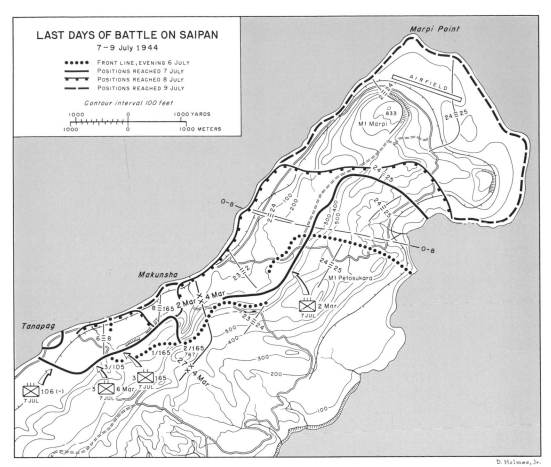

LAST DAYS OF BATTLE ON SAIPAN
7-9 July 1944

●●●●● FRONT LINE, EVENING 6 JULY
———— POSITIONS REACHED 7 JULY
—┬—┬— POSITIONS REACHED 8 JULY
— — — POSITIONS REACHED 9 JULY

Contour interval 100 feet

1000   0   1000 YARDS
1000   0   1000 METERS

MAP 14

D. Holmes, Jr.

the overflow from the charge that had all but overwhelmed the 105th. By 0930 the attached 3d Battalion, 106th, had finally reached the floor of Harakiri Gulch and was mopping up the Japanese still hidden in the caves and ditches. Occasionally, random riflemen who were apparently part of the main enemy counterattack wandered into the area to delay operations, but no serious opposition remained. Shortly after noon, the 1st Battalion, 165th, to the right, was able to advance through the draw at the upper end of the gulch and move into

the plateau to the north overlooking the plain. It stopped there for the night and made plans to descend the cliffs the next day.[83]

Final Victory

In spite of the fact that by nightfall of 7 July the 27th Division had recovered some of the lost ground in the area of the

---

[83] 165th RCT Jnl, 7 Jul 44, Msgs 14, 15, 46; Love, Battle for Saipan, pp. 936-37.

FLAME THROWER BLASTING PARADISE VALLEY CAVE, *an effective method of flushing Japanese.*

counterattack and had at last cleaned out Harakiri Gulch, General Holland Smith decided to relieve most of the Army units from the line. The 2d Marine Division (less detachments)[84] was ordered to pass through the 27th Division and "mop up and destroy enemy elements" remaining in its zone of action. Attached to the Marine division would be the 165th Infantry, as well as the 3d Battalion, 6th Marines, which was now to be released from the control of the Army division. Upon being

passed through, the 27th was ordered into corps reserve.[85] (*Map 14*)

"Mop-up" was the proper word for the activities of most of the 2d Marine Division for the next two days. Along the beach the 6th Marines had an easy time after its jump-off at 1130. In the words of the official report, "Initially, the attack was field day for our troops and slaughter for the Japs." Later in the afternoon, however, the regiment came up against a small pocket of resistance, just southwest of the coconut grove, containing about a hundred Japa-

[84] The detachments were the 2d Marines; 1st Battalion, 29th Marines; and Company A, 2d Tank Battalion.

[85] NTLF Opn Order, 7 Jul 44, NTLF Rpt Marianas, Phase I, Incl A.

nese who had taken refuge in the bed of a small stream that ran down to the sea. Flame throwers, tanks, and self-propelled mounts were brought up to wipe out the enemy, but at nightfall the pocket still remained. By 1830 all units of the regiment had reached the beach, and the next day was spent mopping up and eliminating all enemy in the area.[86]

In the hills and ravines just east of the coastal plain, the 8th Marines spent most of 8 and 9 July in demolition work, since the remnants of enemy consisted of disorganized groups holed up in caves. Every cave had to be investigated, and the few Japanese remaining alive were destroyed or driven out with hand grenades, flame throwers, and TNT charges.[87]

On the division right, the 165th Infantry met similar scattered opposition and dealt with it in much the same way. Delaying its assault on the 8th until the marines could come abreast, the 165th jumped off from its positions north of Harakiri Gulch at 1130. By midafternoon Company I had forced its way through Paradise Valley, where General Saito had established his final headquarters and from which the banzai order had been issued. Apparently not all of Saito's men had joined in the charge, for the caves in the cliffs' sides still harbored enough Japanese to offer stiff resistance to progress through the valley. By 1245 of 9 July forward elements of the regiment reached their destination on the shore, while Company K stayed behind to finish mopping up the caves of Paradise Valley.[88]

The morning of the 8th found the 4th Marine Division poised and ready for its final drive to Saipan's northern tip. On the left, the 23d Marines were on the high ground overlooking Karaberra Pass, through which the regiment would have to advance in order to seize its assigned portion of the shore line north of Makunsha. Following an intense preparation by rockets and tank fire, and assisted by LCI gunboats lying off Makunsha, the 23d Marines forced its way through the pass and by 1205 had rushed across the coastal flats to the sea.[89] On its right, the 23d and 24th Marines kept abreast and secured their assigned zones by about 1530, while the 25th Marines, on the east flank, advanced its lines about 600 yards against no opposition. That night the 1st Battalion, 2d Marines, suffered a series of minor counterattacks that were troublesome in the extreme but that failed to make a dent in the division line. On the 9th, with three regiments abreast (the 23d Marines was pinched out), the 4th Marine Division completed the final lap in a fast sprint to Marpi Point.[90] At 1615, 9 July 1944, Admiral Turner announced Saipan to be "secured." [91]

All that remained was to ferret out the few remaining enemy troops from their scattered hiding places in the caves and gulleys and ravines that littered the northern part of the island. Initially, this task was assigned to the two Marine divisions, with the 165th Infantry still attached to the 4th. These men still had to witness a few horrendous sights before they were through with Saipan. In spite of continu-

[86] 6th RCT SAR FORAGER, pp. 15–16.
[87] 8th RCT SAR FORAGER, p. 9.
[88] 165th RCT Record of Opns FORAGER, p. 9.

[89] 4th Marine Div Opns Rpt Saipan, Annex H 23d RCT Rpt, p. 48; Hoffman, *Saipan,* p. 238.
[90] 4th Marine Div Opns Rpt Saipan, Sec. VI, pp. 36–37; Hoffman, *Saipan,* pp. 239–42.
[91] NTLF Rpt Marianas, Phase I, Incl E, G–3 Rpt, G–3 Periodic Rpt 25.

ous American efforts to induce both military and civilian survivors to give themselves up, the traditional Japanese code of death before surrender prevailed in most cases. Shortly after the declaration that the island was secured, hundreds of civilians leapt from the cliffs of Marpi Point to the knifelike rocks below. At times the waters below the point were so thick with the floating bodies of men, women, and children that naval small craft were unable to steer a course without running over them.[92]

On the 9th many Japanese soldiers swam out to the reefs of Tanapag Harbor and defied capture. 1st Lt. Kenneth J. Hensley, USMC, commanding officer of Company G, 6th Marines, was ordered out with a small flotilla of amphibian tractors to capture or destroy these die-hards. A few surrendered, but most refused to give up. From one reef, to which fifty to sixty Japanese were clinging, machine guns opened up on the approaching LVT's. The Americans returned fire and the force was annihilated. On another reef a Japanese officer was seen beheading his little band of enlisted men with his sword before he himself was shot down by his would-be captors.[93]

For the remainder of their brief stay on Saipan, the marines spent most of their days investigating the caves and wooded sections along the north shore. On 13 July the 3d Battalion, 6th Marines, occupied tiny Maniagassa Island in Tanapag Harbor in a miniature amphibious landing complete with naval gunfire, artillery, and aerial bombardment. They found twenty-nine Japanese soldiers on the island, but encountered no serious opposition.[94] This action brought to an end Marine activities on Saipan. The 2d and 4th Divisions both withdrew to prepare for the assault on nearby Tinian. The Army took over the job of clearing out the last remnants of the enemy. From 31 July through 6 August, the 27th Division conducted a gradual sweeping operation with two regiments abreast from just north of Mount Tapotchau to Marpi Point, thus concluding the organized mop-up.[95] Starting the middle of August and ending in October, the division embarked in stages for the much welcomed trip to the New Hebrides for rehabilitation.[96]

The toll of American killed and wounded was high. Of the 71,034 officers and men that made up Holland Smith's Northern Troops and Landing Force,[97] it is estimated that 3,674 Army and 10,437 Marine Corps personnel were killed, wounded, or missing in action.[98] This total of 14,111 represents about 20 percent of the combat troops committed, or roughly the same percentage of casualties suffered at Tarawa and Peleliu, both of bloody renown.[99]

In exchange, almost the entire Japanese

---

[92] For eyewitness accounts of this episode, see Robert Sherrod, *On To Westward: War in the Central Pacific* (New York, Duell, Sloan and Pearce, Inc., 1945).

[93] NTLF Rpt Marianas, Phase I, Incl D, G–2 Rpt, App. K.

[94] 6th RCT SAR FORAGER, p. 17.

[95] 27th Inf Div G–3 Rpt, G–3 Periodic Rpts 45–50.

[96] 27th Inf Div, Hist of 27th Inf Div, 20 Mar 45, p. 4.

[97] Figure is from TF 51 Opns Rpt Marianas, p. 6.

[98] Army casualty figures are derived from 27th Inf Div G–1 Periodic Rpt, 6 Aug 44, Annex B, and XXIV Corps Final Rpt, S–1 Rpt. Marine Corps figures were compiled by Machine Records Sec, Hq USMC, and published in Hoffman, *Saipan*, pp. 268–69.

[99] Smith, *Approach to the Philippines*, pp. 472–577; Stockman, *The Battle for Tarawa*, p. 67.

garrison of about 30,000 men was wiped out. Far more important, the inner defense line of the Japanese Empire had been cracked, and American forces were at last within bombing range of the enemy homeland.

PART THREE

TINIAN

CHAPTER XIII

American and Japanese Plans

Writing after the war, Admiral Spruance expressed the opinion, "The Tinian operation was probably the most brilliantly conceived and executed amphibious operation in World War II."[1] To General Holland Smith's mind, "Tinian was the perfect amphibious operation in the Pacific war."[2] Historians have—by and large—endorsed these sentiments.[3]

Much of this praise is well deserved, although a close examination of the facts reveals that these, like most superlatives, are somewhat misleading. The invasion of Tinian, like other military operations, was not entirely without flaw. Various deficiences can be charged to both plan and execution. Yet, as an exercise in amphibious skill it must be given a superior rating, and as a demonstration of ingenuity it stands as second to no other landing operation in the Pacific war.

Situated only about 3.5 miles off the southern coast of Saipan, Tinian is the smaller of the two islands. (*Map IV.*) From Ushi Point in the north to Lalo Point in the south, it measures about 12.5 miles, and in width it never extends much more

than 5 miles.[4] In one respect its terrain is not as formidable for would-be attackers than that of Saipan—it is far less mountainous. In the northern part of the island Mount Lasso rises to 564 feet, or only a little more than a third of the height of Tapotchau. Another hill mass of almost the same height dominates the southern tip of the island and terminates in heavily fissured cliffs that drop steeply into the sea. Most of the rest of the island is an undulating plain, which in the summer of 1944 was planted in neat checkerboard fields of sugar cane.

It was indeed the relative flatness of Tinian's terrain that made it such a desirable objective—that and the fact that its proximity to Saipan made its retention by the Japanese militarily inadmissible. Tinian's sweeping plains and gentle slopes offered better sites for bomber fields than its more mountainous sister island, and of course one of the main objectives of the Marianas operation was to obtain sites for air bases for very long range bombers. To a limited extent, the Japanese had already realized this possibility and near Ushi Point had constructed an airfield that boasted a runway almost a thousand feet longer than Aslito's. In addition, smaller fields were located just south of the Ushi Point field and at Gurguan Point, and another was under

---

[1] Quoted in Maj. Carl W. Hoffman, USMC, *The Seizure of Tinian*, Historical Division, Headquarters, U.S. Marine Corps (Washington, 1951) (hereafter cited as Hoffman, *Tinian*), p. III.

[2] Smith, *Coral and Brass*, p. 201.

[3] See Isely and Crowl, *U.S. Marines and Amphibious War*, p. 352; Morison, *New Guinea and the Marianas*, p. 351; Hoffman, *Tinian, passim.*

[4] JICPOA Bull 73-74, 10 May 44, p. 2off.

COASTAL AREA, NORTHWEST TINIAN, *showing White Beach areas, checkerboard terrain inland, and Ushi Point airfield in background.*

construction just northeast of Tinian Town.[5]

But if the island was well suited by nature for the construction of airfields, its natural features were also well disposed to obstruct a landing from the sea. Tinian is really a plateau jutting up from the surrounding ocean, and most of its coast line consists of cliffs rising sharply out of the water. Only in four places is this solid cliff line interrupted. Inland of Sunharon Bay, in the area of Tinian Town on the southwest coast, the land runs gradually to the sea, offering a fairly wide expanse of beach protected by the usual reef line. South of Asiga Point on the east coast there is an indenture in the cliff wall that forms a small approachable beach about 125 yards in length. The northwest coast line offers

other possible routes of ingress through the cliffs over two tiny beaches about 60 and 150 yards in length, respectively.[6]

The peculiar features of the coast line placed American planners in a dilemma. The beaches off Tinian Town were obviously the best suited for a landing operation, but by the same token they were the best fortified and defended. The other beaches, which were little more than dents in the cliff line, were obviously not desirable sites for an amphibious assault of corps dimensions. The risks of troops and supplies being congested to the point of immobility as they tried to pour through these narrow bottlenecks were considerable and alarming. For these reasons, which were just as apparent to the Japanese as to the Americans, defenses on the smaller

---

[5] NTLF Rpt Marianas, Phase III, Incl D, G–2 Rpt, p. 32.

[6] *Ibid.,* Annex A.

beaches were less formidable than those elsewhere.

In the end, the American planners seized the second rather than the first horn of their dilemma, chose the narrow beaches on the northwest coast, and accepted the risks that troops, equipment, and supplies might pile up in hopeless confusion at the water's edge. Having made the choice, the planners were compelled to devise special means of overcoming the accepted risks. This involved working out novel techniques that were radical modifications of standard amphibious doctrine as it had been evolved during the war in the Pacific. Paradoxically then the invasion of Tinian was a "perfect amphibious operation" largely because it was atypical rather than typical— because of its numerous departures from, rather than its strict adherence to, accepted amphibious doctrine.

Plan for the Invasion

From the very outset of the planning for the seizure of the southern Marianas, Tinian had been considered one of the three main targets of the operation. Holland Smith's Northern Troops and Landing Force was ordered to "land, seize, occupy and defend SAIPAN Island, and then . . . be prepared for further operations to seize, occupy and defend TINIAN Island." [7] Consequently, planning for the Tinian phase commenced at the same time as that for the capture of Saipan and was continuous until the very day of the landing on Saipan. By the time Admiral Turner's task force set sail from Pearl Harbor, maps, photographs, and charts of Tinian had been distributed and tentative arrangements had been made for loading and for resupply shipping. While at sea, Holland Smith's staff had more leisure than earlier to concern itself with this phase of the operation, and by the time the ships reached Eniwetok a draft plan was ready for the commanding general. In devising this plan, the staff gave due consideration to the relative merits of the various landing beaches and recommended that a landing be made on northern Tinian in order to make full use of artillery emplaced on southern Saipan.[8]

While the fighting for Saipan was in process, the Americans were afforded ideal opportunities for scrutinizing the island to the south from every angle. Beginning on 20 June, when artillery first bombarded Tinian from southern Saipan,[9] observation planes flew daily over northern Tinian. Frequent photo reconnaissance missions were flown, and many valuable documents throwing light on Tinian's defenses were captured on Saipan.[10] Opportunities for gathering intelligence were almost without limit, and it is doubtful if any single enemy island was better reconnoitered during the Pacific war.

With Saipan secured and the preparations for the next landing in mid-passage, a change in command within the Northern Troops and Landing Force was ordered. On 12 July General Holland Smith was relieved and ordered to take command of Fleet Marine Force, Pacific, a newly created headquarters for all Marine Corps combat units in the theater. The new commanding general of Northern Troops and Landing Force was General Schmidt, who

---

[7] NTLF Opn Plan 30–44, 10 May 44, in NTLF Rpt Marianas, Phase I, Incl A.

[8] NTLF Rpt Marianas, Phase III, p. 2.

[9] XXIV Corps Arty Final Rpt on FORAGER Opn, S–3 Rpt, p. 6.

[10] NTLF Rpt Marianas, Phase III, p. 3.

was in turn relieved of his command of the 4th Marine Division by General Cates.[11] Concurrently, a shift in the naval command structure took place. Admiral Hill, who had served as Admiral Turner's second in command, took over a reconstituted Northern Attack Force (Task Force 52) and thus became responsible, under the Commander, Joint Expeditionary Force (Admiral Turner as Commander, Task Force 51), for the capture of Tinian.[12]

As planning for Tinian went into high gear, it was becoming increasingly apparent to all hands that the original concept of landing the assault troops somewhere in the northern part of the island was sound. Members of the staff of the 4th Marine Division, notably Lt. Col. Evans F. Carlson, the division's planning officer, had already decided that an amphibious landing in this area was desirable. Working independently of the Marines, Admiral Hill had arrived at the same conclusion.[13] All agreed that the Tinian Town area was too well defended to justify an amphibious assault there and that the advantages of heavy artillery support for landings on the northern beaches were too considerable to ignore.

All, that is, but one. Admiral Turner was still not convinced. In his mind, the Tinian Town beaches offered important advantages that should not be lightly dismissed. From the point of view of gradient and inland approaches, the Tinian Town beaches were even more favorable to the attacker than those used on Saipan and certainly far better than Tinian's other beaches. Also, Sunharon Bay offered an excellent protected harbor for small craft and good facilities for unloading supplies, once the beachhead was secured. On the other hand, the beaches in the northern half of the island, argued the admiral, were too narrow to permit a rapid landing of a force of two divisions with full supplies and equipment, and if the weather took a turn for the worse the shore-to-shore movement of supplies in small craft from Saipan might be seriously endangered. In addition, an advance down the full length of the island would take too much time, and the troops would soon outrun their artillery support based on Saipan—an especially dangerous prospect should weather conditions forbid shifting the heavy artillery pieces from Saipan to Tinian.[14]

In the light of these objections and out of ordinary considerations of military caution, General Schmidt ordered a physical reconnaissance of the northern beaches. The task fell to the Amphibious Reconnaissance Battalion, V Amphibious Corps, commanded by Capt. James L. Jones, USMCR, and naval Underwater Demolition Teams 5 and 7, commanded by Lt. Comdr. Draper L. Kauffman, USN, and Lt. Richard F. Burke, USN, respectively. Their job was to reconnoiter Yellow Beach 1 on the eastern coast below Asiga Point and White Beaches 1 and 2 on the northwestern coast. Under cover of darkness the three groups were to be carried part way to their destinations by the high-speed transports *Gilmer* and *Stringham*. Then, launched in rubber landing boats (LCR's), they would be paddled to distances about 500 yards offshore and swim in the rest of the way. The men were charged with the responsibility of investigating and securing

[11] *Ibid.*, p. 4; Smith, *Coral and Brass*, p. 201.
[12] TF 51 Opn Rpt Marianas, p. 2.
[13] Hoffman, *Tinian*, pp. 20, 161.

[14] Ltr, Turner to Comdt USMC, 21 Dec 50, quoted in Hoffman, *Tinian*, p. 21.

Marianas Leaders Confer at Tinian. *Left to right: Rear Adm. Harry Hill, Maj. Gen. Harry A. Schmidt, Admiral Spruance, General Holland Smith, Admiral Turner, Maj. Gen. Thomas E. Watson, and Maj. Gen. Clifton B. Cates.*

accurate information concerning the height of surf, the height and nature of the reef shelf, depth of water, location and nature of mines and underwater obstacles, the slope of the bottom off the beaches, the height and nature of cliffs flanking and behind the beaches, exits for vehicles, and the nature of vegetation behind the beaches. The naval personnel would conduct the hydrographic reconnaissance while members of the Marine amphibious reconnaissance group were to reconnoiter the beaches themselves and the terrain inland.[15]

After dark on 10 July, but well before moonrise, *Gilmer* and *Stringham* got under

way from Magicienne Bay on the east coast of Saipan to take their respective stations off of Yellow Beach 1 and White Beaches 1 and 2. As the rubber boats approached Yellow Beach 1, the men heard sharp reports and thought they were being fired on, but went about their business anyway. Two of the men swam along the cliffs south of the beach and discovered them to be 20 to 25 feet high and unscalable by infantry without ladders or nets. One Marine officer, 2d Lt. Donald Neff, left two of his men at the highwater mark and worked his way along inland for some thirty yards to investigate the possibilities for vehicle exits. Japanese sentries were apparently patrolling the entire area, but the suspected rifle shots proved to be exploding caps being used by construction workers

[15] NTLF Rpt Marianas, Phase III, Incl L, Amph Rcn Bn Rpt, Annex A, pp. 1–2.

nearby. In any case, all hands got back to their ships without being detected.[16]

Meanwhile, on the other side of the island, the reconnaissance of White Beaches 1 and 2 hit a snag. As the rubber boats cast off they were set rapidly to the north by a strong current that they had not been compensated for. Hence the swimmers assigned to White Beach 2, the southernmost of the two, ended up on White 1, while the second group destined for the latter beach were set ashore about 800 yards to the north. This left White 2 unreconnoitered, and next night another group of swimmers had to return to finish the job.[17]

The information gathered during the two nights fully justified the valiant labor expended. Yellow Beach 1 was clearly unsuitable for an amphibious landing. In addition to its natural disadvantages, the beach was strung with strong double-apron wire, and large, floating, contact mines were found anchored about a foot underwater off the reef.[18] On the other side of the island no man-made obstacles were reported on White Beaches 1 and 2. Although White Beach 1 to the north was only sixty yards in length, the bluffs that flanked it for about 150 yards on either side were only from six to ten feet in height and offered enough small breaks to permit men to proceed inland in single file without the need of cargo nets or scaling ladders. From the reef to the shore line the water depth was never more than four feet and the gradient was slight. Of the hundred and fifty yards of White Beach 2, only the central seventy yards were approachable by amphibian vehicles, the flanks of the beach being guarded by coral barriers jutting out

from the reef. Nevertheless, the barriers offered no obstacle to infantrymen, who could scramble over them and wade the rest of the way in. At two hours before high tide the water inside the reef was nowhere more than four feet in depth.[19] In short, although the White Beaches were far from ideal for landing purposes, they were better than Yellow Beach 1, and except for their narrowness offered no known natural or man-made obstacles.

With this information in hand, Admiral Turner's objections to a landing on the northwest coast, however strong they may once have been, were overcome. At a meeting held aboard his flagship on 12 July, General Schmidt made a forceful presentation of the case for the White Beaches. An amphibious assault against the strong enemy defenses in the Tinian Town area would be too costly; artillery could be more profitably employed against the northern beaches; Ushi Point airfield would be more quickly seized and made ready; tactical surprise could be obtained; the operation could more easily be conducted as a shore-to-shore movement from Saipan; and, finally, most of the supplies could be preloaded on Saipan and moved on amphibian tractors and trucks directly to inland dumps on Tinian. Admiral Hill concurred, and Admirals Turner and Spruance gave their consent to a landing on White Beaches 1 and 2.[20]

The next day, 13 July, General Schmidt issued the operation plan that was to govern the invasion of Tinian.[21] General Cates' 4th Marine Division was assigned the task of conducting the amphibious as-

---

[16] *Ibid.*, Annex A; Annex E.
[17] *Ibid.*, Annex B.
[18] *Ibid.*, Annex E.

[19] *Ibid.*, Annexes D and E.
[20] Hoffman, *Tinian*, pp. 23–24.
[21] NTLF Opn Plan 30–44, 13 Jul 44, NTLF Rpt Marianas, Phase III, Incl A.

sault over White Beaches 1 and 2 on JIG Day, which was later established as 24 July. On landing, the division was to make its main effort toward Mount Lasso and, before reorganizing, seize the Force Beachhead Line, which included Faibus San Hilo Point, Mount Lasso, and Asiga Point. Once this area was captured, it was presumed that the beachhead would be safe from ground-observed enemy artillery fire. To accomplish the division's mission General Cates ordered the 24th Marines to land in column of battalions on White Beach 1 on the left, the 25th Marines with two battalions abreast on White Beach 2. The 23d Marines would remain in division reserve.[22]

The assault troops would be carried ashore in the customary fashion in amphibian tractors discharged fully loaded from LST's. Of the 415 tractors assigned to carry troops, 225 were supplied by Army units—the 715th, 773d, and 534th Amphibian Tractor Battalions. The remainder were Marine LVT's from the 2d, 5th, and 10th Amphibian Tractor Battalions. Because of the narrowness of the landing beaches, only one company of amphibian tanks could be employed in the assault, Company D, 2d Armored Amphibian Tractor Battalion (Marine). The battalion was ordered to precede the first wave of troops, fire on the beaches after naval gunfire was lifted, and move to the flanks before reaching land. The 708th Armored Amphibian Tank Battalion (Army) was ordered to stand by off the beaches and be prepared to land and support the infantry ashore.[23]

As before, command of the entire operation was vested in Admiral Turner as Commander, Joint Expeditionary Force (Task Force 51), under Admiral Spruance; General Holland Smith, who still retained his position of Commander, Expeditionary Troops, continued in over-all command of troops ashore. In fact, however, both of these officers had sailed aboard *Rocky Mount* on 20 July to be on hand for the Guam landings, which took place the next day, and did not return to the Saipan–Tinian area until the 25th.[24] During the landing then, Admiral Hill, as Commander, Northern Attack Force (Task Force 52), commanded all naval craft and supporting forces, while General Schmidt commanded the landing forces.[25] Even after Admiral Turner returned, Admiral Hill retained the responsibility "for offensive and defensive surface and air action" in the area and for all practical purposes Schmidt remained in tactical control of the troops.[26]

Because most of the heavy artillery pieces could more profitably be employed from emplacements on Saipan, the 4th Marine Division would carry only 75-mm. pack howitzers in the initial assault. In addition to its own two battalions (1st and 2d Battalions, 14th Marines), it was loaned the two light battalions of the 2d Marine Division (1st and 2d Battalions, 10th Marines). These battalions would be carried ashore in Marine DUKW's. Additional fire power was afforded the division by attaching the 2d Division's tank battalion. Army troops (1341st Engineer

---

[22] 4th Marine Div Opn Order 34–44.
[23] NTLF Rpt Marianas, Phase III, Incl H, LVT Rpt, pp. 1–3.

[24] TF 51 Opn Rpt Marianas, Incl A, pp. 17–19.
[25] NTLF Opn Plan 30–44, Annex I.
[26] TF 51 Opn Rpt Marianas, Incl A, pp. 17–19.

LVT With Ramp

Battalion) would make up part of the assault division's shore party, the remainder being provided by the 2d Battalion, 20th Marines.[27]

To the rest of General Watson's 2d Marine Division was assigned the role of landing in the rear of the assault division once the latter had cleared an initial beachhead and moved inland. Before this, the division was to conduct a demonstration landing off Tinian Town for the purpose of diverting Japanese attention from the main assault to the north.[28]

The 27th Infantry Division, less the 105th Infantry and less its organic artillery, was to remain in corps reserve and "be prepared to embark in landing craft

on 4 hours notice and land on order . . . on Tinian."

One of the main justifications for the final decision to land over the unlikely beaches on the northwestern shore of the island was the feasibility of full exploitation of artillery firing from Saipan. Consequently, all of the field pieces in the area except for the four battalions of 75-mm. pack howitzers were turned over to XXIV Corps Artillery during the preliminary and landing phase. General Harper arranged his thirteen battalions, totaling 156 guns and howitzers, into three groupments, all emplaced on southern Saipan. Groupment A, commanded by Col. Raphael Griffin, USMC, consisted of five 105-mm. battalions, two each from the Marine divisions and one from V Amphibious Corps. It was to reinforce the fires of the 75-mm. pack howitzers and be ready to move to Tinian

---

[27] NTLF Opn Plan 30–44, 13 Jul 44.

[28] This scheme was not part of the original operation plan, but was devised shortly before the assault took place.

on order. Groupment B, under the 27th Division's artillery commander, General Kernan, was made up of all of that division's organic artillery except the 106th Field Artillery Battalion. It was to reinforce the fires of Groupment A and also to be ready to displace to Tinian. Groupment C, commanded by General Harper himself, contained all the howitzers and guns of XXIV Corps Artillery plus the 106th Field Artillery Battalion. It was to support the attack with counterbattery, neutralization, and harassing fire before the day of the landing, deliver a half-hour preparation on the landing beaches immediately before the scheduled touchdown, and execute long-range counterbattery, harassing, and interdiction fire.[29]

In addition to the artillery, the troops would of course have the support of carrier-borne aircraft, aircraft based on Aslito field, and naval gunfire. Although all three supporting arms were to be employed against targets everywhere on Tinian, primary responsibility for the northern half was allocated to artillery while naval gunfire and air took over the southern half. The task of co-ordinating the three was vested in a XXIV Corps Artillery representative at General Schmidt's headquarters.[30]

The most unique feature of the plan for Tinian was its logistical provisions. Because only slightly more than 200 yards of beach were available, it was essential that precautions be taken to avoid congestion. Hence, a supply plan was developed that allowed all supplies to cross the beach on wheels or tracks and move directly to division dumps without rehandling. This entailed devising

a double shuttle system in which loaded trucks and Athey trailers traveled back and forth between the base supply dumps on Saipan and division supply dumps on Tinian, and all amphibian vehicles carrying supplies between ship and shore moved directly to division dumps. The objective was to avoid any manhandling of supplies on the beaches themselves. The solution represented a marked departure from standard amphibious practice and was made possible, of course, by the proximity of Tinian to the supply center on Saipan.[31]

The plan called for preloading thirty-two LST's and two LSD's at Saipan with top-deck loads of all necessary supplies except fuel. Ten LST's were allotted to each Marine division, eight to general reserve, and four primarily to 75-mm. artillery. All amphibian tractors and trucks available, both Army and Marine Corps, were initially assigned to the 4th Marine Division, but after the assault was over were to be distributed between the two divisions. The supplies were loaded on the LST's in slings, and the ships carried crawler cranes on their top decks so that the slings could drop supplies into DUKW's and LVT's coming alongside. To carry out the shuttle system, the plan called for preloading eighty-eight cargo trucks and twenty-five Athey trailers on Saipan to be taken to Tinian aboard LCT's and LCM's. A special provision for fuel supply was made. Seven ponton barges loaded with drums of captured Japanese gasoline and matching lubricants were to be towed to positions off the landing beaches to act as floating supply and fueling points for LVT's and DUKW's. Other fuels for initially refueling the trucks were

---

[29] NTLF Opn Plan 30–44, Annex F.
[30] *Ibid.*, Annexes C, D, F.

[31] NTLF Rpt Marianas, Phase III, Incl F, G–4 Rpt, p. 1.

placed on barges that were to be spotted off the beaches.[32]

One other innovation introduced in the Tinian campaign was a special portable LVT bow ramp. Ten amphibian tractors were equipped with this device so as to provide a means for extending the narrow beach area. The ramps were so constructed that an LVT could drive up to a cliff flanking the beaches, place the ramp in position along the ledge, then back down leaving the ramp to act as a sort of causeway by which other vehicles could get to shore.[33]

Finally, precautions were taken to supply the troops in case of unexpected bad weather after the landing. Plans were made to drop about 30 tons of supplies by parachute and to deliver 100 tons by air daily to Ushi Point airfield as soon as it had been captured.[34]

The Enemy

As already observed, the opportunities for gaining detailed intelligence of Tinian's defenses were superior to those enjoyed by American forces in most Pacific operations. Proof of this superiority lies in the accuracy with which General Schmidt's staff was able to estimate Japanese strength and dispositions. As of 13 July they predicted, on the basis of captured documents, photo reconnaissance, and other intelligence data, that the strength of the Tinian garrison came to 8,350, plus possible home guard units. The main part of this force was believed to consist of the *50th Infantry Regiment* (reinforced)—about 4,000 men—

---

[32] *Ibid.,* p. 2.
[33] NTLF Rpt Marianas, Phase III, Incl H, LVT Rpt, p. 3.
[34] TF 52 Rpt Tinian, pp. 1–3.

and the *56th Keibitai* (*Naval Guard Force*)—about 1,100 men—plus sundry air defense, base force, and construction personnel. The Army troops were believed to be disposed in three sectors, northern, western, and southern, which included respectively the Ushi Point–Asiga Bay retion, the west coast north of Gurguan Point including White Beaches 1 and 2, and the southern part of the island including Tinian Town. The northern and southern sectors were thought to be defended by at least one infantry battalion each, but the western sector where White Beaches 1 and 2 were located had, it was estimated, only one company with one antitank squad. It was predicted that in each of these sectors the Japanese would first try to repulse the landing at the water's edge and would shift two thirds of each defense force from the areas not under attack to the beaches where the actual landings were taking place. A reserve force of one battalion was believed to be located near Mount Lasso, and it too was expected to move to the specific area under amphibious attack. One artillery battalion was thought to be located in the Tinian Harbor area, one battery near Asiga Bay. These estimates, except those pertaining to artillery strength, were remarkably accurate.

The defense of Tinian was in the charge of Col. Takashi Ogata, commanding officer, *50th Infantry Regiment*, which represented the bulk of the Japanese Army forces on the island. Other important units were the *1st Battalion, 135th Infantry;* the *Tank Company, 18th Infantry;* the *56th Naval Guard Force;* and two naval antiaircraft defense units. All together, Ogata had four Army infantry battalions, none of which were straggler units, plus additional

TABLE 1—ESTIMATED STRENGTH OF THE JAPANESE GARRISON ON TINIAN

Unit	Unit Commander	Estimated Strength
Grand total		8,039
Army—total		3,929
50th Infantry Regiment	Col. Takashi Ogata	
Headquarters	—	60
1st Battalion	—	a576
2d Battalion	—	576
3d Battalion	—	576
Artillery Battalion (12 75-mm. mountain guns)	Maj. Katuro Kahi	360
Engineer Company	Lt. Chuichi Yano	169
Antitank Platoon (6 37-mm. antitank guns)	2d Lt. Moto Otani	42
Signal Company	Lt. Hayashi	141
Supply Company	Lt. Kenishi Nozaki	200
Medical Company	Lt. Masaakira Narazawa	130
Fortification Detachment	Capt. Masagi Hiruma	60
1st Battalion, 135th Infantry Regiment	Capt. Isumi	b714
18th Infantry Regiment Tank Company (9 tanks and 2 amphibian trucks)	Lt. Katsuo Shikamura	c 65
264th Independent Motor Transport Company platoon	—	60
29th Field Hospital Detachment	—	200
Navy—total		4,110
56th Naval Guard Force	Capt. Goichi Oya	950
82d Antiaircraft Defense Unit (24 25-mm. antitank guns)	Lt.(s.g.)Kichitaro Tanaka	200
83d Antiaircraft Defense Unit (6 dual-purpose 75-mm. guns)	Lt.(s.g.)Meiki Tanaka	250
233d Construction Unit	—	600
Headquarters, 1st Air Fleet	Vice Adm. Kakuji Kakuta	200
Air units (mostly 523d TOKA)	—	1,110
Miscellaneous construction personnel	—	800

—Unknown.

aThe strength figures for the three infantry regiments given here are somewhat lower than those estimated by NTLF, chiefly because the latter included attached artillery units in its infantry strength estimates. The figure 576 is the actual strength of the *2d Battalion, 50th Infantry,* as of February 1944 (*Headquarters, 2d Battalion, 50th Infantry Regiment,* War Diary, February 1944, NA 27434). It is assumed that the other regiments were approximately the same.

bEstimated on the basis of unit records for May 1944 of *Headquarters, 1st and 3d Companies,* and *Infantry Gun Company* (NA 22237, 27394, 27393).

cShikamura Tai War Diary, 29 April to 23 July 1944 (NA 22831).

Source: These strength figures are derived from NTLF Rpt Marianas, Phase III, Incl A, G-2 Rpt, pp. 24–30 and TF 56 Rpt FORAGER, Annex A, G-2 Rpt, p. 57.

infantry in the *56th Naval Guard Force* and other naval units. For artillery, the Japanese commander had his regimental artillery battalion, the coast artillery manned by part of the *56th Naval Guard Force,* and two naval antiaircraft defense units. The *18th Infantry Tank Company* had nine tanks, which constituted the entire armored strength present. Total personnel strength, as indicated in Table 1, came to a little more than eight thousand officers and men, Army and Navy.

As foreseen by General Schmidt's intelligence section, the Japanese Army plan for the defense of Tinian provided for the disposition of forces in three sectors. (*Map 15*) The northern sector force guarding Ushi Point, Asiga Bay, and part of Masalog Point was the responsibility of the *2d Battalion, 50th Infantry,* and a platoon of engineers; the western sector, containing Mount Lasso and the northwest coast, was guarded only by the *3d Company, 1st Battalion, 50th Infantry,* and an antitank squad. Regimental reserve in the southern sector consisted of the *1st Battalion, 50th Infantry,* less the *3d Company* and less one antitank squad and was located about 3,000 yards southeast of Faibus San Hilo Point. The *1st Battalion, 135th Infantry,* was designated "mobile counterattack force," and was in effect another reserve. Ogata's armored strength came to only nine tanks of the *Tank Company, 18th Infantry,* which was located on the northeast side of Marpo Well with orders to advance either to Tinian Town or Asiga Bay, wherever the landings came. In addition, this company had two vehicles rarely found among Japanese forces, amphibious trucks similar to the American DUKW.[35]

Japanese naval personnel on the island were under the command of Capt. Goichi Oya, who reported to Colonel Ogata. There was another, more senior, naval officer present on the island, but he held no position in the chain of command and had nothing to do with the defense of Tinian. This was Vice Adm. Kakuji Kakuta, Commander in Chief, *1st Air Fleet,* who was responsible only to Admiral Nagumo of the *Central Pacific Area Fleet.* After the loss of most of his planes in the Battle of the

Philippine Sea, Kakuta made several efforts to escape Tinian by submarine. Each time he failed, and in the end he apparently committed suicide.[36]

Captain Oya appears to have made some effort to integrate his command with that of the Army. The *56th Naval Guard Force* was charged with the defense of the air bases, defense of harbor installations and ships in the harbor, and destruction of enemy attack forces. The force was divided into two parts. One was to man the coastal defense guns and antiaircraft weapons and the other, called the *Coastal Security Force,* was to maintain small coastal patrol boats and lay beach mines. No matter what the intentions of either commander, however, it would seem that there was little real co-ordination or even co-operation between Army and Navy forces. There may have been serious interservice friction.[37] This is at least suggested in the captured diary of one Army noncommissioned officer, who wrote:

15 June: The Naval aviators are robbers. There aren't any planes. When they ran off to the mountains, they stole Army provisions, robbed people of their fruits and took cars. . . .

25 June: Sailors have stolen our provisions. They took food off to the mountains. We must bear with such until the day of decisive battle. . . .

6 July: Did Vice-Admiral Kakuta when he heard that the enemy had entered our area go to sleep with joy?[38]

---

[35] NTLF Rpt Marianas, Phase III, Incl A, G–2 Rpt, pp. 8–9.

[36] *Ibid.,* p. 21; 4th Marine Div Opns Rpt Tinian, G–2 Rpt, Special Intel Rpt 4.

[37] 4th Marine Div, Representative Translations Made on Tinian, Record and Research Sec, Hist Br, G–3 Hq USMC, Sec. I, Sec. IX, p. 3.

[38] CINCPAC-CINCPOA Trans 11405, excerpts from the diary of a noncommissioned officer, a member of the *Medical Administrative Unit, Mountain Artillery Battalion, 50th Infantry Regiment.*

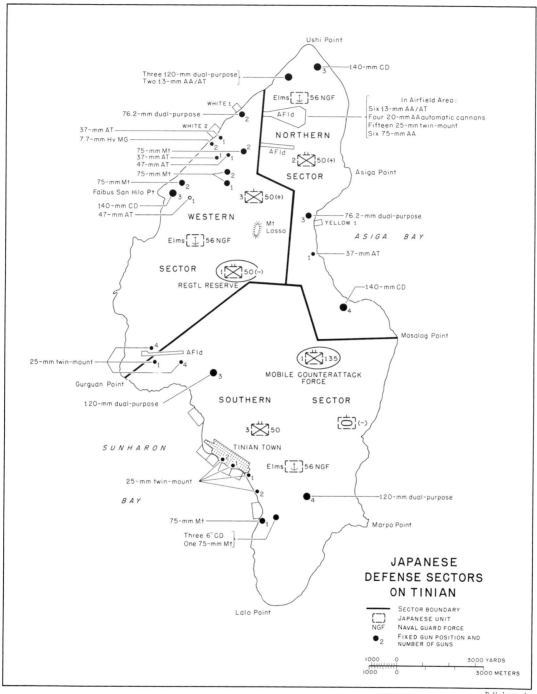

Ushi Point

140-mm CD

Three 120-mm dual-purpose
Two 13-mm AA/AT

WHITE 1

76.2-mm dual-purpose

Elms ⊥ 56 NGF

In Airfield Area:
Six 13-mm AA/AT
Four 20-mm AA automatic cannons
Fifteen 25-mm twin-mount
Six 75-mm AA

AFld

37-mm AT

WHITE 2

NORTHERN

7.7-mm Hv MG

AFld

75-mm Mt
37-mm AT
47-mm AT

2 ⊠ 50 (+)

SECTOR

Asiga Point

75-mm Mt

75-mm Mt

3 ⊠ 50 (+)

Faibus San Hilo Pt

140-mm CD
47-mm AT

3   76.2-mm dual-purpose

WESTERN

YELLOW 1

A S I G A   B A Y

Mt
Lasso

37-mm AT

Elms ⊥ 56 NGF

SECTOR

1 ⊠ 50 (−)

REGTL RESERVE

140-mm CD

4

Masalog Point

4   AFld

25-mm twin-mount

4

1 ⊠ 135

Gurguan Point

3

MOBILE COUNTERATTACK
FORCE

120-mm dual-purpose

SOUTHERN   SECTOR

3 ⊠ 50

⊡ (−)

S U N H A R O N

Tinian Town

2

Elms ⊥ 56 NGF

25-mm twin-mount

1

B A Y

2

120-mm dual-purpose

4

75-mm Mt

1

Marpo Point

Three 6" CD
One 75-mm Mt

JAPANESE
DEFENSE SECTORS
ON TINIAN

Lalo Point

Sector boundary
Japanese unit
NGF   Naval guard force
●₂   Fixed gun position and
number of guns

1000   0   3000 YARDS
1000   0   3000 METERS

MAP 15

D. Holmes, Jr.

Responsibility for coastal defense was divided about equally between Army and Navy. Because of the small number of beaches over which hostile troops could possibly land, the problem was somewhat simplified. Consequently, even with the rather limited means at hand, it was possible for the Japanese to distribute their fixed gun positions so as to place a fairly heavy guard around the only feasible approaches to the shore. The Tinian Town area boasted three British-made 6-inch coastal defense guns, two 75-mm. mountain guns,[39] and six 25-mm. twin-mount antiaircraft and antitank automatic cannons. Just up the coast from Tinian Town in the area of Gurguan Point were three 120-mm. naval dual-purpose guns and nine 25-mm. twin mounts that guarded the northern approaches to Sunharon Bay as well as the Gurguan Point airfield. The northwest coast from Ushi Point to Faibus San Hilo Point, including the area of White Beaches 1 and 2, was quite well fortified, especially considering that the Japanese had no real expectations of hostile amphibious landings in that area. All together, this stretch of coast line contained three 140-mm. coastal defense guns, two 75-mm. mountain guns, two 7.7-mm. heavy machine guns in pillboxes, one 37-mm. covered antitank gun, two 13-mm. antiaircraft and antitank machine guns, two 76.2-mm. dual-purpose guns, and three 120-mm. naval and dual-purpose guns. In addition, in the hills behind and within range of this shore line were two

47-mm. antitank guns, one 37-mm. antitank gun, and five 75-mm. mountain guns. Guarding Ushi Point airfield were six 13-mm. antiaircraft and antitank guns, fifteen 25-mm. twin mounts, four 20-mm. antiaircraft automatic cannons, and six 75-mm. antiaircraft guns. On the northeast coast, between Ushi Point and Masalog Point, were seven 140-mm. coastal defense guns, three 76.2-mm. dual-purpose guns, one 37-mm. antitank gun, and twenty-three pillboxes containing machine guns of unknown caliber. Except for the coastal defense guns, all of these weapons were concentrated in the area of Yellow Beach 1, south of Asiga Point. Finally, inland from Marpo Point on the southeast coast there were four 120-mm. dual-purpose guns.[40]

The most surprising feature of the distribution of fixed positions is the relatively heavy concentration of guns within range of White Beaches 1 and 2. In spite of the fact that General Ogata assigned a low priority to the infantry defenses in that region, it is quite apparent that the Japanese were by no means entirely neglectful of the area. The figures cited here of course give no indication of the damage wrought on these positions by naval gunfire, field artillery, and aerial bombardment before the landing. But had American intelligence estimates of Japanese artillery dispositions been as accurate as they were in other respects, the plan for an amphibious landing over the White Beaches might not have been undertaken so optimistically.

More accurate knowledge of Japanese mining activities off of White Beaches 1 and 2 might also have given the American

---

[39] The JICPOA report cited below, note 45, lists these as 75-mm. M94 mountain howitzers. This must be an error because the Japanese had no 75-mm. howitzers and their Model 94 field piece was a 75-mm. mountain (pack) gun. (War Dept Technical Manual E 30–480, 15 Sep 44, Handbook on Japanese Military Forces, p. 220.)

[40] JICPOA Study of Japanese Fixed Gun Positions, 24 Jul–5 Aug; Hoffman, *Tinian*, p. 15.

planners pause. The reports of the amphibious reconnaissance and underwater demolition groups to the contrary, the Japanese had set up a mine defense of sorts along the northwest coast. Off White Beach 1 they had laid a dozen horned mines, though by the time of the landing these had deteriorated to the point of impotence. White Beach 2 was mined in depth. Hemispherical mines were placed in two lines offshore, conical yardstick, and box mines covered the exits from the beach. All together, more than a hundred horned mines were laid in the area. In addition, there were many antipersonnel mines and booby traps concealed in cases of beer, watches, and souvenir items scattered inland. On the other side of the island, Yellow Beach 1 was protected by twenty-three horned mines and by double-apron barbed wire. In the Tinian Town area a strip about thirty-five yards wide from the pier north along the water's edge to the sugar mill was completely mined. The beach south of the pier was laid with hemispherical mines that had steel rods lashed across the horns. Behind these were conical mines placed in natural lanes of approach from the shore line.

Until the very eve of the landing, the Japanese worked furiously to improve their beach defenses, especially in the Tinian Town and Asiga Bay areas. Even the gathering rain of American shells and bombs failed to stop them entirely, for when the pressure became too great they worked at night and holed up during the day.[41]

Ogata was well aware that an invasion of Tinian was inevitable, and in one respect he was more fortunate than Saito.[42] Unlike the commanding general of Saipan, he had no stragglers to deal with, and his Army troops were well trained, well equipped, and well integrated under a unified command. He had had his regiment since August of 1940. For almost four years before moving to Tinian the unit had been stationed in Manchuria, and, under the semifield conditions obtaining there, Ogata was able to develop a high degree of homogeneity and *esprit*.[43]

Ogata's plan of defense conformed to standard Japanese doctrine at this stage in the war. The enemy was to be destroyed at the water's edge if possible and, if not, was to be harried out of his beachhead by a counterattack on the night following the landing. "But," read the order, "in the eventuality we have been unable to expel the enemy . . . we will gradually fall back on our prepared positions in the southern part of the island and defend them to the last man." [44]

Whichever of the three possible beach areas was hit by the Americans, the bulk of the Japanese forces in the two other sectors was to rush to the point of attack and close arms with the invader. Tinian Town and Asiga Bay were strongly favored as the probable landing beaches, the northwest coast being relegated to third place in Ogata's list of priorities.[45] Thus, when the Americans chose this unlikely lane of approach, they achieved complete tactical surprise—a rare accomplishment in the Central Pacific theater of war.

---

[41] CINCPAC–CINCPOA Trans 11962, excerpts from the diary of Kaneko Tokutaro, noncommissioned officer at *Hq, 2d Bn, 50th Inf Regt*; Shikamura Tai War Diary, 29 Apr to 23 Jul, NA 22831.

[42] 4th Marine Div Representative Trans.
[43] NTLF Rpt Marianas, Phase III, Incl A, G–2 Rpt, p. 25.
[44] *Ibid.*, p. 9.
[45] 4th Marine Div Representative Trans.

CHAPTER XIV

Invasion and Capture

Preliminary Bombardment

Field Artillery

The decision to land the assault infantry troops across beaches on northwestern Tinian had stemmed in part from a desire to make optimum use of artillery based on Saipan. In many Pacific landings such as those at Tarawa, Saipan, and Iwo Jima it had not been, or was not to be, practicable to seize neighboring islands for the purpose of establishing bases for field artillery before the principal landing operations. Hence reliance had to be put entirely on naval gunfire and aircraft for whatever preliminary bombardment was laid down. In these operations some part, and probably a considerable part, of the casualties incurred by the infantry during the amphibious assault phase must be attributed to the limitations inherent in naval and aerial bombardment. The invasion of Tinian, on the other hand, offered an ideal opportunity to supplement these arms with field artillery. Tinian was, in fact, favored with a more prolonged preliminary artillery bombardment than any other island in the Central Pacific to be assaulted by American troops.

As early as 20 June, Battery B of the 531st Field Artillery Battalion was ordered to emplace its 155-mm. guns to fire on Tinian. Lateral observation posts were established on southern Saipan and counterbattery and destructive fires commenced forthwith. Four days later the battalion's other two batteries, relieved of their duties of supporting the troops on Saipan, turned around and began firing to the south. On 8 July, the day before Saipan was declared secured, the other three battalions of XXIV Corps Artillery were ordered either to turn around in their present positions on southern Saipan or to displace to the area of Agingan Point and commence firing on Tinian.[1] Meanwhile, observation planes made daily flights over Tinian to register fires and to accumulate intelligence data for future use. Observation posts had been established on Agingan Point, Obiam Point, and Nafutan Point. All together, from 20 June through 9 July, while the troops were engaged in capturing Saipan, XXIV Corps Artillery fired a total of 331 missions—7,571 rounds—on Tinian, or roughly a fifth of the total it expended on Saipan.[2]

With Saipan officially secured on 9 July, even greater attention could be directed toward the island to the south. Corps artillery increased the tempo of its bombard-

---

[1] The field artillery battalions were the 225th (155-mm. howitzers), the 145th (105-mm. howitzers), and the 532d (155-mm. guns).

[2] XXIV Corps Arty Final Rpt on FORAGER Opn, Phases I and III, S–2 Rpt, p. 8; *Ibid.*, S–3 Rpt, pp. 7–8.

ment. By 15 July all four battalions of the 27th Division artillery had displaced to new positions to fire on Tinian,[3] as had also the two Marine divisions' howitzers (except for the two 75-mm. pack howitzer battalions of each)[4] and the 5th Battalion, V Amphibious Corps Artillery. This represented a total of 156 pieces—two 155-mm. gun battalions, three 155-mm. howitzer battalions, and eight 105-mm. howitzer battalions.[5] Corps artillery had at its disposal nine organic planes plus the additional observation planes of the units attached. Air activity became so heavy at Isely Field that a new airstrip for the exclusive use of observation planes had to be constructed somewhat to the westward.

Except for a brief period on 16–17 July, when ammunition ran low, artillery maintained a steady round-the-clock schedule of fire totaling 1,509 missions or 24,536 rounds. In addition to counterbattery and harassing and general area bombardment, the artillery attempted to burn off cane fields with white phosphorus shells, but without much success because of the heavy rains that immediately preceded the landing.

For the most part, XXIV Corps Artillery confined its efforts to the area north of the line between Gurguan Point and Masalog Point, while aircraft restricted their efforts to the southern half of the island. Naval ships were assigned any targets on Tinian deemed unsuitable to either of the other two arms. Co-ordination of the three supporting arms was assigned to the corps artillery representative attached to General Schmidt's staff. In one instance, an artillery air observer discovered three 140-mm. coastal defense guns on Masalog Point that were within easy firing range of White Beaches 1 and 2, but were masked from field artillery. The battleship *Colorado* was called in and, with its main batteries adjusted by an airborne artillery observer, succeeded in neutralizing or destroying the enemy weapons. Because the spotting plane was not in direct radio contact with the ship, it was necessary for the plane to submit its spotting data to the artillery post by radio, whence they were relayed by telephone to General Schmidt's headquarters, and in turn by radio on another frequency to the firing ship. In spite of this somewhat complicated system of communications, the time lag was so slight as to be insignificant.[6]

Naval and Air Bombardment

Naval guns had harrassed Tinian intermittently since 11 June when Admiral Mitscher's Fast Carrier Force first made its appearance in the adjacent waters. For about a week after Saipan was secured, the job was left almost entirely to field artillery except for night fires delivered on Tinian Town by small naval craft. Then, starting on 15 July, naval gunfire was resumed. Admiral Hill's plan called for daily destructive fire by destroyers on specific targets that were not suitable to air or artillery, gradual intensification of daytime fire by employment of additional destroyers and cruisers, and a continuation of night harassing missions. Commencing on the 16th, seven destroyers began to deliver destructive fire

[3] 27th Inf Div Arty Rpt FORAGER Opn, p. 25.

[4] Each Marine division had two 105-mm. howitzer battalions and two 75-mm. pack howitzer battalions.

[5] XXIV Corps Arty Final Rpt on FORAGER Opn, Phases I and III, S–3 Rpt, p. 9.

[6] *Ibid.*; TF 52 Rpt Tinian, 24 Aug 44, Incl A, p. 61.

155-MM. GUN FIRING AT TINIAN FROM SAIPAN *during night bombardment of the island to the south.*

against targets designated by corps artillery. On the evening of the 17th, additional destroyers commenced harassing fire against the Japanese who were known to be working feverishly at night to install beach defenses in the Asiga Bay area. On the 20th the cruiser *Louisville* was added to the armada, and two days later another cruiser, *New Orleans,* was sent into the line, as were two LCI gunboats whose job it was to pour 40-mm. fire into the many caves that pocked the cliffs along the shore line.[7]

Starting at 0600 on 23 July, the day before the landing, Admiral Hill stepped up

[7] TF 52 Rpt Tinian, Incl A, pp. 58–59.

his preparatory fire with a total of three old battleships, two heavy cruisers, three light cruisers, and sixteen destroyers, distributed in such a way that the island of Tinian would be shelled from every point on the compass. The Navy made no effort to concentrate on White Beaches 1 and 2 —in fact, the ships assigned to that area were fewer in number than in most of the other five sectors into which the waters off the island were subdivided. Deception was given even greater consideration than destruction, and the naval gunfire plan can have given the Japanese no indicaton as to where the amphibious assault would take place. At 1500 all ships ceased fire for an hour to permit aircraft to drop napalm bombs on the wooded area inland of Faibus San Hilo Point, and at 1720 naval fire was again discontinued for an air strike with napalm against the White Beaches area. During the night of 23–24 July destroyers and cruisers kept important road junctions between Faibus San Hilo and Gurguan Points interdicted, while the destroyer *Norman Scott* delivered harassing fire to cover Asiga Bay and all important road junctions on the east side of the island. Another destroyer, *Waller,* covered a last-minute underwater reconnaissance of White Beaches 1 and 2 by Underwater Demolition Team 5, which unsuccessfully attempted to detonate some recently discovered mines. Throughout the day and thereafter during the operation, in order to minimize interference between air and naval gunfire, all ships were directed to deliver their fire from ranges of a maximum ordinate of less than 1,000 feet when possible and to exceed that maximum only after notification by Admiral Hill.[8]

For air support on Tinian, Comdr. Lloyd B. Osborne, USN, who was Admiral Hill's Commander, Northern Support Aircraft, had 358 fighters, bombers, and torpedo planes under his control, mostly Army and Navy. Tinian, like Saipan, had of course felt the might of Marc Mitscher's carrier force early in June, and from then on was subject to an increasing tempo of bombing from naval planes of Turner's and Hill's escort carriers and from Army P–47's from Isely Field. Starting on 22 June, P–47's of the 318th Fighter Group kept the airfields at Ushi and Gurguan Point and the new strip just east of Tinian Town under constant strafing and bomb-

ing attacks. Tinian Town itself was reduced to rubble.[9]

On 22 July, just two days before the invasion, two P–47's dropped on Tinian the first napalm bombs used in the Pacific war. These were fire bombs consisting of jettisonable aircraft fuel tanks filled with a mixture of napalm gel and gasoline. Shortly before the scheduled landing on Tinian, Lt. Comdr. Louis W. Mang, USNR, recently arrived from the United States, easily persuaded Admiral Hill of the efficacy of these new bombs, and, since napalm was in short supply, an order for 8,500 pounds was immediately dispatched to Pearl Harbor. Meanwhile, diesel oil was sometimes used as a less efficient substitute. The new fire bombs were found to be especially effective in burning cane fields and underbrush. During the late afternoon of 23 July thirty were dropped immediately inland and on the flanks of White Beaches 1 and 2 to burn off underbrush cover and destroy enemy personnel that might be located in open trenches and dugouts. In both respects the bombs were successful and their continued employment in the Pacific war was assured.[10]

The Landings

At daybreak on 24 July a motley flotilla of ships and landing craft carrying the 2d and 4th Marine Divisions got under way from Tanapag Harbor for the short trip to Tinian. All together, it included 8 transports, 37 LST's, 2 LSD's, 31 LCI's, 20 LCT's, 92 LCM's, 100 LCVP's, 533

---

[8] *Ibid.,* pp. 62–63.

[9] This account of preliminary air activities is derived from TF 52 Rpt Tinian, Incl A, p. 26, and AAF Hist Div Army Air Forces in the Marianas Campaign, MS, OCMH.

[10] TF 52 Rpt Tinian, Incl A, pp. 93–96.

LVT's, and 140 DUKW's. All of the LST's were assigned to the 4th Marine Division, whose assault troops were nested in their amphibian tractors waiting for the moment when the bow doors would open and their vehicles would crawl out into the water and approach their line of departure. Four of the LST's carried DUKW's, aboard which had been loaded four battalions of 75-mm. pack howitzers. Tanks were stowed in LCT's and LCM's, some to be carried to their destination in the wells of LSD's, others to get there under their own power. The eight transports carried the two regimental combat teams of the 2d Marine Division scheduled to make a diversionary feint at Tinian Town before landing in the rear of the assault troops. The division's other regiment would have to stand by on Saipan until ten of the LST's bound for White Beaches 1 and 2 had unloaded and returned to pick it up.[11] (*Map 16*)

On past the White Beaches to Sunharon Bay steamed the Demonstration Group— the transports carrying the two 2d Marine Division RCT's accompanied by their escorts.[12] The Japanese expected a landing at Tinian Town, and Admiral Hill intended to prolong that expectation as far as possible. Into the water went landing craft lowered from their mother transports; down the cargo nets climbed the marines of the 2d Division, to all appearances bound for the beach.

Ashore, the Japanese reacted immediately and furiously. Flashes from their guns, followed by tremendous geysers of water, kept the marines crouching low beneath the gunwales of their boats as they approached the 2,000-yard line, which marked the inshore limits of their fake attack. Nothing but water and a few shell fragments hit the troops, but the escorting ships were not so lucky. The three British-made 6-inch coastal defense guns located south of Tinian Town struck the battleship *Colorado* and the destroyer *Norman Scott,* scoring twenty-two hits on the former and six on the latter. In this short action the Navy lost 62 killed and 245 wounded before the shore battery could be silenced.[13]

By 1015 the boats and men had been recovered and the Demonstration Group stood up the coast toward White Beaches. The feint had been altogether successful. From Colonel Ogata to Tokyo went the message that more than a hundred landing barges had been repulsed in an attempt to get ashore at Tinian Town.[14] The *56th Naval Guard Force* stuck to its guns that guarded Sunharon Bay, and no part of the *3d Battalion, 50th Infantry Regiment,* abandoned the southern sector to meet the amphibious landing in the north.[15] One Japanese infantryman probably reflected the thoughts and hopes of all when he wrote in his diary, "24 July: Today the enemy began to land on the beach at Tinian. 3 companies were sent out. Our platoon moved into position. . . . Up to 0900 artillery fire was fierce in the direction of Port Tinian but it became quiet

---

[11] *Ibid.,* p. 6; NTLF Rpt Marianas, Phase III, Incl H, LVT Rpt, pp. 1–3.

[12] Unless otherwise noted, the account of the diversionary feint against Tinian Town is derived from TF 52 Rpt Tinian, pp. 30–32; Hoffman, *Tinian,* pp. 43–45; Morison, *New Guinea and the Marianas,* pp. 361–62.

[13] The battery was actually destroyed four days later by the battleship *Tennessee.* Morison, *New Guinea and the Marianas,* p. 362.

[14] Japanese Studies in World War II, 55, pp. 51–52.

[15] 2d Marine Div Rpt Tinian, D–2 Rpt 76; NTLF Rpt Marianas, Phase I, Incl A, G–2 Rpt, p. 41.

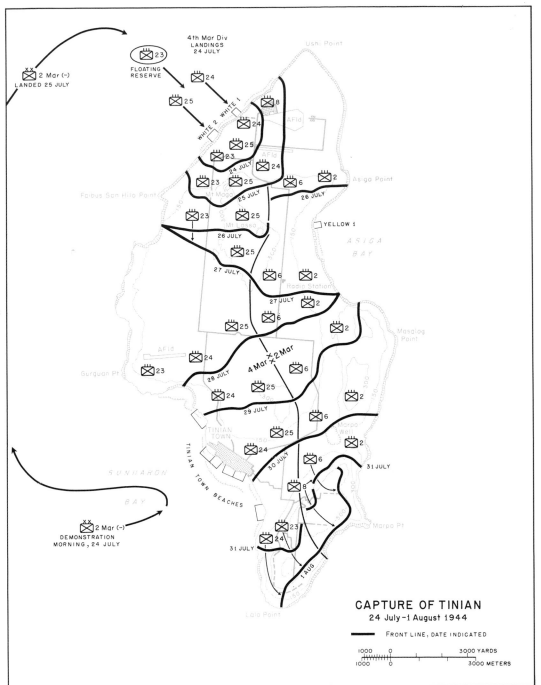

CAPTURE OF TINIAN
24 July–1 August 1944

━━━━━ FRONT LINE, DATE INDICATED

MAP 16

after the enemy warships left. Maybe the enemy is retreating."[16]

Meanwhile, the northwest coast of Tinian which had heretofore been treated with a studied impartiality, began to receive the full force of the attackers' armament. At 0600 one battery of 155-mm. howitzers on Saipan commenced laying down a smoke screen on Mount Lasso to last for two and a half hours. Forty-five minutes later all of General Harper's guns and howitzers burst forth in a massed fire. For fifteen minutes artillery pounded known installations on northern Tinian, likely enemy assembly areas, and avenues of approaches to the beaches. Then, on signal, artillery lifted its fires to the woods and bluffs above the shore from which the Japanese might observe the approach of the assault craft and vehicles.[17]

The chorus of destruction was swelled by Admiral Hill's support ships offshore. Starting at 0530, *Tennessee*, *California*, and *Louisville* opened up on White Beaches 1 and 2 with their main batteries, while *Birmingham* and *Montpelier* together bracketed Mount Lasso from opposite sides of the island. Freshly arrived from Guam, Admiral Spruance's flagship *Indianapolis* took over responsibility for Faibus San Hilo Point, which overlooked the landing beaches from the south. From 0625 until 0640 all ships' fire ceased in order to allow an air strike against the beaches, and more particularly against the recently discovered mines off White Beach 2, which neither underwater demolition swimmers, nor mine sweepers, nor ships'

guns had been able to detonate. Thirty minutes before the scheduled landing time, artillery fire from Saipan shifted to the landing beaches. Throughout this period, one battery of 155-mm. howitzers fired a continuous barrage of smoke shells at Mount Lasso to prevent enemy observation of the landing beaches. Then came the final crescendo of naval bombardment with destroyers abandoning their screening duties to add their five-inch shells to the general destruction.

The first wave was to touch down at 0730, but because of a slight delay in forming the landing waves, Admiral Hill ordered a ten-minute postponement. The formation of landing craft and vehicles followed the pattern by now familiar in the Central Pacific. First in line abreast went the LCI gunboats, six toward White Beach 1, nine toward White Beach 2. Astern came a wave of amphibian tanks, followed in turn by the troop-carrying amphibian tractors. Those bound for the northern landing beach were crewed by marines of the 2d Amphibian Tractor Battalion; the Army's 773d Amphibian Tractor Battalion carried the assault troops to the southern beach. As the gunboats approached shallow water, they turned to port and starboard and took the flanks of the landing area under fire; at 300 yards the amphibian tanks turned toward the flanks and the first waves of amphibian tractors churned through the water to touch shore on White Beach 1 at 0742, on White Beach 2 at 0750.[18]

By comparison with most assault landings in the Central Pacific, the initial in-

---

[16] 4th Marine Div Representative Trans, Sec. VII, Diary of Takayoshi Yamazaki.

[17] XXIV Corps Arty Final Rpt on FORAGER Opn, Phases I and III, S–3 Rpt, p. 11.

[18] TF 52 Rpt Tinian, pp. 33, 65; XXIV Corps Arty Final Rpt on FORAGER Opn, Phases I and III, S–3 Rpt, p. 11.

INVASION CRAFT *make an easy landing on Tinian's White Beaches.*

vasion of Tinian was easy.[19] Within forty minutes after the touch down, the entire assault battalion of the 24th Marines was ashore on White Beach 1, and after a brief fire fight moved rapidly to the first objective line. On White Beach 2, to the south, the 25th Marines faced somewhat heavier odds in the form of scattered land mines and two Japanese pillboxes undestroyed by the preliminary bombardment. Two LVT's were blown up by the mines. As the first wave of marines rushed inland it bypassed the pillboxes, which were subsequently reduced without difficulty. Following the landing of the two assault regiments, tanks and half-tracks moved in on schedule, and in spite of the difficulties involved in landing over the narrow, cliff-flanked beaches,

[19] The account of JIG Day on Tinian is derived from the following sources: 4th Marine Div Opns Rpt Tinian, pp. 16–20, 23–24; Hoffman, *Tinian,* pp. 48–58.

none of the vehicles was lost. By midafternoon DUKW's had succeeded in landing all four of the pack howitzer battalions assigned to the 4th Marine Division, and by late afternoon the reserve regiment (23d Marines), after some delay caused by communications failure, was ashore and in position in its assembly area on the right (south) flank of the beachhead. The two shore parties (1341st Engineer Battalion (Army) on White Beach 1 and the 2d Battalion, 20th Marines, on White Beach 2) had landed all their men and equipment by 1400. Two of the ten special portable LVT ramps were launched late in the afternoon. One capsized when the amphibian tractor struck a coral head, but the other was in proper position before nightfall. Six of the eight remaining ramps were installed the next day, the other two having been swamped in the process.

4TH MARINES WADING TOWARD WHITE BEACH 1 *keep their weapons dry.*

By nightfall of the 24th the 4th Marine Division had established a beachhead about 2,900 yards in width and almost a mile deep in the center.[20] Casualties for the day had been light—15 killed and 225 wounded.[21] Barbed wire was strung along the entire length of the division front, machine guns were emplaced to provide interlocking bands of fire, and pack howitzers were registered to cover the main road from Ushi Point airfield and other likely routes of enemy approach. Amphibian vehicles preloaded with ammunition had made their direct deliveries from ships lying offshore to the front-line troops as scheduled, and the latter were well supplied with reserve stocks of shells, mortars, and bullets. Every precaution was taken against the expected traditional first-night

enemy counterattack. When it came, the marines were ready for it.

Japanese Counterattack
24–25 July

Having failed to stem the tide of the American assault over the beaches, Colonel Ogata now had to put into execution the second phase of his defensive plan—an organized counterattack during the first night after the landing. Whether the Japanese commander was in direct communication with any of his troops other than those assigned to the Tinian Town area is uncertain, but his battalion commanders were well enough indoctrinated to launch the drive on their own initiative. Still under the illusion that the main amphibious assault would eventually be directed against Tinian Town, Ogata kept the *3d Battalion,*

---

[20] Hoffman, *Tinian*, Map 8, p. 3.
[21] 4th Marine Div Opns Rpt Tinian, p. 24.

50th Regiment, in position. The *2d Battalion,* to which had been assigned the northeast sector guarding Asiga Bay, also stayed out of the fight, as did the main body of the *56th Naval Guard Force* manning the coastal defense guns along southern Tinian. Thus the brunt of the counterattack fell to Ogata's mobile reserve battalion (the *1st Battalion, 135th Infantry Regiment*), the *1st Battalion, 50th Infantry,* and sundry naval units stationed in the northern part of the island.[22]

The attack, when it came, consisted of three separate and seemingly un-coordinated thrusts against the American front—one along the western shore against the marines' left, one in the center at the boundary between the 25th and 24th Marines, and a third against the 23d Marines on the American right flank. The first commenced about 0200 and was undertaken exclusively by naval personnel coming down from the north. It lasted almost five hours, but the Japanese failed to penetrate the marines lines at any point and lost an estimated 476 men in the effort.[23]

In the center, Japanese infantrymen struck about 0230. Between the two Marine regiments they discovered a weak spot in the line through which a large body of Japanese poured and then branched out in two directions. One of the enemy groups turned west toward the rear areas of the 25th Marines where it was eliminated after a brief fire fight. The other headed straight for the beach where it was eventually stopped by Marine artillerymen and elements of the 2d Marine Division that had landed only a few hours earlier. The next morning almost 500 dead Japanese were counted in this area.

The third attack was from the south and was preceded by five or six tanks, over half of the entire Japanese tank strength on the island. All the tanks were destroyed before they penetrated the lines of the 23d Marines, against which the attack was directed. The infantrymen following the tanks had no better luck. In the eerie light furnished by naval star shells, the marines quickly disposed of this last group, estimated to number over 270 enemy soldiers.

On the morning of the 25th a total of 1,241 Japanese dead was counted, about 700 identified as members of the two infantry regiments. Later interrogation of six prisoners of war revealed that by the morning of the 25th the *1st Battalion, 50th Infantry,* had been virtually destroyed as a result of the fighting incident to the landing and the counterattack.[24] Another prisoner of war testified that the *1st Battalion, 135th Infantry,* Ogata's mobile reserve, had been "practically annihilated."[25] In the light of this evidence, General Cates' final conclusion seems irrefutable—in the early morning hours of 25 July, the 4th Marine Division "broke the Japs back in the battle for Tinian."[26]

Capture of Northern Tinian

During the next eight days, until the island was finally declared secured on 1 August, the fighting on Tinian resolved it-

---

[22] The account of the counterattack is derived from 4th Marine Div D–2 Periodic Rpt 72, and Hoffman, *Tinian,* pp. 62–68.

[23] This and subsequent figures for Japanese casualties are taken from dead counts made on the morning of 25 July. Since some of the Japanese may have been killed by preliminary naval, air, and artillery fire, the estimates are probably exaggerated.

[24] 4th Marine Div Representative Trans, Note 574, Sec. IX.

[25] 4th Marine Div D–2 Periodic Rpt 73, 26 Jul 44.

[26] 4th Marine Div Opns Rpt Tinian, p. 25.

self into three phases. First, it was necessary to push across to the eastern coast and seal off the entire northern third of the island, including such vital points as Mount Maga, Mount Lasso, and the Ushi Point airfield. Once this was accomplished, both Marine divisions could wheel to the south and proceed at a more rapid pace down Tinian's long axis until they reached the foot of the plateau that dominated the island's southern tip. Finally came the two-day battle for the plateau and the cliffs of Marpo Point that brought the operation to a close.

On 25 July the 4th Marine Division, against only sporadic resistance, spent the day expanding the beachhead in all directions. On the right, the 23d Marines covered about half the distance from White Beach 2 to Faibus San Hilo Point, meeting very few Japanese as they went. In the center, the 25th and 24th Regiments made comparable advances in an easterly and southeasterly direction, the 25th capturing Mount Maga, which lay athwart the division's approaches to Mount Lasso, the highest point of the island. Army P–47's flying from Isely Field, as well as artillery based on Saipan, supported the action. On the left, the 8th Marines (attached to the 4th Marine Division), assisted by tanks and by armored amphibians firing from the water, inched its way through the coral cliffs that lined the west coast north of White Beach 1. Meanwhile, most of the remainder of the 2d Marine Division had come ashore and by midafternoon General Watson had set up his command post inland of White Beach 2.[27]

Marine casualties for the day were low, and enemy opposition, although occasionally fierce, was spotty. Nevertheless, those marines who did make contact with the enemy developed a healthy respect for the caliber of the Tinian garrison. The Japanese here were reported "to be better troops than those encountered on Saipan, with much better marksmanship."[28]

The fact is that immediately after the failure of his night counterattack, Colonel Ogata decided to disengage his forces and establish a new defense line running from Gurguan Point to the radio station inland from the center of Asiga Bay. The brief flurry of artillery fire that the 25th Marines had encountered during their approach to Mount Maga had merely been a delaying action. The bulk of the Japanese troops remaining in northern Tinian were withdrawing to the new line south of Mount Lasso.[29]

On JIG plus 2 (26 July) General Schmidt ordered the 4th Division, now on the right, to continue the attack in a southerly direction and the 2d Division to drive straight toward the east coast.[30] In the 4th Division zone, the 23d Marines pushed down the coast another 2,500 yards to a point well below Faibus San Hilo Point, while the 25th Marines occupied Mount Lasso, which had been entirely evacuated by the Japanese the day before.[31] At Mount Lasso the 25th Marines reported evidence of "a careful, well-planned withdrawal, removing dead and destroying documents. Abandoned posi-

---

[27] This account is derived from 4th Marine Div Opns Rpt Tinian, pp. 25–26; 2d Marine Div Rpt Tinian, p. 2; Hoffman, *Tinian*, pp. 69–77.

[28] 4th Marine Div D–2 Rpt 72. See also 2d Marine Div D–2 Periodic Rpt 74.
[29] Japanese Studies in World War II, 55, p. 52.
[30] NTLF Opn Order 32–44.
[31] 4th Marine Div Opns Rpt Tinian, pp. 26–27.

USHI POINT AIRFIELD, *in the northern portion of Tinian. This field was a major objective of the Tinian operation.*

tions had been well dug-in and carefully planned." [32]

On the corps left, meanwhile, the 8th Marines took over Ushi Point airfield, and its sister regiments sped on to the east coast and prepared to swing south.[33] Thus, in three days, the major tactical objectives of the Tinian invasion had been achieved: Ogata's major counterattack had been beaten off with a consequent loss to him of about one fourth of his force; Ushi Point airfield had been taken and was already in the process of being made operational for American planes; Mount Lasso, the commanding position of the island had been occupied. In the words of the official Marine Corps historian, "Seldom was the victor of any of the Central Pacific con-

quests so unmistakably identified so early in the fight." [34]

Drive to the South

From 27 through 30 July both Marine divisions made rapid advances toward the plateau that dominated the southern tip of the island. Enemy resistance on the 27th and 28th was almost nonexistent, but it gradually stiffened as the Americans approached the Japanese last main defensive line. During the 27th and 28th General Schmidt employed what has been called an "elbowing" technique. That is, on the first day of the attack southward, he held back the 4th Division on the right while the 2d Division surged forward; the second day the roles were exchanged. The ostensible

---

[32] 4th Marine Div D–2 Rpt 73, Annex, D–2 Material for Dispatch Summary 271700.
[33] 2d Marine Div Rpt Tinian, pp. 2–3.

[34] Hoffman, *Tinian,* p. 76.

OPEN TERRAIN OF CENTRAL TINIAN, *which permitted rapid advance toward the hill mass that dominates the southern tip of the island.*

purpose of this tactic was to permit his artillery to concentrate first in support of one division, then of the other.[35]

On the 29th this technique was abandoned, and both divisions were ordered to advance as rapidly within their respective zones as conditions permitted.[36] On the right, the 4th Division on the 30th assaulted a series of well-camouflaged cave positions on the west coast and after reducing them pushed on in and through Tinian Town. Land mine fields on the town's outskirts and along the beaches of Sunharon Bay slowed the advance a little, but the town itself had been reduced to rubble by naval gunfire and aerial bombardment and had been evacuated.[37] On the left,

the 2d Division faced a tougher proposition as it came abreast the Masalog hill mass, but by nightfall of the 30th the area was overrun, and the Japanese were in retreat to the south.[38]

Apparently Colonel Ogata had relinquished his mid-island line of defense almost as soon as it had been established, and on the night of the 29th he moved his command post to a shrine in a cliff near Marpo Point. Seeing his delaying actions crumble before the advancing Americans, he ordered all Army and Navy forces to assemble on the southern tip of the island to defend the ridge line there.[39]

On their part, the Americans in four days had pushed their lines ahead about

---

[35] *Ibid.,* p. 86.
[36] NTLF Opn Orders 35, 36.
[37] 4th Marine Div D–2 Periodic Rpt 77; Hoffman, *Tinian,* pp. 96–97.

[38] 2d Marine Div Rpt Tinian, pp. 3–4; Hoffman, *Tinian,* pp. 98–100.
[39] 4th Marine Div Representative Trans, Sec. IX, p. 5.

155-MM. HOWITZER EMPLACEMENT ON TINIAN

10,000 yards on the left and 4,000 on the right.[40] Coming so soon after the prolonged deadlocks of the Saipan battle, this seemed indeed like a sprint. As General Cates expressed it, the marines were "heading for the barn." [41]

One of the reasons for this rapid movement was the gently undulating terrain of central Tinian, which permitted tanks to be used with far greater effectiveness than had been the case on Saipan. To each regiment was assigned one reinforced medium tank company (eighteen tanks), a platoon of four flame thrower tanks, and two light tanks. Each of the tank companies stayed with its parent regiment throughout the operation, which of course facilitated tank-infantry co-ordination. Also, one infantry regiment of each division was at all times in reserve, thus giving its assigned tank unit an opportunity to repair its vehicles. In addition, communications between tanks and infantry were markedly improved over those on Saipan.[42]

Tinian's terrain also offered more favorable opportunities for the employment of artillery than had Saipan's. Initially, all artillery in support of the 4th Marine Division was based on Saipan except for four battalions of 75-mm. pack howitzers from the 14th and 10th Marine Artillery Regiments. On 26 July the 3d Battalion, 14th Marines (105-mm. howitzers), came ashore, followed the next day by the 105-mm. howitzers of the 4th Artillery Battalion, V Amphibious Corps (attached to the 4th Marine Division), and the two 105-mm. howitzer battalions of the 10th Marines.[43] On 28 July the 419th Field Artillery Group of the XXIV Corps Artillery (155-mm. howitzers) displaced from

---

[40] See Hoffman, *Tinian*, Map 10, p. 87.
[41] 4th Marine Div Opns Rpt Tinian, p. 29.

[42] *Ibid.*, Annex C, Opns Rpt, p. 19; *Ibid.*, Annex K, 4th Tank Bn Rpt.
[43] 4th Marine Div Opns Rpt Tinian, Annex F, 14th Marines Rpt, pp. 4–6; 2d Marine Div SAR, Phase III, FORAGER, Annex, 10th Marines Rpt, pp. 1–3.

Saipan to positions on Tinian, as did one battery of the 106th Field Artillery Battalion (also 155-mm. howitzers). The other two batteries of this battalion were forced to return to their Saipan positions since they were unable to land over the White Beaches because of wrecked ponton causeways there. The XXIV Corps Artillery's 420th Field Artillery Group remained on Saipan throughout, its 155-mm. guns having sufficient range to hit any part of the southern island.[44]

Corps artillery alone fired 1,404 missions, totaling 46,309 rounds, during the assault and capture of Tinian.[45] Added to this, of course, was the Marine divisions' organic artillery, which fired approximately 142,000 additional rounds.[46] As one Japanese prisoner testified, "You couldn't drop a stick without bringing down artillery."[47]

Close air support on Tinian was provided by Army P-47's flying from Isely Field, as well as Navy carrier-based planes. As the two Marine divisions started their drive south from the Mount Lasso line, Army and Navy aircraft alternated in providing air cover in advance of the troops, averaging 175 sorties daily. Admiral Hill's support aircraft commander, Commander Osborne, had the final responsibility for approving and directing all air strikes requested by the Marines on the front line. Under him was the Commander, Support Aircraft Ashore, who was stationed on Isely Field with authority to exercise direct control over the P-47's. Final responsibility for co-ordinating air, artillery, and naval

bombardment resided with a representative from XXIV Corps Artillery at General Schmidt's headquarters.[48]

Only in rare instances were supporting aircraft directly coached into their targets by air liaison parties attached to the infantry. The Navy command was fearful of turning over control of supporting aircraft to the ground troops for a variety of reasons. Neither the air liaison parties nor the pilots were deemed sufficiently trained in the niceties of air-ground co-ordination to risk it. Air-ground communications were uncertain chiefly because of unsatisfactory and insufficient radio equipment. Finally, the danger of decentralizing control of air strikes over such a small target as Tinian was considerable. Once the drive to the south was under way, the marines had on the front lines at all times at least twelve battalions, each with its own air liaison party. The lines themselves were often irregular and of course the front narrowed as the troops approached the southern tip of the island. Under these conditions, to have allowed each battalion to control its own called strikes would have seriously endangered the units on the flanks, and the risk was considered unacceptable.[49]

On Tinian, as on Saipan, the time lag between requests for and execution of air strikes was a cause for dissatisfaction among the ground troop commanders. Even when the planes were on station above the target, half an hour was usually required to complete an air strike, and when the planes had to be flown from their mother carriers or from Isely Field, an hour's delay was more common. One air liaison party had to wait a full nineteen

---

[44] XXIV Corps Arty Final Rpt on FORAGER Opn, Phases I and III, S-3 Rpt, p. 12.

[45] Ibid.

[46] NTLF Rpt Marianas, Phase III, Incl F, G-4 Rpt, and Incl D.

[47] 4th Marine Div Representative Trans.

[48] TF 56 Rpt FORAGER Tinian, Incl I; NTLF Opn Plan 3-44, Annexes C, D, F.

[49] Hoffman, Tinian, p. 128.

hours to get its request honored, but that was exceptional.[50] Nevertheless, General Cates and General Watson were both of the opinion that the execution of air strikes was several cuts above what it had been on Saipan—largely because the pilots had been better briefed, were more familiar with the terrain, and were gaining experience.[51]

Naval fire support during the battle for Tinian was also considered to be an improvement over that for Saipan, again because of greater experience on the part of ships' companies and because of more favorable terrain. Preparation fires were commonly delivered on request of division commanders before the morning jump-off to supplement the field artillery, and counterbattery interdiction and destructive fires were delivered daily on call.[52] In the opinion of Lt. Col. E. G. Van Orman, USMC, who was Holland Smith's naval gunfire officer, "In the occupation of Tinian call fire procedure was carried out much more satisfactorily than at either Saipan or Guam because of experience gained by all hands at Saipan and exchanged and clarified in meetings of all personnel both afloat and ashore prior to J-Day." [53]

Perhaps the most unusual features of the battle for Tinian were the techniques that were improvised for getting supplies over the narrow beaches to the front-line troops both during the initial amphibious phase and later. Responsibility for preparing the beaches themselves and for controlling traffic over them fell to the Army's 1341st Engineer Battalion and the 2d Battalion, 20th Marines (the Engineer regiment of the 4th Marine Division). The former was assigned to White Beach 1, the latter to White Beach 2. Both were landed on JIG Day, at first operating under control of the 4th Marine Division and later (26 July) coming under the direct command of General Schmidt's shore party officer, Col. Cyril W. Martyr, USMC.[54] Also on the 26th the 2d Battalion, 18th Marines (organic to the 2d Marine Division), came ashore to assist at White Beach 2, to work in the division dumps, and later to help unload aircraft at Ushi Point airfield.[55]

To facilitate unloading on the White Beaches, two ponton causeways were assembled on Saipan and on the afternoon of 24 July were towed to Tinian. There they were put to excellent use until the night of 29 July, when the tail of a typhoon that had been building up in the Philippine Sea hit Tinian with full force. The storm broached one of the artificial piers and broke the other in two.[56]

It was during this typhoon that the DUKW's once again demonstrated their outstanding versatility and durability. About half of the 140 amphibian trucks used on Tinian were crewed by Army personnel of the 477th Amphibian Truck Company and the 27th Division Provisional Amphibian Truck Company, the rest were crewed by marines of the 1st and 2d Marine Amphibian Truck Companies. As the seas mounted on the afternoon of 29 July,

[50] 4th Marine Div Opns Rpt Tinian, Annex E, Special Comments and Recommendations.

[51] 2d Marine Div Rpt Tinian, p. 18; 4th Marine Div Opns Rpt Tinian, Annex C, p. 12.

[52] TF 56 Rpt FORAGER Tinian, Incl I, Naval Gunfire Rpt.

[53] Ibid., p. 138.

[54] 4th Marine Div Opns Rpt Tinian, Annex G, 20th Marines Rpt, pp. 1–4; NTLF Rpt Marianas, Phase III, Annex J (2), Engineer and Shore Party Rpt, p. 1.

[55] 2d Bn 18th Marines Rpt, p. 1.

[56] TF 56 Rpt FORAGER Tinian, Incl J, Engineer and Shore Party Rpt, p. 2.

broaching one LST and washing a landing craft control boat up on the beach, it developed that of all the small craft and vehicles present, only the DUKW's were seaworthy enough to operate in the heavy swells, and for the duration of the storm they were solely responsible for overwater supply.[57]

As General Schmidt's supply officer remarked, the DUKW's at Tinian "performed an astounding feat of supply."[58] Equipped with A-frames, they carried most of the artillery pieces from LST's directly to firing positions ashore.[59] They were solely responsible for averting a serious fuel shortage when the typhoon struck, since they were the only means at hand for getting through the surf to fuel barges anchored off the northwest coast of Tinian. Not only did they prove more seaworthy than their sister amphibian vehicle, the LVT, but over Tinian's fairly well developed road system they delivered supplies more quickly to the troops as they approached the southern end of the island and also, of course, wrought much less damage to the roads than did the tracked vehicles.[60]

The DUKW's and LVT's bore the main burden of shuttling supplies and equipment of all kinds from the vessels lying off the beaches straight to inland dumps, or even to the men on the front lines as they pushed farther southward. It was this direct and rapid system of supply, which eliminated manhandling supplies on the beaches, that struck most observers as the outstanding feature of the Tinian battle. In the words of General Schmidt's supply officer:

This operation was in many ways a remarkable demonstration of the fact that preconceived notions and amphibious doctrine can be altered radically on the spot. In effect, a reinforced corps was landed over less than 200 yards of beach and over a difficult reef, and was supplied throughout nine days of heavy combat without handling so much as one pound of supplies in the usual shore party manner. Everything rolled in on wheels. When a violent sea made impossible the landing of trucks, the DUKW's took over all supply, supplemented to a minor degree by incoming air evacuation planes bringing in rations. The troops never lacked what they required at the time it was required.[61]

Tinian Secured

Nightfall of 30 July found the two Marine divisions drawn up on a line just north of the hill mass that dominated the southern tip of Tinian. South of them was about a mile of flat land that terminated in an abrupt wooded escarpment rising to a plateau. Here Colonel Ogata had elected to make his last desperate stand. The area consisted mostly of an oblong mountain mass about 5,000 yards long and 2,000 wide running generally in a northeast–southwest direction. This high ground was something like a huge mesa with the steep ridges and cliffs of its shoulders supporting the comparatively gentle slopes along the

[57] NTLF Rpt Marianas, Phase III, Incl F, G-4 Rpt, Sec. B, pp. 2-3. To supplement this delivery, transport planes from Saipan flew rations to the front-line troops on Tinian.

[58] NTLF Rpt Marianas, Phase III, G-4 Rpt, Sec. B, pp. 2-3.

[59] This particular use of the specially adapted DUKW's had been introduced by the 7th Infantry Division at the invasion of Kwajalein. See Crowl and Love, *Gilberts and Marshalls,* p. 227.

[60] Hoffman, *Tinian,* p. 136.

[61] NTLF Rpt Marianas, Phase III, Incl F, Supply Rpt, p. 4. This statement contains two minor inaccuracies. The beaches were somewhat more than 200 yards in width, and the vehicles that carried supplies inland were tracked as well as wheeled.

top. Of the two long sides, one faced the flat land around Tinian Town, the other met the sea on the east coast. The entire southern tip sloped steeply to the water. Colonel Ogata's defense line was drawn on the forward (northwestern) slopes of the hill mass.

On the morning of 31 July the marines attacked as before with two divisions abreast, the 4th on the right, 2d on the left. Before the jump-off, two battleships (*Tennessee* and *California*) and three cruisers (*Louisville, Montpelier,* and *Birmingham*) fired about 615 tons of shells into the area, and Army bombers dropped about 69 tons of explosives.[62]

On the right the 24th Marines, supported by tanks and armored amphibians, made slow but steady progress against stiffening resistance along the coast line south of Tinian Town, and by the end of the day had advanced about 2,500 yards.[63] The 23d Marines on the division left faced greater obstacles as it came up against the cliff line that marked the northwestern face of the plateau. With the help of supporting tanks, the regiment knocked out a 47-mm. antitank gun in the path of its progress and at day's end dug in at the foot of the cliff, though one company reached the top and spent the night there.[64]

On the left, the 2d Marine Division attacked with three regiments abreast. The two left regiments, 2d and 6th Marines, moved forward to the base of the cliff against only light rifle and machine gun fire, but the 8th Marines was not let off so easy. In its zone lay the precipitous double-hairpin road that offered the most

feasible route to the top of the plateau, and to get even partial command of this artery took a day of heavy fighting and arduous climbing. By late afternoon one company had reached the top of the cliff, followed after dark by most of the two assault battalions of the 8th Marines, but, as night fell, there was a gap of 600 yards on the right and one of 350 yards on the left of the Marine battalions atop the cliff. The time and the situation were ripe for a Japanese counterattack, and it came as expected.[65]

Colonel Ogata personally led the counterattack, which was directed mainly against the 8th Marines atop the cliff. According to one Japanese prisoner of war, Ogata was killed during the charge by American machine guns and was last seen hanging dead over the Marines' barbed wire.[66] About 2300 the Japanese first struck elements of the 8th Marines but were repulsed. Three hours later a force of some 150 of the enemy suddenly rushed the hairpin road up which the marines had been trying to carry ammunition and other supplies. There, the Japanese set up a roadblock, burned two ambulance jeeps, and threatened to cut off the two American battalions on top of the plateau. An hour later a platoon of the enemy moved up the road and attacked from the rear. In a short but furious fire fight they were driven back and their roadblock was eliminated. For the next three hours, 75-mm. half-tracks, mortars, and field artillery kept the enemy at bay, but at 0515 came the final banzai

[62] TF 52 Rpt Tinian, pp. 79–80, 132.
[63] Hoffman, *Tinian,* Map 11, p. 103.
[64] 4th Marine Div Opns Rpt Tinian, pp. 30–31; Hoffman, *Tinian,* pp. 102–07.

[65] 2d Marine Div Rpt Tinian, pp. 5–6; Hoffman, *Tinian,* pp. 107–10.
[66] NTLF Rpt Marianas, Phase III, Incl D, G–2 Rpt, pp. 18, 20, 21. A Japanese study of the operation prepared after the war, on the other hand, has Ogata still alive and leading another counterattack as late as 3 August. Japanese Studies in World War II, No. 55, p. 53.

charge. For a full half hour the attackers charged the Marine lines, but at no point did they penetrate. Daybreak revealed over a hundred enemy dead in an area only about 70 yards square. Later interrogation of prisoners indicated that the entire counterattacking force had numbered between six and eight hundred.[67]

With the failure of this last counterattack, organized Japanese resistance quickly came to an end. By late afternoon on 1 August both Marine divisions had reached the southern edge of the cliff line, and at 1855 General Schmidt declared the island secured.[68] Mopping up, to be sure, was a long and often bloody process.[69] Not until 1 January 1945 were the remnants of the enemy force considered sufficiently disposed of to permit the mop-up troops, the 8th Marines, to be transferred to Saipan. In the three months after Tinian was turned over to the island commander, Maj. Gen. James L. Underhill, USMC, a total of 542 Japanese were reported killed.[70]

All together, the capture of Tinian had cost the invading ground forces a total of 328 killed and 1,571 wounded in action, almost all of them Marine Corps personnel.[71] In exchange, the Japanese sacrificed their entire garrison of more than eight thousand men, most of them killed. More significant than this death toll was the fact that the U.S. forces had succeeded in wresting from the enemy one of the best airfield sites in the Central Pacific. Ushi Point airfield and Gurguan Point airfield, enlarged and expanded, became vital bases for the XXI Bomber Command, which in the spring and summer of 1945 would unleash its very long range bombers against the Japanese homeland with such devastating effect. Significantly, it was from Ushi Point airfield that the B-29 *Enola Gay,* took off on 6 August 1945 to drop the first atomic bomb on the city of Hiroshima.[72]

Tinian was largely a Marine Corps show. A Marine headquarters made the tactical plans and Marine infantrymen carried the main burden of attacking and overrunning the island. Nevertheless, the Army's role was by no means negligible. In the ship-to-shore movement, over half of the amphibian tractors were provided by the Army and crewed by soldiers. Half of the amphibian trucks that landed the artillery and later, during the typhoon, played such an important role in supplying the troops, were Army-manned. An Army engineer battalion acted as shore party for one of the landing beaches. Army artillery played a decisive part in the preliminary bombardment and in supporting the marines after they had landed. Finally, Army P-47's flew continuous close support missions in front of the Marine infantry. Since so much of the success of the operation depended upon artillery based on Saipan, on the efficient work of the amphibian vehicles, on the organization of the supply system at the beaches, and on close air support, it can be concluded that the Army's share in the reduction of Tinian was far out of proportion to the number of its personnel actually committed to the operation.

---

[67] Hoffman, *Tinian,* pp. 109–13.

[68] NTLF Rpt Marianas, Phase III, p. 15.

[69] Pfc. Robert L. Wilson of the 2d Battalion, 6th Marines, was posthumously awarded the Medal of Honor for covering with his own body a live hand grenade on 3 August, two days after Tinian had been declared secured. For a similar feat performed on 30 July, Pvt. Joseph W. Ozbourn, 1st Battalion, 23d Marines, was given the same award. Hoffman, *Tinian,* pp. 98, 117.

[70] Hoffman, *Tinian,* p. 121.

[71] *Ibid.,* App. III, p. 150.

[72] Craven and Cate, *AAF V,* pp. 715–17.

PART FOUR

GUAM

CHAPTER XV

Plans and Preparations

The Island

To the invaders of Guam, southernmost of the Marianas chain, the physiography of the island presented essentially the same problems and challenges that had already been encountered at Saipan—those for Guam were just on a larger scale. Located a little more than a hundred miles south of Saipan, Guam is more than twice its size, measuring 228 square miles in area. From Ritidian Point in the north to the southern coast line, the distance is about thirty-four miles; the width of the island varies from five to nine miles.[1] (*Map V.*)

Guam, like Saipan, is surrounded by coral reefs ranging in width from 25 to 700 yards. Even the lowest of these is covered at high tide by only about two feet of water—a condition that of course made the employment of amphibian tractors mandatory in the projected ship-to-shore movement. Around the entire northern half of the island from Fadian Point on the east coast to Tumon Bay on the west, sheer cliffs rising to 600 feet ruled that area out for landing. In the southern part of the island the shore line cliffs are somewhat less forbidding, but even so in many places, such as at the tip of Orote Peninsula on the west coast, they are still too precipitous to permit rapid movement inland by any large numbers of men approaching from the sea. The southern and southeast coasts, exposed as they are to the prevailing easterly winds, are pounded too heavily by surf to permit easy landing operations. This leaves about fifteen miles of coast line feasible for an amphibious assault, all on the west coast, north and south of Orote Peninsula. At various places in this region, the reef is low enough and the sandy beaches are both wide and deep enough to permit invading troops to get ashore and establish a foothold before assaulting the mountainous terrain inland.

Although nowhere does Guam's mountain range reach the heights of Mount Tapotchau on Saipan, it still presents obstacles of no mean proportions. The northern part consists almost entirely of a coral limestone plateau broken by three elevations, Mount Barrigada (674 feet), Mount Santa Rosa (870 feet), and Mount Machanao (610 feet). The central part, the waist of the island between Agana Bay and Pago Bay, is mostly lowland draining into the Agana River through a wide swamp of the same name. Just south of the waist the land begins to rise again toward the mountain range that runs to the southern tip of the island. Dominating the northern part of this range are Mount Chachao, Mount Alutom,

---

[1] This account of the physical features of Guam is derived from ONI 99, and Military Intelligence Service, War Department (MIS WD), Survey of Guam, 1943.

CLIFF LINE AT TIP OF OROTE PENINSULA

and Mount Tenjo, all inland from Apra Harbor and all attaining more than a thousand feet. East of Agat Bay below Orote Peninsula lies Mount Alifan (869 feet); south of it and inland from Facpi Point is Mount Lamlam, the highest point on the island (1,334 feet).[2]

Though Guam's mountain mass is not so high as Saipan's, its vegetation is lusher, heavier, and thicker. A degree and a half of latitude in this area of the world makes a difference, and Guam is considerably more tropical than the northern island. At the time of the invasion the northern section of Guam was heavily covered with tropical forests, weeds, trailing vines, lianas, air plants, and underbrush—all combining to make foot passage almost impossible except through man-made jungle trails. The mountain tops themselves were mostly bar-

ren volcanic rock covered only with sparse growths of sword grass and scrub. The southern plateau was covered mostly with sword, cogon, and bunch grass and scrub forest, except between Mount Alifan and Mount Lamlam, where timber grew in fairly large stands.

To facilitate passage over and through this rough and forbidding country there were, in the summer of 1944, about a hundred miles of hard-surface road, linked together by single-lane unsurfaced roads and a network of narrow jungle trails cut through the bush. The main road ran from the town of Agat along the west coast to Agana, then northeast to Finegayan, where it split into two parallel branches, each terminating near Mount Machanao near the northern tip of the island. Another branch of the same road ran northeast to the village of Yigo, where it dwindled into a narrow unsurfaced road that continued on almost to Pati Point, on the northeast-

---

[2] Heights of land are derived from Army Map Service, Map, Island of Guam, Scale 1:62,500, Washington, 1944.

Cabras Island   Apra Harbor   Sumay   Orote Peninsula   Agat Harbor

OROTE PENINSULA

ern coast. Also from Agana to Pago Bay on the east coast stretched a main artery that continued south and west along the coast line to Umatac. Umatac and Agat on the west coast were connected only by a dirt road.

Except for the surfaced highways, the roads and trails were normally all but impassable during the rainy season, which lasted from July to November. During this summer monsoon period, 20 to 25 days out of each month were rainy. Mean temperature was about 87° Fahrenheit and average humidity about 90 percent—factors that would increase the discomfort of combat troops, whether American or Japanese.

Plans for the Invasion

Guam was initially included in the list of American targets for 1944 by the Joint Chiefs of Staff directive of 12 March 1944 that ordered Admiral Nimitz to prepare to seize and occupy the southern Marianas.

Like the islands to the north, it offered sites for B–29 bases and, in addition, Apra Harbor was the best ship anchorage in the entire archipelago, having excellent possibilities for development into a small forward naval base. Then too, Guam, like the Philippines, had been an American possession; its native population was presumed loyal to the United States, and its liberation deemed a moral obligation.

Little more than a week had passed since the 12 March directive when Admiral Nimitz issued a preliminary order (dated 20 March) for the seizure of the southern Marianas, including Guam. Saipan and Tinian were assigned to the V Amphibious Corps. To the III Amphibious Corps, commanded by General Geiger, USMC, went the job of recapturing Guam.[3] Gen-

---

[3] Actually at this date the unit was named I Marine Amphibious Corps (I MAC), but on 15 April its designation was changed to III Amphibious Corps. To avoid confusion the latter title is used throughout this volume.

CHART 2—TASK ORGANIZATION FOR MAJOR COMMANDS FOR ATTACK ON GUAM

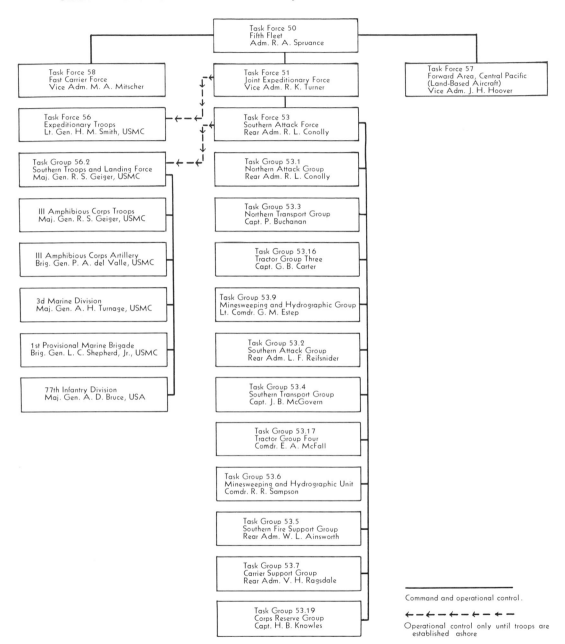

Task Force 50
Fifth Fleet
Adm. R. A. Spruance

Task Force 58
Fast Carrier Force
Vice Adm. M. A. Mitscher

Task Force 51
Joint Expeditionary Force
Vice Adm. R. K. Turner

Task Force 57
Forward Area, Central Pacific
(Land-Based Aircraft)
Vice Adm. J. H. Hoover

Task Force 56
Expeditionary Troops
Lt. Gen. H. M. Smith, USMC

Task Force 53
Southern Attack Force
Rear Adm. R. L. Conolly

Task Group 56.2
Southern Troops and Landing Force
Maj. Gen. R. S. Geiger, USMC

Task Group 53.1
Northern Attack Group
Rear Adm. R. L. Conolly

III Amphibious Corps Troops
Maj. Gen. R. S. Geiger, USMC

Task Group 53.3
Northern Transport Group
Capt. P. Buchanan

III Amphibious Corps Artillery
Brig. Gen. P. A. del Valle, USMC

Task Group 53.16
Tractor Group Three
Capt. G. B. Carter

3d Marine Division
Maj. Gen. A. H. Turnage, USMC

Task Group 53.9
Minesweeping and Hydrographic Group
Lt. Comdr. G. M. Estep

1st Provisional Marine Brigade
Brig. Gen. L. C. Shepherd, Jr., USMC

Task Group 53.2
Southern Attack Group
Rear Adm. L. F. Reifsnider

77th Infantry Division
Maj. Gen. A. D. Bruce, USA

Task Group 53.4
Southern Transport Group
Capt. J. B. McGovern

Task Group 53.17
Tractor Group Four
Comdr. E. A. McFall

Task Group 53.6
Minesweeping and Hydrographic Unit
Comdr. R. R. Sampson

Task Group 53.5
Southern Fire Support Group
Rear Adm. W. L. Ainsworth

Task Group 53.7
Carrier Support Group
Rear Adm. V. H. Ragsdale

Task Group 53.19
Corps Reserve Group
Capt. H. B. Knowles

———— Command and operational control.

←—←—←—←—←—

Operational control only until troops are
established ashore

eral Geiger was to have under his command the 3d Marine Division; the 1st Provisional Marine Brigade, consisting of the 4th and 22d Marine Regiments, reinforced; III Amphibious Corps Artillery; and the 9th and 14th Marine Defense Battalions. The 27th Infantry Division was constituted Expeditionary Troops Reserve for the entire force of the two corps. The 77th Infantry Division, commanded by Maj. Gen. Andrew D. Bruce—still in the United States but scheduled shortly to move to Hawaii—was designated Area Reserve. Twenty days after Saipan was assaulted, the 77th was alerted for movement into the Marianas.[4]

Command relationships between the top commanders for the Guam phase (Phase III) of the Marianas operation were to be in every way similar to those that were obtained for Saipan and Tinian. Under Admiral Nimitz, Admiral Spruance as Commander, Fifth Fleet, was in over-all command. Under him came Admiral Turner, Commander, Joint Expeditionary Force (Task Force 51), and General Holland Smith, Commander, Expeditionary Troops (Task Force 56), whose respective powers and responsibilities on this echelon of command have already been described.[5] The Joint Expeditionary Force was in turn divided into two groups. The first, called Northern Attack Force (Task Force 52), also under Admiral Turner, was directed to land and support the assault troops on Saipan and Tinian. The second, designated Southern Attack Force, commanded by Admiral Conolly, USN, was given the same task for Guam. In like manner, General Holland Smith's Expeditionary Troops was

MAJ. GEN. ROY S. GEIGER

split into two parts: Northern Troops and Landing Force (Task Group 56.1) consisting mainly of the V Amphibious Corps plus the XXIV Corps Artillery and commanded also by General Smith was allocated to Saipan and Tinian; Southern Troops and Landing Force (Task Group 56.2), made up mostly of the III Amphibious Corps, commanded by General Geiger, was destined for Guam. The command relationships between General Geiger and Admiral Conolly were essentially the same as those that obtained between General Smith as Commander, Northern Troops and Landing Force, and Admiral Turner as Commander, Northern Attack Force.[6] Thus, during the ship-to-shore movement, Con-

---

[4] TF 56 Rpt FORAGER, Incl B, G-5 Rpt, pp. 1-5.

[5] See above, p. 33.

[6] TF 56 Opn Plan 2-44, 11 Apr 44; Opn Plan 3-44, 26 Apr 44; III Phib Corps Opn Plan 1-44, 11 May 44, Annex King.

olly was to command the landing force through Geiger. Once Geiger determined that the status of the landing operation permitted, he was to assume command of the troops on shore and report that fact to the task force commander. (*Chart 2*)

Planning for the invasion of Guam was somewhat complicated by the vast distances that lay between the headquarters of the various commanders concerned. General Geiger's III Amphibious Corps headquarters was located at Guadalcanal; General Holland Smith's Expeditionary Troops staff was at Pearl Harbor, as were Admirals Spruance, Turner, and Conolly and their staffs. The 77th Division was still in the United States during the period when the initial plans for the landing were being worked out.

On 29 March, General Geiger flew to Pearl Harbor, where for better than a week he conferred with General Smith and Admirals Turner and Conolly and their respective staffs. A week after Geiger's departure from Pearl Harbor, Admiral Conolly flew to Guadalcanal, where the two commanders completed their planning and ironed out some of the many complicated problems involving naval-ground force coordination in the forthcoming landing.[7]

The upshot of these various conferences was the promulgation of one preferred and two alternate landing plans for Guam. The preferred plan called for simultaneous landings on the west coast by the 3d Marine Division between Adelup Point and Tatgua River and by the 1st Provisional Marine Brigade between the town of Agat and Bangi Point. The landing day (designated

W Day) was tentatively set as 18 June, three days after D Day for Saipan.[8]

To support the troops, Admiral Conolly split his Southern Attack Force into two groups, Northern and Southern Attack Groups. The former, commanded by Conolly himself, was, under the preferred landing plan, to support the 3d Marine Division; the later, to be commanded by Rear Adm. Lawrence F. Reifsnider, USN, would perform the same function for the 1st Provisional Brigade. The provisions for naval gunfire support during and after the landing closely paralleled those established for the Saipan operation. Before W Day, ships and aircraft of Admiral Conolly's Task Force 53 were to co-ordinate their bombardments with scheduled strikes by aircraft from Admiral Mitscher's Task Force 58. On W minus 2 and W minus 1, Task Force 53 was charged with responsibility for close-range support of underwater demolition teams and for destruction of coastal defense guns and antiaircraft and field artillery batteries on the landing beaches and of areas immediately inland. During the evenings ships of Task Force 53 were to provide harassing fires and some time during this period were to conduct a diversionary bombardment on the east coast of Guam.[9]

On W Day itself the first priority for the fire support ships would be counterbattery fire, beginning at dawn, on known and suspected enemy positions. Secondary attention would be paid to local defenses by close-range fire. Third priority would be given to interdiction fire against any roads

---

[7] III Phib Corps Rpt Guam Opn, 3 Sep 44, pp. 1–2.

[8] III Phib Corps Opn Plan 1–44, 11 May 44; Opn Plan 3–44, 30 May 44; Opn Plan 4–44, 9 Jun 44.

[9] III Phib Corps Opn Plan 1–44, Annex C, Naval Gunfire Support Plan.

leading to the landing beaches. Shortly before H Hour naval gunfire was to shift to close support fire on the flanks of the landing beaches. When the leading tractor waves were 1,200 yards from shore, cruisers were to lift their main batteries to the inland areas with an accelerated rate of fire to neutralize mobile batteries and mortars. Five-inch gunfire was to be maintained along the beaches while naval aircraft strafed and bombed the same area. When the leading assault wave of LVT(A)'s was 500 yards from shore, the 5-inch batteries were to shift fire to the near flanks of the beaches. One novel safety factor was introduced into the plans for Guam that had not been prescribed for the other landings in the Marianas. During the period when air and naval bombardment was to be conducted simultaneously, ships were ordered to restrict their fire to a maximum range of 8,000 yards, which meant in effect a maximum shell ordinate of about 1,200 feet. At the same time pilots were instructed to fly no lower than 1,500 feet.[10]

After H Hour, ships were to continue scheduled fires until ordered to stop. Call fires, it was planned, would be available as soon as communication with the shore fire control parties on the beaches was set up, and fire support ships were then to be prepared to deliver harassing fire, interdiction fire, star shell and searchlight illumination, and white phosphorus projectile fire on call.[11]

Admiral Conolly, as Commander, Northern Attack Group, was to control the naval fire in support of the 3d Marine Division's landing over the Asan beaches, while Admiral Reifsnider was to control bombardment of the brigade's beaches in the Agat area. Control of aircraft over both sets of beaches was to be exercised by Admiral Conolly alone through his Commander, Support Aircraft, stationed aboard the task force flagship, the AGC *Appalachian.* This officer was assigned control of combat air patrols, antisubmarine patrols, close air support of troops, and a variety of special missions. He would control not only the planes flown from the carriers attached to Task Force 53 but also planes flown from the fast carriers of Task Force 58 from the time of their arrival over the combat area until their departure for recovery by their parent ships.[12]

Before the arrival of *Appalachian* in the Guam area, an Advance Commander, Support Aircraft, embarked on the cruiser *Honolulu,* would discharge these functions. A standby Commander, Support Aircraft, embarked in Admiral Reifsnider's flagship *George Clymer,* was assigned the temporary additional duty of Commander, Landing Force Support Aircraft. He was to assume this role under the command of General Geiger after the latter had established his command post ashore. The plan provided that when the Landing Force Support Aircraft commander was ready to take control of aircraft (land-based and carrier-based) in direct support of the troops, he was to advise Admiral Conolly and thereafter, under Conolly, would assume control of all support aircraft over Guam. Requests for carrier-based and distant land-based aircraft were to be sent by the Commander, Landing Force Support Aircraft, to Admiral Conolly, who would effect the arrangements for getting the planes on station and notify the Commander, Landing

[10] TF 53 Opn Plan A162-44, 17 May 44, Annex D, Vol. I, pp. 1-15.
[11] *Ibid.*

[12] III Phib Corps Opn Plan 1-44, Annex D, Air Support Plan.

Force Support Aircraft, of their estimated time of arrival at the rendezvous point.[13] This procedure would automatically give the landing force commander (General Geiger), through his air representative, more direct control over the aircraft employed in the support of his troops than was the case at Saipan and Tinian. There the Commander, Attack Force Support Aircraft, afloat, had kept close rein on all troop support missions flown from carriers.

To avoid conflict between air support strikes and field artillery fire, Commander, Support Aircraft, or Commander, Landing Force Support Aircraft, was to request a cessation of fire from the commanding general of III Amphibious Corps Artillery for the duration of the air strike. Further coordination was to be secured through air observers, artillery spotters, and through the air co-ordinator. The function of the latter was to direct scheduled air strikes from the air and to report developments of the ground situation. Marine air observers were to keep General Geiger informed on the ground situation, while artillery spotters would direct Marine artillery fire.

Preliminary air strikes on Guam were to begin on D Day at Saipan and last until W Day minus 1 under direction of the Advance Commander, Support Aircraft. On W Day itself a major air strike was scheduled to last for half an hour, from H Hour minus 90 minutes to H Hour minus 60 minutes. During this period forty-six fighters and ninety-six dive bombers were to bomb and strafe gun positions and beach installations in the two landing areas and surrounding territory.[14]

---

[13] *Ibid.*
[14] *Ibid.*, App. 1.

Change of Plans

Following intensive amphibious training and rehearsals in the Guadalcanal area,[15] the various Marine units of the III Amphibious Corps set sail aboard the transports and LST's of Task Force 53 and arrived at the staging area at Kwajalein Atoll on 8 June. After a brief period allowed for fueling, watering, and provisioning, the convoy put to sea again and by 15 June had arrived at its designated assembly area over a hundred miles to the east of Saipan. There it waited for ten days, cruising idly through the open seas, while higher authorities debated the feasibility of an early landing on Guam.

Originally, W Day for the assault had been tentatively set as 18 June, but events on Saipan and in the adjacent waters made a postponement mandatory. As already indicated, the 27th Infantry Division, at first designated as reserve for the Saipan and Guam phases of the Marianas invasion, had to be committed in its entirety to Saipan. Furthermore, the Japanese *Mobile Fleet* had been sighted steaming toward the Marianas with the apparent intention of giving battle, and it was obvious folly to send the slow-moving troop transports and LST's of Task Force 53 into the waters west of Guam. Hence, Admiral Spruance canceled W Day and ordered Conolly's task force to remain out of danger well to the east of Saipan.

By 25 June the situation ashore on Saipan had improved sufficiently to warrant releasing the III Amphibious Corps from its duties as floating reserve for the V

---

[15] See Major O. R. Lodge, USMC, *The Recapture of Guam*, Historical Branch, G-3 Division, Headquarters, U.S. Marine Corps (Washington, 1954) (hereafter cited as Lodge, *Guam*), pp. 26-28.

Corps. Accordingly, the ships carrying the 3d Marine Division sailed back to Eniwetok where they were followed five days later by the rest of the vessels carrying the 1st Provisional Marine Brigade.[16] By early July, with the Saipan battle over two weeks old, thought could at last be given to deciding on a firm date for the landing on Guam. As a result of conferences among Admirals Turner, Hill, and Conolly and Generals Holland Smith and Geiger, 25 July was recommended. These commanders deemed an earlier attack on Guam inadvisable because, as Admiral Spruance expressed it to Admiral Nimitz, "The character of enemy resistance being encountered in Saipan and the increase over the original estimates of enemy strength in Guam" made the presence of the entire 77th Infantry Division necessary.[17]

Admiral Nimitz was anxious to schedule the assault for 15 July, by which time it was presumed that at least one regimental combat team of the 77th Division could be dispatched to the scene of operations. Nevertheless, he deferred to the judgment of the officers present in the combat area and agreed to delay W Day until the whole of the Army division had arrived at Eniwetok. On 6 July Admiral Spruance was advised that the last two regimental combat teams of the 77th Division to leave Hawaii could reach Eniwetok by 18 July, four days earlier than expected. Consequently, W Day was advanced to 21 July. The 305th Infantry of the 77th Division was constituted reserve for the 1st Provisional Brigade and ordered to land on the Agat beaches sometime after the brigade had gone ashore. The rest of the division

was designated corps reserve and was ordered to prepare to land "about William plus 2 Day on designated Beaches between Agat Village and Facpi Point"—also in the brigade zone.[18]

77th Infantry Division Training and Preparation

For the 77th Infantry Division, the invasion of Guam was to be the first chapter of a distinguished combat record in the Pacific war. Activated in March 1942, the unit spent its first two years in the United States undergoing training in basic infantry warfare and in various specialties such as desert warfare at Camp Hyder, Arizona, mountain warfare in West Virginia, and amphibious warfare in the Chesapeake Bay area. In May 1943 General Bruce assumed command of the division. A veteran of World War I, General Bruce was a graduate of the Infantry School, the Field Artillery School, the Command and General Staff School, the Army War College, and the Naval War College. Before he assumed command of the 77th Division he completed a tour of duty in the Operations and Training Division of the War Department General Staff and commanded the Tank Destroyer Center at Camp Hood.[19]

By March 1944 the division was located at Oahu, and for the next three months it was put through an intensive indoctrination in the techniques of warfare peculiar to the Pacific area under the direction of General Richardson's United States Army

---

[16] TF 53 Opn Rpt Guam, 10 Aug 44, pp. 5–6.
[17] Comdr Fifth Fleet, Final Rpt on Opn to Capture the Marianas, p. 5.

[18] III Phib Corps Opn Plan 1–44, Addendum, 10 Jul 44.
[19] *Ours To Hold It High, The History of the 77th Infantry Division in World War II By Men Who Were There* (Washington: Infantry Journal Press, 1947), pp. 1–40.

Forces in the Central Pacific Area (USAF-ICPA). Infantrymen were trained as flame thrower and demolition men so as to avoid the necessity of relying exclusively on engineers to perform these functions in combat. Officers and noncommissioned officers took a forward-observers course to reduce dependence on artillery personnel. The 706th Tank Battalion trained with the infantry regiments in mutual close-in support, combined maneuver problems, and landing operations. The entire division spent six days at the Unit Jungle Training Center on Oahu. Amphibious training for the infantrymen consisted of net-climbing, embarkation, and debarkation from mock-up ships, transfer of personnel and equipment from LCVP's to LVT's at sea, and landing on beaches in wave formation. Artillery units conducted test landings from LST's and practiced landing operations in DUKW's and LVT's with battalion landing teams. Experiments in loading and landing 155-mm. guns from LCM's, LST's, and LCT's were made. The 77th Division Reconnaissance Troop held four days of practice with destroyer escorts, and part of the 292d JASCO trained with Navy aircraft at Maui. The JASCO's shore fire patrol party conducted destroyer firing exercises at the naval gunnery range on Kahoolawe Island. The only important feature missing from the program was the customary last-minute ship-to-shore rehearsal, which had to be foregone because of the lack of time. For most of the period the XXIV Corps, to which the division had initially been assigned, assisted in the training. Not until 22 June, almost on the eve of its departure from Oahu, was the division released to the V Amphibious Corps, the Marine Corps' administrative

and training command in the Hawaiian area.[20]

At the time the division set sail from Hawaii in the first week of July, it was still a matter of doubt as to how and where it would be employed on Guam. Not until the middle of the month when the troop transports had reached Eniwetok was General Bruce fully apprised of the intentions of his superiors in regard to his unit. This meant that there was very little time before the target date to complete plans and to disseminate them to subordinate units. An additional handicap was the fact that not until they arrived at Guam itself were the commanding general and his staff able to establish personal contact with higher, adjacent, and supporting units.[21]

Despite these difficulties, by 15 July General Bruce was able to promulgate three plans (one preferred and two alternates) for the division's commitment. The plan already devised by III Amphibious Corps had contemplated the seizure of a Force Beachhead Line to extend from Adelup Point along the Mount Alutom–Mount Tenjo–Mount Alifan ridge line to Facpi Point. According to the corps' preferred plan, the 3d Marine Division would land between Adelup Point and the mouth of the Tatgua River and move south to the Apra Harbor area while the 1st Provisional Marine Brigade, with the 305th Regimental Combat Team of the 77th Division attached, would land between the town Agat and Bangi Point and then wheel north to the base of Orote Peninsula.

---

[20] USAFICPA Participation Rpt Marianas, Vol. I, pp. 24, 68, 171, 172, 266, 276, 289–93; Vol. II, pp. 315, 337. See Appendix D for order of battle of the 77th Infantry Division for the Guam operation.
[21] 77th Inf Div Opn Rpt FORAGER, 21 Jul–16 Aug 44, p. 17.

Gearing his own plans to this schedule of operations, General Bruce directed the 2d Battalion, 305th, with a platoon of the 706th Tank Battalion, to assemble at the line of departure two hours after H Hour and be ready to land on order of the 1st Provisional Marine Brigade. The other two battalions of the 305th were free of specific instructions except to be ready to debark and land, also on brigade order. As corps reserve, the 306th and 307th Regiments would land on corps order over the same beaches as the brigade, move to assembly areas, and be prepared to relieve the brigade of the duty of defending the final beachhead line.[22]

The two alternate plans prepared for the Army division's commitment were both based on the assumption that the Marines' preferred plan would be put in effect. One of these contemplated a landing by the 306th and 307th Infantry Regiments near Adelup Point, whence they would move southwest to assembly areas and be prepared to attack either south toward Mount Tenjo or southeast toward Pago Bay. The second called for landings by the same two regiments on the northwestern coast between Uruno and Ritidian Points, from which positions they would move southwest in order to secure from the rear a beachhead at Tumon Bay.[23]

This second plan was particularly dear to General Bruce's heart.[24] He wanted the two regiments of the 77th Division that were in corps reserve (the 306th and 307th) to land at dawn or just before dawn near the northwest tip of Guam about four days after the initial amphibious assault. They would then drive rapidly south and capture a beachhead at Tumon Bay from the rear. They would land without heavy equipment, but once the Tumon Bay beaches were secured necessary supplies and equipment and possibly other infantry elements could be landed there. The concept of the plan, as Bruce expressed it, was "for the 77th Division to become a hammer striking forwards and eventually on the anvil, i.e., the Force Beach Line. Should the enemy divert sufficient forces to halt this Division for any appreciable length of time it should be possible for the 77th Division to become the anvil and the forces occupying the FBL to become the hammer." [25]

Immediately upon his arrival at Eniwetok on 11 July, General Bruce, with characteristic enthusiasm, pressed this scheme on the Marine commanders present. None of them warmed to the proposal, and Maj. Gen. Allen H. Turnage told him he had better drop the idea. The Marines were reluctant to divert the corps reserve to a secondary landing for fear it might be needed to support the assault troops at the main beachheads. Undaunted by this

---

[22] 77th Inf Div Opn Plan I, 15 Jul 44, 77th Inf Div Initial Opn Plans and Adm Orders Guam, Jun–Jul 44.

[23] 77th Inf Div Opn Plan II and III, 15 Jul 44, 77th Inf Div Initial Opn Plans and Adm Orders Guam, Jun–Jul 44.

[24] Throughout his entire World War II service as commanding general of the 77th Division, General Bruce was an enthusiastic supporter of the concept of the "amphibious end run," that is, of secondary amphibious landings to the rear of the

main Force Beachhead Line. During the Leyte operation he succeeded in getting the idea accepted with the result that the 77th Division made a highly successful landing at Ormoc. At Okinawa he tried to persuade his immediate superiors to let his division make a similar landing on the southern coast of the island to the rear of the Japanese main line of resistance, but the plan was rejected.

[25] Hq 77th Inf Div, Alternate Opn Plan Employment 77th Div in Corps Reserve, 14 Jul 44.

cold reception, Bruce sent a despatch outlining his plan to General Geiger, who had already sailed for the Marianas aboard Admiral Conolly's flagship, *Appalachian*. The corps commander rejected the plan on the grounds that it was then too late to make any radical changes.[26]

Loading and Embarkation

77th Division

In the Hawaiian area where the 77th Division loaded and embarked for the Guam operation, its logistical needs were handled by the supply section of General Richardson's headquarters and its subordinate agencies and by Commander, Service Force Pacific, a naval organization. Holland Smith's staff determined the amounts of each class of supplies to be landed initially and supervised or at least checked the tentative loading plans. In the early phases of the logistical planning, it was not considered necessary to provide initial combat supplies to the division because the earlier operation plans did not call for its commitment within thirty-five days of the Marine assault landings.[27] Once the division was designated area reserve and then, in mid-June, alerted for movement to the Marianas, supply activities were naturally accelerated.

General Bruce's first supply order was issued on 24 June and specified the levels of initial supply for each class:

[26] Ltr, Lt Gen Andrew D. Bruce, USA (Ret.), to Gen A. C. Smith, 11 Feb 55, with Incl 2 (copy of FORAGER Notes kept by General Bruce), OCMH.
[27] TF 56 Rpt FORAGER, Incl E, G-4 Rpt, p. 8.

Class I

Rations

Type B	10 days
10-in-1 pack	10 days
Type C	7 days
Type K	3 days
Type D	2 days
Assault candy ration	2 per man
Rations accessory pack	20 days

Water

In 5-gallon containers and 55-gallon drums, 2 gallons per man per day for 5 days; 1 water point unit for each RCT; 2 water distillation units for each engineer combat battalion.

Class II

20 days maintenance of clothing, equipment, and general supplies, bulk clothing and individual equipment carried by RCT's to be equally distributed in all ships and landed early.

Class III

Fuels and lubricants	20 days

Class IV

Chemical Warfare	20 days
Engineer	20 days
Ordnance	20 days
Quartermaster	20 days
Medical	30 days
Signal	20 days

Class V

Antiaircraft weapons	10 CINCPOA U/F
All other weapons	7 CINCPOA U/F[28]

Like the 27th Division before it went to Saipan, and unlike any of the Marine divisions destined for the Marianas, the 77th complied enthusiastically with General Holland Smith's directive that between 25 and 50 percent of all supplies be palle-

[28] 77th Inf Div Administrative Order 1, 24 Jun 44, pp. 1-3. Later the number of days supply of 10-in-1 pack rations was changed to 20. Maj. Gen. Andrew D. Bruce, "Administration, Supply, and Evacuation of the 77th Infantry Division on Guam," *Military Review*, XXIV (December, 1944), 3. For the composition of CINCPOA units of fire, see Appendix B.

tized.[29] All together, the division built about five thousand pallets, but about a thousand of these were dismantled before being loaded aboard ship because they would not fit into available spaces in the holds or because they were too difficult to handle in holds where fingerlifts were not available.[30] In contrast, the marines bound for Guam palletized none of their supplies, partly because they lacked the building materials and equipment to handle them and partly because they were still skeptical as to whether pallets could be satisfactorily hauled ashore over a coral reef.[31]

To lift the more than 18,000 troops and the 21,428 tons of supplies and equipment of the 77th Division from Hawaii to Eniwetok and then on to Guam, the Navy provided seven attack transports, four transports, three AKA's, two AK's, and three LST's. The LST's carried 612 troops and the 53 DUKW's allotted to the division. The DUKW's were the only amphibian vehicles allowed the 77th; no LVT's were taken along since the division was not scheduled to go into the beach in assault.[32]

Loading the vessels was complicated by the fact that the 77th Division had less than two weeks' advance notice as to how many ships would be made available to it and what their characteristics would be. Loading plans therefore had to be sketchy and tentative, since they could not be made final until approved by the commanding officer of each ship. The vessels themselves

did not arrive at Oahu until forty-eight hours before the date set to begin loading. To troops who were about to embark on their first amphibious operation, the delay of course was maddening. One battalion commander later recalled that his transport quartermaster, the troop officer in charge of loading, "worried for 5 straight days without sleep, as did most of his assistants." [33] The 305th Regimental Combat Team was the first of the regiments to be loaded, and it left Honolulu on 1 July. Embarkation was hasty, troops and cargo were loaded simultaneously, and much confusion resulted. The other two regiments had to await the return of transports that had been involved in the first phase of the Marianas operation at Saipan. They did not leave Hawaii until 8 July.[34]

The Marines

The Marine units embarking for the Guam operation had one distinct advantage over the 77th Division in that their assigned shipping was present in their mounting area, the Solomon Islands, well in advance of the embarkation date. Admiral Conolly and his staff arrived at Guadalcanal on 15 April for a stay of nearly a month of preliminary planning with the III Amphibious Corps. The naval forces assigned to Task Force 53 were largely from Admiral Halsey's South Pacific Area and had engaged in the Hollandia operation before putting in to bases in the Solomons on 10 May. Before their return for attachment to Conolly's task force, arrangements had been made to station

[29] TF 56 Rpt FORAGER, Incl G, Transport QM Rpt, p. 15.

[30] 77th Inf Div Adm Order 1, 24 Jun 44; Bruce, "Administration, Supply, and Evacuation . . .," Military Review, XXIV, 6.

[31] III Phib Corps Rpt Guam, Incl A, Supply Rpt.

[32] TF 56 Rpt FORAGER, Incl G, Transport QM Rpt, pp. 515, 517, Incl BB.

[33] Ltr, Col James E. Landrum, Jr., to Gen A. C. Smith, 27 Apr 55, and Incl, OCMH.

[34] Ibid., p. 20; 77th Inf Div Opn Rpt FORAGER, 305th RCT Rpt, p. 12.

them at Guadalcanal, Efate, Espiritu Santo, and Hathorn Sound so as to avoid over-crowding Guadalcanal and Tulagi.[35]

Because of the presence of the ships in the immediate area of the points of em-barkation, there was ample time for the transport division commanders and ship captains to check thoroughly the loading plans of the various units. Such difficulty as was encountered centered primarily around the loading and embarkation of the 1st Provisional Marine Brigade, which had only recently been formed and had not had as much time to prepare detailed plans as had the 3d Marine Division.[36]

More important was the fact that early in May the naval lift allotted to the assault units was unexpectedly ordered to carry more than five hundred troops of Maj. Gen. Henry L. Larsen's Island Command Headquarters Group, which was destined for garrison duties on Guam after it was secured. This raised additional demands on the already limited shipping space, and the result was that the marines had to leave a good number of their organic vehicles be-hind when they sailed from the Solomons. Their supply of amphibian vehicles, how-ever, was not curtailed. The 358 LVT's of the 3d and 4th Amphibian Tractor Bat-talions were assigned respectively to the 3d Marine Division and the 1st Provisional Marine Brigade. Their job, after delivering the assault troops ashore, was to transship cargo and personnel from landing craft over the reef and thence to shore. In addition to these vehicles, the marines were sup-plied with a hundred DUKW's.[37]

Preliminary Bombardment

Naval Gunfire

No matter what the immediate incon-venience to American forces caused by Ad-miral Spruance's postponement of the scheduled landing day on Guam, the long-run consequences of that decision were for-tunate. The postponement of W Day from 18 June to 21 July made possible a more prolonged preliminary air and sea bom-bardment against Guam than against any other island in the Pacific during the war. The marines of the III Amphibious Corps who had chafed and fretted at being con-fined to their ships in the sweltering lagoon of Eniwetok later had good reason to be thankful for their enforced inactivity.

The first American naval shells to hit Guam were fired from ships of a small task group from Task Force 53 on 16 June, the day after the landing on Saipan. For an hour and three quarters, the cruiser *Hono-lulu*, the battleships *Pennsylvania* and *Idaho*, and several destroyers, all supported by planes from accompanying aircraft car-riers, bombarded the west coast of the is-land. The damage done appears to have been negligible, but the raid did alert the Japanese as to the probable American choice of landing beaches in the forthcom-ing invasion.[38]

The enemy ashore mistook the shelling for the usual last-minute preliminary to an assault landing, and one Army lieutenant wrote in his diary:

For the first time I saw the enemy fleet and was under its gunfire. I regret very much that we are powerless to do anything but to look

---

[35] TF 53 Opn Rpt Guam, pp. 1–2.
[36] III Phib Corps Rpt Guam, Incl A, Supply Rpt, pp. 1–3.
[37] Lodge, *Guam*, pp. 21–22. See Appendix E for Order of Battle of III Amphibious Corps (less 77th Division).

[38] CINCPAC–CINCPOA Opns in POA, Jul 44, p. 29; Morison, *New Guinea and the Mari-anas*, p. 377.

at the enemy which came in barely 10,000 meters away. They shelled us steadily for two hours. Our positions were hit fourteen times. Fortunately none was injured. . . . We think that at last the enemy will land tonight, and so we will observe strict alert all night. We were issued hand grenades and are now waiting for the enemy to come.[39]

By next morning, of course, the American ships had disappeared over the horizon, much to the disappointment of the lieutenant, and probably of most of his comrades. Impatiently, he wrote, "If the enemy is coming, let him come. The spirit to fight to the death is high. We are anxiously waiting but nothing unusual has happened so far as dawn breaks."[40]

The next surface ship strike against Guam occurred on 27 June when a small detachment of cruisers and destroyers (Task Unit 58.4.5) from Admiral Mitscher's carrier fleet made a quick run into the waters off Guam and Rota, sank a small harbor tug and two barges in Apra Harbor, and set fire to some oil storage tanks ashore. Three days later Destroyer Division 46 shelled the airfields on Orote Peninsula.[41]

Then, on 8 July, began the greatest single naval bombardment program of the war—greatest at least in terms of time expended. For thirteen days the Japanese garrison on Guam was treated to the most spectacular display of shore bombardment that the U.S. Navy had yet produced.

First to arrive were four heavy cruisers, twelve destroyers, and two escort carriers of Task Group 53.18 commanded by Rear

Adm. C. Turner Joy. The group's primary mission was to destroy coastal defense and heavy antiaircraft guns. Secondary targets were warehouses, command posts, communications facilities, and troop concentrations. Co-ordinating with the planes from two task groups of Task Force 58 that arrived in the area about the same time, the cruisers and destroyers were responsible for one half of the island while the planes bombarded the remainder. At noon each day the two exchanged areas of responsibility. Meanwhile, planes from the two escort carriers flew combat air and antisubmarine patrol. At night each warship delivered harassing fire against the island. On 12 July the battleships *New Mexico, Idaho,* and *Pennsylvania* arrived to add their bit to the fireworks. Two days later Admiral Conolly himself put in his appearance aboard the AGC *Appalachian* and thereafter personally took charge of co-ordinating all naval and air bombardment. The same day, the battleship *Colorado* joined the bombardment force, as did *California* and *Tennessee* on the 19th. By the time the marines arrived to invade the island, a total of six battleships and nine cruisers with their escorting destroyers were saturating Guam with naval shells of all varieties. For this period of thirteen days (exclusive of W Day itself) naval ammunition expenditures against shore targets totaled 836 rounds of 16-inch, 5,422 of 14-inch, 3,862 of 8-inch, 2,430 of 6-inch, and 16,214 of 5-inch shells.[42]

At the invasion of Roi-Namur Admiral Conolly had earned the sobriquet "Close-in Conolly" for his insistence that warships

[39] CINCPAC–CINCPOA Trans 10634, extracts from the diary of 2d Lt Imanishi, Rai 3211 To (*38th Inf Regt, 29th Div*) (hereafter cited as Imanishi Diary).

[40] *Ibid.*

[41] CINCPAC–CINCPOA Opns in POA, Jul 44, p. 29.

[42] TF 53 Opn Rpt Guam, Incl E, Intel Rpt, p. 5; TF 56 Rpt FORAGER, Incl G, Naval Gunfire Support Rpt, p. 71; CINCPAC–CINCPOA Opns in POA, Jul 44, p. 29.

cruise close to shore when firing at land targets.[43] At Guam, he reaffirmed his right to the title, but more important was the systematic procedure he introduced for co-ordinating naval gunfire and aerial bombardment and checking the results of each. A target board of six officers, representing the air, gunnery, and intelligence sections of the staff, was set up to assign primary missions for air strikes and naval gunfire and assess the damages daily before designating the next day's targets. Aerial photographs were taken each morning and on the basis of these damage was assessed and new targets were assigned. In these operations, the admiral's staff was aided by the presence aboard *Appalachian* of General Geiger who, as commanding general of the landing force, naturally had the greatest personal concern about the accuracy both of the bombardment and of the damage reports submitted afterward.[44]

During the later stages of the preliminary bombardment, one additional duty was imposed on the ships present—that of supporting naval underwater demolition teams. All together, three teams were made available for the Guam landings. The procedure was one that had by now become standardized in the Pacific. Swimmers disembarked from their mother APD into LCPR's that took them close to the reef before putting them in the water to swim in the rest of the way to inspect the reef itself. In the meantime, four LCI gunboats lay to just off the reef and fired their 40-mm. and 20-mm. guns over the heads of the swimmers. On each flank of the

LCI(G)'s was a destroyer firing five-inch shells farther inland, while the APD followed astern of the line of gunboats, also firing. After the small boats had picked up their swimmers, the covering ships continued their fire on the beaches in an effort to interdict the area where the enemy was attempting to make repairs.

On 14 July Underwater Demolition Team 3, aboard the APD *Dickerson*, arrived in the area and for three days conducted reconnaissance of the chosen landing beaches and other segments of the western coast line. On 17 July Underwater Demolition Teams 4 and 6 put in their appearance. Actual demolition work began that evening. The obstacles discovered on the Agat beaches were chiefly palm log cribs filled with coral and connected by wire cable. On the Asan beaches wire cages filled with cemented coral were spaced about every five feet. Only occasional strips of barbed wire were found, and no underwater mines. All together, 640 obstacles were blown-up off Asan and about 300 off Agat by hand-placed demolitions.[45] Some of these, at least, had been constructed as recently as 3 July, by which time the Japanese had been tipped off as to the probable landing beaches to be used by the invaders.[46]

Aerial Bombardment

In preparing the way for the amphibious assault on Guam, four main duties fell to the air arms of the Army and Navy. They were to neutralize Truk and the other islands in the Caroline group from which the Japanese might be expected to send

---

[43] See Crowl and Love, *Gilberts and Marshalls,* Ch. XVIII.

[44] TF 53 Opn Rpt Guam, Incl B, Naval Gunfire Support Rpt; Lodge, *Guam,* p. 34; Morison, *New Guinea and the Marianas,* pp. 380–81.

[45] TF 53 Opn Rpt Guam, p. 10; CINCPAC-CINCPOA Opns in POA, Jul 44, pp. 31–42.

[46] Imanishi Diary.

their own aerial strength into the southern Marianas, prevent intervention by Japanese carrier-borne planes, photograph the island, and soften the target itself with an accelerated program of aerial bombing and strafing.

Starting in mid-March and continuing even after Guam had been secured, Army Air Forces bombers of the Seventh, Thirteenth, and, later, Fifth Air Forces conducted a series of devastating raids against the Carolines, chiefly Truk and Woleai. On one occasion, during the last two days of April, they were joined by Admiral Mitscher's Task Force 58, which dropped 748 tons of bombs on Truk while retiring from the Hollandia invasion. The major credit for keeping the Carolines neutralized, however, fell to the Army Air Forces. By the time of the invasion of the southern Marianas, the island of Truk, once the leading Japanese bastion in the Central Pacific, had been rendered virtually useless.[47] A like fate had befallen the great Japanese *Mobile Fleet* at the hands of Task Force 58 during the Battle of the Philippine Sea. By 20 June it was clear that the invaders of Guam need have no fear of serious Japanese threats from the air.

To Task Force 59, commanded by Maj. Gen. Willis H. Hale, AUS, fell the chief responsibility for aerial photographic reconnaissance of the Marianas. Seventh Air Force and shore-based Navy bombers, both under General Hale's command, maintained armed reconnaissance over all the southern Marianas for more than two months before the first landings on Saipan. The first mission over Guam was carried out on 6 May by ten Army B–24's escort-

ing six Navy PB4Y's. Five of the planes were shot down over the target by enemy fighters; six others were damaged. Again on 24 May, 29 May, and 6 June flights of B–24's and PB4Y's made the trip over Guam, taking photographs and dropping token loads of bombs on targets of opportunity.[48] Of the 6 June raid, a Lieutenant Imanishi wrote despairingly, "There were 9 B–24's,[49] but not one of our planes went up to meet them. We felt disheartened. Just how desirous our air force is of fighting is open to doubt."[50]

Desirous of fighting or not, the Japanese pilots stationed on Guam were soon to lose the means of doing so. Shortly after the photographic flight on 6 June, Admiral Mitscher's fleet showed up to begin its methodical destruction of enemy aircraft and air facilities. In the belief that the island would be invaded on 18 June, Commander, Task Force 58, first unleashed his mighty armada of fighters and bombers against Guam and nearby Rota on 11–12 June. In the ensuing air battle, a total of 150 Japanese planes was reported destroyed in the air or on the ground. For the next four days, one or more of Mitscher's task groups carried out strikes against aircraft facilities, runways, coastal guns, and antiaircraft positions on Guam and Rota.[51]

Against this overwhelming naval airpower, the Japanese were almost helpless. Wrote Lieutenant Imanishi, "It is especially pitiful that we cannot control the air. We can only clench our fists with anger and

---

[47] See above, pp. 71–72; Craven and Cate, *AAF IV*, pp. 676–90; USSBS, *The Reduction of Truk.*

[48] Army Air Forces in the Marianas Campaign, Operation FORAGER, Mar–Aug 44, pp. 7–10, MS in OCMH.

[49] Actually there were seven B–24's and four PB4Y's.

[50] Imanishi Diary.

[51] CINCPAC–CINCPOA Opns in POA, Jun 44, pp. 69–93.

watch." [52] At the same time, a Japanese private noted that he and his companions were unable to leave their shelters and help repair the damage because of the bombings.[53] Another enlisted man complained, "The number of enemy planes was said to be more than 500 today, while not one of our planes took to the air. I felt a bitter resentment at the manner in which the enemy stressed his air power." [54]

Yet there was still some fight left in the Japanese air contingent on Guam, for on the evening of 15 June a few planes took off from Orote field to launch a low-level torpedo attack against the American carriers offshore. As a result, two of Mitscher's task groups next day concentrated heavily on Guam to prevent a repetition of the previous evening's attacks.[55] During the two-day Battle of the Philippine Sea, the fields of Guam again received the attention of Mitscher's fliers. Japanese land-based planes still undamaged by previous raids, as well as carrier planes that had flown in from Ozawa's fleet, constituted a threat on Mitscher's flank and rear that could not be overlooked. On the morning of 19 June, before the Great Marianas Turkey Shoot had even gotten well under way, two separate air battles were fought over Guam, both ending in victory for the Americans. Even during the course of the main battle itself, which was fought well out to sea, Mitscher kept one contingent of fighters and bombers over Guam to interdict the air-

fields and prevent any remaining planes from taking off to join Ozawa's carrier planes. All together, about fifty Guam-based planes were destroyed on the 19th alone, and the fields themselves were at least temporarily put out of business.[56] That night, when about fifteen Japanese carrier bombers attempted to make emergency landings there, they found the fields too torn up to do so and, being out of fuel, had to crash.[57]

The raids of 19 June all but delivered the *coup de grâce* to Japanese airpower on Guam. Occasionally, in the weeks that followed, a few Japanese planes flew into Orote from Yap and other islands in the Carolines, but they posed no real threat. On 4 July one of Mitscher's task groups (Task Group 58.3) returned to conduct a daylight raid over the island, and from 6 through 17 July two other carrier groups (Task Groups 58.1 and 58.2) alternated daily in strikes over Guam and Rota. Primary targets were coastal and antiaircraft guns, supply dumps, airfield installations, and the towns of Asan, Piti, and Agat. These strikes were co-ordinated with those of the escort carrier planes and the naval bombardment ships of Admiral Conolly's Task Force 53.[58] On the last three days before the landing, the Japanese on Guam witnessed the full weight of American naval airpower in a mounting crescendo of aerial fury. On 18 July planes from the two task forces flew 662 bombing sorties and 311 strafing attacks, on the 19th the number increased to 874 and 392, and on the day before the landings to 1,430 and 614. The total tonnage of bombs,

[52] Imanishi Diary.

[53] CINCPAC–CINCPOA Trans 10996, extracts from the diary of Leading Pvt Murano, Koko (*2d Bn, 10th IMR*).

[54] CINCPAC–CINCPOA Trans 10802, extracts from the diary of Cpl Susuki, Tai (*Yoshikawa Unit*).

[55] CINCPAC–CINCPOA Opns in POA, Jun 44, Annex A, pp. 81–98.

[56] Morison, *New Guinea and the Marianas*, pp. 257–63, 274–77.

[57] Imanishi Diary.

[58] See above, pp. 320–21.

depth charges, and rockets dropped and launched during these three days came to 1,131.[59]

Assessment of Damage

As night closed in on 20 July, it seemed impossible to those aboard the flagship *Appalachian* that the Japanese on Guam could put up anything but token resistance to the troops that would go in the next day in amphibious assault. Maj. William M. Gilliam, USMC, who was Geiger's naval gunfire officer, reported, "When the morning of the landing arrived, it was known that the assault troops would meet little resistance." [60] Admiral Conolly's staff believed, "Not one fixed gun was left in commission on the west coast that was of greater size than a machine gun." [61]

These conclusions were to prove somewhat extravagant, as the marines next day discovered to their sorrow. Testimony given after the war by Lt. Col. Hideyuki Takeda, IJA, who was a staff member of the *29th Division,* provides a corrective to the American reports on which these optimistic conclusions were based.

Conventional construction, Takeda reported, consisting of buildings reinforced on an emergency basis, was completely destroyed when it received direct hits. Field positions that were hit by shells were completely destroyed, and of those on or near the landing beaches, over 50 percent were demolished. Half-permanent positions in which the hard agent *cascajo* (a type of coral) was used and that were reinforced

with concrete about 50-cm. thick remained in good condition except in cases of direct hits. Those that were hit by shells were more than 50 percent destroyed. Permanent positions with concrete over one meter thick remained in perfect condition even after receiving direct hits. All open naval gun emplacements were completely destroyed before the landings. Of those naval guns emplaced in caves, about half remained operational at the time of the landings, but they were soon put out of commission by counterbattery fire that closed up the cave mouths where they were located. Antiaircraft artillery on the island sustained damage from naval gunfire only once, and so long as Japanese antiaircraft ammunition lasted the Japanese were reasonably safe from American planes. Harbor installations received almost no damage, water pipes received only one direct hit, and power installations were all located in caves and so escaped damage. Most military boats were sunk. Naval gunfire had no effect against construction in the valleys or in the jungle and had very little effect against the interior parts of the island over two and a half miles from the shore line.

American airpower, reported Colonel Takeda, succeeded in knocking out the airfields on Guam but posed little threat to defense positions because there was little bombing of Japanese gun emplacements from the air. By far the most important effect of aerial bombing and strafing was the extreme limitation it placed on Japanese ground movement during daylight hours. However, neither naval guns nor aircraft succeeded in causing any serious interruption in communications on Guam. Takeda could not remember a single case where telephone lines were cut because of naval gunfire. As of 21 July, *Headquarters,*

---

[59] TF 53 Opn Rpt Guam, Incl C, App. 5.
[60] III Phib Corps Rpt Guam, Incl G, Naval Gunfire Support, p. 3.
[61] TF 53 Opn Rpt Guam, Incl B, Naval Gunfire Support, p. 11.

29th Division, in command of the defense of Guam, possessed perfect wire and wireless communications with the *18th Infantry Regiment,* the *38th Infantry Regiment,* the force on Orote Peninsula, forces south of Pago on the east coast, and forces at Tarague on the north tip of the island. Perfect field telephone communication with the *48th Independent Mixed Brigade* was maintained. Headquarters also had uninterrupted wireless communication with Rota, as well as with Imperial General Headquarters in Tokyo.[62]

In spite of the limited effectiveness of American preliminary bombardment, Takeda's testimony does indicate that it produced certain substantial results. Many of the buildings that were destroyed by direct hits, such as hospitals, warehouses, and office buildings in the towns of Piti, Agana, and Agat, housed military personnel and equipment. Takeda's own appreciation of the important role played by American air and sea power in reducing the defenses of Guam emerges through the crude but clear translation of the closing words of his postbattle report:

Among the battle colored by the holy blood of the dead I can find out the only lesson: The powerful air and sea powers make ground forces to defend island unnecessary. That is, the defence of island depending merely upon the isolated and helpless ground forces cannot be existed in the world. If the defence depending only upon the ground forces succeeded it would only be due to the fact that the island was neutralized, troops on it would hardly exist and they could perform their duty to defend the island because the enemy did not land on it.[63]

Intelligence of the Enemy

Considering the fact that Guam had been a U.S. possession for more than forty years, American intelligence of the island's road system and terrain was remarkably incomplete. The War Department in June 1943 had prepared and published a general survey of the island, and in February 1944 the Office of Naval Intelligence circulated a voluminous bulletin containing all kinds of information about hydrographic conditions, ground contours, road systems, weather, and the native population.[64] Neither of these studies was any further up to date than 10 December 1941, the date of the Japanese occupation, nor could the information supplied by American servicemen and native Guamanians who had lived on the island before the occupation give the planners any idea of Japanese defense installations or dispositions. General Geiger asked permission to send in small patrols by submarine to contact natives and "see behind the curtain," but the request was turned down. Hence, for up-to-date data on the activities and progress of the Japanese garrison, reliance had to be placed entirely upon photographic reconnaissance, chiefly aerial.[65]

Not until 25 April, after Conolly's staff had arrived on Guadalcanal, were photographs received, and the first ones were badly obscured by cloud cover. Later, aerial photographs were only fair, but were supplemented by excellent obliques of the coast line taken by the submarine USS

[62] Lt Col Hideyuki Takeda, IJA, Outline of Japanese Defense Plan and Battle of Guam Island, translated by Major Sato, IJA, Incl to Ltr, Col W. S. Coleman to Comdt USMC, 4 Oct 46; Lt Col Hideyuki Takeda, Ltr to Brig Gen J. C. McQueen, USMC, Dir Marine Corps Hist, 20 Feb 52, translated by Thomas G. Wilds, OCMH (both in Records Sec Hist Br G–3, Hq USMC).

[63] Takeda, Outline of Japanese Defense Plan.
[64] MIS WD, Survey of Guam ONI 99.
[65] III Phib Corps Rpt Guam, Intel, p. 3.

Greenling. Maps of the interior, prepared from prewar sources and revised on the basis of these aerial photographs, were fairly good as to scale and azimuth, but only occasionally did they portray ground contours accurately. Changes made by the Japanese in the road system were not indicated on the maps provided the troops; in fact, in the north of the island map locations of the roads were as much as 1,500 yards off from their true positions. Trails were not shown at all.[66]

With the capture of Saipan, a good number of Japanese documents were made available to the planners for Guam and afforded them for the first time some idea of the enemy situation. On the basis of these documents and of interrogations of prisoners of war, the intelligence section of III Amphibious Corps estimated that Guam was garrisoned by a total of 17,673 Army troops and 9,945 to 10,945 Navy, Air, and construction personnel. Although these figures proved to be considerably in excess of actual enemy strength, Geiger's staff correctly predicted that the bulk of the Army troops on the island was composed of the *29th Division* under Lt. Gen. Takeshi Takashima and the *11th Infantry Regiment* under Maj. Gen. Kiyoshi Shigematsu.[67] The principal naval unit on the island was thought to be the *54th Naval Guard Force,* and it was believed that about 2,185 naval air personnel were stationed there as well.[68]

It was assumed, on the basis of these documents and interrogations, that the Japanese would concentrate their defenses around Tumon Bay, Agana, and Agat, all on the west coast. Only two battalions were thought to be garrisoned on the south and southeast coasts. American troops about to invade Guam were warned to expect a large amount of mobile artillery and a determination on the part of the Japanese to exploit the mountainous terrain, which provided excellent observation. The enemy was thought to be holding back (from the beach defense) a mobile reserve of at least one battalion plus supporting weapons in the Agana area. A smaller reserve of about reinforced company strength was believed to be located somewhere inland of Agat.

"It seems evident," concluded Geiger's intelligence section, "that both we and the Japanese have been thinking along the same lines, that is, the beaches we find best for landings are those the Japs find most dangerous to them and have fortified the most." [69] The conclusion was fully warranted.

---

[66] *Ibid.,* p. 1; TF 53 Opn Rpt Guam, 10 Aug 44, Incl E, p. 2.

[67] The *11th Infantry Regiment,* somewhat expanded, had actually been renamed the *48th Independent Mixed Brigade.*

[68] III Phib Corps Opn Plan 1-44, Supplement 4 to Annex B, 9 Jul 44.

[69] *Ibid.,* p. 5.

CHAPTER XVI

The Enemy

The Japanese defense of Guam was much less effective than that of Saipan. Not only did the Japanese have fewer men, less artillery, and fewer tanks than their compatriots on Saipan but they also had a much larger area of land to defend. Nevertheless, they had ideal terrain for the defense and a sufficient force to prevent a rapid or easy conquest of the island.

Guam's defense was commanded initially by General Takashima, Commanding General, *29th Division* and *Southern Marianas Army Group*. In the middle of June General Obata, Commanding General, *31st Army,* reached Guam with his two senior staff officers. He had been in the Palaus, probably because the Japanese expected the next American thrust to be in that area. Once it became apparent that the blow would come farther north, he had hastened to the Marianas, too late, however, to reach his headquarters on Saipan. Instead, he landed on Guam to linger in forced inactivity while the garrison on Saipan went down to defeat. His presence on Guam had very little influence on Japanese tactics there until the death of General Takashima on 28 July, after which Obata assumed direct command.[1]

Troops and Troop Dispositions

In mid-July, on the eve of the American invasion of Guam, the Japanese defenders numbered about 18,500 men. The early preponderance in air and naval strength that the Americans were able to establish in the area resulted in the loss to the Guam garrison of about 900 much needed men, including the *1st Battalion, 10th Independent Brigade*. These troops had been temporarily stationed on Rota and on 8 June had been ordered to return to their parent commands on Guam. By the time the move could be organized, however, the 38-mile stretch of water between the two islands was under close American surveillance, and the transfer was never made.

All together, the American invaders faced an understrength garrison composed of eleven Army infantry battalions, two and two-thirds Army artillery battalions, three tank companies, two Army antiaircraft companies, Army engineers, service troops, and so forth, together with various Navy units, the most important of which were the *54th Naval Guard Force* and the *60th Antiaircraft Defense Unit*.[2]

In early June these forces were spread all over the island as a precaution against

---

[1] Japanese Studies in World War II, 55; TF 56 Rpt FORAGER, Incl D, G–2 Rpt.

[2] See Appendix F for complete Japanese order of battle.

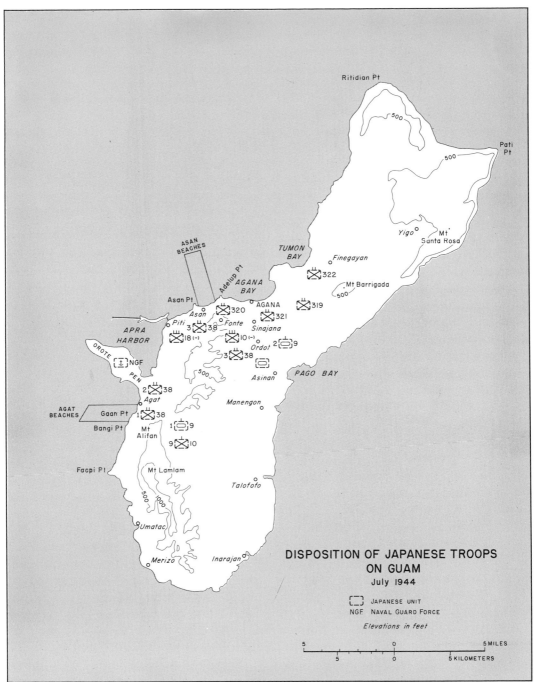

Ritidian Pt

Pati Pt

500

500

Yigo Mt Santa Rosa

ASAN
BEACHES

TUMON BAY

Finegayan

322

Mt Barrigada
500

Adelup Pt

AGANA BAY

Asan Pt

AGANA

Asan 320

319

Piti 3 38 *Fonte*
18(-) *Sinajana*

APRA HARBOR

10(-) *Ordot* 2 9

OROTE PEN

I NGF

3 38

Asinan

PAGO BAY

2 38
Agat

Manengon

AGAT
BEACHES

Gaan Pt 1 38

Bangi Pt

1 9

Mt
Alifan

9 10

Facpi Pt

Mt Lamlam

Talofofo

500
1000

Umatac

**DISPOSITION OF JAPANESE TROOPS
ON GUAM**

July 1944

Merizo *Inarajan*

JAPANESE UNIT
NGF NAVAL GUARD FORCE

Elevations in feet

5   0   5 MILES

5   0   5 KILOMETERS

F. Temple

MAP 17

an invasion from any direction. Guam was divided into four sectors for purposes of defense. In the Agana sector were stationed the four battalions of the *48th Independent Mixed Brigade* and the *3d Battalion, 38th Infantry;* in the area around Agat were the *1st* and *2d Battalions, 38th Infantry;* on the south coast in the Inarajan sector were two battalions of the *10th Independent Mixed Brigade;* and in the northern sector, with headquarters at Finaguayac, was the *2d Battalion, 18th Infantry.*[3]

By July this picture had radically changed. The American naval shelling of Agat on 16 June had tipped off the Japanese as to the probable place of the forthcoming landings, and the postponement of W Day gave them ample opportunity to reorganize their defenses. By mid-July almost the entire garrison had been moved to the west coast between Agat and Tumon Bay. (*Map 17*)

At the time of the American amphibious assault, *Headquarters, 29th Division,* and most of the division's service troops were located at Fonte, as was the headquarters of the *48th Independent Mixed Brigade.* General Shigematsu, Commanding General, *48th Independent Mixed Brigade,* commanded the Agana sector, which stretched along the west shore from Piti to Tumon Bay and included the great majority of the Japanese forces on the island. For purposes of shore defense, the Agana sector was divided into three, perhaps four, beach defense areas. From northeast to southwest, the first of these was at Tumon Bay, where the *322d Independent Infantry Battalion* was located. The *321st Independ-*

ent *Infantry Battalion* defended the area around Agana Bay, and the *320th Independent Infantry Battalion* manned the defenses between Adelup Point and Asan Point, where the 3d Marine Division was to land. In the Piti area was the *18th Infantry Regiment,* less the *1st Battalion,* which was on Saipan. The unit was considerably understrength since some of its personnel and much of its equipment had been lost when one of its ships en route from Japan had been sunk by an American submarine. The *18th Regiment* also had partial responsibility for Asan Point in case the Americans should land there.

The *10th Independent Mixed Regiment,* less its *1st Battalion* and *9th Company,* was in the Fonte–Ordot area. The *319th Independent Infantry Battalion* was inland, east of Agana, in reserve. Two of the three tank units on the island were also in reserve, poised to strike the beachhead with the infantry. These were the *29th Division Tank Unit* at Ordot and the *2d Company, 9th Tank Regiment,* at Sinajana. Also in general reserve was the *Otori Unit,* composed chiefly of naval air personnel reorganized into a jerry-built unit for ground combat. Most of the Army artillery, including the *48th Independent Mixed Brigade Artillery Unit,* formerly the *3d Battalion, 11th Mountain Artillery Regiment,* was disposed throughout the Agana sector. The two batteries of the *10th Independent Mixed Regiment Artillery Unit* had been removed from regimental control and placed directly under the *48th Independent Mixed Brigade.* Certain guns of these batteries were located just inland of Tumon Bay, but the majority were in the vicinity of Agana. The *38th Infantry's Artillery Battalion* was broken up, one battery attached to each infantry battalion, so

---

[3] TF 56 Rpt FORAGER, Incl D, G–2 Rpt, p. 47. The locations of the *3d Battalion, 18th Infantry,* and of the several naval units were unknown.

that the *3d Battery,* attached to the *3d Battalion,* was also in the Agana sector force.

The Agat sector was commanded by Col. Tsunetaro Suenaga, commanding officer of the *38th Infantry Regiment,* whose command post was on Mount Alifan. The *1st Battalion, 38th Infantry,* covered the beaches in the Agat area, and the *2d Battalion* of the same regiment occupied the base of Orote Peninsula. To the rear of the Agat beaches, the *1st Company, 9th Tank Regiment,* was in readiness to counterattack in case of a landing. Also in reserve for the Agat beaches was the *9th Company, 10th Independent Mixed Regiment.* Orote Peninsula was garrisoned by the main body of the *54th Naval Guard Force;* the *755th Air Unit,* reorganized for ground combat; and the two batteries of the *52d Antiaircraft Artillery Battalion,* which was charged with antiaircraft defense of Orote airfield. Since this unit's guns, which were 75-mm. antiaircraft, could be depressed as low as minus seven degrees, they were in effect dual purpose and could be used to supplement the conventional field artillery and antiboat weapons.[4]

Other units, such as service, engineer, and construction units, were scattered throughout the island, some on the west coast, and some inland as far as Santa Rosa. None of these, however, had any

significant combat value. Nor could the Japanese arm the civilian population, most of which appears to have remained at least passively loyal to the United States. As of 10 January 1944, the native Guamanians numbered about 24,000.[5] Slightly over a hundred were of mixed American and Chamorro parentage and had been jailed as soon as the Japanese occupied the island. The rest of the population suffered some organized maltreatment and abuse in the early days of Japanese rule, but this appears to have gradually tapered off. However, rigid food rationing, forced labor, confiscation of property without compensation, exclusion from business enterprises, and a score of lesser deprivations and humiliations kept the native population sullen and restive during the period of Japanese occupation. In June 1943 all able-bodied men between the ages of fourteen and sixty were forced to work for the occupation army, and women were ordered to replace the men in the fields. After the American air raid of 11 June, large numbers of natives fled to the hills. Many were rounded up by Japanese military police and placed in camps near Asinan, Manengon, and Talofofo. The Guamanians were clearly poor raw material for collaborationism, and there is no evidence that the Japanese made any successful attempt to reconstruct them to that end.[6]

Japanese military doctrine for the defense of Guam was essentially the same as that for Saipan. Emphasis was placed on meeting and annihilating the enemy at the

[4] Sources from which the locations of the Japanese units on Guam were derived are as follows: TF 53 Rpt FORAGER, Incl D, G–2 Rpt; Japanese Studies in World War II, 55; Ltr, Takeda to McQueen, USMC; III Phib Corps Rpt Guam, Incl D, G–2 Rpt; CINCPAC–CINCPOA Trans 10194, Opn Orders of Guam Garrison Units, 15–16 Jul 44; 77th Inf Div G–2 Jnl File, Guam Opn; POW Interrogation Rpts made by III Phib Corps, Hq 3d Marine Div, SLF (TG 56.2), and Intel Sec 21st Marines, in Records Sec Hist Branch G–3, Hq USMC.

[5] III Phib Corps Rpt Guam, Incl D, G–2 Rpt 10.

[6] Sources for the description of the lot of Guam's civilians under Japanese rule are William Hipple's report in *Newsweek,* August 21, 1944, p. 35, and Thompson, *Guam and Its People,* p. 160.

TABLE 2—ARTILLERY ON GUAM

Type of Weapon	Estimate of III Amphibious Corps G–2 Report	Estimate of Colonel Takeda
20-cm. coastal defense guns (short Navy guns)	19	16
15-cm. coastal defense guns	8	6
12.7-cm. coastal defense guns	22	
12-cm. coastal defense guns		10
12-cm. dual-purpose guns		16
105-mm. howitzers (M91)	6	
75-mm. mountain and field guns	38	
75-mm. antiaircraft guns		14
57-mm. antitank guns	2	
37-mm. antitank guns	20	
25-mm. antiaircraft guns (Navy)	4	60
20-mm. antiaircraft guns (Army)		12

Source: III Phib Corps Rpt Guam, Incl D, G–2 Rpt; Ltr, Takeda to McQueen, 4 Oct 46. The first column represents the Japanese pieces captured or destroyed before 10 August, the date Guam was officially declared secured. Colonel Takeda's estimate was made in October 1946, more than two years after the battle. Of the two estimates, the first is undoubtedly the more accurate.

beaches. If that failed, an organized counterattack was to be delivered against the beachhead soon after the landing. Finally, if the invaders succeeded in establishing and holding their beachhead line, the Japanese would retire to the hills and fight on from there.

Thus General Shigematsu, in command of the Agana sector garrison unit, which contained the majority of troops on the island, declared on 15 July, "It has been decided that the enemy is going to launch an attack in force at dawn in the region of the Agana sector. When he lands, the Division will be quick to seize the opportunity to attack him in this sector with a powerful force and crush him at the beaches. . . . The Garrison Unit will await its initial opportunity and will completely destroy the enemy landing force upon the beaches." [7] If the infantry units at

the shore line failed in their mission, the *10th Independent Mixed Regiment,* two battalions of the *18th Infantry,* and the *3d Battalion, 38th Infantry,* were ordered to carry out the second phase of the plan —a counterattack in force against the American beachhead in this area.

Supporting Weapons

Artillery on Guam, including coast defense, field artillery, and antiaircraft and antitank weapons, was manned by both Army and Navy personnel. As indicated above, the bulk of the field artillery pieces in July were situated to command the western shore line from Tumon Bay to Agat. Table 2 gives two estimates of the number and type of these weapons. Just how many were still operational at the time of the American landings is not known, and even a comparison of these figures with the assessment of damage wrought by the

[7] CINCPAC–CINCPOA Trans 10194.

preliminary bombardment cited above will provide only a hazy idea of Japanese artillery strength on 21 July.

Japanese tank strength was considerably lower than it was believed to be by American intelligence staffs, both before and after the battle. Although the Americans claim to have destroyed or captured fifty-nine enemy tanks by 11 August, actually there were no more than thirty-eight present at any time, and possibly even fewer.[8] The *1st Company, 9th Tank Regiment,* which was located in the Agat–Orote area, had from twelve to fifteen light tanks. The *2d Company* of the same regiment and the *29th Division Tank Unit,* both situated so as to support the defense of the Asan beaches, had a total of from twenty-one to twenty-three tanks, of which at least ten were mediums.

Fortifications

The main fortified area ran along the west coast from Tumon Bay to Facpi Point and included, of course, Orote Peninsula. Other fortified beaches, on the south and east coasts from Merizo to Pago Bay, had been abandoned before W Day, their defenders having moved to the north. Outside the main fortified area, the airfields were provided local defense by antiaircraft and dual-purpose guns.

The most notable and certainly the most effective fortifications on the island were constructed across the neck of Orote Peninsula, which contained a fairly elaborate system of trenches and foxholes

arranged in depth, together with large numbers of pillboxes and heavy-caliber weapons. Outside of Orote, the prepared defenses were generally hastily constructed and often incomplete. The typical beach defense was arranged, from the seaward side, in four parallel lines: first were obstacles and mines on the fringing reef offshore; second came beach obstacles and tank traps; third were trenches, machine gun positions, pillboxes, heavy weapons, artillery, and coast defense guns on the beaches or immediately inland; and, finally, came the machine guns, heavy weapons, and artillery emplaced on the high ground inland.

Insufficient advantage was taken of the high ground, and except on Orote little provision was made for defense in depth. Even as late as the five-week period of pre-invasion bombardment, the Japanese continued to work frantically on improving offshore obstacles and beach defenses, to the neglect of positions in the rear.[9]

During the first two years of the war, the Japanese had slighted the military development of the Marianas in favor of more forward areas, and almost nothing was done to fortify Guam until early 1944. The beaches had to be protected first, and Guam's large size and numerous possible landing points meant that proportionately greater effort had to be expended at the shore line before work could be commenced on defenses in depth. The time, effort, and materials expended on the south and southeast shores was ultimately wasted when these positions were abandoned. After the assault on Saipan, Guam was entirely cut off from its sources of matériel,

---

[8] TF 56 Rpt FORAGER, Incl D, G–2 Rpt, p. 65; 3d Marine Div Interrogation Rpt 396, Capt Sato, Hideo (CO *24th Tk Co, 29th Div Tk Unit*), Records Sec Hist Br G–3, Hq USMC; CINCPAC-CINCPOA Trans 9304, 9th Tk Rgt Order of Battle.

[9] Ltr, Takeda to McQueen, 4 Oct 46.

and the five-week period of bombardment not only destroyed many of the existing fortifications but also severely hampered efforts on the part of the Japanese to continue construction.[10]

As has been already mentioned, the Japanese relied heavily on coral-filled palm cribs and wire cages to interrupt and impede the approach of landing craft to and over the offshore reef.[11] In addition to these, which were all blown up by American underwater demolition teams, a series of antiboat mines of about forty to fifty pounds was placed along the reef or between the obstacles. The beaches themselves were strung with barbed wire and in some places aerial bombs were embedded in the sand just inland of the wire. Antitank obstacles also were installed on the beaches by lashing coconut logs across trees or setting them vertically in the ground.

The Agat beach defenses were typical of the others. Here was an almost continuous line of open trenches about two feet wide and three and a half feet deep. Running parallel to the shore line approximately fifty feet inland of the high-water mark, these trenches were supplemented by an occasional rifle or machine gun pit about eight feet to their front and by shelters to their rear. Distributed along the beach between Agat and Bangi Point were about twenty-five pillboxes. A strong concrete blockhouse on Gaan Point held two 75-mm. mountain guns, one 37-mm. gun, and positions for machine guns and riflemen. Two concrete emplacements of 40-mm. guns were located between Gaan Point and

Agat only about five feet inland of the high-water mark.[12]

Pillboxes here were constructed of palm logs, sandbags, reinforced concrete, earth, and coral rocks, the majority being simple structures of palm logs covered with earth. They averaged about eight feet square and three feet high, with roofs two feet thick in the center and one foot at the edge. Usually, they had two firing ports about twelve by four inches in size, which allowed only a fairly narrow traverse. The reinforced concrete types were either square or octagonal and located chiefly along the roads. About eight feet across and two to three feet high, their walls were about six inches thick. There were a few masonry pillboxes of coral rocks with walls a foot thick. All the pillboxes on the beaches were mutually supporting against attack from the seaward side, but not against attack from the flanks or rear.

Japanese Situation on the Eve of Battle

The effects of American preliminary bombardment on Japanese defenses has already been described in as much detail as surviving records permit. The devastation was great and widespread, if not as effective as the invaders at first believed. Moreover, the accelerating tempo of naval shelling and aerial bombing and strafing made it almost impossible for the Japanese to repair the damage or to engage in new construction.

Notwithstanding these difficulties, the defenders bent every effort to shore up their crumbling defenses to the last minute before the invasion. But most of the labor,

---

[10] TF 56 Rpt FORAGER, Incl D, G-2 Rpt, pp. 61-63.

[11] See above, p. 322.

[12] MIS WD Mil Rpt 25, Jan 45, p. 31.

JAPANESE BEACH OBSTACLES AT GUAM *were numerous along the northern landing beaches.*

at least along the beaches, had to be performed at night when darkness and the physical exhaustion of the troops slowed progress to a snail's pace. The dilemma was inescapable, as is attested by one Japanese Army lieutenant who complained, "Our positions have been almost completed but they have not been done as we had hoped . . . great effort was put into the construction but we still have been unable to complete the cover. We are in a terrible fix." [13]

The weeks of American bombardment, the prolonged uncertainty, the anxious waiting from day to day while explosions rent the air but no American soldier came into view to be shot at or stabbed with bayonet—all these factors took their psychological toll even on the martial-minded Japanese. They suffered greatly in *seishin* —a word that means not so much "morale" as "psychological well-being." After several days of successive attacks, "scattered outbreaks of serious loss of spirit" occurred. After another week the spirit of some of the men deteriorated so badly that they "could not perform their duties in a positive manner." [14]

This cumulative physical and psychological exhaustion would show up in the days of battle to come. The troops on Guam tended to become more easily disorganized than had their compatriots on Saipan and Tinian. They turned more readily from organized combat to futile and suicidal individual displays of fanaticism.[15]

[13] Imanishi Diary; see also C I N C P A C–CINCPOA Trans 10802, extracts from the diary of Cpl Suzuki, Tai; CINCPAC–CINCPOA Trans 10410, diary of an unidentified soldier.

[14] The quotations are from Ltr, Takeda to McQueen, 20 Feb 52.
[15] III Phib Corps Rpt Guam, Incl D, G–2 Rpt 7.

JAPANESE OPEN-TRENCH BEACH DEFENSES AT AGAT, *where the 1st Provisional Brigade units landed.*

But if their *seishin* was ebbing, the Japanese on Guam remained high in *shiki*—meaning morale in the sense of a willingness to die in combat.[16] This spirit is reflected, with the usual rhetorical flourishes, in the diary of one enlisted man: "I will not lose my courage, but now is the time to prepare to die! If one desires to live, hope for death. Be prepared to die! With this conviction one can never lose . . . . Look upon us! We have shortened our expectancy of 70 years of life to 25 in order to fight. What an honor it is to be born in this day and age." [17]

Against this kind of determination, the task facing the marines and soldiers of the III Amphibious Corps would by no means be light.

---

[16] Ltr, Takeda to McQueen, 24 Jan 52.

[17] CINCPAC–CINCPOA Trans 10802.

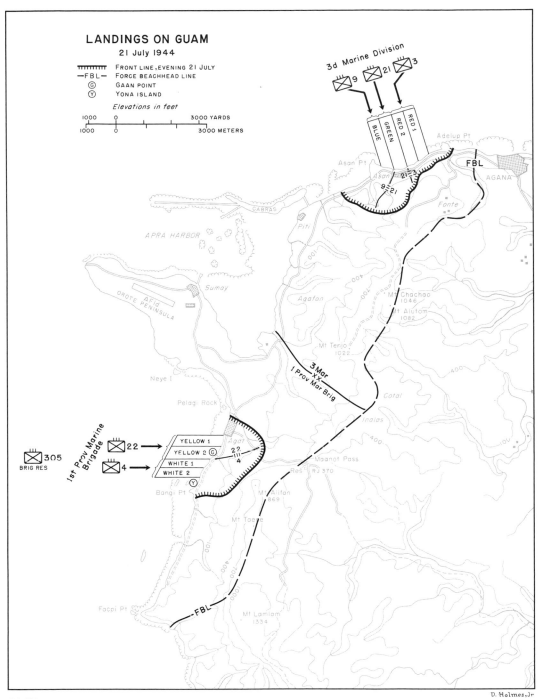

MAP 18

CHAPTER XVII

The Fight for the Beachhead

As evening of 20 July closed in, Admiral Conolly and those around him who were responsible for the invasion of Guam looked forward with high optimism to the success of their enterprise. Reports indicated that "all known major defensive installations in position to interfere with the transports approach and the landing have been destroyed and the assault beaches cleared of obstructions and searched for mines with negative results." [1] The weather forecast for 21 July was excellent. Conolly confirmed W Day as 21 July and H Hour as 0830. To his entire task force he promised, "conditions are most favorable for a successful landing."

Ashore, the Japanese command was not to be outmatched, at least in outward show of confidence. To the men of the *48th Independent Mixed Brigade,* General Shigematsu announced encouragingly: "The enemy, overconfident because of his successful landing on Saipan, is planning a reckless and insufficiently prepared landing on Guam. We have an excellent opportunity to annihilate him upon the beaches. We are dedicated to the task of destroying this enemy, and are confident that we shall comply with the Imperial wish." [2]

W-Day Preliminary Bombardment

The morning of 21 July dawned bright and clear as predicted. The wind was light, the sea calm. At 0530 came the first order to commence fire and for almost three hours the din and smoke of incessant naval salvos filled the air over the transport areas and shot up great geysers of dirt and debris ashore. From their flagships *Appalachian* and *George Clymer,* Admirals Conolly and Reifsnider directed the bombardment of the Asan and Agat beaches, respectively. (*Map 18*) Ships' fire was slow and deliberate, concentrating on the landing beaches themselves, their flanks, and the areas immediately inland. On this day alone the fire support ships would expend a total of 342 rounds of 16-inch shells, 1,152 rounds of 14-inch, 1,332 rounds of 8-inch, 2,430 rounds of 6-inch, 13,130 rounds of 5-inch, and 9,000 4.5-inch rockets. [3]

Twenty minutes after the opening of this tremendous naval bombardment, the first planes appeared overhead to provide cover against possible enemy air or submarine attack. At 0615 a roving patrol of twelve fighters, nine bombers, and five torpedo planes from the carrier *Wasp* made the day's first strike—against tiny Cabras Island lying just off the right flank of the 3d

---

[1] TF 53 Rpt Guam, Incl A, Opns Chronology, p. 11.

[2] III Phib Corps Rpt Guam, Incl D, G–2 Rpt 1.

[3] TF 56 Rpt FORAGER, Incl G, Naval Gun Fire Rpt, p. 71.

First Wave of Landing Craft Heads for Agat Beaches. *Smoke is from pre-invasion naval shelling and air bombardment.*

Marine Division's zone of attack. These and all other planes from Mitscher's Task Force 58, as well as those flown from the escort carriers of Task Force 53, were under the control of Conolly's Commander, Support Aircraft, aboard *Appalachian*. Also on station was an airborne air co-ordinator to direct scheduled air strikes and such other attacks as might later be ordered by the Commander, Support Aircraft.[4]

_____
[4] TF 53 Rpt Guam, Incl A, p. 26; *Ibid.*, Incl C, p. 13.

From 0715 to 0815 planes from Mitscher's fleet bombed and strafed the fourteen miles of coast line from Agana to Bangi Point. During this period of simultaneous attack from air and sea, naval guns were restricted to a maximum range of 8,000 yards to insure that the ordinate of their shells would be no higher than 1,200 feet. Pilots were instructed to pull out of their runs before reaching as low as 1,500 feet—a precaution taken to save American planes from being struck by friendly naval fire while at the same time rendering unnecessary the usual cessation of naval

ASAN'S GREEN AND BLUE BEACHES *stretch from Asan town (left center) to Asan Point (lower right).*

fire during the aerial strikes. Throughout this hour of bombardment, 312 of Mitscher's planes pounded the northern and southern landing beaches and their flanks with a total of 124 tons of bombs.[5]

Over each of the two sets of beaches flew a naval observation plane equipped with parachute flares, which were released when the troop-laden landing vehicles were 1,200 yards (8 minutes) from the shore —a signal to the support ships to step up their fire. Immediately, the support ships

commenced a last mighty bombardment of the beaches and maintained it until the troops were reported to be only 300 yards from the shore. Then all naval fire was shifted inland, to continue even after the first of the marines had touched land. The parachute flares were also the signal for a special H Hour strike by aircraft from Task Force 53. A flight of forty-four fighters strafed the two landing beaches until the first troops were almost ashore, then shifted their attack 1,500 to 2,500 yards inland. This strike was followed by a flight of twenty-four, whose task was to

⁵ TF 53 Rpt Guam, Incl C, p. 13.

keep the enemy down until the first wave of marines could cross the open beaches and gain cover.[6]

From Ship to Shore

In the midst of all this fire and smoke, the ships carrying the assault troops arrived on schedule and took station in the transport areas off the landing beaches. Amphibian tanks and amphibian tractors laden with marines eased their way into the water through the open bow doors of the LST's, transports lowered their LCVP's over the sides, and the LSD's let down their tail gates to permit their tank-carrying LCM's to become waterborne.

The pattern of the ship-to-shore movement was essentially the same for the northern and southern beaches—a pattern, in fact, that had been standardized in the Pacific since the invasion of the Marshalls. Ahead of the first waves of landing vehicles bound for each set of beaches went a line of nine LCI(G)'s firing 4.5-inch rockets and 40-mm. and 20-mm. guns as they came within range of the shore line. Then came a wave of amphibian tanks firing 37-mm. and 75-mm. guns to escort the marines over the reef and onto the beaches. Close astern were the successive waves of amphibian tractors carrying the assault troops, followed at intervals by LCM's embarking tanks. Reserve troops were loaded in LCVP's that would have to stand by at the edge of the reef until the first waves of tractors had debarked their troops and could return to take more men in from the reef.[7]

Off the northern beaches the LCI(G)'s crossed the line of departure at 0806 and commenced firing their rockets when they were about 1,000 yards off the shore line. At 0819 the first wave of troop-carrying LVT's reached a line approximately 1,200 yards offshore. Parachute flares were dropped from the observation plane overhead, and three minutes later the last flurry of intense close naval fire on the beaches began. The tempo of firing of the 5-inch guns increased from five to ten rounds per minute. About 300 yards from the shore the LCI(G)'s ceased their salvos of rockets, moved to the flanks, and, along with the destroyers, kept these areas under fire. By then mortar and artillery fire from shore was falling among the approaching tractors. In spite of the pounding they had been receiving from ships and aircraft, the Japanese were able to bring their pieces to bear on the assault waves and destroy nine of the 3d Marine Division's amphibian tractors.[8] Nevertheless, the waves of vehicles rolled on, and at 0828 the first LVT(A) touched down, two minutes ahead of schedule.[9]

Off Agat, fire from the shore was even heavier. There, the Japanese greeted the invaders with a hail of small arms, machine gun, and mortar fire for the duration of their approach to the shore. In addition, several 70-mm. guns in well-placed concrete blockhouses enfiladed the beaches and fired at the LVT's as they crossed the reef. On Gaan Point, near the middle of the landing area, a 75-mm. field piece and a 37-mm. gun opened fire as did a 75-mm. field piece on Yona Island to the right. One LCI(G) was hit and thirteen am-

---

[6] *Ibid.*, p. 14.
[7] The formation of the landing waves is given in SLF TG 56.2 Opn Plan 1-44, 11 May 44, Annex G, Charts 11 and 12.

[8] 3d Marine Div War Diary, Jul 44, p. 6.
[9] TF 53 Rpt Guam, Incl A, pp. 27-30.

3D MARINE DIVISION BEACHHEAD. *All types of invasion craft in background; first-aid station in foreground.*

phibian tractors were knocked out.[10] Still the landing formation held, and the troops got ashore on schedule.[11] In the zone of the 4th Marine Regiment (and there alone along the entire corps landing zone) the amphibian tractors had been ordered to move a thousand yards inland before disembarking their troops. As on Saipan, this scheme failed, and here as elsewhere during the assault on Guam, the leading waves of

troops dismounted from their LVT's close to the shore line.[12]

The Northern Beaches

The 3d Marine Division plan called for a landing of the assault elements of all three regiments over about 2,500 yards of beach between Asan Point and Adelup Point. From right to left, the 9th Marines was to go ashore on Blue Beach, the 21st Marines on Green Beach, and the 3d Ma-

---

[10] TG 53.2 Rpt Guam, Incl D, p. 2.
[11] 1st Provisional Marine Brig Opn Rpt and SAR Jnl, p. 10.

[12] 1st Provisional Marine Brig War Diary, 1 Jul–10 Aug 44, p. 4.

rines on Red Beaches 1 and 2. On hitting shore, the division was to capture the cliffs and high ground immediately inland and prepare for further operations to the east and southeast. The 9th Marines was to seize the low ridge facing its beach, protect the division right flank, and be prepared to move along the coast to take Piti Navy Yard and Cabras Island if so ordered. In the center, the 21st Marines was to capture the cliff line to its front. On the left the 3d Marines was ordered to secure Adelup Point, Chonito Cliff, and the high ground southeast of the cliff.[13] (*Map VI.*)

On the right, the 9th Marines, commanded by Col. Edward A. Craig, moved ahead steadily against fairly heavy machine gun and rifle fire and by the end of the day had secured a beachhead about 1,500 yards in depth.[14] In the center, Col. Arthur H. Butler's 21st Marines found the opposition only moderate, but the terrain "almost impossible." Ahead lay low cliffs of bare rock mounting to a plateau covered with scrub growth and tangled vines. Intense heat and a shortage of water added to the day's ordeal, but in spite of the natural obstacles as well as enemy mortar and rifle fire, two battalions had made their way to the top of the cliff and tied in with the 9th Marines on the right by nightfall.

It was on the division left that the day's most intense and arduous fighting occurred. Northeast of Red Beach 1 was Chonito Cliff, containing a complex system of cave defenses and offering the enemy a

perfect opportunity to pour mortar and artillery fire on the low ground below. Inland of Red Beach 2 lay Bundschu Ridge,[15] offering the same sort of obstacles. By noon, Chonito Cliff was cleared, but two separate and costly attacks on the ridge to the south failed to make any significant headway, and by nightfall the right flank of Col. W. Carvel Hall's 3d Marines was still out of contact with the 21st Marines in the division center.

The day's casualties on the northern beachhead came to 105 killed, 536 wounded, and 56 missing in action. The cost was more than had been anticipated, yet the results, if far from decisive, were at least hopeful. The beaches themselves were secured, as was Chonito Cliff on the left flank. By late afternoon General Turnage, the division commander, was ashore, and his command post was in operation; division artillery was in position and in the process of registering; division engineers had cut a road to supply the 21st Marines and were at work removing land mines and demolishing cave positions.

The Southern Beaches

According to the operation plan of the 1st Provisional Marine Brigade, the two Marine regimental combat teams would land in assault, and Col. Vincent J. Tanzola's 305th Regimental Combat Team of the 77th Infantry Division would be in reserve. The 4th Marines on the right was to go over White Beaches 1 and 2 north of Bangi Point, establish a beachhead, and protect the brigade right flank. On the left, the 22d Marines was to land on Yellow

---

[13] 3d Marine Div Opn Plan 2-44, 13 May 44.

[14] This account of 3d Marine Division's operations is derived from: 3d Marine Div SAR For-AGER Opn, 19 Aug 44, p. 1; *Ibid.,* Incl L, 3d Marines SAR, p. 1; *Ibid.,* Incl M, 9th Marines SAR, p. 1; *Ibid.,* Incl M, 21st Marines SAR, p. 1; Lodge, *Guam,* pp. 38-47.

---

[15] So named after Capt. Geary R. Bundschu, Commander, Company A, 3d Marines, who later lost his life there.

Beaches 1 and 2, occupy the town of Agat, and then drive north to seal off Orote Peninsula at its base. The 305th Infantry, when committed to action on brigade order, would pass through the lines of the 4th Marines and protect the right sector of the beachhead.[16] (*Map VII.*)

The terrain facing the brigade was far more favorable for the attack than that facing the 3d Marine Division to the north. Low hills and open ground characterized most of the area immediately inland of the landing beaches. In spite of numerous pillboxes still alive with Japanese, both of the assault regiments moved forward rapidly. By early afternoon, the 4th Marines had cleared Bangi Point and Hill 40 just inland and had set up a roadblock supported by five tanks on Harmon Road, which ran east out of Agat. The 22d Marines captured Agat, which had been mostly reduced to rubble by naval and air bombardment but still contained its share of defenders hiding in the debris. Moving out from Agat, the regiment began to receive artillery fire from the hills beyond and suffered some casualties, as well, from a misplaced American air attack. It was also handicapped by the fact that a communications failure kept the reserve battalion (the 3d) afloat until too late to participate in the day's fighting.[17]

Despite these difficulties, by the close of the first day's fighting the brigade had established a beachhead ranging in depth approximately 1,300 to 2,300 yards at the cost of only about 350 casualties. Brig. Gen. Lemuel C. Shepherd, Jr., came ashore before noon and his command post southeast of Gaan Point was in operation by 1350. Defenses were organized in depth against the expected Japanese night counterattack. Artillery was ashore and registered.

Landing the 305th Infantry

The operation plan for the 1st Provisional Marine Brigade had designated the 305th Regimental Combat Team as brigade reserve, to be used at General Shepherd's discretion. Accordingly, the brigade commander had ordered one battalion team (later designated the 2d, commanded by Lt. Col. Robert D. Adair) to be boated and ready at the line of departure by 1030 of the 21st. The other two battalion landing teams would follow the 2d ashore when and as needed.[18]

Actually, the first element of the 77th Division to go ashore was a liaison party of four from the 242d Engineer Combat Battalion, which was attached to the 305th Infantry. Two officers and two enlisted men landed shortly after 0830 on White Beach 1, which they proceeded to reconnoiter. The second group, the first organized element of the division to come ashore, was the reconnaissance party of the 305th Field Artillery Battalion. At 0830 this group was boated in two DUKW's at the line of departure, where it remained for several hours. Finally, the vehicles were ordered ashore, and by midafternoon the reconnaissance party had established itself on White Beach 2.[19]

[16] 1st Provisional Marine Brig Opn Plan 7–44, 11 Jul 44.
[17] 1st Provisional Marine Brig War Diary, p. 4; 22d Marines SAR, p. 3; Lodge, *Guam,* pp. 47–56.
[18] 1st Provisional Marine Brig Opn Plan 7–44, 11 Jul 44.
[19] 305th Fld Arty Bn, Action Against the Enemy, Guam, 21 Jul 44, p. 1; 242d Engr Combat Bn Hist, p. 1, in 77th Inf Div Opns Rpt Guam, 21 Jul–10 Aug 44.

CIRCLING LANDING CRAFT. *The 2d Battalion of the 305th Infantry waited three and a half hours for the signal to go in to the reef.*

Meanwhile, the infantrymen of Colonel Adair's 2d Battalion were climbing down cargo nets from their transports into the bobbing landing craft that were to carry them to the edge of the reef. By 1030 all boats were in position near the line of departure waiting for the signal to go in. For three and a half hours they circled impatiently. At last, at 1405, came the message to proceed to the beach and assemble in an area 300 yards inland from Gaan Point.[20]

Unfortunately, no amphibian tractors were on hand to transport Adair's men over the reef and on to the shore line, and of course their LCVP's were too deep-drafted to negotiate either the reef or the shallow waters inland of it. Over the sides of their boats the men climbed, and waded the rest of the way in water at least waist

deep. Some lucky few were able to pick up rides in Marine LVT's on the landward side of the reef, but most stumbled in over the rough coral bottom, cutting their shoes en route and occasionally falling into deep pot holes. Luckily, no enemy fire impeded their progress, and except for the dousing they got and the exhaustion they suffered the troops of the 2d Battalion, 305th, completed their ship-to-shore movement without injury.[21]

The remaining two battalions of the 305th Infantry encountered even greater difficulties in getting ashore. At 1530 Colonel Tanzola received the message (a

---

[20] 1st Provisional Marine Brig War Diary, Jul 44, p. 4; 305th RCT AAR, 18 Jun–9 Aug 44, p. 1.

[21] S. Sgt. James M. Burns, Narrative of the Guam Campaign, Notes, 21 Jul 44 (hereafter cited as Burns Notes), MS, OCMH. Sergeant Burns headed the historical team attached to the 77th Infantry Division on Guam. See also, AFAS, *Guam,* pp. 33–34. (This account was prepared in large part from the notes and interviews made by Sergeant Burns.)

full hour after it had been dispatched) to land the rest of his regiment immediately. With only enough landing craft available to embark one battalion, he ordered Lt. Col. James E. Landrum, Jr., to boat his 1st Battalion and head for the reef. However, naval officers in charge of boat traffic had not been apprised of these orders and refused to permit the landing craft to proceed beyond the line of departure. Finally, at 1730, General Shepherd settled the matter by ordering the regimental commander to land his combat team at once. Again no amphibian tractors were available and again the troops had to make their way through the water on foot. This time conditions were even more adverse. The tide was full, forcing some of the men to swim part of the way, and night was approaching. It was no easy task in view of the fact that the average infantryman was loaded down with a steel helmet and liner, gas mask, life belt, rifle, bayonet, grenade launcher, light pack, two bandoleers of ammunition, a bag full of rifle grenades hung from his neck, another pouch of hand grenades strapped to his thighs, a two-foot long pair of wire cutters tied to his pack, two canteens of water, a first aid pack, and a machete hanging from his cartridge belt. Nevertheless, the troops reached the beach safely after nightfall, although they were scattered and several hundred yards south of Gaan Point, where they were supposed to touch down. Colonel Landrum gathered the better part of his men together and led them to their designated assembly areas inland. The rest had to spend the night on the beach, since after 2130 Marine military police stopped all movement.[22]

The 3d Battalion, 305th, commanded by Lt. Col. Edward Chalgren, Jr., took even longer to get to shore. Before the landing craft assigned to the 1st Battalion had returned to the transport area, the report came in that an enemy submarine had been spotted in the area, and all the ships of Transport Division 38 put to sea—including *Alpine,* aboard which Chalgren's unit was embarked. Not until 2120 did the ship return, and it was 0330 of the 22d before the bulk of the battalion completed the complicated transfer from ship to landing craft to shore. To expedite the ship-to-shore movement of his battalion, Chalgren borrowed five LVT's from the Marines. One of these acted as control boat while the other four ferried the troops across the reef in driblets. Even so, some elements failed to reach the beach until 0600, and not for another hour was the unit fully reorganized. Meanwhile, Colonel Tanzola and his staff had debarked and reached the reef line, where they, too, found no transportation waiting them. The regimental commander came upon an abandoned rubber raft, commandeered it, and paddled his way to shore while the rest of his staff waded and swam in.[23]

Japanese Counterattack

The American troops that dug in along their beachhead perimeters on the night of 21–22 July were well aware that the odds favored an organized enemy counterattack, probably in the early morning hours. Jap-

[22] Burns Notes, 21 Jul 44; 305th RCT AAR, 18 Jun–9 Aug 44, p. 1; 305th RCT Jnl Record Book, 1 Jul–8 Sep 44, 21 Jul 44; 1st Provisional Marine Brig Opns Jnl, 21 Jul 44, in 1st Provisional Marine Brig Opns and SAR; AFAS *Guam,* pp. 34–36; Ltr, Col Landrum to Gen A. C. Smith, 27 Apr 55, Incl, OCMH.
[23] Burns Notes, 21 Jul 44; Lodge, *Guam,* pp. 57–58.

anese defensive doctrine prescribed such countermeasures and at both Saipan and Tinian the island commanders had rigidly adhered to doctrine. All along the line the troops were alerted to prepare for the expected attack and took such measures as the terrain and their own dispositions permitted. When the counterthrust did materialize, it was surprisingly feeble, at least in comparison with those that the enemy had launched against the invaders of Saipan and Tinian.

In the zone of the 3d Marine Division, whose hold on the beachhead was the most precarious, no critical threat to the Marine lines occurred. Mortar and artillery fire falling on the beaches put a temporary end to unloading about 0230, and enemy patrols probed the front lines throughout the night, but that was all.[24]

Farther south, the Japanese undertook more serious measures. Against the Agat beaches, Colonel Suenaga of the *38th Infantry Regiment* himself led a force consisting of at least two infantry battalions supported by tanks. The brunt of the attack, which started about 0100, fell in the zone of the 4th Marines. In two successive waves, the enemy struck the Marine perimeters around Hill 40 and succeeded in penetrating as far as the pack howitzer positions on the beaches before being destroyed or beaten off. Another force, led by four tanks followed by guns mounted on trucks, came down Harmon Road in an apparent attempt to re-establish positions in the town of Agat. Fortunately, the marines had set up a roadblock, and a platoon of Sherman tanks with the help of a single bazooka quickly disposed of the Japanese armor, after which the enemy infantrymen retreated. About the

same time, another group of Japanese hit the 1st Battalion's lines south of the road, and again succeeded in penetrating the defenders' lines as far to the rear as the artillery positions. Fighting was so fierce in this area that one platoon of Company A was reduced to four men.[25]

It was here, too, that the soldiers of the 305th Infantry got their first taste of close-in combat on Guam. One finger of the Japanese penetration reached the hastily established lines of Companies A and B, and in the fighting that ensued seven Americans were killed and ten wounded in exchange for about twenty Japanese.[26]

On their part, the Japanese lost at least 268 men and 6 tanks during the counterattack.[27] Among those killed was Colonel Suenaga who, after being wounded in the thigh by mortar fire, continued to lead the attack until he received a fatal bullet in the chest. Suenaga's death deprived the Japanese defenders on Orote Peninsula of their commander. Command of the sector passed to Comdr. Asaichi Tamai, IJN, of the *263d Air Unit,* who took over not only the Navy forces stationed on Orote but also the *2d Battalion, 38th Infantry,* guarding the base of the peninsula.[28]

Consolidating the Southern Beachhead 22–24 July

General Shepherd's plan for 22 July contemplated an expansion of the beachhead in three directions—north, east, and south.

---

[24] Lodge, *Guam,* p. 59.

[25] *Ibid.,* pp. 54–55.
[26] Burns Notes, 21 Jul 44.
[27] III Phib Corps Rpt Guam, Incl D, G–2 Rpt 2. Major Lodge estimates the number of Japanese killed to be closer to 600. Lodge, *Guam,* p. 55.
[28] Ltr, Takeda to McQueen, 20 Feb 52. See also Takeda Rpt, 4 Oct 44; Japanese Studies in World War II, 55.

On the right (south), the 4th Marines was ordered to seize Mount Alifan and then push south along the ridge line toward Mount Taene. The 22d Marines was to head in a northeasterly direction and capture an intermediate objective line that ran about 4,000 yards east of Pelagi Rock. The 305th Infantry (less 2d Battalion) was ordered to pass through the left battalion of the 4th Marines and attack toward Maanot Pass, a cut through the mountains over which Harmon Road ran from Agat to the east. The 2d Battalion, 305th, and 2d Battalion, 4th Marines, were to be in brigade reserve.[29]

At the outset of the attack the 4th Marines ran into heavy enfilade fire from the reverse slopes of Alifan's foothills. Once this was neutralized and the marines could approach the mountain itself, the chief deterrent to rapid progress was the terrain. Approaches to the crest were snarled with pandanus roots and led to vertical cliffs covered with thick scrub growth. Enemy resistance, however, was only nominal, and one patrol was able to reach Alifan's summit, where it discovered no evidence of Japanese activity. The patrol then returned to the foot of the cliffs and joined the rest of the regiment.[30]

In the brigade center the 305th Infantry was slow in jumping off because of the many delays incurred in getting ashore the night before. Neither the 1st nor the 3d Battalion had been able to get fully organized until about 0700; the regimental command post was not in a position to direct the attack until an hour later; the 305th Field Artillery was even longer in getting set to go into action. By 1000, how-

ever, all was in order and the regiment, with the 1st Battalion on the right, the 3d Battalion on the left, passed through the left flank of the 4th Marines and launched its attack to capture the high ground over which Harmon Road passed to the east.[31]

During the morning the 305th encountered little resistance, and by 1252 the 3d Battalion was already on the line that had been set as the day's objective.[32] That afternoon Chalgren's men pushed ahead still farther but before night were pulled back to their 1300 positions in order to tie in with the 1st Battalion, which had made slower progress because of the dense underbrush that covered the hills over which it had had to advance. When the regiment dug in, its two forward battalions had firm contact, but a deep gully prevented physical contact with the 22d Marines on the left.[33]

On the brigade left, the 22d Marines pushed off at 0845, ahead of the other two regiments. Until late afternoon, it encountered only moderate resistance. The hill northeast of Agat that had held up the 1st Battalion the day before was easily mounted as tanks cleared the way to the next high ground. When the marines on the left reached the Ayuja River they were temporarily halted when it was discovered that the Agat road bridge across the river had been destroyed. The men were reluctant to ford the river without their supporting tanks, and the tanks could not cross because the river banks were too steep. In

---

[29] 1st Provisional Marine Brig Opns and SAR, War Diary, p. 5; 305th RCT AAR Guam, p. 2.
[30] Lodge, *Guam,* p. 66.

[31] 305th RCT AAR, p. 2; 305th RCT Jnl Record Book 1 Jul–8 Sep 44, 22 Jul, Msgs 65, 66.
[32] 305th RCT Jnl Record Book, 22 Jul, Msgs 71(c), 75.
[33] 305th RCT AAR, p. 2; Burns Notes, 3/305, 22 Jul 44.

4TH MARINES MOVES INLAND TOWARD MT. ALIFAN

the absence of engineers, amphibian tanks were called up to replace the tanks until provision could be made to get the latter across.

This substitution of armored amphibians for tanks was contrary to prevailing Marine Corps doctrine. Experience at Saipan had shown that amphibian tractors, armored or otherwise, were extremely vulnerable to enemy fire when out of the water.[34] Hence, that afternoon General Shepherd sent clear orders to all the units under his command that the amphibians should not be used inland except where absolutely necessary.[35]

In any event, the troops made their way across Ayuja River, some of them reaching a point beyond the Old Agat Road before

they were ordered back to the road itself to tie in for the night with the rest of the 22d Regiment. Later, the 22d Marine Tank Company, after twenty-four hours of labor, constructed a causeway across the river to enable its vehicles to cross over.

By nightfall the brigade, with the 305th Infantry attached, was drawn up along a line extending from the shore near Pelagi Rock, along the high ground northeast of Harmon Road, through Mount Alifan, southwest along the ridge line toward Mount Taene, then west to the sea at Magpo Point. The 4th Marines held this line from its coastal anchor at Magpo Point to Mount Alifan; the 305th Infantry held the area along the foothills northeast of Mount Alifan to a point about 1,200 yards from the Old Agat Road; and the 22d Marines held the area north and northeast of Agat. Approximately 3,000

---

[34] See above, Ch. V.

[35] 1st Provisional Marine Brig Opns and SAR, Jnl, 22 Jul 44, Msg 62.

ASSEMBLY AREA OF 305TH INFANTRY ON 22 JULY

yards of the Force Beachhead Line in the brigade's zone was now in American hands.

It was clear by now that nothing was likely to impede the complete and rapid occupation of the southern beachhead, and, accordingly, General Geiger announced the second objective for the brigade—the capture of Orote Peninsula. Once the Force Beachhead Line had been fully occupied, the brigade was to be relieved by two regiments of the 77th Infantry Division, which would take over defense of the line from Inalas to Magpo Point. This task was to fall to the 305th Infantry, already ashore, and to Col. Aubrey D. Smith's 306th Regimental Combat Team, which was still afloat. The 305th would be released from brigade control, and both regiments were

to be under direct command of General Bruce. The 307th was ordered to remain afloat in corps reserve and be prepared to land anywhere on order.[36]

The night of 22–23 July in the brigade zone was one of relative quiet, disturbed only occasionally by Japanese patrols, whose efforts to infiltrate through the lines were uniformly unsuccessful. The next morning, and throughout the 23d, the 4th Marines on the right (south) made no further effort to advance, but consolidated its positions and prepared to be relieved by the 306th Infantry. That these men were able to go about their preparations undisturbed was partly due to the fact that

[36] 77th Inf Div G–3 Jnl, 22 Jul 44, Msg 1830, CG III Phib Corps to CG 77th Inf Div and CG 1st Provisional Marine Brig.

naval guns and aircraft sealed off most of the possible routes of enemy counterattack. Early in the morning of the 23d observers had spotted a large Japanese troop movement headed from Mount Lamlam toward Facpi Point. The call went out immediately for naval and air assistance, and in response the cruiser *Honolulu,* aided by carrier planes, dispersed the Japanese.[37]

For the other two regiments, the push toward the Force Beachhead Line was considerably facilitated by the landing of field and antiaircraft artillery. By the morning of 22 July, Brig. Gen. Pedro A. del Valle, USMC, had two thirds of the 155-mm. guns and howitzers of III Amphibious Corps Artillery ashore, and the 9th Marine Defense Battalion had succeeded in placing two dozen 40-mm. and 20-mm. guns and a dozen .50-caliber machine guns along the beach between Agat and Bangi Point.[38] Late the same afternoon, Brig. Gen. Isaac Spalding, Commanding General, 77th Division Artillery, set up his command post inland of Gaan Point. By then the remainder of the 305th Field Artillery Battalion was ashore, as were two other artillery battalions, the 304th and 902d. The 305th was ordered to continue to support the 305th Infantry; the 304th Field Artillery Battalion was assigned to close support of the 306th Infantry when it should get ashore; and the 902d was given the mission of general support for the division. The 304th and 902d Battalions were also ordered to be prepared to support the brigade in its forthcoming attack on Orote Peninsula.[39]

Meanwhile, on the 23d the 305th Infantry had made rapid progress, hampered only by occasional enemy patrols. By 1130 the 3d Battalion, on the left, had reached the O–2 line; the 1st was pushing from the Harmon Road along the ridge northeast of the Maanot Pass toward the O–2 line on the right of the 3d. The 2d Battalion moved to Maanot Pass to block the path of possible Japanese approach from the east along the Harmon Road. By early afternoon, as the 305th Infantry was digging in for the night in a deep salient along the O–2 line and the Force Beachhead Line, all of the high ground overlooking Orote Peninsula from the southeast was in American hands.[40]

To the left, the 22d Marines moved more slowly in its northward thrust toward the base of Orote Peninsula. Little resistance was encountered on 23 July until midafternoon, but then, as the regiment attempted to swing across the narrow neck leading out onto the peninsula, the Japanese suddenly came to life. The southern approaches to the peninsula were guarded by marshy rice paddies interspersed with small hills that the Japanese had organized into a system of mutually supporting strongpoints. Moreover, the zone of the 22d Marines approach was exposed to artillery and mortar fire from both Orote Peninsula on the west and Mount Tenjo to the northeast. The Japanese had not failed to make full use of these commanding positions. In spite of heavy concentration laid down by corps and division artillery, assisted by the big guns of the battleship *Pennsylvania,* the marines could do nothing to dislodge the enemy. After a

---

[37] Lodge, *Guam,* p. 66.
[38] *Ibid.*
[39] 77th Inf Div Opns Rpt Guam, p. 3; 77th Inf Div Arty, Daily Summary of Events, 23 Jul 44, p. 4.

[40] 305th RCT AAR, p. 2; 305th RCT Jnl, 22 Jul 44, Msgs 93, 96, 102, 104b, 109.

SMOULDERING JAPANESE TANKS *knocked out on Agat–Sumay Road by U.S. medium tanks.*

wasted, exasperating afternoon sloshing through the rice paddies, the regiment finally drew back a full 400 yards from its most advanced positions and dug in just south of the Old Agat Road.[41]

General Shepherd's plan for action on the 24th contemplated a two-pronged movement, the object of which was to envelope the rice paddy area and establish a firm line across the narrow neck of Orote Peninsula. All three battalions of the 22d Marines were to be committed to the attack. On the right, the 2d Battalion was to jump off from its night positions south of the Old Agat Road, skirt to the right of the marshland, and push north to the town of Atantano, just inland of Apra Harbor.

On the left, the other two battalions were to drive north up the coast along the Agat–Sumay Road in columns of battalions. Once the rear battalion had reached a point on the Agat–Sumay Road about 600 yards from its line of departure, it was to fan out to the right and then head north toward the south shore of Apra Harbor. The lead battalion would continue in a northeasterly direction along the Agat–Sumay Road. If this plan succeeded, nightfall would find the regiment drawn up across the neck of Orote Peninsula from the seacoast to Apra Harbor, with all three battalions abreast. Enemy defenses in the rice paddy area would be enveloped and presumably destroyed or neutralized. To relieve the 22d Marines of the necessity of lengthening its already thinning lines, the 305th Infantry was ordered to shift left

[41] 1st Provisional Marine Brig Opns and SAR, War Diary, 23 Jul 44, p. 7; *Ibid.,* Jnl, 23 Jul 44, Msgs 62, 63b; Lodge, *Guam,* p. 67.

MAJ. GEN. ANDREW D. BRUCE *discussing operational plans with Col. Douglas McNair.*

as far as Old Agat Road, which was to be the new regimental boundary line.[42]

After delaying an hour to permit a longer preliminary naval bombardment, the regiment jumped off as ordered at 1000, 24 July. The battalion on the right, was counterattacked almost immediately and had to fall back to its previous night's positions south of the Old Agat Road. By early afternoon, however, it regained the initiative and was quickly able to reach its

objective at Atantano, where it established visual contact with the 305th Infantry on its right. The other two battalions found the going slower as they felt their way up the Agat–Sumay Road. The road was thickly mined with aerial bombs and subject to heavy enemy artillery fire from Pelagi Rock and Orote Peninsula. Five Japanese tanks appeared and contested the passage but were quickly disposed of by the heavier Shermans that were spearheading the drive. As planned, on reaching the point on the road where the ground to the right permitted a decent foothold, the rear battalion fanned out in that direction. Without too much difficulty it overran the strongpoints that had held up the regiment on the 23d, but as evening approached and the battalion was compelled to dig in, it was still some 400 yards short of its objective on the south shore of Apra Harbor. Meanwhile, on the left, the lead battalion had succeeded in reaching its objective on the west coast of the narrow neck of Orote.[43]

Thus by the end of 24 July, General Shepherd's major objectives had been achieved. The Force Beachhead Line had been captured and was now manned mostly by units of the 77th Division. Orote was sealed off and the time was at hand to launch the drive to capture this vital peninsula that pointed fingerlike into the ocean between the two landing beaches and would constitute a danger to each so long as it remained in enemy hands.

Landing the Reserves

General Geiger's plan to commit the major portion of the 1st Provisional Marine

---

[42] 1st Provisional Marine Brig Opns and SAR, War Diary, p. 8; 1st Provisional Marine Brig Opn Order 15. (See Lodge, *Guam,* Maps 14, 15.)

[43] 1st Provisional Marine Brig Opns and SAR, War Diary, p. 8; Lodge, *Guam,* pp. 68–69.

Brigade to the assault on Orote required that the 77th Division take over the duty of manning the Force Beachhead Line until the peninsula could be secured. Accordingly, he ordered the 305th Infantry to occupy the northern part of the line and the 306th to land and relieve the 4th Marines on the southern part.

Late in the afternoon of 22 July, Colonel Smith, commanding officer of the 306th, had come ashore with Col. Douglas C. Mc-Nair, 77th Division chief of staff, to reconnoiter the landing beaches and assembly areas. Next day the whole regiment made the damp journey from ship to shore. As in the case of the Army troops that had preceded them, the men had to wade in from the reef line carrying all their equipment. The 77th Division as a reserve unit had been assigned no LVT's and its DUKW's had to be reserved for cargo and light artillery. Division headquarters had tried to land the troops at low tide, but overloaded communications and other difficulties in procuring landing craft delayed the ship-to-shore movement until the tide was flooding. Vehicles had to be dragged by bulldozer from the reef to the beach, and most of them drowned out. Almost all of the radio sets, even those waterproofed, were ruined, and one tank disappeared altogether in a large shell hole.

As a result of the delays incident to this slow procedure, only the 3d Battalion, commanded by Lt. Col. Gordon T. Kimbrell, was ashore in time to make its way into the line that afternoon. This battalion, with Companies A and C attached, relieved the 3d Battalion, 4th Marines, in its positions between Mount Alifan and Mount Taene where, after repulsing a small enemy attack, the Army battalion established its perimeters for the night. The

other two battalions of the 306th stayed in their assembly areas.[44]

On the morning of 24 July Lt. Col. Charles F. Greene's 2d Battalion, 306th Infantry, completed the relief of the 4th Marines on the northern part of its line and established contact with the 305th Infantry on the left. Throughout the day Greene's men cleaned out Japanese caves and dugouts in their area. No organized enemy appeared to contest their positions.[45]

General Bruce therefore requested permission to land two battalions of the 307th Infantry so that he could push the Force Beachhead Line still farther east and as far south as Facpi Point. General Geiger denied the request because he considered a further expansion unnecessary and also because he was loath at this time to part with all but one battalion of his corps reserve.[46] Nevertheless, he conceded that the 307th should at least be landed in the area of the southern beachhead, although it was retained under the III Amphibious Corps command. Starting on the morning of 24 July, Col. Stephen S. Hamilton's regiment commenced the uncomfortable trek from its transports to the beach—made even more arduous this time by an untimely storm at sea. By midafternoon, General Bruce himself was ashore at his command post and ready to take over direction of his two regiments on the line.[47]

---

[44] 306th RCT Opn Rpt Guam, p. 2; 306th RCT Jnl, 23 Jul–10 Aug 44, 23 Jul 44, Msgs 2, 4, 6; AFAS, *Guam*, p. 39; Ltr, Lt Gen A. D. Bruce, USA (Ret.), to Gen A. C. Smith, 11 Feb 55, Incl 1, OCMH.

[45] 306th RCT Jnl, 24 Jul 44, Msgs 8, 12, 14, 15, 16; 306th RCT Opn Rpt Guam, p. 2.

[46] III Phib Corps Rpt Guam, Opns Rpt, p. 3.

[47] 77th Inf Div Opns Rpt Guam, p. 5; 307th RCT Jnl, 24 Jul 44, Msg, 1030.

Thus by the end of 24 July, after four days of fighting, the 1st Provisional Marine Brigade, with an assist from the 77th Infantry Division, had captured almost all the ground between the landing beaches and the Force Beachhead Line and had cut off from retreat and reinforcement the Japanese garrison on Orote Peninsula. The 305th and 306th Regimental Combat Teams had taken over all of the line except that section across the neck of Orote Peninsula, where the marines were poised to launch the next major assault. All of del Valle's III Amphibious Corps Artillery was ashore, and most of the 77th Division Artillery was in position to support the advance. Beach defenses from Agat to Gaan Point were manned by the 9th Marine Defense Battalion, and from Gaan Point south to Bangi Point by the 7th Antiaircraft Artillery (Automatic Weapons) Battalion of the 77th Division. Firmly in American hands was a large irregular slice of Guam running from Magpo Point northeast to Mount Taene, north to Mount Alifan, and again northeast to Inalas, where it bent back northwestward to Atantano and then southwest across the neck of Orote Peninsula. Casualties up to the night of 24 July were 188 killed in action, 728 wounded, and 87 missing in the brigade; 24 killed in action, 63 wounded, and 1 missing in the Army division.[48] This was a substantial price to pay, but the figures were not out of proportion when compared to those for most Central Pacific campaigns. Nor were the losses nearly so great as those being suffered at the same time by the 3d Marine Division in its bitter fight for the northern beachhead.

Consolidating the Northern Beachhead 22–24 July

Speaking of the terrain that faced the 3d and 21st Regiments of the 3d Marine Division just inland of their landing beaches, Lt. Gen. Alexander A. Vandegrift, commandant of the Marine Corps, later remarked that it was "some of the most rugged country I have ever seen." [49] Coming as it did from a veteran of Guadalcanal, this description conveys some idea of the nature of the problem facing the marines immediately upon their landing in this zone. Bundschu Ridge and Chonito Cliff were little more than a hundred feet in height, but rose precipitately from the narrow coastal plain beneath.[50] Dense and tangled underbrush covered the approaches to the ridge, and the whole area was striated with deep ravines and gulleys that made contact between the attacking units extremely difficult to maintain and at the same time offered ideal routes for Japanese infiltration. (*See Map VI.*)

On 22 July, while the 21st Marines reorganized, the 3d Marines, on the left, assaulted Bundschu Ridge behind a heavy concentration of artillery and heavy weapons, supplemented by the 20-mm. and 40-mm. guns of the 14th Marine Defense Battalion. A few men reached the top, but only to return to their parent unit before the day's close. By this time Colonel Hall's 3d Marines was a badly battered regiment. In two days fighting he had lost 615 men, and some of his companies were down to 30 or 40 men.[51] On the next day he decided to pit his 1st and 2d Battalions, deci-

[48] Lodge, *Guam,* p. 70; 77th Inf Div G–1 Jnl, 24 Jul 44.

[49] 3d Marine Div SAR, p. 4.
[50] See USAFICPA, Map, Island of Guam, Apra Harbor, Rev., Apr. 44.
[51] 3d Marine Div SAR, p. 2.

mated as they were, against the ridge. To General Turnage he sent the message, "I am going to try and advance up that mess in front of me. What I really need is a battalion whereas I have only 160 men to use on that 500 yard slope." [52] To his great surprise, when his men finally hacked their way to the top on the morning of the 23d, most of the Japanese had evacuated.

Still it was impossible to push on immediately. The cliffs were studded with machine guns that had to be mopped up, and contact had yet to be gained with the 21st Marines on the right. That regiment had made little progress during the day in the face of heavy opposition from enemy pillboxes. Colonel Hall asked for reinforcements from the 77th Division, whose 307th Regiment was still afloat, but General Geiger was unwilling to release his corps reserve.[53]

On the morning of 24 July, two battalions of the 21st Marines attacked up the ravine that lay between the 21st and the 3d Marines to the left. From the cliffs on either side came murderous machine gun fire. On top of this, American naval pilots, called in to make an air strike, were forced to drop their bombs so close to the attacking line that seventeen marines were killed or wounded.[54] That afternoon, two companies of the 3d Marines coming up from the left were able at last to establish contact between the two regiments.

At the close of 24 July the left and center regiments of the 3d Marine Division had, by dint of great effort and many casualties, succeeded at last in establishing a foothold on the first ridge line inland from the sea. Yet, though this victory was by no means a Pyrrhic one, neither could it be considered decisive. Ahead still lay a series of formidable ridges, running roughly parallel to the sea, each one higher than the one before, and all culminating in the mid-island mountain mass, which in this area was dominated by Mount Chachao, Mount Alutom, and Mount Tenjo.

Meanwhile, on the division right, the picture was not so discouraging. On 22 July the 9th Marines moved southwest along the ocean shore against light resistance and occupied Piti Navy Yard. Late the same afternoon a minor amphibious assault of battalion size was sent against Cabras Island. The landing was unopposed and uneventful except that one LVT hit a land mine. The next day the occupation of the island was completed. On the 24th the regiment sent out a patrol south along the Piti–Sumay Road in an attempt to establish contact with the brigade. Covered by amphibian tanks as they moved along the coastal road, the men eventually came under heavy machine gun fire from the inland cliffs, and this, coupled with the fact that they were approaching the edge of the pattern of American fire being directed against Orote, persuaded them to return. Contact between the division and the brigade would have to await another day.[55]

Initial Supply Over the Beaches

If the 3d Marine Division suffered more severely than the 1st Provisional Marine Brigade from enemy fire and nightmarish terrain, it did enjoy one advantage over the troops to the south—the movement of supplies from ship to shore during the early days of the assault was more expeditious.

[52] Quoted in Lodge, *Guam,* p. 62.
[53] III Phib Corps Rpt Guam, Opns Rpt, p. 2.
[54] 21st Marines SAR, p. 3.

[55] Lodge, *Guam,* pp. 62–63.

PONTOON BARGE WITH CRANE *is a fueling station. Alligator is refueling from a barge inside the reef.*

Off the Asan beaches, the lagoon between the shore line and the reef's edge was for the most part dry at low tide and trucks were able to drive to the edge and take on supplies directly from cargo boats and lighters. Off the Agat beaches, however, the abutting reef and the lagoon bottom were underwater at all times, and consequently all cargo had to be restaged to amphibious vehicles several hundred yards offshore. To add to the difficulty, the fringe of the reef was not pronounced, and therefore it was impossible to position cranes on the coral outcroppings as was done at Asan. As a substitute measure, the cranes at Agat were mounted on pontoon barges moored along the line where the shallow water began. Using this system, it was possible for the cargo boats to load LVT's at the rate of 25 tons an hour and

DUKW's at the rate of 40 tons an hour.[56] Another device employed to expedite unloading over the southern beaches was the construction of improvised pontoons made by lashing together two life rafts covered by a platform. Each attack transport of the Southern Transport Group was ordered to provide one of these "barges," each of which had a capacity slightly in excess of one ton. LCVP's could lower their ramps over the floating platforms and transfer their supplies. The rafts could then be floated over the reef and in to shore.[57]

Notwithstanding these emergency measures, the brigade on 21–22 July suffered from a scarcity of supplies, especially ammunition. The main reason, aside from

[56] TF 53.2 Rpt Guam, Incl F, pp. 2, 6.
[57] *Ibid.*, Incl B, p. 12.

the hydrographic difficulties described, was the shortage of amphibian vehicles. Thirteen of Shepherd's LVT's had been knocked out by enemy gunfire during the ship-to-shore movement, and eleven more had been lost later on W Day. The poor roads ashore made it necessary to use a portion of the amphibian tractors to transport supplies directly to the front lines instead of just to the shore line as planned, thus reducing still further the number of amphibian vehicles available for ship-to-shore supply. The DUKW's, of course, took over part of the burden, but many of these during the first two days were occupied with the job of landing artillery pieces and could not be diverted to carrying cargo. Also, some of the DUKW's got mired in the silt that bordered the shore line and others had their tires punctured on sharp coral heads.[58]

Ashore, the movement of supplies inland was further impeded by the congestion resulting because of the narrow dispersal areas, especially on White Beach 1. For the

first two days infantrymen, artillery pieces and their crews, and the members of an LVT repair pool all crowded together in this restricted area, causing confusion and delay.

Admiral Conolly was quick to take cognizance of the shortages suffered by the brigade and ordered his transports to continue unloading throughout the night of 21–22 July and on until midnight of the 22d.[59] Thereafter, ships ceased loading from 2400 to 0530. In order to get supplies and equipment into the hands of the troops that needed them, the admiral was willing to keep his transports at anchor and partially lighted even at the risk of exposing them to enemy air and submarine attacks at night. Partly as a result of these measures, and in spite of the numerous obstacles involved, an average of about 5,000 tons a day was unloaded over the northern and southern beaches during the first eight days of the invasion.[60]

---

[58] *Ibid., passim.*

[59] This order also applied to the transport off the 3d Marine Division's beaches.

[60] COMINCH P–009, V, 15–16; TF 56 Rpt FORAGER, Incl G, Transport QM Rpt, p. 26.

CHAPTER XVIII

The Assault Completed
25–30 July

Late on the afternoon of 24 July, General Geiger issued his orders for the next day's action—orders that contemplated a completion of the assault phase of the invasion of Guam. Commencing at 0700, 25 July, the 1st Provisional Marine Brigade was to press the attack against Orote Peninsula while the 77th Infantry Division (less the 307th Regimental Combat Team, in corps reserve) held the Force Beachhead Line in the southern zone. In the north, the 3d Marine Division was to resume the offensive and seize the high ground overlooking the Mount Tenjo road. Efforts were also to be made to link the two beachheads by establishing firm contact between the Marine brigade or the Army division and the 3d Marine Division.[1]

On the receipt of this order, General Shepherd of the Marine brigade asked for a day's postponement. His troops, he submitted, were greatly fatigued by four days and nights of steady fighting. Moreover, his 4th Regimental Combat Team had not been fully relieved by Army elements until midafternoon on 24 July and needed more time to move north and get into position to launch the attack on Orote. In view

of these representations, General Geiger agreed to delay the assault on the peninsula until 0700 on 26 July.[2]

Meanwhile, the 22d Marines (less 2d Battalion) was directed to capture all unseized ground between Agat Bay and Apra Harbor across the narrowest portion of the peninsula's neck. The 4th Marines was to remain in its current bivouac area and prepare to relieve its sister regiment on order.[3]

While the marines were thus preparing for the final drive against Orote, General Bruce ordered the 77th Division to straighten and improve its defensive lines and take precautions to disperse and camouflage its gun positions. The two infantry regiments on the line (305th and 306th) were to mop up within their defense sectors and carry out security patrols beyond their front lines. On 26 and 27 July, two battalions of the 306th Infantry pushed in a southeasterly direction beyond the Force Beachhead line. Advancing against negligible opposition, they reached Maanot Pass –Mount Lamlam road south of Road Junction 370 and dug in about 1,500 yards from their line of departure. The 305th In-

<hr/>

[1] III Phib Corps Opn Plan 6-44, 24 Jul 44; 77th Inf Div FO 2, 0800, 25 Jul 44, in 306th RCT Jnl, 23 Jul-10 Aug 44.

[2] 1st Prov Marine Brig Opns and SAR, War Diary, pp. 8–9.
[3] *Ibid.*

TROOPS IN BIVOUAC. *305th near the reservoir at Maanot Ridge.*

fantry extended its right flank and tied in with the new position of 306th. Two of the Army field artillery battalions (304th and 305th) would continue to support the two Army infantry regiments on the line, but the other two (306th and 902d) were placed in general support and ordered to start moving toward the base of Orote Peninsula and prepare to fire in advance of the marines next day.[4]

Preparations for the Assault on Orote
25 July

Jumping off at 0800 behind a fifteen-minute air and artillery attack, the 22d Ma-

rines got an early foretaste of the rigors that still lay ahead before the Japanese garrison on Orote could be subdued. (*See Map VII.*) From Neye Island and from the airfield near the end of the peninsula, artillery rained down on the column of the 1st Battalion as it tried to make its way along the coast of Agat Bay to Dadi Beach, while to the north the 3d Battalion ran into a hive of concrete pillboxes supported by well-camouflaged machine gun nests. Enemy tanks appeared at intervals throughout the day to obstruct the attack. By noon the 1st Battalion, 22d, was so depleted that it had to be replaced by the 1st Battalion, 4th Marines. Nevertheless, by nightfall the Americans' front line had been pushed ahead to extend across the narrow neck from Dadi Beach to a point

---

[4] 77th Inf Div FO 2, 0800, 25 Jul 44, in 306th RCT Jnl, 23 Jul–10 Aug 44.

just east of the thick mangrove swamp that lay inland of Apra Harbor.[5]

On the 24th the 307th Infantry landed near Agat. The two other Army regiments on the line consolidated their positions and tied in together by nightfall in the vicinity of the reservoir on Maanot Ridge. Little enemy opposition was encountered, except for some light mortar fire that fell into the ranks of the 2d Battalion, 305th, in the early evening. Contact with the 22d Marines was established during the afternoon, and later Company F of the 307th Infantry was attached to the 305th for the purpose of maintaining contact with the brigade on the left.[6] Meanwhile, an outpost of the 2d Battalion, 22d Marines, made contact with a patrol from the 9th Marines at the bridge that crossed the Big Gautali River. Thus for the first time in six days of fighting a link, although a feeble one, was forged between the northern and southern beachheads.[7]

The Fight in the North
25 July

In the zone of the 3d Marine Division, the prospect on the morning of 25 July was still the same. The 9th Marines on the right faced little opposition and fairly easy terrain; the other two regiments were up against the enemy's only remaining organized defense line (except for Orote Peninsula), which was drawn up along the hellish approaches to the Chachao–Alutom

–Tenjo mountain system. In view of the punishment suffered during the preceding days by the 3d Marines, one battalion of the 9th Marines was attached to the 3d Marines early in the morning. (*See Map VI.*)

During the day the 9th Marines on the right, with the support of the antiaircraft batteries emplaced on Cabras Island, pushed up the coast line of Apra Harbor as far as the high ground overlooking the Aguada River. This advance so lengthened the division's lines that during the afternoon General Turnage ordered the 9th Marines to pull back about 1,500 yards to the north of the Laguas River. The movement was completed by noon of the next day. In the division center, the 21st Marines jumped off in the direction of Mount Tenjo, but the way was barred by heavy enemy artillery, machine guns, and mortars well emplaced on the reverse slopes of the ridge that crossed the marines' line of advance. By nightfall the regiment was still short of the Mount Tenjo road. On the left, the 3d Marines, fighting against moderate opposition, captured a stretch of the Mount Tenjo road in the morning. Ahead of them lay Fonte Plateau. Tanks were requested but were slow in arriving, so Lt. Col. Robert E. Cushman, commanding the 2d Battalion, 9th Marines, which was attached to the 3d Marines, decided to take advantage of the few remaining hours of daylight and advance without them. As night closed in, this one battalion had succeeded in gaining a foothold on the slopes leading up to Fonte. By that time the division lines had been stretched more than 9,000 yards. The regiments and battalions had almost no reserves to call on, and even division had only one depleted battalion in

[5] 1st Provisional Marine Brig Opns and SAR, War Diary, 25 Jul 44, p. 9.

[6] 305th RCT AAR, p. 2; 306th RCT Opn Rpt, p. 2; 307th RCT Hist Records, Summary of Events, p. 1.

[7] 2d Bn 22d Marines Jnl, 21 Jul–21 Aug 44, 25 Jul 44.

reserve.[8] Should the enemy choose this time and place for an organized counter-attack, the situation for the marines could hardly have been worse. Unfortunately, the Japanese did so choose.

Japanese Counterattack
25–26 July

In fact, General Takashima had been planning and preparing for a full-scale counterattack for several days. Units that had remained in the Agana and Tumon Bay areas even after the American landings were withdrawn to the line facing the 3d Marine Division. Commander Tamai on Orote Peninsula was notified to launch an offensive in co-ordination with the main attack in the north.[9] Detailed orders with accompanying maps and overlays were issued to subordinate commanders. Takashima set up his command post in a cave about 325 yards west of Fonte. In preparation for the attack, General Shigematsu, commanding officer of the *48th Independent Mixed Brigade,* moved his command posts to Mangan Quarry, about 540 yards west of Fonte, and Col. Hiko-Shiro Ohashi assembled the *2d* and *3d Battalions* of his *18th Infantry Regiment* in the hill area south of Agana.[10]

According to the plan issued by General Takashima, the *48th Independent Mixed Brigade* would attack on the right against the 3d Marines, who were drawn up before the Fonte Plateau. Simultaneously,

the *2d* and *3d Battalions* of the *18th Infantry Regiment* (from right to left) would come down from the hills and attack toward Asan Point and the mouth of the Nidual River in the sector held by the 21st Marines. On the Japanese left, another unit, probably part of the *10th Independent Mixed Regiment,* was to push down the valley of the Tatgua River against the 9th Marines. At the same time the force on Orote Peninsula was to launch a drive to the east in co-ordination with the main attack.[11]

On the marines' left the attack first fell on the 2d Battalion, 9th Marines, which had succeeded the day before in establishing only the most precarious of footholds on the western slopes of Fonte. Seven times during the night of 25–26 July the Japanese rolled down from the plateau and seven times they were repulsed. By morning the battle here was over, but not before Colonel Cushman's battalion had suffered over 50 percent casualties. In exchange, approximately 950 of the enemy were killed in this single segment of the front.[12]

In the center of the line, Maj. Chusha Maruyama's *2d Battalion, 18th Infantry Regiment,* struck the lines of the 21st Marines in mass and penetrated as far to the rear as the battalion command post and the perimeters of the mortar sections. There, those Japanese that had survived the first onslaught were eventually eliminated with the help of engineers, cooks, clerks, communicators, and any other miscellaneous troops the regiment could throw into the fight.

---

[8] 3d Marine Div SAR, Incl L, pp. 2–3; *Ibid.,* Incl M, p. 2; *Ibid.,* Incl O, pp. 3–4; Lodge, *Guam,* pp. 74–76.

[9] In spite of the heavy American bombardment, Takashima still had good communications with the isolated garrison on Orote.

[10] Ltr, Takeda to McQueen, 20 Feb 52; Japanese Studies in World War II, 55, pp. 48–49.

[11] 3d Marine Div D–2 Periodic Rpt, 26 Jul 44, Incl, Map found on body of Maj Chusha Maruyama, CO 2d Bn, 18th Inf.

[12] 3d Marine Div SAR, Incl L, pp. 2–3; Lodge, *Guam,* pp. 81–82.

About the same time Maj. Setsuo Yukioka's *3d Battalion, 18th Regiment,* also hit the 21st Marines, locating and fully exploiting an 800-yard gap that lay between that regiment and the 9th Marines to its right. Here, in the high ground overlooking the Nidual River, the Japanese set up machine gun emplacements that could rake the flanks of both of the Marine regiments with deadly accuracy. Part of the attack through the gap got as far as the division hospital area. Doctors, corpsmen, and pajama-clad patients set up a makeshift line around the hospital tents and held fast until reinforcements arrived in the morning to put the remaining Japanese to rout. Meanwhile, the division artillery regiment (12th Marines) was busily engaged in hand-to-hand combat with numerous small suicide squads that had infiltrated the rear on 25 July and had timed their attacks with that of the main offensive. All morning the artillerymen beat off these desperate Japanese, some of whom had packs of TNT strapped to their backs, others of whom were loaded with magnetic mines. Around noon, when the fighting had let up, some fifty or sixty dead Japanese were located in the area of the 12th Marines alone. Not until early afternoon were the Japanese machine gun positions that had been emplaced in the gap between the two Marine regiments finally overrun. By that time the attack had spent itself, and the few surviving Japanese were fleeing into the hills.[13]

Meanwhile, on Orote Peninsula, Commander Tamai, according to order, had launched his attack against the 22d Marines. Starting about 2230 a horde of drink-crazed Japanese, mostly naval personnel, armed with anything from rifles to ball bats, swarmed through the mangrove swamps to fall upon the lines of the 22d Marines. Artillery pieces of corps, brigade, and the 77th Division almost immediately commenced fire and kept up at a rapid rate for the next two hours. Pack howitzers were dragged to within thirty-five yards of the infantry front lines to fire point blank at the onrushing enemy. "Arms and legs," reported one observer, "flew like snowflakes." [14] The marines here, and in the zone of the 1st Battalion, 4th Marines, which was guarding the regimental boundary, fought off those Japanese that had escaped the barrage of heavy shells with rifle, hand grenade, and bayonet. The American lines held, and by daylight it was apparent that the attack had failed. Not as well organized as Takashima's counteroffensive against the 3d Marine Division, and more nearly similar to the traditional and suicidal Japanese banzai charge, Tamai's counterattack suffered besides from the fact that the marines in this zone were in better position to resist and were backed by the major part of American artillery on the island.[15]

All together on both fronts, the Japanese lost an estimated 3,500 men in the night counterattack of 25–26 July. In the north, three whole battalions were virtually annihilated. Up to 95 percent of all commissioned officers in the sector defense forces were killed, according to later Japanese testimony. Among these was General Shigematsu, who lost his life on the 26th while futilely trying to rally his decimated brigade around Fonte Plateau. Also numbered among the dead were Colonel Ohashi,

---

[13] 3d Marine Div SAR, Incl L, pp. 2–3; *Ibid.,* Incl O, pp. 4–5; Lodge, *Guam,* pp. 78–88.

[14] Quoted in Lodge, *Guam,* p. 78.
[15] 1st Provisional Marine Brig Jnl, 26 Jul 44; Lodge, *Guam,* p. 78.

JAPANESE AIRFIELD, THE PRIME OBJECTIVE ON OROTE PENINSULA

commanding officer of the *18th Infantry Regiment;* Lt. Col. Ichiro Kataoka, commanding officer of the *10th Independent Mixed Regiment;* and Majors Maruyama and Yukioka, commanders of the *2d* and *3d Battalions, 18th Infantry.* Over 90 percent of all Japanese weapons were estimated to have been destroyed or captured. Radio communications between units on the island, which had remained surprisingly good in spite of the heavy American bombardment, were almost completely knocked out.[16]

On their part, the marines had suffered heavily too, especially the 3d Marine Di-vision. Between 25 and 27 July, the division reported 166 killed in action, 645 wounded in action, and 34 missing in action, mostly as a result of the Japanese counterattack.[17]

At his command post back of Fonte, General Takashima stayed in ignorance of the outcome of the attack until morning of the 26th. After dawn survivors of the holocaust gradually straggled back to headquarters, and the full story of the failure was pieced together before noon. On the basis of these reports, the island commander decided that all hope of expelling the Americans from Guam was lost. The only recourse left to him, as an officer in the Imperial Japanese Army and a man

---

[16] Ltr, Takeda to McQueen, 20 Feb 52; Japanese Studies in World War II, 55, pp. 48–49; III Phib Corps G–2 Rpts 7 and 8; Intel Sec 21st Marines, POW Interrogations 5 and 8.

[17] 3d Marine Div D–3 Periodic Rpts 5–7.

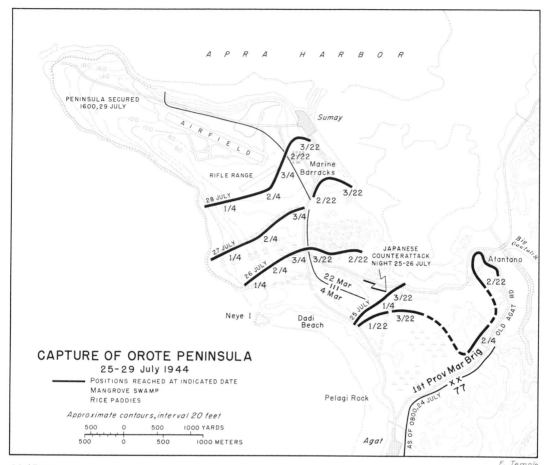

CAPTURE OF OROTE PENINSULA
25-29 July 1944
——— POSITIONS REACHED AT INDICATED DATE
MANGROVE SWAMP
RICE PADDIES

Approximate contours, interval 20 feet

MAP 19

F. Temple

of honor, was to retire with his remaining troops into the interior of the island and inflict as many losses on the Americans as possible until he himself should go down in the inevitable defeat.[18]

The Capture of Orote

Notwithstanding the counterattack of the previous night, the 1st Marine Provisional Brigade was prepared on the morning of 26 July to jump off on time in

---

[18] Ltr, Takeda to McQueen, 20 Feb 52.

the attack on Orote Peninsula. Behind it was the greatest array of artillery pieces yet mustered for any single attack since the beginning of the operation on Guam. Three battalions of General Spalding's 77th Division Artillery were in position and ready to fire along with four Marine battalions from III Amphibious Corps and the 3d Marine Division. Lt. Col. Leo B. Burkett's 902d Field Artillery Battalion first opened fire at 0645 in deep support of the Marine infantrymen and all together during this preparation phase fired a thousand rounds. From 0800 to 0830, the 305th and 306th Field Artillery Battalions, commanded respectively by Lt. Col. Edward B. Leever and Lt. Col. Jackson B. Serfas, joined in the fire. Some batteries fired as many as two rounds a minute per gun. On General Bruce's order, all Army artillery pieces were to direct their fire at least 1,000 yards in front of the advancing marines. Closer support bombardment was delivered by Marine artillery as well as by naval planes and by the 90-mm. guns of the 14th Marine Defense Battalion based on Cabras Island.[19] (*Map 19*)

Jump-off hour for the brigade was 0700, with the 22d Marines on the right, 4th Marines on the left. Enemy artillery fire delayed the 22d Marines for an hour, but the 4th Marines got under way on time and made rapid progress against light resistance. In fact, progress on the left was so rapid that the regiment's right flank soon became exposed. In view of this, Lt. Col. Alan Shapley, commander of the 4th, requested permission to shift to the right and take over part of the 22d Marines zone. The brigade commander agreed, and shortly before noon the regimental boundary was laid down at the Agat–Sumay road. On the right, Col. Merlin F. Schneider's 22d Marines found the going harder. Not only was the unit blanketed by heavy enemy mortar fire but, because most of its front line was blocked by the wide mangrove swamp lying inland of Apra Harbor, all forward movement had to be confined to a narrow corridor along the Agat–Sumay road. By nightfall the regiment's

left flank had reached Road Junction 15 and tied in with the 4th Marines. The rest of the line was bent back to the east of the mangrove swamp.[20]

The next morning the attack jumped off at 0715. Once again progress on the right was delayed because the 22d Marines were compelled to channelize all troops and supplies along the road inland of the mangrove swamp. This narrow corridor had been mined with aerial bombs and was covered by automatic weapons located in well-camouflaged pillboxes. By midafternoon, Colonel Schneider's men had worked their way through the bottleneck, but only to come up against a series of pillboxes and dugouts on the ridge east of the old prewar U.S. Marine barracks. Late in the afternoon marines on the front lines were rewarded with signs that Japanese organized resistance was beginning to crumple. The first harbinger of the breakdown of enemy organization occurred when a lone Japanese officer rushed out and attacked an American tank with his sword. Shortly afterward, another officer, waving a huge battle flag, marched his men up the peninsular road straight into American fire and to certain annihilation. Then, about two hours before dark, after an intensive bombardment by American artillery and naval guns and aircraft, the Japanese in front of the 22d Marines broke and ran—a rare occurrence in the Pacific war. This proved to be the turning point in the battle for Orote Peninsula. Although it was too late in the day for the marines to capitalize fully on this retreat, the 22d Regiment was able before dark to push forward and set up a line within 300 yards of the old

[19] 77th Inf Div Arty Rpt Guam, 26 Jul 44, Msg 23; 77th Inf Div Opns Rpt Guam, Rpt Hq 77th Div Arty, p. 26; 305th Fld Arty Bn Rpt, p. 2; 306th Fld Arty Bn Rpt, p. 6; 902d Fld Arty Bn Rpt, p. 2.

[20] 1st Provisional Marine Brig Opns and SAR, War Diary, p. 10; Lodge, *Guam,* pp. 88–89.

Marine barracks. The 4th Marines on the left had made somewhat slower progress during the day, and a gap existed between the two regiments when they dug in for the night. Fortunately, the Japanese were in no position to exploit the gap.[21]

On 28 July the 22d Marines swept through the barracks ground and on to the outskirts of the village of Sumay. There, they were halted for the night while demolition teams searched the rubble-littered streets for mines that the Japanese had laid in great numbers. On the left, Colonel Shapley's regiment was forced to make its way more slowly through dense scrub growth that concealed several coconut log pillboxes. Marine tanks were called in, but could make little headway because the heavy underbrush restricted observation and frequently made it impossible to fire without endangering friendly troops.

In the face of this difficulty General Shepherd, early in the afternoon, put in a call to 77th Division headquarters for Army medium tanks to reinforce those of the brigade. The request could not be honored in full since only the light tanks of Lt. Col. Charles W. Stokes' 706th Tank Battalion had landed. Five of these from Company D were immediately organized into a platoon under 2d Lt. Charles J. Fuchs and dispatched to General Shepherd, who routed them to the 4th Marines sector to support an attack ordered for 1600. There, they were joined by two Shermans from Headquarters Company, 706th Tank Battalion, which had since come ashore. Two more platoons of Marine mediums were meanwhile shifted from

the zone of the 22d Marines to join the scheduled tank-infantry attack on the brigade left.

Promptly at 1600 Colonel Shapley launched the assault along his whole regimental front. All up and down the line the tanks moved forward cautiously, followed at short distances by the Marine infantrymen. In their zone, the seven Army tanks covered about three hundred yards of front, often firing at ranges of ten to fifteen yards at the reinforced log pillboxes that barred their path. The light tanks of Company D alone expended about 10,000 rounds of .30-caliber ammunition, 100 rounds of high explosive, and 20 rounds of canister. They were credited with the destruction of four pillboxes, numerous dugouts, and about 250 Japanese.[22]

Before this massed Army-Marine armored attack Japanese defenses collapsed, and the infantrymen rushed on and set up their night positions just short of the airfield. One of the strongest enemy defensive lines on the peninsula had been established there to protect Orote field. After the battle, some 250 pillboxes and emplacements were counted in the area taken by the 4th Marines and their supporting tanks.[23]

29 July saw the end of the battle for Orote, except for minor mopping-up activities. Once again tremendous Army and Marine artillery fire, supplemented by naval gunfire, pounded the tip of the peninsula in preparation for the infantry assault. Again the seven Army tanks, this time assisted by six M10 tank destroyers as well as the brigade's own mediums, led

---

[21] 1st Provisional Marine Brig Opns and SAR, War Diary, pp. 11-12; III Phib Corps G-2 Rpt 7; Lodge, *Guam*, pp. 90-91.

[22] 706th Tk Bn Opns Rpt Guam, pp. 3-4; 1st Provisional Marine Brig Opns and SAR, War Diary, p. 12; AFAS, *Guam,* pp. 44-45.
[23] Lodge, *Guam,* p. 93.

MARINE CORPS OFFICERS *with plaque taken from the wreckage of the old Marine Corps barracks on Guam. From left: Lt. Col. Alan Shapley, Brig. Gen. Lemuel C. Shepherd, Col. Merlin F. Schneider, and General Holland Smith.*

the assault. By 1400 Orote airfield had been overrun with little opposition, and an hour later the 4th Marines took over the entire brigade zone, the 22d Marines mopping up Sumay and the cliffs bordering Apra Harbor. The platoon of Army tanks, accompanied by Marine infantry, was dispatched to the tip of the peninsula. On discovering only two live Japanese in the area, they reported back and were released to their parent division.[24]

Orote was now, to all intents and purposes, secured. An estimated 2,500 Japanese had been killed in the process. In exchange, the American attackers had lost 115 killed in action, 721 wounded, and 38 missing.[25]

On the afternoon of the 29th, with appropriate ceremony, the American flag was raised over the skeleton remains of the old Marine barracks. "Under our flag," said General Shepherd, "this island again stands ready to fulfill its destiny as an American fortress in the Pacific." [26] Before the general's words could be fully realized, however, the marines and soldiers of the III

---

[24] 1st Provisional Marine Brig Opns and SAR, War Diary, pp. 12–13; 706th Tk Bn Opns Rpt Guam, pp. 3–4.

[25] 1st Provisional Marine Brig Jnl, 30 Jul 44.
[26] Quoted in Lodge, *Guam*, p. 95.

Amphibious Corps would have more than a week of fighting ahead.

The Capture of Fonte and the
Force Beachhead Line

Whipped though they were and in retreat after their full-scale counterattack, the Japanese in the north were still capable of putting up a strong rear-guard defense while the main body of Takashima's troops prepared to retire into the interior. In their favor, of course, was the fact that that they still maintained possession of the high ridge from Fonte south through Mount Alutom, Mount Chachao, and Mount Tenjo. Fonte Plateau, in particular, was the site of an enemy strongpoint that Takashima refused to yield without a battle. Here, in a hollow depression atop the plateau, lined on all sides with cave-emplaced machine gun positions, the Japanese chose to make the advance of the 3d Marines as costly as possible. The 2d Battalion, 3d Marines, and the 2d Battalion, 9th Marines, would spend three bitter days of fighting before the left flank of the corps Force Beachhead Line could be secured. (*Map 20*)

On the morning of 27 July the attack was first delayed when shells and bombs delivered by American air and artillery fell behind the Marine front lines. Then a force of about 150 Japanese came out of the hills and launched a banzai charge. Once these men were disposed of, the two battalions moved out and by late afternoon reached their day's objective—the power line that stretched across the forward slopes of the plateau. By the following evening the two battalions had pushed up to the rim of the plateau and on the 29th cleaned out

most of the remaining enemy positions in the depression on top.[27]

Sometime on the previous day American machine gun fire had killed General Takashima just as he was about to evacuate to the rear. This left only one Japanese general officer alive on Guam—General Obata, Commanding General, *31st Army,* who had only recently arrived from the Palaus and who, up to this time, had exercised no control over the island's defenses. To him fell the hopeless task of reorganizing the remaining Japanese forces defending Guam's interior against the invaders.[28]

During these three days (27-29 July) the 21st Marines in the division center had kept abreast of the units struggling on Fonte, while on the right the 9th Marines had been assigned the task of capturing Mount Alutom and Mount Chachao. On 28 July Maj. John Lovell's 3d Battalion, 307th Infantry, which on the 26th had moved north along the Old Agat Road to the vicinity of Piti and was then attached to 3d Marine Division, reversed its course and attacked south on the 9th Marines' right, over the same ground it had covered two days before. As the marines pushed their way up the slopes leading to the mountain peaks, they soon spotted elements of the 77th Division atop Mount Tenjo to the south. Meanwhile, General Geiger had moved the boundary between the Marine and Army divisions north so that it ran along a trail leading east from the Old Agat Road through Agafan to the junction of the road between Mount Tenjo and

---

[27] 3d Marine Div SAR, Incl L, 3d Marines Rpt, pp. 3-4; Lodge, *Guam,* pp. 96-102; Lt. Col. Robert E. Cushman, "The Fight at Fonte," *Marine Corps Gazette* (April, 1947).

[28] Ltr, Takeda to McQueen, 20 Feb 52.

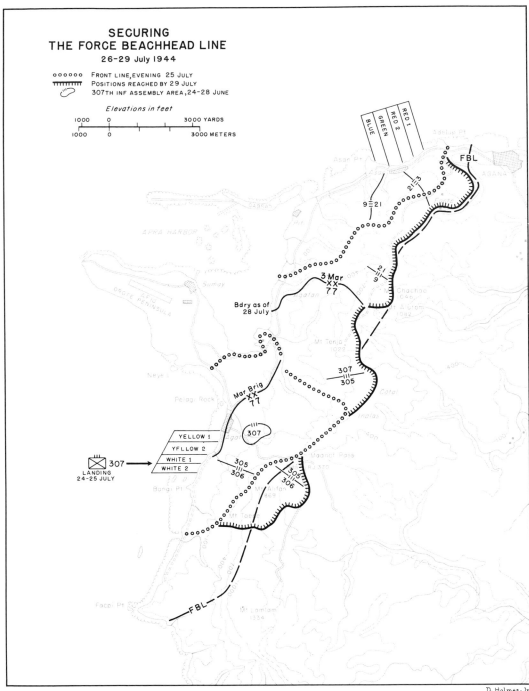

SECURING
THE FORCE BEACHHEAD LINE
26–29 July 1944

○○○○○○ FRONT LINE, EVENING 25 JULY
⊤⊤⊤⊤⊤⊤ POSITIONS REACHED BY 29 JULY
◠ 307TH INF ASSEMBLY AREA, 24–28 JUNE

Elevations in feet

1000   0   3000 YARDS
1000   0   3000 METERS

RED 1
RED 2
GREEN
BLUE

FBL

Adelup Pt

AGANA

Asan Pt

2‖‖3

9≡21

2‖
9

CABRAS

APRA HARBOR

Sumay

3 Mar
XX
77

21
9

Chachao
646

Mt A Liten
934

OROTE PENINSULA

Bdry as of
28 July

Mt Tenjo
1026

Neye

307
‖‖
305

Cotal

Inglas

Pelagi Rock

Mar Brig
XX
77

307

YELLOW 1

YELLOW 2

WHITE 1

WHITE 2

Magpo Pass
RJ 370

⊠ 307
‖‖
LANDING
24–25 JULY

305
‖‖
306

305
‖‖
306

305
‖‖
306

Mt Alifan
869

Bangi Pt

Mt Tenae

FBL

Facpi Pt

Mt Lamlam
1334

D. Holmes, Jr

MAP 20

Mount Chachao. This shift of the original boundary line between the 3d Marine Division and the 77th Infantry Division so as to include Mount Tenjo in the latter's zone had been suggested by General Bruce. He wanted to get his troops on the high ground so that they could work along the ridges rather than push ahead along a line abreast and get trapped in the ravines. Also, to prevent the piecemeal commitment of his division and to preserve its integrity, he wanted to be given the job of capturing Mount Tenjo. The boundary change meant in effect that the 3d Marine Division's right flank would orient its movement to the south while the 77th Division pushed north to establish firm contact along the Force Beachhead Line.[29]

On the 28th the 3d Battalion, 9th Marines, supported by heavy artillery and tank fire, fought its way to the top of Mount Chachao and annihilated an infantry company that had been left behind in the general Japanese withdrawal. At the same time the 1st Battalion, 9th Marines, and the 3d Battalion, 307th Infantry, moved south against light opposition and by 1745 were in contact along the new division boundary with those soldiers of the 77th Division that had meanwhile been moving northwest of Mount Tenjo.[30]

The men who were sighted on Mount Tenjo on the morning of 28 July were members of Company A, 305th Infantry. General Bruce ordered the 305th Infantry to send a company to reconnoiter the approaches to Mount Tenjo. If Japanese were

ANTITANK CREW *of 305th RCT on coastal ridge overlooking Harmon Road.*

not encountered in great number, Lt. Col. Charles F. Learner's 2d Battalion, 307th Infantry, was to occupy the mountain, while Colonel Landrum's 1st Battalion, 305th, was to take and hold the high ground from Cotal south to Inalas. Once Tenjo was in American hands, Colonel Chalgren's 3d Battalion, 305th, was to send out patrols to the north and establish contact with the right flank of the 3d Marine Division.[31]

At 0500 on 28 July, Company A, 305th Infantry, moved out of its assembly area toward Mount Tenjo. The men encountered no resistance on the way except for occasional sniping, and reached the summit

[29] 3d Marine Div SAR, Incl M, 9th Marines Rpt, pp. 2-3; III Phib Corps G-3 Periodic Rpt, 1800, 27 Jul-1800, 28 Jul, overlay; Ltr, Bruce to Gen A. C. Smith, 11 Feb 55, OCMH.

[30] 3d Marine Div SAR, Incl M, 9th Marines Rpt, pp. 2-3; 307th RCT Hist Records, Summary, pp. 1-2.

[31] 77th Inf Div G-3 Jnl, 27 Jul 44, Msg 28; AFAS, *Guam*, pp. 47-48.

at 0815. There they remained until mid-afternoon, when they were relieved by Learner's battalion. While it was waiting, Company A suffered a mishap of a sort that was occurring with alarming frequency on Guam. American planes came up out of the sea and bombed and strafed their own infantrymen. Only the quick thinking of Pfc. Benno Levi, who rushed out from cover under fire to spread identification panels, saved the unit from possible disaster.[32]

With the 2d Battalion, 307th Infantry, in firm possession of Mount Tenjo, Chalgren's 3d Battalion, 305th, according to plan pushed north to establish contact with the southward moving soldiers attached to the 9th Marines. At last, after eight days of fighting, the northern and southern beachheads were firmly joined.

Reconnaissance of Southern Guam

With the repulsion of Takashima's big counterattack and the launching of the drive on Orote Peninsula on 26 July, General Geiger could safely predict a rapid push to the Force Beachhead Line and the termination of the first phase of the battle for Guam. Before initiating the second phase, it was necessary for him to have reliable information as to where on the island the remaining Japanese had withdrawn. All indications pointed to northern Guam as their most likely destination. It was clearly the most logical course for the Japanese command to have taken. Southern Guam was a mass of jungle and mountain, serviced only by roads and trails not wide enough or hard enough to permit the passage of large numbers of troops and vehicles.

It was known that before the American invasion few troops had been stationed in the southern area. From captured documents and interrogations of prisoners of war, it appeared almost certain that the enemy troops were moving north toward Mount Barrigada.

Nevertheless, before the corps commander could finally decide to commit his forces to a northern drive, simple military caution demanded a reconnaissance of the southern section. The reports obtained through aerial reconnaissance were inconclusive since the island's dense jungle made camouflage and concealment of enemy positions and troop movements too easy. Ground reconnaissance was the only alternative. (*Map 21*)

The task fell to the 77th Infantry Division, which had already been conducting limited reconnaissance. General Bruce had prepared an extensive patrolling plan for covering the southern half of Guam, but it first had to be cleared through corps in order to prevent interference from friendly air, naval, and artillery bombardment. Once the clearance was received Bruce assigned the mission to the 77th Reconnaissance Troop, which for the past few days had been guarding Maanot Reservoir. Five patrols, each consisting of five men and each accompanied by a native guide, were ordered to leave from Road Junction 370 early on the morning of 28 July and to penetrate inland south and east up to seven miles. Patrols Able and Baker were to proceed directly east to the coast and return. The other three, Patrols Charlie, Dog, and Easy, would move directly south along the ridge below Alifan, Charlie toward Mount Lamlam, Easy to Umatac, and Dog along the coast below Facpi Point. Within the limits of these general

---

[32] 305th RCT AAR, p. 2; AFAS, *Guam,* p. 49.

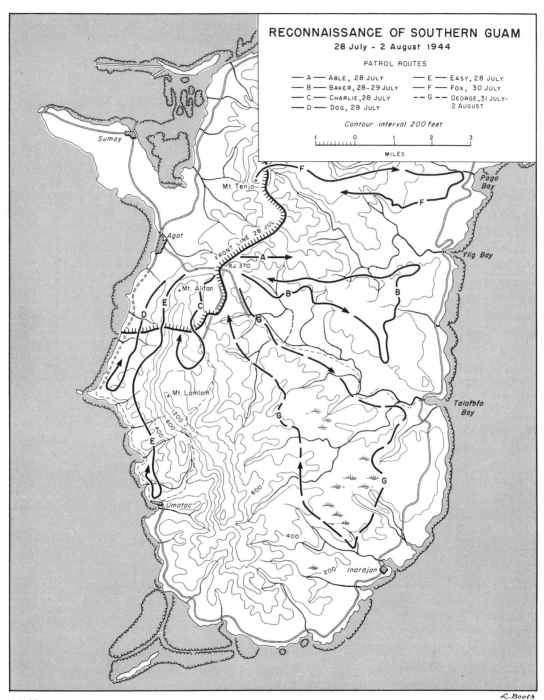

RECONNAISSANCE OF SOUTHERN GUAM
28 July - 2 August 1944

PATROL ROUTES

—— A —— Able, 28 July   —— E —— Easy, 28 July
—— B —— Baker, 28-29 July   —— F —— Fox, 30 July
—— C —— Charlie, 28 July   – – G – – George, 31 July-
—— D —— Dog, 28 July   2 August

Contour interval 200 feet

1   0   1   2   3

MILES

L. Booth

MAP 21

orders, each patrol was to exercise discretion about its own movements. Each was to report by radio every two to three hours and call for artillery support if needed.[33]

Pushing off on order early on the morning of 28 July, Patrol Able got less than half way to Ylig Bay when two of its members as well as the native guide came down with fever and had to return. Consequently, Patrol Baker took over responsibility for the entire area from Ylig Bay to Talofofo Bay. As Patrol Baker started out toward Talofofo, the men sighted a few Japanese, but stayed out of their way and went on to spend the night in a cave overlooking the eastern coast. The next morning they moved north along the coast for about four and a half miles to Ylig Bay, where they were greeted by Chamorros

who informed them that the Japanese had all moved north except for groups of less than platoon size that were still roaming around the southern jungles. With this information, Patrol Baker returned to headquarters.

Meanwhile, Patrols Charlie and Dog reached the slopes of Mount Lamlan, but turned back on receiving rifle fire. Patrol Easy went on to Umatac on the west coast below Facpi Point, found little evidence of enemy activity, and came back on up by the coastal road. Later, on 30 July, two other patrols from the reconnaissance troop (Fox and George) were sent out to reconnoiter Pago Bay and the southeast tip of the island. Both reported negative results.

The reports brought back by the patrols confirmed General Geiger's assumptions: no organized enemy resistance could be expected in southern Guam, the main body of the Japanese had retreated to the north, and it was in this direction that the next American attack would have to be launched.

---

[33] The account of the reconnaissance of southern Guam is derived from the following sources: 77th Reconnaissance Troop AAR Guam, pp. 1–2; AFAS, *Guam,* pp. 57–63; Lt Col F. C. Bridgewater, "Reconnaissance on Guam," *The Cavalry Journal* (May–June, 1945), pp. 46–48.

CHAPTER XIX

Pursuit to the North

The Japanese Withdrawal

When news reached General Takashima of the disastrous defeat suffered by his troops in the counterattack of 25–26 July, he ordered the survivors to withdraw from the Fonte area and to establish a new defensive line farther north. As an intermediate step the troops were to assembly around Ordot, then they were to move north and establish positions along a line between Dededo and Barrigada. While this shift was taking place, a rear-guard force was to be left in the vicinity of Ordot to fight a delaying action until the new defensive line could be established.[1] (*See Map V.*)

Takashima was killed shortly after he issued this order. However, his successor, General Obata, had been kept fully informed of the tactical situation and had no particular trouble taking over. Obata established his headquarters at Ordot on 28 July and remained there for about a day supervising the transfer of troops and equipment to the defensive line.[2] During that time he had under his immediate command in the Ordot area approximately 1,000 Army infantry troops, 800 Navy shore combat troops, and 2,500 others, including the *29th Division Tank Unit,* and

the *48th Independent Mixed Brigade* artillery unit, which had six guns.[3] Just how many other Japanese were scattered through the rest of the island at the time it is impossible to determine.

By the 30th, organized Japanese movement to the north had begun in earnest, and General Obata established his headquarters to the north of the new line at a three-pronged road junction northwest of Mount Barrigada. That same day he reaffirmed his intention to be guided by Takashima's defensive plan. Along the newly prepared line he deployed his troops in two sectors. A right sector unit was located in the vicinity of Dededo, and a left sector unit was placed on the southwest slopes of Mount Barrigada. In case these new dispositions failed to stop the attackers—and Obata must have been aware of the hopelessness of his situation—a final defense line was to be drawn up just below Ipapao. If this too should succumb, Obata designated Mount Santa Rosa as the site of a last stand. A day later he moved his headquarters again, this time to Mount Mataguac, and on 1 August he set up a hastily organized unit to defend Mount Santa Rosa and its environs. This bobtailed organization, called the *Mount Santa Rosa Garrison Force,* was composed entirely of

---

[1] Japanese Studies in World War II, 55, p. 49.
[2] Ltr, Takeda to McQueen, 20 Feb 52.

[3] Japanese Studies in World War II, 55, p. 49.

naval units, including laborers.[4] The entire force was organized into four and a half companies. Three of these were placed under command of a Captain Otori and ordered to defend Mount Mataguac, site of Obata's new command post. The remainder, composed of one company of infantry and two machine gun squads, was assigned to Mount Santa Rosa, where it would construct dummy positions "to fool U.S. troops." [5]

Obviously, the intention of the Japanese commander on Guam was to make the inevitable American victory as expensive as possible. His compatriots on Saipan had succeeded in doing this by orderly withdrawals to the northward where two separate and fairly well-organized lines were drawn across the breadth of the island. Obata apparently hoped to accomplish somewhat the same result, but his problem was more difficult and the means at his disposal less promising. Guam was considerably wider than Saipan and there were fewer men left to defend it. The American troops were hot in pursuit and no delays such as had held up the 27th Infantry Division in Death Valley were to give the *31st Army* commander on Guam an opportunity to reorganize. To add to his troubles, Obata was constantly being harassed by American naval and aerial bombardment.

As postwar Japanese testimony indicates: "The enemy air force seeking our units during the daylight hours in the forest, bombed and strafed even a single soldier. During the night, the enemy naval units attempting to cut our communications were shelling our position from all points of the perimeter of the island, thus impeding our operation activities to a great extent." [6]

Drive to the O-2 Line
31 July-1 August

General Geiger was fully aware of the route of the Japanese retreat and geared his plans accordingly. Late on the afternoon of 30 July, he ordered the 3d Marine Division and 77th Infantry Division to commence the pursuit on the morning of the 31st.[7] The corps commander planned to swing his line across Guam, pivoting on its left flank until he had occupied the waist of the island, and then push north. (*Map 22*) For this he would use both the 3d and the 77th (initially less the 306th Infantry) Divisions. General Geiger established two objective lines, the first (O-1) ran from the shore just east of Agana along the Agana–Pago Bay road to the town of Famja, where the road curved southeast along the high ground south of the Pago River. The second line (O-2) began at a point on the western shore little more than

---

[4] It consisted of the *263d Air Unit*, the *521st Naval Air Unit* with attached personnel, the *217th* and *218th Construction Units*, the *5th Field Hospital*, the *5th Construction Unit*, a weather observation unit, an air depot unit, an air ordnance unit, and the *30th Labor Unit*.

[5] Ltr, Takeda to McQueen, 20 Feb 52; Japanese Studies in World War II, 55, p. 49; POW Interrogation 47, Interrogation of Leading Seaman Shirakawa Yukio, in TF 56.2 Interrogation Rpts; III Phib Corps Rpt Guam, Incl D, G-2 Rpt 12, 311801K–011800K and Rpt 18, 061801K–071800K.

[6] Japanese Studies in World War II, 55, p. 50.

[7] The word pursuit as used here does not imply that the enemy was completely disorganized and routed. Nor does it imply that the attacking troops could move rapidly against few obstacles. General Bruce has suggested that a more accurately descriptive phrase to cover this phase of the battle for Guam would be "pursuit by direct pressure." Ltr, Bruce to Gen A. C. Smith, 11 Feb 55, Incl 1, OCMH.

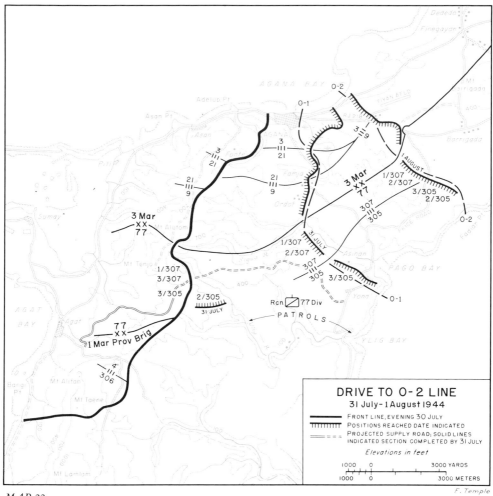

MAP 22

DRIVE TO O-2 LINE
31 July-1 August 1944

FRONT LINE, EVENING 30 JULY
POSITIONS REACHED DATE INDICATED
PROJECTED SUPPLY ROAD; SOLID LINES
INDICATED SECTION COMPLETED BY 31 JULY

Elevations in feet

F. Temple

a mile beyond the O-1 line and ran inland through Road Junction 218, reaching the east coast about a mile west of Fadian Point. The drive was scheduled to begin at 0630, 31 July, with the 3d Marine Division on the left as the hub of the turning maneuver. The 3d Division had but two to five miles to cover from its line of departure, while the 77th Division would have to advance nearly ten miles from the Tenjo–Alifan ridge. In force reserve was the 22d Marines (less 3d Battalion), while the 1st Provisional Brigade (less force reserve but initially plus the 306th Infantry) would hold the Force Beachhead Line, protect the corps right, and continue patrols throughout southern Guam.[8]

In compliance with this plan, General Bruce directed the 77th Division to move off in column of regiments, with its initial

---

[8] III Phib Corps Opn Order 7-44, 30 Jul 44, in III Phib Corps Rpt Guam, Opns Orders.

objective the O–1 line along the high ground south of the Pago River. First to move out would be the 307th Infantry, with 3d Battalion of the 305th Infantry, a reinforced company of the 706th Tank Battalion, and other supporting units attached. Behind the 307th would come the 305th Infantry, less its 3d Battalion, but otherwise similarly reinforced. The 307th Infantry would move east about two thirds of the distance from the Force Beachhead Line to the east coast and then turn north. The 305th Infantry, behind it, would cover the division south flank and turn northeast so as to go into position abreast and east of the 307th Infantry. Thus the division would present a two-regiment front facing north, 305th Infantry on the right, 307th on the left. When the 306th Infantry was relieved from its attachment to brigade, it would follow the division advance. The 105-mm. howitzers of the 902d Field Artillery would give direct support to the 307th Infantry, while the rest of the division artillery would be in general support. The boundary between the 77th Division and the 3d Marine Division roughly paralleled the Sigua River to the point where it joined the Pago River, and from there the boundary continued generally northeast.[9]

The Army Advance

On the morning of 31 July the 77th Division moved out on schedule. The 1st Battalion, 307th Infantry, led the advance, followed by the 3d Battalion, and, finally, by the 2d in reserve. Echeloned to the right was the attached 3d Battalion, 305th Infantry. Encountering no enemy opposition,

the advance moved fairly well. Only the roughness of the terrain and the weight of their loads slowed the troops. Men slid down the steep slopes of ravines and gorges, struggled through tangled undergrowth where it was next to impossible to see other units, and sweated it out in the humid heat. By noon the 305th Infantry, relieved on the final beachhead line by the 4th Marines, had joined the advance, and the 3d Battalion, 305th Infantry, had rejoined its parent regiment.

So far enemy resistance had been non-existent, for the handful of Japanese flushed out of their holes were more concerned with saving themselves than with killing Americans. Shortly before noon, General Bruce pushed up his schedule and ordered the two attack regiments to occupy the O–1 line by that night.[10]

During the afternoon the 77th Division troops moved ahead, still encountering little resistance. The 307th Infantry occupied its section of the O–1 line during the early afternoon, while the 3d Battalion, 305th Infantry, followed by the 1st Battalion, drove farther east toward its assigned objective along that line. As afternoon passed into the dusk of early evening, Capt. Lee P. Cothran's Company I, leading the 305th Infantry's advance, reached the high ground overlooking Pago Bay. Earlier in the day, a patrol from the 77th Reconnaissance Troop had reported that there were no enemy forces in the vicinity. The men of I Company pushed rapidly down

---

[9] 77th Inf Div FO 4, 30 Jul 44, in 77th Inf Div Guam Opn, Overlays.

[10] 77th Inf Div G–3 Jnl, 31 Jul 44, Msgs 1–36; 77th Inf Div G–2 Rpt 8, 31 Jul 44, in 77th Inf Div G–2 Jnl File (Guam), 30 Jul–2 Aug 44; Guam, Opns of the 77th Inf Div, pp. 95–98, MS in OCMH; 77th Inf Div G–3 Rpt, p. 4, in 77th Inf Div Rpt of Opns for the Capture of Guam.

MEN OF COMPANY B, 305TH RCT, *moving out from the high ground along the FBL.*

the trail toward the town of Yona, about 1,500 yards southwest of the mouth of the Pago River, where the company commander sought secure positions for the night. As the lead scouts neared the town, they saw two Japanese run across the trail. The enemy soldiers disappeared into the thick vegetation that bordered the trail just as a squad of the 2d Platoon opened fire. Small arms fire from Yona answered.

Forming a skirmish line, Company I began moving into the town. The Japanese were surprised. Some returned the fire, but others, in varying stages of undress, fled from the village. Those that remained apparently acted as a rear guard to cover the retreat of their comrades, for the Japanese firing at I Company made little or no attempt to move from their huts and dug-

outs. Soon K Company joined the fight and, thus reinforced, I Company moved into and through Yona, ending the brief struggle. Of an estimated 50 to 100 Japanese in the village, five were killed and the rest made good their escape. Shortly thereafter the 1st Battalion joined the 3rd Battalion in the area, and the 305th Infantry dug in for the night along its sector of the O–1 line.[11]

It had been a hard, hot, agonizing march. Luckily only a handful of Japanese had shown up to oppose the advance. There was another compensation. At the town on Asinan, on the south bank of the

[11] Guam, 77th Div (MS), pp. 98–103; 77th Inf Div G–3 Rpt 8, 1 Aug 44; 77th Inf Div G–2 Rpts 8 and 9, 31 Jul and 1 Aug 44, in 77th Inf Div G–2 Jnl File (Guam), 30 Jul–2 Aug 44.

Pago River about a mile from its mouth, troops of the 307th Infantry discovered a concentration camp in which the Japanese had assembled some 2,000 Chamorros. Although the enemy had left the area, the natives were apparently still too frightened to depart, and greeted the men of Company L, first into the area, as liberators. The scene was a moving one, as sick, hungry, but joyful Chamorros exhibited tiny and hitherto hidden American flags. While the troops pressed rations and cigarettes on them, the natives told of their oppression under the enemy and of their constant faith that the Americans would return. "We long time wait for you to come," said one.[12]

The 77th Division advance had been so rapid on 31 July that less than two hours after noon of that day General Bruce ordered the 305th and 307th Infantry Regiments to occupy the O–2 line on 1 August. With the 305th on the right, the two regiments would move out at 0700.[13] The decision to press on with all speed to the O–2 line was based not only on the lack of enemy resistance and the necessity of putting pressure on the enemy before he could reorganize, but on the need to secure a supply route. The Army troops had left the Force Beachhead Line with only small loads of rations in order to lighten their burdens over the rough terrain ahead. Building a supply route behind the advance or landing supplies at Pago Bay proved unfeasible, and it was obvious that the 77th Division would have to be supplied over the main road from Agana to Pago Bay. The Marine advance into Agana

on 31 July placed half of this road in American hands, but not until the O–2 line was seized would the rest of it be secured. If the 77th Division wanted food, it would have to occupy the O–2 line and its half of the cross-island road. "Capture that road," said General Bruce to the 307th Infantry's Colonel Hamilton, "and we'll bring up your breakfast."[14]

With some minor exceptions, 1 August was a repetition of 31 July. The 77th Division's advance was unopposed. Hungry and thirsty now, and somewhat more weary, the men nevertheless made good progress. By noon a portion of the Agana–Pago Bay road had been seized by the 307th Infantry, and soon the promised breakfast was on the way. Meanwhile, some of the troops appeased their hunger with captured Japanese canned salmon and candy. To satisfy their thirst, the men dropped halazone tablets into the unpleasant-tasting creek water. Others, more enterprising, mixed Tom Collinses from captured sake, K ration lemon powder, and sugar.

By evening the 77th Division was safely deployed along the O–2 line. On the right was the 305th Infantry with its 2d Battalion on the right, 3d on the left, and 1st in reserve. Just west of the point where Price Road—the northern branch of the Agana–Pago Bay road—crossed the O–2 line, began the zone of responsibility of the 307th Infantry. That regiment also had two battalions on the line, the 3d on the right, the 1st on the left; its 2d was in reserve. So far, the advance to the north had been easy.[15]

———————
[12] Quoted in Guam, 77th Div (MS), p. 104.
[13] 77th Inf Div FO 5, 31 Jul 44, in 77th Inf Div Guam Opn, Overlays.

———————
[14] Quoted in Guam, 77th Div (MS), p. 114.
[15] Ibid., pp. 114–18; AFAS, *Guam*, Map, p. 76.

The 3d Marine Division Zone

The same was true for the marines. On
31 July Turnage's men jumped off at 0630,
9th Marines on the right, 21st in the center, and 3d on the left. The 9th pushed
through Ordot, eliminating the small enemy detachment that had been left there
to guard supplies and equipment. That
afternoon two Japanese tanks showed up
to give battle but were quickly disposed of,
and by midafternoon Colonel Craig's unit
had dug in on the O–1 line. Craig's only
real problem was one that was to occur
with increasing frequency as marines and
soldiers pressed further into the jungle—
the matter of contact. The 9th Marines
was in physical contact with the Army
division on the day's objective line on its
right, but not with the 21st Marines on its
left. Finally, before nightfall, patrols from
the two Marine regiments met about 300
yards to the left of the 9th Marines boundary, and Craig sent Company C to plug
the gap.[16]

Meanwhile, the 21st Marines had
reached the corps objective line as had the
3d Marines on the left. In the course of
the day's advance the 3d had overrun
Agana, capital city of Guam, and seized
control of the western end of the Agana–
Pago Bay road. All together, the Marine
division had pushed forward more than
5,000 yards. On 1 August a comparable
advance was made against negligible opposition, and the division halted just short of
Tiyan airfield, the 21st Marines, which
had been in the center, being pinched
out.[17]

FORWARD OBSERVERS OF THE 77TH DI-
VISION *check progress of troops near
the Pago River.*

Supply Problems

The chief problem facing Geiger's troops
at this point was supply. The Army and
Marine Corps divisions had both moved so
rapidly on the last day of July and the first
of August that supply dumps were left far
in the rear—as much as sixteen miles in
the case of the 77th Division.

The problem in the Army's zone had
been foreseen and steps were taken in an
attempt to solve it. General Bruce proposed
to construct a main supply route from the
Agat area across the island. From Agat, a
main road ran inland, connecting with
trails that lead southeast to the coast. The
western terminus of the new supply route
that Army planners envisaged would be on
this road about 1,000 yards southeast of
Agat. From this point the new route would

---

[16] 3rd Marine Div G–3 Jnl, 31 Jul 44; Lodge,
Guam, pp. 124–25.
[17] 3d Marine Div D–3 Jnl, 1 Aug 44; Lodge,
Guam, pp. 125–27.

run generally along the high ground to the south of the Pago River in an easterly direction to Yona and Pago Bay. From there, it was planned, the supply route would turn north to follow the advance of the division up the island.

Soon after the 77th Division landed, Companies A and C, 302d Engineer Combat Battalion, began working on the new road. Like the infantrymen, the engineers found nature on Guam to be their worst enemy. The soft clay of central Guam proved an insufficient foundation for the road, and torrential rains and heavy traffic combined to make it a quagmire. Because of the consistency of the ground and the need for speed, once the move out of the beachhead area was begun the engineers could not follow good road-building practice. It was impossible to build roads on a higher level than the surrounding ground, since the soft clay would not support such a route. Instead, after culverts of coconut logs or oil drums had been emplaced, a two-lane road was bulldozed out, excess dirt being pushed to either side. This road was actually below the surrounding ground, and water drained onto rather than off of it. As heavy traffic rutted the road, the bulldozers pushed off the mud until a firm base was reached farther down.[18] "Such a road," commented the S–3 of the 302d, "is soon lost." With no other equipment than that organic to a division Engineer battalion, with the need for speed, and with men and equipment of the unit hard-pressed to complete other

tasks within their mission, the 302d Engineers had its troubles.

The rapid advance of the 77th Division on 31 July made it obvious to General Bruce, "that we could not hope to supply the division over this route."[19] Late that afternoon the 302d Engineers was ordered to abandon its attempt to construct a main supply route across the island. By this time the engineers had built about three and a third miles of road, and their labors had brought them to the southern slopes of Mount Tenjo. Remaining unfinished were nearly six miles of planned road.

The decision to abandon work on the project meant that the 77th Division had to rely on the main Agana–Pago Bay road, which was captured on 1 August. Since this road would also serve the 3d Marine Division and corps artillery, indeed had been doing so since the capture of its western half the day before, the strain on it as the main supply route would be tremendous. The road had once been good. It was hard surfaced and two lane, but the rigors of the weather and poor maintenance had considerably reduced its efficiency, and in the summer of 1944 it was a "tortuous route" requiring constant maintenance.[20]

The steady stream moving along this overloaded supply artery threatened to burst it but, by constant day and night movement of every vehicle the weary supply people could lay their hands on, the situation was kept fluid. In the absence of Japanese air and artillery opposition night movement could be carried out with lights on—a tremendous advantage. By dint of hard work and detailed planning, aided not a little by Japanese inability to

---

[18] 302d Engr Combat Bn (Guam), S–3 Opn Rpt, p. 2. Unless otherwise indicated, this section is based on: the above report, pp. 1–3; Bruce, "Administration, Supply, and Evacuation of the 77th Infantry Division on Guam," *Military Review,* XXIV, 8; Guam, 77th Div (MS), pp. 106–08; AFAS, *Guam,* Map, p. 72.

[19] Bruce, "Administration, Supply. . . ," p. 8.
[20] *Ibid.*

ARTILLERY COLUMN MOVING INLAND *from Agat beachhead over rutted supply road. Construction and maintenance difficulties prevented extension of this road as far as Pago Bay.*

interfere, the Agana–Pago Bay road was made to serve as a main supply route for the whole III Amphibious Corps. "The books would say it can't be done," wrote General Bruce, "but on Guam it was done —it had to be." [21]

The Marine 3d Division was in a slightly more advantageous position as far as supply was concerned because its supply dumps were closer to its own front lines and because the coastal road through Agana was within its zone of action. Nevertheless, traffic along the route was extremely congested and, furthermore, the road had been littered with Japanese aerial bombs and single-horned mines. To im-

prove the situation, the 25th Naval Construction Battalion and the 19th Marines (the Engineer regiment of the 3d Marine Division) concentrated all their efforts on improving existing roads and trails and removing the mines. However, the progress of supplies to the front lines was by no means satisfactory, and on 2 August General Geiger requested that a harbor reconnaissance be made of Agana Bay on the west coast and Pago Bay on the east coast. If these could be opened to boat traffic, some of the heavy load on Guam's poor and inadequate road system might be reduced.[22]

[21] *Ibid.*

[22] III Phib Corps G–3 Jnl, 2 Aug 44; Lodge, *Guam,* pp. 127–29.

To Barrigada and the O–3 Line
2–4 August

On the evening of 1 August General Geiger informed the forces under his command that the enemy, by all indications, had fallen back to the vicinity of the town of Yigo, in the eastern half of Guam, roughly eight miles northeast of the O–2 line. The two divisions were to make all possible speed to regain contact with the Japanese, while Task Force 53 was to work over enemy concentrations in the north with naval gunfire. Geiger's hope was that he could close with the Japanese in northern Guam before they could construct effective defenses there. Each division made ready for its mission. Meanwhile, corps artillery shifted to take targets farther north under fire, and a force of two battleships, five cruisers, ten destroyers, and four LCI(G)'s cruised off Guam's northern coasts to carry out their part of the attack.[23] Since the advance was in the nature of a pursuit, no artillery preparation was to precede it. Since the Japanese were withdrawing northward, corps artillery and naval gunfire support were concentrated on northern targets and neither of the infantry divisions planned a preassault bombardment.[24] Later that night General Geiger issued additional orders, directing the ground attack to begin at 0630, 2 August, with the initial objective a phase line (O–3) crossing the island about four miles northeast of the O–2 line.[25]

77th Division: 2 August

In compliance with these orders, General Bruce directed the light tanks of the 706th Tank Battalion to open the advance with a reconnaissance to the O–3 line. The infantry attack elements of the 77th Division —the 305th and 307th Infantry Regiments—were not to move out until 0700.[26]

The first major objective of the 77th Division drive was the village of Barrigada, in a large clearing about two miles northeast of the center of the divisional position on the O–2 line. The town was important to General Bruce for two reasons. First, about a hundred yards northwest of Road Junction 306, in the center of the town, was a reservoir and pump capable of supplying the thirsty troops with 20,000 gallons of water daily. Up to now streams and creeks had been the main source of water, but there were few watercourses in the northern part of Guam into which the division was moving. Moreover, water points established by the engineers near the beaches were too far away from the front lines for rapid delivery, a situation made worse by the fact that all supplies were carried along the overworked Agana–Pago Bay road. Weapons and ammunition had first priority on this artery, and with two divisions as well as corps troops being supplied along it there was not much room to bring up large quantities of water. On the morning of 2 August, for instance, the 305th Infantry put in an urgent plea for water. "We haven't had any since yesterday," it reported.[27] The capture of the Barrigada

[23] 77th Inf Div G–3 Jnl, 1 Aug 44, Msg 88; Lodge, *Guam*, p. 127 and fn. 33.
[24] For 3d Marine Division plans for the advance, see 3d Marine Div D–3 Jnl, 1 Aug 44, Msg 110.
[25] 77th Inf Div G–3 Jnl, 1 Aug 44, Msg 97; III Phib Corps G–3 Jnl, 1 Aug 44, Msg 2000; 77th Inf Div G–3 Rpt 10, 3 Aug 44, Overlay.

[26] 77th Inf Div G–3 Jnl, 1 Aug 44, Msgs 93, 102.
[27] 77th Inf Div G–4 Jnl, 2 Aug 44, Msg 1. It was not until nearly 1500 that a water point could be moved forward to take care of the 305th Infantry's requirements. *Ibid.*, Msg 5; Guam, 77th Div (MS), pp. 122–23.

reservoir would solve the problem. Furthermore, even before they reached Barrigada, the troops would be in control of the entire length of Price Road, the northern branch of the Agana–Pago Bay road, and thus obtain an additional route over which supplies might be carried to the front-line troops. Seizure of Road Junction 306 would give the 77th Division a link from Price Road to Barrigada, and a direct route from Agana to Barrigada.

The capture of Barrigada was assigned to the 307th Infantry, on the left of the division line. Maintaining contact on its left with the 3d Marine Division, the regiment was to push through the town and continue generally northeast for a little over a mile to seize Mount Barrigada—a jungle-covered mountain, 674 feet in height. With its 3d Battalion on the right, its 1st on the left, and its 2d in reserve, the regiment was to advance in a series of three phase lines to Mount Barrigada. The first of the lines, the so-called C line, would place the as yet uncaptured portion of Price Road in 77th Division hands and, if the marines on the left did their share, breakfast for the 307th could be brought up along Price Road as soon as it was captured. From the C line, with full stomachs, the 307th Infantry would advance on order, the 3d Battalion, on the right, passing through the center of Barrigada, with the 1st Battalion moving up to the west of the town.[28]

The 305th Infantry, to the right of the 307th, would attack northeast at the same time. Responsible for the area between the

307th Infantry and the east coast of Guam, the 305th planned to strike with its 2d Battalion on the right, its 1st in reserve, and its 3d Battalion on the left, in contact with the 307th. The 305th Infantry would advance east of Barrigada and Mount Barrigada, and thus would not, if the plan were followed, be engaged in the fight for the town itself.[29]

Promptly at 0630 on 2 August about a dozen light tanks of D Company (reinforced), 706th Tank Battalion, moved out from the 77th Division lines and advanced in column northwest along Price Road. On the alert for 2,000 Japanese reported north of Barrigada, they turned east at the point where the road from Barrigada met Price Road. No sooner had the tanks made this turn, a little over a mile west of Road Junction 306, than they were fired on by a small group of enemy soldiers. After putting machine gun fire on the enemy and on likely areas of concealment, the reconnaissance force turned and drove back to the division line with their report of contact. It was 0730.[30]

At 0800 the light tanks moved out again on a second reconnaissance. To supplement the armor, General Bruce requested an aerial reconnaissance of the area around Barrigada and northward. The tanks moved rapidly ahead, in close radio contact with the division advance command post, and pushed along the same route they had taken on their first reconnaissance. About 0845 they brushed aside an estimated twenty-five Japanese defending a roadblock

[28] A request by the 307th Infantry that it be allowed to stop once Price Road was secured in order to receive the expected food had been approved by General Bruce. 307th RCT Summary of Events, p. 3, and Overlay Showing Scheme of Maneuver for 2 Aug, in Opn Overlays, both in 307th RCT Guam Opn, FORAGER Rpt.

[29] AFAS, *Guam*, p. 77; 305th RCT S–3 Jnl File, 2 Aug 44, Entry 321 (map showing 3d Battalion routes of advance for 2 August).

[30] 706th Tk Bn Opn Rpt Guam, pp. 5–6; AFAS, *Guam*, pp. 79–80. See also 77th Inf Div G–2 Jnl File (Guam), 2 Aug 44, Msgs 14, 17–24.

at Road Junction 306 and, following orders, by 0900 had turned to continue north on the road to Finegayan. Two thousand yards up the road the tankers found their way blocked by three Japanese trucks. The tankers knocked out the trucks, killing about thirty-five enemy soldiers, then moved back to Barrigada and turned east to investigate matters in that direction. Despite enemy mines and a Japanese pillbox that proved to be undefended, the tanks advanced a few hundred yards with no resistance. When one tank got hung up on a stump, however, the whole column was halted on the narrow road. At this point the enemy put in an appearance in force. About 1045 some 150 Japanese attacked the tanks with hand grenades and 20-mm. and machine gun fire. The tanks returned the fire with a vengeance and managed to drive off their attackers without any American casualties. They then returned to their own lines.[31]

While the tanks had been making their reconnaissance, the attack echelons of the 77th Division moved out. At 0700 the 305th Infantry, on the right, and the 307th Infantry, on the left, crossed the line of departure and began the general advance. From right to left were the 2d and 3d Battalions, 305th Infantry, and the 3d and 1st Battalions, 307th Infantry. Moving forward against little or nor resistance, the men reached C line, securing Price Road, by 0830. Supplies were moved in quickly and 10-in-1 rations issued to the hungry troops of the 307th. While the 307th Infantry was eating and reorganizing, General Bruce sent word to the 305th Infan-

try to hold and reorganize on the C line, abreast of the 307th. Both regiments would resume the attack at 1030.[32]

The plan of attack for 2 August had not called for the 305th Infantry to a halt on the C line. Consequently, sometime between 0930 and 1000 when that regiment received General Bruce's order to halt along C line,[33] the 305th had already sent a reinforced company of the 3d Battalion beyond. Company I, reinforced by the heavy machine guns and mortars of M Company, was advancing in front of the battalion and by about 0930 the point of the company had just reached the edge of a clearing in a small draw about 300 yards southeast of Barrigada. (*Map 23*) Reconnoitering the area, the lead squad of the 2d Platoon came under enemy small arms fire from the direction of the town and took some casualties before it could fall back on the rest of its platoon and form a skirmish line. Soon the 1st Platoon had joined the 2d and a fire fight began between the Americans and what appeared to be a small group of Japanese with a machine gun. The Japanese were well concealed in the thick foliage at the edge of the draw, and attempts to flank the position were halted by effective fire from the same or another enemy machine gun. Company M's machine guns and mortars joined the struggle, but the enemy troops were so well hidden and their fire discipline was so perfect that the American fire had little effect. Moreover, a few enemy riflemen managed to infiltrate the M Company

[31] 77th Inf Div G-2 Jnl File (Guam), 2 Aug 44, Msgs 5, 25-35, 44-49; 77th Inf Div G-2 Rpt 10, 2 Aug 44; 706th Tk Bn Opn Rpt Guam, p. 6. See also AFAS, *Guam*, p. 81.

[32] 307th RCT Summary of Events, p. 3, in 307th RCT Rpt Guam; 305th RCT Rpt Guam, p. 3; 77th Inf Div G-3 Jnl Advance CP, 2 Aug 44, Msgs 3-10.

[33] 77th Inf Div G-3 Jnl Advance CP, 2 Aug 44, Msg 10; 305th RCT S-3 Jnl File, 2 Aug 44, Msg 322.

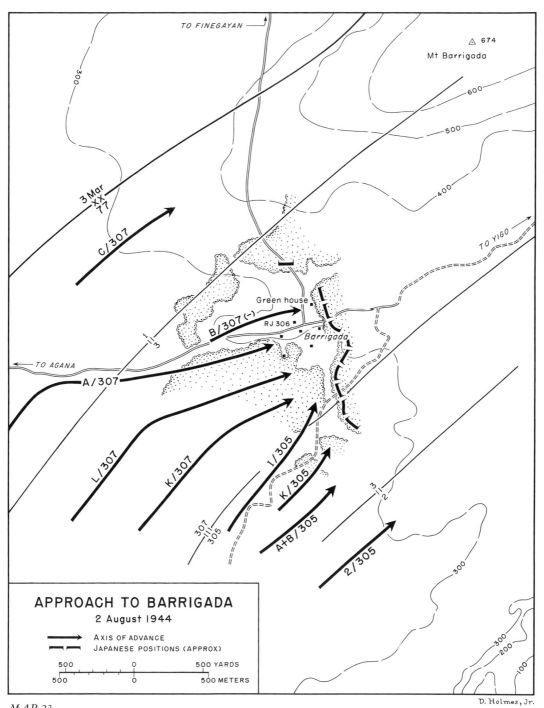

TO FINEGAYAN

△ 674
Mt Barrigada

300

600

500

400

3 Mar
XX
77

C/307

TO YIGO

Green house

B/307 (-)

RJ 306

Barrigada

TO AGANA

A/307

1/3

L/307

K/307

1/305

K/305

A+B/305

3
2

307
305

2/305

300

300
200
100

APPROACH TO BARRIGADA
2 August 1944

AXIS OF ADVANCE
JAPANESE POSITIONS (APPROX)

500   0   500 YARDS
500   0   500 METERS

MAP 23

D. Holmes, Jr.

positions. By 1030 the Americans estimated that a company of Japanese, well equipped with automatic weapons, was dug in in good positions to command the clearing. The presence of these enemy troops, possibly some of the same soldiers who in a few minutes would ambush the tank patrol, was ample proof that the Japanese controlled the road east of Barrigada and were therefore free to bring in reinforcements along that route. At the time, the men of the 3d Battalion, 305th Infantry, were in no position to challenge effectively the enemy control there.[34]

Meanwhile, at 1030 the 307th Infantry and the remainder of the 305th began their advance in accordance with Bruce's orders. On the right, where the Japanese positions had already been discovered, the 305th Infantry built up a line on I Company. On the left, however, the advance of the 307th Infantry had not uncovered the main enemy positions by 1030. It was here, on the left of the 77th Division, that the major action of 2 August was to occur.[35]

The formation of the 307th Infantry was, from right to left, Companies K, L, A, and, in contact with the marines, C. Each battalion kept a rifle company in reserve, and the 2d Battalion was in regimental reserve. The direction of the attack was northeast, aimed at Mount Barrigada, which meant that the 3d Battalion would push through the town of Barrigada while the 1st Battalion would move past it on

the west, in position, if necessary, to flank any Japanese in the town.[36]

As the regimental attack got under way, a number of enemy riflemen opened fire on Company A. The resulting delay in the company advance was in large measure to abort the attack of the 307th Infantry on 2 August.

By the time A Company had driven the Japanese off before it, the rest of the line had advanced beyond it. Drawn slightly to its right by the enemy, and further confused by its poor maps, Company A took up its advance in the wrong direction. Instead of following its assigned azimuth of 45°, the company veered to the right and followed generally along the road linking Price Road and Barrigada, or on an azimuth of nearly 80°. A wide gap between C Company, on the division left, and A Company, which in turn was now moving into the 3d Battalion zone, resulted. Once contact between these units was lost, it was extremely difficult to regain, not only because of the dense undergrowth but also because the 1st Battalion's radio batteries had become so weak that its radios were ineffective beyond a range of two hundred yards.

As the troops approached Barrigada, Company A pushed in on the left of Company L, which in turn crowded K Company over against the 305th Infantry zone. The axis of the 3d Battalion attack was thus shifted away from Barrigada and toward the area south of the town. Company A was moving toward Barrigada, but the three companies were crowded into the center and right half of the 3d Battalion area, in a line not wide enough for two

[34] AFAS, *Guam*, pp. 81–84; 3d Bn 305th RCT Unit Rpt, 2 Aug 44 (with overlay), in 305th RCT S–3 Jnl File 4–11 Aug 44, Entry 419; Ltr, Col Edward Chalgren, Jr., CO 3d Bn 305th Inf, to Hq USMC, 23 Jan 53 (comments on Guam MS), in Hist Br, USMC.

[35] 77th Inf Div G–3 Jnl Advance CP, 2 Aug 44, Msg 14; AFAS, *Guam,* p. 90.

[36] AFAS, *Guam,* p. 130. See also, 307th RCT S–1/S–4 Jnl, 2 Aug 44, Entry at 0955, in 307th RCT Rpt Guam.

companies, much less for three. Moreover, on the left of A Company was a gap of 1,000 yards between that unit and C Company, which was still advancing to the northwest of Barrigada.

By about 1130 Company A reached the edge of the clearing just west of Barrigada and almost immediately was taken under heavy small arms fire by Japanese troops in the town. Deploying on a north–south line near a temple in the southwest corner of the clearing, about 225 yards west of Road Junction 306, the men of A Company began to extend to their right only to run into members of L Company, also moving into the clearing. By the time the Americans could get into line they were squeezed into an abbreviated front. Company A could only bring one platoon to bear on the enemy and, while Company L could place its entire force in action, K Company had almost been driven into the 305th Infantry's zone and was facing that portion of the enemy opposing the 305th, rather than the Japanese in front of the 307th Infantry. Thus the Americans attacking the western half of the Japanese position, like those attacking to the east, were unable to force their way forward into the enemy line.

By about noon, most of the 1st Battalion reserve—a large portion of B Company—had been committed to regain contact with C Company, northwest of Barrigada. The 2d Platoon, B Company, was ordered to drive north around Barrigada, on the left of A Company, and capture a two-story green house with a concrete base that was located less than 200 yards north of Barrigada on the east side of the Barrigada–Finegayan road. From here the platoon would be in a good position to put fire on the enemy flank.

The 2d Platoon, B Company, moved across a large, open, grassy field on the left of Company A. Advancing by short rushes in groups of two or three men, the troops reached Finegayan road without incident. Since they had not been fired upon and all appeared quiet to their front and flank, the men began to cross the road. As the first small group reached the other side, however, an enemy machine gun in the woods east of the green house took the platoon under fire. The men of the 2d Platoon threw themselves into the ditches on either side of the road and sent back a request for a section of machine guns, which was moved up under heavy fire.

It was now nearly 1400. About this time, the weapons of Companies A and L scored a hit and set afire a grass shack on the road east of Barrigada near the point where the light tanks had been ambushed that morning. An enemy medium tank inside was forced to leave in a hurry, and, with three Japanese on top, drove west along the road toward the 307th Infantry's line. Raking the American position with cannon and machine gun fire, the tank moved up the road in the face of machine gun, BAR, and rifle fire. The three passengers were quickly knocked off, but the tank was still undamaged when it reached Road Junction 306 and turned north to confront the men of the 2d Platoon, B Company.

Caught in the open, some of the Americans dashed forward to the house, while the others pressed themselves helplessly against the bottom of the ditch. The tank threw a burst of machine gun fire at the prostrate men, killing one and wounding two, but then turned back to the road junction. Here it turned west again and moved along the Agana road toward Company A, 307th Infantry. A machine gunner emplaced in the temple opened fire on the tank, which retaliated by plunging into the side of the building, shifting gears, and forcing its way out the other side. The tracks missed the American gunner by a close margin, but the roof of the temple caved in and pinned him to the ground. The tank, meanwhile, undamaged but with a piece of thatched roof partially obscuring its vision slit, continued on and into the American lines.

Rifles, machine guns, BAR's, and grenades were powerless against the tank. The three bazookas in the A Company line—the only weapons that might have stopped it—were of no avail since two failed to go off and the gunner of the third was so excited that he failed to pull the safety until it was too late. For a moment the tank got hung up on a coconut log, but even then it remained impervious to American bullets and continued to fire wildly. In another moment it was free again and swept on down the road through a battalion command post and aid station and, about 1415, on through the command post of the 307th Infantry.

So far luck had been with the Japanese tank on its impromptu dash. It had succeeded in raising havoc on the 307th Infantry lines, forcing the men to fall back in search of better cover. Wounded men and scattered equipment marked its trail. What happened to it next is difficult to establish firmly. The tank left the 307th Infantry sector around 1430 and apparently moved west into the 3d Marines' sector, since a lone Japanese tank was destroyed there late in the afternoon by two American mediums.

Since the tank dash was not part of a planned Japanese attack, but rather an ex-

temporaneous move on the part of the driver, the enemy forces made no attempt to follow up their advantage. However, those men of the 2d Platoon, B Company, who had sought shelter in the green house were exposed to the same enemy fire that had opposed the platoon advance across the road. From a pillbox and from other emplacements in the woods, the Japanese sent machine gun and automatic weapons fire through the thin walls of the house. The men were helpless, and a runner made his perilous way back to company headquarters and received permission for the exposed platoon to withdraw.

It was agreed that Company A would cover the withdrawal, but before the 2d Platoon, Company B, could begin to fall back, American artillery fire began to drop around the house. The battalion commander tried desperately to have the shelling stopped, the men in the house who could still move made a dash for safety, and most of A Company also fell back to escape the artillery fire. Enough men stayed, however, to cover the withdrawal of the 2d Platoon, B Company, and the evacuation of the wounded.

It was by then 1500. With the exception of C Company, which had reached a point north and west of Barrigada, the men of the 307th Infantry had been stopped short of their day's objective. The gap in the line was still open and should the Japanese choose to take advantage of it they might inflict heavy damage. Accordingly, Lt. Col. Thomas B. Manuel, who had replaced Colonel Hamilton as regimental commander when the latter was evacuated for illness, asked General Bruce for permission to commit the reserve 2d Battalion (less one company) of the 307th Infantry. This was granted immediately, and Bruce

ordered the 306th Infantry, the division reserve, to send one battalion forward to a
position of readiness should it too be
needed.[37]

Probably General Bruce would have sent
more forces into the 307th Infantry area,
even had they not been requested. The
heavy jungle growth retarding and con-
fusing the advance of C Company had resulted in a loss of contact between Army
and Marine troops in the early afternoon.
General Turnage was forced to commit a
portion of his reserves in an attempt to regain contact. Indeed, shortly after 1400
General Geiger had radioed a terse message
to General Bruce: "You are holding up advance of 3d Mar Div," he said. "Make
every effort to advance your left flank to
maintain contact." [38] General Bruce replied with a brief description of his
difficulties in the 307th Infantry sector. "I
do not," he said, "expect to capture Mt.
Barrigada today." He would consolidate
for the night on a line just north of Barrigada village and attack again the next
morning.[39] To his own troops, after approving use of the 307th Infantry's reserve,
Bruce sent orders to complete the capture

of Barrigada, tie in with the marines, and
hold for the night.[40]

Bruce's realization that he could not take
Mount Barrigada on 2 August was not
based on consideration of the situation on
his left alone, since his advance on the
right had been equally frustrated. By 1330
Company K, 305th Infantry, reinforced
with five light tanks of Company D, 706th
Tank Battalion, moved out in attack. It
had taken the 305th Infantry until that
time to strengthen I Company's position on
the left and deploy in the thick woods.
Company K and the tanks moved from behind Company I and up and parallel to
it. To reach the enemy positions, it was
necessary to cross a slight draw, all fairly
open ground. The attackers adopted a formation in which the tanks took the lead,
each with a small group of infantrymen for
close-in protection, while two platoons of
infantry moved in the rear of the armor.

Four tanks and their accompanying infantry moved across the draw without opposition. As soon as the fifth tank exposed
itself, however, it became a target for machine gun and cannon fire. This had no
effect on the tank, but the ricochets off its
sides hit the infantrymen around it. The
riflemen threw themselves into the dirt,
and the lead tanks tried to return the fire,
but the Japanese were so well concealed
that the tankers could discover no targets
and had to fire blind.

With their accompanying infantry
pinned down, the tanks did not dare to advance farther toward the Japanese positions and shortly thereafter pulled back to
less exposed positions. The men of K Company, hugging the ground in the slight
cover of the draw, were unable to move in

[37] This description of the action of the 307th
Infantry is based mainly on: Guam, 77th Div
(MS), pp. 131–39; AFAS, *Guam,* pp. 84–90,
and Map, p. 82. Also see 77th Inf Div G–3 Jnl
and G–3 Jnl Advance CP, 2 Aug 44; 307th
RCT S–2/S–3 and S–1/S–4 Jnls, 2 Aug 44;
77th Inf Div G–2 Rpts 10 and 11, 2 and 3 Aug
44, in 77th Inf Div G–2 Jnl File; 706th Tk Bn
Rpt Guam, p. 6; 77th Inf Div Arty Rpt Guam,
pp. 8–9; Lodge, *Guam,* p. 129; Ltr, Col Joseph
B. Coolidge to Gen A. C. Smith, 6 Apr 55,
OCMH.

[38] III Phib Corps G–3 Jnl, 1410, 2 Aug 44;
Lodge, *Guam,* p. 128. See also 3d Marine Div
Opn Summary as of 1800, 2 Aug 44, Msg 87, in
3d Marine Div D–3 Jnl, 2 Aug 44.

[39] III Phib Corps G–3 Jnl, 1447, 2 Aug 44.

[40] 77th Inf Div G–3 Jnl, 2 Aug 44, Msg 9.

any direction. There was no indication that the Japanese positions had in any way been reduced, and the Americans still had no precise idea of their location. The tank-infantry attack had gained nothing.

One more attempt was made to knock out these enemy positions with armor. Carrying as a guide an officer of Company I, 2d Lt. Edward C. Harper, who had already crawled forward on his belly to reconnoiter the enemy line, one light tank moved to within five yards of the presumed Japanese position and opened fire with its machine guns. The enemy fire proved to be more effective, however, and Japanese machine gun or possibly 20-mm. bullets hit the tank's trailing idler and drive shaft and put a hole in its armor plating. Unable to move forward, the tank backed, only to have one of its tracks drop off. Thus ended this attempt. Covered by two medium tanks of Company C, 706th Tank Battalion, which had just come up, the tankers jumped out of their vehicle and ran back to safety. The mediums then destroyed the abandoned light tank.

The Japanese position was still intact, and the 3d Battalion, 305th Infantry, did not yet have a clear idea of the enemy dispositions. Accordingly, the riflemen still out in the draw were ordered to fall back, and artillery fire was requested. The men in the draw made their way out by a circuitous route, not without casualties, but the 3d Battalion was denied artillery support on the grounds that shelling might hit 307th Infantry elements on the left.

There was one last chance. Four medium tanks of C Company, 706th Tank Battalion, with Lieutenant Harper again acting as a guide, moved out abreast. Advancing on the enemy position, they fired 75-mm. shells at the Japanese. The fire destroyed some of the enemy's camouflage that had hidden a tank, which the mediums quickly knocked out. Under protection of the tanks several American wounded who had previously been trapped were evacuated, but by this time it was almost dark, and any hope of following up the attack vanished. Moreover, A and B Companies, which had been moving up during the afternoon to join the 3d Battalion attack, had been so delayed by scattered enemy fire that they were not yet ready to begin an attack, even if one had been possible. It was fully dark before the two companies were in position between the 3d and 2d Battalions.

The 305th Infantry thus had little success on 2 August. Only on the extreme right, in the 2d Battalion sector, had its advance been unopposed, though the 2d Battalion had not ventured forward of the line held by the 3d, lest contact between the units be broken.[41]

On the left of the 77th Division, the 307th Infantry was to make one more attempt before dark. Shortly after 1500 the 2d Battalion (less F Company) began to move up to fill the gap in the 307th line. Within an hour or an hour and a half, with Company E advancing to make contact with C Company and Company G pushing toward Barrigada, contact was established along the line. The gap still was not completely filled since the line curved inward, leaving a salient that might still be occupied by enemy troops.

───────────
[41] Guam, 77th Div (MS), pp. 139–44; AFAS, *Guam*, Map 18, p. 91; Ltr, Chalgren to USMC, 23 Jan 53; 706th Tk Bn Opn Rpt Guam, p. 6; 3d Bn 305th RCT Unit Rpt, 2 Aug 44, in 305th RCT S-3 Jnl File, 4–11 Aug 44, Msg 419; 305th RCT, Overlay Showing Situation as of 0900, 3 Aug 44, Entry 359, in 305th RCT S-3 Jnl File, 28 Jul–3 Aug 44.

Late in the afternoon the regimental commander planned to send a small force of tanks and Company G to evacuate wounded from the green house area. The plan called for an enveloping attack. The 2d Platoon was to follow four light tanks of D Company, 706th Tank Battalion, along the Agana–Barrigada road to Road Junction 306 and then, turning north, to approach the house from the south. At the same time the 1st Platoon would move east parallel to the 2d Platoon advance and 200 or 300 yards north of it, to hit the Finegayan road north of the house. The two platoons would thus move around the edges of the open field across which B Company had made its unsuccessful attack a few hours earlier.

Unfortunately for the success of the plan, the officers concerned were not sufficiently briefed. Consequently, when the tanks moved through the 1st Battalion and along the Agana–Barrigada road, the 2d Platoon was not behind them. Instead the platoon leader, following what he believed to be his orders, had begun to move his men across the open field, a move that the planners had specifically meant to avoid. When the 2d Platoon was halfway across the field and still somewhat protected from enemy fire to the east, a runner reached it with the correct orders but it was too late for the infantrymen in the field to move back and catch up with the tanks which had by then almost reached Road Junction 306. Accordingly, the platoon leader decided to continue his advance across the field in an attempt to arrive at the green house simultaneously with the tanks. Moreover, should the tanks be held up at the road junction, he believed his men would be in position to break up any resistance in front of the tank advance.

The platoon leader's plan worked. The 2d Platoon reached the green house just as the tanks arrived. Heavy Japanese fire was coming from the woods, but although the infantry had no way of communicating with the tank crews to designate targets, fire from the tanks greatly reduced the volume of enemy fire. The 2d Platoon soon formed a line just east of the house, and the tanks began evacuating wounded.

Meanwhile, the 1st Platoon, G Company, had moved across the northern edge of the field. Before the 1st Platoon was across the field, the tanks at the house began to fall back with the wounded they had gone to rescue. The volume of American fire was thus noticeably lessened, and from the woods to the north Japanese riflemen and machine gunners, who had remained quiet all day, opened fire on the flank of the two American rifle platoons. Another machine gunner east of the house also began shooting, and the two platoons were caught in a cross fire.

As the men of G Company's 1st and 2d Platoons fell back or vainly searched for cover, the heavy Japanese fire began to take its toll among the exposed Americans. One of the men managed to get back to company headquarters with a call for help, and the 3d Platoon was sent forward to assist. It pushed across the field and into Barrigada village. Leaving a squad at Road Junction 306, the rest of the men advanced north on the Finegayan road pouring a heavy volume of rifle, BAR, and machine gun fire at the enemy. Machine guns and mortars from H Company moved up and joined the fight, and soon two tanks were back to lend their heavier fire.

The rescue force did not know where the 1st Platoon was, and so had concentrated on getting to the 2d Platoon, which was around the green house. Moreover, fearing to hit the 1st Platoon, the force had concentrated its fire to the east, rather than to the north. This sufficed to cover the evacuation of the wounded men of the 2d Platoon. In the gathering dusk, and with their men now low on ammunition, the leaders of the 2d and 3d Platoons withdrew their units, although not without sustaining a few more casualties.

The 1st Platoon, to the north, was still pinned down and still suffering casualties. The rescue force, this time with three tanks and led by the regimental commander, now moved out to the aid of the beleaguered men who were scattered across the northern half of the field, most of them casualties. Covered by heavy fire from the tanks, the rescuers began evacuating the wounded. The 1st Platoon had suffered twenty-six casualties, most of them killed, including the commander, 1st Lt. James T. Whitney. As darkness closed in, the last men of G Company returned to their line of departure and dug in for the night.[42]

With the coming of night, the 77th Division had yet to take Barrigada village. The American line ran roughly from southeast to northwest, with the woods just north-northwest of Barrigada forming an enemy salient. The Japanese positions had been barely dented, although by dark American attacks had developed the enemy defenses fairly well. At least the Americans knew where the Japanese were, which had not been the case twelve hours earlier. To acquire this information had cost a total of 102 casualties: 6 killed, 18 wounded, and one missing in the 305th Infantry, and

22 killed and 55 wounded in the 307th Infantry.[43] The two regiments claimed a total of 105 Japanese killed, almost all by the 305th Infantry. Contact with the 3d Marine Division was at best tenuous, for while a platoon of C Company, 307th Infantry, was with the marines, it was out of contact with the rest of its own company.[44]

On the evening of 2 August the Japanese still controlled most of Barrigada village and the roads leading north (to Finegayan) and east. The 77th Division G-2 section made a cautious estimate that the enemy resistance might indicate that the Americans had struck forward positions of a Japanese line defending northern Guam.[45] On lower echelons, the troops were restless in their foxholes, mindful of the great banzai attack on Saipan that had overrun and ripped up American lines on that island.[46]

The night passed without incident, but General Bruce's plan of action for 3 August was a more cautious one than that of the previous day. This time the 77th Division commander called for an artillery preparation on the enemy before him. Division artillery—supported by a battalion of 155's from corps artillery—would begin firing at 0630. At 0700, as the big guns shifted their fire to targets farther north and northeast, the 305th and 307th Infantry Regiments would renew their attack. General Bruce hoped to push on to Mount Barrigada and the O-3 line, if necessary bypassing and containing resistance at the town of

[42] Guam, 77th Div (MS), pp. 146–55; AFAS, Guam, pp. 93–99; 307th RCT S-1/S-4 Jnl, 2 Aug 44.

[43] 77th Div G-1 Daily Consolidated Rpt of Casualties, Guam, 2 Aug 44.
[44] Guam, 77th Div (MS), p. 141; 3d Marine Div D-3 Jnl, 2 Aug 44, Msg 78.
[45] 77th Inf Div G-2 Rpt 11, 3 Aug 44.
[46] AFAS, Guam, p. 101.

Barrigada itself in order to reach his objective.[47]

There was to be no change in regimental boundaries, but the battalions were regrouped.[48] On the right of the division line, southeast of Barrigada, the 305th Infantry would continue its push to the northeast. Its 2d Battalion maintained its position on the right while on the left the 1st Battalion replaced the 3d, which had done the bulk of the regiment's fighting on 2 August.[49] On the division left, the 307th Infantry was to drive northeast through Barrigada. Its 3d Battalion remained tied in with the 305th Infantry. The 1st Battalion, however, was so spread out that the 2d Battalion, part of which had already seen action on 2 August, replaced it as the left flank unit of the 77th Division. This replacement was actually carried out in the late afternoon and night of 2–3 August at the direction of Brig. Gen. Edwin H. Randle, assistant division commander, present at the regimental command post during the afternoon.[50]

In planning the advance for 3 August, General Bruce gave some attention to the problem of contact between units. On 2 August the main body of his troops had been out of contact with the 3d Marine Division, and the drive northeast through the thick jungles of Guam promised to make lateral liaison progressively more difficult. While Bruce was well aware of this problem and gave it due consideration, he did not feel that it was the primary issue. The Army general subscribed to the theory that, in jungle fighting, close contact between units, though desirable, should not be insisted upon to the sacrifice of rapidity of advance and destruction of the enemy. Under such conditions, according to this theory, it is often preferable to push ahead quickly over whatever trails and roads there are through the jungle and maintain lateral contact only by patrols and connecting files or only where favorable terrain permits.

Bruce had served in Panama in 1933 and while there had developed a set of principles governing jungle warfare, some of which were later incorporated into the Army manual on the subject and all of which he impressed on the 77th Division during training. As he himself later expressed it, "The Japanese were skillful in penetrating 'lines' and attacking flanks and rear. I pointed out that it was far better to get through the jungle regardless of flanks until they [the attacking troops] arrived at a trail or road where liaison and contact could be established with adjacent units. I emphasized the lack of vision in woods or jungle precluded the ordinary concept of fighting in the open. In brief, my idea . . . was to push boldly forward and then take up a strong all around defense at night."[51]

Bruce's thoughts were made clear on the morning of 3 August when he submitted his plan for the day's action to the III Amphibious Corps. "I intend to push hard with my right unit past [Mount Bar-

---

[47] 77th Inf Div Rpt, pp. 4–5; 77th Inf Div G–3 Jnl File, 3 Aug 44, Entry 6; 307th RCT Rpt, p. 3; 307th RCT S–1/S–4 Jnl, Entries at 0618, 0626, 0627, 3 Aug 44; 77th Inf Div Arty Rpt Guam, p. 9; Overlay, 77th Inf Div Arty, Preparation Fires 3 Aug 44, in 77th Inf Div Arty S–3 Jnl File, 3 Aug 44; III Phib Corps Arty Rpt, p. 7.

[48] AFAS, *Guam*, p. 101.

[49] 305th RCT Rpt, p. 3; 3d Bn 305th RCT Rpt, p. 3.

[50] 307th RCT S–1/S–4 Jnl, 1605, 2 Aug–0543, 3 Aug 44, *passim*.

[51] Ltr, Bruce to Gen A. C. Smith, 11 Feb. 55.

rigada] without regard to contact. I suggest 3d Div unit on my left push up past mountain. This may cause a gap which I will fill with my reserve. Otherwise progress will be slow because of the difficult terrain." [52] Almost immediately corps headquarters approved this method of attack, and Bruce was ordered to "keep pushing to hit main enemy body. Do not hold up for small pockets which can be mopped up later." [53] By this time the 77th Division attack was already well under way.

77th Division: 3 August

At 0700 on the morning of the 3d, as 77th Division Artillery shifted to forward targets, the two infantry regiments began to move slowly forward. The 307th Infantry, advancing with Company A, 706th Tank Battalion, in support, reported that the artillery preparation had inflicted numerous casualties on a platoon-sized enemy patrol that had approached the American positions. However, the advance of the 2d Battalion, on the left, was slowed by short artillery rounds that disrupted communications and killed some men in the command post area and wounded others, including the battalion commander, Colonel Learner, who was replaced by Maj. Thomas R. Mackin, battalion executive officer.

The division advance was slow but, initially, steady, for most of the Japanese defending Barrigada had pulled back during the night or under the morning's artillery fire. Only scattered resistance met the Americans as they moved forward, and

in the 305th zone on the right the troops had more trouble with the difficult, heavily wooded terrain than they did with the scattered enemy. On the division left the 2d Battalion, 307th Infantry, pushed through Barrigada clearing it with relative ease but was halted by automatic weapons fire north of the town shortly after 0900. The 3d Battalion was generally astride and east of the Barrigada–Finegayan road, 200 or more yards from Barrigada and in contact with the 305th Infantry. (*Map 24*)

The seizure of the village of Barrigada, anticlimatic after the frustrating struggle of the previous day, put the important Barrigada reservoir in American hands on 3 August. Working rapidly, the 302d Engineers established a water point and had it in operation by 1430 to assure a ready supply for the thirsty troops.

Meanwhile the 3d Battalion, 307th Infantry, supported by the tanks of Company A, 706th Tank Battalion, had pushed farther northeast through the Japanese defenses. The advance was extremely slow, however, because the thick, almost trackless jungle made for hard going. Moreover, at 1130 the battalion commander, Major Lovell, had to be evacuated because of sunstroke and was replaced by his executive officer, Maj. Joseph Hanna. By now the regimental commanding officer and each of the battalion commanding officers had been evacuated because of wounds or illness. On the left (southwest) of the 3d Battalion, the 2d Battalion was still moving extremely slowly, but its right had reached Finegayan road at Road Junction 410, about 1,000 yards from Barrigada. At noon the entire 307th Infantry halted to reorganize for another attack in the afternoon. The 305th Infantry, meanwhile, was east-southeast of Barrigada, pushing very

[52] III Phib Corps G–3 Jnl, 0815, 3 Aug 44.
[53] *Ibid.*, 0830, 3 Aug 44.

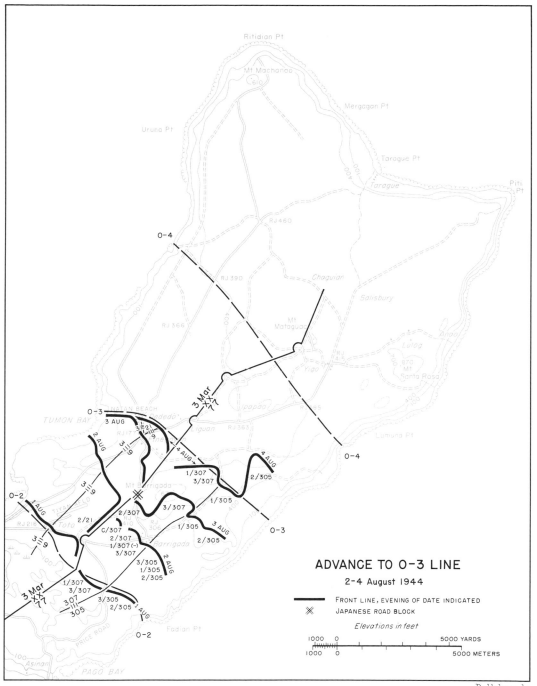

ADVANCE TO 0-3 LINE

2-4 August 1944

▬▬▬ FRONT LINE, EVENING OF DATE INDICATED
✳ JAPANESE ROAD BLOCK

Elevations in feet

MAP 24

D. Holmes, Jr.

slowly northeast through the dense and virtually uncharted jungle.[54]

It had become apparent that the bulk of the enemy resistance was north to northeast of Barrigada in front of the 3d Battalion, 307th Infantry, exactly where General Bruce had expected it. Bruce's original plan had been to continue the push on his right with the 305th Infantry, regardless of how much the 307th might be held up. With conditions now anything but favorable for such a maneuver, the division commander changed his plan to take advantage of the success at Barrigada village. All four division artillery battalions would support an attack by the 307th Infantry with a five-minute concentration and a rolling barrage. The shelling would start at 1330, at the rate of a round per gun per minute. At 1335 it would lift 100 yards and an additional 100 yards every two minutes thereafter, maintaining the same rate of fire. As the artillery fire climbed Mount Barrigada, the infantry would follow close behind to seize the height.[55]

On the heels of the artillery fire, the 307th Infantry attacked. Two platoons of tanks spearheaded the advance, breaking a trail through the thick jungle as the troops moved against scattered resistance on the lower slopes of Mount Barrigada. As the men pushed forward resistance lessened, and by 1500 the 3d Battalion was on the summit, 2,400 yards northeast of the

town of Barrigada. A 400-yard gap lay between K and I Companies, but the regiment had ample time to reorganize and close the gap before nightfall.

Echeloned to the left rear (southwest) of the 3d Battalion was the 2d Battalion. The 2d Battalion's advance had been held up somewhat because it had to resupply itself with water. Company E, for instance, had received no issue of water for at least twenty-four hours. Another reason for the delay was the denseness of the vegetation. The failure of the 2d Battalion to keep up with the 3d had left a gap between the two units and, on the left, the 2d Battalion was out of contact with the 3d Marine Division. In addition to falling behind, Mackin's men had moved somewhat to the right in an attempt to maintain contact with the 3d Battalion. Responsibility for the loss of contact between Army and Marine troops did not lie entirely with the 2d Battalion, 307th Infantry, however. General Bruce's plan and Geiger's approval of it had been passed on to the 3d Marine Division that morning.[56] General Turnage immediately ordered the 9th Marines, on the right of his division line, "to break contact with the 77th and push ahead as rapidly as possible." [57] Thus as early as 0845 on 3 August, contact between Marine and Army units was as good as lost.

[54] 77th Inf Div Rpt, p. 5; 77th Inf Div G-3 Rpt 11, 4 Aug 44; 77th Inf Div G-3 Jnl, 3 Aug 44; 77th Inf Div Arty S-3 Jnl, 3 Aug 44; 307th RCT Rpt, p. 3; 77th Inf Div Arty Rpt Guam, p. 9; 307th RCT S-1/S-4 and S-2/S-3 Jnls, 3 Aug 44; 706th Tk Bn Opn Rpt Guam, p. 6; AFAS, *Guam*, p. 102; 305th RCT, Overlay Showing Situation as of 0900, 3 Aug 44, in 305th RCT S-3 Jnl File, 3 Aug 44, Entry 361.

[55] 307th RCT Opn Rpt Guam, p. 3; 77th Inf Div G-3 Jnl, 3 Aug 44, Entry 43.

[56] 3d Marine Div D-3 Jnl, 3 Aug 44, Msg 17. Unless otherwise indicated, this account of the 77th Division attack on the afternoon of 3 August is based on the following: 77th Inf Div Rpt, p. 5; 77th Inf Div G-3 Jnl, 3 Aug 44; 77th Inf Div G-3 Rpt 11, 4 Aug 44; 307th RCT Rpt Guam, p. 3; 307th RCT S-1/S-4 and S-2/S-3 Jnls, 3 Aug 44; AFAS, *Guam,* pp. 103–04; 706th Tk Bn Opn Rpt Guam, pp. 6–7.

[57] 3d Marine Div D-3 Jnl, 3 Aug 44, Msg 18. III Amphibious Corps was notified of this order. III Phib Corps G-3 Jnl, 0925, 3 Aug.

During the day the 2d Battalion, 307th Infantry, made numerous attempts to regain contact with the 3d Battalion as well as with the Marine division—all unsuccessful. By 1230 General Turnage was worried enough about the gap between Marine and Army troops to rescind his earlier order to the 9th Marines and halt the advance on the right.[58] Meanwhile, the 307th Infantry continued its efforts to regain contact with the 3d Marines and late in the afternoon a platoon of medium tanks with men of the 2d Battalion riding on their decks moved north along the Finegayan road toward the Marine lines. However, Japanese mines and an enemy roadblock less than 1,000 yards beyond Road Junction 410 frustrated the attempt, and the 9th Marines began to protest that Army fire on this roadblock was falling within their positions.[59] Thus at nightfall gaps still remained between the two battalions of the 307th Infantry and between the 307th and the 9th Marines. To fill the latter and protect his right flank, General Turnage released a battalion of the 21st Marines from reserve to the 9th Marines.[60]

While the 307th Infantry was advancing on 3 August with varied success, the 305th Infantry, to its southeast, had continued to push slowly across the thickly overgrown terrain. By this time the tropical rain forest had grown so thick that the only way the men could make any progress at all was by reversing the guns on their medium tanks and tank destroyers and using the vehicles as trail blazers.[61] Struggling through the luxuriant vegetation, the regiment soon found roads dwindling to trails and trails disappearing altogether. Small pockets of enemy resistance in the heavy jungle involved the Americans in a number of minor engagements, with companies or smaller units fighting independent actions. The regimental right did not extend all the way down to the water's edge, but rather held along the top of a bluff, which paralleled the coast about 1,000 yards inland. An attached platoon of the 77th Reconnaissance Troop patrolled the slope of the bluff.[62] By the end of the day the 305th Infantry was southeast of Mount Barrigada, almost on line with the 307th Infantry on its left. The regiments were in contact with each other.

For most of the 77th Division, the day's advance had netted disappointingly short gains of from 2,000 to 2,500 yards, the 2d Battalion, 307th Infantry, having advanced less than 1,500 yards. The reserve 306th Infantry was in position 1,500 yards south of Barrigada. It had not been used to fill the gap between Army and Marine units, though General Bruce had indicated that morning that he might so employ the unit, because the gap was at most 800 yards wide and Bruce felt that it could be closed once the enemy roadblock on the Finegayan road was broken. The 3d Marine Division, meanwhile, had pushed rapidly ahead, held back only on its right flank in order to keep in contact with the 77th Division. Casualties in the two Army regiments attacking on 3 August were four killed and twenty wounded in the 305th Infantry and eight killed and thirty-three

[58] 3d Marine Div D–3 Jnl, 3 Aug 44, Msg 69.

[59] 307th RCT S–1/S–4 Jnl, 1730, 1732, 3 Aug 44.

[60] 3d Marine Div D–3 Jnl, 3 Aug 44, Msgs 66, 69.

[61] Ltr, Landrum to Gen A. C. Smith, 27 Apr 55, Incl, OCMH.

[62] 77th Inf Div Rcn Troop Rpt, p. 2.

wounded in the 307th. A total of 161 enemy dead was claimed by the two units.[63]

Disappointed with the speed of the 77th Division advance on 3 August, General Bruce issued his orders for the next day's operations. He hoped on 4 August to secure Mount Barrigada and pull his troops up to the O-3 line. The attack was to continue at 0700. The only change in the assault formation was in the 307th Infantry sector where the 1st Battalion would push through the 2d to replace it on the regimental left. The 3d Battalion would hold in position until the 1st was abreast of it. The 306th Infantry was to maintain contact with the 305th, follow behind that regiment mopping up the area, and be prepared to turn north toward Mount Santa Rosa once Mount Barrigada had been passed, pinching out the 307th Infantry and replacing it on the line.[64]

77th Division: 4 August

The 77th Division attack got under way on 4 August after a night that saw American lines raided by small groups of Japanese, despite harassing fire placed on enemy-held road junctions by division and corps artillery. Actually, the infantry attack was taken up only by the 305th Regiment, for the 307th Infantry spent the morning reorganizing its assault formation and attempting to regain contact with the marines.

Shortly after 0600 the 1st Battalion, 307th Infantry, began to move through the 2d in order to relieve that unit on the regimental left. Less than three quarters of an hour later, a platoon of the 1st Battalion, with a single tank of Company A, 706th Tank Battalion, in support, set off along the Finegayan road to reduce the Japanese roadblock between Army and Marine positions. The 3d Battalion held firm but sent patrols over the northern part of Mount Barrigada. By 0700, when the 305th Infantry began its attack, the 307th had already made a good beginning in its own sector.

The attempts to gain contact and to pull the 307th Infantry lines abreast of the 3d Marine Division—both part and parcel of the same general scheme to align and tie in the entire corps front—met both tragedy and failure. By about 0800, little more than an hour after the tank-led patrol had set out for Marine positions, it was halted by the same Japanese roadblock that had stopped similar attempts the previous afternoon and evening. The roadblock was well covered by machine guns, and the 2d Battalion commander requested artillery fire to knock out the Japanese position. The request was turned down, and instead Major Mackin was ordered to use tanks to break through the roadblock. A few minutes later a platoon of tanks set off up the road leading an infantry patrol. Shortly after 1030 the tank-infantry force succeeded in smashing the Japanese position as well as a second roadblock a little farther along the road. Just before 1100 the American patrol came upon a third block. Taking no chances, the men in the tanks opened fire immediately, but with unfortunate results. The roadblock was not manned by enemy troops, but rather by Americans of Company G, 9th Marines, who had established the block in accordance with 3d Division orders to protect the right flank of

---

[63] 77th Inf Div G-1 Daily Consolidated Rpt of Casualties, Guam, 3 Aug 44.

[64] 77th Inf Div Rpt, p. 5; 307th RCT Rpt Guam, p. 3; 77th Inf Div Arty G-3 Jnl, 3-4 Aug 44, Msg 16.

the Marine division. The 3d Marine Division had been warned of the approach of the Army patrol and was expecting it; the Army troops, on the other hand, had been told that red smoke grenades would be used as a signal to indicate friendly positions, although Company G, 9th Marines, was apparently unaware of this signal. The marines, recognizing the Army troops, did not fire; the soldiers, not seeing any signal, did. Seven marines were wounded before the Marine company commander, Capt Francis L. Fagan, stopped the action by running down the trail to the Army troops and waving his helmet. Only through this mishap was contact between the two divisions at last re-established.[65]

Even so, it was tenuous and short-lived. The main body of the 9th Marines had picked up the advance again at 0700 that morning and by now was well ahead of the point of contact; there was thus no tie-in of the front lines of Army and Marine units. The 1st Battalion, 307th Infantry, had passed through the 2d by about 0900 and continued to move forward unopposed. Heavy undergrowth, however, blocked the way as the battalion moved very slowly up the western slopes of Mount Barrigada. At 1230 the 1st Battalion was still slightly to the left and rear of the 3d, and not yet in contact with it. On the regimental left contact with the marines was again lost as the assault troops of both services pushed on past the roadblock on Finegayan road. General Geiger therefore

ordered the 3d Marine Division to halt its advance until the 77th Division could straighten its lines and close the gap. He so informed General Bruce, who in turn passed the word on to the 307th Infantry. Shortly after 1245 the 1st Battalion was abreast of the 3d, and the 307th was ready to take up the attack.[66]

Even before receiving General Geiger's prodding message, General Bruce ordered the regiment to drive forward to a trail, roughly paralleling and just short of the O-3 line, which ran generally east out of Finegayan. The division commander suggested that the advance be made in one or two columns per battalion for the drive through the jungle, with the regiment reorganizing along the trail, where it would dig in for the night. A Marine patrol would make contact with the 1st Battalion on the regimental left at a point on the trail about 1,100 yards southeast of Finegayan.[67]

About 1300, as the 307th Infantry prepared to attack, the regiment was a little more than 1,000 yards short of its objective line. With hopes that this attack would be successful, General Geiger directed the 3d Marine Division to continue on to the O-3 line if the left of the 77th Division moved up. It was the hope of the III Amphibious Corps commander to tie down his entire front along the O-3 line that night.[68]

---

[65] 77th Inf Div G-3 Jnl, 4 Aug 44; 77th Inf Div G-3 Rpt 12, 5 Aug 44; Guam, 77th Div (MS), p. 170; 77th Inf Div Rpt, p. 5; 307th RCT S-1/S-4 and S-2/S-3 Jnls, 4 Aug 44; 77th Inf Div Arty S-3 Jnl, 4 Aug 44, Entry 21; Lodge, Guam, pp. 136, 141; 3d Marine Div D-3 Jnl, Entries 17, 21, 59; 706th Tk Bn Opn Rpt, Guam, p. 7.

[66] III Phib Corps G-3 Jnl, 4 Aug 44, Entries of 1222, 1225, 1229; 77th Inf Div G-3 Jnl, 4 Aug 44, Entries 35, 44; 307th RCT S-1/S-4 and S-2/S-3 Jnls, 4 Aug 44, passim; 307th RCT Rpt, p. 4; 3d Marine Div D-3 Jnl, 4 Aug 44, Entries 5, 21, 26, 59; 77th Inf Div Artys S-3 Jnl Worksheet, 3-4 Aug 44, Entry 17.

[67] 77th Inf Div G-3 Jnl, 4 Aug 44, Msg 39; 307th RCT S-2/S-3 Jnl, 1250 and 1252, 4 Aug 44; 307th RCT Rpt, p. 4.

[68] III Amph Corps G-3 Jnl, 1330, 1340, 4 Aug 44; 3d Marine Div D-3 Jnl, Msg 29, 4 Aug 44; 77th Inf Div G-3 Jnl, 4 Aug 44, Msg 47.

During the afternoon the 307th Infantry moved slowly toward its objective. Crossing the line of departure sometime between 1300 and 1400, the regiment moved in columns through the thick jungle against scattered, light opposition. Contact between the two battalions was maintained mostly by radio, although occasional openings in the heavy undergrowth permitted visual contact from time to time. Shortly after 1600, men of the 3d Battalion hit the trail that General Bruce had designated as their objective, and within an hour or so the entire battalion was on it. The 1st Battalion, to the left, was a little slower in coming up, the jungle in its sector being extremely heavy. Medium tanks of the 1st Platoon, C Company, 706th Tank Battalion, strained their engines to knock down trees and break trails through the thick vegetation. By 1800 at the latest, however, the 1st Battalion appears to have been in position.

As usual, there was the question of contact with the marines on the left, and as usual there was no contact. Both the 9th Marines and the 1st Battalion, 307th Infantry, sent patrols along the trail, the marines pushing southeast from and the soldiers northwest toward Finegayan. The jungle was thick and enemy elements engaging the American patrols prevented free movement. As dusk settled on the battlefield, the soldiers and marines, in radio contact with each other, decided to postpone further attempts to make physical contact until the next morning.

Though not in contact with the marines, the 307th Infantry had gained its objective, the trail just below the O-3 line. About 1800 the 3d Battalion was a little too far to the right of the 1st Battalion and out of contact with it, except by radio. By dark, however, the 3d Battalion had extended to its left and made contact with the 1st Battalion.[69]

On the right of the 77th Division, meanwhile, the 305th Infantry moved up to and, indeed, beyond the O-3 line in its zone. Unhampered by problems of contact or of straightening its line, the regiment was opposed only by the difficult terrain and scattered enemy resistance. Attacking at 0700 on the heels of a five-minute artillery preparation, the 305th Infantry made its main effort on the left with its 1st Battalion advancing on a narrow front. On the right, the 2d Battalion moved over a wider area, and patrols covered the 1,000-yard slope of the bluff between the regimental right and the sea. The mission of the 305th Infantry was to seize a strong position on its left on the O-3 line and push on toward the O-4 line so as to allow the 306th Infantry to slip across the front of the 307th Infantry on the left of the division line.

Moving slowly through the thick jungle with tanks and bulldozers clearing the way, Colonel Tanzola's regiment advanced in a column of companies within each battalion. Resistance during the morning was negligible, the biggest problem was to find the way through the jungle. Maps were completely useless when it came to showing trails and roads, and the paths that the Americans followed twisted and turned, branched and forked, stopped dead and started up again with amazing frequency and inconsistency. Perhaps as much time was taken in choosing a route as in following it, and when the men had

[69] 307th RCT Rpt, p. 4; 307th RCT S-1/S-4 and S-2/S-3 Jnls, 4 Aug 44; Guam, 77th Div (MS), p. 169; 706th Tk Bn Opn Rpt Guam, p. 7; 77th Inf Div G-3 Jnl, 4 Aug 44; 3d Marine Div D-3 Jnl, 4 Aug 44, Entries 44, 52, 54.

to push cross country more tanks with dozer blades and more bulldozers had to be called on. Moreover, frequent patrolling on cross trails was necessary in order to maintain contact between nearby units. Not much progress had been made by noon, and by 1300 the regiment had barely pulled abreast of Mount Barrigada's summit.

Shortly thereafter tanks and infantry leading the 1st Battalion advance were halted by dense undergrowth at a bend in the trail they were following. While stopped, one of the men of the point suddenly spotted a small party of Japanese and opened fire. The men in front formed a skirmish line to fight off the enemy at ranges so close that the Japanese, well concealed in the thick woods, could easily reach them with grenades. While the advance squads were so engaged, the remainder of the lead company, Company C, with tanks to beat a path through the undergrowth, circled the enemy position, and fell upon it from the rear. Thus outmaneuvered, the Japanese left some of their weapons and many supplies and hastily retreated. They had been cooking when the Americans surprised them, and when the 1st Battalion moved into the area the food was still warm. The 1st Battalion then picked up the advance again.

During this action the 2d Battalion on the regimental right had continued to push ahead almost unopposed and by 1600 was just short of the O–3 line. As the advance continued, Adair's men shifted more and more to the left because that was where the emphasis of the 305th Infantry attack lay and because the terrain and vegetation forced them that way. By late afternoon the 2d Battalion had moved in front of the 1st to cross the O–3 line. When, about

1800, the two battalions dug in for the evening, the 1st was on the O–3 line on the regimental left and tied in with the 307th Infantry, and the 2d Battalion was about 1,250 yards ahead—one third of the way to the O–4 line. The reserve 3d Battalion was on the southeast slopes of Mount Barrigada, perhaps a mile behind the 1st. Patrols covered the area from the regimental right flank to the sea.[70]

By the night of 4 August the 77th Division had reached the O–3 line and, on the right of the 305th Infantry, had pushed a battalion well forward of the line. The 306th Infantry, under Lt. Col. Aubrey D. Smith, remained in reserve just below Barrigada, conducting reconnaissance and laying plans for its move the next morning to replace the 307th Infantry on the division left.[71] Casualties in the two attacking regiments on 4 August were, for the 305th Infantry, four killed and thirteen wounded, and for the 307th Infantry, nine killed, seventeen wounded, and one missing. The 305th Infantry claimed fifty-nine enemy killed, and the 307th Infantry claimed none at all.

The advance of the 77th Division from the O–2 to the O–3 line had taken three days and had cost about two hundred casualties, of which slightly more than fifty were fatal. It had been an advance against two enemies, the Japanese and the jungle, and it would be difficult to say which of the two had been the more effective in

[70] 77th Inf Div G–3 Jnl, 4 Aug 44; 77th Inf Div Arty S–3 Jnl, 3–4 Aug 44, Entries 34, 53, 57, 79, and 4–5 Aug 44, Entry 8, and Jnl Worksheet, 4–5 Aug, Entry 2; 305th RCT S–3 Jnl File (KC or AG), 5 Aug 44, Entry 378 (overlay showing position as of 0800, 5 Aug); 77th Inf Div G–3 Rpt 12, 5 Aug 44; AFAS, *Guam*, pp. 105–06; 77th Inf Div Rpt, p. 5; Ltr, Landrum to Gen A. C. Smith, 27 Apr 55, Incl, OCMH.
[71] 306th RCT Unit Rpt 13, 5 Aug 44.

slowing the American drive. On the first day the Japanese themselves were the more successful in frustrating the 77th Division attack, although the jungle terrain contributed to the mix-up on the American left. On the following two days it was definitely the thick, heavy undergrowth that thwarted progress. In places the jungle was almost trackless; the few existing trails led nowhere and only served to confuse the troops. The Japanese proved only slightly more than a nuisance, their main achievement being to prevent soldiers and marines from regaining contact with each other, and here of course the almost impenetrable jungle must be given almost equal credit.

The denseness of the Guamanian vegetation, inadequate maps, and aerial photographs obscured by cloud cover, all combined to make the location of individual units a nightmare. Unit commanders rarely knew exactly where they were, and the reports they sent back to higher echelons could not be relied on. This not only hampered attempts to maintain contact between units, but sometimes also resulted in American artillery fire falling on friendly troops. Consequently, even when Japanese shelling hit 77th Division positions the men often refused to believe it was not American fire. General Bruce had to remind his troops that the enemy had heavy-caliber weapons and that the Japanese frequently masked the sound of their own artillery by firing at the same time that the American guns were fired. He warned the infantry regiments to "stop accusing our own artillery of firing on [our] own troops until the 'facts are known.' " [72]

To add to the disagreeableness of the heavy jungle and of the chance of friendly shells hitting them, the men of the 77th Division were faced with other discomforts. This was the rainy season on Guam. Intermittent drizzles, or heavy, drenching showers, fell regularly. When it was not raining, the blazing heat of the tropical sun in the steaming, insect-infested jungle bathed the men in their own perspiration. At night lower temperatures and foxholes filled with water chilled the same troops who had sweated during the day. Flies and mosquitoes tormented them with pestiferous malevolence. One veteran of the campaign later recalled there were "billions of flies—dead Japanese and animals all over —with inevitable results, something new on Guam." Even the frogs, which normally kept Guam's fly population under control, couldn't cope with the stepped up proliferation caused by such wholesale human death and decay.[73] All of nature seemed to combine to make life more difficult for the tired soldiers. As they moved north the sticky red mud, which smeared uniforms, equipment, and hands and faces with a thick dirty coating, gave way to hard coral and limestone five inches below the surface and made foxhole digging a major excavation problem. "The hike was tough," commented one American after a particularly trying day, "the heat terrific, the insects maddening and the digging backbreaking." To add to his troubles he was soon taken under fire by an enemy rifleman who had infiltrated the American lines after dark.[74] There were

---

[72] 77th Div G-3 Jnl File, 4 Aug 44, Msg 16. This general discussion of difficulties in the advance to the O-3 line is based on AFAS, *Guam*, pp. 102-03.

[73] Ltr, Landrum to Gen A. C. Smith, 27 Apr 55, Incl, OCMH.
[74] Narrative of Pvt Connelly, Co E, 305th Inf, quoted in Guam, 77th Div (MS), p. 175.

few pleasures in the life of an infantryman on Guam.

The Marines: 2–4 August

Nightfall of 2 August saw the 3d Marine Division in full possession of Tiyan field but more rapid progress, which might have been expected in view of the negligible character of enemy resistance, was frustrated by the jungle and by the difficulties of establishing contact with the Army troops on the right. On 3 August the 9th Marines on the right of the two-regiment front flushed a covey of Japanese, estimated to be about platoon size, near Road Junction 177, southwest of Finegayan village. Within half an hour the stronghold was overrun by tanks and infantrymen and 105 dead Japanese were counted. By 1300, after a second brief encounter with a smaller number of the enemy, the road junction was secured, and the marines prepared to spend the night in Finegayan. Any further advance was considered impracticable because firm contact with the Army troops still had not been established.[75]

On 4 August the 21st Marines was fed into the middle of the division line, making it again a three-regiment front with the 9th Marines on the right, 3d on the left. To fill the ever widening gap along the division boundary, General Turnage ordered the 3d Battalion, 21st Marines, and 2d Battalion, 9th Marines, to move over and protect his right flank. In pursuance of these orders, the 2d Battalion, 9th Marines, established a roadblock on the Finegayan –Barrigada road, and it was this position

that was fired on by the patrol sent out by the 77th Division.[76]

Later in the afternoon, when it appeared that the problem of contact was still unresolved, General Turnage ordered the 21st Marines to take over the zone of the 1st Battalion, 9th Marines, and halt about a thousand yards short of the O–3 line. The 1st Battalion, 9th Marines, drew up before a roadblock along the Finegayan–Barrigada road, which the Japanese were still defending with antitank guns, 75-mm. guns, machine guns, and rifles. Meanwhile, on the division left the 3d Marines had made good progress against light resistance and had reached the O–3 line from Naton Beach inland to a point north of Dededo.[77]

During the day, for the fifth time since their arrival on Guam, American troops were molested by their own planes. This time two B–25's opened up on the command post of the 3d Battalion, 21st Marines, and strafed other marines along the Finegayan–Barrigada road.[78]

While the two divisions in the attack had been moving through the jungle against what was left of the main line of enemy resistance, the 1st Provisional Marine Brigade had been assigned the duty of patrolling southern Guam to flush the scattered remnants of enemy soldiers lurking there in the bush. All together, three companies were employed, A of the 22d Marines and A and F of the 4th Marines.

Late on the afternoon of 3 August, General Shepherd was ordered to move the entire brigade (less the 1st Battalion, 22d Marines, the 9th Defense Battalion, and

---

[75] 3d Marine Div D–3 Jnl, 2–3 Aug 44; Lodge, *Guam,* pp. 128–29, 137–40.

[76] See above, pp. 402–03; 2d Bn 9th Marines SAR, Guam, p. 6.

[77] 3d Marine Div D–3 Jnl, 4 Aug 44; Lodge, *Guam,* pp. 140–41.

[78] 3d Marine Div D–3 Jnl, 4 Aug 44.

the 7th Antiaircraft Artillery Automatic Weapons Battalion) to the vicinity of Toto, where it would act as force reserve and prepare to support the final push to the north. The excluded units would be formed into a separate task force with the mission of protecting Geiger's southern flank and, with the help of Guamanian volunteers, would continue the job of capturing or eliminating Japanese stragglers still in the southern part of the island.[79]

As the marines and soldiers of the III Amphibious Corps prepared to launch their final drive to the northern tip of the island, General Obata was engaged in a withdrawal to his final defense line. The Dededo–Barrigada line had crumbled before the American attack—in fact it does not appear that the Japanese had had time to set up anything resembling an organized defensive line there at all. From his new headquarters atop Mount Mataguac, to which he had retreated as early as 31 July, the Commanding General, *31st Army,* now summoned his last feeble strength to pit itself against the American juggernaut as it moved inexorably toward Mount Santa Rosa, Mataguac, and Yigo.[80]

[79] 1st Provisional Marine Brig War Diary, 1 Jul–10 Aug 44, pp. 16–18.

[80] Japanese Language Study 55, Opns in CENPAC. See map in original Japanese version.

CHAPTER XX

Guam Secured

By the evening of 4 August, General Geiger had concluded that the Japanese in northern Guam were falling back on Mount Santa Rosa, which is east of Yigo and a good six and a half miles northeast of Mount Barrigada. To deny the enemy enough time to complete his defenses in this area, Commander, III Amphibious Corps, directed his forces to chase and close with the Japanese as rapidly as possible.[1]

77th Division: 5–6 August

The 77th Division plan for 5 August called for the 306th Infantry to replace the 307th on the division left and the 305th Infantry to continue its push to the northeast, sending at least one battalion to the O–4 line, which crossed the island about a mile south of Yigo. The 307th Infantry was to complete the advance to positions assigned the day before and then go into division reserve until its men were sufficiently rested. (*Map 25*)[2]

On the division right, Colonel Tanzola's 305th Infantry floundered ahead through the heavy jungle, the individual units having little or nor idea of their actual positions. The only means the troops had of

obtaining their approximate positions was by shooting flares and, by prearrangement, having their supporting artillery triangulate on the flares. Then the artillerymen would plot the position of the flares on their maps and radio the information to the infantry. The lost and weary soldiers moved slowly through the dense jungle, following thin, winding trails or hacking their way through the thick vegetation. Only an occasional Japanese was encountered, and the jungle as usual proved the great obstacle to the advance. The two forward battalions, 2d Battalion in front of the 1st by more than 1,000 yards, moved in column through the undergrowth and quickly lost themselves in the vegetation. Unable to see more than a short distance around them, each unit was unaware of its location and could not orient itself on the relatively flat terrain nor find its position on the inadequate maps available. Even regimental headquarters was apparently ignorant of the location of subordinate units, nor could artillery spotter planes locate the troops. Late in the morning the 2d Battalion was reported to have reached G line, an advance of about 1,100 yards, and by the middle of the afternoon the battalion thought it had reached the O–4 line, about 2,000 yards farther ahead. The 1st Battalion was thought to be 1,000 or 2,000 yards behind the 2d. The positions

---

[1] III Phib Corps Rpt Guam, p. 7; 77th Inf Div G–3 Jnl File, 5 Aug 44, Msg 2 (C–3 III Phib Corps to CG 3d Marine Div *et al.*).

[2] 77th Inf Div G–3 Jnl, 4 Aug 44, Msgs 68, 69.

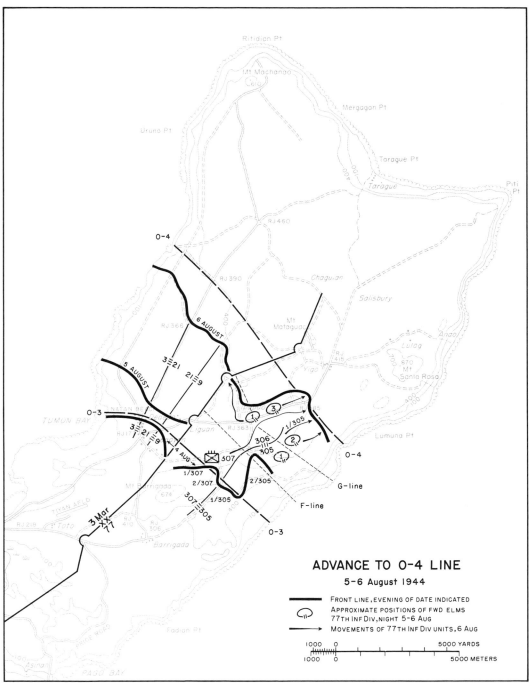

Ritidian Pt

Mt Machanao
610

Mergagan Pt

Uruno Pt

Tarague Pt

Tarague

Piti Pt

400

RJ 460

O-4

RJ 390

Chaguian

Salisbury

400

RJ 366

6 AUGUST

Mt Mataguac

Anao

Lulog

670
Mt
Santa Rosa

3≡21

21≡9

5 AUGUST

RJ
415

Yigo

O-3

TUMON BAY

NATAN BE

Iguan

RJ 363

①

③

1/305

306
ㅣㅣㅣ
305

②

1/305

306
ㅣㅣㅣ
305

①

Lumuna Pt

3≡1
21≡9

RJ17

4 AUG

×
307

O-4

1/307

2/307

2/305

G-line

Mt Barrigada
674

1/305

F-line

307≡305

3 Mar
××
77

RJ 218

Toto

RJ
410

RJ
306

O-3

Barrigada

Fadian Pt

ADVANCE TO O-4 LINE

5-6 August 1944

——— FRONT LINE, EVENING OF DATE INDICATED

◯ APPROXIMATE POSITIONS OF FWD ELMS
77TH INF DIV, NIGHT 5-6 AUG

——→ MOVEMENTS OF 77TH INF DIV UNITS, 6 AUG

1000 0   5000 YARDS

1000 0   5000 METERS

PAGO BAY

D. Holmes, Jr.

MAP 25

were no more than guesses. Indeed, the 2d Battalion began cutting a trail to the coast on a 90° azimuth in an attempt to make an exact determination of its position. At nightfall the map location of the two battalions was still in doubt. They were somewhere east-northeast of the F line, with the 2d Battalion apparently still in the lead. Regimental headquarters and the 3d Battalion were apparently somewhere along the eastern portion of either the O–3 line or the F line.

Heavy rainfall during the late afternoon and evening of 5 August increased the discomfort of the troops. The downpour stopped around midnight, but the night was still dark and overcast. Shortly before 0200, men of Company A, holding the northern portion of the 1st Battalion perimeter, heard the noise of approaching tanks and infantry. American tanks were reportedly in the neighborhood, and the troops assumed that the force they heard was a friendly one moving back from the 2d Battalion. The men in their foxholes kept careful watch, however, and as the full moon came from behind a cloud the Americans saw revealed in its light two Japanese tanks and an estimated platoon of enemy infantry setting up machine guns.

Company A opened fire at once and silenced the Japanese infantry, but the two tanks drove against the line of the perimeter. One cut to the right off the trail, the other to the left, then both drove into the perimeter away from the trail which the 1st Battalion was astraddle. Firing their weapons as they came, the Japanese tanks broke through the defenders and pushed through the perimeter. Once inside, one of the vehicles stopped and threw a stream of fire around the area while the other drove farther on. A platoon of American

tanks from C Company, 706th Tank Battalion, attached to the 1st Battalion, could not fire for fear of hitting the American infantry.

The enemy infantry outside the battalion perimeter had been killed or drive off, but inside the perimeter the Japanese tanks continued to raise havoc. The tank that circled inside the area probably did the most damage as men struggled to escape from its path or threw ineffective small arms fire at its steel sides. Bazooka men were so excited that they neglected to pull the safety pins in their ammunition. Soon the two tanks rejoined and doubled back to the north again through A Company's perimeter. As they left the area a last defiant rifle shot killed a Japanese soldier who had ridden one of the tanks through the entire action.

Behind them the tanks left a trail of ruin. Equipment was smashed or bullet-riddled; one or two jeeps were badly crushed, and the area was a shambles. All six enlisted men in an artillery observation party were either killed or wounded and the officer observer was injured. Casualties in the 1st Battalion, mainly in Company A, were heavy. A total of forty-six men were wounded, of whom thirty-three had to be evacuated; fifteen were killed. The Japanese tanks escaped unscathed, although the losses among the enemy infantry, caught in the first burst of A Company's fire, were probably high.

On the next morning (6 August) the 305th Infantry continued in its attempt to reach the O–4 line. Its 3d Battalion was kept in force reserve in accordance with corps and division plans for pushing the pursuit to the northeast, but the remaining two battalions were able to drive for the

O–4 line. Neither the 1st nor the 2d Battalion knew its exact position.

The 2d Battalion had found and was following a tiny path near the coast that led into "impenetrable jungle" so thick that "a man cannot even step off a trail without cutting."[3] To avoid following this path, the battalion attempted to work to the northwest, and General Bruce gave his permission for the unit to move out of the regimental zone and into the area of the 306th Infantry, if this proved necessary. As the battalion advanced along a narrow trail in a thin column of companies, the lead scout suddenly came face to face with an enemy soldier. The American sent back a warning to the rest of the column, while simultaneously the Japanese shouted the alert to his own unit, the same tank-infantry force that had the night before attacked the 1st Battalion, 305th Infantry, with such success.

The chance meeting started a fierce fire fight. The initial advantage was with the Japanese, for the two enemy tanks were in hull defilade, their 57-mm. cannon and machine guns covering the trail, while the American infantrymen were strung out along the narrow trail in an exposed position. The advantage was ably exploited by the enemy. His machine gun fire raked the trail while shells burst in the trees and sent punishing fragments into the column of American troops. Company E, the lead unit, hastily deployed on both sides of the trail, but the same rise in ground that gave hull defilade to the enemy armor prevented the Americans from locating the Japanese riflemen supporting the two tanks.

The intense enemy fire brought down a number of Americans. Medics attempted to move forward to aid the wounded, and the supporting platoon of mediums of Company C, 706th Tank Battalion, advanced up the trail to hit the enemy. The lead American tank halted, and riflemen formed a skirmish line on either side of it. Heavy machine guns of H Company were brought up next to the tank, but sweeping Japanese fire put these guns out of action before they could fire more than a few bursts. The enemy fire, especially the tree bursts from which there seemed no defense and no protection, soon began to drive the riflemen back from around the tank. The driver of the Sherman, fearing to be left alone, reversed his course and in so doing almost precipitated a panic in the entire American line. However, the battalion executive officer, Capt. Charles T. Hillman, with the aid of a sergeant from H Company, began to rally the troops. Both men were wounded, Hillman fatally, but by their efforts troops of the 2d Battalion were able to form a line just a few yards behind the first American position.

To the American rear, meanwhile, other soldiers were attempting to put the 81-mm. mortars into operation. Tree bursts and continued enemy machine gun fire made this dangerous and difficult, and the heavy jungle overhead made it equally dangerous to attempt to fire the mortars. One piece finally got into action, however, and began lobbing a steady barrage of shells at the Japanese position.

Once the mortar was in action the enemy was finished. Japanese fire began to slacken and then suddenly ceased. Squads of American infantry that had moved out on flanking maneuvers on either side of

---

[3] 77th Inf Div G–3 Jnl, 6 Aug, Msg 10; Ltr, Landrum to Gen A. C. Smith, 27 Apr 55, Incl, OCMH.

the trail closed in on the enemy position without opposition. They found the two Japanese tanks deserted and three dead Japanese.

Most of the Japanese riflemen of this particular tank-infantry team had apparently been killed during the fight with the 1st Battalion the night before. The tanks and few remaining infantrymen would seem to have been attempting to regain their own lines when they encountered the 2d Battalion. Outnumbered, and eventually outgunned, the Japanese had rendered a good account of themselves in the short battle. Casualties on the American side were not as heavy as might have been expected, for only four Americans were killed, but at least fourteen, possibly as many as thirty, were wounded.

Other than this fight, the daylight hours of 6 August witnessed no serious engagements in the 305th Infantry area. A few scattered Japanese were encountered but, as on the previous day, the main enemy force was still the jungle to the north. Both battalions continued to have difficulty threading their way through the heavy vegetation, and both were still unsure of their exact positions. The 1st Battalion, which did not have to retrace its steps, appears to have done less wandering and to have moved rapidly forward northeast in the left half of the regimental zone. Shortly after noon, advance elements were on the O-4 line and in contact with men of the 3d Battalion, 306th Infantry, on the left. By midafternoon the entire 1st Battalion, 305th Infantry, was on the objective line. The 2d Battalion was also moving forward with a clearer knowledge of its location and by dusk, at the latest, it too was on the O-4 line. Its wanderings had brought it to the right of the regimental sector, and it

dug in on the right (southeast) of the 1st Battalion.

While the 1st and 2d Battalions had been advancing to the O-4 line on 6 August, regimental headquarters and the 3d Battalion, in force reserve, had moved to positions on the F line. An attached platoon of the 77th Reconnaissance Troop continued to patrol the open right flank of the 305th Infantry down to the sea. It discovered evidence of enemy patrols in the area, and in a brief encounter with a small Japanese force in midafternoon killed one soldier. One of the enemy patrols that eluded the American patrol, or perhaps some Japanese stragglers from elsewhere in the jungled 305th Infantry area, got as far as the regimental command post before two were killed and the others driven off.

On 5 and 6 August the 305th Infantry had thrashed its way through the heavy Guam jungle, across poorly mapped and unfamiliar terrain, and against sporadic, but on two occasions punishing, Japanese resistance, to positions along the O-4 line. The regiment suffered nearly a hundred men wounded on the two days, and about twenty-five killed. The regiment estimated that it had killed about a hundred Japanese and had knocked out the two enemy tanks that had invaded the regimental zone of action.[4]

---

[4] This account of the advance of the 305th Infantry on 5-6 August is based on: 77th Inf Div G-3 Jnl, 5-6 Aug 44; 77th Inf Div Rpt, pp. 5-6; 77th Inf Div G-2 Rpts 14-15, 6-7 Aug 44; 77th Inf Div G-3 Rpts 13-14, 6-7 Aug 44; 77th Inf Div G-2 Jnl File, 6-7 Aug 44, passim; 305th RCT Jnl File, 4-11 Aug 44 (AG), Msgs 378, 392, 402, 429, 432; 305th RCT Rpt, p. 3; 77th Inf Div Arty S-3 Jnl and Jnl Worksheets, 4-6 Aug 44, passim; 706th Tk Bn Opn Rpt Guam, p. 9; 77th Inf Div Arty Rpt, p. 10; AFAS, Guam, pp. 111-16; Burns Intervs of 2d Bn and Co H, 305th RCT, pp. 371, 414; 77th Rcn Trp Rpt, p. 2.

To the left, the movement of the 306th Infantry around the right flank and in front of the 307th Infantry was impeded more by the thick vegetation and poor trails and the lack of decent maps than by the Japanese opposition. The maneuver would have been arduous under any circumstances, because of the complicated trail net that involved several 90° turns. It was so difficult to keep track of the units within the regiment that a division artillery liaison plane was called on to spot infantry positions.

Colonel Smith's regiment began its move at 0630 on 5 August in a column of battalions, the 1st in the lead, followed by the 3d. It advanced generally unopposed along a trail from the Barrigada area past the east side of Mount Barrigada. By noon the 1st Battalion, 306th Infantry, had reached the trail running east from Finegayan that had marked the 307th Infantry's objective line the previous day. Moving eastward along the trail, the men reached another trail that led north to a juncture with the coral road that ran from Finegayan east-northeast to Yigo. As the 1st Battalion turned north toward the Finegayan–Yigo road shortly after noon, it began to run into a few scattered enemy riflemen. Lt. Col. Joseph A. Remus' men advanced north along the trail against increasing Japanese opposition, and by the time they reached the Yigo road shortly after 1400 the resistance had become quite strong.

The enemy consisted for the most part of individual riflemen and machine gun positions. The Japanese astride the road itself were driven off without too much difficulty, but these or other enemy soldiers filtered through the jungle and struck the flank of Company A, which was leading the battalion advance. The assault, while thrust home with vigor, was not made in great force, and the Americans were able to drive off the enemy as tanks came up to help complete the job. The entire action along the Yigo road took more than two hours before the enemy was finally destroyed or driven off. Company A had been supported by the battalion's 81-mm. mortars and by a platoon of B Company, 706th Tank Battalion, as well as by the artillery. It had killed nearly a score of Japanese while the company itself had lost one man killed and seven wounded.

It was about 1630 before the 1st Battalion could pick up the advance again. Unable to find Road Junction 363, forward elements pushed west a few hundred yards beyond where their map showed the junction to be and then fell back to night positions at a point about where the battalion had first hit Yigo road. The 3d Battalion, meanwhile, had turned east according to plan when it reached the Yigo road in midafternoon. Encountering scattered light resistance, Colonel Kimbrell's troops were able to move only a few hundred yards east along the road and northeast into the jungle before halting for the night.

The day's advance was not sufficient for the 306th Infantry to make contact with the marines, who were still about 1,000 yards to the west of the 1st Battalion. That night, during a heavy rainfall, the Japanese made several attempts to infiltrate the perimeter, but all were beaten back.[5]

---

[5] 77th Inf Div G–3 Jnl, 5 Aug 44; 306th RCT S–3 Jnl, 5 Aug 44; 77th Inf Div Arty S–3 Jnl, 4–5 Aug 44; 77th Inf Div G–3 Rpt 13, 6 Aug 44; 306th RCT Rpt 14, 6 Aug 44; 306th RCT Opns Rpt, Guam, p. 3; 77th Inf Div G–2 Rpt 14, 6 Aug 44; 306th Inf FO 3, 4 Aug 44, Entry 58 in 77th Inf Div G–3 Jnl File, 4 Aug 44; AFAS, *Guam*.

Shortly after 0700 on 6 August the 306th Infantry, according to orders, pushed off again. The 1st Battalion started west on the Finegayan–Yigo road in search of Road Junction 363 and the trail north. The battalion moved slowly, apparently against light opposition. With the aid of an artillery spotter plane it was able to locate the road junction, which it reached shortly after 0900. The trail to the north led through heavy jungle and was evidently not very wide or clear. The battalion turned north to follow it, sending a patrol of company size farther west along the Finegayan–Yigo road in an attempt to make contact with a Marine patrol pushing east along the road. Slowly northward the soldiers pushed, cutting through the thick vegetation that bordered and overgrew the trail. By about 0930 they had encountered a Japanese force about 150 to 200 yards north of Road Junction 363. Company B, leading the advance, engaged the enemy, taking a few casualties. Tanks and supporting weapons were then brought up to drive the rest of the Japanese off.

Continuing in the same direction, Remus' battalion encountered little or no enemy opposition, but by about 1330, when the troops were still roughly half a mile from the division boundary, the trail gave out. From here on the men had to cut their way through the heavy jungle, packing coral limestone down so that vehicles could follow the advance. By 1700 the battalion had reached the division boundary on G line. When the men dug in for the night their perimeter was but 300 yards from that of the 2d Battalion, 9th Marines, and contact, either visual or by patrol, had been established.

Meanwhile, the company of the 1st Battalion that had continued to push west

along the Finegayan–Yigo road had moved easily against little or no resistance during the morning. By about 1100 the Army patrol had met a similar Marine patrol that had pushed east from Marine lines, thus establishing contact about 400 yards west of Road Junction 363.

While the 1st Battalion was pushing north and west, the 3d Battalion drove east along the Finegayan–Yigo road. Kimbrell's men had moved about 1,000 yards up the road from their morning position on G line when, shortly after 0800, the lead scout of I Company noticed the muzzle of an enemy 47-mm. gun in the bushes ahead of him. The infantry column halted and deployed as quietly as possible while a platoon of Shermans of B Company, 706th Tank Battalion, moved up. The enemy position was well camouflaged and the lead American tank discovered it was facing a Japanese medium tank at about the same time that the enemy vehicle opened fire. The first round flattened a bogie wheel on the American tank, but answering fire from the 75-mm. gun on the Sherman was much more effective. Three rounds set the Japanese tank aflame, and the Sherman's machine guns and a quick rush by the American infantry took care of the enemy soldiers around the Japanese tank. Nearly a score of Japanese were killed with no American losses.

With the enemy ambush thus effectively demolished, the 3d Battalion picked up the advance again. By about 1000 it had reached Road Junction 385, just 400 yards from the O–4 line, and within half an hour the men had crossed the objective line and were reported by an air observer to be only about 1,200 yards from Yigo itself. Since an advance up Yigo road by only the 3d Battalion, 306th Infantry, would have exposed the unit to flank attack and disturbed division plans for the next day, the battalion was called back to the O–4 line. Darkness found the 3d Battalion dug in in its assigned position and in contact with the 305th Infantry to its right (southeast).

Thus, on 6 August, the 306th Infantry completed its mission by gaining the O–4 line and establishing contact with the marines. Moreover, Yigo road was now open as far as the O–4 line. Casualties in the regiment on the 6th were two killed and fourteen wounded, mostly in the 1st Battalion. One additional casualty occurred in midafternoon when Col. Douglas McNair, chief of staff of the 77th Division, was fatally wounded by an enemy rifleman while reconnoitering for a new division command post about 600 yards east of Road Junction 363. McNair had gone forward accompanied by an officer from the Reconnaissance Troop armed with a carbine, a sergeant armed with a BAR, and an escort of two light tanks. The party suddenly came upon a small shack almost concealed in the brush and the men thought they detected movement inside. "Spray it, Sergeant," said the Colonel, and the sergeant peppered the shack. But one shot was fired in retaliation and it caught McNair in the chest. He died almost instantly. One of the tanks then rushed forward and demolished the shack and burned it. In the ruins were the bodies of three Japanese soldiers.[6]

Meanwhile, on 5 August, the 307th Infantry had rested and reorganized. The regiment moved forward only a few hundred yards, and so did not reach the O–3 line. Patrols from the 1st Battalion established contact with the marines at the division boundary on the trail east of Finegayan that had been the regimental objective on 4 August. However, this point of contact was still 2,100 yards behind the 3d Division's right flank, which hung in the air.[7]

The next morning, as planned, the men of the 307th pushed off again to the rear of the 306th, with the intention of giving General Bruce a three-regiment front before nightfall. Moving slowly in a column of battalions, 3d leading with 1st close behind it and 2d bringing up the rear, the 307th Infantry followed the same route that the 306th had taken. The rain of the previous night had left the trail muddy and the men sank ankle-deep into the ooze. The jungle continued to hamper off-trail movement. These two factors, combined with the fact that the 307th Infantry had to wait until all elements of the 306th had passed it, made the going slow.

By noon of the 6th the 307th Infantry had reached the trail junction that gave access to the trail leading north to Yigo road. Shortly thereafter, with all 306th Infantry elements passed, Colonel Manuel's regiment continued its advance, going

[6] 77th Inf Div G–3 Jnl, 6 Aug 44; 306th RCT Jnl, 6 Aug 44; 306th RCT Unit Rpt 15, 7 Aug 44; 306th RCT Opns Rpt, pp. 3–4; AFAS, *Guam*, pp. 109–11; 77th Inf Div G–2 Rpt 14, 6 Aug 44; 706th Tk Bn Rpt, p. 8; Burns Combat Interv of 1st Bn, 306th Inf, p. 535; 3d Marine Div D–3 Jnl, 6 Aug 44, Msgs 30, 33, 66, 67; 77th Inf Div Arty S–3 Jnl, 5–6 Aug 44, Entry 55. The account of the details of Colonel McNair's death

is given in Ltr, Brig Gen Isaac Spalding to Gen A. C. Smith, n.d., Incl, OCMH. McNair's death came but two weeks after his father, Lt. Gen. Lesley J. McNair was accidentally killed by friendly bombers in France.

[7] 307th RCT Rpt, p. 4; 3d Marine Div D–3 Jnl, 5 Aug 44; 77th Inf Div G–3 Jnl, 5 Aug 44; 77th Inf Div G–3 Rpt 13, 6 Aug 44; Overlay Showing Summary of Outstanding Events and Areas Secured by 307th Infantry, in 307th RCT Rpt.

north to Yigo road and then turning east to follow the 3d Battalion, 306th Infantry, along this main route. By midafternoon the lead battalion of the 307th Infantry—the 3d—had reached the O-4 line and had tied in with 306th Infantry troops already there. The other units followed, and by nightfall the 3d Battalion, 307th Infantry, was on the O-4 line between the 306th and 305th Infantry Regiments, with the 2d Battalion and regimental headquarters on the Yigo road 800 yards to the rear and the 1st Battalion on the road another 800 yards farther back.[8] The 77th Division now had three regiments on the line. In conformance with plans already issued for the continuation of the attack, General Bruce could throw his entire division (less 3d Battalion, 305th Infantry, which was in force reserve) into the assault.

3d Marine Division
5–6 August

Meanwhile, on the corps left, the 3d Marine Division, attacking on a three-regiment front, was groping its way through jungle just about as thick as that slowing the progress of the Army troops. On the division left and center the 3d and 21st Marines met no organized resistance on 5 August, but on the right the 9th Marines fought hard to clear the remaining Japanese out of the Finegayan area and open Road Junction 177 to permit supplies to move north toward forward dumps at Dededo.

On the 6th the same general pattern was repeated. The two regiments on the west gained as much as 5,000 yards against only nominal opposition. The 9th Marines, pushing north from Finegayan, succeeded in keeping abreast of the rest of the division, though it continued to meet scattered resistance and had to dispose of 700 Japanese defenders in the Finegayan area in the process.[9]

During this movement General Turnage approached the ever worrisome problem of unit contact in much the same manner as had General Bruce. In view of the tremendous difficulties involved in maintaining continuous physical contact in the nightmarish jungles of northern Guam, Turnage ordered his regimental commanders to advance in column along the trails. Patrols were to fan out 200 yards on either side of the trails to wipe out enemy troops that might possibly be lurking in the underbrush, but physical contact was to be established only at indicated points where lateral roads or cleared spaces made it feasible.[10]

Capture of Mount Santa Rosa
7–8 August

By the close of 6 August the final defensive line that General Obata had tried to set up across northern Guam had been pierced and overrun in so many places that it constituted no line at all. Only isolated pockets of Japanese remained to contest the American advance, and these were without adequate weapons, out of touch with higher headquarters, and often virtually leaderless. The Japanese, like their attackers, were harassed and obstructed by the jungle that surrounded them. As

---

[8] 77th Inf Div G-3 Jnl, 6 Aug 44, Msgs 7, 9, 34, 35, 54, 91; 77th Inf Div Rpt, pp. 5–6; 307th RCT Rpt, p. 4; 3d Marine Div D-3 Jnl, 6 Aug 44, Msg 26.

[9] 3d Marine Div D-3 Jnl, 5–6 Aug 44; Lodge, *Guam*, pp. 141–45.

[10] 3d Marine Div Opns Order 16, 6 Aug 44.

MT. SANTA ROSA, *taken by the 307th Infantry on 8 August.*

Colonel Takeda later reported, "They were obliged to fight in the jungle where it was very hard to cooperate and communicate with each other. Therefore they could not fight satisfactorily to show their whole strength. And as the American armoured troops drove along the highways and trails in jungle to cut off the front line into several pockets, our troops were forced to be isolated."[11] So much for the supposed inherent superiority of the Japanese in jungle warfare.

With less than one third of Guam still remaining in Japanese hands, General Geiger issued orders to complete the destruction of the enemy on the island. These

orders—ready since the morning of 5 August, but not made effective until the afternoon of the 6th—called for an all-out attack on the morning of 7 August. Geiger planned to put almost his entire force into the final assault, holding out only one battalion from each division as force reserve. The 77th Division would make the main effort, seizing Mount Santa Rosa and the northeastern portion of the island. On its left and supporting it, the 3d Marine Division would drive northeast to the sea. Finally, on the far left would come the 1st Marine Provisional Brigade, protecting the 3d Division flank and securing the northernmost tip of the island by patrols. The corps commander stressed the necessity for maintaining contact between units, since the Japanese might well mount a last desperate counterattack to spring the crushing American trap. With the Army troops making the main offensive effort, General Geiger for the first time directed that responsibility for maintaining contact would be from left to right—the 1st Brigade would be responsible for maintaining contact with the 3d Division, and the 3d Division would be charged with keeping touch with the 77th. Warships and aircraft—P–47's and B–26's from Saipan—had been softening up Mount Santa Rosa for several days, and the bombardment, reinforced by corps and division artillery fire, would continue on the day of the attack. The corps assault plan was to go into effect at 0730, 7 August.[12]

The corps plan of attack did not reach General Bruce until the late afternoon of 5 August, but in anticipation the 77th Di-

---

[11] Lt Col H. Takeda, Outline of Japanese Defense Plan, 4 Oct 46.

[12] CG SLF to CG 3d Marine Div *et al.* (III Phib Corps Opn Plan 8–44), 050714 and 061324, Aug 44, both in III Phib Corps Opn Orders; AFAS, *Guam,* pp. 117–18.

vision staff had already worked out a scheme of assault to be put into action once the O-4 line was secured.[13] Distributed and explained to subordinate units shortly before noon of the 5th, the division plan fitted in well with the over-all corps scheme.[14] (*Map 26*)

General Bruce's plan of attack—including modifications worked out up to the morning of 7 August—called for a wheeling maneuver on the part of his division, three regiments in line pivoting on their right. The object of the attack was Mount Santa Rosa, a height of nearly 900 feet, in front of the 77th Division. When the wheeling maneuver was completed, Bruce's regiments would have surrounded the mountain on three sides—south, west, and north—pinning the Japanese defenders against the sea.

On the left of the division attack was the 306th Infantry with an attached company of Shermans of the 706th Tank Battalion. The 306th was to advance along the division's left boundary until it had passed Mount Santa Rosa and then swing east to seize an objective area north of the mountain from the town of Lulog seaward to Anao on the coast. Patrols from this regiment would push northeast above the main body to the coast farther north. Since the 306th Infantry had to cover far more ground than either of the other two regiments, it would advance without regard to contact in order to accomplish its mission. On the right of the 306th was the 307th Infantry. For its action in the fairly open, rolling terrain around Yigo, the regiment had a company of medium tanks attached and the 706th Tank Battalion (less two companies) in support. The 307th would continue to attack up the Finegayan –Yigo road to capture Yigo and then swing east and northeast to block the western side of Mount Santa Rosa. In order to hold these gains and prevent any enemy escape, the 307th was authorized to commit all three of its battalions without maintaining a reserve. On the division right the 305th Infantry (less 3d Battalion in force reserve) had only a short distance to cover in its move to seal the southern approaches to Mount Santa Rosa and support the 307th Infantry. In spite of this advantage the regiment was handicapped by having only two of its battalions in the assault and also in having no tanks attached.

The line of departure for the 77th Division was from 400 yards to a mile in front of the 306th and 307th Infantry positions on the O-4 line, with the shortest distance between the two lines on the left, in front of the 306th. The 305th Infantry, with only a small area to cover, would attack from the O-4 line. The 306th and 307th Regiments would begin the advance to the line of departure at 0730; the 305th would remain in position until ordered forward. The 1st Battalion, 306th Infantry, would start for the line of departure half an hour early, at 0700. This battalion had not reached the O-4 line on 6 August, but had halted on the G line, a good 2,000 yards from the O-4 line. The extra half hour was apparently to enable the 1st Battalion to move abreast of the 3d.

H Hour, the time of the general division attack from the line of departure, was set tentatively by General Bruce at approxi-

---

[13] III Phib Corps G-3 Jnl, 5 Aug 44, Entry 098; 77th Inf Div G-3 Jnl, 5 Aug 44, Entry 60. The 3d Marine Division received the order at the same time. 3d Marine Div D-3 Jnl, 5 Aug 44, Addendum to Jnl, Entry 2A.

[14] 77th Inf Div G-3 Jnl, 5 Aug 44, Entry 31; 77th Inf Div Overlay Showing Tentative Future Opns, 5 Aug 44, in 77th Inf Div Overlays.

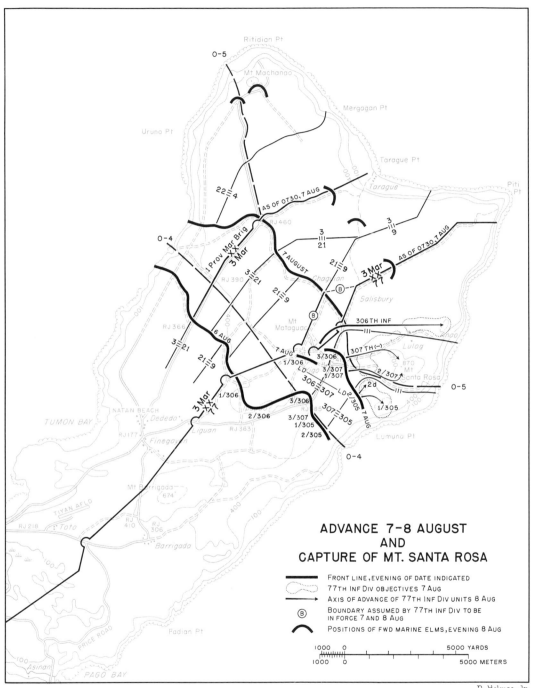

ADVANCE 7-8 AUGUST
AND
CAPTURE OF MT. SANTA ROSA

▬▬▬▬	FRONT LINE, EVENING OF DATE INDICATED
◌◌◌	77TH INF DIV OBJECTIVES 7 AUG
───▶	AXIS OF ADVANCE OF 77TH INF DIV UNITS 8 AUG
Ⓑ	BOUNDARY ASSUMED BY 77TH INF DIV TO BE IN FORCE 7 AND 8 AUG
◖	POSITIONS OF FWD MARINE ELMS, EVENING 8 AUG

1000   0   5000 YARDS
1000   0   5000 METERS

D. Holmes, Jr.

MAP 26

mately 1200. The 77th Division assault was to be supported by a tremendously heavy air, artillery, and naval gunfire preparation. For an hour, beginning at 0900, P–47's and B–26's would bomb and strafe Mount Santa Rosa. Twenty minutes before H Hour division artillery reinforced by corps artillery would begin a barrage lasting until the attack began. All four battalions of division artillery were to fire a round per gun per minute, all concentrations to fall in the zone of action of the 306th and 307th Infantry Regiments. At the same time that the artillery preparation began, a one-hour naval bombardment of the Mount Santa Rosa area would start, with the warships firing from south to north and moving their fire beyond the area immediately in front of the infantry by H Hour. After H Hour division artillery, supported by the corps weapons, was available on call. The immense air, artillery, and naval gunfire preparation, it was hoped, would leave the Japanese defending the Mount Santa Rosa area too weakened or dazed to put up more than a feeble resistance against the 77th Division attack.[15]

The turning maneuver planned for the 77th Division was a difficult one to carry out. Its execution was made even harder by a misunderstanding on the part of Bruce's staff as to the precise location of the boundary between the Army and Marine divisions. Tentative division plans worked out before the receipt of General Geiger's orders used the operational boundaries between the 3d and 77th Divisions prescribed by corps on 2 August. The boundary then established ran along a road that branched off to the northeast from the main Finegayan–Yigo road at Liguan, passed Mount Mataguac, and ended at the junction with Yigo–Chaguian road about 2,000 yards north of the mountain. Since corps had not projected the boundary beyond the end of Liguan road, the 77th Division staff on its own initiative extended the boundary line to the northeast—from the road junction cross-country to Salisbury and thence along the Salisbury–Piti Point Road to the coast.[16] Unless corps called for a change in operational boundaries, this line would stand. Unfortunately for those concerned, a boundary change is precisely what was directed by General Geiger.

The new operational boundary established by corps on 5 August was, beyond the town of Salisbury, exactly as 77th Division planners had assumed: along the road running from that town to the coast. While the Army was responsible for the road, it was to be used jointly by soldiers and marines. In an apparent effort to make as much of this road as possible available to the 3d Division, however, General Geiger shifted the interdivisional boundary below Salisbury eastward to a line that ran from a crossroads southwest of Mount Mataguac to a point on Yigo–Salisbury road midway between the two towns, and from there along the road to Salisbury. Thus a large diamond-shaped area, about two miles long, between Mount Mataguac

[15] 77th Inf Div Overlay Showing Tentative Future Opns, 5 Aug 44, 77th Inf Div Opns Overlay for 7 Aug, dated 6 Aug 44, and 77th Inf Div FO 6, 061900 Aug 44, all in 77th Inf Div Overlays; 77th Inf Div Rpt, p. 6; CG 77th Inf Div, Notes on Plans for 7 Aug, Entry 63 in 77th Inf Div G–3 Jnl File, 6 Aug 44; 77th Inf Div G–3 Jnl, Entries 61, 85, and 86 on 6 Aug, and 2 on 7 Aug 44.

[16] CG SLF to 3d Marine Div et al., 020935 Aug 44, in III Phib Corps Opns Orders; 77th Inf Div Overlay Showing Tentative Future Opns, 5 Aug 44, in 77th Inf Div Overlays.

and Salisbury was transferred from the 77th Division to the 3d Marine Division.

That a new boundary had been drawn was made explicit in the III Amphibious Corps order that the 77th Division received on the afternoon of 5 August. "Boundary," read the order, "between 77th and 3d Mar Div changes . . . ," and then proceeded to describe the new boundary. The boundary was described again further on in the order when a reference was made to use of the Salisbury road. While no overlay accompanied the order, the map co-ordinates, repeated twice, and the use of the word "change" made it quite clear that a new boundary had been established.[17]

Nevertheless, when the 77th Division field order and final overlay for the 7 August attack were drawn up on the afternoon of the 6th, the original boundary line was incorporated in both the order and the overlay.[18] The zone of action of the 306th Infantry, making its sweep around Mount Santa Rosa on the division left, was therefore partially within the 3d Marine Division's operational area.

Promptly at 0700 on 7 August the 1st Battalion, 306th Infantry, began advancing along the Liguan trail toward the line of departure. At 0730 the 3d Battalion, on its right, began to advance cross-country, the 2d Battalion remaining in its reserve position.[19] In the 307th zone, in the center of the division, that regiment's 3d Battalion led the way along the Yigo road on

schedule, with the 1st and 2d Battalions prepared to follow.[20] The two battalions of the 305th Infantry on the O–4 line stood by in position.[21]

By 0900 or a few minutes thereafter, just as American aircraft began pummeling Mount Santa Rosa, the 1st Battalion, 306th Infantry, and the 3d Battalion, 307th, had reached the line of departure. The 3d Battalion, 306th Infantry, advancing overland between them, did not reach the line until 1000.[22] The 305th Infantry, meanwhile, had asked and received permission at 0905 to begin moving its 2d Battalion forward from the O–4 line. Ten minutes later, with a bulldozer cutting the way through the thick jungle, the 2d Battalion moved out to start the regimental advance.[23]

The first resistance of the day was encountered by the 3d Battalion, 307th Infantry, as it moved up Yigo road just before it reached the line of departure. As the battalion began fanning out to occupy a line about 800 to 1,000 yards below Yigo, it received enemy rifle and machine gun fire from concealed positions in the woods ahead. About 0840 the first Japanese fire struck Capt. William B. Cooper's Company I, which was leading the advance. In the face of the enemy fire, it was almost 0930 before I Company could deploy along the line and begin to advance against the Japanese positions. The other companies had bunched up on the road, making it dif-

---

[17] CG SLF to CG 3d Marine Div *et al.* (III Phib Corps Opns Plan 8–44), 050714 Aug 44, in III Phib Corps Opns Orders.

[18] 77th Inf Div FO 6, 061900 Aug 44, and 77th Inf Div Opns Overlay for 7 Aug, dated 6 Aug 44, both in 77th Inf Div Overlays.

[19] 306th RCT Jnl, 7 Aug 44, Entry 2; 306th RCT Unit Rpt 16, 8 Aug 44.

[20] 307th RCT S–1/S–4 and S–2/S–3 Jnls, 7 Aug 44, *passim;* see also 307th Inf FO 6 and Annex to FO 6 (overlays showing scheme of maneuver), in 307th RCT Rpt.

[21] 305th RCT Jnl File, 7 Aug 44, Msg 430.

[22] 306th RCT Jnl, 7 Aug 44, Entries 8 and 11; 307th RCT S–2/S–3 Jnl, entry at 0912, and S–1/S–4 Jnl, entry at 0910; 77th Inf Div Rpt, p. 6.

[23] 77th Inf Div G–3 Jnl, 7 Aug 44, Entry 31.

ficult for the entire battalion to deploy and
for the attached tanks of Company A,
706th Tank Battalion, to move forward.
Nevertheless, once I Company had formed,
it began to push back the enemy. By
shortly after 1000 some of the Japanese
had been killed and the rest were falling
back. The Americans had suffered eleven
casualties, but the 2d Battalion was on the
line and ready to push off.[24]

With all his attack battalions on the line
of departure and the other units moving
forward behind them, General Bruce was
able to set H Hour definitely at 1200. Division units and corps headquarters were
notified accordingly.[25]

The artillery preparation began promptly
at 1138—General Bruce had advanced the
time by two minutes[26]—with the three
105-mm. howitzer battalions of division artillery opening fire on targets in front of
the 306th and 307th Infantry Regiments.
At 1148 the shelling stopped for two minutes and then at 1150 all four battalions
of division artillery and the three 155-mm.
battalions of corps artillery delivered a
heavy ten-minute preparation.[27] To add to
the weight of metal falling on enemy
positions on the forward slope and atop
Mount Santa Rosa, naval gunfire support
vessels were also sending their big shells
crashing inland. Meanwhile, the infantry
and tanks made ready to attack.

The major opposition to the day's advance of the 77th Division was to come in
the center of the 307th Infantry zone of
operations. Here, a tank-infantry assault
had been planned to take advantage of the
relatively open terrain around Yigo. The
706th Tank Battalion (less Companies A
and B) was to spearhead this assault as
soon as the artillery fire lifted at 1200. At
that time the light tanks of Company D
were to push up the Yigo road as fast as
possible and enter the town with C Company's mediums right behind them. The
infantry was to act in close support of the
armor, with the medium tanks of Company
A, attached to the 307th, providing general
support. Once Yigo was seized, the two
companies of the 706th Tank Battalion
were to occupy the high ground east-
northeast of the town, thus opening the
way for the 307th Infantry to swing
against the western slopes of Mount Santa
Rosa.[28]

Co-ordination between the 706th Tank
Battalion and the 307th Infantry was something less than satisfactory. While the plan
for the use of the tanks had been worked
out late on 6 August, it was then too early
to set the time of H Hour. At 0700 on 7
August the tank battalion (less A and B
Companies) began moving from its assembly area to positions behind the 307th
Infantry, prepared to move into the line
as soon as H Hour was announced. At
1040 General Bruce sent word to the 706th
that H Hour would be at noon, but the
message never reached Colonel Stokes, the
tank commander. Not until 1145 did
Stokes get word to report to the 307th
Infantry command post and not until his
arrival, nearly ten minutes later, did he

[24] 307th RCT S-2/S-3 and S-1/S-4 Jnls,
passim; AFAS, *Guam,* pp. 120-21; 77th Inf Div
G-2 Rpt 15, 7 Aug 44, in 77th Inf Div G-2 Jnl
File, 7-10 Aug 44. There is no breakdown on
American casualties; Japanese casualties are un-
known.

[25] III Phib Corps G-3 Jnl, 7 Aug 44, msg in
at 1010; 77th Inf Div G-3 Jnl, 7 Aug 44, Entry
17.

[26] 77th Inf Div G-3 Jnl, 7 Aug 44, Entry 26.

[27] 77th Inf Div Arty S-3 Rpt 14, for period
6-7 Aug 44, in 77th Inf Div G-3 Jnl File, 9 Aug
44, Msg 42; III Phib Corps Arty SAR, p. 9.

[28] AFAS, *Guam,* p. 121.

learn the attack was scheduled to commence at 1200.[29]

With only a few minutes to go before H Hour, the two companies of tanks scheduled to spearhead the attack were still some distance behind the line of departure. At 1155 Stokes radioed Company D, which was to have led the drive, to move up and carry out the plan of action.[30] Meanwhile, the officers of the 3d Battalion, 307th Infantry, poised on the line of departure to follow the tanks, had been growing anxious about the failure of the armor to appear. The battalion commander had orders to follow closely on the heels of the artillery. At 1156 the barrage was falling at a good distance from the line of departure and the infantry commander informed the regimental command post that he was about to move out. Without the tanks, then, at H Hour minus 3 minutes the 3d Battalion crossed the line of departure and began advancing on Yigo.[31]

As the light tanks of Company D pushed hastily forward on Yigo road, they found their way blocked by the confusion of men and vehicles before them. Unable to move through the thick jungle on either side of the road, the tanks had to make their way between soldiers, vehicles, and the company of medium tanks attached to the 307th Infantry. It was thus 1207 before D Company reached the rear of the 3d Battalion, and nearly 1220 before the tanks could pass through the leading infantry and begin to fan out in the more open terrain. The advance by this time had covered about 250 yards from the line of departure without resistance. However, less than 500 yards from the edge of Yigo, the Americans began to meet rifle fire from enemy troops driven south from the town by the volume of the preattack artillery preparation.[32]

Japanese small arms fire increased in intensity as the light tanks of D Company echeloned to the right, and the mediums of C Company moved up along the road behind them. The light tanks overran or pushed by several dugouts and pillboxes, leaving them for the infantry to clean out. Just short of the southern edge of Yigo, D Company swept across a slight rise of ground east of the road and began to receive fire of a heavier caliber from enemy positions concealed in the woods along and west of the road. It was apparent that the Japanese here had weapons too heavy for the light tanks, and a call went back for the mediums. Just as Company C reached the area, the Japanese succeeded in stopping the light tank farthest to the left. A few minutes later a second light tank was knocked out.

The enemy troops were well concealed in the woods to the left, and it was not until its mediums began to receive fire that C Company could determine the location of the Japanese positions. The mediums swung to put fire on the Japanese before following D Company on toward Yigo, but two of C Company's tanks were also knocked out by enemy fire. As the two companies of the 706th began to push into the shell-flattened town, the 3d Battalion, 307th Infantry, attacked the Japanese positions along and west of the road. The infantrymen advanced cautiously into the woods, using rifles, machine guns, and

[29] Burns, Interv with Col Stokes, p. 192; 77th Inf Div G–3 Jnl, 7 Aug 44, Msg 18.

[30] Burns, Interv with Stokes, p. 193.

[31] 307th RCT S–2/S–3 and S–1/S–4 Jnls, 7 Aug 44, msgs in 1112–1206, *passim;* 77th Inf Div G–3 Jnl, 7 Aug 44, Entry 35.

[32] 307th RCT S–1/S–4 Jnl, 7 Aug 44, msgs in at 1207, 1222; 77th Inf Div G–3 Jnl, 7 Aug 44, Entries 35, 41; AFAS, *Guam,* p. 122.

grenades. It was slow work, and at 1330 the troops still had not cleaned out the area. The tanks, with their mission to push through Yigo, had reorganized and were entering the town in force. The attached medium tanks of the 307th were still back with the rest of the regiment, and the task of destroying the enemy defenses was left to Major Lovell's battalion.

Suddenly, unexpected assistance appeared from the west. The 3d Battalion, 306th Infantry, advancing on the west flank of the 307th had heard the firing below Yigo, and Colonel Kimbrell, battalion commander, had taken a platoon of K Company to investigate. The Japanese had neglected to protect their rear and the K Company platoon caught them completely unawares, killing those enemy troops that had not been disposed of by the 3d Battalion, 307th. Other elements of K Company, 306th Infantry, struck enemy positions in the woods farther north, and the entire area south of Yigo was soon cleared.

The Japanese position had been a strong one, built around two light tanks with a 37-mm. or 47-mm. antitank gun between them. In addition, the enemy had been equipped with two 20-mm. antitank rifles and six light and two heavy machine guns. No report on Japanese casualties is available, but undoubtedly they were heavy. There were probably a score of casualties in the 3d Battalion,[33] while the 706th Tank Battalion reported two killed, ten wounded, and one man missing.

By 1408 the leading elements of the 3d Battalion, 307th Infantry, were at the southern edge of Yigo, while the two companies of the 706th Tank Battalion had reached Road Junction 415, some 250 yards farther up the road at the northern edge of Yigo. A quarter of an hour later the tanks reported Yigo clear of Japanese, and the 307th Infantry commander ordered his 3d Battalion to press through the town. By 1450 Yigo was secured, the 3d Battalion had reached Road Junction 415, and the two tank companies had moved unopposed up to the high ground east-northeast of the village.

Now that enemy resistance had been broken, Lovell's 3d Battalion, 307th, moved east along the road from Road Junction 415, the men advancing about 1,000 yards during the late afternoon. The 1st Battalion, ordered up a few hours earlier, also moved through Yigo and followed the 3d. The 2d Battalion moved to Yigo, where Major Mackin, battalion commander, set up his command post. In the village were found fifteen abandoned Japanese trucks and other mobile equipment, as well as several ammunition and food dumps, showing that the site had recently been a major part of the Japanese defense scheme.

No Japanese resistance was encountered during the afternoon. However, the 3d Battalion was mistakenly strafed by American planes in midafternoon though, fortunately for the infantrymen, no one was hurt. Nightfall found the 307th Infantry in control of Yigo and a large area to the northeast, east, and southeast.[34]

---

[33] This figure is obtained by subtracting the number of casualties suffered in the morning from the total casualties for the regiment on 7 August. No breakdown can be made.

[34] 307th RCT S–1/S–4 and S–2/S–3 Jnls, 7 Aug 44; 77th Inf Div G–3 Jnl, 7 Aug 44; 77th Inf Div Rpt, p. 6; 307th RCT Rpt, p. 4; AFAS, *Guam*, pp. 122–25; 77th Inf Div G–3 Rpts 15, 16, 7, 8 Aug 44; 77th Inf Div G–2 Jnl File, 7–10 Aug 44; Msgs, 706th Tk Bn to G–2, and Bomb Disposal Squad to G–2, Nos. 15 and 30, 8 Aug 44, in 77th Inf Div G–2 Jnl File, 7–10 Aug 44; 706th Tk Bn Rpt, p. 9.

BURNING U.S. MEDIUM TANKS *disabled by enemy fire along the road to Yigo.*

While the 307th Infantry fought its way through Yigo on the afternoon of 7 August, the regiments on its flanks were also advancing, although with much less difficulty. The 306th Infantry, to the left, crossed the line of departure on time at noon. With the 3d Battalion on the right, 1st on the left, the regiment advanced against scattered light resistance. Well over a hundred Japanese were claimed killed, while only three Americans were wounded. In its rapid movement up the Yigo road, the 3d Battalion employed a type of tank-infantry tactics peculiarly adapted to the jungles of Guam. To the lead company of infantrymen was assigned a tank platoon. One tank moved through the brush on one side of the jungle trail, a second on the other side, and the remainder followed along the trail about a hundred yards to the rear. The object of this unorthodox formation was to permit the tanks to support each other, protect the lead tanks from mines located on the trail, and widen the trail for the infantrymen who would follow. With each vehicle went four infantrymen on foot to serve as guides, spotters, and protectors. In this manner, the 3d Battalion pushed on through Yigo and then northeast about 900 yards along the Salisbury road. There, it dug in for the night.[35]

The 1st Battalion advanced along the Liguan road to the crossroads southwest of

[35] 306th RCT Rpt, p. 4; 306th RCT Unit Jnl, 7 Aug 44; 77th Inf Div G-2 Rpts 15, 16, 7, 8 Aug 44, in 77th Inf Div G-2 Jnl File, 7-10 Aug 44; 77th Inf Div G-3 Jnl, 7 Aug 44, *passim;* AFAS, *Guam,* p. 110.

Mount Mataguac where the new corps boundary left the trail. Although General Bruce had ordered the 306th Infantry to advance some 600 yards farther up the Liguan trail, the 1st Battalion during the afternoon ran into resistance from about forty Japanese with two machine guns just below the crossroads. With the help of the attached Company B, 706th Tank Battalion, the battalion eliminated the opposition but did not advance much farther. Had the 1st Battalion continued, it would have entered what was actually Marine territory under the new boundaries. This might have caused difficulties, since the 9th Marines had moved past the crossroads along and east of the Liguan trail, in an area that the 77th Division still thought to be within the Army zone of operations. However, since the 1st Battalion, 306th Infantry, had not yet advanced beyond the point of the boundary change, there had been no trouble so far.[36]

On the division right the 305th Infantry (less the 3d Battalion) also advanced unopposed. With bulldozers blazing a trail through the thick jungle, the 2d Battalion covered 1800 yards during the day and by nightfall was digging in about a mile northwest of Lumuna Point. The 1st Battalion, meanwhile, remained with regimental headquarters on the O-4 line, preparing to pick up the advance on 8 August.

No opposition impeded the movement of the 2d Battalion, 305th Infantry, on 7 August. The only untoward incident of the day occurred around 1500 when American aircraft hitting Mount Santa Rosa mistakenly dropped a bomb on F Company, causing some casualties. Presumably, these were the same planes that strafed the 3d Battalion, 307th Infantry, about the same time.[37]

The night of 7–8 August found the 77th Division dug in in positions from which it could launch a final attack on Mount Santa Rosa the next day. Despite the day's successes, there was some apprehension among the Americans as to possible Japanese moves during the night. As early as noon on 7 August, General Bruce had requested permission to move the 3d Battalion, 305th Infantry, then in corps reserve, to Road Junction 415 at Yigo in midafternoon in order to get set for any enemy counterattack. A counterblow at Yigo, either down the Salisbury road or from Mount Santa Rosa, would almost certainly be initially aimed at this important junction. Bruce's request was denied, but that night General Geiger informed subordinate units that he was expecting a counterattack in force and that the 3d Bat-

---

[36] The 77th Division reported to corps that the advance here had actually carried to the point where Bruce had ordered it, that is, 600 yards beyond the crossroads, but the overwhelming weight of evidence indicates that this report was incorrect. 306th RCT Unit Jnl, 7 Aug 44; 77th Inf Div G-3 Jnl, 7 Aug 44, *passim*; 77th Inf Div G-2 Rpts 15, 16, 7, 8 Aug 44, in 77th Inf Div G-2 Jnl File, 7-10 Aug 44; 3d Marine Div D-3 Jnl, 7 Aug 44, *passim*; 306th RCT Rpt, p. 4; 706th Tk Bn Rpt, p. 9.

[37] Regimental casualties for the day, half a dozen killed and more than a score wounded, presumably were taken for the most part by the 3d Battalion, which, in corps reserve, was engaged in flushing out the area around the division command post where Colonel McNair had been hit on 6 August. In this mission the battalion encountered and engaged Japanese estimated to be a company in strength. 77th Inf Div G-3 Jnl, 7 Aug 44, Entries 33, 71; 305th RCT Rpt, p. 3, and atched bn rpts; 77th Inf Div G-2 Rpts 15, 16, 7, 8 Aug 44, in 77th Inf Div G-2 Jnl File, 7-10 Aug 44; 305th RCT Overlay Showing Situation as of 1400, 7 Aug 44, and Overlay Showing Situation as of 0800, 8 Aug 44, Entries 437 and 443, in 305th RCT Jnl File, 4-11 Aug 44.

talion, 305th Infantry, and the Marine battalion in reserve with it were on call.[38]

Fortunately for the Americans, the Japanese mounted no major attacks during the night. Possibly the speed of the American advance during the day, combined with the heavy artillery bombardment that continued as harassing fire during the night, prevented a major enemy counterblow. Whatever the reason, the Japanese made only a few local counterattacks and attempts to infiltrate during the night.[39] The first of these came shortly before 1920 when a small group of the enemy took advantage of the rapidly gathering dusk between sunset and moonrise to attempt to infiltrate the 1st Battalion, 307th Infantry, east of Yigo. Alert infantrymen spotted the Japanese, however, and nine of the enemy were killed trying to penetrate the position.[40]

At 0230 corps sent another warning of a possible major Japanese counterattack to the 77th Division.[41] Within an hour the biggest enemy attack of the night struck the 3d Battalion, 306th Infantry. In the exposed position on the Salisbury road north of Yigo, these men had already been the target of two small enemy probing attacks. The first had been beaten off about the time of the attack on the 1st Battalion,

307th Infantry; the second had come around midnight and, in the bright moonlight, had been repulsed. The final attack against the 3d Battalion began between 0300 and 0330.

This time, the enemy force consisted of three medium tanks and riflemen estimated to be of platoon strength. First came the Japanese tanks, firing their machine guns and cannon into the battalion perimeter. The defenders were safe in their slit trenches from the flat-trajectory machine gun fire, but the high-explosive cannon shells burst in the trees above, raining fragments down on the Americans. Attempts to knock out the tanks with bazookas and flame throwers were aborted by fire from the accompanying Japanese infantry. Two machine gunners finally got the first tank by waiting until it was almost upon them and then closing in with their light machine gun to fire into the tank through an aperture. They burnt out the barrel of their gun, but they also killed all the Japanese in the tank. A rifle grenade knocked out a second tank. This apparently discouraged the occupants of the third tank, since they drove their vehicle off with one of the other tanks in tow. The enemy infantry, deprived of their support, quickly followed. The 3d Battalion, 306th Infantry, had killed eighteen Japanese while itself sustaining losses of six killed and more than a dozen wounded. The enemy attack, the largest of the night, had failed to penetrate the American position guarding the northern approach to Yigo.[42]

[38] 77th Inf Div G-3 Jnl, 7 Aug 44, Entries 37, 48, 77; III Phib Corps G-3 Jnl, 1215, 7 Aug 44. The 77th Division G-2 felt that if the enemy chose to assume the offensive, his attack would come in the manner described above. 77th Inf Div G-2 Rpt 15, 7 Aug 44, in 77th Inf Div G-2 Jnl File, 7-10 Aug 44. See also 77th Inf Div Rpt, p. 6.

[39] 77th Inf Div Rpt, p. 6; 77th Inf Div G-3 Rpt 16, 9 Aug 44.

[40] 77th Inf Div G-3 Jnl, 7 Aug 44, Entry 78.

[41] 77th Inf Div G-2 Jnl File, 7-10 Aug 44, Entry 52 on 7 Aug.

[42] 306th RCT S-3 Jnl File, 8 Aug 44, Entry 3; 306th RCT Unit Rpt 17, 9 Aug 44; 77th Inf Div G-3 Jnl, 8 Aug 44, Entry 6; 77th Inf Div G-2 Rpt 16, 8 Aug, and Entry 3 on 8 Aug, both in 77th Inf Div G-2 Jnl File, 7-10 Aug 44; AFAS, *Guam*, pp. 126-27.

While the Army and Marine troops were forging ahead on 7 August, General Geiger issued orders directing that the pursuit of the enemy be continued at 0730 on 8 August.[43] Later, he added, "Admiral Nimitz arrives 10 August. Push Japs off Guam before then." [44]

The 77th Division plan for 8 August called for a continuation of the drive begun on the 7th. The 306th Infantry would complete its envelopment of the northern flank of Mount Santa Rosa with its 1st and 3d Battalions while the 2d Battalion followed with the command post. In the center of the division line, the 307th Infantry would attack with the 1st and 3d Battalions abreast to seize Mount Santa Rosa; the 2d Battalion was to be prepared to execute an enveloping attack up the southern slopes to bring the assault to a successful conclusion. Finally, the 305th Infantry (less 3d Battalion in corps reserve) would continue to close in on Mount Santa Rosa and seal it off from the south. There was no plan for a division artillery preparation, although all battalions were available for call fire. As directed by corps, the infantry would attack at 0730.[45]

General Bruce's force opened the assault on schedule. In the zones of operations of the 305th and 307th Infantry Regiments, the attack proceeded rapidly and with little or no difficulty. The 305th Infantry, on the

division right, encountered only slight opposition in its short advance to the regimental objective area. The 2d Battalion pushed forward about 1,000 yards to secure the left (northwest) half of the objective area, while the 1st Battalion followed the 2d for a while and then, in the early afternoon, swung east to secure the rest of the objective zone. The 3d Battalion, still in corps reserve, moved forward to set up defensive positions behind the 307th Infantry at Yigo and the important Road Junction 415. Casualties in the 305th Infantry were five killed and six wounded, while the regiment claimed to have killed twenty-five of the enemy.

Like the 305th Infantry, the 307th in the center of the division experienced little difficulty in its drive on 8 August. By H Hour the 1st Battalion had pulled abreast and to the right of the 3d, approximately 1,000 yards east of Road Junction 415. Although the forward displacement of artillery battalions and some confusion as to unit locations prevented a brief artillery preparation requested by the regiment, the two battalions stepped off on schedule unopposed. About 0800, when potential opposition was revealed by a captured document indicating an enemy gun position before the 1st Battalion, artillery fire was quickly brought to bear on the target. By about 0830, when General Bruce arrived for a check at the 307th command post, the attack was well under way. Bruce himself went forward to look over the situation and immediately ordered the regimental commander to throw his 2d Battalion into the planned envelopment from the south. Moreover, to exploit the situation further, he directed that the attached company of medium tanks (Company A), as well as all other supporting

[43] III Phib Corps Opn Order 9–44, 7 Aug 44, in III Phib Corps Opns Orders.

[44] III Phib Corps G–3 Jnl, 7 Aug 44, Entry 0148.

[45] 77th Inf Div G–3 Jnl, 7 Aug 44, Entries 63 and 66; AFAS, Guam, p. 127; 307th RCT S–1/S–4 Jnl, 1803, 7 Aug 44; 307th RCT FO 7, 7 Aug 44, Overlay Showing Scheme of Maneuver for 8 Aug; 306th RCT Jnl File, 7 Aug 44, Entry 30; 306th RCT, Overlay For Future Contemplated Action, in 77th Inf Div G–3 Jnl File, 6 Aug 44, Entry 96; 77th Inf Div Rpt, p. 7.

regimental units, be used in the attack. When the 2d Battalion went into action, the regiment made quick arrangements with the 305th Infantry to prevent a collision between the 2d Battalion, 307th, and the left battalion of the 305th, since the trail that the 2d Battalion was to follow led through the objective area of the 305th Infantry.

With the 307th Infantry attack well under way, twenty minutes after the 2d Battalion had been committed, General Bruce enlarged the regimental mission. The regiment was not only to carry out its earlier mission of seizing Mount Santa Rosa but was also to push on from that height to the sea beyond. Within an hour Bruce also directed all available tanks of the 706th Tank Battalion (less Companies B and C) to join the company of mediums already with the 307th Infantry. By pushing through as fast as possible, the division might well end the fight in short order.

By 1050 the three battalions of the 307th Infantry were on a north–south line about 2,000 yards east of the Yigo area, having covered approximately 1,000 yards from the morning's line of departure. Each battalion was astride a trail leading up the western slopes of Mount Santa Rosa, 3d Battalion on the left (north), 1st in the middle, and 2d on the right. So far Japanese opposition had been negligible, but a prisoner captured by the 1st Battalion—the first taken in over a week by the division—revealed strong potential resistance ahead. Talking freely, the captured Japanese stated that there were 3,000 of his compatriots in caves on Mount Santa Rosa. If this information were correct, the 307th Infantry might be in for a tough fight. Accordingly, the regimental commander, with the immediate approval of

General Bruce who was impatient for the 307th to seize Mount Santa Rosa, ordered a new maneuver to wipe out any Japanese left on that height. The 2d Battalion was to continue with its planned envelopment from the south while the 1st and 3d Battalions were to follow a trail to the northeast until they were due north of Mount Santa Rosa and then attack south to hit the enemy from the north. The result would be a double envelopment that, it was hoped, would crush the enemy between its two wings.

The elaborate preparations proved unnecessary, for if 3,000 Japanese had ever been on Mount Santa Rosa they were no longer there. It is little wonder. Since 3 August, Admiral Conolly's fire support ships had been bombarding the mountain day and night. Seventh Air Force P–47's and B–25's, flying down regularly from Isely Field on Saipan, had intensified the destruction. The infantry and tank advance in the 307th Infantry sector was almost completely unopposed. By 1240 the northern half of Mount Santa Rosa was in American hands, and as the regiment moved to secure the rest of the mountain the 1st Battalion continued to push on to the sea. Shortly before 1400, with the entire height under regimental control, the command post of the 307th Infantry began displacing forward to the summit of Santa Rosa. By 1440 the 1st Battalion commander reported he had reached the cliffs along the sea and could look down into the water. Regimental patrols were ranging over the entire Santa Rosa area. As night fell the regiment was still mopping up small isolated groups of the enemy, patrolling, and digging in. It had not encountered any large force of Japanese. The day's action had cost the 307th Infantry only one man killed and a dozen wounded; less than fifty Japanese were claimed killed.[46]

The relatively easy time enjoyed by the 305th and 307th Infantry Regiments on 8 August was shared in part by the 306th Infantry, but the latter regiment had difficulties arising out of miscalculation as to the location of the division boundary on its left and a failure to observe the regimental boundary on the right. Colonel Smith's regiment jumped off on time from the positions it had secured the night before: 3d Battalion on the right, on the Salisbury road about 900 yards above Yigo; 1st Battalion on the left, in the vicinity of the crossroads southwest of Mount Mataguac marking the point where the boundary change began. The 2d Battalion, near the regimental command post on the Finegayan–Yigo road about a mile below Yigo, was prepared to follow and join the action when necessary. The regimental advance would also be supported by Company B, 706th Tank Battalion, which at that time was still attached.

The two lead battalions of the 306th moved forward unopposed, the 3d advancing along the Salisbury road and the 1st continuing along the Liguan road from the crossroads. The advance of the 1st Battalion led it into the Marine zone, and the fact that the 9th Marines had cleared this area on the previous day probably accounted

for the lack of resistance to the Army battalion. By 0910 the 1st Battalion had advanced about 1,000 yards up the trail, and had been in contact with the marines since 0840. To the east the 3d Battalion had made a similar gain, while the 2d Battalion jumped off in column at 0900 to follow the 3d.

By about 0930 the 3d Battalion was well into its turning movement, cutting a trail east from the Salisbury road at a point about 2,400 yards above Road Junction 415. At the same time, the 1st Battalion apparently was either beginning its turn to the east to follow the 3d or was preparing to begin its turn. It was encountering slight opposition.

About 0955, however, General Bruce, then at the 307th Infantry command post and eager to exploit that regiment's gains, ordered a change in the mission of the 306th Infantry. One battalion was to drive all the way east to the coast, instead of halting on the north side of Mount Santa Rosa; another battalion was to push northeast on the Salisbury road all the way to Pati Point at the far northeast corner of Guam; the remaining battalion would set up a roadblock on the Salisbury road, midway between Salisbury and Yigo where another trail came down from Chaguian to the northwest. Thus the 3d Battalion would continue its drive east; the 1st Battalion, instead of following, would advance on Pati Point; and the 2d Battalion roadblock at the junction of the Chaguian trail and the Salisbury road would protect the rear of the other two battalions.

In its movement to the east, the 3d Battalion and supporting tanks met no opposition. The path they were cutting, however, led the battalion southeast rather than east. A slight southeast movement was necessary,

---

[46] 77th Inf Div G–3 Jnl, 8 Aug 44; 77th Inf Div Rpt, p. 7; 307th RCT Rpt, p. 5; 307th RCT S–1/S–4 and S–2/S–3 Jnl Files, 8 Aug 44; 77th Inf Div Arty Rpt, p. 11; 77th Inf Div Arty S–3 Jnl, 7–8 Aug 44, passim; 77th Inf Div Arty S–3 Rpt 15, period 7–8 Aug 44, in 77th Inf Div G–3 Jnl File, 10 Aug 44; 77th Inf Div G–2 Rpts 16–17, 8–9 Aug 44, in 77th Inf Div G–2 Jnl File, 7–10 Aug 44; Msg, 307th RCT to G–2, No. 23 on 8 Aug, in same jnl; 706th Tk Bn Rpt, p. 10; AFAS, Guam, pp. 117–18.

but the troops went too far and, before they realized it, were in the 307th Infantry zone of operations. By 1110 the battalion found itself on a trail on the northwest slope of Mount Santa Rosa, nearly 1,000 yards south of the regimental boundary and blocking the planned route of advance of the 3d Battalion, 307th Infantry, to the northern flank of the mountain.

The trail that the 3d Battalion, 306th Infantry, now blocked led northeast toward the Lulog area. If the battalion could follow this trail with the same speed as the day's earlier advance, it would soon reach its objective and be out of the way of the 307th Infantry. However, about this time the 3d Battalion's leading elements began to encounter light, scattered, enemy opposition, which slowed the advance. Most of the Japanese had little desire to fight. Still stunned by the terrific artillery, air, and naval bombardment, many of them simply huddled in caves or huts and waited to be killed. A few offered desultory resistance; some committed suicide. When enemy strongpoints were encountered, however, well co-ordinated infantry-tank teams, with flame throwers and pole charges, quickly dealt with the resistance.

The advance of the 3d Battalion, 306th Infantry, was still not fast enough to suit either the 307th Infantry or General Bruce. Meanwhile, the men of the 3d Battalion, 306th, were not too happy when tanks with the 307th accidentally began firing in their direction. This fire was stopped, but the 306th infantrymen were ordered to move out of the area, or at least off the main trail, as soon as possible. By early afternoon the 3d Battalion had either left the trail or advanced far enough to permit the 307th Infantry to secure its oper-

ational area unhindered. Indeed, midafternoon found the 3d Battalion, 306th Infantry, in full possession of the Lulog area and with strong patrols between that point and the sea. By nightfall the entire Lulog-Anao Point area was in the hands of Kimbrell's men.

While the 3d Battalion, 306th Infantry, struggled to keep out of the way of the 307th Infantry, Colonel Smith's other two battalions of the 306th were having difficulties of their own. West of the Salisbury road, the 1st Battalion was moving cross-country unopposed in a general northeasterly direction in what it believed was 77th Division territory. Its aim was apparently to regain the Salisbury road and then follow the road in the direction of Pati Point. About 1030, however, the battalion reported that Marine units on the Chaguian trail—who were actually in what the marines correctly believed to be their own zone—were blocking the Army advance. Moreover, the marines on the Chaguian trail, and along another trail leading from the Chaguian trail northeast toward Salisbury that the soldiers apparently had themselves hoped to follow, claimed that they were going to Pati Point. Reporting this to corps, General Bruce said he had no objection to following the marines on up, but he asked that the 3d Marine Division troops clear rapidly so that the soldiers could continue their mission. This was agreeable to corps headquarters. The marines were directed to move forward rapidly, and the Army troops were ordered to follow.

Shortly after 1100 General bruce decided that if the marines were going to Pati Point in force there was no need of sending more than a small group of Army troops in that direction. By now he had received the report that 3,000 Japanese might still be on Mount Santa Rosa, and in his desire to insure the success of the 307th Infantry's drive he made another change in the orders for the 306th. Instead of setting up a roadblock on the Salisbury road, the 2d Battalion, 306th Infantry, was to follow the 3d Battalion in its advance east, prepared to support the latter or, if necessary, to move to the aid of the 307th Infantry. The 1st Battalion, meanwhile, would send only one company up the Salisbury road, and that solely to maintain contact with the marines. The rest of the 1st Battalion was to join the regimental command post group, which had moved up with the 2d Battalion, apparently to be used as the regimental commander saw fit.

The 1st and 2d Battalions, 306th Infantry, moved to carry out their new assignments. Shortly after noon lead elements of the 2d Battalion moving up the Salisbury road reached the turn-off point where the 3d Battalion had begun cutting its trail to the east that morning. A few minutes later the 1st Battalion (less one company) began moving back toward the regimental command post, just below the junction of the Chaguian trail and the Salisbury road.

Beginning about 1215 and continuing for approximately two hours, troops of the 306th Infantry in the confused area along the Salisbury road found themselves under fire from a quarter they least expected. About 1215, 2d Battalion elements making the turn to the east began receiving rifle and machine gun fire that they thought might have been from Marine weapons. Half an hour later Company F, bringing up the rear of the battalion, was engaged at the junction of the Chaguian trail and Salisbury road by a force that the soldiers were convinced was composed of marines.

Notified of this, the 3d Marine Division replied that it had no troops in that immediate area but that the firing might have been done by some Japanese troops left over from a scrap the marines had had there that morning. By the time this information was relayed back to F Company, however, the fire fight had stopped as mysteriously as it had begun. No sooner was this over than pack howitzer fire began to fall on the regimental command post below the road junction. This time there was no mistake; fragments taken from the wounds of one soldier proved conclusively to be from a Marine weapon. Again, not long after this shelling had been stopped, an Army motor column moving up the Salisbury road came under machine gun fire, which the soldiers again blamed on the marines.

The climax of the confusion came about 1400, when a battalion of the 9th Marines began moving east off the Salisbury road on the trail that the 3d Battalion, 306th Infantry, had cut that morning. Earlier, Marine and Army units had conflicting overlays to show that each was in its own zone of operations, but this time there was no doubt that the Marine battalion was in the Army zone. The Marine commander, however, in the apparent belief that he was still on the Salisbury road, stated that he had permission to be where he was and refused to withdraw. Finally, the 306th Infantry commander was able to persuade a Marine staff officer of the error and the Marine commander reluctantly agreed to turn his battalion around and march it back.

By about 1500 everything appeared to have been straightened out. The shooting had stopped; there were no Army troops in the Marine area; there were no Marine troops in the Army area. The 1st Battalion (less the company charged with maintaining contact with the marines) and the regimental command post group had moved east on the heels of the 2d Battalion, which was now advancing against extremely light and scattered resistance behind the 3d Battalion. Completion of the regimental mission was relatively easy, and at 1715 the 306th Infantry reported itself dug in across the northern face of Mount Santa Rosa. The 3d Battalion had reached the sea at Anao Point; the 2d Battalion was tied in to its west; the regimental command post was at Lulog; and the 1st Battalion was along the trail west of the command post. The day's action had cost the regiment 11 men killed and 24 wounded, while 172 Japanese were claimed killed.[47]

As if the confusion between American units during the daylight hours of 8 August had not been enough, just at sunset the 1st Battalion, 306th Infantry, west of Lulog, and the 3d Battalion, 307th Infantry, to the south on Mount Santa Rosa, were involved in another tragic incident. About 1830 both battalions began receiving mortar fire. This was either Japanese fire or, more probably, fire from American weapons being zeroed in for the perimeter defense that night. Unfortunately, the fire hitting the 306th Infantry troops came from the south, where the 3d Battalion, 307th Infantry, was digging in, while the

shells that landed in the 307th area came from the north, where 306th Infantry troops were preparing their defenses. Both battalions reported a counterattack and opened fire with small arms in the direction of the presumed assault, which only served to increase the illusion of a counterattack. Tanks of the 306th Infantry began shooting, and both battalions called down artillery fire.

Fortunately for those involved, the confusion was short lived. Within the space of a few minutes it became apparent that the troops were exchanging shots with their fellow Americans, and all firing was halted. The 902d Field Artillery Battalion had fired a brief barrage and both infantry battalions had done considerable firing on their own. The result was at least ten casualties in the 3d Battalion, 307th Infantry, and a smaller number of casualties in the 1st Battalion and regimental command post of the 306th Infantry.[48]

The Marines: 7–8 August

On the morning of 7 August, General Geiger for the first time had all three of his units deployed abreast for the attack. The 1st Provisional Brigade, which had spent the past days resting and patrolling southern Guam, was now fed into the line to the left of the 3d Marine Division and made responsible for securing the northwest coast of the island including Mount Machanao and Ritidian Point. The mission

[47] 77th Inf Div G–3 Jnl, 8 Aug 44; 306th RCT Unit Jnl File, 8 Aug; 306th RCT Unit Rpt 17, 9 Aug 44; 306th RCT Rpt, p. 4; Burns interviews with 1st and 3d Bns, 306th RCT (none available for 2d Bn), pp. 506, 537–38, 564, 566–68, 572–73; 77th Inf Div G–2 Jnl File, 8 Aug 44, passim; 706th Tk Bn Rpt, p. 10; 77th Inf Div Arty Jnl, 7–8 Aug, passim; III Phib Corps G–3 Jnl, 8 Aug 44, passim; 3d Marine Div D–3 Jnl, 8 Aug, Entry 29; 307th RCT S–1/S–4 and S–2/S–3 Jnls, 1155, 8 Aug 44.

[48] 77th Inf Div G–3 Jnl, 8 Aug 44, Entries 75–77, 81, 83, and 9 Aug, Entry 3; 306th RCT Unit Rpt 18, 10 Aug 44; 77th Inf Div Arty S–3 Jnl, 8–9 Aug 44, Entries 4–6, 10, and journal worksheet entry at 1917 (from 304th Fld Arty); 77th Inf Div G–2 Jnl File, 7–10 Aug 44, Entry 49, 8 Aug 44.

LT. GEN. ALEXANDER A. VANDEGRIFT *being greeted at Orote airfield by (from the left) Maj. Gen. Henry L. Larsen, General Geiger, and General Holland Smith on 10 August.*

of the 3d Marine Division, in the center of the corps attack, was to continue to push to the north and northeast until it reached the sea in the vicinity of Tarague Point.

The 7th of August was a relatively quiet day for both Marine units. The 3d Division came across a few antitank guns guarding a roadblock in the neighborhood of Road Junction 390 but quickly reduced it without casualties. By 1530 elements of the division reached the O–5 line along the trail that ran southeast from Road Junction 460 to the Yigo–Salisbury road. There, the entire division dug in for the night after a day's advance of about 6,000 yards. On

the left, the brigade's 4th Regiment kept pace and succeeded in occupying a line running due west of Road Junction 460. Pausing there, General Shepherd late in the afternoon brought in the 22d Marines to take over the western (left) half of the brigade line.[49]

The next day the chief obstacle facing the Marines was again jungle rather than Japanese. The only reported fighting in the zone of the 3d Division was around a roadblock manned by nineteen enemy

---

[49] 3d Marine Div D–3 Jnl, 7 Aug 44; 1st Provisional Marine Brig, War Diary, 1 Jul–10 Aug 44, p. 19; Lodge, *Guam*, pp. 149–50.

soldiers. These were quickly eliminated. Nightfall found the division on a line north of Salisbury about a mile and a half from the sea. At the same time the 22d Marines forged ahead up the west coast in the wake of a series of well-placed aerial bombing attacks. By midafternoon marines of the 22d Regiment reached Ritidian Point, the northernmost point of Guam.[50]

The End on Guam

By nightfall of 8 August the end of fighting on Guam was virtually at hand. The gains of the 77th Division around Mount Santa Rosa, the advance of the 3d Marine Division to within a mile and a half of the sea, the occupation by the 1st Provisional Marine Brigade of the entire northwest coast of the island to Ritidian Point—all spelled the doom of the remaining Japanese. That night even Radio Tokyo conceded that nine tenths of Guam had fallen to American troops.[51]

The capture of Mount Santa Rosa by the 77th Division marked the end of organized resistance on Guam, for this was the last Japanese stronghold on the island, and the enemy now had no important rallying spot. Only a little more than 500 Japanese dead were discovered on Santa Rosa, far less than the number of enemy troops there at the beginning of the attack, and far less than General Bruce had expected to encounter. Apparently the extremely heavy preassault bombardment forced most of the defenders to flee the area. The Japanese were denied their last major defensive area on Guam and were driven north into the jungle in a completely disorganized state.

On the evening of 8 August General Geiger ordered the pursuit to continue at 0730 the following morning.[52] Accordingly, on 9 August, the 77th Division moved out on schedule to complete its mission. The 306th Infantry patrols sent northward to the sea to flush the area between Lulog and the north coast encountered only scattered and light resistance. The 307th Infantry on Mount Santa Rosa patrolled vigorously between that height and the seacoast to the east. The 305th Infantry (less 3d Battalion) moved to an assembly area south of Barrigada. Nowhere in the division zone on 9 August was any organized resistance encountered. The same held true for the 10th.[53]

To the west, marines of the 3d Division and 1st Provisional Brigade encountered only a little more difficulty. During the early morning hours of 9 August, the 2d Battalion, 3d Marines, came under attack by five enemy tanks accompanied by infantrymen. The marines withdrew into the jungle without suffering any casualties and by daylight the enemy force had disappeared. That day the 3d Marines gained another 1,500 yards, which put it roughly about the same distance from the sea. At the same time, the 9th Marines completed its particular assignment by reaching Pati Point. On the corps left, the brigade extended its control southeast from Ritidian Point as far as Mergagan Point.[54]

---

[50] 3d Marine Div D-3 Jnl, 8 Aug 44; 1st Provisional Marine Brig, War Diary, 1 Jul–10 Aug 44, p. 20; Lodge, *Guam*, pp. 153–55.

[51] III Phib Corps C-2 Periodic Rpt 19.

[52] III Phib Corps Opn Ord 10-44.

[53] 77th Inf Div Rpt, p. 7; 77th Inf Div G-3 Jnl, 9-10 Aug 44; 77th Inf Div G-3 Rpts 17, 18, 19, 11 Aug 44.

[54] 3d Marine Div SAR, p. 5; 1st Provisional Marine Brig, War Diary, 1 Jul–10 Aug, p. 21; Lodge, *Guam*, pp. 154–57.

The next day, 10 August, with only a small pocket between Mergagan Point and Pati Point left to be occupied, General Geiger at 1131 announced that organized resistance on Guam had ended.[55] The announcement was timed to correspond with the arrival on Guam of Admirals Nimitz and Spruance and Marine Generals Holland Smith and Vandegrift aboard Spruance's flagship *Indianapolis.*

The official conclusion of the campaign did not mean it was actually over, for soldiers and marines were to spend many dreary weeks before they finally cleaned out the enemy-infested jungles and mountains of Guam. Even though all signs of Japanese organized resistance were crushed, General Obata killed (on 11 August), and the island overrun, there still remained unaccounted for a large number of Japanese who had fled into the jungles in small groups and continued to harass the American garrison, even until after the

end of the war. Two officers, who were eventually captured, Colonel Takeda and Major Sato, vainly attempted to organize these survivors, but they remained for the most part isolated stragglers. Almost all were too preoccupied with the eternal search for food to think of fighting, and their weapons and ammunition were saved for hunting until they rusted for want of lubricating oil. American patrols killed a few every day; others succumbed at last to the siren song of American psychological warfare and gave themselves up.[56]

Eventually, the entire Japanese garrison on Guam, numbering about 18,500, was killed or captured. In exchange, American casualties as of 10 August 1944 came to 7,800, of whom 2,124 were killed in action or died of wounds. Of this total, the Army accounted for 839, the Navy for 245, while the remaining 6,716 were marines.[57]

---

[55] 77th Inf Div G-3 Jnl, 10 Aug 44, Entry 31.

[56] Lt Col H. Takeda, Outline of Japanese Defense Plan, 4 Oct 46.

[57] Lodge, *Guam,* App. III, pp. 178-80.

PART FIVE

CONCLUSION

CHAPTER XXI

Fruits of Victory

The Allied decision to invade and capture the three major islands of the southern Marianas was made with three main objectives in mind. First, it was hoped that the enemy fleet or a sizable part of it might be flushed and decisively defeated. Second, the islands of Saipan, Tinian, and Guam were considered desirable as forward naval bases, even though they were not favored with first-rate harbors. But most important, the southern Marianas were ideally located for use as bases from which the newly developed very long range bombers could bombard the Japanese homeland. The islands were, as the wartime phrasemakers put it, "anchored aircraft carriers" from which the aerial war against Japan could be pressed with hitherto unequaled intensity.

The first of these objectives was of course achieved with Spruance's victory over Vice Adm. Jisaburo Ozawa's *Mobile Fleet* in the Battle of the Philippine Sea. Although a large part of the Japanese Fleet escaped destruction because of Spruance's determination not to leave the landing force at Saipan unprotected, the battle was nevertheless a decisive victory for the Americans. Sustaining only minor losses, the U.S. Fifth Fleet and its supporting submarines sank three carriers and two fleet tankers and damaged two carriers, a battleship, three cruisers, and a tanker. Equally

if not more important were the tremendous losses of planes and trained aircraft personnel suffered by the enemy. All together, 476 Japanese planes were destroyed in the Battle of the Philippine Sea, and the total number of aviators lost was about 445.[1]

In the words of Professor Samuel Eliot Morison, "The Battle of the Philippine Sea contributed as much to victory as if Ozawa's fleet had been destroyed; for without its air arm the fleet was crippled, and the six carriers that survived were useful only as decoys . . . ."[2] Fleet Admiral King was of the same opinion. Commenting on the affair long after the war, he wrote:

Spruance accomplished more lasting results than he or anyone else realized at the time, for the great loss of Japanese naval aircraft in the Battle of the Philippine Sea crippled Japanese naval aviation for the remainder of the war. Planes could be replaced, but pilots could not, and, as was discovered later in the year at the Battle for Leyte Gulf, the Japanese no longer had the trained and seasoned aviators that were necessary for successful operations against our fleet.[3]

The second objective of the campaign— to provide secondary naval facilities for the

[1] Morison, *New Guinea and the Marianas,* p. 321.
[2] *Ibid.,* p. 318.
[3] King and Whitehill, *Fleet Admiral King,* p. 559.

LST's, LCI's, Small Boats, *and other vessels at Tanapag Harbor carried much of the shipping required by the stepped-up tempo of action in the Pacific in May 1945.*

fleet—began to be realized shortly after the islands were secured. At the time of their capture, none of the southern Marianas possessed adequate sites for fleet anchorages, and, in fact, the only truly protected anchorage in the entire area was Apra Harbor at Guam. Nevertheless, on both Saipan and Tinian it did prove feasible to set up various other naval facilities important to the further prosecution of the war in the central Pacific. On Saipan, a naval seaplane base was constructed at Tanapag Harbor, small-boat and LVT repair units were established, and the pier at Garapan was enlarged to permit its employment as a major ammunition dock. Farther inland, naval construction battalions built a large tank farm to house aviation gasoline and

diesel and fuel oil, a naval supply depot, sundry administration buildings, several hospitals, fleet recreation areas, and an ammunition depot. On Tinian, an airfield was constructed for the use of naval patrol planes, and a tank farm similar to that on Saipan was built. In addition, two railways were set up for use in landing craft repair, and Tinian Harbor was dredged and supplied with docking facilities for eight Liberty ships.[4]

Guam, with its relatively large land mass and protected harbor, was to be the scene of more ambitious base development proj-

[4] Department of the Navy, Bureau of Yards and Docks, *Building the Navy's Bases in World War II: History of the Bureau of Yards and Docks and the Civil Engineer Corps, 1940–1946,* 2 vols. (Washington, 1947), II, Ch. 28.

ects. On 9 August, the day before the official announcement that the island was "secured," Admiral Nimitz made known his plans to use Guam as a base for the Pacific Fleet and as forward headquarters for his Pacific Ocean Areas command.[5] As a result, Apra Harbor was dredged and given the additional protection of a lengthy breakwater. An extensive tank farm was erected, several major supply depots were established, and hospitals and administration buildings were constructed. Early in 1945 Nimitz' forward headquarters was set up on the island, and by the end of the war the naval base at Guam was capable of supporting a third of the U.S. Pacific Fleet.[6]

The major construction effort on all three islands was of course devoted to laying out airfields and other facilities for the very long range bombers, the Army Air Forces' B-29's. In the minds of many U.S. strategic planners this had been, after all, the compelling reason for launching the Marianas Campaign. The first B-29 airdrome to be completed was Isely Field on Saipan.[7] Work started on 24 June 1944 and by mid-December Saipan boasted two B-29 runways plus storage space for sixty spare bombers at nearby Kobler Field.

The first of the very heavy bombers arrived on the island on 12 October, and on 24 November B-29's flew the first mission against Tokyo.[8]

On Tinian, two fields were developed. The first, North Field, on the site of the old Japanese airdrome near Marpi Point, was ready for use by February 1945, and the second, West Field, just above Tinian Town, became operational the next month. On Guam, North and Northwest Fields, located inland of Ritidian and Pati Points, respectively, were put into operation between January and June of 1945, and the first mission from Guam to Japan was launched in late February. In addition on Guam, Harmon Field above Agana was commissioned for use as headquarters of the XXI Bomber Command.

Starting on 24 November 1944 and continuing through early August of 1945 when the atomic bombs were dropped on Hiroshima and Nagasaki, the home islands of Japan were subjected to a mounting crescendo of B-29 raids, all flying out of the five airfields in the Marianas. Japan's industrial plants were flattened, her shipping was mined and sunk, and her cities were laid waste.

Without attempting to allocate responsibility for the ultimate defeat of Japan among the various agencies, services, and weapons that contributed to that end, it is more than clear that the Marianas-based B-29's played a major role. Certainly, that was the opinion of many responsible Japanese leaders. Prince Fumimaro Konoye later reported, "Fundamentally, the thing that brought about the determination to

---

[5] CINCPAC-CINCPOA Ser. 000650, 11 Aug 44. 44.

[6] Bureau of Yards and Docks, *Building the Navy's Bases in World War II*, II, Ch. 28; *The War Reports of General of the Army George C. Marshall, Chief of Staff, General of the Army H. H. Arnold, Commanding General, Army Air Forces, Fleet Admiral Ernest J. King, Commander-in-Chief, United States Fleet, and Chief of Naval Operations* (Philadelphia & New York, J. B. Lippincott Company, 1947), p. 685.

[7] For reasons unknown, the XXI Bomber Command changed the original spelling to Isley, although the field derived its name from Comdr Robert H. Isely, USN, a navy pilot who had been killed during the assault on Saipan. (See Craven and Cate, *AAF V*, p. 515.)

[8] Information on the construction of B-29 bases in the Marianas is derived from Craven and Cate, *AAF V*, pp. 512-25, and Bureau of Yards and Docks, *Building the Navy's Bases in World War II*, II, Ch. 28.

HARMON FIELD, GUAM, *where headquarters of the XXI Bomber Command opened,* 16 December 1944.

make peace was the prolonged bombing by the B–29's." According to Premier Kantaro Suzuki: "It seemed . . . unavoidable that in the long run Japan would be almost destroyed by air attack so that merely on the basis of the B–29's alone I was convinced that Japan should sue for peace." [9]

Even before the bombs began to drop, many Japanese were aware that the loss of the Marianas, and especially of Saipan, was a crucial, if not the decisive, turning point in the war. The most immediate repercussion was the fall of Premier Tojo and his entire cabinet. Japanese leaders were aware of the tremendous potentialities of the B–29 (although not of the atomic bomb), and they fully realized that with the loss of the Marianas those potentialities could be quickly brought to bear against Japan. Prince Naruhiko Higashikuni, Commander in Chief of Home Defense Headquarters, later stated:

The war was lost when the Marianas were taken away from Japan and when we heard the B–29s were coming out . . . . We had nothing in Japan that we could use against such a weapon. From the point of view of the Home Defense Command, we felt that the war was lost and said so. If the B–29s could come over Japan, there was nothing that could be done.[10]

Postwar testimony in the same vein was volunteered by such high ranking officers as Fleet Admiral Nagano, Chief of the Naval General Staff and Supreme Naval Advisor to the Emperor; Vice Adm. Shigeru Fududome, who had served as Chief of Staff, *Combined Fleet*, Commander, *Second Air Fleet*, and Commander, *10th Area Fleet;* Vice Adm. Shigeyoshi Miwa, Commander in Chief, *Sixth (Submarine) Fleet;* and Capt. Mitsuo Fuchida, Air Staff Officer to the Commander in Chief, *Combined Fleet*.[11]

The Japanese high command had realized from the beginning the strategic importance of the Marianas in the Empire's defensive system. It was for that reason that the high command ordered the *Combined Fleet* to intercept or frustrate the landing on Saipan. The thorough defeats that Japan suffered during the Marianas campaign on the sea, on land, and in the air proved irreparable.

To be sure, other battles remained to be fought before the Japanese could finally be induced to surrender. General MacArthur's return to the Philippines would cut Japan's vital line of communications to the Netherlands Indies and secure important naval and air bases. The U.S. Navy's victory in the Battle of Leyte Gulf would reduce to virtual impotence the remnant of the Japanese Fleet that was left afloat after the Battle of the Philippine Sea. The capture of Iwo Jima by Admiral Nimitz' forces would greatly facilitate the bombing of the home islands from bases in the Marianas. And, finally, the successful invasion of Okinawa would bring American forces to the very doorstep of Japan.

Out of the long sequence of campaigns and battles that took place in the Pacific between 7 December 1941 and 15 August 1945, it is of course impossible to isolate any single one as "decisive" in bringing about the defeat of Japan. But certainly, by any reasonable standard of judgment, the campaign in the Marianas must be

[9] AC/AS Mission Accomplished: Interrogations of Japanese Industrial, Military, and Civil Leaders of World War II, Washington 1946, pp. 39–40.
[10] AC/AS Mission Accomplished, p. 18.

[11] USSBS, *Interrogations*, II, Naval Nos. 80, 115, 72, 99.

rated high in the order of events that led to the success of American arms. Admiral King often spoke of the Marianas as "the key to the Pacific War." [12] Purists might quarrel with his choice of the definite article, but few would deny that victory in the Marianas was *a* key and a very important key to the door that led to the defeat of the Japanese Empire in World War II.[13]

In the campaign in the Marianas, the U.S. Army played an important, although not the major, role. The Army contributed two reinforced divisions, a corps of artillery, and sundry other troops, numbering 39,280 officers and men. In addition, the Seventh Air Force provided three squadrons of P–47 fighters, a detachment of P–61 night fighters, and a squadron of B–25 medium bombers to fly tactical missions in support of the ground troops. By comparison, the Marine Corps contributed 85,824 officers and men—or three reinforced infantry divisions, a provisional brigade of two regiments, a corps of artillery, and various other troops.[14]

Army casualties came to 4,523 killed in action, dead of wounds, and wounded in action. Of these, 3,666 were incurred on Saipan and Tinian, 857 on Guam. Total Marine Corps casualties came to 19,272 killed in action, dead of wounds, and wounded in action. Of these 10,437 took place on Saipan, 1,892 on Tinian, and 6,943 on Guam.[15] The ratio of casualties

to total troops employed was roughly 1 to 9 for the Army and 1 to 4.5 for the Marine Corps. The higher proportion of casualties suffered by the Marine Corps can be explained largely by the fact that the marines were given the initial task of assaulting the beaches on all three islands, were in action for a longer time than either of the two Army infantry divisions, and were almost solely responsible for the fighting on Tinian.

The role of the Navy in the Marianas campaign was of course fundamental. Admiral Spruance's Fifth Fleet softened up the targets and kept the battlefields isolated once the troops were ashore. Naval vessels transported the troops to the islands, supplied them when they got there, and kept up a continuous program of naval bombardment against enemy troops and installations. Naval aircraft provided the great bulk of aerial support both before and during the land battles.

Without doubt the outstanding feature of the campaign in the Marianas was the skillful manner in which the separate services and the component arms of the U.S. forces were co-ordinated. Perhaps more than any other type of warfare, amphibious operations require a harmony of action, a precise meshing of the multitudinous gears that comprise the whole of the assault machinery. Land, sea, and air forces must be combined in the proper quantities at the proper time and place.

---

[12] King and Whitehill, *Fleet Admiral King*, p. 557.

[13] See Butow, *Japan's Decision to Surrender, passim.*

[14] These figures are derived from TF 56 Rpt FORAGER, Incl A, G–1 Rpt, pp. ˙3–23; *Ibid.,* Incl C, G–3 Rpt, pp. 8–9; NTLF (TF 56.1) Rpt Marianas, Incl C, G–1 Rpt, pp. 2–5.

[15] These figures are to be understood as approximate only. Casualty statistics submitted by various units are so uneven and at times so con-

tradictory as to render impossible an absolutely precise statement of the number. The figures here given are derived from studies, made by the Marine Corps Historical Branch, G–3, U.S. Marine Corps Headquarters, which contain the most accurate and up-to-date data available. They are contained in Hoffman, *Saipan*, App. III, p. 268–69; Hoffman, *Tinian*, App. III, p. 150; Lodge, *Guam*, App. III, pp. 178–80.

By the summer of 1944, the U.S. Army, Navy, and Marine Corps had had sufficient experience in joint operations to be optimistic about the success of future landings in the Pacific. Victory in the Marianas brought confirmation to the belief that current amphibious doctrine was sound and could be employed, with modifications, against any Japanese-held island or land mass.

To be sure, all was not perfection. There were still some "bugs" in the machinery, some failures of performance. Also, the Smith versus Smith affair on Saipan was alarming to those who had hoped for perfect teamwork between the services. Nevertheless, the relief of General Ralph Smith and the interservice controversy that ensued should not be allowed to obscure the fact that for the most part co-operation between the separate U.S. services was excellent. Had it been otherwise, victory in the Marianas would have been neither so rapid nor so complete.

Appendix A

Total Strength—66,779

Unit	*Estimated Strength*
Northern Troops and Landing Force Troops	2,296

Lt. Gen. Holland M. Smith, USMC (to 12 July 1944)
Headquarters and Service Battalion, V Amphibious Corps (less detachments)
Signal Battalion, V Amphibious Corps (less detachments)
Motor Transport Company, V Amphibious Corps (less detachments)
Headquarters, Provisional Engineer Group, V Amphibious Corps
Headquarters, Provisional LVT Group, V Amphibious Corps
7th Field Depot (less detachments) (reinforced)
Medical Battalion, V Amphibious Corps
31st Field Hospital
2d Provisional Portable Surgical Hospital
3d Provisional Portable Surgical Hospital
Air Warning Squadron 5 (less detachments)
Detachment, 680th Air Warning Company
Detachment, 726th Air Warning Company
Detachment, 763d Air Warning Company
Detachment, Company C, 101st Signal Battalion
Mobile Communication Unit, Central Pacific
Amphibious Reconnaissance Battalion, V Amphibious Corps (less detachments)

2d Marine Division	21,746

Maj. Gen. Thomas E. Watson, USMC
Headquarters Battalion
Tank Battalion
Service Battalion
Motor Transport Battalion
Medical Battalion
2d Marines (less 1 battalion)
6th Marines
8th Marines
10th Marines (artillery)
18th Marines (engineer)

Attached Units
2d Amphibious Tractor Battalion (LVT)
1st Battalion, 29th Marines (reinforced)
1st Amphibious Truck Company
18th Naval Construction Battalion
2d Joint Assault Signal Company (JASCO)
2d 155-mm Artillery Battalion
715th Amphibious Tractor Battalion (LVT(A))

Unit	*Estimated Strength*
5th Amphibious Tractor Battalion (LVT)	
2d Provisional Rocket Detachment	
4th Marine Division	21,618
Maj. Gen. Harry Schmidt, USMC (to 12 July)	
Headquarters Battalion	
Tank Battalion	
Service Battalion	
Motor Transport Battalion	
Medical Battalion	
23d Marines	
24th Marines	
25th Marines	
14th Marines (artillery)	
20th Marines (engineer)	

Attached Units
708th Amphibious Tank Battalion (LVT(A)) (Army)
10th Amphibious Tractor Battalion (LVT) (less Company A and plus Company C, 11th
    Amphibious Tractor Battalion)
773d Amphibious Tractor Battalion (LVT) (Army)
534th Amphibious Tractor Battalion (LVT) (Army) (less Company A less 1st Platoon)
1st JASCO
121st Naval Construction Battalion
2d Amphibious Truck Company
311th Port Company (Army)
539th Port Company (Army)
4th 105-mm. Artillery Battalion (howitzer) (V Amphibious Corps)
1st Provisional Rocket Detachment
Detachment, Air Warning Squadron 5
Detachment, 7th Field Depot

1st Battalion, 2d Marines (reinforced)	1,084
1st Battalion, 2d Marines	
Company A, Amphibious Reconnaissance Battalion, V Amphibious Corps	
XXIV Corps Artillery	2,682
Brig. Gen. Arthur M. Harper, USA	
Headquarters and Headquarters Battery	
1st Provisional Gun Group (155-mm. gun, Army)	
2d Battalion, 55th Coast Artillery	
32d Coast Artillery Gun Battalion	
225th Field Artillery Howitzer Group (155-mm. howitzer)	
145th Field Artillery Battalion	
225th Field Artillery Battalion	
477th Amphibious Truck Company	
Provisional Antiaircraft Artillery Group	949
864th Aircraft Warning Antiaircraft Battalion (less detachments)	
Battery A, 751st Antiaircraft Battalion	
Battery B, 751st Antiaircraft Battalion	
27th Infantry Division	16,404
Maj. Gen. Ralph C. Smith, USA	
Headquarters, 27th Infantry Division	
Headquarters, Special Troops	

Unit   *Estimated*
                                                                               Strength

Headquarters Company
Military Police Platoon
27th Division Band
27th Cavalry Reconnaissance Troop
727th Ordnance Company
27th Quartermaster Company
105th Infantry
106th Infantry
165th Infantry
Headquarters, 27th Division Artillery
104th Field Artillery Battalion
105th Field Artillery Battalion
106th Field Artillery Battalion
249th Field Artillery Battalion
102d Engineer Battalion
102d Medical Battalion

    Attached Units
38th Field Hospital
98th Portable Surgical Hospital
295th JASCO
762d Tank Battalion
766th Tank Battalion
1165th Engineer Group headquarters
34th Engineer Battalion
152d Engineer Battalion
1341st Engineer Battalion
94th Bomb Disposal Squad
95th Bomb Disposal Squad
88th Chemical Battalion
604th Quartermaster Graves Registration Company
Detachment, 534th Amphibious Tractor Battalion

Source: TF 56 Rpt FORAGER, Incl C, G–3 Rpt, pp. 8–9; NTLF Rpt Marianas, Phase I, Incl C, G–1 Rpt, pp. 2–5; 4th Marine Div Opns Rpt Saipan, pp. 3–4.

Appendix B

Pacific Ocean Area Unit of Fire for Ground Weapons

(Rounds Per Unit of Fire)

Weapon	Total Rounds
.30-caliber carbine	45
.30-caliber rifle	100
.30-caliber BAR	500
.30-caliber machine gun	1,500
.12-gauge shotgun	25
.45-caliber automatic revolver	14
.45-caliber submachine gun	200
.50-caliber machine gun	600
20-mm. antiaircraft machine gun	540
27-mm. antitank or tank gun	100
37-mm. antiaircraft gun	270
40-mm. antiaircraft gun	270
57-mm. antitank gun	90
60-mm. mortar	100
81-mm. mortar	100
4.2-inch chemical mortar	100
75-mm. howitzer field or pack	300
75-mm. self-propelled tank gun or LVT howitzer	150
75-mm. gun	100
3-inch self-propelled or antitank gun	50
90-mm. self-propelled or antitank gun	125
105-mm. M3 (short barrel) howitzer	150
105-mm. field howitzer	200
105-mm. self-propelled or tank gun howitzer	100
4.7-inch antiaircraft gun	75
155-mm. M1 howitzer	150
155-mm. M1 gun	100
8-inch howitzer	100
240-mm. howitzer	60
75-mm. gun	300
3-inch antiaircraft mobile	150
Hand grenade	1 per EM
Rifle antitank grenade launcher	2M9AT grenade
2.36-inch antitank rocket launcher (bazooka)	6 rockets

Source: TF 56 Rpt FORAGER, Incl E, G–4 Rpt, Incl A.

Appendix C

Japanese Order of Battle on Saipan[a]

Army

Unit	Commanding Officer	Strength
Headquarters, 31st Army	Lt. Gen. Hideyoshi Obata	1,100
43d Division		
Headquarters, 43d Division	Lt. Gen. Yoshitsugu Saite	268
118th Infantry Regiment	Col. Takeshi Ito	2,605
135th Infantry Regiment	Col. Eisuke Suzuki	3,000[b]
136th Infantry Regiment	Col. Yukimatsu Ogawa	3,650
43d Division Signal Company	Capt. Yoshimitsu Washizu	223
43d Division Transport Company	Capt. Mitsuo Yamamoto	94
43d Division Ordnance Company	Capt. Yoshihiro Murase	99
43d Division Field Hospital	Lt. Col. Ikko Fukayama	500
43d Division Intendance Duty Unit	Lt. Hideo Okawa	2,500
47th Independent Mixed Brigade		
47th Independent Mixed Brigade Headquarters	Col. Yoshiro Oka	227
316th Independent Infantry Battalion	Capt. Susumu Eto	618
317th Independent Infantry Battalion	Captain Sasaki	618
318th Independent Infantry Battalion	Major Nagashima	618
47th Independent Mixed Brigade Engineer Unit	1st Lieutenant Yoneya	188
47th Independent Mixed Brigade Artillery Unit	Captain Yamane	323
Miscellaneous Units		
1st Battalion 18th Infantry Regiment	Capt. Masao Kubo	600
(reorganized and re-equipped stragglers; the main body of the regiment was on Guam)		
3d Battalion 9th Independent Mixed Brigade		578[c]
(destined for Pagan, the unit was caught on Saipan)		
3d Independent Mountain Artillery Regiment	Lt. Col. Tsune Nakashima	845
16th Shipping Engineers Regiment (less one company)	Maj. Masaichi Tsunekawa	450
7th Independent Engineer Regiment (less one company)	Col. Fukujiro Koganezawa	600
11th Independent Engineer Regiment (straggler unit)		200
9th Tank Regiment (less two companies)	Col. Takashi Goto	550
4th Independent Tank Company (straggler unit; no tanks)		118
25th Antiaircraft Artillery Regiment	Lt. Col. Jitsunori Niiho	600
43d Independent Antiaircraft Company	1st Lt. Kiichi Kimishima	136[d]

[a]Unless otherwise indicated, this order of battle is based on NTLF Rpt Marianas, Phase I, G–2 Rpt, 12 Aug 44, App. J, dated 1 Sep 44.

[b]NTLF G–2 Report gives 2,200. According to *135th Infantry Regiment* War Diary, May 1944 (NA 27445), the total number, as of 31 May 1944, was 3,914, of which approximately 900 were on Tinian.

[c]This unit is not listed in NTLF G–2 Report. The numerical strength is estimated from the known battalion strength of the *48th Independent Mixed Brigade* on Guam.

[d]NTLF G–2 Report gives the number as 150. *4th Independent Antiaircraft Company* War Diary, May 1944 (NA 22761), gives the number as 136.

Army

Unit	*Commanding Officer*	*Strength*
44th Field Machine Cannon Company	1st Lt. Takahiro Hasagawa	105[e]
14th Independent Mortar Battalion (straggler unit)	Capt. Tatsuo Jinnai	580
17th Independent Mortar Battalion (straggler unit)	Capt. Hajime Matsunami	350[f]
20th Independent Mortar Battalion (straggler unit)		387[g]
115th Airfield Battalion (straggler unit)		269
23d Field Airfield Construction Unit (straggler unit)		392
14th Hangar Maintenance Section (straggler unit)		250[h]
60th Anchorage Headquarters	Colonel Saito	81[i]
1st Independent Security Unit		54[i]
Detachment, 15th Infantry Regiment (straggler unit)		182[i]
9th Expeditionary Unit		908
(a straggler unit; part was reorganized as *318th Independent Infantry Battalion*, the rest remained stragglers)		
150th Infantry Regiment (straggler unit)	Col. Keize Hayashida	300
264th Independent Motor Transport Company	Capt. Tadaomi Iwama	120
278th Independent Motor Transport Company	1st Lt. Shozo Arima	183[j]

Navy

Central Pacific Area Fleet Headquarters	Vice Adm. Chuichi Nagumo	502
5th Base Force Headquarters	Admiral Takahisa Tsujimura	
(this headquarters was combined with *Central Pacific Area Fleet Headquarters*)		
55th Naval Guard Force	Capt. Sanji Takashima	2,000
Yokosuka 1st Special Naval Landing Force	Lt. Comdr. Tatsue Karashima	800
5th Construction Department	Rear Admiral Tsujimura	456
5th Communications Unit	Lt. Comdr. Shinasaku Miyazaki	369
41st Naval Guard Force (straggler unit)		400
Saipan Branch, 4th Fleet Supplies and Accounts Department	Comdr. Makota Mihara	45
1st Branch, Truk Transportation Department	Comdr. Akiyoshi Mizumoto	
Saipan Harbor Master Department	Ens. Shoichi Takahashi	100
Saipan Branch, 4th Naval Stores Department	Comdr. Akiyoshi Mizumoto	

Total Estimated Strength on Saipan

	Army	*Navy*	*Total*
NTLF G–2 count	22,702	6,960	29,662
Revised count	25,469	6,160[k]	31,629

[e]NTLF G–2 Report gives the number as 150. *44th Field Machine Gun Cannon Company* War Diary, May 1944 (NA 27395), gives the number as 105.

[f]NTLF G–2 Report gives the number as 580. CINCPAC-CINCPOA Translation 10931, a file of orders and tables showing troop movements and locations of units in the Central Pacific Area, gives the number as 350.

[g]This unit is not mentioned in NTLF G–2 Report. The number is derived from CINCPAC-CINCPOA Translation 9696, handwritten tables showing the approximate number of men receiving supplies in sectors under the *31st Army.*

[h]NTLF G–2 Report gives the number as 139. CINCPAC-CINCPOA Translation 9883, file of shipping headquarters orders March–May 1944, gives the number as 250.

[i]Not listed in NTLF G–2 Report. This figure is taken from CINCPAC-CINCPOA Translation 9696.

[j]NTLF G–2 Report gives the number as 120. CINCPAC-CINCPOA Translation 9696 gives the number as 183.

[k]In the revised count, the number of Navy personnel is reduced because the NTLF G–2 Report mistakenly identified certain Army units as Navy organizations.

Appendix D

Organic Units

Headquarters and Headquarters Company, 77th Division
Headquarters Special Troops
Military Police Platoon
77th Division Band
777th Ordnance Company
77th Quartermaster Company
77th Reconnaissance Troop
77th Signal Company
302d Engineer Combat Battalion
302d Medical Battalion
305th Infantry Regiment
306th Infantry Regiment
307th Infantry Regiment
Headquarters and Headquarters Battery, 77th Division Artillery
304th Field Artillery Battalion
305th Field Artillery Battalion
306th Field Artillery Battalion
902d Field Artillery Battalion

Attached for Guam Operation

292d JASCO
132d Engineer Combat Battalion
233d Engineer Combat Battalion
242d Engineer Combat Battalion
36th Field Hospital
95th Portable Surgical Hospital
706th Tank Battalion
7th Antiaircraft Battalion
404th Ordnance Company
88th Chemical Battalion (Company A)
92d Bomb Disposal Squad
Base Censor Detachments
2218th Pacific Ocean Area Transport Quartermaster Team
Detachment 1st Information and Historical Section
Photo Assignment Units, 3116th Signal Service Battalion
Counter Intelligence Corps Detachment
Interrogator, Interpreter, Translator Team

Source: The information on the units comprising the 77th Division at Guam is taken from *Ours to Hold it High,* pages 431–33, and from the Order of Battle Branch, War Histories Division, Office of the Chief of Military History.

Appendix E

Order of Battle of III Amphibious Corps (less 77th Infantry Division) for the Guam Operation

Southern Landing Force Troops
    Headquarters and Service Battalion, III Amphibious Corps (less detachments)
    4th Ammunition Company
    III Amphibious Corps Signal Battalion (less detachments)
    Detachment, Argus 17
    Detachment, Marine Air Warning Squadron 2
    Detachment, 246th Aircraft Warning Company
    Communications Unit 41
3d Marine Division (reinforced)
    3d Marine Division
    14th Marine Defense Battalion (less 155-mm. Seacoast Artillery Group, 2 batteries 90-mm. antiaircraft guns, 1 platoon searchlight, detachments, Headquarters and Service Battery)
    1st Armored Amphibious Tractor Battalion (less Companies A and B)
    3d Amphibious Tractor Battalion (reinforced)
    2d Ammunition Company (less 4th Platoon)
    III Amphibious Corps Motor Transport Battalion (less Company C—DUKW's)
    Detachment, III Amphibious Corps Signal Battalion
    2d and 3d War Dog Platoons
    3d JASCO
    25th Naval Construction Battalion
    2d Aviation Engineer Battalion
    Detachment, 5th Field Depot
1st Provisional Marine Brigade (reinforced)
    1st Provisional Marine Brigade
    9th Marine Defense Battalion (less 155-mm. Seacoast Artillery Group, 90-mm. Antiaircraft Group, detachments, Headquarters and Service Battery)
    4th Amphibious Tractor Battalion (reinforced)
    2d Ammunition Company, 4th Platoon
    1st Armored Amphibious Tractor Battalion, Companies A and B
    III Amphibious Corps Motor Transport Bn—DUKW's, Company C
    1st War Dog Platoon
    53d Naval Construction Battalion
    5th Field Depot (less detachments)
    III Amphibious Corps Medical Battalion (reinforced)
Corps Artillery
    1st 155-mm. Battalion (howitzer)
    7th 155-mm. Battalion (gun)
Garrison Force
    3d Marine Division (when released by III Amphibious Corps)
    14th Marine Defense Battalion (less above detachments)
    9th Marine Defense Battalion (less above detachments)

2d Aviation Engineer Battalion
25th Naval Construction Battalion
53d Naval Construction Battalion
Company B, 2d Special Naval Construction Battalion
Communications Unit 41
Detachment, Argus 17
Detachment, Marine Air Warning Squadron 2
Detachment, 746th Aircraft Warning Company
Army Defense Troops
5th Field Depot

Source: III Phib Corps Opn Plan 1–44, Annex A, pp. 1–2.

Bibliographical Note

The primary sources for this volume are the official records of the U.S. Army, Navy, and Marine Corps and the various strategic planning agencies both American and Allied. The draft narratives and reports of interviews prepared by Army field historians during or shortly after the campaign constitute an almost equally important source of information. During the preparation of the volume, most of the leading participants in the campaign were consulted and their letters and comments on the early drafts of the manuscript have proved invaluable. The various services have prepared special studies of the campaign, or particular aspects of it, and these have been most useful, as have the many works published since World War II, especially the official Marine Corps histories and the semiofficial history of naval operations authored by Samuel Eliot Morison. Finally, Japanese records, both in the original and in translation, have been exhaustively examined.

Official Records

Strategic Planning

The records relating to strategic planning on the highest Allied and U.S. levels were maintained by the Combined Chiefs of Staff (Allied) and U.S. Joint Chiefs of Staff and its subordinate committees, particularly the Joint War Plans Committee and the Joint Strategic Survey Committee. Copies of these records were kept for the Army by the Strategic Policy Group of the Operations Division and are identified by the initials ABC. They are in the custody of the World War II Records Division, National Archives and Records Service (NARS). Other papers on planning for the Marianas Campaign are to be found in the OPD central files, also World War II Records Division, NARS.

U.S. Army

The official U.S. Army records form the backbone of this study. The three general types most frequently consulted were operation plans (or field orders), after action reports, and unit journals. The after action reports include those of the highest theater command, Headquarters, U.S. Army Forces in the Central Pacific Area (USAFICPA); the XXIV Corps Artillery; and the 27th and 77th Infantry Divisions and their component regiments and battalions. The unit journals—on the level of division, regiment, and battalion—with their minute-by-minute record of combat actions as reported to and seen by the various unit commanders, are for the most part the most reliable and complete of all official records. Generally speaking, the lower the unit, the more detailed is the official journal. Most of these records are in the custody of World War II Records Division, NARS, although many administrative files and some unit journals are in the Kansas City Records Center, AGO.

Another important source of information on the operations of the 27th Infantry Division on Saipan and especially the events leading to the relief of Lt. Gen. Ralph Smith is the Buckner Report, with its many annexes (designated exhibits), a copy of which is located in the World War II Records Division, NARS. General Ralph Smith himself submitted to the Commanding General, USAFICPA, a special preliminary report and Brig. Gen. Ogden J. Ross prepared a special "summary of operations of the 27th Infantry Division on Saipan." Both of the latter are located in the World War II Records Division, NARS.

U.S. Navy

For the U.S. Navy, the same types of records have been used, except that it has not been felt necessary to consult ships' logs, which are the naval equivalent of the unit journal. Naval action reports[1] consulted include those of the Commander in Chief, U.S. Fleet, and Chief of Naval Operations; Commander in Chief, U.S. Pacific Fleet, and Commander in Chief, Pacific Ocean Areas (monthly from February through August 1944); Commander, Fifth Fleet; Commander, Joint Expeditionary Force Marianas; Commanders Task Forces 52 and 53 and their subordinate commands; and in some few cases individual ships' reports. All World War II U.S. Navy records are located in the Classified Operational Records Branch, Naval History Division, and copies of most of

those used in this volume are to be found in the World War II Records Division, NARS, or in the Records and Research Section, Historical Branch, G–3, Headquarters, U.S. Marine Corps.

U.S. Marine Corps

Marine Corps action reports and daily journals have been covered in the same manner as those of the Army, except that it has not been felt necessary to consult Marine battalion reports and journals. Most frequent use has been made of the reports of Headquarters Expeditionary Troops (Task Force 56); Northern Troops and Landing Force (V Amphibious Corps); Southern Troops and Landing Force (III Amphibious Corps); 2d Marine Division; 4th Marine Division; 3d Marine Division; the 1st Marine Provisional Brigade; and the appropriate regimental reports and journals. These records are located in the Records and Research Section, Historical Branch, G–3, Headquarters, U.S. Marine Corps.

Interviews, Field Histories, and Letters

Each of the two Army operations described here was covered by a field historian and a team of specialists sent by Headquarters, U.S. Army Forces in the Central Pacific Area, to accompany the troops during the fighting on Saipan and Guam. For Saipan the historian was Capt. Edmund G. Love; for Guam, S. Sgt. James M. Burns. Each took extensive notes and made reports of interviews in the field, and each prepared draft narratives of the operations he covered. These manuscripts are filed in the Office of the Chief of Military

---

[1] Army and Navy nomenclature differs here. The same type of report that is called "after action report" by the Army is called "action report" by the Navy. The U.S. Marine Corps usually employs the Navy term. Other variations used occasionally are "special action report," "operations report," and "participation report."

History (OCMH), Department of the Army.

Early drafts of this volume were submitted to a large number of Army, Navy, and Marine Corps officers who played significant roles in the campaign. Many of them, in response, submitted suggestions, corrections, and additional information, all of which was invaluable in the preparation of the book in its final form. They are:[2] Col. Leonard A. Bishop, AUS (Ret.); Lt. Gen. Andrew D. Bruce, USA (Ret.); Admiral Richard L. Conolly, USN (Ret.); Col. Joseph B. Coolidge, USA; Lt. Gen. Pedro A. del Valle, USMC (Ret.); General Graves B. Erskine, USMC (Ret.); Brig. Gen. Charles B. Ferris, USAR; Maj. Gen. Wallace M. Greene, Jr., USMC; Maj. Gen George W. Griner, Jr., USA (Ret.); Vice Adm. Harry W. Hill, USN (Ret.); General John R. Hodge, USA (Ret.); Lt. Gen. Robert Hogaboom, USMC; Brig. Gen. Gerard W. Kelley, USAR; Brig. Gen. Redmond Kernan, Jr., AUS (Ret.); Col. Gordon T. Kimbrell, USA; the late Fleet Admiral Ernest J. King, USN; Col. James E. Landrum, Jr., USA; General of the Army Douglas MacArthur; Fleet Admiral Chester W. Nimitz, USN (Ret.); the late Vice Adm. Lawrence Reifsnider, USN; Lt. Gen. Clark L. Ruffner, USA; General Harry Schmidt, USMC (Ret.); General Lemuel C. Shepherd, Jr., USMC (Ret.); General Holland M. Smith, USMC (Ret.) Brig. Gen. Isaac Spalding, USA (Ret.) Admiral Raymond A. Spruance, USN (Ret.); General Allen H. Turnage, USMC (Ret.); and Lt. Gen. Thomas E. Watson, USMC (Ret.).

---

[2] Ranks are those held as of the time of completion of this volume.

Special Studies

Among other sources used were several special studies prepared after the campaign, either under the official auspices of particular commands or by individuals attached to the historical sections of the various services. In the first category are: Headquarters, Central Pacific Command, Target Saipan; A Story of XXIV Corps Artillery; and Army Air Forces Historical Division, Army Air Forces in the Marianas Campaign. Copies of both manuscripts are in OCMH. Individual special studies consulted are Roy E. Appleman, Army Tanks in the Battle for Saipan, MS in OCMH; 1st Lt. Russell A. Gugeler, FA, Army Amphibian Tractor and Tank Battalions in the Battle of Saipan, 15 June–9 July 1944, MS in OCMH; Lt. Grace P. Hayes, USN, The War Against Japan, MS in JCS Historical Section; Lt. (j.g.) A. O. Van Wyen and Lt. (j.g.) W. G. Land, Office DCNO, Naval Air Operations in the Marianas, 11–20 June 1944, copy of MS in Records and Research Section, Historical Branch, G–3, Headquarters, U.S. Marine Corps.

Japanese Records

The major collection of captured Japanese military records, amounting to about 7,000 linear feet, was returned to Japan in 1958. Before they were returned these records were in the custody of the National Archives and Records Service, Washington, D.C. Except for a small group of selected operational records reproduced by the Navy Department, there are no substantial collections of Japanese military records now remaining in the United States.

After the war the G–2 Section of General Headquarters, Far East Command (GHQ, FEC), directed a group of former Japanese Army and Navy officers to prepare a series of special studies of Japanese operations, based on their personal recollections and on available official records in Tokyo. These were translated, edited, and incorporated into a formal numbered series of Japanese Studies now on file in the Office, Chief of Military History. Those used in the preparation of this volume are Study Number 55 (Operations in the Central Pacific) and Study Number 75 (History of the Army Section, Imperial General Headquarters, 1941–1945).

A large collection of translated captured enemy records is contained in the bulletins and translations prepared during the war by Headquarters, Commander in Chief Pacific Fleet and Pacific Ocean Areas, and by the Joint Intelligence Center, Pacific Ocean Areas (JICPOA). Complete collections of both are deposited in the Classified Operational Records Branch, World War II, Office of Naval History, and the Records and Research Section, Historical Branch, G–3, Headquarters, U.S. Marine Corps. The 4th Marine Division also collected a series of "representative translations made on Tinian," which is deposited in the same place. Of particular use in understanding and evaluating Japanese defensive operations on Guam were two letters from Lt. Col. Hideyuki Takeda, IJA, one addressed to the Commandant, U.S. Marine Corps, dated 4 October 1946, and the other to Brig. Gen. J. C. McQueen, USMC, dated 20 February 1952. Both are also to be found in the Records and Research Section, Historical Branch, G–3 Division, Headquarters, U.S. Marine Corps.

Published Works

Appleman, Roy E., James M. Burns, Russell A. Gugeler, and John Stevens. *Okinawa: The Last Battle.* UNITED STATES ARMY IN WORLD WAR II. Washington, 1948.

Arnold, H. H., General of the Air Force. *Global Mission.* New York: Harper & Brothers, 1949.

Bartley, Lt. Col. Whitman S., USMC. *Iwo Jima: Amphibious Epic.* Historical Branch, G–3 Division, Headquarters, U.S. Marine Corps. Washington, 1954.

Butow, Robert J. *Japan's Decision to Surrender.* Stanford, Calif.: Stanford University Press, 1954.

Cass, Bevan G. (ed.). *History of the Sixth Marine Division.* Washington, 1948.

Craven, Wesley Frank, and James Lea Cate (eds.). *The Army Air Forces in World War II,* Vol. IV, *The Pacific: Guadalcanal to Saipan, August 1942 to July 1944.* Chicago: The University of Chicago Press, 1950.

————. Ibid., Vol. V, *The Pacific: Matterhorn to Nagasaki, June 1944 to August 1945.* Chicago: The University of Chicago Press, 1953.

Crowl, Philip A., and Edmund G. Love. *Seizure of the Gilberts and Marshalls.* UNITED STATES ARMY IN WORLD WAR II. Washington, 1955.

Department of the Navy, Bureau of Yards and Docks. *Building the Navy's Bases in World War II; History of the Bureau of Yards and Docks and the Civil Engineer Corps, 1940–1946.* 2 vols. Washington, 1947.

Halsey, Fleet Admiral William F., USN, and Lieutenant Commander J. Bryan, III, USNR. *Admiral Halsey's Story.* New York and London: Whittlesey

House, McGraw-Hill Book Company, Inc., 1947.

Heinl, Lt. Col. Robert D., Jr., USMC, and Lt. Col. John A. Crown, USMC. *The Marshalls: Increasing the Tempo.* Historical Branch, G–3 Division, Headquarters, U.S. Marine Corps. Washington, 1954.

Historical Division, War Department. *The Capture of Makin, 20 November–24 November 1943.* AMERICAN FORCES IN ACTION SERIES. Washington, 1946.

————. *Guam: Operations of the 77th Division (21 July–10 August 1944).* AMERICAN FORCES IN ACTION SERIES. Washington, 1946.

————. *Small Unit Actions.* AMERICAN FORCES IN ACTION SERIES. Washington, 1946.

Hoffman, Major Carl W., USMC. *Saipan: The Beginning of the End.* Historical Division, Headquarters, U.S. Marine Corps. Washington, 1950.

————. *The Seizure of Tinian.* Historical Division, Headquarters, U.S. Marine Corps. Washington, 1951.

Isely, Jeter A. and Philip A. Crowl. *The U.S. Marines and Amphibious War.* Princeton: Princeton University Press, 1951.

Jane's Fighting Ships, 1944–45. New York: The Macmillan Company, 1947.

Johnston, Richard W. *Follow Me!: The Story of the Second Marine Division in World War II.* New York: Random House, 1948.

Joint Army-Navy Assessment Committee. *Japanese Naval and Merchant Shipping Losses During World War II By All Causes.* Washington, 1947.

Kenney, George C. *General Kenney Reports, A Personal History of the Pacific War.* New York: Duell, Sloan and Pearce, 1949.

King, Fleet Admiral Ernest J. and Walter M. Whitehill. *Fleet Admiral King, A Naval Record.* New York: W. W. Norton & Company, 1952.

Lodge, Major O. R., USMC. *The Recapture of Guam.* Historical Branch, G–3 Division, Headquarters, U.S. Marine Corps. Washington, 1954.

Love, Edmund G. *The 27th Infantry Division in World War II.* Washington: Infantry Journal Press, 1949.

Miller, John, jr. *CARTWHEEL: The Reduction of Rabaul.* UNITED STATES ARMY IN WORLD WAR II. Washington, 1959.

————. *Guadalcanal: The First Offensive.* UNITED STATES ARMY IN WORLD WAR II. Washington, 1949.

Milner, Samuel. *Victory in Papua.* UNITED STATES ARMY IN WORLD WAR II. Washington, 1957.

Morison, Samuel Eliot. *History of United States Naval Operations in World War II*, Vol. III, *The Rising Sun in the Pacific, 1931–April 1942.* Boston: Little, Brown and Company, 1948.

————. *Ibid.*, Vol. IV, *Coral Sea, Midway and Submarine Actions, May 1942–August 1942.* Boston: Little, Brown and Company, 1949.

————. *Ibid.*, Vol. V, *The Struggle for Guadalcanal, August 1942–February 1943.* Boston: Little, Brown and Company, 1949.

————. *Ibid.*, Vol. VII, *Aleutians, Gilberts and Marshalls, June 1942–April 1944.* Boston: Little, Brown and Company, 1951.

————. *Ibid.*, Vol. VIII, *New Guinea and the Marianas, March 1944–August*

1944. Boston: Little, Brown and Company, 1953.

Myers, Denys P. *Handbook of the League of Nations.* Boston and New York: World Peace Foundation, 1935.

Office, Chief of Naval Operations, Division of Naval Intelligence. ONI 29, *Palau, Mariana Islands.* Washington, 11 May 1942.

————. ONI 99, *Strategic Study of Guam.* Washington, 1 February 1944.

Ours To Hold It High: The History of the 77th Infantry Division in World War II By Men Who Were There. Washington: Infantry Journal Press, 1947.

Pomeroy, Earl S. *Pacific Outpost: American Strategy in Guam and Micronesia.* Stanford, Calif.: Stanford University Press, 1951.

Proehl, Carl W. (ed.). *The Fourth Marine Division in World War II.* Washington, 1946.

Robson, R. W. (comp.). *The Pacific Islands Year Book, 1942.* Sydney, Australia: Pacific Publications, Limited, 1942.

————. *The Pacific Islands Handbook, 1944.* New York: The Macmillan Company, 1946.

Romanus, Charles F., and Riley Sunderland. *Stilwell's Mission to China.* UNITED STATES ARMY IN WORLD WAR II. Washington, 1953.

Sherrod, Robert. *On to Westward! War in the Central Pacific.* New York: Duell, Sloan and Pearce, Inc., 1945.

Smith, Holland M. *Coral and Brass.* New York: Charles Scribner's Sons, 1949.

Smith, Robert Ross. *The Approach to the Philippines.* UNITED STATES ARMY

IN WORLD WAR II. Washington, 1953.

Sprout, Harold and Margaret. *Toward a New Order of Sea Power.* Princeton: Princeton University Press, 1940.

Stockman, Captain James R., USMC. *The Battle for Tarawa.* Historical Division, Division of Public Information, Headquarters, U.S. Marine Corps. Washington, 1947.

Thompson, Laura. *Guam and Its People.* Princeton: Princeton University Press, 1947.

United States Strategic Bombing Survey, Chairman's Office. *Japan's Struggle to End the War.* Washington, 1946.

————. (Pacific), Naval Analysis Division. *The Campaigns of the Pacific War.* Washington, 1946.

————. (Pacific), Naval Analysis Division. *Interrogations of Japanese Officials.* 2 vols. Washington, 1946.

————. (Pacific), Naval Analysis Division. *The Reduction of Truk.* Washington, 1947.

The War Reports of General of the Army George C. Marshall, Chief of Staff, General of the Army H. H. Arnold, Commanding General, Army Air Forces, Fleet Admiral Ernest J. King, Commander-in-Chief, United States Fleet and Chief of Naval Operations. Philadelphia and New York: J. B. Lippincott Company, 1947.

Zimmerman, Maj. John L., USMCR. *The Guadalcanal Campaign.* Historical Division, Division of Public Information, Headquarters, U.S. Marine Corps. Washington, 1949.

List of Abbreviations

AAF	Army Air Forces
AAR	After action report
ABC	American-British Conversations
Adm	Administrative
AFAS	American Forces in Action Series
AGC	General communications vessel
AK	Cargo ship
AKA	Cargo ship, attack
Amph	Amphibious
AP	Transport
APA	Transport, attack
APD	Transport (high speed)
App	Appendix
Armd	Armored
Arty	Artillery
Atchd	Attached
BAR	Browning automatic rifle
BLT	Battalion landing team
Bn	Battalion
Br	Branch
Brig	Brigade
Bull	Bulletin
C–3	Operations officer or section of a Marine amphibious corps
CCS	Combined Chiefs of Staff
CD	Coastal defense
CEC	Civil Engineer Corps
C&GS	Command and General Staff
CG	Commanding general
CINCPAC	Commander in Chief, U.S. Pacific Fleet
CINCPOA	Commander in Chief, Pacific Ocean Areas
CINCSWPA	Commander in Chief, Southwest Pacific Area
CM–IN	Classified message, incoming
CM–OUT	Classified message, outgoing
CNO	Chief of Naval Operations
Co	Company
CO	Commanding officer
CofS	Chief of Staff
Comdt	Commandant
COMINCH	Commander in Chief, U.S. Fleet

CP	Command post
CTF	Commander Task Force
D–2	Intelligence officer or section of a Marine division
D–3	Operations officer or section of a Marine division
DCNO	Deputy Chief of Naval Operations
Div	Division
DUKW	Amphibian truck, 2½ tons
Elms	Elements
Env	Envelope
FBL	Force Beachhead Line
FEC	Far East Command
Fld	Field
FMF	Fleet Marine Force
FO	Field order
FTP	Fleet Training Publication
Fwd	Forward
G–1	Personnel section of divisional or higher staff
G–2	Intelligence section of divisional or higher staff
G–3	Operations section of divisional or higher staff
G–4	Supply section of divisional or higher staff
G–5	As used in this volume, refers to the Marine section of divisional or higher staff responsible for tactical planning for an assault from its inception to the time of issue of the final operations plan
Gen	General
GSC	General Staff Corps
H&S	Headquarters and Service
Hist	History, historical
Hq	Headquarters
I and H Sv	Information and Historical Service
IJA	Imperial Japanese Army
IJN	Imperial Japanese Navy
IMR	*Independent Mixed Regiment*
IMTFE	International Military Tribunal for the Far East
Incl	Inclosure
Inf	Infantry
Intel	Intelligence
IPS	International Prosecution Section
JANAC	Joint Army-Navy Assessment Committee
JASCO	Joint Assault Signal Company
JB	Joint Board
JCS	Joint Chiefs of Staff
JICPOA	Joint Intelligence Center, Pacific Ocean Areas
Jnl	Journal
JPS	Joint Staff Planners
JSSC	Joint Strategic Survey Committee
JWPC	Joint War Plans Committee

LIST OF ABBREVIATIONS

LCI	Landing craft, infantry
LCI(G)	Landing craft, infantry, gunboat
LCM	Landing craft, mechanized
LCR	Landing craft, rubber
LCT	Landing craft, tank
LCVP	Landing craft, vehicle and personnel
LD	Line of departure
LSD	Landing ship, dock
LST	Landing ship, tank
Ltr	Letter
LVT	Landing vehicle, tracked
LVT(A)	Landing vehicle, tracked, armored
LVT(A)(1)	Landing vehicle, tracked, armored (Mark I) ("Water Buffalo," turret type)
LVT(A)(4)	Landing vehicle, tracked, armored (Mark IV)
Min	Minutes
MS	Manuscript
MID	Military Intelligence Division
MIS	Military Intelligence Service
Msg	Message
Mtg	Meeting
NA	National Archives
NARS	National Archives and Records Service
NR&H	Naval Records and History
NTLF	Northern Troops and Landing Force
OCMH	Office of the Chief of Military History
OCNO	Office of the Chief of Naval Operations
ONI	Office of Naval Intelligence
OPD	Operations Division, War Department General Staff
Opn	Operation
Pac	Pacific
PC	Patrol craft
Phib	Amphibious
POA	Pacific Ocean Areas
POW	Prisoner of war
Rad	Radiogram
Rcn	Reconnaissance
RCT	Regimental combat team
Regt	Regiment
Rpt	Report
RS	Records Section
S–2	Military intelligence section of a unit not having a general staff
S–3	Operations and training section of a unit not having a general staff
SAR	Special action report
SC	Signal Corps

Sec(.)	Section
Ser.	Serial
SLF	Southern Landing Force
SWPA	Southwest Pacific Area
TF	Task Force
TG	Task Group
Tk	Tank
TQM	Transport quartermaster (officer)
Trac	Tractor
Trans	Translation
U/F	Unit of fire
USA	U.S. Army
USAF	U.S. Army Forces
USAFICPA	U.S. Army Forces in the Central Pacific Area
USAFMIDPAC	U.S. Army Forces, Middle Pacific
USMC	U.S. Marine Corps
USMCR	U.S. Marine Corps Reserve
USN	U.S. Navy
USNG	U.S. National Guard
USNR	U.S. Naval Reserve
USSBS	U.S. Strategic Bombing Survey
WD	War Department
WDC	Washington Document Center
WDCSA	War Department Chief of Staff, U.S. Army
WDGO	War Department General Orders
WPD	War Plans Division

Glossary of Code Names

CARTWHEEL	Operation for the seizure of the Solomon Islands—New Britain–New Ireland area
FORAGER	Operations for the capture of the Mariana Islands
GALVANIC	The Gilberts–Makin operation
GRANITE	Nimitz' plan for operations in 1944
ORANGE	Prewar plan of operations in event of war with Japan
QUADRANT	First Quebec conference, August 1943
RAINBOW	Various plans prepared between 1939 and 1941 to meet Axis aggression
RENO	MacArthur's plans for advancing along north coast of New Guinea and thence to Mindanao
SEXTANT	International conference at Cairo, 22–26 November and 3–7 December 1943
TRIDENT	International conference at Washington, 12–25 May 1943

Basic Military Map Symbols*

Symbols within a rectangle indicate a military unit, within a triangle an observation post, and within a circle a supply point.

Military Units—Identification

Antiaircraft Artillery . . . .

Armored Command . . . .

Army Air Forces . . . .

Artillery, except Antiaircraft and Coast Artillery . . . .

Cavalry, Horse . . . .

Cavalry, Mechanized . . . .

Chemical Warfare Service . . . .

Coast Artillery . . . .

Engineers . . . .

Infantry . . . .

Medical Corps . . . .

Ordnance Department . . . .

Quartermaster Corps . . . .

Signal Corps . . . .

Tank Destroyer . . . .

Transportation Corps . . . .

Veterinary Corps . . . .

Airborne units are designated by combining a gull wing symbol with the arm or service symbol:

Airborne Artillery . . . .

Airborne Infantry . . . .

*For complete listing of symbols in use during the World War II period, see FM 21–30, dated October 1943, from which these are taken.

Size Symbols

The following symbols placed either in boundary lines or above the rectangle, triangle, or circle inclosing the identifying arm or service symbol indicate the size of military organization:

Squad . . . .   •

Section . . . .   ••

Platoon . . . .   •••

Company, troop, battery, Air Force flight   I

Battalion, cavalry squadron, or Air Force squadron . . . .   I I

Regiment or group; combat team (with abbreviation CT following identifying numeral) . . . .   I I I

Brigade, Combat Command of Armored Division, or Air Force Wing   X

Division or Command of an Air Force   XX

Corps or Air Force   XXX

Army   XXXX

Group of Armies   XXXXX

EXAMPLES

The letter or number to the left of the symbol indicates the unit designation; that to the right, the designation of the parent unit to which it belongs. Letters or numbers above or below boundary lines designate the units separated by the lines:

Company A, 137th Infantry . . . . A⊠137

8th Field Artillery Battalion . . . . ⊡|8

Combat Command A, 1st Armored Division . . . . A⬯|I

Observation Post, 23d Infantry . . . . ⩘23

Command Post, 5th Infantry Division . . . . ⊠5

Boundary between 137th and 138th Infantry 137
                                                                    —III—
                                                                     138

Weapons

Machine gun . . . .   •→

Gun . . . .   ●

Gun battery . . . .   ⊥⊥⊥

Howitzer or Mortar . . . .   ◆

Tank . . . .   ◇

Self-propelled gun . . . .   ◖●

UNITED STATES ARMY IN WORLD WAR II

The following volumes have been published or are in press:

Index